ITALY
for the Gourmet Traveler

ALSO BY FRED PLOTKIN

The Authentic Pasta Book

Eating Healthy for a Health Baby
(with Dana Cernea, M.D.)

Opera 101: A Complete Guide to Learning
and Loving Opera

Recipes from Paradise: Life and Food
on the Italian Riviera

Italy Today: The Beautiful Cookbook
(with Lorenza de'Medici)

La Terra Fortunata: The Splendid Food and Wine
of Friuli-Venezia Giulia

Classical Music Unbuttoned:
A Complete Guide to Learning and Loving Classical

ITALY

for the Gourmet Traveler

FRED PLOTKIN

WITH PHOTOGRAPHS

BY THE AUTHOR

KYLE CATHIE LIMITED

For my parents,

BERNICE AND EDWARD,

EACH OF WHOM HAS SPENT TIME WITH

ME IN ITALY AND ENCOURAGED

MY PASSION FOR IT

First published in Great Britain in 1997 by
Kyle Cathie Limited
122 Arlington Road, London NW1 7HP
general.enquiries@kyle-cathie.com
www.kylecathie.com

This revised edition published in 2006

10 9 8 7 6 5 4 3 2 1

ISBN-10 1 85626 666 4
ISBN-13 978 1 85626 666 6

© 1996, 2003, 2006 by Fred Plotkin

Maps by Mary Reilly

A Cataloguing in Publication record for this title is available from the British Library.

Printed in Singapore by Star Standard

Avrai tu l'universo,

Resti l'Italia a me

You may have the universe,

But let Italy remain mine

—from *Attila,*

music by Giuseppe Verdi,

libretto by Temistocle Solera

CONTENTS

Contents | vii

ACKNOWLEDGMENTS

I first visited Italy in 1973 and have lived, traveled, studied, and worked there for much of the time since. Everyone I have ever encountered in Italy has contributed in some way to the ideas and information contained in *Italy for the Gourmet Traveler*. This book is the product of their many voices and smiling faces and talented hands. Yet certain individuals have been especially helpful, and I wish to express my gratitude to them herein.

This book benefited from the constant interest and assistance I received from five dear friends: Laura Bellinazzo, Patrizia Cantini, Pasquale di Lena, Gilberto Polloni, and Roberto Visentin. I have shared many wonderful meals and bottles with them, and each has been an oracle who has taught me things about Italian food, wine, culture, history, and traditions that even most Italians don't know. *Italy for the Gourmet Traveler* is as much theirs as it is mine.

Thanks also to many individuals in regions around the country: In Liguria, Lorenza and Roberto Volpini; In Piemonte, Chiara Castino, Elio Archimede, Ennio Ranaboldo, Andrè Fucci, Riccardo Tagliabò, Carlo Vischi, Carmen Wallace; In Valle d'Aosta, Elisabetta Allera, Massimo Balestra; In Lombardia, Stefano Palazzi, Nicoletta Dozio, Sonia Politi, Claudio Riolo; In Veneto, Giancarlo Voglino; In Trentino, Lucinda Addison, Joan Bloom of Hill & Knowlton, Serena Colombaro, Stefano Girelli; In Alto Adige, Teresa Delaney of Relais et Chateaux; In Friuli–Venezia Giulia, Walter Filiputti and Patrizia and Lorenza, Rossana and Riccardo Illy, and all the kind people in this wonderful region; In Emilia-Romagna, Alice Fixx; Renzo Cattabiani, Leo Bertozzi, and Mario Zannoni (the Garibaldi, Cavour, and Mazzini of the Consorzio del Formaggio Parmigiano-Reggiano); Giuseppe Morini; Luca Panzavolta; Dr. Rocco Bagnato; Dr. Lorenzo Sassoli de Bianchi; Gianni Grassilli; In Toscana, Emanuela Stucchi; Senator Riccardo Margheriti, Pasquale di Lena, and the capable staff at the Enoteca Italiana; Giovanni Battista Gorio; the Colombini family at the Barbi winery in Montalcino for their assistance on wine tourism; Doreen Schmid; Ursula Thurner; In Marche, Maria Bertone Gazzetti; In Lazio, Maurizio Accinni, Margherita Cardillo of Alitalia; In Campania, Alfredo Papoff; In Abruzzo, Piergiorgio D'Andrea; In

Molise, Angelina di Lena, Zio Mario, Zia Lilina, Carmella e Antonio; In Sicilia, Giselde Cantaro.

Thanks also to the Gruppo Ristoratori Italiani, the Ordine Ristoratori Professionisti Italiani, and the Gruppo Italiano Vini.

In the United States, I have received assistance and encouragement from numerous individuals and institutions:

The staff at the New York office of the Istituto di Commercio Estero/the Italian Trade Commission, Giorgio Lulli, Hermelina Ressa, Maria Woodley, and others have opened many doors for me in my quest to go down the *strada* less traveled to find the Italy less known.

Mary K. Hartley at Italian Government Tourist Office (ENIT) is a kindred spirit who has provided me with all the facts, figures, and documentation that an effective travel guide requires.

Foodcom and the International Olive Oil Council, especially Arlene Wanderman, Linda Russo, and Dr. Fausto Luchetti, have been constant companions in my ongoing appreciation of the olive and its oil.

The Oldways Preservation and Exchange Trust in Boston is an ardent defender of gastronomic and cultural traditions in Italy and elsewhere. Sara Baer-Sinnot, Greg Drescher, K. Dun Gifford, Robin Insley, Paul Krohn, and Sarah Powers all do this work with great talent and dedication.

Tony May of San Domenico restaurant in New York and Dr. Lucio Caputo, the U.S. representative of the Ente Fiere di Verona, have enabled me to meet many talented chefs, wine makers, and food growers all over Italy.

Marta Lotti of Alitalia has a ready smile and warm voice and has been a source of great help and reassurance.

Elizabeth Kane has been a wonderful friend who has provided constant professional and personal support and encouragement in this project.

Nancy Bachrach and Karen McAndrew played a key role in the production of this book, and I thank them both.

In the creation of this book Jennifer Josephy, my patient and enthusiastic editor, has been there every step of the way. She understands my passion for Italy and my desire to make this book a written and visual expression of that. My thanks to her, to Abigail Wilentz, Sue Betz, and everyone else at Little, Brown and Company who participated in the genesis of *Italy for the Gourmet Traveler*.

David Black, as always, has been the sort of agent authors dream of. My thanks to him and to Susan Raihofer, Marah Rhodes, and Lev Fruchter in his office.

Katharine Pollak brought great artistry to the developing of my photographs, and I am grateful for her patience and sensitivity.

A raise of the glass to the *Italiano Come Me* gang: Carol, Faith, Nancy, Corby, and Ed.

And, finally, special thanks to Michelle K. Jones, who, at least as regards my life as a writer about Italy, made me the man I am today.

ITALY

for the Gourmet
Traveler

Garibaldi with a Fork

Wherever you travel in Italy, you are sure to see the name Giuseppe Garibaldi (1807–1882). There may be a Via Garibaldi, a Piazza Garibaldi, a Bar Garibaldi, or any number of civic institutions named for the man who is often thought of as the George Washington of Italy. Along with Giuseppe Mazzini (1805–1872) and Camillo Cavour (1810–1861), Garibaldi was the leader of the *Risorgimento* (the "Revival" or "Resurgence") that led to the unification of the Italian peninsula's many city-states, kingdoms, duchies, papal territories, and especially the lands under foreign domination. The movement, which began in 1815, was in full throttle by 1840, but it took until 1870 for the Italian nation to be formed.

With changes resulting from wars and treaties in the twentieth century Italy as we know it is somewhat different from that of 1870. Only in 1954 did the Italian republic acquire the composition it has today. What is notable is that by the time you read this book, Italy may have reconfigured yet again. With the founding of the Second Republic in 1994, several Italian regions have made loud noises about separatism or, at the very least, more autonomy. Political corrupton has continued unabated, and the economy has struggled since the creation of the euro. The message here for you, the gourmet traveler, is to reject immediately your notion of Italy as a country in which there is a uniformity of taste, culture, language, and history from region to region.

When Italy was unified in 1870, it was an amalgamation of peoples extending from the Alps (near France, Germany, Switzerland, and the Austro-Hungarian Empire), past the great Venetian republic and the royal House of Savoy, to the noble city-states in the center of the peninsula that were at their zenith in the Middle Ages and the Renaissance, through Roma and its papal territories, to the deep south, with cultural and historic influences drawn from ancient Greece and the Maghreb in North Africa. Although railroads, television, and telecommunications have encouraged Italians from around the peninsula to see and hear one another, there is no question that a person's self identity is strictly local. If you meet a woman from Siracusa in Milano, she will identify herself at least as *siciliana*

Faenza, Emilia-Romagna

if not *siracusana*. Back in Sicilia she will always refer to herself as a native of Siracusa. In this book I will refer to the cities and regions by their Italian names, since this is how you will refer to them in Italy.

Many Italians you meet now have roots in two or more regions. A woman I am fond of lives in rural Toscana, but has parents and grandparents from Napoli, Firenze, and Milano. So she draws on all of these sources in her sense of self. I have other friends in Toscana who can trace their ancestors back to the Renaissance. If you ask them where in the region they are from, they will detail that on one side of the family there are relatives from Siena, Poggibonsi, Volterra, and San Gimignano, while on the other side they came from Arezzo, Greve, Radda, and Castellina. All of these towns are very near to one another, yet citizens of one have a strong sense that they belong to that town only and not another. So a *toscano* who has roots in eight towns is really something of a mixed breed in the eyes of other *toscani*.

In Italy there is something called *campanilismo,* drawn from the word *campanile,* or "bell tower." It refers to the idea of extreme devotion to one's own town. Since practically every village in Italy has a church and a bell tower—whose chimes once told the time and dictated the rhythms of life in the town—one's point of reference seldom extended beyond hearing range of the bells. A *campanilista* is a person with a strong attachment to his hometown, and you will meet one wherever you go. Italians rarely profess a sense of national pride, except when Italy's soccer team is competing in the World Cup. A *campanilista* will tell you that the *salame* or pasta typical of his town is the best in Italy, and certainly better than the almost identical one from the nearest town. There is a centuries-old enmity between the peoples of Parma and Reggio Emilia (twenty-eight kilometers [eighteen miles] apart) as to who produces the better cheeses, hams, and *salami*. One of the great pleasures for gourmet travelers is going from town to town and making their own determination about where the food is better.

So when Garibaldi, Mazzini, Cavour, were leading the drive for unification—with powerful support from Giuseppe Verdi, many of whose operas were clear calls to arms to throw out the Austrians who occupied much of the north—they had to convince many disparate peoples to join together. While Mazzini and Cavour were thinkers and politicians, Garibaldi was a military man of action. He gathered an army of one thousand volunteers (known as the *Mille*), who marched from Sicilia up the peninsula to fight for unification. Just as in the eastern United States one can point to many places where George Washington slept, there are hundreds of Italian towns with plaques on buildings where Garibaldi slept. And wherever he slept, he ate.

In the years that I have spent living and traveling in Italy, I have come to think of myself as a Garibaldi with a fork. I have slept and eaten in most of the towns he visited, and many he didn't, taking notes on everything I ate and drank. I know that I often surprised and delighted locals with my strong interest in and affection for their foods, customs, history, and dialects. Much of this acquired *campanilismo* will be shared with you in this book, along with the encouragement to go and discover these places for yourself. Do I have a favorite place? Of course. You will probably figure out which it is as you read this book, but I remind you that there are at least fifty other cities that I would happily visit and dine in whenever given the chance.

When you plan your first visit to Italy, you will likely put Roma, Firenze, and Venezia at the top of your list, perhaps adding Milano and Napoli as well. These destinations make sense because they are all world-class cities with great history, art, architecture, culture, and food. I have visited each of these places at least once a year for two decades. Yet, to have a fuller understanding of Italy's culture, character, and cuisine, you must also plan to include regional capitals and smaller towns in your itinerary.

A traveler making a return visit to Italy might be well advised to base himself in one or two towns in one geographic part of the country and use these as bases for travel to nearby places. For example, someone who likes big cities might choose to stay in Genova and Torino while visiting the regions of Liguria and Piemonte. If you prefer smaller cities, you might pick San Remo and Alba to use as bases to explore these regions. The logic of selecting cities to use as bases comes in the fact that you can unpack your bags and settle into a hotel room for a few days, which is more comfortable than being an itinerant. More important, if you live in a neighborhood for a time, you begin to get a sense of the rhythms and traditions of a place, and it will start to feel a little bit like home. Because the vast majority of

Italians are unusually warm and gracious, you will find that shopkeepers and the coffee man at the bar will recognize and greet you when you come back to buy some fruit or a cappuccino. This is part of the joy of being in Italy.

If you have more time, you can choose two geographic zones to explore. So after Liguria and Piemonte, you might head south to Abruzzo and Molise to experience a completely different Italy. En route you can stop in Firenze or Roma to deepen your acquaintance with those ever-fascinating cities. My advice to you is to resist the desire to spread yourself too thin. Your visit to Italy will be much more meaningful if you get to know a few places well instead of setting foot in ten cities in two weeks. I fully understand that not everyone gets to Italy as often as I do, but since this country arguably has the longest and most complex political, cultural, and gastronomic history of any nation in the world (its only rivals could be China and India), you cannot expect to take in as much during a visit here as you might in most other places. Remember: Italy is a young nation made up of many ancient independent states, each with centuries of its own art, culture, and tradition.

In modern Italy there are twenty regions, although I will be featuring twenty-one in this book. This is because two northern provinces, those of Trento and Bolzano, are merged into one region called Trentino–Alto Adige. Yet they are significantly different enough that, for the purposes of this book, I have chosen to separate them. The Trentino is predominantly Italian-speaking and has sufficiently distinct food and wine to merit independent consideration. The Alto Adige is German-speaking, and its citizens feel strong bonds to Switzerland, Germany, and particularly Austria, to which it belonged for many years. The cities there are referred to by both their German and Italian names (Bozen/Bolzano, Meran/Merano, Brixen/Bressanone). When you visit the Alto Adige, you will be hard-pressed to find much about it that is Italian.

Let me explain how Italy is arranged geographically. This knowledge is central to your understanding of the country, so you should make an effort to learn it. This is especially important if you plan to travel to smaller places. Each of the twenty regions has a capital city. (In the Trentino–Alto Adige, the cities of Trento and Bolzano are the capitals.) Every region is divided into provinces, which have capitals as well. Then there are many small cities and towns in each province. A corresponding example in America are cities, counties, and states: Miami is a city in Dade County in the state of Florida. The difference is that in Italy the county (or province) always bears the name of the provincial capital.

Every provincial capital in Italy has a two-letter abbreviation. For example, the capital of Lombardia is Milano, whose abbreviation is "MI." But this is also the capital of the province of Milano, one of eleven provinces in Lombardia. So Milano has three separate governments: city, provincial, and regional. The other provinces in Lombardia are Bergamo (BG), Brescia (BS), Como (CO), Cremona (CR), Lecco (LC), Lodi (LO), Mantova (MN), Pavia (PV), Sondrio (SO), and Varese (VA). In each province are many smaller towns. For example, the town of

Broni, which produces excellent sparkling wine, is in the province of Pavia. So on all mail and in all references to Broni, you will see it listed as "Broni (PV)." In spoken Italian, when one talks about the hinterlands of a province, an adjective is formed using the name of the capital. So if you are going for a drive *nel bresciano*, you are traveling in the countryside of the province of Brescia. These adjectives often denote dialects or styles of cooking as well, such as *bergamasco, comasco, cremonese, lodigiano, mantovano, milanese*, or *pavese*. Gastronomes know certain dishes by these names, such as the breaded veal cutlet fried in butter that is universally called *cotoletta alla milanese*, or simply *una milanese*.

Until 1994, all license plates in Italy had the initials of the car's province of residence. It was always great fun on long drives to identify where the nearby car was from and to peer in at the passengers. Sometimes drivers from towns that are historic rivals, such as Firenze and Siena, would get into a playful auto rally at 160 kilometers (100 miles) per hour. The new license plates are bland and anonymous, but do save money. The plate now lasts for the life of the car and does not have to be changed if the owner moves from one province to another. But many Italians mourn the gradual disappearance of regional license plates, as I do.

In your travels you will gradually come to realize how distinct every region— and, for that matter, every province—is. If you think of the Veneto, your first thoughts are of the singular and exotic seaport city of Venezia (VE). But there is also Padova (PD), the economic hub of the region with one of the greatest food markets in Italy. In the province of Padova one also finds the Colli Euganei, hills full of little resort towns with popular mud and mineral-water spas. The Veneto is also the graceful city of Verona (VR), whose province is one of the biggest wine producers in Italy. Nearby Vicenza (VI), the home of the great sixteenth-century architect Andrea Palladio, has some of the most outstanding villas in the world. Rovigo (RO), south of Padova, is in a flat valley of the Po, Italy's largest river. Rovigo's province draws cultural and culinary influence both from the Veneto and neighboring Emilia-Romagna. Treviso (TV), a half hour's journey north of Venezia, has a marvelous food and wine culture that is highlighted by superb vegetables. Farther north is Belluno (BL), capital of the province that includes Cortina d'Ampezzo and many of the most popular ski resorts in Europe.

So the Veneto gathers within its borders high Alps, rolling hills, the shores of the Adriatic sea, one of northern Italy's famous lakes (Lago di Garda, in the province of Verona), and broad plains flooded with many of the rivers that flow from farther north and west. The region is intensely industrialized but is also one of the most high-powered agricultural areas of Italy. It produces excellent fish from lakes, rivers, and the sea. Animals are raised to produce meat, and milk that becomes butter and cheese. Game caught in the Alps appears in regional dishes, as do tiny birds that are served on beds of polenta. Many of the Veneto's wines are world-class, and its thermal stations provide delicious mineral water. Its orchards and gardens yield some of the finest apples, cherries, grapes, asparagus, corn, and lettuces in Italy. The Colli Berici, hills near Vicenza and Verona, sprout wonderful truffles and wild mushrooms. Many of the region's ingredients go into some of the finest baking in Italy: breads, cereals, pastries, and cookies.

The gourmet traveler can spend weeks exploring the gastronomic and economic riches of the Veneto without ever venturing into another region. This is also the case in other regions, including Liguria, Piemonte, Lombardia, Friuli–Venezia Giulia, Emilia-Romagna, Toscana, Campania, Puglia, Sicilia, and Sardegna. In developing the ideas for this book, I decided to select one city in each region that gathers within its walls much that embodies the character, history, and gastronomic personality of the region. I refer to this city as the "Classic Town." With three exceptions (Trento, Bologna, Roma) I have avoided regional capitals, since these larger cities often are administrative centers that have lost some of their local character. In addition to the three regional capitals, I have selected seven provincial capitals and eleven provincial cities. My thinking here is that if you want to travel to several Italian regions, stopping only in one or two towns in each, you might choose to follow my suggestions to get a strong sense of the cuisine, wine, and culture of each region. These cities are not only superb food centers, but each will be fairly representative of the history, culture, terrain, and temperament of the region. I found that some of these places (Cogne, Bologna, Norcia, Larino, Nuoro) are the very essence of their regions. Others (San Remo, Alba, Cremona, Sulmona, Amalfi, Martina Franca, Tropea, Siracusa) are microcosms of much of the best of their region and are in every case delightful. Here is the list:

THE CLASSIC TOWNS OF ITALY

Liguria: San Remo
Piemonte: Alba
Valle d'Aosta: Cogne
Lombardia: Cremona
Veneto: Treviso
Trentino: Trento
Alto Adige: Brixen/Bressanone
Friuli–Venezia Giulia: Udine
Emilia-Romagna: Bologna
Toscana: Siena
Marche: Urbino

Umbria: Norcia
Lazio: Roma
Abruzzo: Sulmona
Molise: Larino
Campania: Amalfi
Puglia: Martina Franca
Basilicata: Matera
Calabria: Tropea
Sicilia: Siracusa
Sardegna: Nuoro

Many lovers of Italy—*campanilisti* by birth or adoption—may quibble with some of my choices, but I stand by them. I will add the caveat that no city can be completely emblematic of a region, but in every case you will be richly rewarded by a visit to the town I propose. In the Veneto, for example, Padova has its wonderful market and a great *caffè* that should not be missed. Bassano del Grappa draws from many terrains—mountains, hills, sea, rivers, plains—in its cuisine, culture, and flavor, representing a cross section of the Veneto's many aspects. Yet I selected Treviso. Its foods, wines, and particular style are some of the region's finest. It is not far from Venezia and has some of that city's canal culture. But it also has a strong sense of the mainland's industriousness, its architecture, and its devotion to hearty eating. Fish and meat have equal status at the Treviso table, representing the two principal domains (sea and land) that have shaped the Veneto. Treviso has enough examples of some of the region's best dishes that you will come away well fed and knowing more about the Veneto than when you arrived. Of course, the traveler will learn about the real Italy not only in Classic Towns but in secondary cities in regions, such as Cosenza in Calabria and Rovereto in the Trentino. Any place I have listed as "Not to Miss" in a region should command your attention.

Italian eating was once completely geared to agriculture and seasonal availability of foods. Although modern food-storage techniques and importation have made many ingredients available year-round, Italians still tend to eat many foods at the time of the year when they are fully ripe and available from local farmers. This is not merely a question of faithfulness to traditions. Whether they realize it or not, Italians are striking a blow in defense of flavor. The peaches that must travel from South America in January can never match a freshly picked local peach in July.

Because of this awareness of seasons and flavor, urban Italians, more than most other peoples, often display a basic knowledge of agriculture. Food is also produced closer to urban centers (I even know of a vineyard in the city of Venezia), so that most city dwellers have seen the plants that give them their food. The arrival of seasonal foods is often celebrated with a festival, called a *sagra*, that has ancient roots both in pagan culture and in the Church. The idea is to thank the land and the deities for the food. This is not unlike Thanksgiving as celebrated in North America, but with two important differences. Thanksgiving is an observance of general bounty rather than the celebration of the arrival of an ingredient. Also, Thanksgiving is a family holiday, while a *sagra* is observed publicly by the extended family of an entire town. In this book, *sagre* and other festivals are listed under the category "Folklore." Many of these events date back centuries and will give you profound insight into the spirit of the people of a particular place. Some regions, such as Abruzzo, are particularly rich in folklore, and you will be well advised to make attendance at these events your primary means of discovering the region.

Almost every dish in Italy has local roots and is best eaten in its place of origin. While spaghetti with fresh tomato sauce can be found throughout the country, nowhere is it more delicious than in its native Campania. Tomatoes that grow in the local volcanic soil have an irreplaceable flavor, and the people of Campania have an innate knowledge of how to use them.

But all is not rosy. While veneration of freshness and quality is still greater than in most any other country, there have been changes in the way Italians acquire and consume their foods. Supermarkets have made serious inroads as food suppliers, often undercutting the prices charged by the neighborhood merchant. More Italians than ever have been drawn to frozen, canned, and packaged foods because of their perceived convenience.

Wines have changed from what would be produced for local sale and consumption within a year (in most cases) to something of much more sophistication. There was always great wine in Italy, but in recent years it has adapted to more international tastes. Italy trades places with France for number one in sales volume and ranks number two in earnings. There used to be many grape varieties seldom seen beyond a small part of a province. *Vivai* (nurseries) have increased the number of varieties available to wine makers, but dozens of native Italian grapes have been almost wiped out. The desire of some Italian wine makers to compete in international markets has led them to uproot their old, family grapes and plant Cabernet Sauvignon and Chardonnay in their place. But how much of these two grape varieties does the world need?

Some regions, especially Friuli, have worked hard to bring back native varieties. Enzo Morganti, the late, great head of the San Felice winery in Toscana, dedicated a whole plot of prime terrain strictly to the growing of grapes that had nearly vanished from Tuscan vineyards. Who will drink these wines? Per capita consumption is way down in Italy and most everywhere else. In Italy, wine once was a food. It would be consumed with lunch and dinner, and a long siesta was taken in the afternoon. Now it is something of a fancy beverage that is sipped delicately. This is not an issue of alcoholism. Italy has had little problem with excessive alcohol consumption, except in the northeastern part of the country. Besides, wine costs too much and is consumed too slowly to be the drink of choice for alcoholics. In Italy, the decline in wine consumption is due, in part, to an accelerating lifestyle in which people eat on the run and families do not automatically dine together. A study published in May 1995 revealed that 45 percent of all Italians now have the television on when they consume meals at home.

There has been, in the minds of many, a phenomenon that Walter Filiputti, an innovative Friuli wine maker and keen observer of trends, calls a "culinary blackout." By this he means that a generation of young people has lost touch with most food and wine traditions and is imitating the eating habits of young people in other industrialized nations. Twenty years ago, international fast-food companies such as McDonald's had little success in Italy, while they had already penetrated France, Britain and Germany. Now McDonald's has entered Italy and has even occupied a desirable site on the main square of Bologna, the city many consider the gastronomic capital of Italy. There are now McDonald's and other fast-food chains throughout Italy, including those that purport to serve Italian fast food. Many Italians are alarmed by this, though some young people embrace it as part of globalization. You can strike a blow by frequenting places listed in this book that promote *la vera cucina italiana*.

This statement is not meant as a singular attack on McDonald's: it does provide a certain kind of service and offers a reliable if not terribly exciting product, and the company has done more than most in supporting important children's charities. Nonetheless, the arrival of fast food in Italy is a radical and disturbing change. As young people lose touch with the land, the food, and the rhythm of the seasons, much of what makes Italy special will disappear. But there are promising signs. Groups such as Arcigola-Slow Food, an organization founded in Piemonte that now has adherents throughout the country, came about to defend the irreplaceable virtues and traditions of cooking, eating, agriculture, and social interaction at the table. This is not a reactionary movement, but a desire to keep vital and healthy a heritage, much as some New Yorkers might organize to save landmark buildings that too often face the wrecking ball in the name of "progress." Many Italians who made money in Italy's economic boom have returned to the land. They have built farms and wineries with the intent of reclaiming and preserving the country's enogastronomic heritage.

After a brief and unbecoming flirtation with French-influenced nouvelle cuisine, Italians have acquired more self-confidence in their own cooking, thanks in part to the great amount of positive feedback that the nation receives from abroad: Italian cuisine is the most popular "ethnic" food in the world. Pizza and pasta can be found around the globe, as can many other Italian dishes. Yet nowhere does Italian cooking equal what you can find in its native country. This is because the quality and freshness of the ingredients can seldom be equaled abroad. Also, when talented chefs cook Italian food in other nations, they are often sorely tempted to adapt flavor, portion size, and the organization of meals to local tastes. So while there are many Italian restaurants in New York and other cities that turn out delicious dishes, I have never felt that the experience of eating in Italy has been reproduced outside of Italy. One thing I would like you to pay attention to is the particular way Italians eat. This is discussed in the next chapter, "Eating in Italy," and concerns the accumulated intelligence, tradition, appreciation of flavor, understanding of texture, and *abbinamento* (proper matching of flavors and textures, along with pairings of foods and wines). These are things I hope you will learn and use when you return home.

What do I love about Italy? I love its wonderful, warm, sometimes-irascible, always challenging, and often-inspired people. They give their nation vibrant life, even as they engage in polemics and watch their nation lurch from crisis to crisis. This book is a gathering of much of what makes Italy special. My intention was not merely to write a restaurant guide. Here is a book about the sensuality of Italy, expressed through its food, wine, and quality of life. More to the point, this is about living Italy, as opposed to all the guidebooks that lead you to inanimate tourist attractions and stores selling gloves and souvenirs. I want to take you to the Italy that you can see, taste, smell, touch, and hear. Music, flavors, fragrances, beautiful scenery, art, food, and people are all sources of pleasure, known in Italy as *piacere*. While the rest of the world veers to standardization, sterilization, and mass-marketing, Italy can still offer much that makes you feel alive, human, and sensual. Much of what is most unique about Italy is the pursuit of pleasure and the skill of Italians to do this.

While there are some generalizations one can make about Italians, the more you read (and the more you travel), you will discover the ways people in each town are unique. You will get to know each town we visit in this book through its culture, festivals, traditions, and special foods. For example, Parma is famous for many foods, including its Parmigiano-Reggiano cheese. We will start with a discussion of the product, visit where it is made, discover where you can buy it, where you can taste it in local cooking, and perhaps have a recipe or two that you can use to make traditional *parmense* dishes at home. This approach represents a continuum that will give you the kind of knowledge and sensation that you simply cannot acquire using a restaurant guide. As a result, every time you taste genuine Parmigiano-Reggiano (as opposed to the insipid product that is often found in gourmet stores outside of Italy) in a dish, you will have a sensory flashback to the time you spent in Parma. My sense memory is such that with a single bite or whiff of an extraordinary food or dish, I am immediately transported back to some pleasurable moment spent alone or in delightful company. This is the sort of continuum that I happily experience and hope you will develop. My approach to travel in Italy (and everywhere else, for that matter) is to be open to sensory experiences, human contact in all of its forms, and to allow myself to feel everything rather than merely fulfill a checklist of attractions I must see. This is not meant to denigrate the wonder one feels in the presence of a much-visited church or painting, or the giddy delight that comes in doing something touristy such as a ride in a gondola down a Venetian canal. I only caution against visiting a must-see attraction—Michelangelo's *David*, for example—simply because you think you are supposed to. This would rob you of the pleasure and the awe that this great human achievement can provoke.

I hope that you experience pleasure and learn some of the Italian skill in pursuing it at the table during your travels. Most restaurant guides to Italy list famous and very costly "temples of gastronomy" or eateries that offer cheap but filling tourist menus, but this book is intended to direct you to the flavors that Italians grew up with and cherish. While there are some expensive restaurants listed (particularly in big cities, where prices tend to be higher), I have made a great effort to direct you to moderately priced restaurants so that you can get more mileage out of your budget. But I have never compromised quality for price. You might find some very inexpensive places intimidating because they just don't seem like the sort you would enter. But here you will also find great food, character, and hospitality. Let go of some of your preconceived notions, and you will be rewarded with a great experience.

In most major towns I take you to a food market, that inimitably festive place that teaches you about food, customs, and life in Italy. I also list many stores where you can buy extraordinary local products and kitchen equipment. In most of Italy, much of the artisanal work you see has its roots in the kitchen. These were originally items of necessity that have evolved into objects of beauty. Whether they are gleaming copper pots, sturdy wooden spoons to stir polenta, or the wonderful ceramics, china, and glassware that one finds throughout the country, these are still essentially practical items whose design originated in functional needs. You will find listings throughout this book for interesting places in many towns to purchase these items and modern kitchen equipment that reflects the latest thinking in Italian aesthetic and industrial design. Italian handicrafts or housewares make fine gifts, reminders of your own trip, or perhaps will enable you to cook typical or unusual dishes at home.

I have also listed good bookstores in several cities. You might be lucky enough to have access to a kitchen during your stay, and, after using the recipes in this book, you might want local cookbooks that will introduce you to the recipes of a region. Bookstores also have good travel, art, and history sections, plus maps. A command of Italian is not necessary to appreciate some of these. A lot of these stores also carry books in English, German, and French.

Some of the listings in this book may seem repetitive—why, for example, would I list stores in twenty cities where you could buy an espresso maker? The answer is that you may be visiting only one of these cities on your trip.

In Italy, the mind and all the senses are always engaged. Everything there has a meaning and occupies a place that is part of a larger whole. The Italophile is a person who seeks to understand what all of this means. So being a gourmet traveler in Italy, a Garibaldi with a fork, is not only about eating in well-regarded restaurants and shopping. It is about making connections with a culture, a lifestyle, a philosophy, a people, and their fascinating history. To do that, this book also includes visits to wineries and farms that serve meals and sometimes offer lodgings. Here you can come into direct contact with people who produce the foods Italians eat. There are also many unusual museums that other books do not list. They honor particular products such as wine, pasta, salt, and olive oil, or objects such as glass, wine labels, or umbrellas. These museums are as much about the people who produce these things as about the items themselves.

There are more ways to meet the Italians. You might want to go to cooking school as part of your visit to Italy. I have listed more than forty schools in cities, on farms, in the Alps, and by the sea. Classes are given in Italian, English, or German in most places. Check before enrolling. Even if you do not speak Italian, you might find these classes interesting because they have not been adapted for foreigners, but rather are intended to teach Italians their own cuisine. You will learn a lot by observation. These classes usually cost much less than the fancier ones that are geared to foreigners. On the other hand, those classes for foreigners are usually held in gorgeous settings and take into account the particular interests and needs of the visitor.

You will read profiles of people I admire who can give you insights into their passion for food, for wine, for life. There are the bread bakers of Larino who played an important social role in the life of the town. There is the frog lady of Robbio, who catches frogs as has been done for centuries. There is the wife of the olive-oil producer who will tell you the real way oil should be used in cookery. There are countesses, opera stars, fishermen, nuns, sybarites, master ice-cream makers, and vintners all waiting to meet you.

This is my Italy and I want it to be yours. *Andiamo!*

A Few Words about this Updated Edition

As you know, life is change. Since this book was first published in 1994, it has received two revisions. I have made more than 30 additional visits to Italy, during which time chefs have come and gone, businesses have changed hands, and prices have risen. A place that once was a charming little trattoria might have put on airs and hiked the cost of a meal. In some cases, people I described in prior editions have died. You might still find them mentioned in this book as a tribute to their important contributions to Italian food culture.

The most notable change recently was the replacement of the Italian lire with the euro. The arrival of this new currency was accompanied by huge leaps in the costs of raw materials and labor. Restaurateurs have had to handle this adaptation while at the same time endeavouring to maintain quality at a manageable price. Readers of previous editions of *Italy for the Gourmet Traveler* know that I do not list prices because they would be obsolete as soon as this book goes to print. I maintain that you will be better served if I list prices as follows: inexpensive; moderately inexpensive; moderate; moderately expensive; expensive; very expensive. If you have a currency that trades favorably with the euro, such as the British pound, Swiss franc or Japanese yen, you will find prices in Italy quite agreeable. Holders of euros may find good deals in Italy compared to their own countries. Currencies such as the U.S., Canadian and Australian dollars, as well as the South African rand and the Indian rupee, may find prices somewhat higher. You will quickly discover what an inexpensive, moderate or expensive meal will cost you.

If you have comments, recommendations or updates for future editions of this book, kindly send them to fspinnyc@hotmail.com.

Eating in Italy

The reason so many people around the world profess a fondness for Italian food is that they have been able to eat a facsimile of it in their hometowns. As a result of decades of Italian migration to countries throughout Europe, North and South America, and Australia, it is possible to eat Italian food everywhere. When we think of Italian food, it is typically an adaptation of Neapolitan food—spaghetti, tomatoes, garlic, mozzarella cheese, pizza, rustic red wine—plus a few dishes from other parts of the country that have become internationalized: fettuccine Alfredo, veal Milanese, chicken cacciatore, shrimp "scampi." But these bear little resemblance to what the original dishes were.

Some people who go to Italy are actually disappointed that a dish with the same name as what they tasted at home doesn't taste like what they already know. In Roma, fettuccine Alfredo is made with egg noodles, Parmigiano-Reggiano cheese, and sweet butter, but there is no cream added. In Milano, a veal chop or cutlet is dipped in egg, then lightly breaded and gently fried in butter. It is not, as often happens in America, thickly breaded and deep-fried in oil or shortening. *Pollo alla cacciatora,* while most famous in Piemonte, is found in various regions in different guises, although there usually are mushrooms, tomatoes, and chicken among the ingredients. As for the seafood dish, "scampi" means "shrimp" in Italian, so that "shrimp scampi" means "shrimp shrimp."

So your first rule for eating in Italy is to cast aside all preconceptions and approach dining afresh. For example, portions in Italian restaurants abroad are bigger than those in Italy. For many tourists in Italy, especially those from the United States, there is the feeling of being gypped because portions do not overflow on a plate. This is because in Italy the dish might be one course in a meal that has three or four, while in the States that bowl of pasta might be the whole meal. But more on that later.

It is a misconception to think that all the Italian emigrants we meet in foreign countries came from southern Italy. It is true that natives of Campania, Abruzzo, Molise, Puglia, Basilicata, Calabria, and Sicilia left their homes in greater numbers than citizens of other regions, but there are special Italian communities throughout the world. Ligurians and Piedmontese are numerous in northern California; there is a community of Tuscans in Wisconsin; Mendoza, the wine-making center of Argentina, is full of Friulians; many residents of the valleys of Bergamo and Brescia found their way to Brazil; and there are immigrants from the Valtellina and the Trentino–Alto Adige in Australia.

Another reason that Italian food was easy to reproduce in foreign lands is that many of the basic ingredients were available to immigrants. Pasta, olive oil, wine, and certain cheeses could be imported, and most of the other raw materials existed already. How do we explain this? One of the most crucial turning points in world history was also an important factor in Italian cuisine. When a Ligurian sailor named Cristoforo Colombo (Christopher Columbus) was sent by the king and queen of Spain in search of riches in India and he wound up in the Americas, he found many foods that did not exist in Europe at that time. Imagine that there were no tomatoes, potatoes, cornmeal, sweet or hot peppers, green or other beans, zucchini, pumpkin, turkey, or chocolate on the Italian peninsula in 1491. This means no tomato sauce, no pizza as we know it, no potato gnocchi, no polenta, no Tuscan bean salad, no stuffed zucchini or peppers, no *tortelli* filled with pumpkin, no turkey with prosciutto and Parmigiano, and no exquisite chocolate from Torino! The cooking of pre-Columbian Italy was a very different proposition than what we know today. But the reason that Italian food is so outstanding is that cooks in Italy had the innate creativity and resourcefulness to take unknown ingredients and find a way to bring out their best characteristics. So the second important concept for you to understand is that the guiding principle of Italian cuisine is to honor the flavor of an ingredient by letting it shine, rather than submerging it in a combination with other ingredients and then drowning it in a sauce. While there certainly are numerous exceptions to this rule (such as the *cialzons* pasta of Friuli, which has forty ingredients), you will find wherever in Italy you go that individual flavors are so memorable because they are so palpable.

Chefs in Italy are very concerned with what is called the *materia prima*, or "basic materials." It has often been observed that even when Italy was a poor nation, the people ate better than wealthier Germans, Americans, and even most Frenchmen. This is because the *materia prima* was so good that the taste of the final product had to be special. Many Italians, despite ever-busier lives, still go to market most every day to buy the freshest ingredients available. And their knowledge of terrain and geography far exceeds that of most other peoples. So they will look for potatoes from Avezzano (Abruzzo), onions from Tropea (Calabria), peppers from Cuneo (Piemonte), cherries from Marostica (Veneto) or Vignola (Emilia-Romagna), mozzarella from Benevento (Campania), lentils from Castelluccio (Umbria), peas from Lazio, oranges from Sicilia, and so forth. It is not that these shoppers are vulnerable to marketing and publicity, but rather that they understand that soil and climatic conditions do affect the flavor of a product. So the air that cures the prosciutto of Langhirano (Emilia-Romagna) is different from that which cures the ham of San Daniele (Friuli) or Carpegna (Marche). The soil in which the artichokes of Liguria grow is different from the terrain that yields those from Lazio. Lesson number three is that you must follow the rules of the season, the marketplace, and the region you are in. Become a culinary geographer, develop an acquaintance with Italian food products and the places they come from, and you will better know what to eat where and when. As a general assumption, if you go to a local market and there is a lot of a good-looking food being sold—asparagus, let's say—it would be wise to order asparagus when you go to a restaurant for a meal.

In the early 1980s, when I was writing *The Authentic Pasta Book*, my editor and I decided that the best way to introduce readers to the many different cuisines of Italy was to arrange my book into regional chapters. At that time, most Americans recognized only the names "Toscana" and "Sicilia," and maybe "Sardegna." The regions of Lazio, Campania, Friuli, Liguria, and Molise were unknown. The first time I mentioned that I was in love with Emilia-Romagna, it was assumed that this was the name of my girlfriend.

Things have changed. My book and others by Italy-loving colleagues have now taught readers that Italy is a republic in name only; rather, it is an agglomeration of ancient duchies, city-states, fiefdoms, and colonies with more than a hundred dialects and native cuisines. Parma and Reggio Emilia have been fighting for centuries over who makes the better cheese, the one we know today as Parmigiano-Reggiano (usually shortened to "Parmigiano" or "Parmesan"). Wherever you go, you will find there is great pride in local ingredients or products with ancient lineage. In my view, there is seldom a "best" in anything; it is more of a pleasure traveling about and learning the differences for myself. Similarly, I think by now it is counterproductive to look for something "authentic" when searching for flavors or preparations of food. Food is a living, evolving thing, and the notion of what is classic is a very subjective one. So I would rather point you to specific and distinctive things that I have discovered and hope that you will appreciate them on their own terms rather than comparing them with a long-lost ideal that may not relate to how Italians eat now anyway.

As you journey in Italy, you will see evidence of the challenges the country faces in supplying its kitchens. It is 75 percent mountainous, which means that every meter of arable land has to be cultivated. In Liguria, for example, perched above the sea are precarious terraces of planted ground that must be climbed with great effort. Italy has thousands of kilometers of shoreline, yet the Mediterranean is overfished and polluted, so seafood must now come from farther away to reach Italian tables. Restaurateurs are required to indicate on the menu that a product was frozen (*surgelato*) when purchased, so that the consumer can make an educated decision. You see, the state in which an ingredient arrives in a restaurant kitchen is of much greater interest to Italians than to most other peoples.

Aside from markets and waterfronts, one of the best ways to learn about Italian food is to visit the farms where it is grown. Throughout this book there are indications for farms that sell their products, serve meals, and sometimes offer lodging. This comes under the general heading "Agritourism," and in practically every chapter you will find the name and address of the regional office that can send you listings of farms that might receive you in the places you are heading. They are seldom fancy (except for certain wineries), but the welcome will be genuine, and prices are usually very convenient.

Dining Out

There are many ways to eat in Italy, from the most simple to the most formal. Each mode is agreeable and is sure to provide pleasures. Although I have wandered into many good meals in Italy, it is smart to make a reservation *(una prenotazione)* if at all possible. This assures that the restaurant will be open when you plan to dine. It also means that the restaurant is looking forward to receiving you and giving you the best possible service. It often happens that people travel all the way to a restaurant in a small town only to find that there is not a table to be had.

Credit cards have gained increasing acceptance in Italy, but there are still many places that do not accept them. For almost every eating place I have included in this book you will find listings of which cards are accepted.

Almost every restaurant in Italy closes for a day or a day and half each week. A blue-and-red sign is usually displayed that says *Chiuso per turno* and indicates the closed day. You will find these closed days indicated in practically every listing in the book. A disproportionate number of places close on Sunday or Monday, so I have tried where possible to give you alternate choices for those days. If you see *Chiuso per ferie*, it means that the restaurant is closed for vacation. In big cities this will usually be July or August. In resort areas this will be during low season. For example, many alpine places are closed in November. If you see *Chiuso per lutto* on a black-bordered sign, this means that a restaurant is closed because of a death in the family. These three signs also appear in store windows as applicable.

My idea of what makes a good restaurant is that you feel that the food has been cooked for *you.* All other considerations are secondary to this essential tenet. Let us begin with the fanciest eating places and work toward the simplest. *Il ristorante* (literally, "the place at which one is restored") is the top of the line. *Ristoranti* in major cities can be very expensive, although some are moderate in price. The menu will reflect the particular talents of a chef or the foods of the region you are in. Major cities have restaurants where you can sample foods of another region In Milano, for example, there are restaurants I often dine in that have the food of Trentino, Piemonte, Toscana, Puglia, Sicilia, and Sardegna. In the phone book they will be listed as being of a region, such as "Ristorante Sardo." In almost every Italian city of any size there is now a Chinese restaurant, more often than not called La Grande Muraglia (the Great Wall), but you have not traveled all the way to Italy to eat Chinese food. Roma and Milano have a few restaurants representing the cuisines of other nations, but not nearly to the extent that New York, Toronto, London, or even Paris do.

In France a restaurant aspires to be a temple of gastronomy, in which elegant waiters serve elaborately conceived and prepared dishes in very formal settings. The Italian counterpart is generally less ambitious. Decor will be pleasing, but seldom elaborate. Only classic restaurants such as Il Cambio in Torino have stunning decor. Service will typically be gracious and attentive, though not stiff. When Italian waiters attempt to imitate their more arch German or French counterparts, they usually look foolish doing it. Being a waiter in Italy is a respected profession, done with dignity, professionalism, and pride. It is expected that you will treat waiters with respect, rather than as servile people. You should refer to a waiter as "Signore" when you speak to him (not *cameriere* [waiter] as many travel books advise). In return, you will receive a level of genuine interest and care that is unmatched in most countries. It is rare that one finds a waitress in formal restaurants, but if you do she is "Signorina" if she is a young woman and "Signora" if she is somewhat older or has a wedding ring on her finger.

In a *ristorante* there will usually be a printed menu and wine list with prices indicated. Sometimes restaurants will give a menu with prices to the person who made the reservation and menus without prices to the guests. Next to certain dishes, especially fish, seafood, Florentine steak, and preparations with truffles, there will not be a price, but rather the letters *s.q.*, which mean *secondo quantità*, (according to the amount consumed), or *p.v.*, or *prezzo da vedere* (price to be determined). Other restaurants will indicate the amount per *etto* (100 grams, or 3½ ounces). So in Alghero, in Sardegna, where the local specialty is lobster, the price might be, for example, 20,000 lire for 100 grams of lobster. In a restaurant you might be shown a fish, a steak, or perhaps a truffle before deciding to order it. But when there is no price indicated, you can ask "Quanto costerebbe, più o meno?" ("How much would it cost, more or less?") and you will have an answer. It is better to do this before ordering than after you have eaten. Almost all restaurants are honest in their pricing when the bill comes, and the few I have encountered that are dishonest I have challenged. In Italy, the fear of *brutta figura* (looking bad) will usually shame someone into rectifying the problem. But the same applies to the diner. Rudeness, crass behavior, or being unusually demanding is also viewed as *brutta figura,* and while the offending persons will probably not be asked to leave a restaurant, they will not be welcome back either. Remember, dining is not only about nourishment, but about enjoyable interchange with restaurateurs and with one's dining companions.

There is an expression, *A tavola non si invecchia* (At the table one does not age), that speaks to the notion of the good feelings that come with dining, whether at home or in any sort of eatery. Italians, unlike Americans, do not adopt special restaurant manners, but instead approach a restaurant meal as a source of pleasure and sociable relaxation. They are dining, not dining out. One of the joys of eating in Italy is to observe the behavior of diners nearby. Each *mise-en-table* seems to be a small drama, whether tragic or comic. I delight in watching four generations of a family carry on precisely as they would at home. Small children are doted upon and given relatively free rein in terms of self-expression. Elderly relatives are closely watched to see that they are eating as they should. Everyone plays and laughs, with an occasional outburst of anger.

It is also common in Italy for male friends to go out for dinner as a group while their wives and girlfriends stay home. This is a legacy of the days when Italian women did not go out unaccompanied. One thinks of Fellini's *I Vitelloni* (1953), in which Alberto Sordi seems to be on a continuous night out with the boys. While his modern contemporaries are less randy, the tradition of men going out for a good meal endures.

The trattoria is generally a notch below the *ristorante* in price, but the food is often just as good, if not better. A *ristorante* may have certain fancy ingredients, such as truffles and lobster, but otherwise many preparations in a trattoria might be similar to those in a *ristorante*. Most trattorias are family-run and have a casual and welcoming spirit about them. One family member will run the kitchen while the other supervises the dining room. Children, grandparents, aunts, and uncles all help out in one way or another. Frequently the diners in a trattoria are neighborhood regulars who know the owners and enjoy the food and the special reception they receive going somewhere familiar. But you will almost always find the same welcome if you are a first-time diner. As I have mentioned elsewhere, Italians are among the warmest, most genuinely hospitable people anywhere. In the north and center, you will always receive a friendly and gracious reception. In the south, a visitor is treated with utmost respect. Southerners believe it is an honor to receive a guest, and you might be startled (and maybe feel a bit ill at ease) at the lengths that are gone to for making you feel welcome.

Roman trattorias are in a class by themselves. The food is earthy, the gentle white wine flows, the walls are invariably decorated with paintings of greater or lesser quality, and you usually feel as if you are in a family's dining room with friends and neighbors dropping in all night. You will probably get in a conversation with people at another table, who will pour you some wine and perhaps invite you for coffee or a *gelato* (ice cream) somewhere. It is almost impossible not to make a friend when you dine in a Roman trattoria, except, of course, if you eat in the many that cater primarily to tourists.

You can usually spot a tourist restaurant or trattoria because a standard multilingual menu will be posted outside that is identical to that of restaurants all over town. This is particularly egregious in Firenze, which probably has the lowest-quality meals in *ristoranti* and *trattorie* of any city in Italy. This is because the city has become so beholden to tourism and most of its eateries compete for that trade. Most menus offer the same items, which are often prepared indifferently for an undiscriminating public. Florentines have their secret haunts where they eat excellent local dishes, and these are the places I recommend. In a tourist restaurant there will usually be a *menu turistico*, which is a set meal of the most mundane dishes—spaghetti with tomato sauce, breaded veal cutlet, green salad, and fruit salad. The preparation may be good, but why travel around Italy eating these same dishes in every town? One thing that frequent travelers in Italy like to do is look for unintentionally funny translations, such as "pig chop" *(braciola di maiale)* or "bowel soup" *(zuppa di trippa)*!

You might encounter a *menu a prezzo fisso*. This is like the French *prix fixe*, in which the chef will select daily specials and create a set-price menu at

Cuneo, Piemonte

a slightly promotional price. This is a good option if the dishes appeal to you. Bear in mind that in tourist areas some trattorias post a *menu a prezzo fisso* that is actually a *menu turistico* in disguise. On all menus you should look for the words *compreso, incluso,* and *escluso*. The first two suggest inclusion, the third implies exclusion. Also, something *escluso* might be *non compreso*. Excluded items might be beverages *(bevande* or *bibite)* or *servizio e coperto*. *Servizio* usually implies the money that will go to the waiter, and it usually is about 10 to 12 percent of the bill. Unlike waiters in countries where the main part of their income is derived from tips (and where they are often forced to grovel or behave insincerely), waiters in Italy receive a salary that is filled out by the *servizio* that is included in your check. Therefore, the kind treatment you usually receive is sincere and not driven by the need to be tipped. You do not need to leave an additional tip *(una mancia)*, but if the service has been good, it is customary to leave two or three thousand lire on the table. *Il coperto* is a dicier and more archaic concept. This is a charge levied by the restaurant for the cost of the bread and the clean tablecloth. We all know that by now these costs should be included in the price of a meal, but it is a convenient way for a restaurant to glean a few extra lire. Since very few restaurants have yet moved to change this, it is something people still pay because they do not want to *fare una brutta figura* and complain. In most restaurants and trattorias the *coperto* is just small enough not to merit a complaint, but it is still an annoyance. I usually remind American visitors to Italy that the price you pay on a menu, plus *servizio e coperto,* is all you pay. There is no tax (which is included in the price), and you are not put in the position of determining how much to tip.

In many trattorias and *osterie* (described below), a menu only appears if a diner asks for it. In some places, there may be no printed menu at all. The waiter or proprietor simply recites the day's offerings, which are typically based on the cook's mood and the morning market. This, I believe, is a positive thing: I would rather have an inspired chef using the freshest ingredients than one who may be tiring of making the same old standbys. Regular patrons of a trattoria know more or less what things will cost, but this is awkward for a tourist who may not. In general, you should dine in places where a menu is posted, unless money is no object.

The issue of prices is important in deciding where to eat. Italians talk about *il rapporto qualità/prezzo,* which suggests what value you are getting for your money. Because the structure of a meal in Italy is different than that in countries where diners usually order one dish large enough to make a meal, it makes no sense to compare prices from one country to another. Prices change everywhere (although they seldom go down), so I have chosen instead to list price categories with each dining place I recommend to you. Because this book will be read by anyone who knows English, the idea of "expensive" varies. Someone from Stockholm or London might consider dining in Italy a bargain, while a native of Chicago or Sydney would think otherwise. So I created my price terminology based on the idea of Italian food value for Italian money, and if your currency is trading well against the lira, you can judge accordingly. Middle-class travelers will probably want to dine at restaurants that have the word "moderate" in the price category. The categories, which are self-explanatory, are "inexpensive," "moderately inexpensive," "moderate," "moderately expensive," "expensive," and "very expensive." The range of eating places in this book extends from private homes and farms to the most expensive restaurant in Venezia. There are some expensive restaurants that are very much worth the price, and I have indicated this in listings when a restaurant is quite special. Conversely, if I have indicated that a restaurant is inexpensive, this does not mean the food is bad. My standards are very exacting, so an inexpensive restaurant will have flavorful, carefully prepared food at very low prices.

An *osteria* (sometimes called *locanda*) is often the best place to get good value for your money (but be careful not to go into one of those expensive restaurants that call themselves *osterie* in an effort to be casually chic). The *osterie* I have recommended are the real thing. The original purpose of an *osteria* was to serve wine and appropriate food to go with it. This being Italy, the food is usually very good. It might be a soup or a simple pasta dish followed by roasted meat or poultry, or slices of excellent cold cuts *(salumi)* and cheese.

In an *osteria* you often sit at tables with other people and invariably become fast friends. One of my wishes for the readers of this book is that they have frequent contact with the sort of everyday Italians that tourists seldom meet. I have made friendships with so many Italians I dearly love (and whom I know love me) and have had many more experiences in which I have a brief and pleasurable encounter with someone and then we each go on our way, gratified with the knowledge that there is yet another nice person in the world. This may sound trite, but one of Italy's great virtues is the way its people relish human contact. When you shop in a food store, pay a bill at a bar, or sit next to someone on a bus, there is a moment of contact that is made sweet by the tendency of most Italians to want that moment to be a nice one. So this book is not merely the memory of wonderful meals but of happy encounters that I know you will have too. You do not need to speak Italian for these encounters to be meaningful. A smile, a *buon giorno,* a *grazie,* are all you need. Italians are grateful when you attempt to communicate in their language and will never be critical of any errors you might make. If you attempt to learn some of the language before your trip, you will be handsomely rewarded for your effort.

A more urban version of the *osteria* is the *enoteca.* This word has several meanings, but you will be able to determine what kind of place you are entering with a quick glance. An *enoteca* might be a wine bar where light food is served. If I do not want a full meal, I often stop in an *enoteca* for a glass of wine and *spuntini* (light snacks). Such wine bars are indicated in listings throughout this book. An *enoteca* might also be a shop that sells bottles of wine. A third type of *enoteca* is usually operated by a consortium of wine producers and showcases their particular product. (For example, the *enoteca* in Barbaresco, in Piemonte, is the place to taste the wine that goes by that name.) An *enoteca pubblica* or *enoteca regionale* (such as that in Dozza in Emilia-Romagna) showcases the wines of a zone or region. You can read more about *enoteche* in the following chapter, which is dedicated to Italian wine.

Another place to have good food at modest prices is to eat at a farm or an *agriturismo.* In the Trentino and Alto Adige these are known as a *maso.* The selection is often limited, but the food can't be fresher, and you have the occasion to dine in someone's home. There are a few of these (such as the Maso Cantanghel in Civezzano in the Trentino) that have become quite fancy and have fabulous food that ranks with the best of the region.

At some point in your visit to Italy you should eat at a pizzeria. This is not a place to stand up and eat a slice with a soft drink, but rather where you would come in the evening (Italians never have pizza during the day) and have an individually baked pie made to order with the ingredients you select. The pie is big enough for one person and, with a beer or mineral water (not wine), you have a filling and inexpensive meal. In Napoli, where pizza was born and still is better than anywhere else, pizzas are traditionally baked in a wood-burning oven *(forno a legna)* and topped only with fresh tomatoes, mozzarella cheese, a few drops of olive oil, and a basil leaf. This is called a *pizza Margherita* and is hard to beat. Other typical pizzas are *alla marinara* (tomatoes, garlic, anchovies), *alla napoletana* (tomatoes, garlic, oregano), *alle quattro stagioni* ("four seasons," mozzarella, tomatoes, and usually one-quarter each of ham, mushrooms, and olives), *prosciutto e funghi* (ham and mushrooms), *salsiccia* (sausage), *ai frutti di mare* (with seafood), and

Social interaction is part of market life in Siracusa and all over Italy

capricciosa, which means the pizza is made at the whim of the *pizzaiolo* (pizza maker). I always ask what the caprice might be, in part because I've had some rather funky pizzas, such as one in Trentino with papaya, bananas, and pineapple.

In recent years, pizzerias have begun to supplant the traditional trattorias by preparing a small menu of pasta and other standard dishes. In general, they slightly undercut the price of the trattoria, but also are less demanding about quality. The food is usually acceptable to tasty, but not special. This development is cause for alarm, because the trattoria fills a crucial gastronomic and social role in Italian life, and once it disappears it will not return. So my advice is to go to a pizzeria for pizza and a trattoria for other food.

In Liguria and in some coastal cities in other regions you may see a *friggitoria* (fry shop) that serves local specialties. While not exactly a fast-food restaurant, the *friggitoria* is a place to taste strictly local dishes while standing up or walking down the street. Many people in Liguria buy food at a fry shop that they take home and have with vegetables and other dishes. More common than the *friggitoria* are the *rosticceria* (literally, "roasting place") and the *tavola calda* (hot table). The *rosticceria* dates from a time when not everyone had the proper facilities at home to do roasting and is more common in central and southern Italy. The *rosticceria* is a great place to buy a roast chicken or something more exotic, such as duck, goose, or rabbit. It also sells roasted potatoes and sautéed greens, such as spinach and escarole. I have had countless great meals that were purchased at a *rosticceria* and washed down with some good local wine. The *tavola calda* is not an American-style cafeteria. It is more like a kitchen from which you can purchase prepared foods such as baked pasta, risotto, baked or roasted meats, and vegetables that can be casually eaten standing up, at a table, or taken out. There is no waiter service. The *tavola calda,* like the *rosticceria,* is an institution that is disappearing as fast-food chains make inroads in Italy, which is a shame.

Another vanishing institution is the *mensa.* This is usually more cafeteria style and is connected to a university or a place of work. Railway workers have a *mensa* near most major train stations, and large factories have *mense* as well. A *mensa* is almost always subsidized, so prices for nourishing, though unastonishing, meals are amazingly cheap, even now. Usually you need a *tessera* (identification card or monthly pass) to dine at a *mensa,* but there are occasional exceptions, especially at universities.

In big cities, especially Milano, you can have a decent lunch at a *paninoteca,* or "sandwich shop." It used to be that all Italians took at least two, and often three, hours for the afternoon meal. They would eat and then rest before returning to work. This tradition was originally rural and dictated by the fact that the heat was at its most intense in the afternoon. In most cities, the lunchtime is still at least ninety minutes, but the workaholic *milanesi* often take thirty minutes before returning to their offices. The *paninoteca* usually has sandwiches made of the best meats, fish, vegetables, and cheeses and is better than you would expect. The *panini* (sandwiches) are often premade, and you just point to what you want. I always ask for mine to be made on the spot, especially in places where mayonnaise has been squirted from a tube onto sandwiches that were made two hours before.

Bars and caffès will become some of your favorite places during your stay. An Italian bar has nothing in common with bars in Dublin or Hamburg or San Francisco. An Italian bar is the place where you can go for a breakfast of a cappuccino and a fresh brioche or *cornetto* (croissant), the two most typical breakfast rolls. Italians usually don't drink cappuccino after ten in the morning, preferring to have *un caffè* (an espresso).

In a 1994 study done in Germany, France, Britain, Spain, and Italy to determine how citizens of these countries spend their leisure time, Italians placed highest in two categories. One was having sex, which 83 percent reported they like to do as often as possible. Italians were also far and away the most avid coffee drinkers. They placed second, just behind the French, in wanting to spend time with their families. They ranked with the other Europeans in terms of smoking, watching movies and videos, and dining out. They devote somewhat less time to drinking tea and reading books. Based on my experience, Italians spend even more time drinking coffee than having sex. There is the breakfast coffee, the social coffees throughout the day, the one that follows lunch, and perhaps one after supper. As a people, Italians are animated, but they are not necessarily hypercaffeinated. The jolt that comes in an espresso is a lot milder than that which you get from a big cup of American coffee. Also, the idea of "the bottomless cup" does not exist in Italy, so Italians actually consume much less caffeine than Americans.

When an Italian offers you a coffee, it is a gesture of graciousness and friendship to the visitor or the friend. You get into a brief quarrel over who pays, and then you politely lose and say *grazie*. If you want to extend the gesture, you simply say, "*Offro un caffè*." The offer of a coffee is not necessarily a pretext to something else, but is simply another one of those Italian moments of human contact lived to the fullest.

Bars also sell thin sandwiches called toasts, which are two slices of crustless white bread that enclose one slice of ham and one slice of cheese and are heated. To me, a toast is useful for staving off hunger if I wind up missing lunch, but I would never go out of my way to eat one. Many bars also have *tramezzini*, thin triangular sandwiches that might have tuna, mozzarella and tomatoes, or vegetables and boiled eggs as a filling. If there is a *paninoteca* around, its offerings are usually preferable to bar sandwiches. If a bar is called a *bar-pasticceria*, this is a bakery that also sells coffee and tea. There are many of these listed in this book, and I don't regret the research one bit. A *caffè* is usually a bar with tables and waiter service, for which you will pay a higher price. *Caffès*, such as those of Torino and Trieste, are often fancy and very beautiful, and you can linger at your table for as long as you wish. There are many places that call themselves bars that have table service, too.

There is a particular method to going to the bar. You enter, look around for what you might want to consume, and then go to the cashier *(la cassa)* and recite your choices. Behind the cashier will be a list with two sets of prices: *al banco* (standing at the bar) or *al tavolo* (seated). Unless you really plan to stop for a while and watch the world go by, it makes more sense to have your drink at the bar. After your order is rung up, you pay for it and receive the receipt *(lo scontrino)*. You take the receipt to the bartender and tell him what you want. It is customary to place a one-hundred- or two-hundred-lire coin on the bar as you place your order. In the past, the bartender would tear your receipt and take it away. Now there is a law that *you must take the receipt with you as you leave*. This system intends to create fiscal responsibility, but has been overdone. A sixteen-year-old boy in southern Italy forgot to take his receipt for an orange juice and was slapped with a hefty fine. Many Italians were outraged that such infractions were being punished while government ministers were stealing millions from state coffers.

In addition to coffee, you can get tea, tisanes (herbal infusions), chamomile tea (thought to promote sleepiness), milk, beer, *cioccolata calda* (thick hot chocolate), mineral water (which you can purchase by the bottle to take away), bottled juices (apricot, peach, and pear), or freshly squeezed *spremuta* (orange, grapefruit, or lemon juice). Wine is available by the glass, and it is common to meet at a bar in the early evening during the *passeggiata* (promenade or walk) and have a wine or an *aperitivo,* accompanied by little salted crackers (which are seldom good) or by the delicious snacks and canapés that better bars serve. Among the popular cocktail-hour drinks are Campari, vermouths by Cinzano, Riccadonna and Martini, and Punt e Mes. Stronger drinks include grappa, as well as imported Scotch, gin, and whiskey. Italians seldom have the strong stuff, and those bottles often languish on shelves for months. Whether you buy liquor or soft drinks ("Coca-Cola" is *una Coca*), you will probably not see ice unless you ask for it *(Vorrei un po di ghiaccio, per favore)*. Italians think ice would dilute the flavor of drinks, while Americans like the burning cold of cubes in their mouths. Some bars also sell ice cream, but I prefer to have my gelato in a *gelateria*.

The coffee boom in the United States does Italian coffee a disservice. Coffee beans do not benefit by being flavored with nut oils, berries, or mint. There are very few places in America that make good espresso or cappuccino, although Italian coffee giants such as Lavazza and Illy have led educational campaigns in the United States that have had some good results. A good espresso should fill a demitasse cup only halfway. It should be freshly brewed with very hot water and beans that have just been ground. Usually a well-made espresso (which Italians call *un caffè*) will have a *crema*, a slight orange-brown foam on top. If you want a

Giusti, in Modena, Emilia-Romagna, is one of Italy's top food stores

more intense coffee, this does not require more coffee; rather, you use less water. This is called a *caffè ristretto*. Conversely, if you want it less intense, you ask for a *caffè lungo*. This has more water, but the amount of coffee used is always the same.

When many Italians receive their *caffè*, they reflexively add sugar, even though excellent coffee is spoiled if something is added to it. In the past, coffee would be sugared to camouflage less-than-perfect quality. Coffee consumed without sugar is called *amaro* (bitter), which is a misnomer. The best coffee has a naturally sweet flavor. Do not expect a lemon peel with your coffee. This is a practice in America left from the days when poor Italian immigrants could not afford good coffee, so they had to improve the flavor of their drink by infusing it with lemon. You should try to develop taste buds in Italy that respond to unadulterated coffee.

There are other coffee drinks in Italy, although fewer than in America. A *cappuccino* (meaning "little hood") is an espresso in a large cup that has a hood of foamed milk on top of it. Many Italians ask for *un cappuccio*, instead of using the diminutive. Despite what you might think, a cappuccino does not have whipped cream, except in Trieste, where a little dollop is sometimes added. A *cappuccino triestino*, with or without the whipped cream, is foamed milk atop an espresso in a demitasse cup. A *caffè latte* is like what the French call café au lait. This is coffee, sometimes "lengthened" with hot water, to which heated milk is added. Unlike a cappuccino, the coffee and milk in a *caffè latte* are blended. The flavor combination of coffee and milk is about fifty-fifty. A *caffè freddo* is a glass of chilled espresso. In the summer, in Roma and farther south, you can get a *caffè latte freddo*, which is cold coffee (often sugared) to which cold milk is added. It is refreshing and delicious, but somehow its appeal has not spread north. In Milano, they make it in a shaker with hot espresso, cold milk, and ice, and it is a failure. A *caffè macchiato* (stained coffee) is an espresso stained with a little milk. Conversely, a *latte macchiato* is a glass of milk to which a little coffee has been added. A *caffè corretto* (corrected coffee) is an espresso to which a shot of grappa or other strong alcohol has been added. If you want any of these drinks decaffeinated, add the word *decaffeinato* to your order, such as *un cappuccino decaffeinato*. The typical request for a decaffeinated espresso is *Caffè Hag* (pronounced Kah-Fay Ogg), which is always served in an orange cup. Finally, there is *caffè d'orzo*, which is a beverage made of toasted barley that supposedly approximates the flavor of real coffee. If you believe that, I have a leaning tower in Pisa I would like to sell you.

Food Shopping

If you have not found enough food in all the places I have mentioned above, you can go food shopping instead. Stay away from supermarkets, which are profoundly uninteresting. Opt instead for specialties shops, where the owners carefully select or produce their wares and sell them with great pride. Here is a list:

Alimentari. An all-purpose food store that sells some bread, milk, cheese, cold cuts, and perhaps a little fruit and some vegetables. Sort of the equivalent of the corner grocery. Certain bigger *alimentari* have a substantial selection.

Bottiglieria. A store in which to buy wine, mineral water, beer, juices, and other bottles.

Caseificio. A cheese producer.

Confetteria. A confectionary shop, with candies and *confetti* (special almond candies often used at weddings and other special occasions).

Drogheria. A dry-goods store that is often great fun. There are coffees, teas, cookies, cereals, flours, candies, seeds, detergent, soaps, and all kinds of other things of interest that will tell you about the tastes and preferences of the town you are visiting.

Enoteca. This is a store that sells wines by the bottle. Sometimes, it is a wine bar that also sells light food.

Erboristeria. An herb shop. A particularly Italian institution that sells herb-based products such as teas, soaps, herb oils for cooking or medicinal purposes. Many *erboristerie* will concoct special combinations to respond to medical conditions you might have. The best *erboristeria* I know is in Ravenna, but there are many good ones throughout Italy.

Frutta e Verdura. Fruit and vegetable seller.

Gastronomia. A fancy food shop, often with elegant prepared foods. You can buy them and feast on flavors at a fraction of the price you would pay in a restaurant for a similar dish.

Gelateria. An ice-cream parlor.

Latteria. A dairy shop, selling fresh milk, cheeses, and butter.

Macelleria. A butcher shop, often also selling cold cuts. You will notice that many Italian butcher shops sell canned food for dogs and cats. This is a legacy of the time when people bought scraps to feed their pets. When industrial pet food was introduced to Italy, it fell to butcher shops to continue the tradition of selling it.

Panetteria (or *Panificio*). A bread baker that sometimes sells plain cakes and cookies *(biscotti)* as well. In general, the standard bread of a town (such as *pane toscano* in Firenze) is sold at an artificially low price to make it affordable to everyone. Specialty breads are not price fixed, so prices float to what the market will bear.

Pasticceria. A bakery for cakes and cookies. Some also have a coffee bar.

Pastificio. A pasta shop, usually featuring fresh pasta *(pasta fresca)*.

Pescheria. A fish seller. A *mercato ittico* is a fish market.

Pizza a Taglio. Some shops sell squares of pizza by the slice. This is a form of fast food, but once you taste fresh, oven-baked pizza, pizza by the slice will be a disappointment.

Pizzicheria. Similar to an *alimentari*.

Polleria. A poultry store for chicken, turkey, pheasant, duck, quail, goose, and sometimes rabbit.

Salumeria (or *Salsamentaria*). The place to buy *salumi* (cold cuts). These include salami, prosciutto, and mortadella, and usually some cheeses, too.

Salumificio. A producer of salami and sausages.

Tabaccaio (or *Tabaccheria*). Technically, this is a tobacconist, but it is a store you should know even if you don't smoke. It is government regulated, and many of the items sold are taxable. In a nation where many citzens, from the prime minister on down, have been known to underpay their taxes, the *tabaccaio* is a revenue producer. Aside from cigarettes, salt is sold here, and the profit goes to a government monopoly. Nontaxed items include postage stamps (it is faster to buy them here than in long, slow post-office lines), postcards, stationery, and candy bars. You can always recognize a *tabaccaio* because a black sign with a large white T hangs above the portal.

Torrefazione. A coffee roaster. You can buy freshly roasted coffee beans here. You should not grind them unless you plan to use all of the coffee very soon. It is always preferable to have a coffee grinder at home and only grind beans as you need them.

Vini e Olii. This is an old-fashioned store that sells wine and olive oil.

IL MERCATO

Whatever you do, always seek out the market in a city, even if there is nothing you intend to buy. There is little to compare with the festive animation of sellers hawking their wares, flirting with and cajoling potential shoppers. This is where people meet to exchange news and information about children, parents, spouses, friends, and lovers. Markets are where Italians cement their sense of community that comes through interaction and through the attachment to food that summons thoughts of meals past and those yet to be had.

When you see the market, you have a sense of how people in this place eat. The more you visit, the more differences you will detect. For example, at the San Benedetto market in Cagliari in Sardegna, notice how much meat is sold in comparison with all of the fruits and vegetables in the market of San Remo in Liguria. A general observation is that you will see food in a more natural state than you are used to. Dead animals hang from hooks with their fur and feathers still on. Butchers will, if asked, clean and trim meat, poultry, and game. Dirt will often be attached to the roots of certain vegetables. You will be amazed at the artistry with which many food sellers arrange and display their products. This is yet another example of the importance Italians give to aesthetics in a way that few other peoples do.

Some cities, such as Bologna, Genova, Firenze, and Padova, have old indoor markets where citizens enjoy gathering. Other places, such as Asti, Bozen, Trento, Modena, and Palermo, have outdoor markets on piazzas and streets that are just as beguiling. If you live in a place for a few days, you will start to know some of the vendors. Before long, they will be adding that extra piece of fruit to your bag in gratitude for your patronage and in an effort to maintain it. These are the people who educated me about the proper handling and use of ingredients, and many of the recipes I've learned first came to me in the market. Despite what you may have heard, bargaining for food is discouraged. Prices are set and posted. If you don't like them, go to another stand.

In most cities there is a clothing and housewares market that comes to town once a week, and this day is even more animated than the others. This is a good place to pick up gloves, sweaters, umbrellas, coffee makers, and all the wonderful little gadgets that are so useful in Italian kitchens.

È l'ora di mangiare (it's time to eat).

The Italian Meal

LA PRIMA COLAZIONE (BREAKFAST)

Breakfast is a light meal of cappuccino, a roll, and perhaps fruit juice. These are invariably better at a bar, and even if a hotel serves breakfast, I tend to go to a bar instead. In most cases hotels now offer sliced ham, salami, plain cheese, and yogurt along with mediocre coffee, stale rolls, and very sour juice. This is not a happy way to start the day. I sometimes make a sandwich of the cold cuts and cheese and pack it for a snack during a day of touring. And then I breakfast at a bar or *pasticceria*.

PRANZO OR COLAZIONE (LUNCH)
AND CENA (SUPPER OR DINNER)

Before we discuss what to eat for lunch and dinner, it is important that you understand *when* to eat. Once upon a time, a traveler had to plan very carefully to be near a place to eat at the time when meals were being served. If that moment was missed, there was not much to choose from except a small sandwich at a bar and perhaps an ice cream. Things have changed somewhat, but if you want to eat a real Italian meal (as opposed to fast food), some planning is still required. As a general rule, the afternoon and evening meals start and end earlier in the north and commence and finish progressively later the farther south you travel. So your lunch in Bozen might be served at 12h, while in Siracusa it may not come until 14:30h.

Lunch used to be the principal meal of the day. This was determined by agricultural hours: a farmer would rise at dawn to milk cows, collect eggs, and so on. He would work in the fields all morning and develop quite an appetite. His lunch would be substantial, filling him up and, with wine, making him drowsy. An afternoon nap (and perhaps more) would follow. As the heat of the sun diminished later in the day, he would return to his labors, do the evening milking, and work until there was no more light. The urban equivalent of this was that a substantial meal would be had either at home or at a trattoria or *mensa*. This would be followed by a nap or a stroll before returning to work. In general, lunch in the north would begin as early as 12h or 12:30h, and the return to work would happen sometime between 14h and 15h. In the center and south, the closing time might be later, and the return to work might not happen until 16h or 17h.

Dinner (or supper) used to be a lighter meal than the one at midday. It might include soup followed by vegetables and sliced meat or cheese. Alternatively, people would have a pizza. I always believed that this was one of the reasons that Italians, despite all the wonderful food available to them, tended to be quite trim. They went to bed with stomachs that were not stuffed and therefore did not store calories as they slept. When I lived in Bologna in the 1970s, I had a regime of a light breakfast, substantial lunch, light supper, and I was never more fit.

But the type of dining I have just depicted was only one aspect of eating in Italy in the past. Poverty once meant that in poor areas throughout the country a single grain-based course would be eaten to fill up on. In the center and south it was pasta; in the north it was rice or polenta. These would be flavored with vegetables, inexpensive fish, or bits of meat and gravy. In parts of the south, this style of eating persists to this day. Read more about this in the chapter about Molise.

The traditional meal for those who were more *benestante* (well off) consisted of a *primo* (soup, pasta, or rice), a *secondo* (a protein, such as meat or fish), a *contorno* (a salad or vegetable side dish), and then a *dolce* (dessert, almost always fruit). The portions for all of these are relatively small, so that at the end of the meal the diner feels satisfied, but not stuffed. The *primo-secondo-contorno-fruit* became the standard meal in the postwar era as affluence arrived in most of the nation. A meal always ends with a cup of espresso, which serves as the final punctuation mark and leaves a pleasant flavor in the mouth.

A larger meal might start with an *antipasto* (appetizer) before the *primo* and *formaggio* (cheese) before the dessert. Of course, there are regional variations in this practice. *Antipasti* are more common in Piemonte and Puglia, while the cheese course is typical in a meal served in Lombardia or Sardegna. A strong alcoholic drink (grappa, *amaro*, or *digestivo*) might be offered after the coffee.

Nowadays three significant phenomena have affected the traditional *primo-secondo-contorno-fruit* meal. First, the lunch period has shrunk, particularly in many northern cities, as the workdays have lengthened. Quicker meals are consumed at or near the office rather than at home. As part of this, less wine is now consumed during the day, and that which is consumed is of better quality than wine in the past, when it was more a nutrient than a beverage. The faster lunch means that the evening meal has taken on added importance in terms of socializing as well as nutrition. In this regard, northern Italians have begun to conform with people in other nations.

With greater affluence, Italians now eat more elaborate meals when they dine out, with fancier wines and ingredients being part of the conspicuous consumption. On special occasions or at business meals, a dinner may include six or more courses and numerous wines, each selected to accompany one or two courses.

The currents of diet and weight consciousness have swept through Italy, although Italians still tend to be thinner than northern Europeans. As a reaction to these currents, many Italians have rejected the standard four-course meal in favor of something lighter. This might mean eating only a dish of pasta and a piece of fruit at lunch and soup, salad, a piece of cheese, and fruit at dinner. This certainly is healthy eating, but one misses the gentle progression of the four-course meal. It has also taken its toll on restaurateurs. As people arrive who order less, the revenue goes down. Some restaurateurs have made it known that they will serve full meals only. You must remember that in Italy, most good places to eat do not think in terms of "turning over" a table. That is, if you make a reservation for 20h, the table will be yours for as long as you want it, and the restaurant does not count on seating other diners there at 22h. So a restaurateur must make whatever income he can from what you and your guests eat.

It is notable that prices for dining have pulled either to the inexpensive or expensive extreme as restaurateurs have struggled to stay solvent. The inexpensive places are either pasta and pizza joints with adequate food or those with imaginative cooks who have looked back to the tradition of peasant cooking and reintroduced delicious dishes that use inexpensive ingredients. On the opposite end, fancy restaurants charge more for elaborate dishes, and it becomes an event, rather than a normal meal, to go there. In this book, of course, you will find delicious food to fit all budgets, with moderately priced places in abundance.

One other thing to remember: on Sundays and most religious holidays the major meal is always lunch. If you go to Sicilia during Easter, you might see women carrying legs of lamb to early mass to be blessed. Other family members go to church later on while *mamma* is home cooking the lamb and the rest of the Easter lunch.

My dining recommendation is that you try to follow the customary Italian model, at least at the start of your visit. Have a light breakfast and spend the morning being a tourist. This can mean visiting museums and monuments or devoting time to being a gourmet traveler by visiting markets, special stores, and points of interest I have described so that you will have a better sense of *living* Italy. If you need a lift in the late morning, have a brief snack at a bar. At around 13h you should sit down for a standard lunch. Eat as slowly and as leisurely as you like, and then either take a stroll or go back to your hotel for a nap or a refresher. In the late afternoon, visit the sites that are open (many in Italy are open only in the mornings) or go shopping. You can also simply wander directionless around a town, for you are sure to make discoveries that will be memorable in part because they are your own. If your plans call for you to travel from one town to another, you might like to do it after lunch, provided you have not had too much wine if you are driving. When you reach the next town, check into your hotel, unpack your bags, then come out in the early evening for the *passeggiata*. If you have not changed towns, you should still program a walk during the *passeggiata*, which, along with market time, is the best occasion to get to know a town and its people. Think in terms of a light supper at around 20h, or later in the deep south. The evening alternative is pizza, which I often have if I am running to an opera or a concert. Late in the evening you might get a small ice-cream cone or an herbal tea before going to bed. If you follow this program, all of the walking will more than make up for the caloric consumption, and you will fit perfectly in that new Italian wardrobe you have purchased.

Let us now look at the different parts of an Italian meal and some of the typical dishes that might be served.

ANTIPASTO (APPETIZER)

Many of the dishes that used to form the center of a meal in poorer times are now served in small portions at the start of the meal to get the appetite going. Many are cured meats or stuffed vegetables. In Emilia-Romagna it is almost unheard of to start a meal without having delicious prosciutto, salami, or mortadella first.

Cold cuts are called *salumi*, and a dish of sliced cold cuts is called *affettato misto*. Do not confuse *salumi* with *salame* (plural *salami*). A *salame* (what English speakers call salami) is a tightly packed casing with various meats (usually pork) and spices that is dried and then sliced. There are many names around the country for local *salame*, so you need only ask for *salame locale*. In Toscana this often contains fennel seeds, while in the south it is frequently spiked with dried *peperoncino* (chili pepper). Many *salame* fans say the best is made in Felino, in the province of Parma. Do not be put off if a restaurant proudly displays *salame di Felino*. It is not made of cat!

Prosciutto cotto is boiled ham, to be sliced paper-thin. *Culatello* is the best boiled ham, made of pork rump, and almost all produced in Parma. *Spalla cotta* is boiled pork shoulder, a less expensive cut. You will be amazed to find that you can distinguish among the different boiled hams. *Prosciutto crudo* is exquisite air-cured ham that is one of the great flavor sensations you will ever know. It, too, should be served paper-thin (the Tuscans too often slice it thick). It matches perfectly with *melone* (cantaloupe) or with *fichi* (fresh figs). Most people say the best *crudo* comes from Parma, although a vocal minority prefers the prosciutto from San Daniele in Friuli. There are also good prosciutti from Carpegna in the Marche and from the Valle d'Aosta, where it is cured with herbs.

Pig products are used in other ways. Mortadella is a large, smooth pork sausage from Bologna. It is pink and often contains cubes of fat and even pistachio nuts. It is served in slices or chunks and is delicious. Its bastardized poor relation is what Americans call bologna, but mortadella is sublime, and bologna is baloney. In the Dolomites, speck is smoked bacon, often served in slices. *Pancetta,* popular in the center and south, is unsmoked bacon and is cooked, often with eggs or tomatoes to dress pasta. *Lardo* is lard, made fragrant with herbs and often sliced very thin. It melts on the tongue and is delicious.

There are many popular versions of raw beef that are either salt cured *(carne salada)* or air cured *(carpaccio* and *bresaola).* Smoked breast of goose *(petto d'oca affumicato)* or duck *(petto di anatra affumicato)* is popular in Lombardia and other parts of the north.

Many meat antipasti are served with *sott'oli* (oil-cured vegetables such as olives, mushrooms, artichokes, and tomatoes) or *sott'aceti* (vegetables cured in vinegar, such as carrots, celery, peppers, and onions). Raw vegetables are called *pinzimonio.* They come before the meal in some parts of the country, while in others they serve to cleanse the palate toward the end. *Bagna cauda* is a popular dip for raw vegetables in Piemonte. It is made of hot olive oil and anchovies, sometimes with a bit of truffle. A *tortino* is a baked tart or quiche usually containing vegetables and cheese. Vegetables grilled *(alla griglia),* baked *(al forno),* or stuffed *(ripieni)* are becoming more popular all the time.

In coastal areas, *insalata di mare* is chilled cooked seafood removed from its shell and tossed with lemon juice, olive oil, and perhaps some parsley. Unless well made, this dish can be rubbery. Certain seafood, such as clams and mussels, can be filled with bread crumbs and other flavors and then baked. These, too, would be referred to as *al forno.*

Il Primo (the First Course)

Many of the foods for which Italian cuisine is so famous come in the category of the *primo.* These include soup, pasta, risotto, and polenta. It is often customary to have soup at the evening meal in place of a grain-based *primo*. In much of the country, *minestra* is another term for *primo* and is indicated as such on the menu. This is confusing, because *minestra* also means soup. *Minestrone* is a bigger soup—in other words, a soup with many ingredients. The most famous soup is probably *pasta e fagioli*, pasta-and-bean soup. There are many variations in the type of pasta and beans used, depending where in Italy you are. *Brodo* is a broth, usually of chicken or capon. It might be served with noodles as a soup or used as a cooking liquid for pasta, especially in Emilia-Romagna. In Bologna a popular *primo* is tortellini served in capon broth. *Crema* and *passato* are terms that suggest a velvety soup, usually vegetable based, rather than one full of chunks of ingredients. It often has light dairy cream added, but this is not an absolute. *Zuppa* sometimes means "soup" and often implies a substantial one that is thick with ingredients. *Zuppa di trippa* is tripe soup. Beware—certain dishes with the word *zuppa* appear elsewhere in the meal. *Zuppa di pesce* is a fish stew that sometimes appears as a *primo* but is hearty enough to be a main course or a whole meal. *Zuppa inglese* is a dessert that is loosely translated as "trifle." This is sponge cake soaked *(inzuppato)* with rum and arranged in layers with jam, chocolate, and custard.

PASTA

The most famous *primo* of all, and arguably the world's favorite food. Noodles of one type or another exist in cuisines of many nations, and Italian noodles have made their way to every nation on earth. Unfortunately, the knowledge of how pasta shapes should be matched with particular sauces and how pasta should be cooked and served has not traveled well. I live in New York, one of the best restaurant cities in the world, yet there are very few places in my hometown that make pasta as well as the average Italian cook. Pasta in Italy is served in relatively small portions, unless it is intended as the only course in a meal. Much less sauce is put on pasta than you would expect, so when you toss the noodles they will be coated in sauce and little will be left at the bottom of the plate. A small amount of freshly grated cheese is then put on top. In America, so much cheese is put on pasta that it dries out the sauce and makes the dish heavy.

Pasta is divided into two categories: *pastasciutta* and *pasta fresca*. *Pastasciutta* is dried pasta, which is boiled until it is *al dente* (chewy) and then tossed with a sauce. Therefore, the flavoring is outside the pasta. *Pasta fresca* is fresh pasta that is cut into noodles and served with sauce, or cut in sheets, filled with different ingredients, folded, cooked, and then covered lightly with butter, cream, or broth. So with these, the most interesting flavoring is often inside the pasta.

Pastasciutta is made of flour and water in an almost infinite variety of shapes. The most famous are the long strands called *spaghetti*, which are native to Napoli. *Spaghetti, linguine, trenette,* and other strand pastas are used with smooth vegetable sauces as well as sauces of seafood or vegetables that have small bits in them that can be gathered in the strands. An unusual strand popular in the Veneto and other parts of northeastern Italy are *bigoli,* very long strands of whole wheat pasta, usually served with either an anchovy sauce or a duck sauce.

Maccheroni (what English speakers call macaroni) are just as popular as strand pastas. These dried tubular pastas come in endless forms and have many names, such as *penne* (quills), *rigatoni* (large pasta with ridges), and *maccheroncini* (tiny macaroni). Tubular pasta goes well with creamy sauces and chunkier meat sauces, which come under the general name *ragù.* When you see the word *ragù* by itself (or *alla bolognese*), it implies a special sauce made in Bologna with beef, pork, chicken livers, tomatoes, milk, and other flavors. Otherwise, a *ragù* is a tomato-based meat sauce with the name of the meat. So *ragù di piccione,* for example, is a sauce made with squab.

In addition to strand and tubular pastas, there are countless other shapes of dried pastas that are regional specialties. *Cavatelli* (or *cavateddi* or *cavatieddi*) are curled pastas found throughout the south. *Orecchiette* are ear-shaped pastas used in Puglia. You should not think that dried pasta is inferior to fresh. It is useful because it can be stored in a pantry and then used when needed to make a perfect dish. With a few ingredients, a good sauce can be made to toss with dried pasta. So when Italians gather to make an impromptu meal, it is often called a *spaghettata,* a big dish of quickly made spaghetti.

Pasta fresca is most typical of Emilia-Romagna, although it is now produced almost everywhere. *Pasta fresca* is made with flour and eggs and sometimes a little water. Sheets of fresh pasta are called *sfoglia,* which can be cut into squares and rectangles to make *cannelloni* and *lasagne,* which can be baked with cheese, sauce, meat, and vegetables. When *sfoglia* is cut (*tagliare* means "to cut" in Italian), the result is *tagliatelle, tagliarini, tagliolini,* and other noodles of various widths. In Roma, noodles similar in thickness to tagliatelle are called *fettuccine.* Very broad noodles in Toscana are called *pappardelle.*

Sfoglia is also cut into little squares, circles, and triangles that are filled with meat, cheese, herbs, or vegetables, or some combination of these ingredients, and then folded. When pasta is filled it is called *pasta ripiena.* The most famous are *ravioli,* native to Genova, but there are also *agnolotti, anolini, tortelli, tortellini, tortelloni, cappellacci, cappelletti, balanzoni, pansôti,* and many more. Cheese-filled pastas are often dressed with a tomato or meat sauce, while meat-filled pastas might be served in broth, *alla panna* (in cream), or, most commonly, with butter and either sage, mushrooms, or truffles. Bologna is the epicenter of *sfoglia* and *pasta ripiena,* although most places in the terrain north of Bologna have interesting local *pasta ripiena.* In Liguria, it is often filled with herbs. Along the shores of the Adriatic it is frequently filled with fish. In Lombardia much of the filled pasta contains meat. Mantova and Cremona make *tortelli di zucca,* containing pumpkin, ground macaroons, and minced *mostarda* (fruit that has been pickled with mustard seed).

Certain special pastas do not quite fit into either category, but are worth trying. *Gnocchi* are among the oldest pastas known. To call them dumplings is misleading because dumplings are generally heavy, and gnocchi are pillow light. Dumpling-type gnocchi are made either with riced potatoes and flour or entirely with flour. In Trentino gnocchi are called *strangolopreti* (priest stranglers). *Gnocchi di semola* are disks made with semolina that are baked with cheese and butter. These are much loved in Roma, as are all types of gnocchi. In fact, Romans eat gnocchi every Thursday, and you might want to do the same. Small gnocchi are *gnocchetti*. In Trentino, Alto Adige, and the northern Veneto, you will find *canederli*, which are large dumplings made of bread and flavorings such as cheese, herbs, speck, prosciutto, or liver. *Canederli* are served one or two per portion, either in soup or topped with melted butter and cheese.

Pizzoccheri are buckwheat pasta typical of the Valtellina in Lombardia. They may be fresh or dried, and after being cooked they are combined with cheeses, garlic, and cabbage or spinach and then baked. *Passatelli* are native to Romagna and are consumed in much of central Italy. They are made of cheese, egg, bread crumbs, flour, nutmeg, and lemon. The dough is either formed into little dumplings or pushed through a press to form cylindrical lengths. *Passatelli* are cooked and served in broth.

POLENTA

There has always been a form of cereal used in cooking throughout Italy, but especially in the central and eastern parts of northern Italy. For centuries this cereal was the staff of life, a substitute for bread, and it became the ideal counterpart to whatever it might be paired with: a little gravy, a bit of fish, a small game bird, melted cheese, or sugar and cinnamon as a dessert. This was the way the poor ate for centuries, and only with postwar affluence did things change.

Until the exploration of the Americas, the cereal that was usually consumed was made with millet, chickpeas, or buckwheat. Maize arrived in Venezia in the early sixteenth century in the aftermath of Columbus's voyages and was used to make cornmeal, the basic ingredient of polenta. (We know that Raphael painted a corncob in 1516, soon after it came from America.) Soon the other cereals went out of fashion, and polenta became the staple from Bergamo (which for a time was under Venetian sway) all the way to Udine. As a generalization it can be said that the farther west one goes the softer the polenta is eaten. In Lombardia it is preferred creamy and often is infused with cheese. In the Veneto it often is cooled and then cut in rectangular pieces. This brick might be served at room temperature or reheated or even grilled. But this is only a generalization: firm polenta can be had in Bergamo and soft polenta is served in Udine.

Making polenta the old-fashioned way is labor-intensive: large cauldrons are filled with cornmeal and water, and the mixture must be stirred continuously with a large wooden implement. As the cereal thickens it becomes more difficult to stir. Nowadays there are instant polentas that are easier to make, but the notion of this cereal as a product of hard work speaks to a different era when more time was spent in the kitchen and food was often a gratefully received reward for effort. Polenta now appears in small pieces as part of an antipasto, in larger amounts with cheese, mushrooms, or sauce as a *primo,* or in a piece or a creamy dollop as a side dish to slow-cooked meat or fish.

RICE

Polenta is not the only starch staple in the territory of the former Venetian Empire. Rice is used for risotto and soups throughout the Veneto, but particularly in Venezia (which imported it from Asia centuries ago), Padova, Vicenza, and Verona. But rice gains in prominence in Lombardia and Piemonte, the two regions where most of it is grown. The city of Vercelli is Europe's largest rice market, and you can read more about rice history and cultivation under the heading for that *piemontese* city. Much of Italy's best rice is grown in the Lomellina, a fertile district in the province of Pavia. There are four lengths of rice, from the short *originario,* through *semifino, fino,* and *superfino,* this last more than .6 cm./one-fourth inch long. Of the many varieties of rice, the best for risotto are Arborio, Baldo, Carnaroli, and Vialone Nano.

Risotto is another misunderstood dish that is seldom as good abroad as it is in Italy. In other countries risotto is often a mushy rice dish with various ingredients added. True risotto should be made with rice that is lightly toasted in butter and then cooked with broth that is added a little at a time. The rice must be regularly stirred as much of the broth is absorbed. The starch from the rice goes into the liquid to make it creamy. When the rice is cooked (usually after twenty-five minutes), grated cheese is stirred in, and the rice is served. The final result should be firm rice in a creamy sauce that you can eat with a fork.

The variations in risotto come in the ingredients with which it is flavored. There is a restaurant in Milano, La Risotteria, that has eighty-five different risottos in its repertoire. The most famous risotto is *alla milanese,* made with saffron. Another popular way to make risotto is to use wine instead of broth. This can be a robust red such as Barolo or Amarone, or something as delicate as Champagne or spumante. Wherever you travel in northern Italy you will find risottos made with an astonishing range of ingredients: fish, seafood, meat, poultry, vegetables, and herbs. There was a recent fad in which fruits such as strawberries were used to flavor risotto. This was an unwelcome affectation that is thankfully going out of style.

If you go to a restaurant and are told that it will take between twenty-five and thirty-five minutes for you to receive your dish of risotto, take this as a good sign: it is being made from scratch. Many restaurants now parboil rice and finish it with ingredients once an order is placed. When risotto is made from scratch, restaurants often require that it be an order for at least two diners to make the effort worth it. In Milano, when there are leftovers, they make delicious *risotto al salto,* little cakes of risotto that are fried in butter until they are crunchy.

There are other uses for rice in Italy. *Paniscia,* or *panissa,* is found in the provinces of Novara and Vercelli. This preparation is usually drier than risotto and contains rice, sausage, beans, and other flavors. *Insalata di riso* is made during the summer with cold cooked rice and chopped fresh vegetables, prosciutto, chunks of cheese, and sometimes *sott'aceti*. *Bomba di riso, sartù di riso,* and *timballo di riso* are baked rice casseroles that use either poultry or meat plus vegetables. *Arancini di riso* are rice balls that contain a little cheese and ground meat and are served with tomato sauce. *Arancini* are popular in Sicilia, Campania, and other parts of the south. *Torta di riso* is a rice cake that often contains ricotta cheese. *Gelato di riso* is ice cream that contains cooked rice. Gelateria Vivoli in Firenze makes a good version of this.

Il Secondo or *la Pietanza* (the Entrée, or Main Course)

Italians have always been creative and economical cooks, employing every possible protein source in their cuisine. While Americans stick to beef, veal, lamb, pork, chicken, turkey, fish, and seafood, Italians have looked much further to find suitable proteins. The thinking in this dates back to a time when meat sources were scarce. When a pig was slaughtered (usually once a year), every imaginable part was used. In Modena the trotter would be stuffed with minced meat and boiled. This dish is called *zampone* and is always eaten at New Year's with lentils, owing to a superstition that this brings money and good luck.

In our discussion of *salumi* above, you learned where much of the rest of the pig went. But the same thinking applies to cattle and sheep. The choicer cuts are sold at high prices in small quantities (this is why veal cutlets are so thin). The less popular parts are slow-cooked with wine and vegetables or made into sausage and pâtés. Among the many animal parts you will encounter that you do not normally eat at home are what Romans call the fifth quarter. After an animal is drawn, quartered, and butchered, the fifth quarter (the animal's innards—brains, tongue, heart, lungs, kidneys, intestines [tripe], pancreas [sweetbreads], liver—plus the head, feet, and tail) is removed to use for cooking. These parts frequently appear on menus, usually at lower prices, and are delicious and nutritious. If you must watch your fat intake, remember that organ meats are often very high in cholesterol.

Italians are also big consumers of birds such as chicken *(pollo)*, rooster *(gallo)*, capon *(cappone)*, duck *(anatra)*, turkey *(tacchino)*, goose *(oca)*, squab *(piccione)*, pheasant *(fagiano)*, guinea fowl *(faraona)*, and quail *(quaglia)*. Many dishes in the repertoire call for the boneless breast *(petto)* of these birds. *Petti* are often prepared as veal cutlets might be, but there are many additional methods as well.

In the search for protein, different animals, such as rabbit *(coniglio)*, hare *(lepre)*, kid *(capretto)*, horse *(cavallo)*, pony *(puledro)*, frogs *(rane)*, snails *(lumache)*, deer *(cervo)*, and wild boar *(cinghiale)*, became popular in much of the country. Although most people can afford not to eat these foods anymore, they still choose to because they like the flavor and feel connected to tradition.

The decision as to whether a particular animal would make a suitable thing to eat is always personal and often emotionally charged. Some people regard animals such as horses as a natural part of the food chain, while others develop strong emotional attachments to certain animals and would never consider eating them. This decision is purely subjective. Why, for example, would many people refuse to eat horse but would happily eat cow or lamb? Some people would be appalled at the idea of eating rabbit, while for others it is second nature. There is also the issue of an old animal versus a younger one. There is an old proverb: *Quando un contadino mangia un pollo, o è ammalato l'uno o è ammalato l'altro.* (When a peasant eats a chicken, either one or the other is sick.) In other words, since chickens provide eggs, killing one only makes sense if the chicken is sick or if it is needed to make a sick person well.

The recipes in the Veneto that employ horse meat are the result of necessity that has evolved into a legacy and a tradition. The annual horse show in Verona draws many equine admirers, many of whom could not envision that the animal they are beholding might be their next meal. But in other parts of Verona and in much of the Veneto, cooks prepare a horse-meat sauce to serve on pasta or a *pastissada de caval* (depending where you are, this is either a salad with strips of horse meat or a horse-meat stew). Should this be abandoned because affluence means it is no longer necessary to eat horse meat? That is up to you, but I have detailed all of this so you understand why such a broad range of meats is consumed in Italy.

Meats in Italy are braised or stewed *(brasato, stufato,* or *in umido),* grilled *(alla griglia* or *ai ferri),* fried *(fritto),* sautéed *(saltato* or *in padella),* baked *(al forno),* and roasted or broiled *(arrosto).* A *casseruola* is a casserole. For reasons of economy and health, meats such as veal or beef are sliced very thin to make *scaloppine* or a paillard. When thin pieces of meat are rolled and filled, these are *involtini.* A *spiedino* is a skewer that has chunks of meat and vegetables (not unlike shish kebab).

Italians also eat a much broader range of fish and seafood than do Americans and many northern Europeans. These include tiny baby fish that are cooked whole as well as enormous ugly fish with delicious meat. In the north a lot of river trout *(trota)* and lake fish are consumed, while in the south magnificent swordfish *(pescespada)* and tuna *(tonno)* are staples. Throughout the country you will see *stoccafisso* and *baccalà,* dried cod and dried salted cod, which have been imported from Norway for five hundred years. This inexpensive ingredient was a staple of the poor, who developed many dishes. When handled correctly, the dried fish is soaked and rinsed enough to rid it of most of its natural or added salt. It is then fried or slow-cooked. Although the Catholic Church long ago lifted the rule of no meat on Fridays, one still sees cod on menus that day in most of Italy. Fresh anchovies *(alici),* dried anchovies *(acciughe),* and sardines *(sarde)* are economical fish that appear in many guises, especially in the south and in Liguria.

In Emilia-Romagna, sturgeon *(storione)* is popular. Centuries ago the Jews of Romagna were the only people who ate sturgeon eggs until everyone else found out how good caviar can be. In Sardegna, *bottarga* is the dried eggs of tuna or mullet. They are tossed with pasta or served in slices with lemon. Eel *(anguilla)* is consumed in much of Italy.

Raw and cooked seafood is eaten all over coastal Italy and is also found in the interior. Because it is now unsafe to eat raw shellfish anywhere in the world, I strongly discourage you from doing so. But cooked seafood is wonderful: lobster *(aragosta)* from Sardegna, prawns *(scampi* and *gamberoni)*, smaller shrimp *(gamberi* and *gamberetti)*, mussels *(cozze* and *muscoli)*, clams *(vongole* and *arselle)*, octopus *(polpo* or *polipo)*, squid *(calamari)*, cuttlefish *(seppie)*, and more. There are fish and seafood stews that are called different things depending where you go. Some names include *zuppa di pesce, brodetto, cacciucco,* and *cassola.* As I mentioned elsewhere, when fish and seafood are bought frozen *(surgelato)* by a restaurateur, this must be indicated on a menu.

Il Contorno (the Side Dish)

In general a *contorno* is eaten either as an accompaniment to a *secondo* (potatoes or beans, for example) or is consumed after the *secondo.* This is particularly true with salads. The idea is that you want the flavors of the salad or other vegetables to stand out rather than compete with the taste of the meat or fish.

One of the joys of dining in Italy is the amazing range of vegetables, almost all of superb quality. Many Italians dote on *primizie,* the first vegetables of the season, because of their delicacy and flavor. Some vegetables are eaten raw; others are cooked, and then many of these are cooled. It is customary to drizzle a little olive oil over some, while others (such as chilled cooked spinach) taste great with fresh lemon juice. Each region has vegetable specialties: tomatoes in Campania, eggplants in Sicilia and Calabria, artichokes and peas in Lazio, fava beans and chicory in Puglia, sweet peppers in Piemonte, radicchio and asparagus in Veneto, beans in Toscana, and so on. You will discover these as you see them turn up on menus. The glossary contains the names of just about every vegetable you will encounter in Italy (at least those that grow in the ground or on bushes).

Potatoes may be roasted (*al forno,* usually served with salt and rosemary), fried *(patate fritte),* boiled *(patate bollite),* and then served hot or cool. When cooked, they are delicious topped with olive oil. Mashed potatoes are called *purè* and go well with boiled meats and *zampone.*

I want to make a special mention of salads. *Insalata* (salad) or *insalata verde* will be all greens. *Insalata mista* will contain greens, tomatoes, and perhaps onions, carrots, cucumbers, or other vegetables. The word *insalata* comes from *sale* (salt). Originally lettuces were highly salted when they were dressed, in part because Italians (especially Romans) have a fondness for salt. There is an old expression:

Insalata, ben salata	Greens, well-salted,
poco aceto, molto oliata	little vinegar, well-oiled
mille volte rivoltata.	tossed one thousand times.

In other words, take some salad greens (carefully washed and dried, I should add), sprinkle over them a healthy amount of salt and a touch of vinegar. At this point the greens are lightly tossed. Then enough oil is poured on top to cover the leaves, and the greens are tossed repeatedly so that the ingredients are well combined. This is unlike a French or American dressing, which is usually prepared in a cruet and then poured over the greens. I don't think I have ever seen an Italian use measuring spoons while preparing a salad dressing. Everything is measured by the eye and the touch of the hand. If you want your salad (or anything else) without salt, say, "Senza sale." If you want just a little salt, say, "Con poco sale." In many trattorias, small cruets of oil and vinegar are placed on the table so you can make your own dressing. Unfortunately, in some parts of Italy (especially those where not much oil or vinegar is produced) the quality of the oil and vinegar in the cruets is often middling.

Il Formaggio (Cheese)

We all have heard the famous lament of Charles de Gaulle about how hard it was to do his job: "How can one govern a nation that produces 365 different cheeses?" Well, one official count determined that there are 451 cheeses in Italy, which must explain why Italy has had more than fifty governments since World War II. But these ungoverned people eat magnificent cheese!

There is a saying in Lombardia: *Il magnar non vale un'acca se alla fine non sa di vacca.* Loosely translated: "A meal is worthless if it doesn't taste of milk at its conclusion."

There are rivers of cow's milk in Lombardia, and much of the nation's best cheese is produced there. But every Italian region makes cheese from the milk of cows, sheep, and goats. You will find these listed in the regional chapters, but a few merit listing here. Parmigiano-Reggiano is the king of cheeses, the best of the best, and an ingredient I would take to a desert island. Pecorino is sheep's-milk cheese, made all over, but at its best in Sardegna and Toscana. It can be eaten young or aged. Gorgonzola is a sublime blue-veined cheese from Piemonte and Lombardia. Ricotta is made of curds that are cooked twice. It is tightly packed but delicate and is very nice at breakfast on bread. Taleggio is a creamy, rich cow's-milk cheese from Lombardia. Mozzarella is from Campania. While it is most often made from cow's milk now, the very best is *mozzarella di bufala,* from the milk of water buffalo. Fontina (from the Valle d'Aosta) and Montasio (Friuli) are excellent mountain cheeses. Mascarpone is a buttery sweet cheese from Emilia and Lombardia that is often used in making desserts such as *tiramisù*.

Il Pane (Bread)

Bread is placed on the table at an Italian meal to nibble on while you wait for your first course. Italians do not butter their bread at meals, and you should not do so either. Nor do they dip bread in olive oil, which is an affectation created in the United States. Bear in mind that Italians almost never eat bread while consuming their *primo*. This is because the starches would be redundant. It is more common, though, to take a piece of bread once you are done with your pasta to scoop up whatever little sauce remains in a bowl. This was once considered inelegant, but now everyone does it. Bread varies radically throughout Italy. In the Alps there are many rye breads. In Piemonte there are *grissini* (breadsticks). Liguria has focaccia. Emilia-Romagna has bone-dry breads that go well with that region's rich foods. Toscana has salt-free bread that often has olive oil in it. Lazio and Abruzzo have large loaves of delicious *pane casareccia* (home-style bread). The bread in Molise is fabulous (read about it on page 531). Sardegna makes very distinct breads, including the crisp *pane carasau.*

La Frutta e I Dolci (Fruit and Desserts)

There is a particular tradition/superstition in Italy that the first time you eat a fruit of a season, you make a wish. Italians chart the passage of time with the annual arrival of fruits and vegetables. When fruits come into season, such as cherries in June or grapes in September, they are consumed with great delight because they are at the peak of their flavor and beauty. When you order *frutta* for dessert, what typically happens is that a bowl of fruit that could inspire Caravaggio is placed before you along with a bowl of cold water. You select the fruit, wash it carefully (except for bananas and citrus), and then peel it with a knife. You might then use a fork to cut it in pieces, or simply use the knife, as Italians do with great dexterity.

Many restaurants prepare a fruit salad each day called *macedonia*. To keep the apples and pears that are the foundation of a *macedonia* from discoloring, a lot of fresh lemon juice is squeezed onto the fruit. By the end of the day, some *macedonie* may be mushy and sour, so you might want to inspect the fruit salad before ordering. But it is generally true that fruit salad in Italy is much better than its American cousin. Another popular dessert is *sottobosco*. This delicacy is a fruit salad of small wild berries such as strawberries, raspberries, blackberries, blueberries, and currants. When served this way, they are only topped with a bit of lemon juice and, if you want, some sugar. These berries are also called *frutti di bosco* and might be served over ice cream or with *crespelle* (crepes).

Italian ice cream *(gelato)* is generally considered the best in the world. While many restaurants have decent ice cream, I tend to buy ice cream at a *gelateria.* The best *gelaterie* are those that make their own product. This will be indicated by the words *artigianale* or *produzione propria.* Italian ice cream is different from others because it is lower in fat and has much more intense flavor. It is made of whole milk (no cream), fresh eggs, sugar, and whatever flavor is selected. No self-respecting *gelataio* would use artificial flavors or colors, so that your palate must adjust to recall what real flavors taste like. Strawberry *(fragola)* is made with real berries that are pureed, which distinguishes it from ice cream made with berries that are virtually frozen and suspended in chilled cream. Italian ice cream is usually divided into two categories: fruit-flavored and cream. The former is self-evident. The latter includes flavors such as chocolate, coffee, nuts, and vanilla. These ice creams have a creamier texture than fruit ice creams. Practically every ice-cream flavor you might encounter is listed in the glossary. When you buy a cup *(coppa)* or a cone *(cono)*, it is customary to ask for two or three flavors. The larger the cup or cone, the more flavors you can have. So the idea is to order flavors that go together well. Fruit flavors go well with others, and cream flavors are well matched with one another. But there is room for crossover: while coffee and strawberry might be strange, chocolate and banana or coconut or pear are delicious.

There are other cold delights: *semifreddo* means "half cold." This is ice cream to which whipped cream has been added. It is often chilled in blocks and served in slices with a sauce. *Granita* is what has been bastardized in the United States as Italian ice. In fact, granita is a liquid (usually coffee or sugared lemon juice) that has been frozen and then allowed to partially melt. It is light on the tongue, strong in flavor, and great on a hot day. *Sorbetto* is fruit sorbet, and it often appears midway through a multicourse meal as a palate cleanser. A *frullato* is not really a dessert, but often can be had at a *gelateria.* This is a drink made of pureed fruit with some milk and ice added. It is not the same as a milk shake because milk is only a supporting character in the *frullato.*

Cakes and pastries have become part of Italian meals in recent years, but I think they are better suited to the afternoon tea or coffee break. Apple strudel is ubiquitous in regions that used to be under Austrian control. Friuli and Veneto have delicious cakes with nuts and spices. Most northern and central regions have creamy desserts such as *tiramisù* (soaked ladyfingers with espresso, cocoa powder, and mascarpone), *creme caramel* (caramel custard), *bonet* (a chocolate, coffee, or nut pudding made in Piemonte), and *budino di mandorla* or *di cioccolato* (almond or chocolate pudding). Southern Italy, especially Sicilia, makes sumptuous desserts with liqueurs, nut creams and pastes, and lots of ricotta cheese. These are delicious, but too heavy to end a meal. In Sardegna, *seadas*, or *sebadas*, look like ravioli. They are filled with sweet cheese, fried, and topped with honey. In fancy restaurants, you might be served tiny pastries called *mignon* or *piccola pasticceria*. In Sardegna, you are often served *dolci sardi,* which are made with marzipan.

In recent years there has been a boom in the production of excellent dessert wines. These are usually accompanied by dry cookies called *biscotti* or *amaretti.* In Toscana, slightly sweet *vin santo* is always served with crunchy almond cookies called *cantuccini.*

Il Vino (Wine)

Throughout most Italian meals, wine forms a pleasurable accompaniment that enhances the flavors of everything you eat. The following chapter is devoted entirely to Italian wine.

Acqua Minerale (Mineral Water)

It used to be that water in Italy, especially the south, was not safe to drink. Mineral water from protected sources was bottled and served at meals. Every water has a label full of technical data about the mineral makeup of the contents of the bottle, and there will be a small essay by a university professor about the potential healthful properties of the water. Minerals are essential to proper body functioning, and this is a good place to get them. Usually at a meal you will order *vino e acqua,* and then will have to specify if you want *gassata* (carbonated) or *naturale* or *non gassata* (uncarbonated) water. Some brands, such as Ferrarelle, are naturally sparkling and are called *frizzante.* Water is bottled as a half liter *(mezzo-litro)* or as a liter *(un litro).* It is generally inexpensive and worth ordering. If you travel about, especially in hot weather, you expend a lot of fluids and minerals, and *acqua minerale* is the perfect way to replace them. As you travel through Italy, you will discover waters that appeal to you. My favorite is Acqua di Nepi from Lazio, which is creamily *frizzante,* but does not have a strong mineral taste. Water from a tap is called *acqua del rubinetto,* it is now drinkable, and there are some areas in Italy where it is excellent, including parts of the Alps, the province of Parma, Norcia, and Lazio. You might see the words *acqua non potabile* on trains, in some rest rooms, and at certain fountains. This means that the water is not drinkable.

Il Caffè (Coffee)

Coffee is discussed in detail earlier in this chapter. Remember that at the end of a meal, only an espresso is served, not cappuccino, whose foamy milk does not sit well on a full stomach.

Il Digestivo (Digestive Liqueur)

There are many *digestivi* made in Italy. These are derived from herbs and are often quite bitter. If you order *un amaro* (a bitter at the end of your meal), you will get a bitter digestive liqueur. Some famous *digestivi* are Averna (from Sicilia), Ramazzoti (Milano), Braulio (Valtellina), Centerbe (Abruzzo and Molise), Amaro Lucano (Basilicata), and especially Fernet Branca, which is found everywhere.

Grappe e Distillati (Grappas and Distilled Spirits)

Grappa, a byproduct of the wine making process, was a beverage of the poor. It is now one of the fastest-growing beverages in Italy and abroad. In former times, wine would be given to the lord of the land, and the peasants would keep the skins, with which they would make a coarse, powerful beverage called grappa. It was meant to keep them warm through the winter and, with its sugar content, provide energy as well. In those days, skins from all grapes (no matter what wine they produced) were thrown together in one batch to make grappa. Until the mid-1950s, grappa and polenta were sustenance for the poor in northeastern Italy, especially in Veneto, Friuli, and Trentino. The middle class and the wealthy in Italy would never have thought of drinking grappa, which was considered rustic and backward.

This has changed in the past twenty years. The need for heat and energy from food is no longer so urgent, but in the northeast some people began to have a sip of grappa at the end of a meal. As the general level of taste and affluence rose, there was a desire for a more sophisticated postmeal drink with flavor and delicacy. Gradually, the *grappa del contadino* of once upon a time disappeared, replaced by an elegant distilled beverage made from high-quality grapes. The revolution was probably led by the Nonino family, who acquired the skins from leading wine producers in their native Friuli to make grappa. The Noninos' theory was that the skins from better wine grapes would make better grappa. They then pioneered the use of *monovitigno* grappas (that is, the skins from only one type of grape—Refosco, for example—would be used to make a grappa, so that flavors became more distinct). Giannola Nonino was also the first to use unusual bottles, many inspired by old medicinal containers, to store the grappa, making the product seem special. She also had a further knack for marketing, putting her radiant face with those of her three gorgeous daughters on all promotional materials, making a beverage identifiable with its creators as few had previously done. Other fine producers, such as Maschio in Veneto and Pisoni in Trentino, maintained quality and rode the wave of grappa's ever-increasing popularity.

Nowadays, it seems that every wine maker in Italy wants to make a few extra lire with his leftover grape skins, so grappa is being produced in Campania, Sicilia, Liguria, and other places. Most of this is not very good, and you would be wise to start your acquaintance with grappa by sticking to that produced in the regions that know it best. A similar but distinct beverage is *acquavita*, a distillation of fruit such as apples, raspberries, cherries, pears, plums, and apricots. This is found throughout the north, and the best ones are quite costly.

To taste grappa or *acquavita* correctly, do not drink it as you would other beverages. Wine and beer briefly pass the mouth and then go down the throat. This should not be done with grappa or *acquavita*. Usually these drinks are served in a small glass, which you should hold by the stem. Swirl the liquid gently so that some of its fragrance wafts up to your nose. Then take a tiny sip onto your tongue, raise it to your palate, and let it evaporate. The fragrance and flavor will permeate your mouth, throat, and nasal passages. If the beverage is of high quality, you will have a pleasant sensation and will not cough. Let this sip slowly disappear and focus meditatively on that taste. Pause a bit and sense the *ritorno*, the flavor that comes back into your mouth a few minutes later. A good grappa will have its best flavors come up; a bad grappa brings back its worst elements. Then take another little sip and repeat the process.

How long does grappa keep? You should store your bottle in a dark, cool place. There will be some evaporation through the years. One experienced grappa maker told me that although he would not say it for the record, grappa matures and changes somewhat in the bottle. By this he meant that some of the more aromatic grappas—those made of some white-wine grapes—will become rounder and less fragrant as they age.

Paying the Bill

Now that we have had a sumptuous meal, it is time to pay the bill. You will ask the waiter for *il conto per favore*. In general it will take a few minutes to come because Italian waiters don't tote up a check in advance as Americans do, since there is no rush to get you out. Therefore, allow more time in Italy to get the check and then to pay it. Remember that the *servizio* (the tip) is included, but you might choose to leave a few euros more if your waiter has served you well.

A reminder: after paying the bill, you must take the check with you. This is a recent law that intends to encourage fiscal responsibility. It seems silly, but you should comply. If nothing else, the check, with its address and phone number printed on it, will serve as a reminder of where you ate. A receipt is called a *fattura*. A more formal receipt is a *ricevuta fiscale*. The *fattura* is sufficient for your needs.

Hotel Dining

If you are staying at a resort in the Alps or at the shore, especially in a rural setting, your hotel might be the only place to eat. When you book your stay, you will be asked whether you want *mezza-pensione* or *pensione completa*. The former is breakfast and a second meal (usually supper); the latter is breakfast, lunch, and supper. Prices for a full pension usually are not much more than those for a half pension. Stays at hotels with meals often represent very good value if you are on a limited budget, unless the hotel has a very fancy kitchen.

Before booking your stay, you should make your decision based on what you want out of your vacation and how much you normally eat. Dining hours in hotel restaurants are more limited than elsewhere, so you need to get into the rhythm of the place you are in. Therefore, if you want to take a long hike but are expected for lunch by 13h, you need to plan to return in time. Hotel menus often have fewer selections than others, but the food can be very good. I have listed numerous hotel restaurants throughout this book. When you order wine and mineral water at a hotel, your room number will be written on the bottle's label. If you have not consumed everything at one meal, the beverage will be saved for you for the next meal. If you are not residing at a hotel, you can still dine in most of them, although it is wise to reserve ahead of time.

Smoking

In 2005 Italy took a step that many Italians and foreigners thought would never happen: smoking was banned in all restaurants and bars. The rule also applied to cinemas, theaters, and other places of public assembly. At first, observers were certain that Italians would anarchically rebel against these new laws, so I can report with considerable pleasure that the new rules have been widely embraced. There has been a shift in recent years in Italian society from individual expression to what Italians call *un senso civico* in which a sense of public good is factored into questions of the personal pursuit of pleasure. This is not political correctness, which is both onerous and odious, but rather a sense of courtesy and respect for others. My personal objection to smoking is not about denying someone else the pleasure of a smoke, but rather that, as an asthmatic, smoke to me is what sugar is to a diabetic. In most countries, when I make this analogy and conclude saying, "You would never put sugar in the water of a diabetic, would you?" the point is quickly made. But one does not have to be asthmatic to have a problem with smoke, especially in places where food and wine are served. In 2005, following the passage of the new legislation, I visited eleven Italian regions. Without exception, owners of restaurants, pizzerie, bakeries, bars, ice-cream parlors, and other places where food is prepared all were thrilled with the new regulation. The reason is simple: smoking can mask the palate and dull the senses of smell and taste. Suddenly, customers—

whether they smoke or not—began to show more interest in what they are savoring. The owner of a simple *osteria* in Udine told me that many clients have asked whether he hired a new chef.

If you are a smoker, there are still many outdoor places to indulge in tobacco, although *al fresco* tables at *caffès* and restaurants are not among them. Some hotels have now designated rooms for smokers and there are designated areas in many public places where a cigarette or cigar may be enjoyed. It is not my intention to tell smokers not to smoke if they wish, but to ask them to acknowledge that their smoking does indeed have serious impact on the health of others as well as the ability to enjoy what they are eating and drinking. If a balance can be struck and mutual respect proffered, this problem is no problem whatsoever.

There are only certain situations, such as officially organized tastings of wine and food, in which a no-smoking policy exists, because it is acknowledged that smoking impairs the senses of taste and smell required for effective tasting. If you have asthma, allergies, or real problems with smoke, I suggest that you carry your inhaler or other medication and try to procure a table out-of-doors or near a window. In large restaurants you might ask to sit far from the smokers, *lontano dai fumatori* (lone-tah-no die-ee foo-ma-tor-ee), although this will be hard to accomplish in a small neighborhood trattoria or osteria.

The Land of Wine

For Aristotle, the eternal puzzle about wine was its ability to make the loquacious taciturn and the taciturn loquacious. I could go on for days, weeks, years, about the glories of wine, but I am not customarily taciturn. The notion of my describing the history and nature of Italian wine in one chapter is not unlike asking Leporello, servant to Don Giovanni, to recount all of his master's dalliances one by one. In fact, the randy Don, at the moment we meet him in Mozart's opera, had already had 2,065 different partners. This number is more or less equal to the number of different wines thought to be produced in Italy today.

It is a commonplace to mention that the ancient Greeks named the southern part of the Italian peninsula Enotria, or Land of Wine. It is also generally thought that the Greeks brought viticulture to Italy. This may not be true, since we have every reason to believe that the Etruscans were drinking wine when the Greeks arrived. But the Greeks were probably the first to understand the potential for mass cultivation of vines for the production of wine on the Italian peninsula. The regions of southern Italy that the Greeks colonized—from Puglia to Sicilia—are still areas of mass wine production today. In Magna Graecia, as this area was later known, archaeologists have found traces of *enodotti*, pipelines constructed by the Greeks to move wine to the ports, from which it would be shipped back to Athens. Wine and oil were stored in amphorae, long terra-cotta containers that had a characteristic twin handle on top and a pointed bottom that was inserted in a hold in a ship.

The Greeks planted what has come to be called *Vitis vinifera*, or grapes suitable for wine production. Grape varieties for wine production have found the Italian soil congenial ever since. Whether grapes came from the eastern Mediterranean, North Africa, or, in later centuries, from France, Hungary, and many other lands, they have contributed to the nearly endless variety of wines that have been produced in Italy. By several estimates, the Italian soil has played host to more than one thousand grape varieties.

It is probably impossible to know exactly what the wine tasted like back then—it certainly was different from what we drink today—but I can think of two possibilities. One is the Malvasia delle Lipari that is produced on a few islands off the

northern coast of Sicilia. This amber-colored wine has hints of honey and eucalyptus in its flavor. When Homer's reference to the wine-dark sea echoes in my
ears, this is the wine I think of. Malvasia delle Lipari is usually served for dessert
but, oddly enough, is also used for cooking squid, among other things. I imagine
that some forerunner of Malvasia fueled many a bacchanal.

Another wine with undisputed Greek roots is Aglianico. This robust red, high
in alcohol and with a raisinlike flavor, is a descendant of an ancient vine that was
Greek in origin. The name Aglianico derives from the word "Hellenic."

When the Romans gained control of the Italian peninsula, they expanded their
influence north, bringing significant changes to viticulture. Their lasting contribution was the unification of the cultivation of vines, wheat, and olives. This combination produced what we think of today as the great trinity of Mediterranean
agriculture. Ever since, wine, bread (and pasta), and olive oil have been linked in
the cuisines of the Italian peninsula.

As Christianity spread throughout Italy, wine took on another significance.
The Mediterranean trinity also had a religious connotation. Wine, of course, represented the blood of Christ, and bread the flesh. Oil was thought of as a balm or
as an *unto*. This term suggests "grease," but also, in religious terms, "anointment."

Since antiquity, Italy has always experienced a struggle between the sacred and
profane (or pagan) ways of life. Of course it is usually those in the sacred camp
who determine what (or who) is profane and what is not. (This is as true today as
it was 1,500 years ago!) But this is an important thing to consider. Throughout
Italian history, production of wine has usually tied in with pagan celebrations that
observe the completion of a successful harvest. These observances still exist today,
perhaps in a more subdued and sometimes touristic form. Many of the most interesting and authentic are indicated under the heading "Folklore" in the city and
town listings in each regional chapter. But this question of sacredness and profan-
ity forces us to look at the two ways that wine has been viewed throughout history.
In the Greco-Roman context wine is a pleasurable libation and perhaps a truth se-
rum *(in vino veritas)*, while in Christian terms it is connected to sacraments.

Wine was used in religious observances in the Middle Ages, and not simply
sipped from a chalice. Wine was often consumed heavily by parishioners throughout
services. Many priests and monks became expert wine makers, developing techniques that improved quality and storage. We know, for example, that Badia a Coltibuono in Toscana was a medieval abbey where excellent wine was produced. It must
be noted that the Church played a crucial role in saving Italian wine making during
the early Middle Ages. In that period, Italy suffered centuries of invasions by barbarians who ravaged the terrain, including most of the vineyards. Many priests, monks,
and nuns replanted vines within church walls, preserving them for future generations. This custodial function was an essential act in the history of Italian wine.

Another important religious contribution to wine history is that as Christianity
spread to northern Europe sacramental wine and wine-making traditions followed

along. Whatever areas beyond the Alps that the Romans had not covered with grapevines, the Catholic Church managed to reach. One other note about sacramental wine: a priest once told me that sometime in the nineteenth century many churches in Italy switched from red sacramental wine to white because spillage had stained too many marble floors in beautiful cathedrals.

Throughout most of history, wine in Italy was only produced in amounts sufficient for local consumption. A person with a piece of land would make enough for himself and his family, with perhaps a little left to sell or exchange for some other product. Landed peasants produced wine for the *signore* of the land, giving him the best and reserving some average wine for themselves.

In certain regions of Italy, a degree of codification and naming of wines began to develop in the late seventeenth century. For example, in the Tuscan town of Carmignano, where Leonardo da Vinci occasionally ate and drank, the "recipe" for the local red wine was defined in 1716. Carmignano wine was a forerunner of Chianti, which also uses a blend of grapes. The formula for Chianti itself was described by Baron Bettino Ricasoli at the end of the nineteenth century, at which time there was a movement to define and make distinct many of Italy's better wines. In 1924, a consortium of Chianti producers created the seal of the *gallo nero* (black rooster) that implied and guaranteed certain standards of *tipicità*, or the typical nature of the wine. This is an important theme that I will discuss below.

Italian viticulture has always been defined by the nation's great range of terrain, altitude, climate, and exposure to sun. The same grape will grow differently if planted in the Italian Alps, the fertile plain of the Po River valley, or the arid expanses of the deep south. For that matter, the same grape will grow differently if planted on one side or the other of a hill in Piemonte. It is often thought the hill with the best exposure to the sun will yield the grapes that would produce the finest wine. In three of Italy's best wine regions there is a local word for this sunny side of the hill: *bricco* in Piemonte, *ronco* in Friuli, and *poggio* in Toscana. When you see these words on a label, you know that the wine you are about to drink came from a sunny hill. What the variations in climate, terrain, exposure, and types of grape mean is that Italy offers a boundless variety of wines, but it resists categorization and standardization.

The nineteenth century also saw the rise of wine journalism in England, which spread the word about good wines and created demand for importation. This journalism also created certain standards of prejudice and misinformation that must be struggled against to this day. As French wine received laudatory praise and extensive coverage, the assumption was, by extension, that Italian wine was inferior. In fact, it may not have measured up to *French* or *English* standards of what a wine was supposed to be, but it surely was good enough to enjoy with superb Italian food.

As these notions of wine spread to America, Italian wines had another potential market in which they were wrongly considered inferior. To this day, many Italian wine producers make the same mistake as many foreign journalists: they reinforce the Italian enological inferiority complex. That is, they believe that Chianti is inferior to Bordeaux, and the wines of Piemonte are inferior to those from Burgundy.

Until the 1960s, most Italian wines shipped abroad were Chianti from Toscana, inexpensive reds from Piemonte, white Frascati from Lazio, and Orvieto from Umbria. Much of this was sent to places where there were large immigrant communities from Italy and was intended to provide the flavor of home. For non-Italians in other countries, these were the first contact with Italian wines and still remain the point of reference. Typically, young lovers on a shoestring would drink a bottle of cheap Chianti from a straw-covered flask as they shared spaghetti by candlelight. These same people, thirty years later, often still think that Italian wine is that innocent Chianti from their youth and that real wine of any stature must come from France or perhaps certain producers in California.

In recent times, the psychological pressure to measure up to France and California has propelled many Italian wine producers to uproot the traditional grape varieties they knew and replace them with Chardonnay and Cabernet Sauvignon, those ubiquitous twins of the international wine circuit. This is a tragedy, because so many special wines are disappearing. Every time a local grape with a particular charm and history is uprooted, we all suffer the loss of a piece of our culture.

Why are native vines being uprooted? Because of the twentieth-century phenomenon of the wine trade that promoted certain few familiar wines and led to less interest in others. In the name of commerce, producers in Italy and elsewhere who wished to sell abroad rushed to make the wines they thought were in demand abroad. In Europe in the early and mid–twentieth century, much of the basic wine used on the Continent (in nonproducing countries) was imported from Algeria and usually relabeled in France. With the war in Algeria in 1962, that supply was cut off. Italy was one of the countries that stepped in to take advantage of the demand.

Part of the rise in postwar Italian agriculture was the result of advances in technology and research. Grapes were grown to produce better wine, and machines were invented to gather grapes and transform them into wine. This does not negate the presence of the wine maker, who must make all sorts of decisions that will affect the quality of the final product: when to pick the grapes, how long they should be fermented and at what temperature, whether wine should be stored in stainless-steel tanks or wooden barrels (or both) and for how long. Technology permitted the wine maker to have more control over the product once he made his decisions.

Wine is an expression of a terrain, of climate, of the grape, and of the man or woman who makes it. From year to year there will be certain variations as these conditions change. Large industrial wine makers ("industrial" is not a negative judgment; it is a description of a segment of wine making in every country) strive for a consistency of flavor and style that has already found a market niche. So the variations in climate and grape quality will be taken into account as they vinify a wine to resemble those of previous years. Consumers who buy industrial wine look for consistency, not variation.

Strolling through vineyards is a pleasant part of wine tourism

Smaller, individual producers will have more variety in their product from year to year. This is what we mean by "good years" and "less good years." Those of us who follow wine closely pay a lot of attention to these changes. They represent not only the story of wine but also the lives of the people who make it. In every country the wine industry is full of personalities who influence the taste and decision making of other producers. It should not surprise you that Italy, which is so full of fascinating individuals, should be full of characters in the wine world.

For example, there are superstar enologists such as Maurizio Castelli, Walter Filiputti, Giorgio Grai, and Ezio Rivella who travel about the country selling their services and commanding high fees. Their styles and preferences influence even those who never meet them. In fashion, for every Coco Chanel or Giorgio Armani, there are dozens of unknowns who design clothes influenced by the masters. Similarly, if a small wine maker tastes a wine by Grai or Rivella, that may affect the way he looks at his own product.

Then there are the talented charismatic producers who make good-to-superb wines but also are at the leading edge of marketing and promotion. These men were often the ones who gave their regions prominence and definition in the national and international wine market. These include Livio Felluga, Marco Felluga, Mario Schiopetto, and Vittorio Puiatti in Friuli, Alois Lageder in Alto Adige, Giorgio Lungarotti in Umbria, and, most famous, Angelo Gaja in Piemonte, who is an international superstar whose excellent wines command astronomical prices.

There is another category that I call the "wine maker–scholar." This is someone who has a great passion for the land and for the study of grapes and their potential. These are often men and women who devote great amounts of time, effort, and expense to rediscovering grapes that fell into disuse as many Italians lunged headlong into the world market with Chardonnay, Cabernet Sauvignon, and a dozen or so Italian varieties. So it is to the great credit of these wine maker-scholars that they continue to *valorizzare* (to give value and worth to) Italy's wine heritage at a time when some of their colleagues consider profit the only virtue. To name a few of the leading wine maker-scholars is not intended to neglect the many hundreds of other producers who approach their work with love and seriousness of purpose. Two of the titans of Italian wine scholarship—Enzo Morganti of San Felice (Toscana) and Renato Ratti in Alba (Piemonte)—have died, and they are sorely missed. They are irreplaceable. I knew Morganti and was very fond of him. He was a great mentor to Leonardo Bellaccini, who continues the tradition. I know Ratti's son Pietro, who is growing into someone his father would be proud of. Two other producers deserve mention in this category: Girolamo Dorigo and his former wife, Rosa Bosco, in Friuli and Antonio Mastroberardino in Campania, universally acknowledged as the greatest wine producer in southern Italy. What I find notable is that I can always identify a wine by San Felice, Ratti, Dorigo, Bosco and Mastroberardino in the glass. Each has a unique personality and classicism that make it distinct and rewarding every time I encounter it.

Then there are the iconoclasts, too many to mention, whose philosophies and personalities are expressed in their wines. Many of these are gimmicky and geared to a perceived niche in the market. But others are the products of people who have very strong views as well as knowledge of their materials at hand. They produce memorable wines that are singular and worth discovering. These include the Tiefenbrunner family in the Alto Adige, Fausto Maculan in the Veneto, and Josko Gravner in Friuli.

Noble or ancient families throughout the country, particularly in Toscana, produce distinguished wines. At the other end of the social scale (but not necessarily in quality) are the cooperatives and *cantine sociali* (collective wineries) in which small growers pool their grapes and make a product that is bottled and sold with a label indicating the name of the cooperative. Many co-op wines are inexpensive and drinkable; others are excellent. Many of these co-operatives provide a social function in addition to the economic one. At Castelgreve in Toscana, the winery is in a centuries-old building that also has a social center and a theater where concerts and plays are given. There are more than three hundred grape growers who are members of this cooperative, and they work with a collective spirit in the best sense of the term.

The majority of Italian wine producers (in number, if not output) are family concerns with small plots of land that they work themselves. This is where one finds the great variety and personal expression that are hallmarks of Italian wines. In Piemonte, Alto Adige, and Friuli, most wines are produced this way, and they are of very high quality. In Toscana one finds a combination of estates and small family producers. Other regions have family wineries whose products' quality ranges from discreet to outstanding.

The large industrial wineries, as I mentioned above, turn out a consistent product at a fair price. They respond to a significant segment of the national and international market and should not be disregarded. Aside from anything else, they provide the work and income that keep families and communities stable. To name a few, there are Zonin and Folonari in Veneto, Ca' vit, Casa Girelli, and Ferrari in Trentino, Gancia and Martini & Rossi in Piemonte, Riunite in Emilia-Romagna, Fazi-Battaglia in Marche, Corvo in Sicilia, and some of the members of the Gruppo Italiano Vini.

All of these entities, from the cooperatives to the families to the noble estates to the industrial wineries, make wine that in some way represents a history, a philosophy, or a segment of the market. How can these thousands of wines be defined, described, and distinguished? This was the challenge Italy faced as it attempted to become a major exporter in the early 1960s. In 1963, a law was passed that established the *Denominazione di Origine Controllata* (popularly known as DOC). This was modeled on the French *Appellation Controlée*, which, to paraphrase Matt Kramer in his writings about wine, describes the "somewhereness" that every wine has. In general, the DOC law, despite its bureaucratic implications, has had a very positive effect. It gave wine producers and regions a very specific sense of themselves and their products. It defined how many grapes could be grown per hectare and which grapes would be used to produce specific wines.

These efforts to assure quality were quickly felt. The combination of increased demand and more sophisticated agricultural techniques led to a boom in production and sales. In the early 1960s, Italy exported 2.4 million hectoliters of wine. By the middle of the decade, exports rose to 9.7 million hectoliters per annum, and, in the early 1970s, the figure rose to 13.4 million. At first the boom was more psychological than financial. Prices fetched abroad were low, and, as of 1970, only 5 percent of the Italian wines sold abroad were DOC. But it was an important first step.

The struggle for quality saw results in the 1970s that continued in the 1980s. More technological innovations made it possible to standardize quality and remove eccentric impurities and anomalies from the product. More wines were given DOC recognition, so that by now there are more than 250 of them. For most wine sellers and consumers, a DOC wine came to be seen as a guarantee that acceptable minimum standards were met. Sales of Italian wines boomed in the late 1970s, and the esteem in which they were held grew as well. Italy now exports more wine than any nation on earth.

By the 1970s, however, it was decided that a separate category, DOCG *(Denominazione di Origine Controllata e Garantita)* should be created to single out certain wines that are of such unmistakable high quality that they should not be grouped with DOC wines and their implication that minimum standards are being met. The DOCG wines include Barolo and Barbaresco in Piemonte; Brunello di Montalcino, Carmignano, and Chianti Classico in Toscana; Albana from Romagna; and Taurasi in Campania. If you purchase a DOCG wine, you are acquiring something that is special and consequently more costly than simpler wines.

An osteria *is a great place to drink and eat with Italians. Pavia, Lombardia*

As important as these DOC and DOCG laws are, some producers have begun to chafe in recent years at having to conform to DOC standards, not because they feel they are too high, but rather because they might be too confining. They have felt that their creativity has been hampered by the guidelines. Through them, a new breed of wine has been born that is modestly referred to as *vino da tavola,* or "table wine." But many of these wines are hardly simple table wines. This is particularly the case in Toscana, where some producers have chosen to ignore DOC provisions and make wines according to the formulas that they find desirable. The result has been a generation of wines known as the Super-Tuscans, which are of extraordinary flavor and quality and often command astronomical prices. The Italian government has proposed giving DOC status to these new wines, thus codifying and "valorizing" (as the Italians like to say) these wines, too.

A raging debate in the Italian wine world concerns the use of wood for wine production and storage. Before the technological revolution in the postwar era, almost all wine was made in wooden vats, transferred to wooden barrels to ferment and then to age. In those years, you must bear in mind, most wine was consumed within a year, and then the barrels were used for the next vintage. Wood was intended to mellow certain wines (such as Barbera) that naturally have a high acid content. Wine was drawn directly from the barrels or was decanted into bottles or much larger demijohns for home use or for sale locally.

In the postwar era stainless-steel tanks were introduced. These were considered more sanitary and also guaranteed more evenness in the product. The advantage of stainless steel was that temperature could be controlled during fermentation, a valuable advance that gave the wine maker more control of the final result. Steel tanks were often thought to be more hygienic. Many wine makers chose to store their wine in steel tanks until it was time to bottle, without the wine's ever touching wood. Others felt that the wine would improve if stored for a period in wooden barrels, as the wood might impart some of its flavor and fragrance to the wine. And, where necessary, the wood could soften a wine that was highly acidic.

According to some DOC regulations, certain wines, especially big reds, must spend a specified minimum amount of time in wood before being bottled, because it is felt that wood is part of the special character of that wine. But some wine makers decide to leave wine in wooden barrels for months or even a year longer than the DOC minimum. Once bottled, some wines go to market almost immediately. Others, especially the better wines, receive further aging in bottles before going to market. Wines that are aged do not bring immediate financial return to producers, which is why they are often more expensive. These factors—steel versus wood fermentation, storage and aging, bottle aging, and so on—are why we see variations even in wines that may have the same name.

The 1980s saw the arrival of the *barrique* rage. *Barriques* are very small, expensive barrels made of oak that usually come from France or Slovenia. Many wine producers thought it was preferable (or at least necessary to remain competitive) to buy these barrels to age their wines. Part of the *barrique* phenomenon is due to the fact that California wine producers evolved a particular style of Chardonnay that is aged in oak that has a distinct and often-pleasing vanilla flavor. But this style did not necessarily translate to European wine production, and I believe that many Italian grape varieties were sacrificed by putting them in extensive contact with wood. Drinking them was shocking: one tasted the tree, not the grape.

I am not against wood: many reds and a few whites improve by having some contact with it as part of their finishing process. Proper use of barrels and *barriques* can give wine real character. But the wood should be an accent, not the dominant flavor. There are many wines, especially whites, that never touch wood and are none the worse for it. Part of what must happen is that wine consumers need to understand that just because a grape is named, for example, Chardonnay, it will not always taste the same. The quality of the grapes grown, the soil that feeds the vines, the amount of rain and sun in a particular place, will all affect a wine's flavor even before the grapes are picked. Then there will be all sorts of variations according to the taste, preferences, and talents of the wine maker. So a typical California Chardonnay will not resemble one from Australia, South Africa, Chile, Spain, France, or many regions of Italy. One of the best Chardonnays I know is Les Cretes, made in Aymavilles in the Valle d'Aosta. This wine is fresh, lively, full of fruit, with no sense of wood, and it in no way resembles the oaky wines of the Napa Valley.

You will develop your own preferences as you drink wine in Italy. Just remember that if a wine maker spends more time bragging about the price of his *barriques* than the quality of his grapes, his values are probably not in the right place.

Two current developments in the Italian wine world are the leveling-off of consumption in Italy and abroad and the integration of Italian agricultural customs and laws into those being forged by the still-expanding European Union (EU). As people drink less wine—even in Italy it has evolved from a food into a prized beverage—demand for better wines sold at moderate prices has increased. This has created a small crisis among some wine makers who invested heavily in technology and excellent new vines only to find that they have to lower their prices to compete with wines from countries with lower production costs. Eventually, this will shake out, and Italian wine producers, in order to survive, will find a way to achieve what is known as *il rapporto qualità/prezzo* (a relationship between quality and price).

Many women in the Italian wine business were in the vanguard of recognizing the slowing growth and the drive for quality at a moderate price. Some of these women formed an important organization called *Le Donne del Vino* (the Women of Wine). At the core of their philosophy is *poco, ma buono* (little, but good). As people, especially young people, learn that drinking small amounts of wine is good and good for them, there may be an upswing in consumption of this quality product. It is unfortunate that Italian young people, like those everywhere, seem to prefer Coca-Cola as their beverage.

For the most part, alcohol abuse is not a problem in Italy. Unlike countries where hard drinking is a social sport and there are many tragic consequences, Italy has seen little of this outside of the northeastern part of the country. The Etruscans, the Greeks, the Romans, and the Christians knew that wine is a product to be enjoyed, whether that enjoyment comes through Dionysian indulgence, through Apollonian study and analysis of this marvelous gift of the earth, through religious veneration, or, in the wisdom of Le Donne del Vino, through the simple pleasure of enjoying a fine glass during a meditative moment. Of course, there are certain people who, for medical, religious, or social reasons, should not—or find it preferable not—to drink any alcohol. This is fine, but does not mean that others have to conform to the behavior of those who abstain. The so-called New Puritanism has created hysteria and paranoia about consumption of alcohol that have swept up quality wine as well. This is a shame. Wine is too costly and precious to use as a means of inebriation, yet it has been associated with other alcoholic beverages that some people use as a drug. As with anything else of this type, education about proper ways to consume wine is essential.

The issue of integration into the EU is more troubling. I have always believed in open markets, but by creating continent-wide standards, the Europeans are negating, or at least ignoring, local conditions, traditions, and taste. What may be good for Brussels may not be good for Canelli or Locorotondo or Montepulciano. For example, in northern European countries with less sunlight, sugar is often added during wine fermentation because not enough sugar developed in the grapes when they were on the vine. Italians do not add sugar, but instead use cooked musts if additional grape sugar is deemed necessary for fermentation. Should this way of doing things, which is sensible and has worked well for years, be abandoned to please bureaucrats? I don't think so.

Another evolving change in Italy and throughout the world is the naming of wines. The EU has begun to push for standardization, which will be difficult to achieve and will wipe out a lot of tradition and culture in the process. Should wines be named for the ground in which the grapes were grown, for the grapes themselves, or for the wine's producer? For example, in Piemonte, many wines are named for the towns they are from (Barolo, Barbaresco) or for the grapes from which they were made (Barbera, Dolcetto, Nebbiolo, Freisa). In Toscana, wines may be named for their grapes and towns (Vernaccia di San Gimignano), for zones (Chianti), or sometimes they are given names that have meaning to the producer (Sassicaia or Belcaro). There is no particular standardization in this, and Italy and the rest of the wine world are moving glacially toward a resolution of the issue because each country has proprietary interests it wants to protect.

The most likely result will be to list the name of the grape on a label if the wine is made of only one variety (Merlot, for example), and then attach its place of origin. So you might see "Merlot del Veneto" or, more specifically, "Merlot del Lison-Pramaggiore, Veneto." Part of the problem is that grapes come in different clones even if they have the same name. So the Chardonnay planted in one vineyard may be different from the one grown next door. Then there is the issue of national provenance of a grape. The European Union has decided that the Tokaj from Hungary is the only grape that can have that name, so that Tocai, the most popular white grape in Friuli, will have to be renamed. It will likely have the much-less-romantic or evocative name of Friuli Bianco, which is generically descriptive but has none of the historical weight and local significance that Tocai del Friuli does. When one enters a bar in Friuli to order a *tajut*, this local-dialect term implies a small glass of Tocai, and everyone understands its meaning and shares in its significance. It gives a sense of oneness and belonging with a place, a people, and a history. When generic names replace those that have meaning and connect people to their land, their home, and their traditions, the fabric of memory will unravel, and we will all be poorer for that.

These are some of the essential details in the history of Italian wine. There are many ways for you, the gourmet traveler, to come into contact with the Italian wine world. One of the recent positive developments has been the linking of wine and tourism. In some countries, this represents little more than an opportunity to get drunk at a winery. In Italy, however, there are many wineries that open their doors at certain times of the year so that visitors can discover how wine is made. This national movement began in Montalcino in Toscana and quickly spread. Most Italian regions now have a representative who can supply you with details about visiting wineries. These contacts are listed in regional chapters under the heading "Wine Tourism."

In some cases, it is possible for travelers to stay at farms and wineries. This is part of the burgeoning agritourism movement. One eats with farm families, observes the rhythms of agricultural life, and finds genuine relaxation and hospitality. Most regions can furnish you with an *agriturismo* directory. Prices range from very reasonable to somewhat expensive (at certain Tuscan estates). There are some *agriturismo* farms that offer meals but not accommodation. This makes for a nice afternoon excursion to the countryside if you are staying in a city.

Another aspect of wine tourism that has developed in recent years is the Wine Road. One of the delights of wine is that it usually grows in places of great beauty, so it is a pleasure to drive or cycle down a road in a district of wineries. I will suggest a few itineraries in the regional chapters. In Italian, the road is called *La Strada del Vino;* in the German-speaking Alto Adige it is *Die Weinstrasse;* in the French parts of the Valle d'Aosta it is the *Route des Vins.* Tourist offices can provide details of Wine Road itineraries. Some wineries also sell food at informal stands that you can snack on as you have a glass. In Friuli and Alto Adige the food offerings are often quite substantial and delicious. The *frasca* in Friuli is an old tradition. This is a winery that cooks meals to serve at outdoor tents or gardens, often attracting large crowds.

Another means of learning about wine is to visit an *enoteca.* This rather wide-ranging term has different meanings in different contexts. Let's start with the Enoteca Italiana in Siena. This special institution plays an important role in the dissemination of information about all of the wines of Italy through its publications, special events, and imaginative nonpartisan leadership. When a wine is awarded DOC or DOCG status, the announcement is made at the Enoteca Italiana. The *Settimana dei Vini* (Wine Week) held at the Enoteca in early June is one of the great annual events on the wine calendar. You can read more about the Enoteca on page 412. It is a worthy destination that you should visit when you go to Siena, which I have designated as the Classic Town for Toscana.

Several regions have an *enoteca regionale* where you can go to learn about, taste, and purchase wines. A particularly outstanding one is the Enoteca Regionale di Emilia-Romagna, in a historic castle in Dozza, not far from Bologna (Classic Town for that region). Then there are many wine towns that have *enoteche* for you to become acquainted with the local product. Piemonte in particular is very well served by its local *enoteche,* although there are good ones throughout the country. You will find all of these listed in the regional chapters. *Enoteche* are good starting points for local wine tourism: they can provide you with information on agritourism and addresses of producers you can visit. Many of these *enoteche* are outgrowths of local consortia *(consorzi)* of producers who set standards and do collective promotion for all the wines made by their members. Two famous consortia are those of Chianti Classico in Toscana and of the spumante sparkling wine in the province of Asti in Piemonte.

The *enoteca* also implies a wine shop or bar, owned by private individuals and not in any way an entity of producers or regional governments. Instead, these *enoteche* are wonderful places to gather to share in the pleasure of wine. Some are conventional wine stores that only do tastings on special occasions. Many others are places where you go for a glass of wine. (Some also sell bottles to take home.) Many prepare good food, usually quite inexpensive, that you can enjoy with your glass of wine. This is particularly true in the Veneto, in cities such as Venezia and Treviso (Classic Town for the region).

A slightly more elaborate *enoteca* is known as the *osteria*. This nice old word suggests open doors and the receiving of guests. This is a very casual, welcoming, usually inexpensive place with a friendly host, pleasing wine, honest food, and good feelings. It often has long tables and is a nice place to meet Italians. A prototype, I think, is Osteria i Malardot in Torriana, near Rimini, at the border of Romagna and the Marche (see page 378) but there are excellent ones across the country.

Throughout Italy there are wine museums that document the history of wine making in the nation or in the zone. One of the best is the one built by the Lungarotti winery in Torgiano (Umbria). Many regional chapters have listings of wine museums.

For wine professionals, a visit to Vinitaly, the nation's premier wine trade fair, is essential. It is held in Verona at the beginning of April each year. It is to Italian wine what the Cannes Film Festival is to the movie business. Almost every wine maker in the country is there offering tastings of recent vintages and attempting to sell his product to owners of *enoteche,* to restaurateurs, and to wine importers from around the world. The huge pavilions of the Verona fairgrounds are set up with hundreds of stands, usually grouped by region. The event lasts four or five days, and even the most organized and dedicated taster can try only a fraction of what is available. But a visit to Vinitaly is the most graphic way of seeing how huge and varied the Italian wine industry is. Traditionally, the public is allowed to attend Vinitaly one day during the fair, usually Sunday. See page 250 in the Veneto chapter for more details.

Wine in Italy is an ongoing joy. When the usually somber and dour Henrik Ibsen was asked to explain why his play *Peer Gynt* was so full of humor, vivacity, and love of life, he explained that it was written in Amalfi (our Classic Town for Campania) "under the influence of the wine cup." Wine brings people together and fosters socialization, meditation, and reflection. I have made many friends in the wine world because these are people who share their love of the land and one of its most sublime products. As you can tell, wine does indeed render me loquacious, if not poetic. If you develop a serious interest in Italian wine, I commend to you the writings of Burton Anderson, Victor Hazan, Matt Kramer, and other experts.

Traveling in Italy
(and Dining en Route)

Le Ferrovie dello Stato (FS)—the Italian State Railways

Once, when one traveled on Italian trains, it was the custom to bring hampers of food for the journey. Trips were long because of slow trains and all-too-frequent delays of up to eight to twelve hours, further aggravated by unexpected strikes. Distances once seemed greater when people traveled infrequently. Although fares were cheap, wages were also low, so that a long train trip from south to north in search of work was a significant expense. At train stations one saw tearful farewells as families passed luggage through windows to the one passenger who jumped on early to grab seats.

Trains were once divided into compartments of eight seats (later reduced to six). There was a long corridor that connected all of the compartments in a railway car. In the corridor were drop-down seats under windows that opened. Pasted on the windows were admonitions in Italian, French, German, and English not to lean out the window, which people nonetheless did, most often in train stations. When passengers were seated in the corridors it was difficult to shimmy past them, especially with luggage. You would slide the glass door of a prospective compartment, look at a seat, and timidly ask "È libero?" to find out if the seat was free. Anyone seated in the compartment would look up and examine the questioner and usually shrug. One did not want to be rude to a fellow passenger, but the cars were often cramped, and people liked to carve a little space for themselves for the journey.

Only later were many Italian trains reconfigured to use long rows of seats, airplane style, with tray tables and a single aisle. The new trains have picture windows and climate-controlled cabins (an unnatural notion if ever I heard one).

Because journeys were long and slow and it was difficult to get food en route, passengers packed meals before departing. This food was less expensive, familiar, and reminded the traveler of *mamma* back home. The food hampers of once upon a time contained loaves of bread, packages of sliced *salame* and prosciutto, fragrant cheeses whose scent became invasive after two hours on board, olives, peaches, apples, cookies, lemons to refresh oneself, water, and homemade wine. I used to wonder why a family of four always had food for twelve. This is because, owing to customary Italian hospitality, it was a given that the food would be shared with whomever else was riding in the cabin. Everyone who traveled made the same assumption, and each person packed in the little compartments would take part in a grand ritual of sincere hospitality. And there was enough food in these rail cars for a wedding.

These long trips usually occurred as families went to see relatives who had emigrated north or, on the occasion of the very frequent elections, as the migrants returned home. Voting is compulsory in Italy, and low fares are instituted to allow people to go home for elections. These travelers mingled freely and amiably with the millions of tourists who came to Italy each year. For foreigners a train trip was often the most enduring contact with locals, who invariably offered a meal and frequently an invitation to come visit. It was through many of these invitations that I've met people from every corner of Italy and have been able to learn about local foods and gather recipes.

There was also once a great romance about train stations. In the 1970s I used to go to the Bologna station at night to see trains come from the south of Italy, or the national expresses from France, Holland, Switzerland, Germany, Austria, and Yugoslavia. Then one would see phantomlike trains from the Eastern Bloc, full of gaunt, thirsty, impoverished people who would be agog at the animation of the Bologna station. Most of them were heading to Roma for an audience with the pope. These holy pilgrimages have changed little since the Middle Ages.

Each Italian train station had its own character. It often reflected the character of the city it was in. Torino Porta Nuova was airy and sedate. Firenze Santa Maria Novella was sleek and busy, but not oppressive. Roma Termini fulfilled the dictum that all roads lead to Rome. It was a hive of activity: priests and nuns arrived from all over Europe, sharing trains with tourists and pilgrims. Flacks and touts from hotels and pensions tried to convince you to follow them, cab drivers vied for your business (at a price, of course). Wide-eyed Italians from tiny villages gaped and blinked at the frenzied pace of their mythic capital.

Large stations had an *albergo diurno,* which was an institutional but dignified place to stop for a shower or a nap before resuming a journey. It was popular with the backpack set, who would sleep on train trips to save money on hotels. The *alberghi diurni* still serve the same function, usually quite capably, but there is a whiff of danger in some of them, especially when one sees the occasional drug addict there getting a fix. Little train stations around Italy were (and are) particularly endearing. Throughout Liguria, train stations brim with flowers and perfume. In San Vincenzo in Toscana, each ticket is still manually franked by the ticket vendor (in most of Italy tickets are now computer printed and must be punched in the little

The castle on Lago di Toblino, Trentino

yellow meters in every station before you board the train). Some stations in provincial capitals such as Cuneo and Mantova have changed little in sixty years and are charmingly quaint.

Sadly, life in Italian train stations changed forever in August 1980, when a bomb was planted by neo-Fascists in Bologna Centrale. More than eighty people were killed (including a friend of mine), and many were injured. The romance and innocence of train travel were gone, and all kinds of things changed. Capital investment resulted in new rails and trains, and redesigned stations with heightened security. A new style of station evolved that was clean, airy, and impersonal. Examples of these can be found in San Remo, Savona, Pescara, and Cosenza.

Nowadays the Italian train system is faster and more expensive, although it is still very modest in cost compared with trains in most European countries. If you purchase a supplemental fare for one of the high-speed trains, you can go from one major city to another in less time. This has brought the peninsula closer together, but has also meant a reduction in the number of trains that ply the local routes. Passengers on longer trips now travel with a sandwich, an orange, and a bottle of mineral water, all of which will be consumed by oneself. Gone are the hampers of food of once upon a time. Conversation is still polite, but more general and less likely to result in further contact. In my view, this is part of the invasive presence of the bureaucratic European Union, which, in the process of standardizing things, has robbed countries of many local traits. Railways conform to European standards, which are comfortable but impersonal. Italy, by contrast, has always been spontaneous and more intimate. The Italian word for "privacy," in fact, is *privacy* and was recently borrowed from the British and carries an Anglo-Saxon connotation. Previously, Italians were not nosy or intrusive, but simply cordial and sociable.

While I would not go out of my way to dine in a train station, sometimes it is the only option. Good meals can be had at many Italian stations while waiting for your train. Not long ago at the cafeteria of Pisa Centrale I had an excellent plate of rigatoni with prosciutto and peas in a tomato-cream sauce that would do any trattoria proud. It was followed by salad and cheese and was washed down with good Chianti. Prices for such a meal are generally inexpensive to moderately inexpensive.

In the past it was possible to buy *cestini*, baskets of hot food, from vendors with pushcarts on railway platforms. If you leaned out of your train window in Bologna and proffered a little money, you would be handed a basket with lasagne or tortellini, roast chicken, tender vegetables, fresh fruit, bread, and wine. The *cestini* have largely disappeared, though you can buy a sandwich and wine or mineral water at most station bars.

On many trains, especially those that go from Venezia or Milano through Bologna and Firenze to Roma, there is a dining car where very good meals can be had at moderate to moderately expensive prices. Pasta and *secondi* are often made to order in a small kitchen on board. Service is typically fine, as is the wine. Most major trains also have a man who pushes a small cart with prewrapped sandwiches, small bottles of water and soda, plus commercial ice cream, candy, and mediocre coffee. The offerings from this cart are often of questionable freshness and uninviting flavor.

What is my recommendation for dining on long train trips? In Italy I always travel with a simple fork, knife, and spoon, plus a small corkscrew. Before going on a long train trip, I go to a good *gastronomia* or *salumeria* and buy more food than I could possibly consume, plus a good bottle of wine. On the train I recreate the warm treatment I received for years by offering food all around, striking a blow for hospitality and perhaps making new friends as well (www.trenitalia.it).

Volare: Flying in Italy

Italian commercial aviation is quite safe, and flying is the quickest, most convenient way to get from one end of the country to the other. It is also quite expensive, so if you are purchasing a ticket from a foreign city, you might try for a fare that includes your flight to Italy as well as one or two air transfers within the country. If you are coming from North or South America, Asia, Africa, Australia, or New Zealand and are not going to Roma or Milano as your first destination in Italy, you have two options. You can fly to Roma on Alitalia or another airline and take a connecting flight. Or you can fly to another European city, such as London,

Paris, Amsterdam, Frankfurt, Zurich, Vienna, Copenhagen, or Madrid, and catch a connecting flight to your preferred city. Among the Italian cities with European air links are Torino, Genova, Verona, Venezia, Trieste, Bologna, Pisa, Firenze, Napoli, Palermo, and Olbia.

Travelers from North America should take note that Delta Airlines has nonstop flights to Venezia from New York and Atlanta. Venezia's Marco Polo Airport is small and well run. There are ferries and very expensive water taxis that will transport you to the Piazza San Marco in about an hour. If you want to go elsewhere in the Veneto or Friuli and are not renting a car, you will have to catch a bus to the Mestre railway station for train connections. Bologna and Torino airports are now served directly from New York on Eurofly, making it possible to avoid connecting in Roma or Milano.

The best way to reach Sardegna from the Italian mainland is by air, because the ferries, which cost more or less the same as a flight, take thirteen hours. Italians take the ferries if they need to transport automobiles that they will use in Sardegna. If you plan to drive there, arrange for a rental car at the Cagliari, Aighero, or Olbia airport.

Milano is served by two airports that receive flights from most of the world. Its Linate Airport is to the east of the city, close by, and is connected to all of Italy and most of Europe. The central city is easily reached by bus or taxi. Linate also has almost hourly service to Roma on the nation's busiest air route. This is the equivalent of the New York to Washington shuttle in the United States. The other airport, Malpensa, is northwest of the city, a full hour or more away, and is served by transcontinental airlines from Asia, Oceania, Africa, and the Americas. Travelers to Milano should be aware that both Malpensa and Linate are closed periodically in autumn, winter, and early spring when the city is blanketed with dense fogs. Flights are rerouted to Genova or sometimes Torino or Bergamo, and shuttle buses are arranged.

The airport situation in Roma is much better. The city's Leonardo da Vinci Airport (also called Fiumicino) has been successfully expanded in recent years and service has been upgraded. After flying to Italy, you can make convenient connections for virtually every Italian city equipped with an airport. The Leonardo Express train connects the airport with Roma Termini. There are good bars and restaurants at Fiumicino, so it is possible to eat well if you need to stay for a couple of hours between connecting flights. (See page 480 for more details.)

I have a tradition whenever I travel to or from Italy by plane. Upon landing I repair to the nearest bar at the airport for a double espresso. This not only gives me a small jolt of energy to face the next part of my trip, but is a transfusion of Italian flavor that puts me in the right frame of mind for my coming visit. Upon departure, usually in the late morning, I have a cappuccino, brioche, and fruit juice (apricot, pear, or peach) to leave a nice taste in my mouth and stave off hunger in the air, where food is often late in arriving and seldom pleasing. On numerous occasions before a transatlantic flight, I have purchased a nice little basket of food from Peck in Milano or Volpetti in Roma to enjoy in the air. It is far better than any airline meal and extends the flavor of Italy in my mouth for a few more hours. Remember that you cannot bring fresh fruits and vegetables, sliced *salumi* and other uncooked meats, and soft cheeses through U.S. Customs, so finish everything before you land or leave it on the plane. Better still, if you have a lot of food, share it with a seatmate.

La Strada: Italy by Road

In researching this book I decided that almost every place listed should be accessible to all readers, so relatively few of the destinations I have included are reachable only by car. Also, I believe that the isolation of an automobile diminishes the likelihood that you might have meaningful contact with Italians.

The chief virtue of traveling by car in Italy is the nearly complete freedom an auto provides. You can journey to far-off vineyards or country restaurants at will. Renting and operating an automobile in Italy is an expensive proposition. Car-rental costs are among the highest in Europe, and gasoline *(benzina)* is exorbitantly expensive. The reason gas is so high is that the government chose long ago to make the sale of *benzina* a form of regressive tax collection. What many travelers do is rent a car in France, Germany, or Austria and then collect coupons at the Italian border that will exempt them from many gas taxes.

European cars in general, and Italian cars in particular, are designed to get many more kilometers per liter (miles per gallon) than their American counterparts, so that a tank of gas will take you farther than you might expect. But there are many places you cannot go. Venezia, of course, is car-free. You must drive over the railway bridge and park at the Piazzale Roma, taking a vaporetto (ferry) or an expensive water taxi to your hotel. Parking is pricey at the Piazzale Roma garages, and the queues are interminable in tourist season. Almost every major Italian city has a *centro storico* (historic center) that is off-limits to all vehicular traffic except cars of residents, taxis, buses, and emergency vehicles. You must park your car outside the city center and go into town by foot or some other means. Parking in Italy is very competitive, and the many street signs are indecipherable, so you may very well wind up with a parking ticket. The police will notify your car-rental company, and the cost will be added to your credit-card bill.

If you plan to concentrate your touring in major cities or any town served by bus or rail, a rental car is probably an unwise expenditure. If, however, your vacation plan is to drive through the Alps, the lake district, the Apennines, the countryside of Piemonte, Toscana, Umbria, or the deep south, a car will enable you to journey more easily. You will find that Italians are audacious but safe drivers who like to speed and change lanes freely. They will not endanger you, but they will not enjoy idling behind you either. Accident rates in Italy are lower than those in France, Belgium, Germany, Austria, Spain, Portugal, and Greece. Drunk driving is only a problem in northeastern Italy, where grappa is more frequently consumed. Beware, too, of fogs in much of northern Italy during the colder months of the year.

Most visitors who get into accident trouble do this because they are lost and focus more on directions than on their driving. Italian signage is very confusing for the uninitiated. On small roads in the city or the country there are blue or black signs pointing to particular towns. These signs are often not visible until you are close to them, which means that you will hold up traffic as you try to read up to ten signs before finding the one that leads to your destination. It often happens that your sign (to Volterra in Toscana, let's say) does not appear at each intersection, forcing you to guess whether to turn left or right or to go straight ahead. A good idea is to look at a map before you leave and learn the names of a few nearby towns and where they are in relation to Volterra. If you see those names on the signs, you will have a better sense of where you are. As you travel, bear in mind that yellow signs will direct you to businesses, hotels, restaurants, and agricultural estates, but not to cities or towns. So if you are looking for a particular restaurant in Volterra, watch the yellow signs as you near the town.

As you drive in small towns and along back roads, remember that most of these byways were paved long before the invention of the automobile. Houses hug the side of the road and, in towns, you seldom have a clear view before making turns that you would easily do at home. Observe stop signs religiously and, if you need to see if any traffic is coming from left to right, inch your car forward just enough to have a view before turning. And remember that *senso unico* means "one way."

The Italian superhighway, called the autostrada, is excellent. It is much better paved and maintained than most American highways, and only those in Germany are considered superior to it in Europe. An autostrada has the letter *A* and a number (A1, A2, and so on), and most signage is green. There are seldom speed limits, so you can get from place to place quickly. Tolls are high on these roads, but if you have invested in a rental car, you will not find the tolls an undue expense.

A secondary road, usually called a *strada statale*, often is near the autostrada but is slower and toll free. These roads are also more interesting, as they take you through small towns and villages and let you see the real Italy. Many a *strada statale* (labeled S.S. on navy-blue signs) was laid out by the Romans, including the famous Via Emilia that runs from Piacenza through most of the towns of Emilia-Romagna to Rimini on the Adriatic Sea.

For dining when you make auto trips, consult this book for restaurants I have listed throughout the country. Plot your itinerary so that a particularly enticing restaurant will be within reach when it is mealtime. It is wise to call ahead to reserve, because you don't want to make significant detours for naught. On the autostrada there may be an Autogrill, which often serves very good food, such as prosciutto, pasta, roast veal, vegetables, fruit, and ice cream. Surprisingly, you can also drink wine, beer, brandy, or grappa at these restaurants before going out on the road. This would be unheard of in North America, but very few Italians abuse alcohol and then drive. Beware, as I said, of the Veneto and bordering areas, where drunk driving is a problem. Many highway restaurants also have stores that sell fabulous food products such as Parma hams and cheeses, olive oils, balsamic vinegar, breads, cakes, and wines that would only be found in fancy gourmet shops in other countries. If you are driving through and have forgotten to buy something before you reach the border, stop at one of these excellent shops on the autostrada.

Another way to journey the back roads of Italy is by bus. I am not referring to motorcoach tours, which, I believe, deny the traveler the chance to discover a town or country in his own way, but to the many bus lines that traverse the parts of Italy where railways might not go. Buses are indispensable in the Alps, Toscana, Umbria, Marche, and in much of the south. They cost slightly more than trains but are still a bargain and are almost always clean, efficient, and punctual. Once, on a very hot day in Basilicata, a bus driver decided that no one would want to travel in such heat, so he canceled his run. I, of course, was waiting at an intermediate stop and had no way of knowing the bus would not come, so I wound up sleeping in a barn as the guest of a friendly farm family. This is a very rare exception, and you should not let it deter you from bus travel, especially in central and northern Italy.

One important way that buses are preferable to trains is that they will usually take you to a city center, while a train might not. A train station in cities might be central, but not near the main square, where a bus might go. Hill towns such as Orvieto and Siena have their train station in the valley below town, and you must find other means to reach the center. Check before deciding which means to use as you plan a trip to a particular destination. A few terms: *Autobus* means "bus," and usually refers to bus lines within cities (such as the number 64 in Roma that takes you to the Vatican). *Corriere* is typically a bus that frequently traverses the same route, such as the one between Firenze and Siena. *Pullman* is the general term for buses that go from town to town or make long-distance journeys.

Italy on Two Wheels

Anyone who has seen the 1979 film *Breaking Away* knows about the romance of cycling in Italy. Cycling is a popular sport in much of Italy, especially the north, but it also is a good way to get from one place to another. Italian bicycles are excellent, and you might want to purchase a *bicicletta* in the first town you visit. The bicycle has always been a popular mode of travel there and, in the days before affluence came to most of the citizenry, it was the only way to go. Moreover, it often meant transportation to a job and therefore a better life. (Think of the towering and tragic 1940s film *The Bicycle Thief* to understand what this means.)

In many cities where the central zones are closed to vehicular traffic, Italians get around by bike. I always marvel at the number of fit elderly Italians who travel about on a bike, and I try to use their example as motivation. If you are concerned about gaining weight during a gastronomic sojourn of Italy, cycling from meal to meal is a good alternative. Ciclismo Classico is an American company that organizes very good itineraries, including a few that are geared to visits to wineries or places of interest to food lovers. These include visits to cooking schools in Bologna, Piemonte, and Puglia. Contact Ciclismo Classico, 13 Marathon Street, Arlington, Massachusetts 02174, tel. 617/6463377 or 800/8667314, fax 617/6411512.

In beach towns and in cities, the *motorino* (moped) has always been popular. It was usually the first step up from the bicycle, and in the past one would see father, mother, and child all on the same vehicle. In Roma you often see a man zooming through town on his *motorino* while his girlfriend sits sidesaddle behind him, legs dangling and high heels pointing. The *motorino* is also the vehicle of the teenager, and it can be noisy. But it is often the fastest way to get around town, and you might use one (it can be rented) if you feel confident about driving in Italian traffic. It is the law that you must wear *una casca* (a helmet) if you ride a *motorino* or a motorcycle *(motociclo)*, which is more powerful than a *motorino*.

Tours

If you are reluctant to venture on your own as a gourmet traveler in Italy, you can take an organized food or wine tour, such as those offered by Mediolanum Tourist Service in Milano. This firm offers packaged tours that visit different food and wine zones of the country, and it can also customize a tour to your particular interests. Contact Mediolanum Tourist Service, Corso Matteotti 1, 20121 Milano, tel. 02/76013676, fax 02/783516. Ask for Carla Galli Falsitta or Giovanna Gelmini.

In the USA, the Smithsonian Institution (www.SmithsonianJourneys.org) creates excellent tours with comfortable hotels, fine food, and knowledgeable study leaders. In Italy the focus may be cooking, art, automobiles, or the performing arts. I have led a couple of opera and food seminars for the Smithsonian in Italy, one in Emilia-Romagna and Veneto, the other in Le Marche. These tours are especially suited for people who want a strong learning component as part of their trip to Italy. They attract an international clientele with many Europeans, Asians, and North and South Americans.

Merion Cultural Tours (www.Merion-culturaltours.com/index.php), based in Genova, puts together excellent custom-made tours specializing in the opera and the visual arts, gardens and villas, food and wine throughout Italy. They deal with individuals, although their primary focus is for special-interest groups.

In the United States there are two food tour operators of note:

Sally Maraventano, Cucina Casalinga, 171 Drum Hill Road, Wilton, Connecticut 06897, tel. or fax 203/762-0768;

Judy Ebrey, Cuisine International, P.O. Box 25228, Dallas, Texas 75225, tel. 214/373-1161, fax 214/373-1162.

Now that you know how to travel in Italy, it's time to go there. *Andiamo in Italia!*

Liguria

REGIONAL CAPITAL:
Genova (GE).

PROVINCIAL CAPITALS:
Imperia (IM), La Spezia
(SP), Savona (SV).

TOURIST INFORMATION:
Assessorato al Turismo di
Liguria,
Via Fieschi 15,
16121 Genova,
tel. 010/54852632.

Agritourism:
Agriturist Comitato
Regionale,
Via T. Ivrea 11/10,
16129 Genova,
tel. 010/5531878.

For many visitors, Liguria (the Italian Riviera to you) is the quintessential Italian region. Little mountain towns perch high over the stunning blue Mediterranean. The 343-kilometer (220-mile) coastline is dotted with romantic fishing villages, rocky cliffs, sandy beaches, and a couple of industrial ports that send Italian goods to the four corners of the world. As beautiful as Liguria is to look at, the olfactory sense is at least as gratified as the visual. Flower growing is one of the most important Ligurian businesses. The mountain valleys are covered with the basil, rosemary, thyme, and marjoram that provide the fragrance in Ligurian kitchens. Unlike in the rest of northern Italy, garlic *(aglio)* is a key player in Ligurian cuisine. A sauce called *agliata* is close at hand when fish, meat, or vegetables are served.

When you mention the name "Liguria" to most Italians, they usually remark about the frugality of the locals. They are occasionally called the Scots of Italy and, in one form or another, are thought to be as tight-fisted as the rest of the Italians are generous. There is some truth in this but, as with most stereotypes and clichés, it is much exaggerated. The fact is that subsistence has always been difficult in Liguria. The sea is not as rich and generous in these parts as it is farther south and west. There is very little level soil for the type of agriculture on a grand scale that one sees in Emilia, Lombardia, or Puglia. The paucity of level land makes every arable patch valuable, and Ligurians have learned how to make the most of limited resources.

As great seafarers, Ligurians are notable for having developed preparations that can be consumed during long voyages. Dried ravioli were the pasta of choice on Genovese vessels of the late Middle Ages. Dried codfish, much of it imported from Norway, has been a central component of Ligurian sailors' foods for five hundred years. Anchovies and sardines preserved in olive oil were other staples.

As you might expect, all of this dried and preserved food can become tiresome rather quickly. It is notable then that the food of the Ligurian terra firma is probably the most fragrant and delicate in all of Italy. The combination of pasta, vegetables, fruit, oil, wine, herbs, bread, fish, and small amounts of meat and cheese makes Ligurian food the ideal choice from the point of view of health as well as flavor. Although the fabled Mediterranean Diet is (mistakenly, I believe) associated with Toscana, you need only look at the robust octogenarians pedaling their bicycles up and down hills to know that we can all learn something from the way Ligurians eat. Ligurians place fruit and vegetables at the center of their eating priorities, which is one explanation of why they are such a healthy people. (They live longer than other Italians, who vie with Iceland and Japan for the world's longest life expectancy.) A visit to the San Remo market, the Mercato Orientale in Genova, or the better shops of La Spezia will show you how extraordinary Ligurian fruit and vegetables are.

Eating in Liguria

As the description above suggests, the food of Liguria is unusual and delicious. It does not divide into categories as neatly as do those from other regions, because so many Ligurian specialties are consumed away from the dinner table. Many of these are found in *friggitorie* (fry shops) that produce Liguria's equivalent of fast food (which puts all others to shame). For the purposes of this book, these specialties will be listed under the traditional categories of an Italian meal. If you wish to deepen your knowledge of Ligurian food, please read my *Recipes from Paradise: Life and Food on the Italian Riviera*.

ANTIPASTI

Acciughe Marinate. Fresh anchovies marinated in lemon juice.

Cappon Magro. A composed salad of various cooked fishes combined with assorted greens. The ingredients are stacked in layers in a bowl lined with vinegar-soaked rusks. The salad is then dressed with a sauce made of anchovies, garlic, pine nuts, capers, olives, olive oil, parsley, and then decorated with hard-boiled eggs and pieces of lobster and shrimp.

Frisceu. Fish and vegetable fritters.

Gianchetti (sometimes called *Bianchetti*). Tiny anchovies or sardines, boiled or fried.

Muscoli Ripieni. Mussels stuffed with breadcrumbs, herbs, and cheese.

BAKED GOODS

Farinata. Chickpea-flour crepes, baked throughout the day and sold hot in wedges.

Focaccia. Liguria's famous bread, made with olive oil and often with flavorings such as cheese, onions, rosemary, olives, or salt.

Sardenaira (also called *Pissadella*). A flat tart topped with tomatoes, olives, onions, and anchovies.

PRIMI

Pastas such as lasagne, *trenette* (long, flat cousins of spaghetti), and gnocchi are served with pesto, the famous sauce made of fresh basil, pine nuts, garlic, olive oil, and Pecorino cheese.

Corzetti. An ancient Ligurian pasta with a figure-8 shape modeled after a coin used in the medieval Republicca di Genova. It also comes in disks with the imprint of a decorative stamp.

Mesciüà. The special soup of La Spezia, made with chickpeas, white beans, *farro* (spelt), olive oil, and pepper.

Minestrone alla Genovese. Vegetable soup spiked with pesto.

Pansôti con Tocco di Noci. Triangles of pasta filled with greens or herbs, topped with a walnut sauce that has a hint of curdled milk.

Picagge con Salsa di Carciofi. Tagliatelle with an artichoke sauce.

Ravioli con Preboggion. Filled with herbs.

Ravioli di Magro. Filled with ricotta cheese.

Sbira. Tripe-and-potato soup.

Tocco de Carne. Meat sauce.

Tocco de Noxe. Walnut sauce.

Trofie. A Genovese pasta tossed with string beans, boiled potatoes, and pesto.

SECONDI

Ligurians stuff all sorts of vegetables (zucchini, lettuce leaves, cabbage leaves, tomatoes, eggplants, artichokes, peppers, and so on) with all kinds of fillings, including meat, herbs, cheeses, nuts, and other vegetables. If you see the words *ripieno, ripieni,* or *farcito* following the name of a vegetable, this means that it is stuffed.

Buridda. A stew made with the best local fish.

Cima alla Genovese. Veal breast stuffed with organ meats, herbs, cheeses, vegetables, pine nuts, and pâté. It is rolled, boiled, chilled, and sliced thin.

Condiggion (or *Condion*). A salad made with vegetables, rusks, and *bottarga.*

Coniglio con le Olive. Rabbit cooked with olives and herbs, a specialty of the province of Imperia. Rabbit is prepared in many ways in Liguria.

Frittate. Omelettes made with various vegetables, herbs, or fish. Served cool.

Funghi. The inland areas of Liguria are full of wild mushrooms that are prepared in many ways, often as a main course. When prepared *alla genovese,* the mushrooms are cooked with potatoes, garlic, and parsley.

Pesce. A general term for "fish," which might include *sarago* and *orata.* These are served grilled or broiled and are central to Ligurian cooking.

Scabecio. Fried fish served with a marinade based on vinegar and herbs.

Tomaxelle. Veal rolls filled with marjoram, parsley, garlic, wild mushrooms, pine nuts, cheese, and egg.

Torta Pasqualina. An Easter dish made with thirty-three layers, one for each year in the life of Christ. Made with pastry layers, vegetables, cheeses, and eggs.

Triglie alla Genovese. Red mullet baked in white wine, fennel seeds, capers, and tomatoes.

DOLCI

Marrons Glacés. Candied chestnuts, invented in Genova around 1790, when the city was under French domination.

Marzipani Quaresemali. Confections served during Lent made with almond paste, cocoa, vanilla, and mint.

Pandolce Genovese. The local equivalent of Milano's famous yeast cake that includes currants and pine nuts.

Pasta Genovese. What we call genoise.

The stone bridge of Dolceacqua

The Wines of Liguria

Liguria, with its steep slopes and difficult soil, is not the most congenial terrain for viticulture. Yet wine has always been available in abundance, because most of the region borders on Piemonte and some of it adjoins Toscana, the two Italian regions where much of the greatest wine production—quantitatively and qualitatively—takes place. The nearness of these great wine-producing regions means that many grape varieties are available; more than one hundred varieties may be found in the small vineyards of Liguria. The leading Ligurian grapes are Pigato, Vermentino, and Rossese. Ligurian wine is influenced by its neighbors in an important way. In Piemonte most wines are made from a single grape (Dolcetto or Nebbiolo, for example), as are the wines of western Liguria (Riviera Ponente). Tuscan wines are usually blends of several grapes, as are those in eastern Liguria (the Lunigiana and the Cinqueterre).

The visitor to Liguria should make an effort to sample the region's wines, most of which marry perfectly with its delicious and delicate cuisine. Only a few Ligurian wines—particularly Rossese di Dolceacqua, Pigato, Vermentino, and the whites of the Cinqueterre—have achieved fame beyond the region, but because of limited production they are hard to find and often pricey.

Wine figures centrally in Ligurian gastronomy and social customs. One drinks white wine (especially Coronata, the white wine of Genova) while consuming freshly baked focaccia. Many Ligurian dishes feature a splash of wine to give flavor to the recipe. Until recently, one would see a *pirrone,* a typical wine bottle, on every fishing boat. A *pirrone* has an unusually long neck and narrow mouth. It is designed so that one can drink from it without placing one's lips on the rim. The *pirrone* provided wine for all of the fishermen and would be passed around while waiting for the fish to bite.

There are four principal wine-producing zones in Liguria:

Rossese di Dolceacqua. This wine is often referred to simply as Dolceacqua. The name means "Sweet Water," but is a reference to the name of the pretty little town it comes from, not the taste of the wine. Dolceacqua, north of Ventimiglia and a stone's throw from the French border, produces a flavorful, full-bodied DOC red that goes well with the rabbit dishes popular in the area. When the Rossese is aged for at least a year and its alcohol content rises from 12 percent to 13 percent, the wine can be called Rossese Superiore.

Riviera Ligure di Ponente. The provinces of Imperia and Savona produce most of the top wines in Liguria. Pigato is made of a grape of the same name. This lightly fragrant white with a slightly bitter almond taste goes beautifully with Ligurian seafood dishes and savory baked goods. Good Pigato comes from near Albenga and will be called Pigato Albenganese. Vermentino from this area is slightly more fragrant and fruity than its cousin in the Lunigiana. The Rossese, a light ruby red, is dry and quite drinkable. A fuller red is Ormeasco, similar to the Dolcetto of Piemonte, made of a grape that has been grown in a small area of the province of Imperia since 1300. Ormeasco Scia-trac is a lighter, pinker version of the red. Ormeasco is honored with a festival in late August in the town of Pornassio.

Cinqueterre. The wines of the Cinqueterre, five beautiful little villages in the hills just north of La Spezia, require great effort to produce. Tiny vineyards dot the slopes. Grapes are collected by hand and placed in small baskets that are carried to wineries by workers or on the backs of donkeys. I have occasionally seen Ligurian women carry these baskets on their heads. A delicate straw-colored DOC white wine called Bianco delle Cinqueterre is made using Albarola, Bosco, and Vermentino grapes. When these grapes are dried and the resulting wine is aged at least a year, Sciacchetrà, or Schiacchetrà, a sweet-dry dessert wine, is made that is at least 17 percent alcohol. It is sold by the bottle and, rarely, by the glass in a few bars and *caffès.*

Colli di Luni. The zone known as the Lunigiana is a mountainous area covering the point where Liguria, Toscana, and Emilia meet. A ruby-colored fragrant red, Rosso dei Colli di Luni, is made of Sangiovese and other available grapes, including Canaiolo, Pollera Nera, and Ciliegiolo. The area's white *(bianco)* is made of Ligurian Vermentino, Trebbiano, and other grapes. In addition, Vermentino, a wine made entirely of the grape of that name, is a delicious, dry white with a slightly almond taste. The wines of the Lunigiana were renowned in Roman times and were a particular favorite of Pliny.

Alassio (Savona)

Alassio is an old seaside town whose renown is based largely on the fact that it has one of the prettiest beaches in Liguria. While most of the Italian Riviera is rocky, Alassio has a long stretch of fine sand. Its most famous restaurant is La Palma (tel. 0182/40314). This place is highly touted in Italian food circles, although it is more famous for being famous than for the quality of its food. To my taste it is coasting on past glory, charging astronomical prices that create an expectation that cannot be met. More in keeping with the style of Alassio was a little meal I had at a place called the Albatros on the small promenade next to the beach. Here you can have inexpensive focaccia, *farinata*, or *panissa fritta* (fried chickpea meal) with toppings such as cheese, prosciutto, *crema di carciofi* (artichoke puree), sausage, mushrooms, Ligurian watercress, or other ingredients. These foods can be washed down with a beer or some local wine. It turns out that this building (Passeggiata Italia 4) was once the residence of Amilcare Ponchielli, composer of *La Gioconda*.

To discover the Alassio of the locals rather than the town that caters to tourists, one must go one block inland. Start at the Piazza Ferrero, a very sweet little square within earshot of the sea that is flanked by the Via Cristoforo Colombo and the Via XX Settembre. The square is filled with tables from the Caffè-Pasticceria San Lorenzo (closed Wednesday), which claims to have the true *baci d'Alassio*, the local baked specialty. These *baci* are chocolate cookies filled with hazelnut cream, honey, and chocolate. Stop in for one with a cup of coffee. The owner, Franco San Lorenzo, greets everyone with carefully chosen endearments: *bella, ciccia, bambola*, and so forth. In addition to the *baci*, most of the other pastries are quite delicious.

A few blocks down the Via XX Settembre is the Piazza Matteotti, a small square that is the domain of Balzola (closed Monday). This *caffè* and bakery has been there since 1902. Women in pink uniforms and tall net caps serve coffee, afternoon tea, and cocktails, along with the many baked goods of the house. Balzola also has a good version of *baci d'Alassio*. Once past the Piazza Matteotti, the Via XX Settembre becomes the Via Vittorio Veneto, the main thoroughfare for the daily *passeggiata*, even though it is narrower than the other major arteries. At 15:30h the Via Veneto is desolate, yet within two hours it is jam-packed with people.

Albenga (Savona)

Albenga attracts very few visitors compared with nearby Alassio, but it is really much more interesting. This city of 21,000 people was once Albium Inguanum, capital of the Ligurian Inguani, the ancient inhabitants of the region. Albenga later became a Roman stronghold, and the town plan is of Roman design. Wander through the city's small squares and peer at its many pleasing nooks and crannies. The Museo Civico Inguano has documentation from the pre-Roman era and is worth a visit.

BAKERY

Pasticceria Pastorino, Via Genova 30, tel. 0182/150293. Open 8–13h, 16–19:30h; closed Monday.

The renown of this little bakery spread far beyond Albenga soon after it opened in 1899, thanks to its three special cookies. The *amaretti di Albenga*, made with hazelnuts instead of the customary almonds, come in a green wrapper. After they won prizes in Paris and Rome in the 1920s, their legendary status was sealed.

Artichokes from Albenga

The *inguani al rhum*, in a red wrapper, are overpoweringly rummy and probably not to everyone's taste. The *delizie al cioccolato* and the *delizie al caffè*, which come in brown wrappers, are very flavorful, mouth pleasing confections.

DINING

Osteria Sutta Cà, Via Ernesto Rolando Ricci 10, tel. 0182/53198. Closed Thursday evenings and Sunday. All credit cards. Moderately inexpensive.

Simple, delicious Ligurian cuisine in which local vegetables are dazzling protagonists.

WINE

Enoteca del Vascello, Via Gian Maria Oddo 16, tel. 0182/51374. Open 9–12h, 16–19:30h. Closed Thursday afternoon and mid-January.

An excellent source for Ligurian wines and olive oils.

Albisola Superiore (Savona)

Albisola is the birthplace of two famous popes. Julius II was the famous mentor and tormentor of Michelangelo. Sixtus IV was the man for whom the Sistine Chapel was named.

DINING

Trattoria da Marietta, Via Schiappapietra 17 Ellera, tel. 019/49059. Closed Thursday and Christmas–January 6. MasterCard, Visa. Moderate.

This lovely place is what eating in Italy is all about. The welcome is warm and genuine, there is no pretense or formality, yet great care goes into the preparation and the serving of the food. The clientele comes from all strata of local society: fishermen,

schoolteachers, lawyers and pensioners. The current owner is the delightful Graziella Saettone, niece of the original proprietor. At lunch, the dishes are fairly standard—pasta with pesto, roasts— though you can be assured of tasty food at a fair price. But if you come for dinner, you can look forward to some of the great dishes of Liguria, all prepared authentically. The *pansôti con salsa di noci* are a must. The herb stuffing (called *preboggion* in local dialect) is full of complex and alluring flavors, all set off by the sweet-dry character of the walnut sauce. *Coniglio al timo* (rabbit with thyme) is a worthy specialty for a *secondo* and, if you are visiting from February through late May, ask for *agnello con i carciofi,* succulent lamb with local artichokes. If you call to reserve (which is always advisable) you might place an advance order for *buridda,* the great Ligurian fish stew. The trattoria is in the village of Ellera, a few kilometers from Albisola Superiore on the road to Sassello.

Ameglia (La Spezia)

Ameglia, in the Luni Hills above La Spezia and the sea, is a little paradise even in Italy, a nation full of *piccoli paradisi.* The fresh air, the astounding views, and the relaxed environment promote feelings of *starbene* (well-being). Nearby towns such as Montemarcello and Sarzana Marinella are just as pleasing.

DINING
Trattoria dai Pironcelli, Via delle Mura 45, Montemarcello, tel. 0187/601252. Closed Sunday and Wednesday. All credit cards. Moderate.

The cooking at this trattoria is classically Ligurian: "poor" ingredients drawn from an unyielding sea and a difficult soil are transformed into dishes of exquisite flavor. Thyme, oregano, and basil give fragrance to many foods, including pasta sauces, bread, peppers, eggplant, tomatoes, onions, cuttlefish, and fresh anchovies. Also worth trying are *tagliatelle bastarde,* fresh pasta made with a combination of chestnut and white flours. The wines to choose are local Lunigiana reds and whites or perhaps a white from the Cinqueterre. Fresh fruit or simple *crostate* (jam tarts) are ideal desserts in a delicious and healthful meal.

RESTAURANT, HOTEL, AND COOKING SCHOOL
Locanda dell'Angelo, Viale XXV Aprile 60, Località Sarzana Marinella, 19031 Ameglia (SP), tel. 0187/64391 or 64392.

Angelo Paracucchi opened the charming Locanda dell'Angelo in 1975. Since then, travelers have gone there for the beauty of the spot, the restful comfort of the *locanda*'s thirty-seven rooms, and the wonderful food. Signor Paracucchi offers cooking courses for two months each year, typically in low tourist season or when he doesn't have other commitments (he also cooks at the Carpaccio restaurant in Paris). Each course lasts a week, beginning on Monday morning and ending on Saturday. Angelo presents different dishes each day, drawing both from inspiration and the foods that are at their peak that morning. The cuisine shows Ligurian and Tuscan influences along with Angelo's own taste, which emphasizes lightness as well as intense flavor. For example, sautéed monkfish with citrus and grilled vegetables may not adhere to a particular regional cuisine, but it is as beautiful to taste as it is to look at. Classes are taught in Italian, although non–Italian speakers will probably be able to learn a lot through observation and by keeping a pocket dictionary at hand. The cost, at this writing, was slightly more than 2 million lire per week, including classes, all meals, and a lovely room at the inn. Because the class

schedule changes each year, contact the school to find out when Angelo is teaching.

Borgomaro (Imperia)

OLIVE OIL

Azienda Agricola Frantoio Borgomaro, tel. 0183/54031.

Laura Marvaldi makes a wonderful oil.

Camogli (Genova)

For its sweetness, graciousness, and unmatched beauty, Camogli is a microcosm of much of what is special about Liguria. It is little corrupted by tourism, and I encourage visitors to tread lightly. Its Sagra del Pesce is one of my favorite of all folkloric events. This is real life, not a touristic creation.

BAKERY

Rocco Rizzo, Via della Repubblica 136.

Rocco and Grazia Rizzo turn out some of the best focaccia in Liguria and serve it to local customers with radiant smiles that show the pride they take in their superb breads. Rocco creates delectable new breads and pastries all the time, based on inspiration and local ingredients. Grazia makes everyone feel welcome and special, so that going to the Panificio Rizzo is a positively addictive experience.

BAR

Bar Primula, Via Garibaldi 140.

Here is my idea of the perfect Italian *caffè*. The cappuccino is heavenly, the view of the sea is splendid and the sounds of waves and church bells are music to the ears. A seat at an outdoor table guarantees a panorama of small-town Italian seaside life. Tasty brioche and fresh-squeezed juices make for a lovely breakfast. Decent food is served through the day, but that is not the main reason to come here. The homemade ice creams at the Primula are divine, especially those based on fresh local fruit. Another notable flavor is *panera*, which is like cappuccino ice cream.

DINING

Da Paolo, Via San Fortunato 14, tel. 0185/773595. Closed Monday. All credit cards. Moderately expensive.

Camogli is not a great restaurant town. Locals eat at home or travel to the superb restaurants of nearby Recco. Tourists tend to sit at outdoor tables and pay little attention to what they are eating. Any place in Camogli with a view of the sea tends to serve mediocre food. Da Paolo does not have any view so, consequently, people go there for the food. A fisherman in the family brings in the catch each day and that is what determines the menu.

La Cucina di Nonna Nina, Via Molfino 126, San Rocco, tel. 0185/773855. Closed Wednesday. MasterCard, Visa. Moderate.

San Rocco perches above Camogli in a gorgeous setting. Buses from Camogli leave periodically from the stop in front of the CARIGE bank on Via della Repubblica. While in San Rocco, be sure to visit the church and leave a little offering as you take a medal of San Rocco, the patron saint of dogs. These medals, blessed by the priest, are proudly worn on the collars of many Italian canines in

San Rocco for blessing and thanks for their fidelity and friendship. The place to eat in San Rocco is Nonna Nina, a charming restaurant that offers typical local cuisine. If you stay past the last bus, the restaurant can summon a taxi for you.

FOLKLORE

Sagra del Pesce, tel. 0185/771066.

It is said that San Fortunato, the local patron saint, interceded during the Second World War to permit boats loaded with fish to return safely to Camogli through mine-filled seas. On the first night of the festival, in the second weekend of May, bonfires are built on the beach and fishing boats put out to sea. On the following day they return after a full night of fishing. Villagers set up a huge frying pan (4 meters/13 feet in diameter) in the port, and an astonishing amount of fish is fried and served to the public. (It tastes all right, but this is not why you attend.) This event, which remains more folkloric than touristic because of the palpable significance it holds for the locals, is worth attending if you are nearby.

Castelnuovo Magra (La Spezia)

DINING

Trattoria da Armanda, Piazza Garibaldi 6, tel. 0187/674410. Closed Wednesday, two weeks in September, and Christmas –New Year. No credit cards. Moderately expensive.

This locale has been in business since 1908. I would make the journey here just for the *lattughe ripiene in brodo*, lettuce filled with eggs, vegetables, and cheese and then braised in broth. This delicate dish, with the fragrances of local herbs, melts beautifully in the mouth, sending waves of flavor across the palate. *Panigacci* (crepes) are pleasing; the minestrone is soothing. The homemade *tagliatelle verdi* with lamb sauce are filling and tasty. The local *salumi* are excellent: some spicy, others sweet. Pan-cooked lamb, mutton, and kid are all delicious. The wines are the best of the Lunigiana, many of which you can purchase at the *enoteca* in the Palazzo Comunale.

Ristorante Bianchi Livia, Vallecchia, tel. 0187/674104. Always open. No credit cards. Moderately inexpensive.

Above Castelnuovo Magra on the road leading to the Apuan Alps is Vallecchia, where you can find Ristorante Bianchi Livia. Here are simple, well-prepared foods, a cuisine that is both rustic and restorative: pickled onions, artichokes, and peppers, *panigacci* with cheese, lasagne with herbs, roast chicken, or rabbit; local wines by the glass. This is a nice place to come before or after a hike in the surrounding hills.

ENOTECA

Enoteca Liguria e della Lunigiana, Palazzo Comunale (Palazzo Ingolotti Cornelio), tel. 0187/675166, fax 0187/670102.

This *enoteca* is operated by the town, which endeavors to promote Colli di Luni wines, oils, and cheeses by local producers.

Cervo (Imperia)

Cervo is yet another of the singular and extraordinary places that Italy seems to possess in endless abundance. Here is a classic hill town that also stands just above the sea, so that you have divine maritime views in one direction and beautiful mountain scenery in the other. Although it is close to some of the finest beaches in Liguria, Cervo remains relatively unexplored and would merit a visit even if it didn't have one of the region's best restaurants.

DINING

Ristorante-Bar San Giorgio, Via A. Volta 19 (Cervo Alto), tel. 0183/400175. Closed Tuesday. All credit cards. Moderately expensive to expensive.

Caterina, the lady who does the cooking here, is one of those chefs who makes dishes that are distinctly personal but done with such passion and assurance that the diner can only smile with grateful admiration. In this regard I consider her a sister of Rita d'Enza at the Ristorante Gallura in Olbia (Sardegna) and Signora Maria at the Ristorante Il Pellicano in Roma. Caterina is a warm and beautiful woman, and you would never believe, when you see her, that she has been working since 1959. She and her son Alessandro have a lovely restaurant with comfortable inner rooms and a terrace with astounding views of mountains and sea. These elements both supply Caterina with ingredients such as seafood, superb vegetables, herbs, wild mushrooms, and game. Every dish I have eaten here is outstanding, and I encourage you to arrive with friends and a big appetite. There is an outstanding list of Ligurian wines too. Caterina makes most of the cakes and cookies you will taste here, and some of these are also sold for you to take away.

Chiavari (Genova)

ENOTECA

Enoteca Bisson, Corso Giannelli 28, tel. 0185/314462. Open 8:45–12:45h, 15:30–19:30h; closed Sunday.

A traditional place to buy Vermentino and other local wines. This *enoteca* also sells wine from elsewhere in Italy and France. In addition, one can buy oils, vinegars, honey, jams, olives, and good *salami*.

Cinqueterre (La Spezia)

There was a time when the Cinqueterre were virtually unknown. The five towns—Corniglia, Manarola, Monterosso, Riomaggiore, and Vernazza—were accessible only by boat or on foot until relatively recently. They were beautiful, otherworldly, and romantic. With the arrival of trains in the towns and automobiles on the road above them, they were no longer a secret. I visited them before they were discovered by travel writers and tourists, and they were treasurable. They still are charming, but tourism has definitely arrived, and the little piazzas now fill up in summer with transient visitors. Monterosso in particular has become a destination because it has the most attractive beach. The other towns do not have too many hotel facilities, so you might choose to make your base in either La Spezia or Monterosso and commute on the trains that frequently connect them. The Cinqueterre produce a DOG white wine and the well-known and, in my view, overrated dessert wine Sciacchetrà. You will discover that the Cinqueterre are the domain of small cats who are uniquely able to scale the walls and terraces that climb up from the shore. These cats skip over cobblestones and fit into small crevices. Their dexterous capabilities leave dogs anxious and confused. The sounds of fighting cats echo from places unseen on the other side of walls and hedges.

Corniglia

Corniglia is the least-visited of the five towns but has the best view. Good food is served at Cantina de Mananan, Via Fieschi 117, tel. 0187/821166, no credit cards accepted, moderately priced.

Manarola

Manarola remains unscathed by tourism. There are a few little stores and eateries. Small fishing boats crowd the tiny harbor, and many more sit in dry dock.

DINING

Rictorante Marina Piccola, Via Discovolo 38, tel. 0187/920103. No credit cards. Moderately expensive.

In nice weather one dines at outdoor tables under a canopy. In keeping with the casual feeling of Manarola, during my visit the waiter here wore a T-shirt and had a day-old growth of beard. Almost all the other diners were fishermen, young and old. They were dressed in the timeless outfits of cotton shirts and blue jeans (which are Ligurian in origin: when Ligurian immigrants went to California during the 1840s Gold Rush, they wore trousers made of a material called Blu Genova, which Levi Strauss renamed "blue jeans"). Aside from a few voices, the only sound was that of water splashing up against the docks. Except for some television antennas and power lines (and the prices on the menu), this could have been the 1930s. The pesto is excellent, as are the *muscoli ripieni*. Grilled fish is very good, and the wine is from the Cinqueterre cooperative. A good meal, but the setting, the atmosphere, and the genuineness are priceless.

Monterosso

BARS AND SOURCES OF WINE
Enoteca Ciak, Via Roma 4, tel. 0187/817315.

Cinqueterre wine from all the major producers, plus tall skinny bottles of pricey Sciacchetrà. It sells elixirs made with Ligurian herbs, plus local olive oil, which is made in Monterosso. There is honey from Corniglia, large jars of anchovies, plus jars of pesto, olives, olive paste.

Bar-Enoteca 5 Terre, Via Fegina 94.

For tasting local wine by the glass and buying by the bottle. Near the train station.

Caffè-Latteria Giuliana, Via Fegina (on the waterfront).

A hangout for the women of the town. A good source for Cinqueterre wines.

FOOD STORE
Il Frantoio, Via Gioberti 1.

Farinata, focaccia al formaggio, and pizza.

Riomaggiore

The international population of youth and student travelers, and backpackers of all ages, have a very effective word-of-mouth network, and many of these itinerants seem to find their way to Riomaggiore. The reason for this is a white-haired woman with a wool cap and bedroom booties trimmed in fake fur who is universally known as Mamma Rose. Like her namesake in the musical *Gypsy* (who formed troupes of dancers and vaudevillians by picking up stray young people along the road), the Mamma Rose of Riomaggiore comes to the train station to meet almost every train (there are about fifty a day!) to nab backpackers as they step onto the platform. They stay at her hostel for about 25,000 lire a night and have the use of a communal kitchen. For a shower or the toilet one must go to the roof, where facilities are separated by shower curtains. But things do work out, and strangers get to know one another well. This is a very valid form of travel and the only option for many people. Passing encounters are enjoyed; occasionally lasting friendships are made.

Communal meals are part of the scene at Mamma Rose's (most of the young guests refer to her retiring, nameless husband as "Papa Rose"). The two main *alimentari* on the Via Cristoforo Colombo have a steady clientele of young people who come in for a package of spaghetti, some vegetables, oil, mineral water, wine, bread, and perhaps some pesto that they will prepare in Mamma's kitchen. I have occasionally slipped into Riomaggiore for a night to reconnect with this kind of travel experience and to enjoy cooking meals for a happy band of assorted souls who will disband ten hours later. If you have been dining in restaurants for two weeks and have a hankering to cook, this might be the place for you, if you don't mind the rough accommodation. There are a few trattorias at the lower end of Via Colombo that are all of similar quality and price and, though not expensive, are out of the budget range for some of Mamma's brood.

A wonderful thing to do in Riomaggiore, especially at sunset, is to walk on the Strada Panoramica. As you exit the train station, there is a sign to the left leading the way. I, however, would recommend the opposite route: from the train station make a sharp right and walk through the railway tunnel that leads to town. Walk up the Via Colombo, stopping for a few provisions if you plan to picnic up above. Continue up the relatively steep street until you reach the tiny square with the small, pretty church of Nostra Signora Assunta in Cielo. If it is open, pay a visit. In this square are a few doorways. If they are open you will see storerooms with barrels and demijohns full of Cinqueterre wine. Turn your back to the church, and you will see signs leading to the *posta* (post office), *chiesa* (the main church of town), and *carabinieri* (police). Walk up to the *chiesa*, visit it if it is open, then continue. As you go along, new views of the town will be revealed, and you will soon get a superb view of the sea. After stopping at the panoramic terrace, walk over the railway tunnel you walked through before, down a few steps, past Mamma Rose's place, and back to the train station. With stops to admire the scenery, this walk will take about forty-five minutes. Do this trip in reverse if you plan to end up at one of the trattorias on the Via Colombo.

WINE COOPERATIVE

Cooperativa Agricoltura di Riomaggiore, Manarola, Corniglia, Vernazza e Monterosso, Località Groppo—Cinqueterre, tel. 0187/920435, fax 0187/920076.

Ristorante Ripa del Sole, Via de Gasperi 282, tel. 0187/920143. Closed Monday. All

credit cards. Moderate.

Many of the small grape growers of the Cinqueterre sell their grapes to this cooperative, which produces much of the wine sold in these parts bearing the name "Cinqueterre." You can stop by for tasting or purchases.

Vernazza

This is still a lovely place that the influx of tourists has only somewhat compromised, primarily because there are very few beds for them to sleep in. On a recent afternoon in late October I was able to sprawl on the slate rocks near the port and bask in the warmth of the setting sun as middle-aged Englishwomen and young Swiss men braved the cold waters. Local fishermen sat at the dock mending nets and cutting bait for the next morning's expedition. Others offered boat rides to the few tourists around. The main street is the Via Roma, which looks like a stage set for an opera. Shuttered windows can open to reveal family vignettes. People call across the narrow street from one window to another. As in much of Liguria, laundry flaps in the wind, and the occasional sock or brassiere threatens to be dislodged by the next strong gust from the sea.

DINING

Trattoria Baretto, Via Roma 29. No credit cards. Moderate.

A good pick for fresh pasta, *acciughe fritte* (fried fresh anchovies), and stuffed mussels.

Gambero Rosso, Piazza Marconi 7, tel. 0187/812265. Open daily in summer. No credit cards. Moderate.

You can take in the harbor scene from an outdoor table. Service slows down when tourists flood in, and the kitchen can be inconsistent.

Gianni Franzi, Via Visconti 2,
tel. 0187/812228. Closed Wednesday,
January, and February. No credit cards.

Foodies and travel writers have worn down the threshold to Gianni and Dea Franzi's restaurant. The food is very good, but you

will hear more English and German than Italian.

WINE

Cinqueterre wine is sold at the cooperative on Via Roma 13.
Closed Wednesday.

Dolceacqua (Imperia)

This precious little town (population 1,850) eight kilometers (five miles) from the sea sits undisturbed except for the occasional busload of French tourists who stop by for a ten-minute photo opportunity. One French visitor did stop here for a longer time: in February 1884 Claude Monet visited Dolceacqua, a town he described in his diary as extraordinarily picturesque, adding "the place is superb; there is a bridge that seems to be a jewel of lightness." To me, the thirty-three-meter (about one-hundred-foot) bridge that spans the Nervia River looks like spun sugar. The bridge was built after the collapse of a previous one in the fifteenth century. On one side of the bridge is the Borgo Medioevale, the medieval quarter that is a miniature version of the pinecone-shaped Pigna quarter of San Remo. A mention of the Borgo can be found in sources dating back to 1177. The gourmet traveler comes to Dolceacqua to sample the silken red wine, Rossese, one of only four DOC wines in Liguria. Although Rossese can occasionally be purchased in other places, it is a special experience to drink the wine—in combination with regional dishes—on the soil where the grapes are grown. Local cuisine is infused with luscious olive oil and pungent herbs.

DINING

Ristorante Re, Via P. Martiri 26,
tel. 0184/206137. Closed Monday and
November 1–December 15. All credit cards.
Moderately inexpensive.

All of the guidebooks cite Ristorante Gastone (Piazza Garibaldi 2, tel. 0184/206577) as the restaurant of choice, but it is closed on Tuesday, the day I visited Dolceacqua. According to Sylvie, a French artist I met who followed Monet's footsteps to Dolceacqua and stayed, the food at Ristorante Re rivals that of Gastone. I certainly had a

good lunch there while seated at a picture window overlooking the bridge and the medieval quarter. While Sylvie and I discussed art and opera, delicious food issued from the kitchen where Signora Bruna was cooking. First came *tagliolini al pesto.* The sauce was unusual in that it was less a blend of ingredients than a suspension of fresh basil leaves in fruity oil, with palpable bits of garlic and pine nuts. The *tagliolini* were fresh and well made. Next came a delicious local specialty, *coniglio alle erbe.* Succulent chunks of rabbit were cooked in olive oil and flavored with a handful of local aromatic herbs, juniper berries, and abundant grated carrot. Next came a green salad with lots of chicory that tasted as if it had just been picked. To my surprise, the house wine was Dolcetto rather than Rossese di Dolceacqua, but I ordered some of the local wine. Although it is not a major-league wine, it had charm and flavor and went perfectly with the rabbit. Dessert was an absolutely luscious Williams pear that dissolved in the mouth into a sort of cream that was a beautiful match for the last drops of the Rossese. A rich cup of coffee was served with a semisweet chocolate from Piemonte.

ENOTECA

The Rossese di Dolceacqua cooperative is at one corner of the little square at the base of the Borgo Medioevale. Tasting and purchases are possible from 10:30h to 12:00h and 15h to 19h. Be sure to visit the little green, pink, and gold church across the way.

SHOPS FOR WINE,
OIL, AND HERBS

Mino Dure, Via P. Martiri 41.

A producer of delicious olive oil. Wine and herbs also available. If the shop is closed, go to the shoemaker next door or ring the buzzer for Ottonello in the building above.

*Luigi Maccario, Via P. Martiri 46,
tel. 0184/206147.*

Herbs, oil, wine, olives, pasta sauces, vegetables packed in oil.

Genova

La loro flotta è così grande	So great is their fleet
che per tutto il mare si spande	that it covers the entire sea
Così ricche son le lor navi	Their ships are so rich
che ognuna ne vale due delle altre.	that one is worth two of anyone else's.
E tanti sono i genovesi	And so many are the Genoese
per il mondo così sparsi	in all corners of the world
che ovunque vadano o abitino	that wherever they go or live
là costruiscono un'altra Genova.	they build another Genoa there.

—ANONYMOUS THIRTEENTH-CENTURY POET

Genova la Superba is the largest port in Italy and one of the nation's most maligned cities. Genova is said to have the largest medieval quarter in Europe. It also has magnificent palaces, sensational food, and, yes, a fair amount of industrialization that is probably the first thing most people notice. But I find this to be a city full of hardworking, clever people who are very welcoming to the rare visitor who comes their way. The medieval quarter may be a little frightening by night to those who do not know their way around, but by day it is fascinating and memorable.

Come to Genova with an open mind and a big appetite. Even the city's detractors admit that the food here is divine. Take a walk on the Via San Vincenzo, Via Colombo, and the Via Galata to discover some of the better food shops in Genova.

A word about addresses in Genova: Blue or black numbers are for residences; red numbers are for businesses. In older neighborhoods, where new coats of red paint come infrequently, it is often hard to tell whether a number is for a home or a store.

BAKERY

Caffè-Pasticceria Klainguti, Piazza Soziglia 98–100R, tel. 010/296502. Closed Monday.

The most famous bakery in Genova was founded by Swiss bakers in 1828. Enticing specialties are displayed in the windows, and it is nearly impossible to walk by. It proudly displays a note from Giuseppe Verdi, who praised a sweet brioche made here, called the Falstaff ("Your Falstaff is better than mine!" he cheered).

CORZETTI STAMPS

Corzetti (also called *corsetti*), a classic *genovese* pasta, is increasingly difficult to find. Many Ligurians I spoke to while researching a forthcoming cookbook about their region's fabulous cuisine did not even know what corzetti are. In fact, there are two types. One is a small, figure 8–shaped dried pasta that one can find in specialty shops. The other is made by cutting squares of fresh pasta and then stamping them on both sides with a wooden stamp that has ancient Ligurian designs. They might be floral or maritime or represent the cross of San Giorgio, one of Genova's favored saints. There are two good sources for corzetti stamps in Genova, both in the old city center. These stamps make distinctive gifts for a cook back home or perhaps for your own kitchen. Both shops can ship the stamps to you, but this will add to the cost.

La Bütteghetta Magica, Via della Maddalena 2R, tel. 010/296590. MasterCard, Visa.

Daniela Tinello owns this marvelous, crowded shop filled with all sorts of Ligurian cooking equipment. You can get a marble mortar and a wooden pestle to make pesto, or buy a *pirrone,* the typical wine decanter that fishermen pass about on the boat as they wait for the fish to bite. There is also the largest selection of *stampe* for corzetti that I have seen in Liguria. Prices are moderately expensive for these handmade items and will be even more costly if you select one made of olive wood. But they are beautiful and will give you much satisfaction.

Granone & Monchieri, Vico del Filo 10R, tel. 010/2471294. No credit cards.

This is an excellent woodworking shop where corzetti stamps can be made to order. Prices are about half those at La Bütteghetta Magica, and if you place a special order you know that your stamp will be distinct.

DINING

Trattoria Vegia Zena, Vico Serriglio 13-15R, tel. 010/299891. No credit cards. Inexpensive to moderately inexpensive.

I discovered this wonderful little restaurant by following my nose to the place that sent wonderful fragrances out to the street, a little lane leading to the Via Gramsci and the old port. The name is *genovese* dialect for "Old Genova" and the cook sticks to tradition, with a few dishes from Sardegna thrown in for good measure. The kitchen is in full view of the clientele, most of whom are local and return here because they know they will eat well and receive friendly service. Pasta with pesto or seafood is excellent, as are the *moscardini*, baby octopus braised in tomato and pepper. For dessert, have a *seadas*, a delicious cheese-filled Sardinian *raviolo* that is fried and then topped with honey.

Antica Osteria del Bai, Via Quarto 12, tel. 010/387478. Closed Monday, March 1–10, and August 1–15. All credit cards. Moderately expensive.

In the district of Quarto on the outskirts of Genova is this eatery that has been in business for well over a century. The owners proudly inform you that Garibaldi dined here in 1869 before leaving for Sicily with the Mille to fight for Italian unification. The specialties are traditional Ligurian pastas: ravioli, *pansôti, corzetti.*

Antica Osteria di Vico Palla, Vico Palla 15r, tel. 010/2466575. Closed Monday and in mid-August. All credit cards. Moderately inexpensive to moderate.

A casual setting with delicious food in the oldest part of Genova. The soups and pastas are wonderful.

Trattoria da Giglio.

See "A Walk on the Via San Vincenzo, the Via Colombo, and the Via Galata," below.

Trattoria da Maria, Vico Testadoro 14, tel. 010/581080. Closed Monday evening, Saturday and three weeks in September. No credit cards. Very inexpensive.

This little trattoria near the opera house has been in business since 1946 and little has changed. I go here for the food, the environment, and the sense that there are precious few places left in Italy like this, and this was the kind of restaurant that nourished me in my youth.

Trattoria del Liberale, Via Monte Fasce 91, tel. 010/395248. Closed Friday. No credit cards. Inexpensive to moderate.

A Genovese institution just beyond the city center. You will first remember the view from 600 meters (more than 1,800 feet): on a clear day you can see Corsica. Yet the food and ambience will stay with you as well. The trattoria is run by Ada Barbagelata, a member of the fourth generation of family owners that began with Giacomo Vallebona in 1891. All the food here is classically Ligurian: stuffed vegetables, fresh pasta, grilled meats, and a wonderful *fritto misto*.

FRIGGITORIE

The *friggitoria*, the fast-food stand central to the eating culture of Liguria, is usually a storefront with a small kitchen that turns out delicious snacks to eat there or take away. You can buy a slice of *torta pasqualina, farinata*, focaccia, or small vegetable snacks. Here are two popular *friggitorie*, although you will probably enjoy finding new ones on your own: Antica Sciamadda at Via San Giorgio 14r; and Raggio on Via Galata.

First weekend of June: Regatta storica. One of the most exciting and beautiful folkloric events in Italy. Each year, as they have for centuries, boatmen from the ancient maritime republics of Amalfi, Genova, Pisa, and Venezia compete. The regatta is held in a different one of these four cities each year. Check with the tourist office for information. Hotel rooms will be hard to come by.

Food Shops:
A WALK ON THE VIA SAN VINCENZO,
THE VIA COLOMBO,
AND THE VIA GALATA

This district, not far from the Brignole train station, is full of enough interesting food shops to teach you about local taste and attitudes. There will be slight detours, but this is essentially a circular walk.

Pasta Fresca Borreani, Via San Vincenzo 51R, tel. 010/562860.

Fresh genovese pasta is considered among the best in Italy. Take a look at the *tagliolini* made of spinach pasta, as well as the tiny *raviolini di carne, triangoli magri* (cheese-filled pasta triangles), gnocchi, *pansôti, pizzoccheri, gnocchi verdi, trofie di Recco*. The shop also sells pesto, walnut sauce, tomato sauce, and wild-mushroom sauce.

Bottiglieria Ferruzzo, Via San Vincenzo 60R.

A source for wine, of course, but notice how much Scotch whiskey it stocks. The *genovesi*, who are often parsimonious, are described as the Scots of Italy. The people of Genova, mostly of Celtic origin, have an ancient commercial and ideological affinity with the British Isles.

Trattoria da Giglio, Via San Vincenzo 64R.

An old-style *friggitoria* selling *torte* made with beetroot, onions, fried cod, and basic pasta dishes.

PaniŠcio Mario, Via San Vincenzo 61R.

Divine focaccia here comes in many types: olive, cheese, potato, sage, onion, tomato, eggplant, zucchini, and many more. When I tasted the onion focaccia, hot out of the oven, I began to hear choruses of angels.

Bar-Pasticceria Panarello, Via Galata 67R. Closed Sunday afternoon and Monday.

Sells *ciambelline* (light, fragrant doughnut-shaped pastries), tiny *pandolcini, cobelletti* (crown shaped and filled with delicious apricot jam), crunchy fan-shaped *ventagli, pinolati* (pine-nut cookies), *anicini* (anise rusks). Serves good coffee with a tiny piece of good chocolate. A good place for breakfast.

Sementi Ronco, Via San Vincenzo 100R (next to black 42).

A wall full of wooden drawers, all with glass windows. Each drawer contains seeds. Buy some here to grow Ligurian herbs at home.

Vini e Liquori Bressler, Via San Vincenzo 130R, tel. 010/565783. Open 7:30–20h.

The gentlemanly proprietor serves Ligurian wines by the glass. You can also buy them by the bottle.

Rossi, Via San Vincenzo 132R, tel. 010/540956. Closed Monday morning in July and August, and Sunday.

A pleasing shop with teas, oils, honeys, cakes, and candies. The Ligurian honeys include *mandorle* (almond), rosemary, *tiglio* (lime), and chestnut. A specialty found here is Stroscia di Pietrabruna, a sweet crunchy bread with olive oil. Other Rossi stores are at Via Galata 30R and Via Cesarea 21R, which has the largest selection. Rossi ships worldwide.

Al Frantoio, Via San Vincenzo 158R, tel. 010/591725.

A great source for Ligurian olive oil, arguably the world's finest.

Now, when you see the Albergo Carletto, turn a sharp left onto the Via Colombo.

L'Arte Bianca, Via Colombo 50R.

A *gastronomia* specializing in unusual pastas. *Triangoli di asparagi* (triangles filled with asparagus), *triangoli di rucola* (arugula), *principesse* (little round ravioli filled with prosciutto and cheese), *pansôti*, ravioli filled with fish, *rotolo* (rolled pasta) filled with speck and radicchio. There are also focaccia and many stuffed vegetables.

Just past the Old Time Bar (26R Via Colombo), turn right and head to the Mercato Orientale. This is a marvelous market, one of my favorites in Italy, that you should wander about slowly to take in all of the details. Above all, make note of how universally high the quality is at every stand. Notice stand 69, which has a wall full of different types of eggs. Upstairs there are more stalls, including a simple-looking *gastronomia* that sells superb Ligurian olive oil. Exit from the market onto the Via Galata, making note of the Salumeria Balleardi on the way out.

Rosticceria Pietra, Via Galata 39R.

Good stuff, including cheese-filled crepes, roast chickens, and stuffed vegetables. Most of the prepared dishes are Ligurian classics.

Pasta Fresca Danieli, Via Galata 41R.

Many pasta types, including several you have not yet seen on this walk. Note the coin-shaped *corzetti del Levante* and the various pastas flavored or filled with herbs. Sells outstanding sauces, too.

Primizie, Via Galata 44R.

Tiny, choice fruit and vegetables that appeal particularly to Ligurians who know and prize flavor. One can also find *primizie* in the Mercato Orientale.

You will now reach the Piazza Colombo:

#9–11: Chicco Cafe.

A coffee roaster where you can buy beans.

#13: Vinoteca Sola.

Wines of all types, including a good selection from Liguria.

#17–19–21: Tarigo.

All sorts of housewares. Nothing fancy, but all practical.

At this point I would keep walking up the Via Galata for another coffee and pastry at Bar-Pasticceria Panarello and think about the range of interesting, high-quality food and wine that the people of Genova feast on.

SWEET SHOP
Confetteria Romanengo, Via Soziglia 74/76r, tel. 010/297869.

Since 1780, this shop has produced candies that are considered the finest in Liguria and, some say, the best in all of Italy. Who will ever know? Nonetheless, a visit here is essential during your stay in Genova. Romanengo is best known for candied fruit because the quality of the fruit is so outstanding that little sugar and no colorings or preservatives are used. This is what candied fruit should taste like. There is also excellent chocolate, often filled with freshly made nut creams. Giuseppe Verdi used to receive regular shipments from Romanengo.

Imperia

Imperia is one of the youngest provincial capitals in Italy, having been established in 1923, at the dawn of the Fascist era, when Mussolini attempted to foster notions of empire in Italian minds. The name of a river valley became a useful excuse to create a town connoting empire. In fact, Imperia was created by combining two smaller towns, Porto Maurizio and Oneglia. Although Imperia is the capital of the westernmost province of Liguria, it is not as well known as such smaller towns as San Remo, Bordighera, Dolceacqua, Taggia, and Ventimiglia. Imperia is the seat of the Valle d'Impero (Valley of the Empire), named for the Impero River that runs from the uplands to the sea. In this valley is the greatest concentration of agricultural activity in Liguria. Characteristically sweet olives produce an oil that is described as *fruttato* because of its fruity flavor. The oil of this area, to many connoisseurs, exceeds in quality even the famous oils of Toscana. Visit the olive museum in town. The Valle d'Impero also produces famous artichokes and many other vegetables and fruits of high quality. Local pasta making has always been excellent.

Restaurants in Imperia are good places to discover the local agricultural splendor if you are unable to travel to the smaller towns. The province of Imperia is the center of Italy's great flower-growing industry (the area is often called La Riviera dei Fiori), so you should not be surprised to see hothouses perched in the hills. With beautiful beaches, attractive little seaside towns, and a few ancient hill towns, the province of Imperia is also a great magnet for tourism.

ENOTECA

Enoteca Lupi, Via Monti 13, Oneglia, tel. 0185/21610, fax 0183/276090. Open 7:45–12:30h, 16:30–20h; closed Wednesday afternoon, Sunday, and last two weeks in August.

A great source for all of the big and little wines produced in the Valle d'Impero. This *enoteca* also has a vast selection of wines from all over Italy. The Lupi brothers, Angelo and Tommaso, make their own olive oil in an old granite press as oil was made once upon a time. Right across the street is a little shop that sells *farinata*, olives, and other Ligurian edibles.

FOLKLORE

Festa al Parasio.

Throughout July, various events, including music, dance, plays in local dialect, and stands selling tasty foods.

OLIVE MUSEUM

Museo dell'Ulivo Fratelli Carli, Via Garessio 11, tel. 0183/27101. Open 9–12h, 15–18h; closed Sunday and Tuesday.

This small, beautifully arranged museum will inspire anyone who never understood the ancient relationship between the olive tree and Mediterranean peoples. You will also see oil-making equipment from ancient times to the present.

La Spezia

The provincial capital for the southeastern part of Liguria is a much-maligned place, but only by those who do not know it. I find Spezia (as locals call it) a friendly town with delicious food. The surrounding area has some of Italy's most spectacular scenery. La Spezia is generally thought of as a port with some industrial development (which it is) and as one of the principal bases of the Italian navy. Yet to me it has the air of a college town more than a rough port such as Napoli, Genova, Marseilles, or Piraeus. The prevailing atmosphere is relaxed, friendly, and sociable. The Via del Prione has an excellent, vibrant *passeggiata* full of young people. Many of these are sailors who parade in their blues and whites, admiring the pretty girls (and boys) of La Spezia. Be sure to take part in the *passeggiata* when you visit. You will notice a plaque on Via del Prione 45: QUI, NELL'ESTATE DEL MDCCCLIII IN UNA ANTICA LOCANDA DELL'ANTICO BORGO, A RICHARD WAGNER SI RIVELÒ UNO SPLENDIDO ACCORDO MUSICALE E PRESE FORMA IL PRELUDIO DELL'ORO DEL RENO. This is a rather florid way of saying that on this site in the summer of 1853 a splendid musical chord was revealed to Wagner that led to the creation of the prelude to *Das Rheingold*. I wonder what it was in La Spezia that let out a long E flat that so captivated Wagner. But one of the hallmarks of genius is to take inspiration where you can find it.

Caffè Cavour, Corso Cavour 125, tel.
0187/20333. Open 5:30–21h; closed Sunday.

A smart bar in the center of town that serves an excellent cup of coffee with a little piece of fine chocolate on the side.

DINING

Casalini, Via del Prione 191. Closed
Wednesday afternoon and Sunday.

A casual place for good Ligurian fast food—*focaccine* with olives, cheese, tomatoes, and such. A popular spot during the *passeggiata*.

Trattoria Toscana da Dino, Via da Passano
19, tel. 0187/21360. Closed Sunday eve-
ning, Monday, and two weeks in July.
American Express, Diners Club, Visa.
Moderate to moderately expensive.

The atmosphere at this restaurant, which attracts a lot of businesspeople, is congenial and efficient. There are white walls with handsome wood trim. All is pleasing, correct, professional. Service is by waitresses who wear crisp navy-and-white striped blouses, navy skirts, a white apron, and a white towel draped over one shoulder. The food is a combination of Tuscan and Ligurian, two cuisines that are well matched in their use of vegetables and good olive oil. The meat dishes are Tuscan, while the fish is more Ligurian. You can start with *trofie al pesto,* perfect pasta with a sauce in which the basil leaves are not pounded as completely as usual. It is served with a curl of butter and is quite good. The *frittura mista* has all sorts of flavorful fish and seafood battered in a delicate sauce and fried in delicious light oil. Fish such as *branzino* (sea bass) and *orata* are beautifully grilled. Vegetables are excellent, and desserts are good. The *tiramisù* is made with mascarpone (as it should be), but lacks the flavor of coffee, a key element. The house wine is average, but there are good selections in bottles. Because da Dino attracts such a large business clientele, you will observe a different element than what you see in more touristic or family restaurants. For example, a staff composed only of waitresses is unusual because most food servers in Italy are men, except in certain family-run trattorias. When I last came here, in 1994, all the diners were men. The portable phone of one of them sounded, and six men reached for their phones like gunfighters reaching for their holsters. However, the man who received the phone call asked forgiveness from all the other diners in the room before engaging in his conversation. Manners are not completely extinct.

Osteria all'Inferno, Via Lorenzo Costa 3
(near the fruit and vegetable market),
tel. 0187/29458. Open 12–14:45h,
19:30–22:30h; closed Sunday. No credit
cards. Inexpensive.

Go down several steps (not quite to hell), walk past the kitchen, and turn right, into a large room with low vaulted ceilings supported by two central pillars. There are long tables at which you sit on benches or rickety chairs. This place, in business since 1905, is immensely popular and draws diners from all strata of La Spezia society. People at one table will talk about a sailing race while at another the topic will be women's literature in Latin America. With only two tiny windows, this is not a place to come to if you are sensitive to cigarette smoke. But Osteria all'Inferno has a style and ambience that visitors to Italy seldom encounter. The list of typical Ligurian dishes is long, but not everything is available each day. The *mesciüà* is a local specialty. A very good *secondo* is *seppie con piselli,* perfectly cooked cuttlefish with sweet peas in a sauce brimming with basil and pepper, an interesting taste combination that works beautifully. The choice of wine is limited. Instead of having coffee here, go around the corner to the Caffè Cavour.

FOLKLORE

Festa di San Giuseppe, tel. 0187/770900.

Since 1565, La Spezia has held a festival on March 19–21 in honor of Saint Joseph. The original intention of this festival was to promote commerce. Nowadays, more than eight hundred stands are erected that offer food and wares not only from the city of La Spezia but all the little towns in the nearby Cinqueterre and Luni Hills.

FRUIT AND VEGETABLES

Giuseppe Panattoni, Piazza Garibaldi 23, tel. 0187/31278.

This is a very old-fashioned fruit store, dating from a time in Italy when bananas were sold as a special precious commodity. Because bananas were imported from Africa or the Caribbean they were much more expensive than the luscious fruit that grows in the nearby Luni Hills. Inside the store are large, ancient posters from Chiquita, Dole, and Del Monte. The store also carries dried fruit, canned and jarred fruit, and fruit juices. While you might not buy anything here, it is a fascinating throwback to another time. More likely you will buy fruit and vegetables at the nearby La Primiziera at Via Fiume 10.

SWEET SHOP

Casa dei Dolciumi, Via Tommaseo 9, tel. 0187/39296. Closed Sunday.

Every kind of packaged, boxed Italian candy you would want as well as jars and baskets full of individual candies fill the shelves from floor to ceiling.

WINE

Casa del Vino, Via Biassa 65, tel. 0187/25450. Closed Wednesday afternoon and Sunday.

Roberto Risso is a serious young man who is finding his way in the wine world. The selection here is not vast, but the wines are chosen with great care and taste. He also has pâtés from Piemonte and excellent Ligurian and Tuscan vegetables packed in olive oil.

Lavagna (Genova)

ENOTECA

Enoteca Franca, Via Roma 86, tel. 0185/393643. Open 9–13h, 16–20h.

Although this place sells wines from throughout Italy, the main reason to come here would be to sample Vermentino, Pigato, Albarola, and other Ligurian wines. You can also purchase pesto and local jams—the apricot is particularly good.

Levanto (La Spezia)

DINING

Trattoria Gritta, Via Vallesanta, tel.
0187/808593. Closed Wednesday. Moderate.

Seafood pastas are a specialty at this trattoria.

ENOTECA

La Cantina Levantese, Piazza Massola 3.
Open 8–13h, 15–20h.

Rosso and Bianco di Levanto are available for tasting or purchasing. The white is much fuller than the delicate one produced in the adjacent Cinqueterre.

FOLKLORE

Festa del Mare (Festival of the Sea).

In late July processions and feasts honor San Giacomo, the patron saint of fishermen.

Noli (Savona)

FOLKLORE

Regatta Storica, tel. 019/748931.

On the second weekend of September a

procession heads to the main piazza in the old part of town. Then the four rural districts of Noli compete in a colorful race in *gozzi*, traditional Ligurian boats.

Pegli (Genova)

DINING

Trattoria Vetta, Viale Modugno 62,
tel. 010/683611. Closed Wednesday.
No credit cards. Inexpensive.

Pegli is a little town just west of Genova. Above Pegli one reaches the Alture (Heights) di Pegli, a quiet spot full of fresh air and crowned by a beautiful stand of mimosa trees. For a special inexpensive meal as part of a daytime excursion from Genova,

this is a nice place to come. *Torta pasqualina* and stuffed vegetables are good, as are the traditional Ligurian pastas. But you might also try the *taglierini con i funghi porcini*, a flavorful departure from all the basil and nuts you have been eating throughout Liguria. Fish here is good, but I have enjoyed following pasta and mushrooms with succulent grilled meats. Fruit is the dessert of choice.

Portofino (Genova)

DINING

Trattoria Stella, Molo Umberto 13, tel.

0185/69007. Closed Wednesday.
All credit cards. Moderate.

*Trattoria U Batti, Vico Nuovo 17,
tel. 0185/69379. Closed Monday.
All credit cards. Moderate.*

Both of these trattorias serve good *pansôti con salsa di noci, trenette genovesi,* and seafood.

Portovenere (La Spezia)

DINING

Taverna del Corsaro, Passeggiata Doria 102, tel. 0187/900622.

The Maietta family members are expert seafood cooks, using the best of the daily catch in this fabled port. Try *tagliolini* with scampi or *buridda San Pietro,* a great fish stew.

Recco (Genova)

DINING

*Manuelina, Via Roma 278, tel. 0185/75364.
Closed Wednesday and in January.
All credit cards. Moderately expensive.*

About one kilometer east of town is this very popular restaurant that has been an institution since 1855. It was an *osteria* frequented by sailors and fishermen, and Marconi dined here often while doing his experiments nearby that led to the invention of the radio. In the past fifty years Manuelina has been discovered by tourists foreign and domestic, but the food quality, I am told by those who would know, has not diminished. You can watch *focaccia al formaggio di Recco* being made while you se-

lect from a predominantly seafood menu. The pesto is good here, too.

*Ristorante Vitturin, Via dei Giustiniani 50, tel. 0185/720225. Closed Monday.
All credit cards. Moderate.*

A good place to try *focaccia al formaggio di Recco* and a bowlful of *corzetti.* A restaurant in every way equal to Manuelina.

FOLKLORE

Festa della Focaccia.

On the fourth Sunday in May the great bread of Liguria is honored with a festival in Recco, home of a delicious cheese that is served melted atop the focaccia.

San Remo (Imperia)
Classic Town

So famous is San Remo that it is a victim of a certain degree of reverse prejudice. Many travelers who claim to be in the know don't go there, assuming that it is passé. This town was an important stop on the international circuit in the nineteenth century, when wealthy Britons and royalty from all over Europe made San Remo and nearby Bordighera the winter resort of choice. Tchaikovsky came here to restore his pulmonary health after too many Russian winters. From 1860 until the 1930s, elegant hotels, villas, and a glittering casino were built to cosset the blue bloods who flocked here. There is a beautiful Russian Orthodox cathedral that was frequented by many émigrés who arrived after the Russian Revolution. With the changes in politics, style, and economics after the Second World War, chic tourism in San Remo declined. It was soon replaced by package tours and day-trippers who came to gawk at the fading splendor. In an attempt to restore San Remo's image, city fathers created a song festival that is held each winter and attracts attention throughout Italy. Aspiring singers of popular songs compete in a national telecast, and a recording of the top songs and performers is released each year. Any winter visitor to San Remo will also be aware that this city is the leading flower market in Italy. The terraces and hothouses from Alassio to Ventimiglia produce a dazzling variety of flowers that are sold in the San Remo flower market. Make an early morning visit (starting at 6h) part of your stay.

Yet there is another San Remo that has existed through the centuries. This has always been a typically Ligurian seaport, drawing a living from the riches of the sea and the agriculture of the hills behind the town. The Festa del Marinaio, a folkloric event held every August 15, reasserts San Remo's ancient links to the sea. Life goes on as in many Ligurian cities, with people shopping for food, meeting in bakeries, bars, and along such popular thoroughfares as the Via Palazzo. Join in and you will get a sense of real life in a town on the Riviera. For the food lover, San Remo has a wonderful market—the Mercato Comunale—that becomes an object lesson about the way the people in this part of the Mediterranean shop and eat. Spend a full morning there after you've visited the flower market.

La Pigna (the pinecone), the ancient neighborhood that stands above the market, is a hill with labyrinthine streets and alleyways that evoke a Liguria of six hundred years ago. Modern life has stubbornly made a few incursions into La Pigna. As you walk by small doors and even smaller windows behind which people live, the only source of illumination will be the gray glow from a black-and-white television. Nowhere is there any pretense of desire to prettify *(imbellire)* this quarter. Walls crumble, steps are worn away from centuries of being trod upon. In the absence of cars (save the occasional passing *motorino*), footsteps and voices become more audible. Sounds and smells of cooking issue from kitchens, including that of Trattoria Il Mulattiere (see "Dining," below). Voices speak in Italian, in local dialect, and, as happened centuries ago, occasionally in Arabic, now that immigrants from the Maghreb have moved into poorer neighborhoods all over Italy. The trek into La Pigna is quite a climb, one not recommended for the faint of heart. Yet it is made daily by many of the amazingly fit superannuated residents. If you have put on pounds in other cities, here is a good place to work them off.

DINING

Bacchus, Via Roma 65, tel. 0184/530990. Closed Sunday. Visa. Moderately inexpensive.

Homemade dishes to go with good wine. There are *torte di verdura* (vegetable tarts), focaccia, *panissa* (chickpea tart), *verdura ripiena* (stuffed vegetables), tripe with beans, and *buridda.*

Cantine Sanremesi, Via Palazzo 7, tel. 0184/572063. Closed Sunday and July 1–15. No credit cards.

This old haunt in the city center is now run by the dynamic Renzo Morselli, who makes everyone feel welcome and assures that delicious food keeps issuing from the kitchen to accompany the wine he pours at the bar. Occupy a seat elbow to elbow with the locals and enjoy the Ligurian equivalent of fast food. The house specialty is *sardenaira*, the local bread, which is a cross between focaccia and pizza. It is made with onions, tomatoes, black olives, and a bit of anchovy. Another star on the small menu is the minestrone spiked with pesto. Other dishes enter and exit the repertoire according to the season and the mood of the cook. These include *zuppa di acciughe* (anchovy soup), *baccalà, seppie, farinata*, and various types of focaccia. Coffee is available. The music played here varies between classical and favorites from San Remo festivals of old. An autographed picture of Luciano Pavarotti once occupied a place of honor on the bar.

Hostaria de la Costa, Via Romolo Moreno 12, La Pigna, no tel. Closed Friday. No credit cards. Inexpensive.

This is a much simpler affair than Il Mulattiere (below), if that is possible. A cart is rolled over with antipasti in a bowl, and you help yourself. There are chopped tomatoes, beans with onions, sardines, olives, and pickled mushrooms and cabbage. All taste like home, because this is home. This small room has six tables, twenty chairs, and a kitchen where Maria Pia cooks whatever she has. You get to take in all the sounds and smells of a kitchen: running water, chopping, boiling, frying, and so on. As you serve yourself antipasti, Tullio puts an unmarked bottle of wine on your table for you to pour. He will tell you that this place has welcomed guests for meals since 1581. The vaulted ceilings, brown with age, attest to centuries of cooking and smoking. Son Gianni may come over for a chat until your stew of rabbit and olives arrives, accompanied by couscous that is much too wet. Dessert will be fresh fruit and homemade cookies, along with a grappa made by Tullio. The food is not outstanding, but the pleasure in coming here is Tullio. He can talk about religion, literature, and music with insight. The names Voltaire, Pushkin, Paganini, rolled off his lips in quick succession on the night of my visit. His older brother Domenico was a friend and classmate of Italo Calvino, one of Italy's great writers. If you read Calvino's stories, there is a Domenico in several of them—this is Tullio's brother. While talking to me about literature, he chatted with another visitor about the afterlife. What happens when you dine here is that you inevitably become involved in conversations with everyone else. For a more authentic food experience, go to Il Mulattiere. But if you speak some Italian and want to spend an evening in the company of new friends, come to Tullio.

Trattoria Il Mulattiere, Via Palma 11,
La Pigna, tel. 0184/502662. Open 10–15h,
18:30–24h, meals served only during
normal dining hours; closed Wednesday.
No credit cards. Moderately inexpensive.

Here is a dining experience like no other. This is about as close as you will come to eating in someone's home without receiving an invitation. The trattoria is the front two rooms of a family's home. The woman of the house cooks what she has purchased in the market that morning, along with ingredients brought in from the family's piece of land in the hills outside of town. What you eat is also what she serves to her children in the back room. She will arrive and tell you what is available, and you make your selections. Part of what I like about Il Mulattiere (the Mule Driver) is that the room is full of artifacts from the family's farm. The rooms are practically a museum of rural Ligurian agricultural history, except that there is nothing self-conscious about how they are arranged. You are surrounded by the history of someone's family. You will see photographs of a recent grape harvest. Hanging above your head are antique baskets that were used to gather grapes during the harvests. The wine is homemade and arrives in an unlabeled bottle. What is lacking in sophistication here is compensated by much character and loving care. Under the public phone (that is also the family phone) there is an old demijohn once used to cart wine for sale. There are also ancient photos of turn-of-the-century San Remo when it had streetcars. I particularly like the photograph of one family member wearing a full baseball uniform. In another he is drinking a Fanta while leaning against a batting cage. San Remo has a baseball field, and here, as in other parts of Italy, America's national pastime is quietly taking hold.

When the woman comes to tell you what is for dinner, she brings *sardenaira* for you to munch on, along with a small blue-and-white Chinese bowl holding a dozen black and green olives made fruity with a few drops of homemade oil. While awaiting your first course (which might be pasta with pesto or a Gorgonzola sauce), let your eye wander around the room. Notice the wooden benches and the umbrella holder full of canes that are used to hike in the hills. Nearby is a tailoring form dressed with a pink-and-white-striped shirt with a long white apron, a lace blouse with long sleeves, and an olive-green vest. This was a typical outfit worn by peasant women until the late 1930s. You might realize that the music being played is a mixture of Broadway musicals, Italian love ballads, recent hits from the San Remo festival, traditional Italian folk melodies, disco, the Rolling Stones, Harold Arlen, Fats Waller, Tito Puente, and Igor Stravinsky.

The *trenette al pesto* are wonderful. The pasta is perfectly cooked, and the pesto is unlike most you will encounter. If the sauce lacks the bright perfume of very fresh basil, it is compensated by fruity olive oil, a palpable crunch of pine nuts, and the assertive flavor of freshly grated Pecorino. Soon it is time to order a *secondo*, and the choice is *arrosto* (roast veal) with *funghi porcini* or *nasello bollito* (boiled whiting). On my visit I order the latter. While my fish is cooking my eye goes to the antique harnesses that were once used to lead donkeys about to do plowing or carting. You will notice the baskets that were attached

Funghi porcini *are staples in the kitchens of Liguria*

to their backs to carry newly gathered grapes or herbs. As I realize that no one else has arrived to sit at one of the eight tables here, I am roused by the sound of a bell on the door. This bell used to hang around a donkey's neck. Neighbors come and go. They might be simply making a social call, or perhaps have come to collect plates of hot food that they had called ahead to order. Later in the evening they will return with empty plates and contented smiles. An old man comes by for some wine and to flirt with Signora.

The whiting arrives, perfectly cooked and filleted. The fish flakes at the touch of a fork and bursts with flavor. I bypass the mayonnaise with chopped basil that accompanies the dish and simply use lemon as a condiment. Just as good is a dish of yellow peppers cooked in the wonderful oil. Then comes a bowl of freshly picked arugula. Since the little cruets on the table contain commercial-smelling vinegar and oil (not the one used for cooking), I opt for simple lemon as a dressing, and the arugula sings. Every dish is an exemplar of flavor and color. Dessert is a gorgeous red pear, nice green grapes, and a piece of apricot tart. Signora then gets busy with people who wander in and out and does not ask if I want coffee. About thirty minutes later, one of the old men who has stopped in brings me a cup made in the family coffeepot.

This rare immersion into Italian family life, into a neighborhood, and into rural Ligurian folkways cannot be given a price, and the memory of it enriches me still. It is easier to reach Il Mulattiere than other parts of La Pigna. From Piazza degli Eroi Sanremesi, find Via Giordano Bruno or Via Morando. These will lead straight to Via Palma.

Nuovo Piccolo Mondo, Via Piave 7, tel. 0184/509012. Reservations essential. Closed Sunday, Monday, and July. No credit cards. Moderate.

Trattoria incredibly popular for its delicious food. I love the excellent pesto and the *coniglio alla sanremasca* (braised rabbit with olives and herbs).

FOOD STORES

De Angelo Il Salumaio ed Il Casaro, Piazza degli Eroi Sanremesi 54.

A superb assortment of cheeses, with a particularly strong selection from nearby Piemonte. Also excellent prosciutto and *salumi*.

King George Aromi e Sapori, Piazza degli Eroi Sanremesi 28, tel. 0184/ 541884, fax 0184/541888.

This quiet, chic store facing the flower market stands in stark contrast to the hustle and bustle of the stores and streets in the old quarter of San Remo. Outside you can buy roses, basil, and cheeses from the countryside. Inside, the *aromi e sapori* (fragrances and flavors) run more toward jams from England, pasta made with truffles (from the excellent Tartuflanghe company in Alba, Piemonte), teas from India and China, and expensive Sauternes, Burgundy, and champagne from nearby France. But this store is also a good source for some of the best local olive oils that are hard to find once you leave the province of Imperia.

Da Franca—Gastronomia Casalinga, Piazza degli Eroi Sanremesi 51.

Good prepared foods. The dishes here change daily, but might include tripe, stuffed sardines, boiled octopus, trout, breaded *funghi porcini*, sautéed yellow peppers, sweet-and-sour onions, roast rabbit, focaccia, and gnocchi. The store also sells containers of fresh pesto to use at home.

A WALK DOWN THE VIA PALAZZO

This street is the main thoroughfare that connects one end of the Via Matteotti (which runs parallel to the sea and is the street to which most visitors confine themselves) and the Piazza dei Eroi Sanremesi, site of the city market and entryway to La Pigna, the fascinating old quarter of the city. The Via Palazzo is now closed to vehicular traffic, making it the natural meeting place of the citizens of San Remo. There are many intriguing shops for the food lover. Here are a few, starting from the piazza and heading toward the sea.

#7: *Cantine Sanremesi.*

A wonderful spot for lunch or a snack — not to be missed. (See "Dining," above.)

#11: *Salumeria Francesco Ponzo.*

Here is a beautiful display of *salumi* and pasta. Genovese *salame* or something from Piemonte is what to pick here.

#15: Casa del Parmigiano.

As you would expect, a good place to buy cheese.

#20: "Drinks."

Despite its silly name, a good source for wine.

#35:

Here is a fine bakery if you want to purchase local breads such as *pane del mari-naio* (sailor's bread), focaccia, *pan dolce*, and fresh breadsticks with olives.

Pasticceria Primavera.

A few doors down on the left is a sumptuous bakery. Beautiful cookies and biscuits are the specialty here, but cakes are also quite appealing.

This is the corner of Via Palazzo and Via Cavour. If you turn left and head up the Via Cavour, this is a way into La Pigna.

MARKET
_____

Mercato Comunale, near Piazza degli Eroi Sanremesi. Open May 1–September 30, Monday–Saturday 6–13h, 16:30–19:30h; October 1–April 30, weekdays 6–13h, Saturday 6–13h, 16–19h.

On Tuesday and Saturday there is an outdoor market surrounding the Saracen tower next to San Remo's covered market, adding more color to the area. Here you can purchase clothes, housewares, and leather goods. Nearby is the Piazza degli Eroi Sanremesi, with more good food stores. One often hears about the fabled Mediterranean Diet that supposedly guarantees health and well-being along with delicious flavor. What one sees of this diet in America, Germany, and other countries is a mere approximation of the real thing. Although certain ingredients can be sent from Mediterranean countries to any corner of the world, others are irreplaceable. Newly picked fruits and vegetables, local nuts and seeds, fresh young cheeses, just-caught fish, fragrant herbs, simple wine, pure oil, and fresh breads are all best found near the place they are born. The perfect place to see and buy these foods is the market of San Remo. The sheer variety and unimpeachable quality of food here is breathtaking. We are also reminded that for us to embrace the Mediterranean Diet we have a long way to go. We must have *materia prima* (original ingredients) of this stature, and we must have a highly developed sense of taste and the knowledge of what good food is. These attributes are innate in most of the people in San Remo.

The covered market of San Remo is a large rectangular space with a vaulted ceiling. In the center one finds almost ninety stands of fruits, vegetables, nuts, and seeds. On the sides of the room are "boxes," little stands with other products. The stands and boxes are all numbered—not necessarily sequentially or conspicuously—and what follows is a list of intriguing vendors whom you should look for during your visit. It is arranged in the order of a meandering walk, and you can find them at your leisure.

Box 28: Da Nuccio.

All manner of bread. The fragrance announces the place even before you see it. Nearby, at Da Milena, is *pan di Triora*, a traditional bread from the Ligurian mountains.

Box 5: Il Pane.

More good bread and La Mollica (the Crumb) at box 15 across the way has even more inviting breads and good cookies.

Box 21: Polleria da Marco.

Fresh poultry, but also has roast chickens with no added fat but loaded with fresh Ligurian herbs. It also grills *galletti* (baby roosters) and chicken and turkey thighs.

Box 24: Polleria da Sclavo.

No grill, but it does have large hampers of brown eggs. There are eggs in plastic containers that are given the most favored display. These are *uova da bere*, eggs so fresh and flavorful that they are meant to be eaten raw (or, as Italians say, to drink).

Stand 84, Opposite box 26: Gianna.

A *salumeria* that has some of the best produce in the market. See if it has *uva fragola da Ceriana* (tiny black grapes). There is also perfect spinach and broccoli, stunning tall green beetroot, and big mean-looking tomatoes called *cuor di bue* (ox's heart).

Near this stand, under an overhang marked COLTIVATORI DIRETTI, the displays are less arresting (and less well lit), but no less important. In most markets, food sellers buy from farms and suppliers, and their quality depends on their contacts, their taste, and whom they buy from. But *coltivatori diretti* are actually the people who raise the crops. They do not engage in the sort of spirited salesmanship that other food sellers do, preferring simply to stand by their produce and let it speak for itself. And it does. Here are fresh basil, rosemary, and lavender that were picked this morning. You will also see tiny zucchini flowers for stuffing with cheese and herbs. Look for figs from someone's tree, or whatever else a farmer might bring in. The point to draw from this section is that everything is at the peak of freshness. It may not always be cosmetically perfect, but the flavor and fragrance are.

Go back to the main room. Stand 11 has a good selection of walnuts, chestnuts, olives, and sun-dried tomatoes, all of local origin. So does stand 42, which also has a large selection of beans and greens. Stand 45 has all kinds of wild mushrooms. And stand 19 has garlands of garlic and red peppers strung around the scale. These are but a few impressions from a vast number of vendors who will delight you with their animated cries and their genuine pride in their wares.

Santa Margherita (Genova)

FOLKLORE

Festa di Primavera.

At some point in February a spring festival is declared. Fritters of all kinds are made and served to townspeople who gather around bonfires on the beach. The bonfires are considered a farewell to winter and a greeting to spring.

BAKERY

Astengo, Via Montenotte 16r, tel.
019/820570.

Famous above all for its amaretti.

DINING

Antica Trattoria Bosco delle Ninfe, Via
Ranco 10, tel. 019/823976. Closed Sunday
evening and Monday. No credit cards.
Moderate.

Good Ligurian specialties, including
farinata, *corzetti*, cod fritters, *cavoli*
ripieni (stuffed cabbage), and cakes.

Ristorante da Enzo, Via Santa Lucia
9–11r (near Torre Leone Pancaldo, the
1519 landmark), tel. 019/37752. Closed
Wednesday. No credit cards. Inexpensive.

A trattoria with nice food. The pasta is
delicious, and the restaurant makes an
excellent *insalata mista*.

Vino e Farinata, Via Pia 15r, no
telephone. Closed Sunday, Monday, and
during part of August and September.
No credit cards. Inexpensive.

A characteristic place to eat fresh hot
farinata washed down with the house rosé
wine. Other specialties include *frittelle*,
chickpea soup, *cima alla genovese*, and
stuffed sardines. The restaurant also sells
farina di ceci (chickpea flour), so you can
make your own *farinata*.

FOOD STORE

Salsamentaria Antica, Via Pia 39.

Aside from the cheeses and *salumi*, this
is an excellent source of *sott'oli*: tiny

artichokes, sun-dried tomatoes, sliced
funghi porcini, all packed in great olive
oil. *On Via Paolo Boselli:*

#5:

This *panetteria* has many breads made
without fat, such as *ciabatte*, *ossa* (shaped
like bones), *toscano* (long loaves with
rounded ends), *sardo* (triangular), *lingua*
sarda (long, tongue-shaped).

#10: Libreria G. Moneta.

A good source for cookbooks.

#11: Gastronomia Teresa.

An excellent selection of olives from
around the Mediterranean. There are also
good cheeses and items to take away, such
as frittatas and vegetable tarts.

ICE CREAM

Gelateria Superfrutto, Piazza Armando
Diaz.

The cream ice creams—chocolate,
nocciola, *crema*—are good; the fruit ice
creams are excellent, with palpable
chunks of fruit giving real flavor.

MARKET

Savona's market is held on Monday
next to the Piazza del Popolo. There is
some food, many flowers, and a vast
array of cookware.

WINE

Paolo Mighetto e Figli Vini d'Asti,
Via Vacciuoli 23.

A nice wine bar near the Duomo, with
many bottles for sale.

Sestri Levante (Genova)

DINING

Polpo Mario, Via 25 Aprile 163, tel. 0185/480203. All credit cards. Moderate to moderately expensive.

Deservedly popular for the fish dishes based on the daily catch by the restaurant's own fisherman. Don't miss the *polpo con le patate*, delicate octopus and potatoes.

Taggia (Imperia)

FOLKLORE

Festa di San Benedetto, tel. 0184/43733.

On Saturday night in mid-February bonfires are lit along with special fireworks called *firgari*. On Sunday afternoon there is a costumed parade evoking historical events. Food, wine, and music are in abundance.

Il Ballo della Morte (The Dance of Death).

This ancient event is part of the July 18 feast of Santa Maria Maddalena del Bosco. A series of religious observances culminates in a wild group dance, followed by distribution of bunches of lavender.

Vall'Aurea (Imperia)

OLIVE OIL

Olio Ardoino, tel. 0183/23660.

Nanni Ardoino is considered by many to be

the region's finest taster of olive oil. His own product, made here, is absolutely wonderful. The family business was founded by his grandfather Giuseppe in 1870.

Ventimiglia (Imperia)

Ventimiglia is not, it must be conceded, the prettiest town in Italy. As the border city with France, it is a major shopping destination for French people looking for Italian clothes, food, and vermouth. Prices for clothes are competitive in Ventimiglia; those for food are less so.

DINING

Trattoria Colombo, Via Cavour 85, tel. 0184/351310. Closed Monday, late June, and early July. All credit cards. Moderate.

Ventimiglia is more a commercial center than a tourist destination. The food, in my experience, is not the best on the Riviera,

and I would choose to eat either in San Remo or Dolceacqua. However, it is possible to have very good grilled or roast fish at the Trattoria Colombo. This is a rather anonymous-looking place on one of the main thoroughfares of town (and not far from the train station). The father of the owner is a fisherman, so that you can be assured of the best fish available. I tried *branzino al forno con le olive,* an oven-roasted sea bass with olives that was rich and flavorful, but definitely not for people who don't like their fish fishy. If the only available fish is frozen, this will be indicated on the menu as *surgelato.*

FOOD STORES
Salumeria Walter, Via della Repubblica 1A.

An excellent selection to make a meal as you sit by the sea or drive to the mountains.

Dried *peperoni* catch the eye, as does *panettone genovese.* There are also cheeses, *salumi,* and olives. This is a good place to buy local olive oil if you are not going up to the hills.

Centro Alimentari, Via Ruffini 10E.
All credit cards.

A vast selection of cheeses, *salumi,* wines, pastas, chocolates, and some fresh fruit. It also sells a lot of vermouth, which is so popular with the French.

Pesto alla Genovese

Once upon a time, pesto was invariably made by hand using a mortar and pestle. The name implies the act of using the pestle. This is still the classic and preferred method, but modern times have even reached certain kitchens in Liguria. It is now a given that much of the pesto you taste is made in a blender. Handmade pesto is indeed better because the ingredients have been worked less, but blender pesto is fine as long as you use the finest, freshest ingredients available. This pesto may be tossed with spaghetti, *maccheroni,* linguine, or the classic Ligurian pastas, *trofie* or *trenette.*

For 4 servings of pasta
1 large bunch fresh basil leaves
4 cloves garlic, peeled
1 teaspoon pine nuts
5 to 6 tablespoons extra-virgin olive oil,
   preferably Ligurian
¾ cup freshly grated Pecorino Romano

Do not wash the basil. Simply wipe the leaves carefully with paper towels or a clean cloth to remove any dirt. Discard the stems.

Classic Method: Place a few leaves of basil in a mortar. Add a clove of garlic and crush the leaves and garlic against the sides of the mortar using the pestle. Add a few more leaves of basil and another garlic clove, and repeat the process. Once you

have crushed all of the basil and garlic, add the pine nuts. Crush until the basil, garlic, and pine nuts are well blended. Add a tablespoon of olive oil and combine with the ingredients in the mortar. Then add the Pecorino Romano a little at a time, stirring with a wooden spoon. Then stir in some more oil, a tablespoon at a time. Your goal is to have a thick, creamy sauce. If you choose not to use all of the oil, that is fine.

Blender Method: Place all of the ingredients in a blender. Blend at high speed for 1 minute. Then lift the lid carefully, and scrape the sides of the blender cup using a rubber spatula. Check the consistency of the pesto, which should be thick and creamy. Blend for a few more seconds if you think the pesto should be a bit thinner, but don't overdo it. A few cooks, after making blender pesto, add a touch of heavy cream to the sauce, but this is not essential.

Cook's Note: In Genova it is traditional to boil a peeled potato along with the pasta. This potato is then chopped into chunks and tossed with the pesto and pasta. The *genovesi* often add a few slivers of cooked string beans as well. Some cooks add a bit of hot water from the pasta pot to dilute the pesto just before it is tossed with the noodles.

If you are making minestrone or another vegetable soup, stir a tablespoon of pesto into each portion for an exquisite treat.

Wine: Pigato, Vermentino, or Vernaccia di San Gimignano.

Zucchine Ripiene
Stuffed Zucchini

Serves 4
4 medium zucchini
1 tablespoon unsalted butter
3 tablespoons finely minced onions
150 grams/⅓ pound ground veal or lean beef
60 grams/⅛ pound prosciutto crudo, minced
2 large eggs, lightly beaten
60 grams/¼ cup unseasoned bread crumbs
80 grams/⅓ cup freshly grated Parmigiano-Reggiano
¼ teaspoon freshly ground black pepper
⅛ teaspoon salt (optional)
Several fresh basil leaves, carefully wiped and torn into small bits (do not cut)
1½ cups tomato sauce or puree

Preheat the oven to 180°C (350°F). Set a large pot of cold water to boil. When it reaches a boil, add the zucchini and cook for 5 minutes. Remove them from the pot, let cool for a couple of minutes, and then slice them in half lengthwise. Carefully scoop out the pulp, making sure not to break the shell of the zucchini. Place the pulp in a large mixing bowl and set aside. Melt the butter in a large skillet. Add the onions and sauté for a few seconds. Then add the veal or beef and cook gently for 1 minute, pushing the meat around the pan so that it cooks evenly and does not stick. Add the prosciutto and continue cooking until the meat is thoroughly browned. Drain all the cooking fat, and add the meat-and-onion mixture to the zucchini pulp. Add the eggs, bread crumbs, Parmigiano-Reggiano, pepper, salt, and basil leaves to the bowl and combine with a wooden spoon. Once the mixture is well blended, spoon it into the 8 zucchini halves. Pour the tomato sauce into a large baking dish that has been lightly greased with olive oil. Carefully place the stuffed zucchini into the dish and bake for 15 to 20 minutes, or until the filling is browned but not overdone. Serve hot or warm with a bit of the tomato sauce from the dish.

Variation: I like to add a little fresh lemon zest or a few drops of fresh lemon juice to the mixture. Some cooks like adding a few sultanas to the mixture as well.

Wine: Rossese di Dolceacqua or Chianti.

Piemonte

Not to Miss in Piemonte

ALBA *(Classic Town)*　　　　**ASTI**

CUNEO　　　　　　　　　　**TORINO**

THE WINES OF PIEMONTE

REGIONAL CAPITAL:
Torino (TO).

PROVINCIAL CAPITALS:
Alessandria (AL), Asti (AT),
　Biella (BI), Cuneo (CN),
　Novara (NO), Vercelli (VC).

TOURIST INFORMATION:
Assessorato Regionale al
　Turismo,
　　Via Magenta 12,
　　10128 Torino,
　　tel. 011/57171.

Wine Tourism:
Movimento del Turismo del
　Vino, Consorzio Turistico
　Alba, Bra, Langhe, Roero,
　Piazza San Paolo 3,
　12051 Alba (CN),
　tel. 0173/361538,
　fax 0173/361524.

Migliaia, milioni di individui lavorano, producono e risparmiono nonostante tutto quello che noi possiamo fare per molestarli, inceppparli, scoraggiarli. È la vocazione naturale che li spinge; non soltanto la sete di denaro. Il gusto, l'orgoglio di vedere la propria azienda prosperare, acquistare credito, ispirare fiducia a clientele sempre più vaste, ampliare gli impianti, abbellire le sedi, costituiscono una molla di progresso altrettanto potente che il guadagno. Se cosi non fosse, non si spiegherebbe come ci siano imprenditori che nella propria azienda prodigano tutte le loro energie e investono tutti i loro capitali per ritrarre spesso utili di gran lunga più modesti di quelli che potrebbero sicuramente e comodamente ottenere con altri impieghi.

"Thousands, millions of individuals work, produce and save despite all that we can do to bother, obstruct and discourage them. It is natural vocation that propels them, not only thirst for money. The taste, the pride in seeing one's own company prosper, the acquisition of credit, inspiring faith in an ever-growing clientele, enlarging installations, beautifying offices, all constitute a form of progress just as powerful as earning money. If this were not the case, how would one explain why there are entrepreneurs who, in their own companies, lavish all their energies and invest all their resources to derive profits that in the long run are more modest than those that they could certainly and easily obtain with other investments."

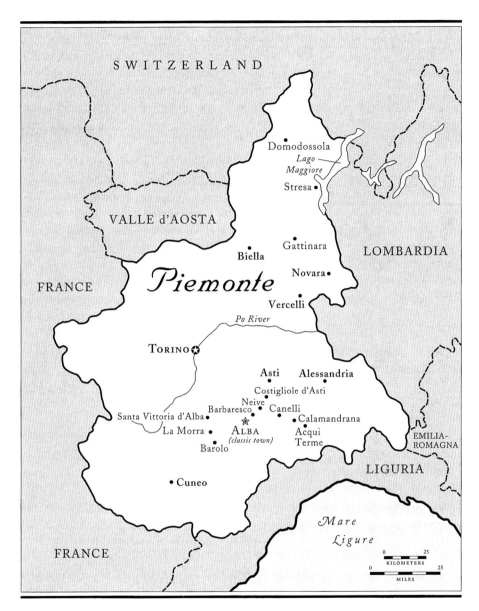

These famous words by Luigi Einaudi, publisher, scholar, and *uomo piemontese*, hang framed on a wall of the Caffè Torino on the Piazza San Carlo in Torino, the capital of Piemonte. But they can be recited by people throughout the region. While they are emblematic of a philosophy that one finds throughout Italy, they are You can receive an excellent brochure indicating more than sixty wineries in the area that receive visitors for tastings and, in some cases, those that serve meals and offer lodging (for a price, of course). Also listed are good hotels and restaurants in the wine-producing zones.

particularly applicable in Piemonte. The people of this region work hard, save, invest, build, and create and take great but quiet pride in their endeavors. It is seldom acknowledged outside of Italy how passionately Italians care about work. In fact, the opening words of the Italian constitution are "Italy is a nation founded and based on work." And nowhere is this truer than Piemonte. Almost every *piemontese* family, from the powerful Agnellis, who own FIAT (Italy's largest automobile maker and producer of 37 percent of the nation's gross national product), to the smallest farmers, subscribes to this philosophy. So bars and *caffès* in Torino are made beautiful by their owners, wine makers in Asti and Alba lavish great care on their products, and restaurateurs in Cuneo devote time and attention to making memorable meals for their customers. I have often heard Italians from other regions remark that the *piemontesi* are cold technocrats. This is a misunderstanding: the people of Piemonte may fastidiously devote themselves to work, but they also know how to derive pleasure from life. The wines of the region are among the best in the world. The terrain yields magnificent truffles and superb fruits and vegetables. The coffee, chocolates, and baking of Piemonte are as good as one can find in Italy. And because the people of this region do not go out of their way to beat their own drums, Piemonte remains one of the great underdiscovered regions for the gourmet traveler in Italy.

Eating in Piemonte

For a region that is one of the most industrialized in Italy, Piemonte also is intensely agricultural. Aside from the production of magnificent wines, all sorts of crops are grown that have found their way into a rich and varied cuisine. Wheat is the most cultivated grain, followed by corn, then rice (in Vercelli and Novara), and rye (in the province of Cuneo). Cuneo also produces excellent beef, veal, and rabbit, while the northernmost reaches of the region are alpine and are full of game. Frogs in the canals that flood the rice paddies are prized in local cooking. Snails are also popular and are especially delicious when cooked with Gorgonzola cheese.

There is extensive cultivation of superb fruit and vegetables throughout the region. The provinces of Alba and Asti are rich in white truffles, one of the world's most expensive and luxurious ingredients. Hazelnuts, walnuts, and chestnuts are abundant and play a central role in the cuisine of Piemonte, especially in the wonderful desserts. In former times, many dishes that now use olive oil from Liguria employed hazelnut and walnut oil. Chocolate and coffee are used with great skill in this region, especially in Torino and Alba. There are two important strains in *piemontese* cuisine. The first is the strong peasant and agricultural tradition that has given people throughout the region an innate understanding of ingredients and their uses. The other influence is the fact that Piemonte was, from the fifteenth century until 1861, part of the royal House of Savoy. The Savoy lands extended from the Monferrato in the eastern part of the region well into territory on the opposite side of the French Alps. This means that French taste and style are felt in the kitchens of Piemonte. More important, as a royal seat, Torino developed a taste for elegant and elaborate cuisine and presentation that one still encounters in restaurants and food stores today.

ANTIPASTI

Bagna Cauda. A plate of raw vegetables, especially *cardi* (cardoons), served with a hot dipping sauce of olive oil, garlic, and anchovies.

Caponet. Zucchini flowers or cabbage stuffed with ground beef, sausage, eggs, parsley, garlic, Parmigiano-Reggiano, then dipped in eggs and sautéed in butter.

Carne Cruda. Raw veal that is sliced very thin or chopped. Served with oil, salt, pepper, and lemon.

Lardo. Delicately sliced herb-scented lard.

Salame de la Duja. A soft *salame* that is preserved in lard. A specialty of Novara.

Vegetables. All kinds are served raw, cooked, or preserved in oil or vinegar. They are also combined with cheese and baked as little cakes called *tortini*.

PRIMI

Agnolotti. Large, filled pasta, typically with meat, but also vegetables or cheese.

Agnolotti del Plin. From Alba, tiny, delicious filled pasta often served with melted butter and truffles.

Cisrà. Chickpea soup.

Gnocchi alla Bava. Potato dumplings with melted cheese.

Paniscia (or Panissa). Typical of Novara and Vercelli, this is a rice dish with sausages, beans, and different vegetables.

Risotto. A silky combination of rice cooked with numerous ingredients, such as saffron or mushrooms, vegetables, fish, cheeses, or wine.

Tajarin (Tagliarini). Very thin egg noodles.

Tofeja. Pork-rind-and-bean soup.

SECONDI

Bollito Misto. Up to seven meats carefully boiled and served with sauces called *bagnet verde* (parsley, garlic, anchovies) and *bagnet rosso* (tomatoes, basil, sweet red peppers, onions, and garlic). In the Langhe it is typical to have boiled veal alone with *cogna*, a sauce of pickled fruit, particularly grapes.

Brasato. Braised beef or veal. Usually the word *brasato* is linked with the name of one of Piemonte's fine wines, such as Barolo. *Brasato* is cooked over a minuscule flame for many hours.

Finanziera. A specialty of Torino. Made with chicken livers and gizzards, cockscombs, porcini mushrooms, minced veal, and Marsala. It often is served with soufflés. It was named for bankers and financiers, who wore a traditional costume called *la finanziera*.

Fritto Misto (also called *Fritto Misto all'Italiana*). A platter of fried foods, including calf's liver, sweetbreads, brains, veal cutlet, baby lamb chops, sausage, zucchini, eggplant, artichokes, apples, pears, bananas, grapes, and semolina fritters.

Grive. Meatballs made with calf's brains, pork liver, nutmeg, bread crumbs, cheeses, eggs, and juniper berries.

Stracotto. Very slowly cooked beef.

FORMAGGI

Bra. An ancient cheese typical of the town of Bra in the province of Cuneo. It can be had young or aged, when it is a bit sharp. Made of cow's milk but often mixed with milks from sheep and goats.

Castelmagno. Cow's-milk cheese, produced in the village of Pradlèves, that graced the tables of kings from Charlemagne to Vittorio Emanuele II.

Gorgonzola. Originally from Lombardia, most is now produced in Novara. This is a blue-veined cheese of exquisite flavor.

Murazzano. A specialty of the Langhe, made either of sheep's milk or a blend of sheep's and cow's milk.

Raschera. An alpine cheese made of cow's milk, sometimes mixed with sheep's milk. Sharp when aged.

Toma. A generic term for a whole group of cheeses that are made throughout Piemonte. Each is named by its place of origin, such as *toma della Valle di Susa* or *toma del Pesio.* Many tend to be white to golden and have a gold crust.

Tomini. Little soft cheeses, often made with goat's milk and dressed with olive oil and herbs.

DOLCI

Torta di Nocciola. Hazelnut cake.

Baci di Dama. Sandwich cookies of almonds or hazelnuts with a chocolate filling. Some *baci* are made with red wine, too.

Amaretti, Albesi, Astigiane. Macaroons, many flavored with wine, rum, or other liqueurs.

Pesche Ripiene. Fabulously flavorful peaches filled with a stuffing of cocoa, sugar, eggs, and amaretti.

Pere Cotte al Vino. Pears cooked slowly in Barolo or another excellent wine.

Cioccolati. Piemonte makes a vast assortment of chocolates, but *gianduia* (a mix of chocolate with hazelnut paste) is the most famous. *Gianduiotti* are little gold-wrapped pieces of *gianduia.*

Bonet. A custard made with milk, eggs, sugar, cocoa, amaretti, and sometimes coffee.

OTHER SPECIALTIES

Coffee. In Torino coffee is an institution and the *caffès* that were built to serve it are monuments to a whole culture. In a *torinese caffè,* one drinks excellent coffee, eats fine chocolate or pastries, and engages in pleasurable social interchange.

Grissini. These are breadsticks, which are native to the region. If you expect stubby little sticks you are in for a surprise. *Grissini* made in bakeries or homes can be the length of a small table.

The Wines of Piemonte

The distinguishing characteristic of the wines of Piemonte, aside from their almost universally high quality, is that most of them are produced on family estates that have small parcels of land. There are thirty-seven DOC wines in Piemonte and four DOCG wines (Barolo, Barbaresco, Gattinara, and Moscato d'Asti). The two leading native white-grape varieties are Cortese di Gavi (which also produces a wine called Gavi di Gavi) and Arneis di Roero, lesser known and very fine.

Brachetto. A light, slightly red sparkling wine from Acqui Terme that is one of the most popular new aperitif wines. It matches particularly well with chocolate, an unusual taste sensation.

Grignolino and *Freisa.* Other native *piemontese* grapes that produce light reds.

Dolcetto. Another native grape, although Ligurians say it was originally theirs, Dolcetto has become a very popular medium-weight red. There are seven varieties, each with a different geographic designation (Acqui, Alba, Asti, Diano d'Alba, Dogliani, Langhe Monregalesi, Ovada).

Barbera. The most popular native grape in Piemonte, at least in terms of how much is produced. It is ruby red, and when it is young it can be quite acidic. As it ages it smoothes somewhat and develops orange glints in its color. There are four different DOC Barberas, each representing a different geographic designation (Alba, Asti, Colli Tortonesi, and Monferrato).

Nebbiolo. The outstanding grape of Piemonte. While Sangiovese is the backbone of Chianti in Toscana, Nebbiolo is the grape that makes most of Piemonte's top wines (it is called Spanna in provinces of Vercelli and Novara). DOC wines Gattinara, Carema, Barbaresco, and Barolo are all made with Nebbiolo. Many wine lovers consider Barolo Italy's best wine, while others are partial to the slightly lighter Barbaresco. These wines are produced in limited quantities in their

DOC zones, so that they can command high prices. If you are in Alba, go to the town of Barbaresco and Barolo to discover these wines where they are made.

Other Red Wines. These include Ghemme (Spanna, Vespolina, and Bonarda Novarese) and Gattinara (Spanna, Bonarda di Gattinara).

Moscato. A straw-colored sweet grape that produces the hugely popular sparkling wine (often called spumante) produced in Asti and Canelli. Bad examples in the past have left the impression that spumante is sugar water. In fact, genuine Moscato smells like a basket of flowers or a bowl of peaches and apricots. It is immensely pleasing and is the perfect way to end a meal.

Vermouth. A native drink of Piemonte made of red or white wine flavored with fifteen herbs.

This is only the most cursory overview of the wine landscape in Piemonte. To learn more, look into the writings of Matt Kramer, Burton Anderson, and Victor Hazan.

Acqui Terme (Alessandria)

BAKERIES AND SWEET SHOPS

Acqui Terme is known not only for its wines, but also its sweets and biscuits. Amaretti in Acqui are made with both sweet and bitter almonds and have a flavor all their own.

Amaretti Gallerotti, Corso Italia 59.

Famous for *boeri* (sweets made with chocolate and cherries).

Pasticceria da Rita, Piazza Bollente 5.

Typical amaretti (sweet and bitter almonds, sugar, and egg whites).

Pasticceria Porro, Corso Italia 43.

Homemade marrons glacés, *torrone* (nougat made with hazelnuts), meringues, cookies, and, especially, Acquesi al Rhum (amaretti with lots of rum).

DINING

Ristorante Alfredo, Piazza Matteotti 3, tel. 0144/56586. Moderately inexpensive.

A *rosticceria/enoteca* where one can have delicious local peppers with Ligurian olive oil or fresh goat cheese served with a jam made of the musts of Barolo, Dolcetto, or Brachetto grapes. There is also a moist *torta di nocciola* with good zabaglione.

ENOTECA PUBBLICA

Enoteca Regionale di Acqui Terme, Piazza Levi, tel. 0144/770273, fax 0144/57627. Open 10–12h, 15–18:30h, Thursday 15–18:30h; closed Monday, Wednesday, and first two weeks in January.

In the Palazzo Robellini opposite the city hall, one can taste all the regional wines, but especially Gavi, Dolcetto, and the delightful Brachetto d'Acqui, a light red wine often consumed as an *aperitivo* or a dessert. It is an unusually fine match with chocolate and with *amaretti di Acqui*. Brachetto has become a very chic wine in Italy in recent years, and the price of its grapes is higher even than that for those used to make Barolo.

Alba (Cuneo)
Classic Town

I thought long and hard before deciding that Alba, rather than Asti, should be designated the Classic Town for the region of Piemonte. Asti has its famous spumante and its outstanding market. It is the main town of the Monferrato, a zone full of vineyards, truffles, and good restaurants. But I think you will find that the hilly Monferrato does not touch the soul in the same way as the sweetly rolling slopes of the Langhe, the zone of which Alba is the principal town. Alba also has a fair amount of truffles (and Italy's largest truffle market), and the nearby wine towns produce Barolo, Barbaresco, Dolcetto, Barbera. Visit La Morra, Neive, Treiso, Santa Vittoria d'Alba, Gallo d'Alba, Barolo, and Barbaresco for fantastic food and wine in beautiful settings. Also, if Asti has the pretensions of a provincial capital, Alba remains a contented smaller community that happily conserves much of the best of Piemonte.

BAKERIES AND SWEET SHOPS

Pasticceria Cheinasso, Corso Langhe 88, tel. 0173/497259.

Famous above all for its *torta di nocciole*.

Io... Tu... e i Dolci, Piazza Savona 12.

The name is a play on words from the title of a popular 1970s film, *Io, Tu e gli Altri (I, You, and the Others)*. The shop makes delicious chocolate-covered hazelnuts.

Sacco, Via Cavour 9.

Hazelnut cakes, rum macaroons.

Bar-Pasticceria Cignetti and Bar-Pasticceria Pettiti.

See "A Walk down the Via Vittorio Emanuele," overleaf.

BARS AND CAFFÈS

Caffè Calissano, Piazza Risorgimento 3. Closed Wednesday.

Comfortable and gracious, with good coffee, pastries, and ice cream.

Casa del Caffè, Via Macrino 1. Open 7:15– 12:30h, 14:30–19:30h; closed Monday.

For serious coffee drinkers. A large roasting machine is in the front, as are sacks of beans for show. But you purchase from plastic containers that preserve the aroma of the beans. In the back is a bar for tasting.

DINING

Osteria dell'Arco, Piazza Savona 5, tel. 0173/363974. Closed Sunday. All credit cards. Moderate.

Delicious food. You can have risotto or *tajarin* with truffles (in season). I am a big fan of *coniglio all'Arneis*, tender rabbit cooked in white wine. There are all kinds of rich desserts, but I was very happy with the *pere al Moscato*, perfect pears poached in dessert wine.

Ristorante La Capannina, Loc. Borgo Moretta, Strada Profonda 21, tel. 0173/442097. Closed Monday. No credit cards. Moderately inexpensive.

This restaurant claims to have invented sliced *carne cruda*, the raw veal antipasto that is so popular in the Langhe. La Capannina is in a green park near a stream.

Il Vicoletto, Via Bertero 6, tel. 0173/ 363196. Reservations essential. Closed Monday and late July–mid-August. American Express, Visa. Moderately expensive.

There is no sign to indicate that you have arrived at Il Vicoletto, but it is worth looking for. An excellent restaurant that produces all the classic dishes of the area.

Vineria dell'Umberto, Piazza Savona 4, tel. 0173/441397. Open 20–24h; closed Monday and in August. No credit cards. Moderately inexpensive.

This is a welcoming place for good food and excellent wine. The main reason to come here, as the name suggests, is to sample wines from a list that contains nearly two hundred selections. The wine cellar's strength, not surprisingly, is in the wines of the Langhe, the hills that surround Alba so go for Dolcetto, Barbera, Barbaresco, and Barolo. There is tasty food here, too, including *tagliarini (tajarin)*, *vitello tonnato*, *agnolotti*, *stracotto*, and chicken.

Osteria Lalibera, Via Pertinace 24a, tel. 0173/293155. Closed Sunday, Monday lunch, three weeks in February and the last two weeks of August. All credit cards. Moderate.

If you hew to *piemontese* classics rather than dishes from elsewhere, you will eat very well. I like the *peperone* with tuna and capers, *vitello tonnato*, *agnolotti dal plin*, and *bonet*.

A WALK DOWN
THE VIA VITTORIO EMANUELE

One of the main thoroughfares of Alba contains many shops and stores that merit your attention. If you can't fill your truffle requirements on the Via Vittorio Emanuele, then you are truly insatiable.

#5: Cignetti.

A wonderful old *bar-pasticceria* (since 1878) famous for its *torrone*, a nougat made with almonds or hazelnuts. Also try the *albesi al Barolo*, wine-flavored macaroons.

#9a: Pasta Fresca Corino.

Agnolotti del plin and other local pastas.

#16a: Pasticceria Berta. Open 7–1h; closed Monday.

Ice cream, *albesi*, *torta di nocciola*.

#18B: Polleria Ratti.

An excellent poultry store that also sells cheese, wine, and truffles.

#19:

Behind here is the courtyard that contains the Mercato del Tartufo on Saturday in October, November, and December.

#25: Pasticceria Pettiti.

Chocolate truffles and Sacher torte are specialties.

#26: Ponzio Tartufi, tel. 0173/440456.

A vast selection of truffle products: pastas, oils, rice, cheeses scented with truffles, pâtés, spreads, sauces. Many of the products come in jars and make perfect gifts for people back home.

#27: Aldo Martino.

Excellent fruits and vegetables. It specializes in *primizie*, the first vegetables of the season. Truffles and *funghi* are also available.

FOOD STORES

See "A Walk down the Via Vittorio Emanuele," above, for more suggestions.

Enoteca Peccati di Gola, Via Cavour 11. Open 8–13h, 15–20h; closed Monday. All credit cards.

A fine source for wines, truffles, *funghi porcini*, truffle paste, and superb cheese.

LIBRARY

Biblioteca Civica G. Ferrero.

Although this is a general city library, it happens to have an unusually strong collection of books in many languages about Italian gastronomy. This is because the nearby Ceretto winery, producer of fine Barolo, has established a prize recognizing excellence in books about the culture of food and wine from a historical, scientific, gastronomic, or sociological point of view. All books that are considered for this prize wind up on the shelves of the Biblioteca Ferrero.

MUSEUM

Civico Museo Archeologico e di Scienze Naturali F. Eusebio, Via Paruzza 1, tel. 0173/290092. Open 9–12h, 15–18h, Friday 9–12h; closed Sunday and Monday.

This museum has an excellent collection of glassware and housewares from ancient times. You can see the influence of these shapes on the designs we have today. Also, there is a marble relief from the second century A.D. of a *capretta accovacciata* (goat). This is important for food historians because it indicates that *toma* cheese was already made in these parts at that time.

TRUFFLES

See "A Walk down the Via Vittorio Emanuele," above, for more suggestions about buying truffles. Also see the listing for TartufLanghe in the town of Piobesi d'Alba. This company's excellent products are available in several stores in Alba.

Mercato del Tartufo, courtyard just past Via Vittorio Emanuele 19. Open Saturday morning, October–December.

One of the most evocative settings in Piemonte. Truffle hunters go into the woods of the Langhe district accompanied by dogs who are primed to sniff out the perfume of truffles buried just below the ground. While October may still be sunny, by November and December the market is often shrouded in fog, which lends it a timeless romance. Prices are, of course, expensive, and certain few sellers will attempt to hold together pieces of truffle with toothpicks. But this is the distinct minority among people who are basically scrupulous.

Tartufi Morra, Piazza Pertinace 3, tel. 0173/290072, fax 0173/362266.

Truffles, truffle paste, oils, pâtés, and pastas. Also, foods made with truffles.

WINE

Enoteca Albese Il Crutin, Via Cuneo 3, tel. 0173/293239. Closed Sunday, Monday, and August.

A good source for wines of this area, plus fine information about these wines.

Enoteca Fracchia & Berchialla, Via Vernazza 7, tel. 0173/440508. Closed Sunday, Monday, and August. MasterCard, Visa.

An excellent source for local and national wines, plus fine oils and vinegars.

Fuori Orario, Corso Torino 4, tel. 0173/440747. Open 18h until it seems like it's time to close; closed Sunday and mid-August.

On the outskirts of town is this friendly wine bar with light snacks such as sandwiches and plates of cheese and *salumi*.

Alessandria

BAKERIES

Pasticceria Gallina, Via Vochieri 46.

Specializes in cookies such as *baci di dama*.

Pasticceria Giraudi, Via San Lorenzo 102.

Specializes in chocolate desserts.

DINING

Ristorante Arcimboldo, Via Legnano 2, tel. 0131/52022. Open evenings only; closed Sunday and first two weeks in January.

No credit cards. Moderately expensive.

A rather elegant place, with good Piedmontese food as well as *prosciutto di alce* (elk). Although this is not a humble restaurant, it does not have a printed menu or wine list, which might cause you problems if your language skills are limited. Nonetheless, the service is friendly and unpretentious, so you need not feel intimidated in attempting to find out what food there is to eat.

Asti

The city of Asti is synonymous with Italy's most famous sparkling wine, known as Asti Spumante. It is made of Moscato grapes. The wine is produced in wineries all over the Astigiano, most famously perhaps in the town of Canelli. The red wines produced in Asti's province are probably more central to the area's sense of self. Barbera d'Asti is a highly acidic red wine that startles tasters who are new to it. Once you understand how the acid and the natural sugars in this wine interact in the mouth, you will better comprehend why this wine is so well regarded. Many other wines are made in these parts, most of them suited to the province's flavorful cuisine based on cheeses, meats, vegetables, and truffles. There is also good baking in Asti, although many of the city's bakers like to spike cookies and pastries with heavy doses of rum. The main attraction of Asti, however, is its market, which I rank fifth in Italy in terms of interest and fascination, exceeded only by those of Bologna, Padova, Genova, and San Remo.

BAKERIES AND SWEET SHOPS

Pasticceria Giordanino, Corso Alfieri 254. Closed Monday.

Since 1912 this has been Asti's top bakery. There are all sorts of pastries, cakes, cookies, and especially Astigiane, little amaretti drenched with flavors such as rum, maraschino, Grand Marnier, Amaretto di Saronno, and grappa. Giordanino merits a visit for its ambience, with old Marsala bottles lining top shelves, two small Venetian chandeliers hanging from a vaulted ceiling, and fancily packaged baked goods on display throughout the crowded, pretty shop.

Pasticceria Martinengo del Tirulè, Portici degli Armaioli (near Piazza Statuto).

Nice fruit tarts, marrons glacés, and *baci di dama.* There is no pretense to fanciness, but the pastries are good and genuine.

DINING

L'Angolo del Beato, Via Guttuari 12, tel. 041/531668. Closed Wednesday, first ten days in January, and first ten days in August. All credit cards. Moderate to moderately expensive.

Here is a charming restaurant with very good *piemontese* food, fine wines, and good service. The *gnocchi alla bava* goes well with Barbera d'Asti. The meats, cold or hot, are also tasty.

Il Convivio, Via G. B. Giuliani 3 (off Via Polletta and Piazza Statuto), tel. 0141/54188. Open 12–14:30h, 19–24h; closed Sunday. No credit cards. Moderately inexpensive.

This place, with very nice food and wine, proves yet again that one can eat very well in Italy without spending lots of money. All the dishes I tried here are tasty, but I want to single out the *rabaton,* typical of the town of Mandrania (near Alessandria). These are gnocchi made of spinach and ricotta, but without flour. They are served with Parmigiano-Reggiano and a little butter and cream. The house red, the Barbera d'Asti made by the Cantina Sociale di Nizza Monferrato, has a very Italian taste. By this I mean that it is what Italians who are not slavish to fancy trends would choose to drink. It is amazingly inexpensive and very good.

Trattoria al Mercato, corner of Campo del Palio (the lower piazza that serves for the Asti market). Open for lunch and dinner; closed Sunday. Inexpensive.

The kitchen closes when the clientele dwindles, so do not plan on a late meal at this very old, very authentic trattoria. No one there knows how long this site has been serving food (it is also a *locanda* with rooms to let), but entering here one immediately senses a certain slice of Italian life of forty, sixty, or eighty years ago. The walls are virtually bare; the tables are long and plain. The room is lit only with exposed, long fluorescent lightbulbs. The clients are real locals. Invariably they speak in dialect, so your Italian skills won't help you. The place is particularly lively on Wednesday and Saturday—market days—when people come in for a bracing glass of red wine and some simple food. Signora Rosalba, who presides with great cheer and warmth, will cook spaghetti or rice using local greens such as chard or arugula. Dishes vary daily according to what she selects in the market. Second courses might include *bollito misto* or *tacchino arrosto* (roast turkey). In a country where these old places disappear or have been spiffed up and designed to look old-fashioned, a place like the Trattoria al Mercato should be preserved under endangered species legislation.

Ristorante da Aldo di Castiglione, Via Giobert 8, tel. 0141/354905. Closed Thursday and at times in the summer. All credit cards. Moderate.

Piemonte is well-represented with *bagna cauda*, *agnolotti*, excellent *anatra al forno* (roasted duck) and *mousse di torrone* (nougat).

FOOD STORES

Most food stores in Asti close on Thursday afternoon, and all are shut on Sunday.

Alta Gastronomia, Via Garibaldi 18.

A wonderful little emporium with delicacies such as *passato di marrons glacés* (chestnut puree), *bagna cauda*, *sugo alla monferrina* (rabbit and tomatoes, for dressing pasta), cheeses, small sacks of Vercelli rice, and fresh ravioli filled with truffles. The *gastronomia* also sells local wines.

I Buteghin, Corso Dante 14. Closed Monday afternoon.

A source for oils from all over Italy, plus vinegars, capers, jams, honeys, and a sauce of radicchio for pasta.

Polleria V. Carosso, Portici Gabriele Capello (near Piazza Statuto).

Next to the Pasticceria San Secondo is this poultry shop of extreme simplicity that usually has a basket of very fresh eggs on display, a pleasing sight.

Tutto Formaggio di Franco e Silvia, Portici Gabriele Capello (near Piazza Statuto).

A wonderfully fragrant shop that has excellent cheeses at good prices and an outstanding *torta di ricotta*, a cheesecake.

MARKET

On Wednesday and Saturday mornings at dawn, the Campo del Palio, the Piazza della Libertà, and the Piazza Alfieri, adjacent squares in the center of town, fill with hundreds of vendors of all kinds of food, seeds, flowers, clothes, shoes, housewares, and just about anything one could want to buy that can be carried home. The huge Campo del Palio has most of the food vendors, along with shoe sellers. There is also the Trattoria al Mercato, which you should not miss (see "Dining," above). On the Piazza della Libertà, the small piazza connecting the two big ones, is the 1925 (Fascist era) Mercato Coperto. This lively covered market, open daily (except Thursday afternoon and Sunday), has enticing food beautifully displayed. Compared with covered markets in many other towns, this market is relatively small. Notice how merchants and customers like to meet for coffee or a glass of wine at the two bars in this building. As you go up to the Piazza Alfieri, you will pass seed and flower sellers before reaching the clothing and housewares market. These three squares comprise one of the most entertaining market experiences you will have anywhere. In Bologna and Padova there are permanent stalls, and the selection is better, but the Asti market feels like a caravan of merchants who arrive twice a week to sell their wares and then mysteriously move on by the early afternoon.

SPECIALTY SHOP
M. Ajmo, Via Garibaldi 31.

This lovely shop sells dried beans, seeds, and old-style wine labels (Freisa, Nebbiolo, *moscato,* and so on) for people who make their wines at home. This store is charming, genuinely *vecchia Italia.*

TRUFFLES
Mercato del Tartufo, Via Cavour 42 (near Caffè San Carlo). Open Wednesday and Saturday at 4h during the autumn truffle season.

This is the truffle market. People hereabouts say there is a relationship between the quality of wine and the quality of truffles in a given year. That is, when rainfall is sufficient to produce great wines, there probably is not enough rain to yield a bumper crop of truffles. By contrast, years with more rain may result in less-than-optimal wine but compensate with a bounty of truffles. Years with a scarcity of rain, sadly, result in a scarcity of both great wine and truffles.

WINE
Enoteca Boero, Corso Dante 37.

Excellent source for wines of Piemonte. You can sample many by the glass. Next door, at the store called L'Enotecnico, is an imposing collection of wine-making machinery, glassware, books, and videos on making wine, grappa, and vinegar.

Barbaresco (Cuneo)

DINING
Trattoria Antica Torre, Via Torino 8, tel. 0173/635170. Closed Wednesday and mid-July– mid-August. No credit cards. Moderate.

Good *piemontese* cuisine is available at this trattoria next to the Enoteca Regionale. Your check will be high if you order a very expensive wine; otherwise, you can have wonderful wine without spending a king's ransom. The meats are all well prepared, which is a good thing, since you want food that will marry well with the fabulous Barbaresco wines that are available.

ENOTECA PUBBLICA
Enoteca Regionale del Barbaresco, Via

Torino 8a, tel. 0173/635251. Open 9:30–12:30h, 15–19h; closed Monday, January, and first week in July.

In the deconsecrated Church of San Donato you can taste and purchase wine from every producer of Barbaresco.

Barolo (Cuneo)

DINING
Locanda nel Borgo Antico, Piazza del Municipio 2, tel. 0173/56355. Closed Wednesday. Diners Club, MasterCard. Moderate to moderately expensive.

Classic Piemontese cuisine, slightly lightened and updated, but not corrupted. Good tasting menus are designed to accompany splendid Barolo wines.

ENOTECA PUBBLICA
Enoteca Regionale di Barolo, Castello

Comunale (Piazza Falletti), tel. 0172/ 56277. Open 10–12:30h, 15–18.30h; closed Tuesday.

Many wine drinkers consider Barolo to be Italy's best wine, although producers of Brunello di Montalcino may certainly challenge this assertion. But serious wine drinkers need to come to Barolo to pay homage the way the pious travel to visit the shrine of a favorite saint. This *enoteca* is full of wine to be tasted and purchased, and there are exhibitions as well.

Calamandrana (Asti)

BAKERY
Pasticceria Saracco, Via Roma, tel. 0141/ 75194.

Very good *biscotti* and amaretti that go beautifully with a good glass of *moscato*.

DINING
Da Violetta, località Valle San Giovanni (2.5 km/1.5 miles north of Calamandrana), tel./fax 0141/769011. Closed Wednesday, Sunday evening, Tuesday evening, three weeks in January, and the first ten days of August. Mastercard, Visa. Moderate to moderately expensive.

When you dine at Da Violetta, you taste wonderful Piemontese cuisine. Above all, Maria and Carlo Lovisolo make you feel like a member of the family who has come home for a meal. I first dined here with Michele Chiarlo, one of Piemonte's finest wine producers (especially known for his peerless Barbera). I have returned since on my own and with great joy. If there is a particular Piemontese dish you wish to try, you can ask Maria to prepare it if you reserve in advance. Chances are it will be in her repertoire. The *frittatine* of onion or Swiss chard are divine, so are the *tortino di carciofi* (artichoke pie), and the best roast beef I have ever sampled.

Canelli (Asti)

This is the home of Gancia, the large spumante producer, whose plant is at one end of town and whose villa towers above Canelli from the other end. The reason to come to Canelli is the Moscato grape.

BAKERY, BAR, ICE CREAM

Pasticceria Sergio Bosca, Piazza A. d'Aosta 3, tel. 0141/823329. Open 8–13h, 16–20h; closed Monday.

A good cappuccino and a warm, fresh brioche make a perfect breakfast. I also am very fond of the *gelato di moscato*, an ice cream made of the grape that made Canelli great.

DINING

Ristorante San Marco, Via Alba 136, tel. 0141/823544. Closed Tuesday evening, Wednesday, and July 20-August 20. Visa.

Moderately expensive.

The restaurant serves carefully prepared classical *piemontese* dishes. Save room for the excellent selection of cheeses.

WINE

Enoteca Regionale di Canelli, Via Roma 4, tel. 0141/831372. Open 9:30–12:30h, 15:30–19:30h; closed Monday.

Here is a place to sample and purchase local wines, especially Moscato and Barbera. Nice selection and a friendly staff. A cellar has one room of old wine-making equipment.

Carema (Torino)

WINE

Cantina dei Produttori "Nebbiolo di Carema," Via Nazionale 28, tel. 0125/85256. Open 9–12:30h, 14:30–19:30h.

Vines were first planted in Carema by the Romans, who were on their way to what is now Aosta. Carema wine was more renowned thirty years ago than it is now. Because it is of such small production, it cannot compete with the much larger supply of reds, such as Dolcetto and Barbera, from elsewhere in Piemonte. But it is worth getting to know.

Cioccaro di Penango (Asti)

DINING AND HOTEL

Ristorante da Beppe, Locanda del Sant'Uffizio, tel. 0141/916292, fax 0141/916068. Closed Tuesday, most of January, and mid-August. Diners Club, MasterCard, Visa. Expensive.

The mother of owner Beppe Firato ran a simple *osteria* nearby that was popular with workers. In the late 1980s they purchased this space (a former convent) and turned it into a charming hotel with quiet, lovely rooms. The pretty grounds, the swimming pool, and the tranquil setting make this a popular weekend retreat for people from Milano and Torino. The restaurant is reason enough to travel here. Chef Leandro Varvello is a master of flavor. One of his calling cards is the *antichissima tartrà,* a very eggy custard flavored with sage served with sautéed artichokes. So is the *tortino di funghi e patate,* a delicate tart of potatoes and wild mushrooms. One of the best pasta dishes I have tasted anywhere is the *gnoc-* *chetti piemontesi di fonduta al tartufo nero e bianco.* The tiny gnocchi are like clouds, and they are tossed in a light Fontina-cheese sauce and topped with shavings of black and white truffles. I can go on and on about the great food, but I must mention one dessert, the rich and wonderful *budino borghese di cioccolato e caffè,* a silken pudding with chocolate and coffee flavors. This is an expensive restaurant, but worth the price.

Costigliole d'Asti (Asti)

DINING

Ristorante Guido, Piazza Umberto I 27, tel. and fax 0141/966012. Reservations essential. Open evenings only; closed Sunday, holidays, first three weeks of August, and December 23–January 10. Expensive to very expensive.

Many people say this is the best restaurant in Piemonte, and there are more than a few who say it is the best restaurant in Italy. I suspect that I have eaten in more places in Italy than most of the so-called experts, and I seldom engage in the business of declaring bests, especially as regards restaurants, because there are so many variables that change over the course of time. I have dined at Guido three times and consider it an excellent restaurant with fine food, wine, and service. The ambience is a bit too monumental for my taste, but it is certainly a comfortable room. Two dishes that I would single out are the exquisite *agnolotti di Costigliole* and the *stracotto di bue al Barbera,* soft buttery ox slow-cooked in Barbera wine.

ENOTECA PUBBLICA

Cantina dei Vini di Costigliole, Via Roma 9, tel. 0141/961661. Open Friday 10–12h, Saturday and Sunday 10–12h, 15–18h.

Typical wines of the area, especially Barbera d'Asti and Moscato d'Asti.

Cuneo

Cuneo is a town of great charm and real gastronomic interest. As the provincial capital of the region that many oenophiles say produces the best wine in Italy, it could rest on those laurels. But it also is famous for the quality of its food, including delicious peppers and other vegetables. Cuneo has excellent markets, top-quality food stores, and several very good restaurants. What I especially like about Cuneo is its people. In general the natives of Piemonte are somewhat reserved and formal in comparison with other Italians. The *cuneesi,* by contrast, are particularly warm and easygoing, at least in my experience. They are proud of their town and its strong anti-Fascist tradition. Wherever one walks, particularly on the Via Roma, one sees plaques that record the bravery of local sons and daughters in the fights against Fascism and Nazism. Cuneo is neatly laid out on a plateau that offers fine views of the Stura River valley on one side and that of the Torrente Gesso on the other. There are many good food stores, bars, *caffès*, and bakeries worth visiting in Cuneo. Most are open 8:30h to 12:30h, 16h to 19:30h, Monday through Saturday (and are closed on Thursday afternoon).

BAKERIES AND SWEET SHOPS

Pasticceria-Confetteria Botasso, Via Roma 37a, tel. 0171/692223. Open 8–13h, 15–19h; closed Monday (except in summer).

A source for *cuneesi al rhum*, rum-soaked macaroons that are a local specialty. Among the other delicacies are *torta contadina* (hazelnut cake), *basin* (chocolate-covered hazelnuts), *baci di Cuneo* (sandwiches of a hazelnut cookie and an almond cookie with chocolate in the middle). A special gift here is called the *scatola di attrezzi*, the toolbox. This contains chocolate hammers, horseshoes, nails, and keys.

BARS AND CAFFÈS

Bar Pietro Bruno, Via Roma 28. Closed Sunday.

More than one hundred years old, this is a very nice *caffè* that evokes another time.

Caffè Torrefazione Fantino, Corso Nizza 28.

A snappy bar with outdoor tables under a portico. A very good coffee is served here with a milk chocolate and a tiny glass of sparkling water. At cocktail hour there is a great range of nibbles to accompany your *aperitivo*, including finger sandwiches with truffle butter.

BREAD

Panettiere Basso Guido fu Fiorano, Via Santa Maria.

Wonderful fragrances in this shop that sells good, basic bread.

DINING

Osteria della Chiocciola, Via Fossano 1, tel. 0171/66277. Reservations essential. Closed Sunday, the first two weeks of January, and in mid-August. All credit cards. Moderate.

Tasty, straightforward Piemontese dishes, prepared with care and served with pride.

Tre Citroni, Via Bonelli 2, tel. 0171/602048. Closed Sunday, part of June, and part of September. All credit cards. Moderately inexpensive to moderately expensive.

There has been a restaurant on this site since the 1860s. Tre Citroni has a moderately priced *menu degustazione* that is hard to beat if you are hungry. This is an eight-course meal with three wines. You can also have a moderately inexpensive *colazione del lavoro* (working lunch) of five courses and

The peppers of Cuneo are among Italy's best

one wine. There are also many dishes à la carte that are moderate to moderately expensive. This is a good opportunity to sample many of the typical dishes of Cuneo as well as the specialties of this kitchen. One of these is the *patè di tonno* (tuna pâté). About one thousand years ago, Ligurian merchants began to sell salt, tuna, cod, and anchovies in Cuneo, and these ingredients were absorbed into the local cuisine. These all figure in this restaurant's tuna pâté. Other specialties include *carne cruda di vitello in insalata* (raw veal with greens), a flan of *funghi porcini*, baked stuffed peppers, *frittatina di cipolla* (a delicate onion omelette), *tajarin* with a meat sauce that is slow-cooked for seven hours, potato gnocchi with a sauce of tuna and tomatoes, *finanziera, coniglio con salsa di peperoni* (rabbit with a sauce of Cuneo's wonderful peppers), and special cheeses such as Castelmagno, Raschera, and Murazzano. The restaurant has 750 different wines, including 60 Barolos, many at moderate prices. The owner, Sguazzin Giobatta, is very passionate about food and wine, and is a nationally renowned cheese expert. He is also the rare restaurateur who does not charge cover and service.

Ristorante al Vecchio Zuavo, Via Roma, tel. 01/62020. Closed Wednesday. No credit cards. Moderately inexpensive.

A restaurant has been operated here since the early eighteenth century. A simple menu with good food, well prepared. Nice ambience.

FOOD STORES

Gastronomia Andrea's, Via Roma 37.

Prepared foods plus excellent *salumi* and many delicacies from abroad. There is also a fine selection of wines from the province of Cuneo.

Casa del Parmigiano da Franco, Via Roma 53. Closed Monday morning, Thursday afternoon, and Sunday.

Cheese, of course, and very good indeed.

Gastronomia Ariano, Via Pascal 2 (at the corner of Piazza Tancredi Galimberti).

Fancy *salumi* and special cheeses.

MARKETS

There is a large fruit and vegetable market with outstanding produce on the Piazza Virginio. It is open Monday (6–10h, 12–18h), Tuesday (6:30–12h), Thursday (6–10h, 12–18h), Friday (6:30–12h), and Saturday (6–16h). On the Piazza Seminario is a covered food market on Tuesday and Friday mornings. Surrounding it is another market of clothing and housewares.

SPECIALTY SHOPS

Fontana Gourmet, Via Roma 60. MasterCard, Visa.

Kitchen equipment, some basic, some very high quality, all here to serve a city that really takes food seriously. Coffeemakers, pasta machines, grills, griddles, pots, and pans.

Drogheria Musso, Via Roma 42B.

A wonderful old shop with all kinds of flours, pastas, salts, herbs, cereals, honeys, jams, powders, sugars, syrups, oils, coffees, wines, and spirits. A real storehouse of treasures.

Erboristeria Officinalis, Via Santa Maria 6 (near Piazza Virginio). Open 15:30–19:30h, *Friday and Saturday 10–13h; closed Sunday.*

Herbs are used to make personalized tisanes and oils that are geared to particular needs you might have. A visit here will remind you how seriously many Italians view the effects herbs have on their health.

Roma 62 Ferramenta, Via Roma 62.

Among the vast collection of novelties in this metalworking shop is an excellent selection of knives.

Dogliani (Cuneo)

BAKERY
Pasticceria della Ferrera, Via Vittorio Emanuele 18, tel. 0173/70587.

If you love hazelnuts as much as I do, Dogliani is the place to be. This bakery features all sorts of cookies and cakes made of *nocciole.* Closed Wednesday.

WINE
Enoteca Pubblica, Palazzo Comunale *(Piazza San Paolo 9), tel. 0173/70107. Open Sunday 10–12h, 15–19h.*

This building was originally a convent built for Carmelite nuns around 1500.

Enoteca La Griva, Via Vittorio Emanuele 43.

Fine wine, good cheeses, and *salumi.* Also sells truffles.

Domodossola (Novara)

DINING
Trattoria Piemonte da Sciolla, Piazza della Convenzione 4, tel. 0324/242633. Closed Tuesday evening, Wednesday, and last twenty days in August. Diners Club, Visa. Moderate. Domodossola is near the Swiss border and attracts diners and shoppers from Switzerland who want a touch of Italy. Many of them come to this old trattoria that was founded years ago by Angelo Sciolla as a meeting point for poets, artists, and thinkers who were drawn by Angelo's good

wine. Angelo is gone, but Giorgio Patrone continues the tradition. Delicious specialties include *gnocchi di castagne* (chestnut gnocchi), *cuchela* (made with potatoes, beans, sausages, and *pancetta,* all cooked in a casserole), goose, *spezzato di montone al ginepro* (chunks of mutton flavored with juniper berries), *mus* (polenta cooked with milk and flavored with poppy seeds and wild fennel). Most of the dishes are quite wonderful and evoke the tastes of alpine Piemonte. Save room for a cheese course after your *secondo.* Many of these cheeses are homemade or from small cheese makers of the area. You should also taste *marun,* cookies made of chestnut flour and rum. Good wines. This place is particularly animated on Saturday, when people from the surrounding valleys come to Domodossola for market day.

Gallo d'Alba (Cuneo)

BAKERY
Pasticceria Marengo, tel. 0173/262071.

The specialty here is the *gallesi al Barolo,* some of the best cookies you will ever taste, made with hazelnuts, egg whites, cocoa powder, vanilla, and Barolo wine. Two are sandwiched together by a cream of chocolate, chestnut cream, and a touch of rum.

Gattinara (Vercelli)

DINING
Albergo Ristorante Impero, Corso Garibaldi 81, tel. 0163/833232. Closed Friday. MasterCard, Visa. Moderate.

The restaurant in this hotel serves eggy *tagliolini* and *brasato al Gattinara.*

ENOTECA PUBBLICA
Piazza Italia 6, tel. 0163/834070. Open 10–12:30h, 16:30–19:30h; closed Monday and January 8–31.

Above all, the place to taste Gattinara wine.

Gignese (Novara)

UMBRELLA MUSEUM
Museo dell'Ombrello e del Parasole, Piazza Museo dell'Ombrello, tel. 0323/20067. Open April 1 to September 30 from 10:30–12h; 15–18h. In the other months, visits on Sundays may be arranged by appointment.

While the umbrella is not strictly gastronomic, there is something very suggestive and beautiful about this object which does, after all, figure in many of the loveliest *caffès* in piazzas throughout Italy. In addition, the umbrella does speak to something particular in this part of the country. When I think of the rice-growing areas of Piemonte and Lombardia, with their moist air, thick sweet-salty fogs, and the luminous skins of the women who live here, the umbrella also comes to mind. Everyone carries one in the event of rain, so it is not only an object of utility but a thing of beauty.

Grinzane Cavour (Cuneo)

ENOTECA PUBBLICA, MUSEUM, AND RESTAURANT
Castello di Grinzane, Via Castello 5, tel. 0173/62159. Open summer 9–12h, 14–18h, winter 9:30–12:30h, 14:30–18:30h; closed Tuesday and January.

A comprehensive display of the wines of Piemonte is presented in this old castle. You can taste, see exhibits about wine making in the region, and dine at the moderately expensive restaurant, where classic *piemontese* cuisine is the rule.

La Morra (Cuneo)

DINING
Azienda Agricola Fratelli Revello, Frazione Annunziata 103, tel. 0173/50276. Reservations essential. Open daily; closed mid-January to mid-February. No credit cards. Moderate.

Here is an unusual opportunity to dine at a winery with fine food and wine. Mariarosa Revello produces classic *piemontese* cuisine. If you want a *finanziera* or *bagna cauda* you must order it when you reserve your table. Otherwise, there are delicious tiny *agnolotti del plin*, *vitello tonnato*, tongue, fabulous *maiale al latte* (boneless pork slow-cooked in milk), *brasato al Barolo*, and good seasonal desserts. When I dined here in early summer, there were perfect *pesche ripiene*. The Revellos make good wine and happen to be a lovely family.

ENOTECA PUBBLICA
Cantina Comunale di La Morra, Via Carlo Alberto 2, tel. 0173/509204. Open 11–12:30h, 14:30–17:30h; closed Monday and Tuesday.

The *enoteca* is housed in the palace of the *marchesi di Barolo*.

TRUFFLES
Piumatti, Via XX Settembre 18, tel. 0173/50257.

Dario Salvano, Via Vittorio Emanuele 7, tel. 0173/509178.

WINE MUSEUM
Renato Ratti S.a.s., Frazione Annunziata 7, tel. 0173/50185, fax 0173/509373.

Renato Ratti was one of the great wine maker–scholars. He wrote extensively about wine and was routinely consulted by writers and wine makers who benefited from his great erudition. Ratti, who produced a superb Barolo, also collected ancient wine-making devices that bespeak a simpler, much more imprecise approach than we know today for turning grapes into wine. He created a museum that is connected to the winery, certainly worth visiting if you are in the area. The Ratti winery is now administered by young Pietro Ratti, who is doing a fine job of filling the shoes of his very famous father. Ratti wines are still first-rate, and Pietro, who speaks excellent English, has embraced much of his father's scholarly respect for wine. The museum can be visited by appointment only, so be sure to call ahead.

Neive (Cuneo)

DINING

La Contea, Piazza Codto 8, tel. 0173/67126. Reservations essential. Closed Sunday evening, Monday, and late January to mid-March. All credit cards. Expensive.

Claudia and Tonino Verro have quite a following. Theirs is a restaurant with very good food, a welcoming setting, and the kind of service that leaves one feeling warm and happy long after the meal is over. Claudia also makes superb preserves, which you can buy. I am going through a jar of jam made of Barolo grapes as I write this chapter, and it brings back nice memories. Be advised that this is a well-known restaurant, and when things get busy sometimes the kitchen slips a little (but just a little). This is also an inn with delightful rooms.

ENOTECA PUBBLICA

Bottega dei Quattro Vini di Neive, Palazzo Comunale (on Piazza Italia). Open Saturday and Sunday 10–12h, 14:30–18:30h.

This *enoteca* is set up in the wine cellar of an old palace that is now the town's city hall. It is dedicated to four wines: Barbera, Barbaresco, Dolcetto, and Moscato.

Nizza Monferrato (Asti)

DINING

Ristorante Le Due Lanterne, Piazza Garibaldi 52, tel. 0141/702480. Closed Monday night, Tuesday, and late July to mid-August. All credit cards. Moderate.

Wonderful *bollito misto, finanziera, bagna cauda, agnolotti dal plin,* gnocchi, cheeses, and *bonet.*

No'vara

This is a town that is not well known outside of Italy, but is a comfortably affluent place midway between Milano and Torino. It is a good example of a wealthy provincial capital city in northern Italy whose citizens live quietly and well. Its territory includes the Piemontese side of Lago Maggiore, and it is also in the middle of the rice belt between Vercelli and Pavia, so this grain has a place of honor in local cooking. The classic *novarese* dish is *paniscia,* which is not so much a risotto as a combination of rice, sausage, and other available meats, cheeses, vegetables, and flavors.

There are seasonal and local variations from kitchen to kitchen and town to town in the province, but it certainly should be tasted once. Novara chefs also make risotto, using local flavors such as Barbera wine, frogs, or Gorgonzola cheese. Although Gorgonzola had its origins just outside of Milano, in Lombardia (where it was first described in the year 879), Novara has now become the chief center of production. This famous blue-veined cheese is one of Italy's best. The presence of mold deters many people from enjoying its exquisite flavor. It comes either as the gold-colored *dolce* (sweet) or the sharper-tasting *piccante,* which is whiter. This cheese is a particularly congenial taste match with pears and walnuts, and a delicious risotto can be made with these three ingredients. If you want to see where Gorgonzola is produced, you can visit Panagani (Via Bartolino da Novara 3, tel. 0321/692100), a producer on the outskirts of town. The bakers of Novara use rice flour in some of their breads and cookies, but are most famous for the simple but delicious *biscotti di Novara,* which you can find at some of the bakeries listed below.

BAKERIES

Biscotteria Camporelli. Closed Wednesday afternoon and Sunday.

Since 1852 this firm has produced the classic *biscottini di Novara,* light confections made simply of eggs, sugar, and flour, but with exquisite results. To reach Camporelli, go down the Vicolo Monte Ariolo from the Corso Cavour, and when you reach the Enoteca Lombardi, turn left into the courtyard, and you will see this small shop across the way.

Fabbrica di Biscottini, Vicolo del Contado (just off Corso Cavour). Open 15:30–20h.

Aristide Barberis is the last individual artisan making *biscottini di Novara.* His great-grandfather began making cookies in this antique *forno* in 1820. Because Signor Barberis has no heirs, he is the last of the line. He makes other cookies as well, and you should pay a visit to witness a style of life and work that is nearly extinct. And do buy some cookies.

Pasticceria Bar Bertani, Corso Cavour 5, tel. 0321/629811.

Here since 1860, this is a good place for breakfast. There is a variety of pastries to go with good coffee. The *pasticceria* also makes a Bertariso, a typical cookie made of rice flour. It makes its own version of *biscottini di Novara,* which you can compare with those of Camporelli. There are a few outdoor tables and a large inner room for afternoon tea in the cold months.

Castoldi, Via Prina 8. Open 7:45–19:30h; closed Sunday.

A bakery since 1858, a bar and bakery since 1937, this is a good place for breakfast in the old center of town. Also good for afternoon tea in the back room. The specialty is *crema Chantilly.*

Pasticceria Sebastiano, Via Fratelli Rosselli 28B. Closed Monday.

Opposite Novara's Teatro Coccia, this is a very fancy bakery that makes elaborate and flavorful cakes that contrast sharply with the humbler butter-eggs-flour-sugar baking of the older tradition.

DINING

Ristorante Monte Ariolo, Vicolo Monte Ariolo 2/A, tel. and fax 0321/623394. Closed Saturday afternoon, Sunday, and August. All credit cards. Moderate.

Local dishes such as *paniscia* and *gnocchi al Gorgonzola*.

FOOD STORES

Most food stores in Novara are closed on Wednesday afternoon and Sunday.

Casa del Parmigiano, Corso Italia 11.

The huge wheels of cheese in the window tell you that you have come to the right place.

Drogheria, Corso Italia 19.

This store without a name is an interesting artifact from another era. Run by an elderly couple, the store sells only canned goods: vegetables, fish, coffees, and such. The display is simple and spare, with no gesture toward an aesthetic that would attract customers. This is very rare in Italy, but the lesson of this store is that it dates from a time when there was little fresh food in the winter and people of limited means had to stock up on items to see them through. As you walk through affluent Novara, pause here and reflect on how Italy has changed.

Gastaldi, Via Omar 16, tel. 0321/26647.

This *gastronomia* has been in business since 1940 and has a superb selection of *salumi*, cheeses (especially Gorgonzola), cooked vegetables, meats, fish, and fruits.

Salumeria Ge. Ba., Corso Cavour 10B.

A small shop with good fragrances of roast chicken and meats, stuffed vegetables, lasagne, and *paniscia*. It also sells *salumi* and cheese.

Salumeria-Gastronomia Maroni, Via degli Avogadro 1.

A small selection, but very high quality. Has *salame della duja*, the local specialty that is swirled in lard for extra flavor. There is also excellent Gorgonzola.

ICE CREAM

Gelateria Capriccio, Via Negroni 2/E, tel. 0321/392759. Open 7:30–24h; closed Sunday.

An extensive selection, although the "cream" ice creams (black chocolate, hazelnut, coffee, *gianduia*, eggy *crema*, *malaga* [rum raisin]) are much better than fruit ice creams such as apple, peach, berry, watermelon, and cherry.

Gelateria "Cream's Garden," Via Solferino 2/E, tel. 0321/34481. Open 9:30–24h.

Although the Capriccio, above, is more famous among the people of Novara, I prefer this place. The fruit flavors are unusually refreshing, including citron, lemon, apple, and mint (which tasted like mint, not like toothpaste).

WINE

Enoteca Lombardi, Vicolo Monte Ariolo 4/A (off Corso Cavour), tel. 0321/35815. Open 9–12:30h, 16–19:30h; closed Monday morning and Sunday.

Massimo and Alfredo have a good selection and offer tastings by the glass. They also sell oil, pâtés, and truffle products.

Piobesi d'Alba (Cuneo)

TRUFFLES

*TartufLanghe, Strada Provinciale 9,
tel. 0173/619347.*

This company makes a superb line of truffle products, including sauces, pâtés, pastes, truffle pasta, flavored oil, and the ingredients to make truffle risotto packed in one jar. All of these products make excellent gifts, and the prices are reasonable for food of this quality.

Revigliasco (Asti)

COOKING SCHOOL AND
RESTAURANT

*Piazza Vittorio Veneto 2, 14010
Revigliasco (AT), tel. 0141/208210.*

Roberto Boggio, the guiding spirit of this sanctuary of classical Piedmontese cookery, must have to tell people all the time that no, he is not Roberto Baggio, Italy's great soccer star who once played for Juventus in nearby Torino. But Boggio is a star on his own turf. The restaurant is moderately expensive, but the food is impressive. At the school you can learn how to make typical foods that the people of the area eat on special occasions such as Easter and Christmas. Boggio is also a great source of information about the historic gastronomic traditions of Piemonte.

Santa Vittoria d'Alba (Cuneo)

If you remember the film *The Secret of Santa Vittoria,* starring Anna Magnani, Virna Lisi, Anthony Quinn, Sergio Franchi, and Giancarlo Giannini, this is where it took place. During the Second World War, fine wines, arms, and townspeople were safely hidden under the mountain where Cinzano has its cellars.

DINING

*Vineria del Muscatel, Strada Statale
68—Cinzano, tel. 0172/478237.
Open 20–2h; closed Monday, Tuesday
evening, and in August. No credit cards.
Moderate.*

Facing the Cinzano plant and museum is the Muscatel restaurant. The Vineria is a wine bar that also serves good food, especially the antipasti.

MUSEUM

*Archivi Storici Santa Vittoria—Cinzano,
Strada Statale 63. Open 10–12h;
closed Tuesday and Thursday. (For
information contact Cinzano in Torino,
tel. 011/6300406.)*

This is one of my favorite museums for the gourmet traveler. It not only elegantly and amusingly tells the story of an august family firm, but reflects the rise of Italian industry, economic development, and style.

A Cinzano has produced wine at least since 1568. By the mid–eighteenth century the family attempted to produce champagne in Piemonte, and in the nineteenth century Cinzano began its industrial expansion, building factories and cellars and offering work to locals. Operations were divided between Torino and Santa Vittoria, and the company made sparkling wines and vermouth. There are fifteen herbs used to flavor wine to make it vermouth. The dominant one is artemisia, also known in English as wormwood. Its German name, *Wehrmuth*, was corrupted into the Italian as *vermuth* (and English as "vermouth"). There is a collection of herbs in the archives of this museum that demonstrates how they can be applied. Much of the ex-

hibit is dedicated to the exploits of Giuseppe Lampiano (1860–1944), who traveled to fifty-four nations selling Cinzano to city sophisticates and tribal chieftains. Lampiano was hired by Enrico Cinzano because of his "self-possession, unscrupulousness, and his oratory skills." The outrageous photographs that Lampiano sent back to Italy of himself serving Cinzano vermouth to native peoples bespeak the imperialism so typical of that era. They are wonderful windows into the not-too-distant, yet very remote, past. This museum is not particularly a promotional effort for Cinzano, but rather a marvelous homage to the past. It is done with great style and class, the very elements that burnish the image of Cinzano products.

Stresa (Novara)

CULTURE

Stresa Musical Weeks, Via R. Bonghi 4, tel. 0323/31095; fax 0323/3256128049.

Each year in August and September a festival of orchestras, chamber music groups, and solo musicians is held in the civic auditorium in Stresa. While other festivals in Italy are free-wheeling and socially active (such as Verona or Pesaro), the Stresa Festival is more formal, owing to the preponderance of audience members from Switzerland who drive down for the evening.

DINING

Ristorante Emiliano, Corso Italia 48, tel. 0323/31396. Closed Tuesday and late November–late December. All credit cards. Expensive.

Although we are on the Piedmontese side of Lago Maggiore, this restaurant's name describes its chef and owner, Corrado Felisi, who hails from Parma in Emilia. The result of this happenstance is that one finds a cuisine that features the best of Emilia and Piemonte, plus a few intriguing combinations. Among the antipasti are *culatello* from Parma and wonderful Piedmontese vegetable antipasti that vary with the season. Also worth trying is *lavarello*, the typical fish of Lago Maggiore. In an intriguing example of Emilian-Piedmontese cross-pollination, there is delicious homemade *mostarda* (pears, figs, and oranges cooked in white wine and flavored with dried mustard) served with various Piedmontese cheeses. With your coffee sample the *margheritine di Stresa*, typical cookies of this lakeside town.

*Ristorante Verbano, Isola dei Pescatori,
tel. 0323/33129. Closed Wednesday (except
May–October). All credit cards. Moderate.*

You need to take the boat from Stresa to beautiful Isola dei Pescatori, the island of fishermen in the middle of Lago Mag- giore. As you might expect, the specialty here is fish of the lake, which is very well prepared. Save room for the *torta di limone*, the house's famous old lemon cake that puts a nice finishing touch on a fish dinner. This is also a rustic hotel with twelve rooms.

Torino

After Bologna, I believe that Torino is the most underrated major city in Italy. It receives very few tourists, yet it is full of style, glamour, personality, magnificent art, and culture. It has many of the finest *caffès* anywhere, wonderful promenades, a strong sense of history, of the value of work, and of itself. To those who do not know it, Torino represents industry, especially the automobile. True, this is a city of engineers and factory workers, but these are in industrial suburbs. The phenome- non of immigration from southern Italy in the postwar era to jobs in factories cre- ated two Torinos: the gracious old city of the *piemontesi* and that of the newcomers with other customs, dialects, and family systems. Which is the real Torino? The city would not be what it is without the labor from elsewhere that helped power the industrial buildup. The children of these immigrants—born and raised in Torino— attempt to assimilate, but there is the pull of home. In recent years, with the arrival of immigrants from North Africa, some southern Italians in Torino have joined with northerners in a sense of unease and disdain toward the foreigners.

Life in Torino is gracious, in part because many of its citizens have exquisite manners. In looking at Torino, you should remember that it was a city whose years of greatness came in the nineteenth century, much later than other Italian cities. So its taste, decor, and outlook are those of that era, and in this regard it has more in common with Paris and Vienna than with Roma or Venezia. You should devote much of your visit to the *caffès* of Torino, which set a standard for all of Italy (only Trieste, Venezia, and Firenze have more than one *caffè* that can rival those of Torino). This city also produces much of Italy's finest chocolate. In fact, chocolate for eating as we know it today (in bars and individual pieces) was created in Torino. Look for *gianduia*, a magical blend of chocolate and hazelnuts. In small candy form these are called *gianduiotti*. In Torino you will find that coffee and chocolate are often combined. Torino is also famous for its vermouth, the herb-and-wine drink that was born here and later married with gin to form the beloved martini. On the Piazza Castello, at the corner of Via Pietro Micca, you will notice a plaque above a telephone booth: A. B. CARPANO, NEL 1786 IN QUESTA CASA, CREÒ IL SUO VERMUTH PRIMO DI UNA INDUSTRIA TIPICA E TRADIZIONALE CHE MOLTO CONTRIBUÌ ALLA FAMA E AL PRESTIGIO DI TORINO NEL MONDO.

(A. B. Carpano, in this house in 1786, created the first vermouth with typical and traditional industry that contributed greatly to the fame and prestige of Torino in the world.) Torino's newspaper, *La Stampa*, is usually ranked in the top three in Italy, along with Milano's *Corriere della Sera* and *La Repubblica*. Much of the world focused on Torino in the winter of 2006 as it hosted the Winter Olympics. It is rare for such a large city to be chosen for these games, but Torino is near the great mountains of Piemonte and the Valle d'Aosta. I can imagine no better hot chocolate to warm up after an icy sport competition than that found in Torino.

BAKERIES AND SWEET SHOPS

Caffè Pasticceria Baratti & Milano.

See "Bars and Caffès," below.

Caffe Confetteria al Bicerin.

See "Bars and Caffès," below.

Pasticceria Neuv Caval d'Brons.

See "Bars and Caffès," below.

Liquoreria-Caffè Platti.

See "Bars and Caffès," below.

Confetteria Avvignano, Piazza Carlo Felice 50, tel. 011/541992. Closed Monday morning and Sunday.

This has been a sweet shop since 1883, but the gorgeous decor dates from 1926. There is a whole range of sweets—many *torinese*, some not—especially chocolates.

Falchero, Via San Massimo 4 (just off Via Po), tel. 011/830024. Closed Monday, ten days in early January, and three weeks in August.

Famous for tiny, fresh, creamy *pasticcini* that weigh about ten grams (less than half an ounce) and contain relatively little sugar, so you can taste the flavors of the other ingredients. Falchero makes more than sixty varieties and produces them every two hours. Needless to say, no preservatives are used. They are expensive but worth it—many *torinesi* consider these the best little pastries in town. The wife of the baker told me that places like this are disappearing because, she thinks, even in Piemonte people are no longer willing to toil as they once did.

Peyrano, Corso Moncalieri 47 (Il laboratorio, where the chocolates are made, is found on the quiet side of the Po River).

Peyrano is generally considered the best chocolate maker in Torino, the city where eating chocolates were first made. They can be purchased at Pfatisch (closed Sunday afternoon and Monday) on Corso Vittorio Emanuele II 76 or Via Sacchi 42 (to the right of the train station).

Confetteria Pasticceria Fratelli Stratta, Piazza San Carlo 191, tel. 011/541567. Open 10–13h, 15–19:30h; closed Monday morning and Sunday. American Express, Visa.

One of the most famous sweet shops in Italy. Since 1836 this wonderland has been a source for chocolates, *confetti* (candied almonds), beautiful pastries, marrons

Bicerin is one of the great caffès *in Torino*

glacés, candied fruits, tiny bottles, and pretty packages closed with ribbons and bows. Stratta does not use preservatives in its products, so it does not ship: sugar crystallizes, and the owners feel that if their products are a few days old they will not be in pristine shape. So you need to visit the shop to try these products at their best. Their *gianduia* is delicious, and I recommend you try at least one *turneis*, a chocolate filled with chestnut cream and a touch of rum. Stratta supplied its products to the House of Savoy and to Cavour and named one of its sweets *merenghetti di Cavour* (meringue and chocolate cream with hazelnuts).

BARS AND CAFFÈS

Caffè-Pasticceria Baratti & Milano, Piazza Castello 29, tel. 011/511481. Closed Monday.

This *caffè*, which opened in 1875, is known for its quiet elegance. Its gracious rooms are ideal for taking coffee or tea with delicious pastries.

Caffè Confetteria al Bicerin, Piazza della Consolata 5, tel. 011/518794. Open 8:30–19:30h, Saturday and Sunday 8:30–12:30h, 15:30–19:30h; closed Wednesday.

A landmark that should not be missed. In business since 1763, it is Torino's oldest *locale* in continuous operation and has a distinct history. *Caffè*s by tradition were frequented only by men who came to exchange ideas or conduct business. Because this place was opposite the Santuario della Consolata, it became a place where women felt they could come for coffee following communion at the basilica across the piazza. Bicerin is notable too because it has always been owned and operated by women. It was also frequented by Cavour, who accompanied the royal family to church but, not being religious, would pass the time at the Bicerin. Nietzsche, who lived on the Via Carlo Alberto, was a regular, as was Alexandre Dumas. Giacomo Puccini, after observing the transport of prisoners across the square, reintroduced that image in his opera *Manon Lescaut.* The evocative facade dates from around 1800, while within it looks as it did more than two hundred years ago. You may see the word *acquacedrataio;* originally this place served water flavored with citron as a cooling refreshment. The Bicerin is named for its most popular beverage, a combination of hot coffee, chocolate, and light cream. The name is often thought to imply *bicchierino* (little glass), but this is mistaken. The word comes from *torinese* dialect and means "something delicious." The *caffè* makes fresh zabaglione and, in the summer, *cioccolato freddo,* a light, delicious chocolate drink. There is also Ratafia, a liqueur made of cherries and other flavors. For pastries to go with your beverage, try a rum-soaked *sorriso di Torino* or the delicious *torta di nocciola,* hazelnut cake that is brought from La Morra.

Casa del Caffè, Piazza Carlo Felice 49 (near the train station). Open 6:30–24h; closed Monday.

Opened in 1920, this *caffè* has chandeliers and a carved-wood bar. Notice the arching half-moon mirrors and painted-glass depictions of bare-breasted brown women picking bright red coffee beans. The motif is continued on the cups, which have coffee plants with red berries. This *caffè* sells good breakfast pastries and has huge glass bowls of *gianduiotti* to eat with your coffee. Many *torinesi* say this bar has the best coffee in town. It is very good, but one can taste its equal at many *caffès* around town.

Caffè Mulassano, Piazza Castello 15, tel. 011/547990. Open 7:30–1h; closed Sunday.

This is a real classic, one of the most beautiful *caffès* in a city full of beautiful *caffès*. It opened in 1907 and reflects a taste for the exotic that influenced art and design in Torino during that time. Look at the wonderful carved-wood walls and ceilings. Note the old cash register and, at the bar, the twin spigots serving glasses of water. The spigots are part of a construction supporting a plant that dominates the room. Every part of the walls is decorated, including many carvings depicting grapes.

Liquoreria-Caffè Platti, Corso Vittorio Emanuele II 72. Open 7:15–21h; closed Friday and fifteen days in August. MasterCard, Visa.

Opened in 1875, this *caffè* was a favorite of Cesare Pavese, one of my favorite Italian writers. He also translated many English-language classics into his native language. Platti serves delicious *crostate,* fruit tarts with fresh apricots, currants, blueberries, apples, pears, and so on. It is also well known for its house liqueur, Rabarbaro, made from rhubarb.

Pasticceria Neuv Caval d'Brons, Via Roma 157 (Piazza San Carlo), tel. 011/545354. Open 7:30–1h; closed Wednesday and five days around August 15.

The Caval d'Brons produces wonderful pastries, chocolates, and ice cream to accompany your coffee. It makes tiny *piccola pasticceria* (usually there are four or five per hundred grams, here there are eight to ten) called *mignon* that are as beautiful as they are delicious. The ice cream here is richer than any I have tasted in Italy, and perhaps anywhere. The *nocciola* is overflowing with the flavor of Piedmontese hazelnuts and has extravagant amounts of butterfat. A small cone or cup is all that anyone would want, but it will be unforgettable. The oval-shaped front room is an elegant place for a quick coffee; the room in the back is very welcoming in winter for sitting down for a casual coffee and cake. Outside there are many tables under the portico with waiter service. There is a small, very expensive restaurant upstairs that serves good food at lunch and dinner (closed Saturday lunch, all day Sunday).

Caffè San Carlo, Via Roma 144 (Piazza San Carlo). Open weekdays 8–1h, Saturday 9:30–2h, Sunday 9:30–1h.

Opened in 1837. A perfectly square room, a neoclassical hall of twelve mirrors with a huge Venetian chandelier above. Two wonderful friezes frame the room: one Della Robbia blue with gold cameos, the other green and cream with putti and birds. The room looks like something Napoleon would have cherished. This gorgeous place is terribly marred, however, by the gigantic Haagen-Dazs ice-cream display on one side that you see as you enter the room and another hexagonal display case to the right. Many *torinesi* have avoided this *caffè* since the American ice-cream company moved in, but you should visit it to admire the room and understand what appealed to the *torinese* aesthetic 150 years ago. To the right of the main room is a wonderful salon, all mirrors, painted glass, and marble tables.

Caffè Torino, Via Roma 204 (Piazza San Carlo). Open 7–1h; closed Sunday.

Opened in 1903. Outside, under the portico, are soft padded chairs. Within, there is a long carved-wood bar on the left, and on the right is a display case with chocolates, tiny pastries, *gelatine* (candied fruit), and breakfast pastries. The walls are covered in a floral fabric, and the ceiling is carved wood. Behind this display are four smart rooms of glass, mirrors, wood, and small paintings. This section is a moderate to moderately expensive restaurant. I come to the Caffè Torino for coffee and pastries only. In the rear a curving grand staircase of twenty-eight steps leads to an upper room that is used in winter.

Bar Zucca, Via Roma 265, tel. 011/531694. Open 7–21h; closed Sunday.

Since 1928, one of *the* places in Torino for cocktail hour. When you have a cocktail *della casa*, wine, spumante, vermouth, or soft drinks, you can snack on all sorts of canapés, including little brioches spread with mascarpone and topped with shavings of truffle.

COFFEE SCHOOL

Avviamento alla Degustazione del Caffè/ Lavazza Training Center, Luigi Lavazza S.P.A., Strada Settimo 410, 10156 Torino, tel. 011/2398525 or 2398562, fax 011/2398431.

In a city that has some of the most wonderful *caffè*s in the world, it should not surprise you that Torino has the largest coffee company in Italy. While Trieste has several excellent companies, led by Illycaffè, in Torino Lavazza is to coffee what FIAT is to automobiles. Lavazza has 45 percent of the

Italian market, and 80 percent of the market in Piemonte. The company has been a trendsetter in terms of coffee research and analysis; coffee roasting, packaging, and marketing; corporate support of the arts; and education and training about coffee making. It offers a free class—available in English by arrangement—for everything a restaurateur or bar owner needs to know about grinding coffee; making espresso, cappuccino, and other coffees; tasting to understand beans and blends; storing coffee; and operating and maintaining coffee machines. This is a very interesting and valuable course that is available to professionals only (it is not a tourist attraction). To take the class, you must arrange in advance by contacting the company.

COOKING SCHOOLS

Il Melograno, Piazza Vittoria 9, 10141 Torino, tel. 011/830037.

This is a serious cooking school with courses that run from September through May. Students come from throughout Piemonte to develop skills for use in restaurants and homes. In June and July, however, the school's director, Romana Bosco, organizes weeklong food trips to rural Piemonte and to other Italian regions for intensive study of the local cuisine and enology. Students stay in villas, on farms, or in intriguing hotels. Most courses are in Italian, although the trips provide enough to engage those who do not speak the language. Reserve far in advance.

Scuola di Arte Culinaria, Via Marco Polo 37, 10129 Torino, tel. 011/500266.

Courses last from one to ten days and usually focus on specific topics. Emphasis is on the use of olive oil in cooking, including ways that it can be substituted for butter and other saturated fats. Courses in Italian.

CULTURE

Teatro Regio, Piazza Castello 215, box office tel. 011/8815241, fax 011/8815214.

This is the main theater in Torino, which needed substantial rebuilding after the Second World War. Historically, the theater has had famous failures and brilliant successes, and it does attract a knowledgeable and sophisticated audience for operas and concerts. A night at the Regio paired with a fine meal or a coffee at one of the gorgeous *caffè*s nearby is a classic *torinese* evening.

DINING

Ristorante del Cambio, Piazza Carignano 2, tel. 011/546690 or 543760. Closed Sunday and in August. All credit cards. Expensive.

This classic *torinese* restaurant is, as you might expect, elegant and gracious. It has a very formal dining room with gold brocade, silver candelabra, red banquettes, and paintings of putti and goddesses. Opened in 1757, it was Cavour's preferred dining spot—in the rear on the right side of the dining room you can see a marker indicating his table. Il Cambio is frequented by business types, old *torinese* families, tourists who cherish food and history, and is the traditional place to fete a child who has just graduated from university. The food is classic *piemontese: bagna cauda, finanziera, agnolotti, risotto al Barolo, brasato,* and *fritto misto alla piemontese* (liver, veal, sausage, lamb, eggplant, zucchini, apple, sweet cheese, and bits of chocolate). The food is very good to excellent, the wine list is outstanding, and the service is topflight.

Trattoria Valenza, Via Borgodora 39, tel. 011/5213914. Closed Sunday, Monday lunch and in August. No credit cards. Moderately inexpensive to moderate.

This trattoria in a working-class neighborhood little known to tourists and even most *torinesi* offers traditional Piemontese preparations. Don't let the casual environment mislead you about the cooking, which is done with great seriousness.

Trattoria dai Saletta, Via Belfiore 37, tel. 011/6687867. Closed Sunday and in August. All credit cards. Moderate.

Since I first wrote about this restaurant years ago, many journalists, chefs, and critics have descended on it. I am glad to report that the quality remains high, with an exceptional amount of care given to the sourcing of superb ingredients and preparing them to great advantage.

Trattoria L'Oca Fola, Via Drovetti 6g, tel. 011/4337422. Open Monday through Saturday evenings. Closed in part of August. MasterCard, Visa. Moderate.

Torino is building a new underground rail system and turning the Porta Susa station into its terminal for high-speed trains to Milano and France. Suddenly, restaurants in this neighborhood are in demand, and this is a very good choice for specialties of Piemonte.

FOOD STORES

Food stores in Torino close on Wednesday afternoon and Sunday.

Gastronomia Baudracco, Corso Vittorio Emanuele II 62, tel. 011/545582.

People from all over Torino patronize this wonderful *gastronomia* near the train station. I can think of no better meal to have on a train journey than one made of provisions gathered here. I have also made meals for picnics on the Po River with dishes from this shop. The *gastronomia* makes its own *prosciutto cotto*, tongue, *salami*, sausages, smoked beef (called Cavour), *vitello tonnato*, and pastas. There is excellent fish, plus vegetables, mushroom preparations, and desserts. There are several sauces made of herbs, nuts, capers, fish, and mushrooms that can be served atop many of the prepared foods sold here. You can also buy superb cheeses, peach jams from Alba, rice from Vercelli and Novara, bread and breadsticks, cookies and cakes, and fine wines from throughout the region.

Gastronomia Steffanone, Via Maria Vittoria 2 (just off Piazza San Carlo).

Since 1886 this small, classy *gastronomia* has provided good food and service to the people of Torino. Not a large selection, but high quality.

Paissa, Piazza San Carlo 196, tel. 011/518364.

A beloved old store for wines, spirits, jams, cakes, cookies, spices, teas, coffees, honeys, packaged goods. Paissa also sells its own *gianduia*. The choice ranges from the most sublime to the most banal.

A WALK DOWN THE VIA LAGRANGE

Not far from the train station is the Via Lagrange, the best street to come to if you only visit one in Torino for food shopping. It used to be that this was an all-food thoroughfare, but some august old places, such as a tripe store, have been shuttered, and now the street hosts clothing boutiques and trendy shops. Still, there is enough here to please the serious eater. Note that several adjacent shops have the same address. Many stores are closed on Wednesday afternoons, on Sundays, and in August.

#34: Salumeria Rosticceria Castagno.

A vast array of prepared foods that wind up on tables throughout Torino. I like the cooked vegetable antipasti and the roasted meats.

#34: Pasticceria Bar Certosio. Closed Monday.

A good place to stop for coffee during your food shopping. Excellent cookies, fruit tarts, *crostata,* and the house specialty, *cupoloni,* a panettone-like cake.

#36: Ottino.

Since 1919 this has been a source of truffles, wild mushrooms, and game.

#36A: Baita del Formagg.

If there is a better cheese store in Torino, I have not found it. A symphony of cheeses from Piemonte, Valle d'Aosta, and Lombardia forms the core of the selection: *paglierine, robiole delle Langhe, tumin d'Chivass, tome d'Alba, tomini chaiverani, robiole savioarde, toma di Bra, toma di Lanzo,* Fontegidia, and Gorgonzola are just the crème de la crème. There are also fine cheeses from throughout Italy, plus France, England (cheddar and Stilton, which are hard to find in Italy), Switzerland, and Germany.

Also available are jars of sauces, quality pastas, truffle butter of the store's own production, oils, *aceto balsamico* (balsamic vinegar), and vinegars made of sherry, Bordeaux, and raspberries.

#38A: Macelleria Castagno.

Superb meats. Worth a visit even if you don't intend to buy.

#38C: Scanavino Due.

Beautiful fruits and vegetables arranged in a window display with a painterly eye.

#39F: Pastificio de Filippis.

Good fresh and dried pastas and sacks of rice, all enticingly presented. Less interesting for its prepared foods, although it does have good *tortine* (a sort of quiche) made with different vegetables and herbs.

Just up the street, at the corner of Via Soleri, is Gelateria Gatsby's, open Monday through Saturday from 8h to 24h. This is one of the most popular ice-cream parlors in Torino, notable especially for its soft ice creams. The flavors are not as intense as one finds in typical Italian gelati, so Americans will be reminded of ice cream from home.

A VISIT TO THE PAST ON THE VIA SAN TOMMASO AND THE VIA BARBAROUX

Not far from the Piazza Castello you can find a collection of old stores that will tell you about the Torino of a century ago. In addition, some nice new shops have opened, making this a special place to spend an hour shopping and tasting. The Via Barbaroux also seems to be a gathering place for very old prostitutes who sit in chairs on the street. At this point their role is more folkloric than entrepreneurial.

#10 Via San Tommaso: Pastificio Elia.

All kinds of fresh pasta, including Torino's beloved *agnolotti* and *tajarin*. Next door is the site of Luigi Lavazza's first shop for roasting and selling coffee.

#12B Via San Tommaso: Antica Pasticceria Lenzi.

Many kinds of cookies, plus real breadsticks, *ciambelline* (round sugar cookies), and cookies and cakes made of cornmeal.

#13 Via San Tommaso: Latteria Bruna Bera.

Run by three wonderful women who sell cheeses, eggs, oils, jams, and jellies. The ladies make it a delightful place to shop.

Corner of Via Barbaroux and Via San Tommaso: Peruquet Uova e Burro.

In business since 1882, here is the classic butter-and-egg man of yore. Opposite is the Caffè alla Contrada, an *enoteca* where you can try local wines in the company of rather brusque and rustic types whom I suspect to be old acquaintances of the ladies seated down the street.

#11 Via Barbaroux: La Ruota. Open weekdays 7–14h, 16–21h, Saturday 7–14h. Inexpensive.

An unpretentious *tavola calda* serving excellent roast chicken, chickpea crepes, and cooked vegetables. A good place for a take-out lunch.

#12F Via Barbaroux: Peracchione.

A superb cheese store that has been in operation since 1921. There is a wonderful milky fragrance in the air as you select from Piedmontese specialties such as *toma, robiola, tomini, fiorone di capra*, as well as fresh milk and yogurt.

FRULLATI

Cremeria Frullati Vartuli, Piazza Castello 51.

In a small glass kiosk is one of the better *frullato* makers I know. What makes its *frullato* so good is the high percentage of fruit and the relatively low amount of milk, making these basically creamy fruit juices rather than fruity milk shakes.

ICE CREAM

Pasticceria Neuv Caval d'Brons.

See "Bars and *Caffès*," above.

Gelateria Pepino, Piazza Carignano 8, tel. 011/542009. Closed Monday.

The Piazza Carignano, not far from the Piazza San Carlo, is an opulent nineteenth-century square that has the palace where King Vittorio Emanuele II, who was a key figure in the unification of Italy, was born. The piazza also has the Teatro Stabile di Torino and the gorgeous Ristorante del Cambio, the most classically Torinese restaurant (see "Dining," above). The Gelateria Pepino has been here since 1884 and is often called the favorite *gelateria* in town. It has many outdoor tables, and inside are about a dozen little round tables next to smart crushed-velvet banquettes.

WINE

Enoteca Casa del Barolo, Via Andrea Doria 7, tel. 011/532038.

A huge selection of the wines of Piemonte.

Enoteca Delsanto, Corso de Gasperi 21, tel. 011/594706. Closed Sunday.

More than a thousand wines, plus grappas, spirits, and even mineral water.

Paissa.

See "Food Stores," above.

Parola, Corso Vittorio Emanuele II 76. Closed Monday morning and Sunday.

Since 1929, the owners have sold wines from Piemonte, the rest of Italy, France, Chile, and California.

Treiso (Cuneo)

DINING

Osteria dell'Unione, Via Alba 1, tel. 0173/638303. Closed Sunday evening, Monday, and two weeks in August. No credit cards. Moderate to moderately expensive.

Seven kilometers (about four miles) from Alba is this well-regarded trattoria that happily went its own way and served good food and wine at fair prices. Then it was discovered by some food writers who enshrined it in their top-ten lists, and boom! It is now very difficult to get a table. One does eat very well here, and if you are in Alba it is worth a visit. But if you cannot get in, there are plenty of other good restaurants in the area. One of them is the Trattoria Belvedere, at Frazione Cappelletto 3, tel. 0173/630174 (closed Wednesdays; no credit cards).

Vercelli

Vercelli is the largest rice market in Europe. As you gaze at the flat landscape outside of town, you will see what people here call the *mare a quadrate*, or the sea divided in squares. Through the seasons the aspect of the rice fields changes: flat dry land yields to areas that are flooded, which then produce green sprouts that may soon grow taller and golden in color. In the autumn, fog enshrouds the area, giving way to a winter stillness before the cycle begins again. What might be called a dull flatland is, if you pay attention, really a thing of beauty.

In the city of Vercelli, you should look for the Piazza Ernesto Zumaglini. If possible, go there on Tuesday or Friday morning, the market days for rice farmers. They gather to buy and sell machinery, seeds, and other rice-related products. On the same piazza, at #13, is the administrative office of the Consorzio Agrario di Vercelli, the rice farmers' guild. Next door, at #14, is the building devoted to regional agricultural administration. On the first floor (one flight up) is the Ente Nazionale Risi, the national organization that governs and promotes rice cultivation. On the main floor is the Borsa Risi, the commodity exchange for rice in Europe and the place where the destinies of Vercelli's rice farmers are determined. You will notice that the squares around this building are full of banks and insurance companies, all of which rely on as well as affect the fate of the rice farmers.

To learn more about Vercelli and rice, take a walk near the train station. Behind it you will see a very old *riseria*, Eurico, which is still in use. It was built here so that railcars could roll directly to the plant and sacks of rice could be loaded and immediately sent to Milano, Torino, and elsewhere. This is a typical example of the industrialization of northern Italy at the beginning of the twentieth century. It merits a brief look for a sense of Italian industrial design of nearly a hundred years ago. That was a time when railways were more central to the transport of goods than they are today. Before leaving the station area, take a couple of minutes to walk to the park to the right of the station as you face it. Here you will find a monument to *le mondine* (the rice weeders), women who performed much of the labor in the rice fields. The story of *le mondine* is an interesting and sad chapter in local history. These were poor women, many of them from the provinces of Ferrara and Ravenna in Romagna, who were brought to Vercelli to work in the fields weeding, transplanting, harvesting by hand, and cleaning the rice. They remained from April to late October, working long hours six or seven days a week. If you drive around the province of Vercelli you will see some crumbling brick structures that were the dormitories where *le mondine* slept on straw mats. These women were often taken advantage of sexually by the owners of certain rice plantations and even by some of the farmers and landed employees who supervised them. Many of these women became pregnant and, as a result, many children with Vercellese fathers were raised in Romagna by relatives of *le mondine*. Believe it or not, this system continued until the late 1960s. The sufferings of *le mondine* were vividly depicted in the classic 1948 neorealist film *Riso Amaro (Bitter Rice)*, in which Silvana Mangano was unforgettable as a *mondina*.

BAKERY

Pasticceria Paola, Via G. Ferraris 96, tel. 0161/255588. Closed Monday.

A source for *bicciolani,* the typical spice cookies of Vercelli. They are made of flour, cloves, nutmeg, lemon zest, pepper, butter, and sugar. They are very hard and intended for dunking in wine or tea. If ever you see them chocolate covered, this is not the original article.

DINING

'l Nos Gal (Albergo Europa), Via Santorre di Santarosa 16, tel. 0161/66847. Closed Wednesday and in August. No credit cards. Moderate.

The main reason to come here is for local rice dishes, which vary according to the season. *Panissa* is the Vercelli equivalent of Novara's *paniscia,* which is rice with sausage and other flavors based on the preferences of the chef. Pastas are homemade. An autumnal specialty is *oca con le verze,* goose with Savoy cabbage.

RICE

Although rice is sold at most food stores in Vercelli, if you want to specialize or visit a rice producer, some suggestions are listed below.

Consorzio Agrario Provinciale di Vercelli: Corso Randaccio 23, tel. 0161/501514.

A bit out of the city center, the Consorzio sells rice from many local producers as well as equipment and supplies they need for their work.

Riseria Viazzo: Via Thaon de Revil 30, tel. 0161/301223 or 301838.

On the periphery of Vercelli, you can purchase rice from one of the best-regarded producers.

The following are other good rice producers in the province of Vercelli who sell their product directly to the public:

Tenuta Carpi: Livorno Ferraris (VC), tel. 0161/477832.

Piero and Michele Rondolino produce an excellent rice that is vacuum-packed for freshness, although it is still possible to buy it in cloth sacks too.

Azienda Agricola Principato di Lucedio: Trino Vercellese (VC), tel. 0161/81518.

SAI Agricola—Tenuta Veneria: Lignana (VC).

SAI Agricola is a large organization that sells the product of many rice producers. The rice at Tenuta Veneria is considered one of the best and can be purchased directly.

WINE

Tutto DOC, Via Crispi 3, tel. 0161/66528. Closed Sunday.

Wines of Piemonte and the rest of Italy, along with those of France, Australia, New Zealand, South Africa, and the United States.

Tajarin con Gorgonzola e Noci
Thin Fresh Noodles with Gorgonzola and Walnuts

Serves 4 as a main course, 6 as a primo
150 grams/6 ounces Gorgonzola
¼ cup light cream
1 tablespoon unsalted butter
450 grams/1 pound fresh taglierini or
  tagliolini
50 grams/2 ounces unsalted walnut meats,
  chopped or broken in little pieces

Set a large pot of cold water to boil. When the water reaches a boil, add a pinch of salt. While the water for the pasta is coming to a boil, separately heat the Gorgonzola, cream, and butter in a double boiler so that it forms a velvety sauce. Do not bring the sauce to a boil or let it scorch the pot. Cook the pasta briefly in the boiling water until al dente. Drain it in a colander, then add the pasta to the sauce in the double boiler. Toss in the walnut pieces, stir so that the ingredients combine thoroughly, and serve immediately.

Wine: Gattinara, Carema, or Dolcetto.

Pere Martine al Vino
Pears Baked in Wine

In Piemonte and the Valle d'Aosta, the most exquisite pear is the Martina, also called Martin Sec. When cooked very slowly in wine, it becomes a scrumptious dessert.

Serves 4 to 6
4 to 6 plump Martina pears (in their absence,
  use ripe Bosc pears)
1 bottle Barolo, Barbaresco, Moscato d'Asti
Sugar to taste (optional)

Wash but do not peel the pears. Place them in a heavy-bottomed pot and pour in the wine to cover the pears completely. (You should not pick a pot that is too broad or the pears will not be submerged in wine.) Add the optional sugar, cover the pot, and cook over the lowest possible heat for 5 to 6 hours. When the pears are cooked, the wine sauce will be like a syrup and the flesh of the pear will be guava colored. If you use Moscato d'Asti, the flesh of the pear will be golden. Serve at slightly cooler than room temperature.

Valle d'Aosta

**REGIONAL AND
PROVINCIAL CAPITAL:**
Aosta (AO).

TOURIST INFORMATION:
Regione Valle d'Aosta,
  Assessorato Turismo,
    Piazza Narbonne 3,
    11100 Aosta,
    tel. 0165/303725,
    fax 0165/40134.

Agritourism:
Assessorato Regionale
  Agricoltura,
    Ufficio Agriturismo,
    Piazza Deffeyes,
    11100 Aosta,
    tel. 0165/553392.

 The Valle d'Aosta is the roof of Europe, a mountainous region par excellence. It is formed by chains of Alps that are snow-capped year-round. Monte Bianco (Mont Blanc), Cervinia (the Matterhorn), and Monte Rosa tower over the region, but there are many peaks that are less famous but no less imposing. Much of the region—Italy's smallest—is occupied by the nation's largest natural reserve, Gran Paradiso National Park. And a big paradise it is, too. The park is named for one of the mountains in the park, which happens to be the highest peak completely within Italy (4,375 meters/13,324 feet).

This was once the royal hunting ground for the House of Savoy. They came for the ibex and chamois, which now are protected by law within the confines of the park. Among the birds are the Le Duc owl and the royal eagle, which is brown and white and lives in pairs. The royal couples change their nests every two years. The ermine and hare that live in the park change colors with the season: they are brown in the summer and white in the winter. The park is full of rare alpine flora, many of which give their flavor and perfume to local honey. There are hundreds of different flowers, many not seen anywhere else.

Despite the formidable natural obstacles of this region, it has been populated since ancient times. The inhabitants were known as the Salassi, who were here 2,500 years ago. Not many traces of them are left, but it appears that they were drawn by the min-

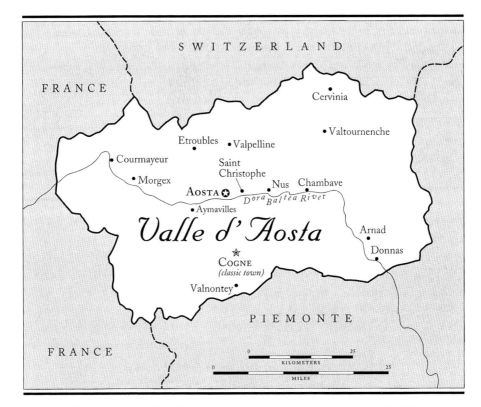

eral wealth in the area. The Romans arrived around 143 B.C. and lived in more or less peaceful coexistence with the Salassi for a while. Yet when they rebelled they were crushed by Roman might and sold as slaves. The Romans made their headquarters at Augusta Praetoria, whose name evolved to "Aosta." The city became and remains the most important in the region. It is laid out in customary Roman fashion, with principal roads that connect to larger trade routes and important squares that were and are gathering places for the populace. The Romans built an arena and aqueducts, the remains of which may still be seen. It is a remarkable juxtaposition of images: Roman ruins in an alpine setting.

Following the fall of the Roman Empire, Aosta and its region came under the influence of the Church and became deeply religious, as they still are today. The rural churches are austerely beautiful and are the focal points of tiny mountain communities. Contact with neighboring France grew as religious figures arrived to lead congregations in the Middle Ages. The region fell under the domain of the Savoy family, which governed the mountain terrain of what is now Savoy and Burgundy in France and Piemonte in Italy. Through the centuries many castles were built on mountaintops, hillocks, and plateaus, so that when you travel through the region today they look like many little Valhallas. The Valle d'Aosta is fully bilingual, and the culture is a mix of Italian and French (unlike the Alto Adige, which feels like a German region under Italian occupation). When the Savoys moved their capital to Torino in 1563, the Valle d'Aosta became a playground for that family. The Valle d'Aosta was a province of Piemonte until 1948, when it was granted autonomous status in recognition of its particular cultural and linguistic mix. This region is the least populous in Italy, with only 115,000 citizens in a nation of 57 million.

Eating in Valle d'Aosta

This region's cuisine is simple and made of ingredients that its terrain can provide. Cows graze on mountainsides when there is grass, so that cheeses made of summer milk are especially delicious. Cow's milk is used to make the butter, cream, and various cheeses (particularly *Fontina*) that are central to the cooking of the region. These milky flavors form a soothing canvas on which other regional ingredients can play a leading role. These include wild mushrooms, game, beef, blueberries, raspberries, chestnuts, apples, pears, honey, and herbs. There is also good freshwater fish from rivers and lakes, and even these are sometimes cooked with cheese. The region's ingredients are combined by cooks in ways both practical and imaginative.

ANTIPASTI

There are very few traditional antipasti in this region. With affluence in recent years, however, the hams and sausages that used to be the centerpiece of a meal have been relegated to its start. They are quite formidable: *mocetta* (leg of veal, chamois, mountain goat, or ibex, cured like prosciutto); *prosciutto di San Marcel* (made with eighteen aromatic alpine herbs); prosciutto from Bosses, sweet, delicious, and hard to come by; *lardo d'Arnad* (lard with herbs); *boudin de Morgex* (blood sausage filled with beets, potato, lard, spices), *tetetta*, or *teteun* (cow's udder, cooked and sliced thin), and typical sausages made of beef, pork, red wine, garlic.

PRIMI

More than most Italian regions, soup (locally called *seuppa*) is an important first course. Most of the soups are made with bread, broth, vegetables, and cheese. There is also *zuppa di castagne*, made with chestnuts and rice boiled in milk, which is popular in the autumn. In the winter many soups are made with a milk base. *Zuppa di Arey* is a specialty of Gressoney: milk, sugar, chopped roasted walnuts, red wine, breadsticks, cinnamon, egg yolks, nutmeg, and salt make for an unusual combination. Fontina cheese is melted with crepes or gnocchi or served atop polenta. When the cheese is melted into the polenta while it cooks, the result is *polenta concia*. The most popular pasta is probably *tagliarini*, also called *tajarin*. Rice is used somewhat, but mostly in soups.

SECONDI

Carbonada is the most famous meat dish: salted rump steak cooked with onions, butter, bacon, cinnamon, salt, pepper, and wine. It is slow-cooked and served with polenta. *Cotoletta alla valdostana* appears often on menus, but it is difficult to find a good version. At its best, this is a veal cutlet dipped in egg and bread crumbs, fried in butter, and then finished with a slice of prosciutto and a layer of melted Fontina. This should be a simple dish, but it is often sloppily done in touristy restaurants, although not the ones I have recommended in this chapter. Other veal and beef dishes appear regularly on menus. Game is popular, including *capriolo* (venison) that is browned in grappa and cooked with fresh tomatoes. *Camoscio* (chamois) is ubiquitous, as is *capretto* (kid).

FORMAGGI

There is a local expression in the Valle d'Aosta: *Il formaggio fresco ha tre fondamentali qualità: toglie la fame, la sete e lava i denti.* (Fresh cheese has three fundamental qualities: it cuts hunger, it cuts thirst, and washes the teeth.) People in this region like fresh young cheese that still tastes of milk. Whether they eat cheese plain or use it in cooking, it is the milkiness that comes through rather than a more evolved taste such as in Gorgonzola or Parmigiano-Reggiano. When one thinks of the cheese of this region, *Fontina* is the name that comes to mind. Fontina is not only the most famous cheese in the Valle d'Aosta, but it is one of the finest cheeses made in Italy. Once you discover its unique buttery-nutty flavor and its smooth, melting texture, you will be hooked. This was a cheese born for eating, but it has also been used for melting in the past three hundred years. It is melted to make fondue *(fonduta)* and all sorts of sauces. In fact, anything this cheese is melted on tastes better. The term "Fontina" is almost seven hundred years old, and from what we know the product is very similar to the one made seven centuries ago. Each year 3.5 million kilos (7.7 million pounds) of Fontina are produced. Of this, 97 percent is consumed in Italy, mostly in the north and center. Since production cannot be expanded, there is little likelihood that more cheese will be shipped abroad. In many markets in northern Europe and the United States there is imitation Fontina from Scandinavia. This bears no relation to the real thing. Scandinavian cheese has a red rind, while real Fontina has a light brown rind.

Once you become acquainted with Fontina, you will be able to detect differences in flavor. From June to early October, cows graze in the upper valleys of the region. For the rest of the year they are fed hay. Since the cheese takes three months to mature, the Fontina you eat from October 1 to January 1 will be a summer cheese, which is slightly higher in fat than the cheese made from cows feeding on hay. Most people eat Fontina when it is young, but some older natives of the region like to age the cheese for up to a year and use it for grating. The consortium of Fontina producers distributes a small free pamphlet with recipes for

Fontina and *fonduta* (which has been sold in cans since 1980; it is convenient, but I prefer melting the cheese myself).

Other cheeses include cow's-milk *toma* (easily digested and low in fat), soft *robiola*, and *tomini*, which are made of goat's milk.

OTHER FLAVORS

Apples (especially the renette), pears (particularly the Martin Sec), and wild berries are delicious in these parts and find their way into jams and desserts as well as serve as flavorings for the meat course. The honeys of this region are special, since the bees have quite a flavor palette to draw from: *millefiori* (a thousand flowers), raspberries, blueberries, and chestnuts. In fact, chestnuts are more popular here than in most regions. For the Valle d'Aosta, the chestnut was once a food of the poor even while it was a gourmet item in the rest of Italy. It was known as *il pane del bosco* (the bread of the forest), because it would be dried, ground, and used as flour. You will find chestnut flavor in Valle d'Aosta dishes for all parts of the meal.

Walnut oil is a particular delicacy of the valley, used by the people who grow the nuts. Most of what is sold goes to France, where the demand for it still exists. If you are in the town of Villeneuve in March, look for the *frantoio* (oil press) of Mario Gerogy and Lauretta Perrier. The press they use was made in 1716 and still produces a fine oil from the walnuts brought by the eighty growers in the area. Mountain herbs are used sparingly in local cooking, but they do appear in omelettes and are used for curing prosciutto. Many breads are made of rye flour, which is grown in these parts. The bread is usually called *pane nero* (black bread). There are also good breadsticks made by hand by some regional bakeries.

LA GROLLA

Throughout the region there is an ancient tradition of hospitality and friendship known as *la grolla*. This is a hand-carved wooden vessel that has two, four, six, or eight spouts. Many in the Valle d'Aosta say *la grolla* is a linguistic corruption of *graal*, or "grail," and that it is a descendant of the drinking cup that was used by the Knights of the Holy Grail. Other people say that this association is apocryphal and that *la grolla* is a purely local creation that bespeaks the kinship of a small population huddling together against the harshness of winter. In fact, the people of the region refer to this vessel not as *la grolla* but *la coppa di amicizia* (the cup of friendship). Nowadays, a *grolla* that you buy in a crafts store such as the I.V.A.T. (Institut Valdôtain de l'Artisan Typique) in Aosta or Cogne will look like what people used long ago. A *grolla* used today is usually a maple-wood (in the past it was made of walnut) chalice with one spout. Does this bespeak the solitary nature of man at the threshold of the millennium or the preoccupations of bacteriologists? I think it is simply a matter of convenience. The purpose of *la grolla* is to contain *caffè valdostano* (or *cafe valdôtain*), a combination of coffee, locally made grappa, and sugar. Tourists like to drink this after a day on the ski slopes, and it is usually served in an individual *grolla* or cup. But some bars and refuges in ski areas offer a multispouted *grolla* filled with spiked coffee, so that it is still possible for you to imbibe with friends as if you were a Knight of the Holy Grail. If you buy a *grolla,* the people here advise that you only need wash it with water because the alcohol disinfects it.

The Wines of Valle d'Aosta

At approximately 900 meters (2,800 feet), the vineyards of the Valle d'Aosta are the highest in Europe. This elevation meant that they were not ravaged by phylloxera in the nineteenth century and early twentieth century as were most of the vines of Europe. Because this is not the most congenial terrain for grape growing, great skill and effort are required to have any yield. And since the supply is so limited, the wine of this region tends to be more expensive than that in most of Italy. In fact, many restaurants sell more wine from Piemonte than the Valle d'Aosta for that very reason.

The grape growers of this region are called vignerons, and they have learned to grow grapes among stones so that the stones will reflect warmth and light up to the plants. Red wines from near the border of Piemonte are often based on clones of Nebbiolo, the popular grape of the neighboring region. Donnas, Arvier, and Chambave are the leading towns for red wines, while Muscat de Chambave *(moscato bianco)* and Blanc de Morgex are the best-known whites. The most popular strong alcoholic beverage is Genepy, a juniper-berry distillate with a light gold color. It is firewater to be sure, but good examples such as the one made by Vertosan are delicate and full of good flavor.

Aosta

BAKERY
Pasticceria Chuc, Via S. Anselmo 104.

Good apple cake and strudel, but notable above all for delicate cookies and biscuits of all types.

CAFFÈ
Caffè Nazionale, Place-Piazza E. Lanoux 9. Open until 2h; closed Monday.

Not to be missed. Most of the beautiful, historic *caffès* of Italy—such as those of Torino, Trieste, and Firenze—are well known and documented, but not the Caffè Nazionale. This hidden jewel on the main square of Aosta has been in operation since 1886. Much of its decor dates from the beginning of the twentieth century. It is done in high Jugendstil: many of the chairs are originals, with slightly faded but still gorgeous fabric. Within the *caffè* is another room that you must see: long ago there was a church on this site, and a chapel remains. It was built as a private sanctuary for the dukes of Aosta to retreat for prayer. You will immediately notice the painted ceiling, which has been divided into ten ribbed segments, like a fan. Each contains a crest representing a district in the Valle d'Aosta. There are additional rooms, and one can also sit at an outdoor table during warm weather. There is live music on the weekends. The current ownership does not appreciate what it has, so it has filled one of the rooms with advertising displays. This place should be declared a landmark and its original interior preserved.

CHEESE SHOPS

Maison de la Fontine, Via De Sales 14.
L'Angolo del Formaggio, Via
Trottechien 13.

DINING

Hotel Europe, Place-Piazza Narbonne 8, tel. 0165/236363, fax 0165/40566. Closed Sunday. All credit cards. Expensive.

This is a snug hotel that gracefully combines old and modern, drawing on the best of both. The same applies to the restaurant. There is a *valdostano* menu using classic ingredients in new, lighter ways. Try, for example, the *fagottino di cavolo con la fonduta*—delicately cooked, still-flavorful cabbage used as a wrapper to enclose equally delicate sausage. This is topped with a light Fontina sauce that manages to preserve flavor while avoiding richness. The whole dish is garnished with fresh mint. The kitchen is full of fresh herbs that enliven the sometimes-heavy flavors of *valdostano* food. But they also appear on the general menu, which features top regional cuisine from all over Italy. There might be *casonsei*, filled pasta from

eastern Lombardia, topped with sage and butter. Or a risotto with the very Roman flavors of aged Pecorino cheese and fresh mint.

Trattoria degli Artisti, Via Maillet 5–7, tel. 0165/40960. Closed Sunday and Monday, two weeks in June, and two weeks in November. All credit cards. Moderately inexpensive to moderate.

Don't miss the *antipasto del camino*, with mocetta, prosciutto, salame, and lardo. The soups, crepes and pastas are good here and frequently enriched with *fonduta*. I am a big fan of the *brasato al Blanc de Morgex*, beef slowly stewed in white wine.

La Cave, Via Challand 34, tel. 0165/44164. Open 10–15h and 18:30–22h, closed Sunday. All credit cards. Inexpensive.

An excellent wine bar with superb wines and beautifully chosen and maintained cheeses and salumi, and one can enjoy them outside during fair weather.

Ristorante Vecchio Ristoro, Rue-Via Tourneuve 4, tel. 0165/33238. Open 12:30–14:30h, 19:30–24h; closed Sunday. American Express, MasterCard, Visa. Moderate to moderately expensive.

A charming place near the city museum. In summer, exhibits there are open until 23h, so you can walk off your supper. One can have a typical Valle d'Aosta set meal, a less expensive tourist menu, or an even less costly set meal selected by the restaurant. It is also possible to order à la carte so that you can devise your own meal. The typical regional meal starts with a plate of antipasto (*lardo, mocetta, boudin,* prosciutto), followed by *crespelle con Fontina.* This delicate crepe is filled with fluffy Fontina and served with a Fontina cream sauce. This dish will gladden your heart before clogging the arteries that lead from it! This is followed by *zuppa di orzo e fagioli* (barley-bean soup). The main course is *carbonada* with polenta. Dessert is a fruit tart. The *ristorante* also makes a nice *sorbetto di mele,* apple sorbet with Calvados. Good wines from the Valle d'Aosta and Piemonte.

Valle d'Aosta cows

FOLKLORE
Bataille des Reines.

The regional championship of the battle of the cows is held on the third Sunday in October at the Croix Noire Stadium. Preliminary heats take place throughout the region (eight in the spring, six in the summer, and five in the fall). While people cheer as heifers knock heads, the meaning of this event is deeper. The annual battle has gone on since the seventeenth century and honors the animal that has been the backbone of the regional economy and sustenance. Cattle breeders strive to improve the stock, encourage agriculture, uphold traditions and folklore, and, of course, to attract tourists. The owners of the winning cow are treated to feasts, presented with barrels of wine, and sometimes even receive the cow who lost the final match.

Fiera di Sant'Orso.

Since the year 1000 this fair, the most important in the region, has been held on the last two days of January. Local crafts are sold, performances of local music, plays, and dances fill the streets, and mulled wine is served to help you stay warm. Aosta holds a summer version of this fair in August, but the real one to see is the winter one.

FOOD STORES

Most, though not all, food stores in Aosta are closed on Thursday afternoon and Sunday.

Il Negozietto, Passage Louis Vescoz 2.

Take a deep breath: off the Via Porta Praetoria, this tiny *latteria* near the Roman theater has been selling excellent milk, cheese, and butter since 1866.

L'Orticello, Rue-Via Aubert 44.

Outstanding fruits and vegetables, including huge, fresh *funghi porcini* when available.

Salumeria-Charcuterie La Valdôtaine, 16 Place Emile Chanoux, tel. 0165/42388. Open 8:30–13h, 15:30–19:30h; closed Thursday afternoon and Sunday (except in summer; plans are to soon be open Sunday morning year-round).

Guido and Marco are the friendly and lively proprietors of this fine store that stocks most of the best products of the Valle d'Aosta. These include *mocetta* of veal and chamois, delicious *prosciutto di San Marcel, lardo d'Arnad, boudin* and other sausages. There is a chamois *salame* called *mignon di camoscio* that is ideal to stick in your pack as you begin a mountain hike. Cheeses include Fontina and various *tome,* some made of goat's milk. Unusual jams are stocked, such as rose, Williams pear, chestnut, plus the typical berry flavors, and honey from Adriano Berti, a top producer. All sorts of wines and spirits, including Genepy di Artemesia Spicata, the local favorite.

HANDCRAFTS AND HOUSEWARES
I.V.A.T., Via Xavier de Maistre 1,
tel. 0165/40808.

A good place to buy *la grolla* or other quality crafts of the region.

Mario Picchiottino, Via S. Anselmo 99,
tel. 0165/262551. Open summer 9–20h,
other seasons 9–12:30h, 15–19:30h; closed
Monday morning and Sunday (except
during Easter, Christmas, and summer).

Signor Picchiottino is an artisan who works in copper. While the more rustic items—platters with ducks, dogs, and sleepy drunks, for example—are kitschy, you should not overlook the many handmade items of real quality and beauty that will find use in your kitchen. There are polenta pots; casseroles; a still (if you make your own spirits); old-style coffeepots (with aluminum insides); molds for puddings, gelatins, and cakes; colanders; pizza pans; an *oliera* (olive-oil can); ladles; skillets. According to Mario's very charming sister, it is easy to clean copper: use a solution of apple or other clear vinegar and salt, then wipe the copper dry with a towel.

WINE
La Bonne Bouteille, Via S. Anselmo 62,
tel. 0165/40772.

Enoteca le Grand Paradis, Via S. Anselmo
121, tel. and fax 0165/44047.

Each has a good selection of Valle d'Aosta and Piemonte wines, as well as Genepy Valle d'Aosta and other spirits. A good selection of honeys and jams, too.

Arnad

The local specialty is delicately spiced *lardo* that melts in your mouth. There is a folkloric festival on the last Sunday in August to celebrate it. A good purveyor is Marilena Bertolin, Via Nazionale 11, tel. 0125/966127.

DINING
Azienda Agrituristica Lo Dzerby, Loc.
Pied de Ville, tel. 0125/966067. No credit
cards. Open weekends in May, June, July,
and September and daily in August.
Inexpensive.

A way to taste delicious food and wine produced right here on the farm. The lard and sausages are not to be missed.

Aymavilles

WINE

Les Cretes Chardonnay, made in Aymavilles, is the best Italian Chardonnay I have tasted anywhere. It is full of freshness, fruit, and the character of the grape and is not encumbered by flavors of wooden barrels. I tasted this wine three times throughout the region, but did not visit the winery, whose fax is 0165/902274.

Chambave

WINE

Società Cooperativa "La Crotta di Vegneron," Piazza Roncas 2, tel. 0166/46670. Open 9–12h, 14–17h; closed Thursday. No credit cards.

Chambave Rouge is a decent red, but most people want to try the *moscato passito* dessert wine. Next door is the Ristorante-Bar La Crotta, which is part of the cooperative. Good, moderately inexpensive food is served.

Azienda Vinicola Ezio Voyat, Via Arberaz 13, tel. 0166/46139.

As the most renowned wine maker in the region, Signor Voyat's wines are quite special and are produced in such limited quantity that demand far outstrips supply.

Champorcher

FOLKLORE

Festa del Pane Nero.

In the old quarter of town are antique ovens that are used to make a typical black bread of the town in the last ten days of July.

Festa del Sargnun.

A mid-August tasting and celebration of the soft local cheese, made with cow's milk and flavored with herbs.

Cogne
Classic Town

Cogne is a friendly town in the middle of the Gran Paradiso National Park. Once upon a time this was a mining center with one of the largest iron deposits in Europe. There is a museum *(Museo delle Miniere)* that recalls this heritage, but the main reason to come here now is to base yourself in a place where you can taste the flavors of the Valle d'Aosta and work off that good food by hiking in some of the Continent's most spectacular scenery. In addition to mountains, rushing rivers, unusual flowers, and animals, you might also see the *ru*, ancient irrigation canals that provided water to grow grapes, wheat, and rye. It is possible to engage

Parco del Gran Paradiso, near Cogne

guides (inquire at the tourist office in the Municipio on the Place E. Chanoux), or you can follow the well-marked trails. Each trail is color coded, so you won't lose your way. The signs indicate the length of each hike in distance as well as in the time it takes to make the journey. If you have time for only one, you should probably take the hike to Valnontey, which I describe below.

BAKERY

Pasticceria Perret, Rue-Vja Bourgeois 59. Open summer 8–12:30h, 15:30–21h, winter 8:30–12:30h, 15–19h; closed Monday.

The specialty is *mecoulin*, a cake similar to panettone, but without candied fruit. One eats this at breakfast with coffee or later in the day topped with cream. This was originally a Christmas cake, but it is now available year round. The bakery also makes *tegole*, biscuits of almond, hazelnut, egg whites, and sugar. *Crema di Cogne* is a sweet made with eggs, sugar, heavy cream, and cocoa powder.

DINING

Ristorante Lou Ressignon (Da Arturo), Rue des Mines de Cogne 23, tel. 0165/ 74034. Open 12–14:15h, 19:20–21:15h; closed Monday evening and Tuesday, though it is often open daily in high seasons; closed in November and ten days in early June. All credit cards. Moderate.

If I were to direct you to only one restaurant in the Valle d'Aosta, this would be the place. It is run with great warmth and care by Arturo Allera; his wife, Jose; their son, Davide; and their lovely daughter, Elisabetta. So well known is this place that it is usually called Da Arturo

(Arturo's place). "Lou Ressignon" is local dialect for "midnight snack." Originally, this was a tavern with food and dancing that offered tasty snacks. There is still dancing on some nights (22h to 2h) on the floor below, where a grill turns out good light food. But let's talk about the restaurant upstairs: The antipasti are all excellent—homemade *mocetta* and *tetetta,* plus *prosciutto di San Marcel* and divine *carne cruda alla Gressonara* (paper-thin slices of beef topped with a pungent anchovy-rich *bagna cauda*). There are all the typical soups of the region, many of which are hard to find outside private homes. The simple and wonderful soup of this town is *soupetta à la cogneintze* (rice, broth, crusts of bread, Fontina). There are excellent pastas, crepes with Fontina, and polenta dishes. One of the signature dishes is *pennette alla Ressignon,* perfectly cooked tiny penne with an intense tomato sauce, plus bits of *prosciutto crudo,* zucchini, and peppers. The sauce is loaded with flavor, but has no palpable chunks of vegetables that alter the texture. This is pasta cooking at its best in a region where pasta is not even native. Second courses include local trout, beef braised in wine, *carbonada,* whole *funghi porcini,* and a classic *bistecca alla valdostana.* Here a boneless steak is breaded, cooked, and topped with *prosciutto cotto* (not *crudo,* as one usually finds), and Fontina. The *camoscio con polenta* is superb: chamois cooked in a sauce of red wine, juniper berries, and a bit of pepper. The chunks of meat are absolutely tender and full of flavor. The polenta that came with this dish is as tasty as you will ever encounter. You also can have a classic *fonduta* made with excellent Fontina. To cleanse my palate, I had a nice green salad

dressed with *agro di mele,* the typical apple vinegar of the region. The typical dessert is silken *crema di Cogne* served with *tegole,* the local cookie. The wine list is excellent, and prices are very reasonable for such good quality. There is Les Cretes Chardonnay and other fine wines from the Valle d'Aosta, as well as good selections from Piemonte (try the Angelo Gaja Dolcetto), Trentino–Alto Adige, and Friuli. You do not need to order mineral water here. The tap water is sweet and clean (it lends its characteristics to all the dishes made at this restaurant). Your meal will end with good coffee and a glass of Genepy. Service is excellent.

La Brasserie du Bon Bec, Rue-Via Bourgeois 78, tel. 0165/749288. Closed Monday (except in July and August). No credit cards. Moderate.

Another good restaurant if you want to take a break from—or can't get into—Lou Ressignon. A nice little dish is *tartiflette,* using matchstick potatoes, *pancetta,* and, of course, Fontina.

FOLKLORE
La Veillà.

This event is held annually in mid- to late July and sometimes into August. From early evening until midnight one can walk in the small streets near the church and see displays of local crafts such as lace, woodworking, and wrought iron. There are also stands selling *la seupetta,* the local soup, plus chamois braised in red wine and served with polenta. The event has ancient origins. For centuries people used to gather during the winter months in the stable. While the women spun wool or made lace, the men sculpted *cornailles*, pieces of wood carved to look like cows. As people worked they told stories of folkloric and religious origin, which were passed from one generation to another.

GASTRONOMIA

Salumeria-Panetteria Gerard, Via

Bourgeois 51. Open 8–12:30h, 15–19h.

Fine products of the region, including *mocetta* of chamois, beef, and *asino* (donkey), *prosciutto di San Marcel, lardo d'Arnad*, cheeses, wines, honeys, *funghi porcini*, breads and cakes, and *tegole* cookies.

A HIKE TO VALNONTEY

There is a paved road that is used by cars that makes an easy, if less interesting, hike. This is recommended for people with walking difficulties or those who are concerned about not being on the main road. There is plenty of scenic beauty to behold from a distance, but if you want to see alpine flora and fauna up close, you should take hiking trail 25, which runs along a river and through stands of trees that lead to gorgeous mountain scenery. It is a distance of 1,534 meters (5,033 feet), and the time it takes—for trekkers from the big city who will stop to catch their breath and gawk at the scenic splendor—is about one hour. It is a hike of moderate exertion. To find trail 25, first locate the *municipio* (city hall) on Place E. Chanoux. On the left side the Rue de Grand Paradis (the paved road) commences. On the side with the parking lot one sees a stone monument with a cross. Here the trail, which is marked with light blue tracks, begins. As you walk along the path you become aware of the silence—the only audible sounds are the rushing water, the murmurs of the forest, the tread of your foot, and perhaps your slightly labored breathing. But the silence is exhilarating. Once in Valnontey, which is not especially pretty, you can walk another ten minutes up to the Giardino Alpino Paradisia to see an extensive collection of alpine flora. These are the flowers that give their flavor to the *millefiori* honey that is made in these parts.

If you wish to stay in Valnontey and use it as a base for exploration higher up, consider Le Petit Dahu (Frazione di Valnontey 22, 11012 Cogne [AO], tel. 0165/74146; no credit cards), run by Cèsar and Ivana Charruaz. Cèsar organizes hikes, picnics, and small meals at their *baita* (mountain hut) up in Valmiana. You can take meals at the hotel—they are very good (moderate prices).

LACE

Les Dentelles de Cogne, 50 Rue dr. Grappein, tel. 0165/749282. Open summer, Monday–Saturday 9–12:30h, 15–19:30h; winter, Saturday and Sunday

9–12:30h, 14:30–19h, peak winter weeks, Thursday–Sunday.

The lace of Cogne (called *dentelles* in French, *pizzi* in Italian) is unlike any lace found in Italy. Nuns from Cluny in France passed through this area around 1600 and taught the locals to make lace as they made it. The women who work here often wear elaborate black costumes trimmed with lace. To make the lace they use *fuselli*, wooden spools that are moved piece by piece in a predetermined order to make the distinct patterns of Cogne lace. In the back of the shop is a small museum documenting this lace's history with pictures and samples of antique lace and local costumes. This store is to the left of Cogne's beautiful cathedral, which dates from the 1200s.

It is much more decorated than most alpine churches and merits a visit. Pope John Paul II, who often summers nearby, has said mass in this church.

WINE

Rue-Via Bourgeois 50, tel. 0165/74151. Open 9–12:30h, 15–20h; Closed Monday, Tuesday, and Wednesday morning in low season.

Most Valle d'Aosta wines, liqueurs, and jams, as well as good wines from Piemonte, Lombardia, Trentino, and Friuli.

Courmayeur

This is one of the most popular ski resorts in Italy, with its position on the sunny side of Mont Blanc, Europe's highest mountain. I have visited Courmayeur once a decade since the 1970s, and while the natural splendor of the surroundings remains unchanged, the town has been built up substantially, so that it now has the air of a posh international resort. This makes it a good destination for fine food even if the town has lost most of its *valdostana* character. More than any town in the region, Courmayeur has excellent food stores that can provide you with breads, cakes, produce, wine, chocolate, and prepared dishes that you can take on mountain hikes.

CAFFÈ

Caffè della Posta, Via Roma 51, tel. 0165/842272.

Right in the center of town is this cozy place that has had a following since 1911. Until 1938 it was also a *drogheria*, selling all sorts of packaged goods that arrived at the nearby post office (hence the name) at this alpine outpost. After the Liberation in World War II the Posta became the command center for the American military. In postwar years, as Courmayeur became a very fashionable ski resort, the Posta welcomed such notables as King Farouk and Errol Flynn, who spent more time at the bar than on the slopes.

DINING

Caldran Solaire, Via Roma 122, tel. and fax 0165/844609. Open 12:30–14h, 19:30–22h; closed Tuesday in low season. American Express, MasterCard, Visa. Moderately inexpensive to moderately expensive.

A very pleasant, homey restaurant, with outdoor dining in warm weather. Soups include the local *zuppa alla courmayeurense*, in which many vegetables are cooked with bread and melted Fontina. Also try the *zuppa di cereali*, made with *farro*, rye, barley, chickpeas, and green peas. The restaurant makes very good *polenta concia* (with Fontina melted into the cornmeal as it cooks). There is also a delicious *fonduta*. For dessert, local chestnuts figure in many preparations, as does chocolate. There is a decent *menu turistico*.

Pierre Alexis 1877 Ristorante, Via Marconi 54, tel. 0165/843517. Closed Monday (except in August), Tuesday afternoon December–March, and October and November. All credit cards. Moderate to moderately expensive.

Owner Serafino Cosson runs a very popular restaurant with good and imaginative cooking. One reason to come here is the apple menu, which begins with a salad with apples, followed by *tagliolini* with an apple-based sauce. Then comes a pork fillet with apple and for dessert a baked apple with chocolate. The *menu valdostano* has many of the region's specialties, and there is a tourist menu if you are watching the lire.

FOOD STORES

Le Bien Faire: La Maison de la Fromage de la Vallée d'Aoste, Via Roma 120, tel. 0165/844634.

A source for cheese, it also sells good baguettes if you are in a French mood.

Da Ettore—Il Salumaio, Via Monte Bianco 10.

Sells Valle d'Aosta specialties such as *mocetta* and *prosciutto di San Marcel*, as well as *salumi* from all over Italy. Excellent quality and a very nice proprietor.

Pastificio-Gastronomia Gabriella, Passaggio dell'Angelo (just off Via Roma 92).

Fresh pasta and prepared foods, including hot pasta, vegetables, salads, and homey cakes. A good choice if you want hot food without going to a restaurant.

Gourmandises, Via Roma 44. Closed Wednesday morning and Sunday. MasterCard, Visa.

A fine selection of wines from the region as well as a huge assortment of chocolate, jams, dried *funghi porcini*, canned pâtés, and a special local candy called Monte Bianco made with almonds, hazelnuts, and chocolate.

Da Peaquin, Piazza G. Brocherel.

Excellent fruit and vegetables, artfully displayed.

Panetteria La Spiga, Via Roma 19.

Excellent bread and traditional cakes. There is flat, crunchy *pane di segale con semi di finocchio* (rye with fennel seeds), nice round loaves of *pane di segale*, and, on the back wall, bins of breadsticks made in many flavors, including spinach, basil, *peperoncino*, tomato, onion, *integrale* (whole wheat). There is an unusual *torta di noci* (nut cake) with pine nuts, almonds, walnuts, and peanuts (this last is not a typical ingredient in Italian cookery). The *torta di Courmayeur* is a yeast cake with dried figs, hazelnuts, almonds, walnuts, and raisins.

Donnas/Donnaz

This town is famous for its pleasing red wine, made of local grape varieties: Picco-tendro, Freisa, Neyret, and Vien de Nus. This was the first wine in the Valle d'Aosta to be awarded DOC status. It is made by a cooperative and is available for purchase all over town.

DINING

Les Caves de Donnas, Via Roma 99,
tel. 0125/807737, fax 0125/807512. Closed
Thursday and first two weeks in October.
MasterCard, Visa. Moderate.

Indoors and outdoors, this restaurant serves regional specialties to taste with the town's wine.

Etroubles

FOLKLORE

Viellà di Etroubles and Bataille des Reines.

Two local traditions during the last ten days of July. In the first, black bread is baked and served with whipped cream. While this is going on, you can watch the "battle of the queens," which sounds oper-atic but is really a harmless butting contest between a black cow and a brown-and-white-spotted cow. The winner receives a bell hung on a decorative collar and, as queen for a day, is free to wander around town. She goes on to compete in the re-gional championship in Aosta.

Sagra della Fontina.

A festival celebrating the region's favorite cheese on the first Sunday in September.

Gignod

FOLKLORE

Festa de Teteun.

On the third weekend in August, while some people are clog-dancing, you can taste the local specialty, *teteun* (also called *tetetta*), which is cow's udder, cooked with salt and spices and sliced thin. Don't knock it until you've tried it.

Gressan

APPLE VINEGAR

Agrival, 3 Hameau de Resselin.

Delicious *agro di mele.*

Lillaz

This town is 4 kilometers (2.5 miles) from Cogne, which makes it a good place for lunch after a morning hike.

DINING
Lou Tchappè, tel. 0165/74379. Closed Monday (except in July and August), June, and November. Moderate.

One of the specialties is *soça du Tchappè*, a soup made of meat, cabbage, potatoes, leeks, garlic, and sage.

Morgex

This town is famous for two products. The *boudin de Morgex* is a blood sausage with beets, potato, lard, and spices that goes nicely with Morgex's white wine, Blanc de Morgex. These vineyards are the highest in Europe.

WINE
Cave du Vin Blanc de Morgex et de La

Salle, Località Les Iles—Frazione La Rulne, tel. 0165/800331.

Nus

FOLKLORE
Carnevalaccio di Nus.

Held during the Carnival period in the five days preceding Ash Wednesday, this is a reenactment of Carnival as it was celebrated in 1300. Seigneurs, or lords, dressed in traditional costume descend from the castle to the blaring of trumpets and the pounding of drums. When the procession is over, 1,500 liters (about 400 gallons) of minestrone are served for free. Try to sample Passito di Nus, a very special dessert wine made of Malvoisie grapes, available locally.

Saint Christophe

FONTINA CHEESE
Cooperativa Produttori Latte e Fontina, Loc. Croix-Noire 10, Saint Christophe (AO), tel. 0165/35714 or 40551, fax 0165/236467.

This is the headquarters of the regional producers of Fontina. You can contact them for information or recipe books about the cheese. If you are in the area (not far from Aosta) this is a good place to buy very fresh, perfect cheese straight from its producer at the point of sale on the grounds of the cooperative.

Saint Pierre

AGRITOURISM
Azienda Agricola Les Ecureuils,
Frazione Homené Ste. Marguerite,
tel. 0165/903831. Reservations essential.
Open Friday, Saturday, and Sunday.

One can sleep at this beautiful alpine spot or simply travel up for a meal. The owners raise various animals (goats, rabbits, geese, turkeys, chickens), which figure in the meals. One can also have lard, sausages, and homemade breads made of whole wheat, potatoes, or chestnuts. There are good vegetable soups. The farm is most famous for its goat cheeses, which are considered the best in the region. It also sells mohair for coats and sweaters. There are twelve beds and fifteen places at the table.

Sarre

BREADSTICKS
Panificio Antico Forno, Frazione St.
Maurice 43, tel. 0165/257518.

Various types of breadsticks are made here: *all'acqua senza grassi* (with water, no fat), *all'acqua con strutto* (with water and lard), *al burro* (butter), *all'origano* (oregano), *al latte* (milk), *alle noci* (walnuts), *alle cipolle* (onions), *alle olive,* and *al sesamo* (sesame).

Valpelline

This town is famous throughout this small region for its soup, *zuppa à la valpellinentse.* In the last days of July, the town holds La Sagra della Seupa à la Valpelenentze, with masses, games, dances, and, of course, soup.

Zuppa à la Valpellinentse
Soup from Valpelline

Serves 4
8 slices of the best black or dark wheat bread
you can find
Unsalted butter
200 grams/7 to 8 ounces Fontina, sliced
thin
½ Savoy cabbage (you may substitute another
delicate green if you wish), torn in bite-
sized pieces

½ cup freshly grated grana or Parmigiano-
Reggiano
4 cups good beef stock

Preheat the oven to 180°C (350°F). Butter the slices of bread on both sides and place them on a baking sheet. Place it in the oven and toast the bread only until it becomes slightly crisp, but not burned. Remove the bread from oven. With butter, lightly grease a large baking dish of cast iron, terra-cotta, or heat-resistant glass. Place a layer of bread on the bottom, top with a layer of Fontina, then a layer of cabbage.

Repeat. Then cover the second layer of cabbage with the grated cheese. Pour the broth over all and then bake, uncovered, in the oven for 10 minutes.

Tartiflette

As prepared in La Brasserie du Bon Bec in Cogne.

Serves 4

6 large potatoes

200 grams/7 to 8 ounces pancetta

1 tablespoon unsalted butter

150 grams/5 to 6 ounces Fontina, coarsely
grated

Preheat the oven to 200°C (400°F). Wash but do not peel the potatoes. Cook them in boiling water, but be sure that they remain firm. Let them cool; peel and cut them into matchstick-sized pieces. Cut the *pancetta* into strips. Combine the *pancetta* with the potato sticks. Melt the butter in a large skillet, add the potatoes and *pancetta*, and cook until the potatoes are almost golden but not crisp. Transfer the mixture to a baking dish, spilling away the fat, if you wish. Cover with the Fontina and bake in the oven for 4 to 5 minutes. Serve immediately.

Wine: Donnaz.

Lombardia

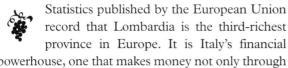

 Statistics published by the European Union record that Lombardia is the third-richest province in Europe. It is Italy's financial powerhouse, one that makes money not only through industrial production and banking, but also in agriculture. The region has by far the highest yields per hectare or acre of any in Italy.

Milano, the region's capital and Italy's second-largest city, is also the national trendsetter in most things. Almost all of the major publishing houses and newspapers are there, so that Milanese opinion is often the point of departure for national debate. La Scala has been the Italian national stage since 1778, a place not only for excellence in opera, ballet, and symphonic music, but also where Garibaldi led the drive for Italian unification in the nineteenth century. Milano is the fashion and design capital of Italy, and perhaps the world, the place where Armani, Versace, Ferré, Gae Aulenti, Ettore Sottsass, and hundreds of others less famous contribute to the ongoing effort to create, innovate, and challenge perspective. The city is a magnet for the best, the brightest, and the most elegant, so that the people of Milano are often a visual and intellectual delight.

Milano is also a great academic center, a pioneer in medicine, and a hotbed of political activity. The city has given Italy many of its leading politicians in recent years—in my view a dubious distinction. Bettino Craxi was prime minister during much of the 1980s. He did some good for Italy, but also led it into some of the most mind-boggling corruption the na-

REGIONAL CAPITAL:
Milano (MI).

PROVINCIAL CAPITALS:
Bergamo (BG), Brescia (BS), Como (CO), Cremona (CR), Lecco (LC), Lodi (LO), Mantova (MN), Pavia (PV), Sondrio (SO), Varese (VA).

TOURIST INFORMATION:
Ufficio Regionale del Turismo di Lombardia, Via Marconi 1, 20123 Milano, tel. 02/870016.

Agritourism:
Agriturist Comitato Regionale, Viale Isonzo 27, 20135 Milano, tel. 02/5468387

tion had ever seen. Craxi died in exile in Tunisia and his reputation has never recovered. Silvio Berlusconi, a billionaire industrialist and media magnate who benefited greatly from Craxi's actions, had the nerve to run for prime minister in 1994 by forming an alliance with neo-Fascists and separatists. In the ashes of the corruption scandals (in which Milano came to be known as Tangentopoli, or City of Bribes), Italians rejected the major political parties and selected Berlusconi, despite his lack of governmental experience, his arrogance, and the many unanswered questions about how he, his family, and his holdings profited during the period of the scandals. His first stab at governance was a failure, but he clawed his way back, using his three television networks and other media holdings to create a favorable image. He returned to power in May 2001 and his leadership has been divisive and damaging for Italy.

Umberto Bossi is the founder of the Lega Lombarda (Lombard League), now the linchpin of a regional confederation called the Lega Nord. This group preaches regional autonomy, if not total separation, from the rest of Italy, asserting that the north is honest and hardworking while the south is lazy and corrupt. One of the Lega's mottos is *Roma ladrona, il Nord non perdona* (Roma is a big thief; the north will not forgive). As most of the recent corruption in Italy took place because northern industrialists bribed politicians from all over the country, Bossi's assertion is weak. The Lega Lombarda's attitude has an underlying current of racism and greed in its belief that the north pays for everything in Italy while southerners are poor, selfish, and tend toward criminality. The standard of living is far higher in the north than elsewhere in Italy because most of the wealth has been kept and invested there. It is also true that much of Lombardia's industrial expansion in the postwar era was achieved thanks to the labors of workers who emigrated from southern Italy.

The sad truth is that almost all Italian political leaders are despicable and reprehensible, no matter where they sit on the ideological spectrum. They inflict great harm on, and arouse massive mistrust among, the vast majority of Italians all over the country who are honest, fair, and very hardworking. The politics of greed infected Italy in the 1980s much as it did in the United States, where it was institutionalized by government policy. When citizens of nations find ways to revile rather than respect, abuse rather than share, these nations are destined for decline and perhaps civil war.

These observations aside, I do not want to leave a negative impression about Lombardia. It is, in fact, one of my favorite Italian regions. It has a remarkable solidity, an undying commitment to excellence, lots of superb food, and some of Italy's most varied and beautiful scenery. Its many cities are noble and proud, its people industrious, creative, open, and kind. Within two hours of Milano in any direction is an amazing range of climates, terrains, foods, and cultural treasures.

I like to describe Lombardia in horizontal bands, starting in the southern part of the region and moving north. The provinces of Pavia, Lodi, Cremona, and Mantova are the heart of Padania, the rich agricultural plain of the Po River that extends to Piemonte, Emilia-Romagna, and Veneto. Foodwise, this is the white belt of Italy, which favors rice, butter, cheese, and cream. Lombardia's cheeses are among the best in Italy, and risotto is its classic *primo piatto*. Although rice is predominant, Lombardia also has many typical fresh pastas of exquisite delicacy, including *tortelli di zucca, marubini, casonsei,* and *pizzoccheri,* second only to those of Emilia-Romagna. Cremona, the Classic Town for Lombardia, is among the foremost centers of cuisine, agriculture, and the arts in all of Italy. Mantova is just as wonderful, but, as a city that borders the Veneto and Emila-Romagna, it is less classically Lombard than Cremona. Pavia has one of Italy's top universities, where the likes of Alessandro Volta (who studied and described voltage), playwright Carlo Goldoni, and this author have studied. Outside of Pavia is the Certosa, a Carthusian monastery that is one of the most beautiful in Italy. The broad fertile fields, the big old stone houses, and the huge disks of baled hay form a typical Padania landscape that I find very beautiful and soothing.

The band north of Padania is the industrial plain that has Milano as its center. "Industrial" should not imply ugly. While there has been a desecration of the air (Milano, in a prealpine valley, has terrible air pollution) and some of the land, there is still much beauty. Milano has more green than any other Italian city, plus splendid architecture, one of the most magnificent Gothic cathedrals in the world, fabulous museums and artwork, the most beautiful window displays you will ever see, elegant *caffè*s, and an old, traditional cuisine that can be sampled at restaurants such as Al Matarel. The provinces of Brescia, Bergamo, Varese, and the Brianza zone (north of Milano in the southern parts of the provinces of Como and Lecco) are all similarly industrial and very rich. Brescia and Bergamo are the strongholds of the Lega Lombarda, which taints some of their appeal, but they are cities of great historical and gastronomic interest. In those two cities polenta, usually served soft and creamy, is a staple.

The next band to the north is the beautiful Lake District. Despite the northerly setting (it is on a latitude similar to that of Montreal), this area's climate is tempered by the lakes, so that lemons, olives, and other beautiful trees and plants make unexpected appearances. The Lombard portion of the district is the largest, including the eastern shore of Lago Maggiore, almost all of Lago di Como, and the western shore of Lago di Garda. There are many other lakes that are less well known, including Lago d'Iseo, which has become very popular, and Lago di Monate in the province of Varese. This is one of the deepest lakes in Italy and has very clean water, and the surrounding farming zone produces some of the nation's best butter *(burro di Monate)*. The Lake District offers serenity, visual pleasure, and a great weekend if you have done intensive urban sight-seeing all week.

The northernmost band, near the Swiss border, has Alps that cover parts of the provinces of Varese, Como, Lecco, Bergamo, Brescia, and the entire province of Sondrio. Much of this province is often called the Valtellina (Valley of Teglio), and it is a world apart from the rest of Lombardia. It is a region that has been blessed with natural splendor but assaulted by mud slides, avalanches, and a soil much less generous than in the rest of the region. Yet skiing and all of the summer and winter mountain sports are wonderful there. The *valtellinesi* have the genuine character of hardworking mountain people (they more resemble the citizens of the neighboring Trentino than the dynamic Lombards to the south). The Valtellina also has superb food, including *pizzoccheri, funghi porcini,* game, cheeses, mountain berries, and excellent red wines. My favorite city there is Chiavenna, and I love the small town of Madesimo very high up in the mountains at the Swiss border. The Valtellina is the best-kept secret in the fascinating region of Lombardia.

One can easily spend a two-week vacation in Lombardia—Italy's most populous region—and never tire of its terrain, its cuisine, its people, and its culture. It is rich in lucre, to be sure, but it is rich in many other ways, too.

Eating in Lombardia

ANTIPASTI

Bresaola. Air-dried fillet of beef, a specialty of the Valtellina. It has become immensely popular, especially when served with shards of Parmigiano-Reggiano and chopped greens such as arugula. In this form it is also eaten as a *secondo*. *Bresaola* should always be sliced paper-thin.

Oca. Goose is a specialty of Mortara. It can be made as a *salame*, or goose breast can be smoked.

Salame Mantovano. A lightly garlicky, crumbly *salame*, delicious in risotto.

Salame Milanese. Fine-grained *salame* made of pork, garlic, and spices.

Sciatt. Folded, deep-fried buckwheat fritters filled with *bitto* cheese. A specialty of the Valtellina.

Violin di Carna Secca. Similar to *bresaola*, but made with goat meat.

PRIMI

Agnoli. Meat-filled pasta typical of Mantova.

Busecca. A tripe soup that is a specialty of Milano.

Casoncelli (Casonsei or *Casunsei).* Folded pasta filled with beef, veal, pork, or sausage, spinach, potatoes, mortadella, plus Parmigano-Reggiano or grana. Served either in rich broth or with melted butter, they are found in eastern Lombardia, especially Bergamo and Brescia. The fillings and preparations vary somewhat from place to place.

Marubini. Cremonese *tortelli* filled with braised beef, roast pork, roast veal, grana cheese, and eggs.

Minestrone. A specialty of Milano, but popular throughout the region. This is a rich vegetable soup with greens, beans, legumes, and pasta. There are seasonal variations, but this is an eternally satisfying *primo*, because the cooks of Lombardia emphasize variety as well as freshness in selecting the ingredients.

Pizzoccheri. Buckwheat pasta that is typical of the Valtellina. It is usually served with Savoy cabbage, potatoes, whole garlic, and melted *bitto* cheese.

Polenta. Cornmeal mush that is served either as a *primo* or as a *contorno*. It is popular throughout the region, but especially in the provinces of Bergamo, Brescia, and Sondrio.

Polenta Taragna. Soft polenta with melted cheese and butter.

Riso al Salto. Leftover *risotto alla milanese* is panfried with butter to make a tasty, crunchy *primo*.

Risotto. A silky combination of rice cooked with numerous ingredients, such as saffron or mushrooms, vegetables, fish, cheeses, or wine.

Risotto alla Certosina. Made with frog's legs, perch fillets, and vegetables.

Risotto alla Milanese. Classic risotto flavored with saffron.

Zucca *fills the* tortelli *of Cremona and Mantova*

Tortelli. Folded pasta filled with different ingredients depending on the town you are in and the preferences of the cook. Many *tortelli* are filled with meat, cheese, potatoes, or green vegetables. An exquisite type, *tortelli di zucca,* is a specialty of Mantova and Cremona. This dish is made of pumpkin or orange squash, ground amaretti cookies, and *mostarda.* Typically, *tortelli* are served with melted sweet butter, grated Parmigiano-Reggiano or grana, and occasionally a few sage leaves.

Zuppa Pavese. Broth with a raw egg on toast floating in it. The egg cooks in the broth. This soup was created in 1525 to give strength to Francis I (Pavia was under French domination) in the Battle of Pavia. The French lost to Spain, but the soup survived.

SECONDI

Asparagi alla Milanese. Boiled asparagus topped with a fried egg and grated Parmigiano-Reggiano.

Bollito Misto. A cart of assorted boiled meats, usually including beef, veal, tongue, pork, and sausages. Served with *mostarda* and various sauces.

Cassoeula. A stew of Savoy cabbage, sausage made from pork belly, and other less familiar parts of the pig. Served with polenta.

Cotoletta (Costoletta) alla Milanese. A delicate veal cutlet (or sometimes chop), dipped in egg and bread crumbs and sautéed in butter. In Lombardia, you will taste the genuine article, not the poor substitutes found elsewhere.

Luccio in Salsa. Pike in a piquant green herb sauce. A specialty of Mantova.

Lumache. Snails, prepared in many ways.

Mondeghili. Cabbage filled with minced veal, potatoes, Parmigiano-Reggiano, and nutmeg.

Ossobuco. Shin of veal cooked very slowly and served with a sauce called *gremolata* (a sauce of lemon peel, garlic, and parsley). You should eat the marrow, too—I save it for last.

Rane. Frogs. More precisely, this refers to frog's legs, often called *cosce di rana.*

Röstin Negàa. Veal chops and potatoes baked for four hours in white wine.

FORMAGGI

If I were forced to choose only one region as the source for my cheese, it would be Lombardia. The exquisite richness and variety of Lombardia's cheeses give special flavor and character to its cuisine.

Bel Paese. A very mild, industrially made cheese. It was invented in 1906 by Egidio Galbani, whose company still produces it. You are probably familiar with Bel Paese, and you may want to taste it again as a point of departure for the more towering cheeses of Lombardia.

Bitto. A cow's-milk cheese from the Valtellina. When young, it melts beautifully and is used in *pizzoccheri* and *polenta taragna.* When aged, it is used for grating.

Gorgonzola. The famous blue-veined cheese, originally from a town of the same name just outside Milano (and now reachable on the city's subway system). Most Gorgonzola is now made in Piemonte, but it is very popular in Lombard cuisine. It can be smeared onto raw vegetables as an antipasto, melted and tossed with pasta, placed over polenta as a *primo,* or served with pears and walnuts as a dessert. There are two types of Gorgonzola: *dolce* (a slightly sweet version that is golden yellow) and *piccante* (a sharper version that is white). I have noticed that people of Cremona like to drizzle a little honey on their Gorgonzola when they eat it as a dessert.

Grana. A granular cheese that is the Lombard version of Parmigiano-Reggiano. Fine versions are made in Lodi and Cremona. It is certainly very good cheese, but when given the choice, I opt for Parmigiano-Reggiano.

Mascherpone (Mascarpone). A sinfully rich, wonderfully sweet and creamy dessert cheese, available only in cooler months. It is one of the prime ingredients in *tiramisù,* but can also be consumed as is or blended with a bit of brandy.

Panerone. A slightly bitter cheese typical of Mantova and found only in the winter.

Parmigiano-Reggiano. Although this divine cheese is primarily produced in Emilia-Romagna, part of the delimited production zone is in the province of Mantova.

Robbiola. A cheese of ancient origins whose name is thought to derive from the Latin *rubium,* which refers to the red crust this cheese often develops. Another theory is that the name derives from Robbio, the town where it is most famously produced. It could certainly be that both sources are accurate. There are also many *robbiola* cheeses produced in the province of Bergamo. They are wonderfully rich and creamy. When aged, they become firmer and a bit piquant.

Stracchino. The word derives from *stracco,* or "exhausted." Cows who made long journeys for grazing would be milked at the end of these travels. The resultant cheese is straw yellow and rich. This is yet another wonderful Lombard cheese. There is a tradition in the province of Milano of eating *stracchino* on Christmas Eve with *mostarda* from Cremona.

Taleggio. A cheese similar to *stracchino,* found primarily in the province of Bergamo.

In addition to the famous cheeses above, you will find many more, mostly made from cow's milk, with names such as Asso, Bagoss, Balon, Bernardo, Branzi, Cingherlino, Crema, Crescenza (a popular soft cheese), Presolana, Puina, Quartirolo, Scimud, Silter, and Val Brandet.

DOLCI

Crema del Lario. A mixture of cream, lemon, and dry liqueur popular at Lago di Como.

Miascia. A cake made with milk, stale bread, butter, sugar, eggs, pears, apples, lemon peel, grapes, raisins, and rosemary.

Mostaccini. Spicy biscuits from Crema.

Panettone. The classic yeast cake of Milano, with egg, saffron, raisins, and sometimes candied fruit. It is ubiquitous at Christmastime, when it is consumed with sparkling wine. It is now possible to find panettone during much of the year.

Torrone. Nougat, a specialty of Cremona. There are documents that report that at banquets in ancient Roma there was a popular sweet made of honey, almonds, and egg whites. The *cremonesi* tell you that *cremonese* legions brought this delicacy to the capital, but we will never be sure. We are certain that in 1441 there was an elaborate celebration for the wedding of Francesco Sforza and Bianca Maria Visconti in which a dessert made of almonds, honey, and egg whites was served in the shape of the *torrione* (the gigantic bell tower next to Cremona's cathedral, the largest in Italy—118 meters [389 feet]). The tower is now referred to as the *torrazzo.* Nobles from throughout Europe attended the wedding, and soon requests arrived to send the sweet to courts all over the Continent.

Torta di Tagliatelle. A Mantova specialty made with thin egg noodles and almonds. It is crunchy and unusual.

Torta Paradiso. An eggy cake that is a specialty of Pavia.

Torta Sbrisolona. A wonderful crumbly and crunchy cake that is a specialty of Mantova, made with cornmeal, flour, almonds, wine, and lots of butter.

OTHER LOMBARD FLAVORS

Mostarda. Whole fruit pickled with mustard seed. A specialty of Cremona and Mantova. There are slight variations in *mostarda,* depending on the available fruit and whether the fruit is cut or left intact. *Mostarda* is served with sliced *salumi,* with *bollito misto,* or is minced and blended into the filling of *tortelli di zucca.* Some of the fruits used are cherries, quinces, plums, figs, and watermelon.

The Wines of Lombardia

Since Lombardia is sandwiched between Piemonte, Veneto, and Trentino, three of the foremost wine-producing regions in Italy, you might expect that it, too, would be a formidable wine maker. In truth, there are some very good wines made here, ones that compete very favorably in national comparisons, but this region's agriculture really is about foodstuffs. Yet you could drink very well strictly on local wines if you make a visit to Lombardia.

There are six notable wine-producing zones. The Valtellina, in the province of Sondrio, produces most of my favorite Lombard wines. It is characterized by its use of Nebbiolo—the noble grape that gives us most of the great reds of Piemonte—yet which here is sometimes called Chiavennasca. The basic DOC is called Valtellina or Valtellina Superiore. The latter is usually denoted by the district in which it is grown: Grumello, Sassella, Valgella, and Inferno. All are delicious.

The Oltrepò Pavese, the district "beyond [south of] the Po River" in the province of Pavia, has made wonderful wine for a long time but has only recently gained the acclaim it deserves. The problem has been that much of the wine was sold inexpensively in *osterie* along the banks of the Po and the Ticino, which left the impression that it is unremarkable in quality. But recognition has come, and quality has begun to rise further. Good reds include Barbera and the slightly fizzy Bonarda. Many white varieties are planted here, the most successful, I believe, being the Riesling Italico. The Oltrepò is best regarded for its sparkling wines, which are delicious. Towns such as Broni and Stradella produce outstanding *moscato* that easily holds its own in comparison with the more famous wines from Asti.

The third major wine-producing area is the province of Brescia. Here is the Franciacorta zone, which gives us excellent reds and whites and an outstanding sparkling wine. The foremost producer of reds and table whites is Ca' del Bosco, and the best sparkling wine (often called Italy's best) comes from Berlucchi. Both Ca' del Bosco and Berlucchi are national leaders in quality and in prestige. There are seventy wineries in Franciacorta, so you are sure to drink well in this area. Closer to the city of Brescia, charming DOC reds called Cellatica, Botticino, and Capriano del Colle are found. Along the Brescian shores of Lago di Garda one finds wines reminiscent of the light, agreeable ones produced across the lake in the province of Verona. Ever more popular is the white Trebbiano di Lugana, produced on the southern shores of the lake.

The other three wine zones of Lombardia are less notable, but good wine can be found locally. The Valcalepio DOC in the province of Bergamo results in a good red. The Colli Mantovani (province of Mantova) produces a good Lambrusco that rivals that made across the border in Emilia. And there is actually a tiny DOC in the province of Milano called San Colombano that makes a nice little red.

Bergamo

Bergamo is a wealthy, conservative city that balances a reverence for its past with its love of affluence. The old city, Bergamo Alta, is on a tall hill that casts its shadow on the town below. Bergamo Alta feels like a quiet hill town, so that the contrast with bustling, sprawling Bergamo Bassa, below, is acute. The lower town could be a quarter in Milano with dense traffic and animated shoppers. There are fancy restaurants, expensive stores, and monumental architecture of recent vintage. To me, Bergamo Bassa should be given some consideration, but much of the time should be spent in the upper town. After an evening rain shower, when all of its buildings and monuments shine under evocative illumination, Bergamo Alta is especially silent and beautiful.

BAR-CAFFÈ

Caffè del Tasso, Piazza Vecchia 3, Bergamo Alta, tel. 035/237966.

One of Italy's most historic caffès. Opened in 1476 as a tailor shop, it became a bar in 1581 and has been a place to meet for a drink ever since. This is where the followers of Garibaldi (of whom there were many in Bergamo) would meet before going to battle. On one of the walls you will see an edict from the 1850s that prohibits rebellion and insurrection. This caffè is elegant, not stuffy, with a rear room with intimate booths.

CULTURE

Teatro Donizetti, Piazza Cavour 14, tel. 035/249631, fax 035/217560.

Bergamo is the birthplace of Gaetano Donizetti (1797–1848), composer of such

bel canto classics as *Lucia di Lammermoor* and *L'Elisir d'Amore.* The opera house is named in his honor, and there is a festival of his works in September and early October. There is also a year-round calendar of performances by all composers. The city is also the home of commedia dell'arte, whose comic/tragic characters and stories are familiar to all Italians.

DINING

Trattoria Tre Torri, Piazza Mercato del Fieno 7A, Bergamo Alta, tel. 035/244366. Closed Wednesday (except in summer). American Express, MasterCard. Moderate.

A lovely restaurant in a beautiful urban setting. There is delicious polenta with cheese, filled pastas, sausages, and carefully prepared vegetables.

La Cantina, Via Ghislanzoni 3, Bergamo Bassa, tel. 035/237146. Closed Sunday. MasterCard, Visa. Moderate.

Amy Todisco, from the United States, is the very friendly host here. Her husband, Giorgio, works wonders in the kitchen with a broad menu using polenta, rice, soups, many cheeses, beef, turkey, and good vegetables. The famous dessert, real American brownies, are made by Amy. Good wines.

Da Vittorio, Viale Papa Giovanni XXIII, Bergamo Bassa, tel. 035/218060. Closed Wednesday and three weeks in August. All credit cards. Very expensive.

A famous, elegant restaurant that has fancy dishes. People in Bergamo who go for a big night out go to Da Vittorio, so there is a certain formality here that you will either welcome or reject, depending on your mood.

Taverna Valtellinese, Via Tiraboschi 57, Bergamo Bassa, tel. 035/243331. Closed Monday. All credit cards. Moderate.

If you can't get to the Valtellina, this is the place to go for valtellinese specialties.

Bar Donizetti, Via Gombito 17a, Bergamo Alta, tel. 035/242661. Closed Tuesday and between Christmas and New Year. Moderately inexpensive to moderate.

Massimo Locatelli offers outstanding meats, cheeses, and sweets and pairs them with wonderful wines from Lombardia and throughout Italy.

Taverna Colleoni, Piazza Vecchia 7, Bergamo Alta, tel. 035/232596, fax 035/231991, colleonidellangelo @uninetcom.it. Closed Monday. All credit cards. Moderately expensive.

Elegant and beautiful, with refined food and service.

Brescia

Caffè-Pasticceria Capuzzi, Via Giovanni Piamarta (corner of Via Musei). Closed Monday.

A charming *caffè* with its own Roman ruin (part of a column). Outside, if you go down Via Musei to Vicolo del Fontanone and turn right and go up the ramp, you will see much more of Brescia's Roman legacy. Farther down the Via Musei are even more ruins.

Caffè Floriam, Piazza della Loggia. Open 7–24h; closed Wednesday.

With outdoor tables, this is a great place for people watching.

Osteria dell'Elfo, Piazza del Vescovato 1d, tel. 030/3774858. Open 11–2h; closed Sunday (although a different day is being considered). MasterCard, Visa. Moderately inexpensive.

Go down the steps past the bar with many good snack foods (fritters, pieces of fried fish, meatballs) and take a labyrinthine trek to a nice room with about ten tables and a large counter laden with excellent cheeses and *salumi*. You can order tasty dishes, including tripe, *casoncelli*, lake fish, *ravioli di trota*, snails, and from an extensive selection of fine wines. My favorite place to eat in Brescia.

Osteria al Bianchi, Via Gasparo da Salò 32, tel. 030/292328. Closed Tuesday evening and Wednesday, and part of July. MasterCard, Visa. Moderately inexpensive.

Delicious homey food including *salumi*, homemade pastas, and braised meats. Save room for *torta sbrisolona* with your last sips of wine.

Osteria del Quartino, Via Fabio Filzi 92, tel. 030/383574. Closed Saturday lunch and Sunday, and in August. All credit cards. Moderate.

Start by choosing a red wine you have never heard of from the wonderful list and then select meats, pasta, polenta, and cheeses to discover how the wine changes character with each new pairing.

Trattoria La Grotta, Vicolo del Prezzemolo 10, tel. 030/44068. Closed Wednesday and in August. Moderately inexpensive to moderate.

This well-regarded establishment in central Brescia makes formidable *casoncelli* (meat-filled for most of the year but with chard in the summer), delicious soups, rabbit, polenta, and then serves excellent local cheeses to pair with great wines.

Cernobbio (Como)

DINING

Trattoria del Vapore, Via Garibaldi 17, tel. 031/510308. Closed Tuesday. MasterCard, Visa. Moderate to moderately expensive.

If the Grand Hotel Villa d'Este, which many people consider the most beautiful in Italy, is not within fiscal reach, you might choose to dine at the nearby Trattoria del Vapore. The flavors here are of the fish of Lake Como. The daily risotto—often perfumed with local fish—is always a good pick to start with, although the *zuppa di orzo* (barley soup) is also very good. Then proceed to *il pesce del giorno* (the fish of the day), and you will be gratified. If you want to stick to land, there are various *brasati e stufati* (braised and stewed meats). The wine list here is very good.

Chiavenna (Sondrio)

Sondrio may be the capital of the Valtellina, but I find Chiavenna a more interesting town. It is also the place to catch the bus to Madesimo, an idyllic town high up at the Spluga Pass at the Swiss border. The Valtellina is a lovely alpine region with excellent food and wines. It is much less known than the Dolomites of the Trentino–Alto Adige or the peaks of the Valle d'Aosta, but no less beautiful. The Valtellina (the name means "Valley of Teglio," one of the main towns) was created by the flow of the Adda River. The valley runs east–west, with vineyards on the right bank of the river to capture the most sunshine. The Valtellina is subject to variable weather but, with its warm days and cool evenings, is an excellent place to grow grapes.

DINING

Al Cenacolo, Via Carlo Pedretti 16, tel. 0343/32123. Closed Tuesday evening, *Wednesday, and in June. Visa. Moderate to moderately expensive.*

This is one of my favorite restaurants in Lombardia and the first one I would go to for a taste of the Valtellina. Part of its charm is its setting. One enters from the street into a handsome dining room with glass doors that lead to a tiny terrace that hangs, seemingly without support, over a rushing river. In the spring, when the alpine snows melt, the power of the river is so strong that it is sometimes difficult to carry on a conversation. But it is a memorable way to dine. If you cannot get a table outside, dining within is also very pleasant. One of the special antipasti is a terrine made of game. The *pizzoccheri* are exemplary, and the soups are excellent. Among the *secondi*, I recommend *capriolo* and all sorts of game. A dessert I am especially fond of is a gelato of fresh plums to which some grappa has been added. The wines are well chosen; service is friendly but correct.

Como

DINING

Osteria del Gallo, Via Vitani 16, tel. 031/272591. Open morning until about 19h; closed Sunday and evenings. No credit cards. Moderately inexpensive.

A very traditional *osteria*. Everyone from students on a break to elderly card players stops in here for good wine by the glass or, if they plan to stay a while, *al metro* ("by the meter," for which you pay a set price and drink as much as you want). There are excellent cheeses and *salumi* (especially the *bresaola*), hearty soups, and a daily special *secondo* and dessert.

Cremona
Classic Town

The region has such a variety of landscapes, no city can fully encapsulate all that Lombardia is. Yet Cremona is a special place that embodies many of its region's values: purposeful hard work, quiet solidity, piousness, and belief in commerce, love of culture, and art. Although opera reaches its zenith at Milano's Teatro alla Scala, the first great opera composer, Claudio Monteverdi (1567–1643) was from Cremona. So too is Mina, Italy's foremost popular singer, whose status as a living legend is comparable to that of Barbra Streisand in the United States. For anyone who loves the violin, Cremona is Mecca. This is where Antonio Stradivari (1644–1737), maker of the finest stringed instruments ever crafted, was born and worked. He was the inventor of the cello *(violoncello)*. Other fine violin makers in Cremona were Amati and Guarneri. In the city hall are several of these violins, which are played every day to keep them in tune. Be sure to visit the violin collection in the Palazzo d'Arte. I suspect that the creativity of the *cremonesi* is in part a product of their substantial cuisine. Most agricultural statistics indicate that the farms in the province of Cremona are the most productive in Italy. This is in the middle of Padania, the fertile plain of the Po River valley. There are beef cows and dairy cows. The former wind up as the *secondo* at many *cremonese* meals. The latter produce rivers of milk, used to make several wonderful cheeses plus butter and cream. Cremona is every bit as important a milk producer as Wisconsin, and information and techniques are routinely exchanged. A special flavor here is *mostarda*, which gives a special tang and sweetness to many of the dishes in *cremonese* cuisine, including *tortelli di zucca and bollito misto*. The food of Cremona surely is not light, but it is more subtle than one would expect from a place that relies on the cow for much of its sustenance. Cremona also vies with Benevento in Campania and a few other towns as the home of the popular *torrone*. Where it was created is a matter of debate, but there is no doubt that the version made in Cremona is the most famous. Most food stores in Cremona are closed on Sunday and on Monday afternoon.

BAKERIES

Pasticceria Lanfranchi, Via Solferino 30. Closed Monday.

This pink and white shop has small glass cases that contain pastries that are displayed—as they should be—like precious jewels. It also sells *torrone* and a specialty called *pan Cremona*, an airy, eggy, chocolate brick speckled with a few almonds.

Pasticceria-Forno Volpi, Corso Mazzini 15.

Crunchy *grissini*, good focaccia (including one made with Gorgonzola), gnocchi, fresh noodles, and filled pasta. The real attraction are the *crostate* made with cherries, apricots, and other fruit.

BARS

Caffè-Gelateria Pierrot, Largo Boccaccino at Via Solferino.

Coffee, pastries, ice cream, torrone.

Bar del Teatro, Corso Vittorio Emanuele 50.

A nice place to go during the day or at intermission of a performance at the Teatro Ponchielli, across the way.

CULTURE

Teatro Comunale Amilcare Ponchielli, Corso Vittorio Emanuele 52, 26100 Cremona, tel. 0372/407273.

Although Claudio Monteverdi, the first great opera composer, was born in Cremona, the local theater is named for Amilcare Ponchielli (1834–1886), whose most famous work is La Gioconda.

DAIRY PRODUCTS

Latteria Sociale di Piadena, Corso Matteotti 86

In the United States, cows are often fed alfalfa. Italians feel alfalfa will change the flavor of the milk and favor grass and grain. To see how the taste is different, buy some milk here, and perhaps some grana or other cheese. Piadena is a major diary town in the province of Cremona.

DINING

Cascina Nuova, Via Boschetto 51, tel. 0372/460433 or 626123. Open daily. Inexpensive.

This farm at the doors of the city dates back to 1920. In addition to having six beds for people who wish to lodge here, the farm serves meals. There are good *tortelloni* and *agnolini* for primi, while snails and chicken are delicious secondi. This is a delightful way to get a sense of life on a provincial Cremonese farm without going far from town.

Trattoria Mellini, Via Bissolati 105, tel. 0372/ 30535. Reservations essential. Closed Sunday evening, Monday, and July. No credit cards. Moderately inexpensive to moderate.

A 20-minute walk from the city center brings you to this small restaurant whose chief attraction is the food provided by cows: excellent beef, whether grilled, braised, roasted or broiled, and a fine selection of cheeses.

Ristorante Centrale, Vicolo Pertusio (just off Via Solferino). Closed Saturday. No credit cards. Moderate.

Places like this are becoming extremely rare in Italy and may be gone by the time you try to find them. Older citizens are drawn to the warm simplicity of the food and service and revel nostalgically in the fragrant broths and good meats and vegetables.

La Sosta, Via Sicardo 9, tel. 0372/ 456656. Closed Sunday evening, Monday and from mid-July to mid-August. All credit cards. Moderate.

Dishes based on meat are excellent here. Ground salami fills the *gnocchi vecchia Cremona*, duck flavors bigoli

pasta, and various boiled meats are served in an exquisite *bollito misto*. Good vegetables and cheeses complete a typically substantial Cremonese meal.

Hosteria 700, Piazza Gallina 1, tel. 0372/ 36175. Closed Monday evening, Tuesday, and a week in mid-August. All credit cards. Moderate.

Lovely pasta dishes such as *marubini* cooked in three broths, chestnut gnocchi in a taleggio cheese sauce, as well as *risotto con stinco di maiale* (pork shank). Among the many fine secondi is *storione al limone* (sturgeon from the Po river in a lemon sauce) and *maialino al latte* (pork cooked in milk).

La Locanda, Via Pallavicino 4, tel. 0372/457835, fax 0372/457834. Closed Tuesday and in much of August. All credit cards. Moderate.

Straightforward cooking in a restaurant that also has nine rooms to let. So you can enjoy a robust meal with lots of wine and then repair to your bed.

Porta Mosa, Via Santa Maria in Betlem 11, tel. 0372/411803. Closed Sunday, in August and at Christmas-time. All credit cards. Moderate.

This is a small restaurant, so reservations are essential. Very high quality cooking comes at a fair price. The pork, the duck, the sturgeon, and truffles in season are all delicious. Save room for a first-rate cheese platter, including the rarely seen *Parmigiano-Reggiano di vacche rosse*, the King of Cheeses, made with milk from native red cows.

SALUMI

Salumeria Paolo Saronni, Via Aselli 1.

Since 1936 this has been a source for fine *salumi* and *mostarda*. *Salame cremonese* is flavored with garlic and is soft and melting in texture (it must be refrigerated). *Cotechino* sausage here is dense and studded with black pepper and should be eaten hot.

TORRONE

Sperlari, Via Solferino. Closed Sunday (except in December) and Monday afternoon.

Sperlari was the first commercial producer of *torrone*, which it has been making since 1836. It can either be hard and crunchy or soft and rich. Classically it is eaten as is, but it can also be covered with chocolate or other flavorings. Sperlari's windows are a sight to behold: with beautifully arranged platters of candy, wine, *torrone* and cakes. Within is an immense selection of all of these products, as well as *mostarda*.

Pasticceria del Duomo, Largo Boccaccino (at the base of the Duomo).

Handmade *torrone*, plus *torta sbrisolona* and *mostarda*.

WINE

Centro Eno Gastronomico di G. Posio, Via Mercateio 16, tel. 0372/24473. Closed Monday morning.

Sells wine and wine-making equipment.

Lecco

A new provincial capital on the eastern shore of Lago di Como. The city is known to every Italian because it is the setting for most of the action in Alessandro Manzoni's *I Promessi Sposi* (1826, translated into English in 1828 as *The Betrothed*), the most famous Italian novel.

DINING

Ristorante Pizzoccheri, Via Aspromonte 21, tel. 0341/367126. Closed Wednesday, August, and Christmas New Year's. Moderate.

The Valtellina is straight up the eastern shore of Lago di Como from Lecco. If you cannot journey there, this restaurant will give you a fair sampling of some of that area's specialties. There is good *zuppa di orzo* and pretty good *pizzoccheri*. A nice light *secondo* is *bresaola* with Parmigiano and arugula and fresh mushrooms. There is also fine venison, grilled pork chops, and cheeses. The house wines are good examples of Valtellina reds. A delicious dessert is the *torta di crusca*, a tender bran cake.

Mantova

Mantova was one of the most splendid duchies during the Italian Renaissance and has always been a city of great sophistication and splendor. It is all the more impressive because it rises from an agricultural plain a bit removed from the main currents of traffic and commerce. Lovers of Verdi's opera *Rigoletto* know all about the Duke and the court at the Ducal Palace. This is one of the most magnificent palaces in Italy, and it should be visited. I commend to you the Sala degli Specchi (Room of Mirrors), where concerts by the likes of Monteverdi were given every Friday. The Sala dei Cavalli (Room of Horses) has a ceiling that should be examined in detail. Notice, in the six paintings of fruits and vegetables, the lettuces, onions, apples, pears, grain, garlic, turnips, and, especially, pineapples, which must have come from afar. To visit the palace you must take a tour, which lasts a little more than one hour. Signs in each room are in Italian and English.

BAKERIES
Panificio Freddi, Piazza Cavalotti 7, tel. 0376/321418. Closed Monday afternoon.

Everything you need in *mantovano* breads, pasta, and desserts. There is the famous *torta sbrisolona* and a cake called *elvezia*, with almonds, eggs, sugar, butter, rum, and chocolate. There is good *torta di tagliatelle* that also comes in a single serving. The delicious *salame di cioccolato* looks like a salami but is made of chocolate, crumbled cookies, candied fruit, and almonds. There is a large choice of *tortelli*, including the classic *zucca* and the unusual radicchio filling. There is also a huge selection of breads.

Pasticceria Caravatti, Piazza Erbe 16.

A place for coffee, *sbrisolona*, and *elvezia* since 1865.

Panicio Cavalli, Via Verdi.

Excellent *sbrisolona*.

BARS AND CAFFÈS
Caffè Roberta, Via Pescherie 34 (corner Via XX Settembre). Closed Sunday.

A good place to drink a cup of coffee and to purchase beans. Above the bar are a few lines, called *Il Caffè*, by Gabriele D'Annunzio:

Nero come la notte	Black as the night
Amaro come il dolore	Bitter as pain
Forte come lapassione	Strong as passion
Bruciante come il desiderio	Burning as desire

Bar-Confetteria La Ducale.

See "A Walk in Old Mantova," below.

Caffè TCS, Via Verdi 26.

A good tasting place for serious coffee drinkers.

CHOCOLATE
G. Zanini, Via Verdi 9–11.

An old, pretty chocolate shop.

DINING
Grifone Bianco, Piazza Erbe 6, tel. 0376/365423. Closed Tuesday, Wednesday lunch, and part of July. All credit cards. Moderate.

There is a general menu and a *menu mantovano*, with homemade *salame*

A typically foggy day in Mantova near the Via delle Pescherie

mantovano, tortelli di zucca or *agnoli* in broth, *luccio in salsa* or *stracotto,* then *sbrisolona.* There are other fine dishes, too, and a set menu that is an excellent value.

Antica Trattoria Cento Rampini, Piazza Erbe 11, tel. 0376/366349. Closed Sunday evening, Monday, last week of December, and first two weeks of August. American Express, MasterCard, Visa. Moderate to moderately expensive.

Mantovano cuisine in a nice setting.

Aquila Nigra, Vicolo Bonacolsi 4, tel. 0376/350651. Closed Sunday, Monday, late December–mid-January, and three weeks in August. All credit cards. Expensive.

Mantova's most famous restaurant serves excellent food. There are *mantovano* classics and lighter interpretations, such as

petto di piccione all'aceto balsamico e miele (breast of squab with balsamic vinegar and honey).

Osteria Ochina Bianca, Via Finzi, tel. 0376/323700. Reservations essential. Closed Monday, Tuesday lunch, mid-August, and first week in January. MasterCard, Visa. Moderate.

Delicious dishes, especially the various risottos using fine local rice, lake and river fish, *salumi,* and vegetables. This place is especially charming and has gained a national reputation among food lovers.

Trattoria Due Cavallini, Via Salnitro 5, tel. 0376/322084. Closed Tuesday and in August. American Express. Moderately inexpensive.

A wonderful old-style trattoria that serves genuine *mantovano* food. One novelty is the *bevr in vin,* a mixture of broth and Lambrusco wine that is a flavor of once upon a time. There is also excellent fresh pasta, boiled meats, and desserts such as *sbrisolona* and rice cake.

FOOD SHOPPING

Mantova's market is on the Piazza Erbe. There are a few stalls selling fruit, vegetables, seeds, bulbs, and cheese. Under the portico are meat stores. There has been a market here for centuries, and it makes a nice setting for the Ristorante Grifone Bianco (see "Dining," above).

Gastronomia Jotti, Piazza 80 Fanteria 8, tel. 0376/329350. MasterCard, Visa.

An elegant and appealing emporium with classic *salame mantovano, cotechino, pane-rone* cheese, local Lambrusco wine, and many excellent prepared dishes. These in-clude *risotto alla mantovana* (with *salame mantovano*), *tortelli di zucca, mostarda* made with apples, *luccio in salsa verde mantovano* (pike with a sauce of green peppers and an-chovy), *cappone Bartolomeo Stefani* (sweet-and-sour capon, a Renaissance dish), and many excellent cakes, pastries, and pud-dings. You can gather the fixings for many good meals here. Armando Jotti also sells all the local brands of rice and *bretelline di riso* (tagliatelle made of rice flour). You will notice, above the cash register, a photo-graph of Armando with Pope John Paul II.

Gianni-Giancarlo Virgilio, Via Verdi 40.

Milk, butter, and cheese from local cows, plus excellent *salumi.*

Lo Spiedo.

See "A Walk in Old Mantova," below.

A WALK IN OLD MANTOVA

Although you will not always realize it, Mantova is surrounded by lots of water—the Mincio River, many canals, and the Po, not very far away. When the rice paddies are flooded, things are even wetter. In the autumn and winter heavy fogs shroud the city's palaces, obscuring details but creating a romantic atmosphere. The waters of Mantova provide many fish, and they appear on the city's menus.

After a coffee at the Caffè Roberta, go down the Via Pescherie (Street of the Fisher-ies). This was the street where fish shops were in former times, and cooked fish were sold directly from the stalls. Part of the street is over a canal from which some fish were drawn. There is one fish stall left, continuing the tradition.

Pescheria Lanfranchi, Via Pescherie. Open 8:30–13h, 16:30–19:30h; closed Monday afternoon and Sunday.

There is a fine selection of local fish, sev-eral of which are carefully cooked. The *luccio in salsa* is worth trying if you have not tasted it elsewhere. The shop has no plastic forks, so come prepared.

Then walk over the covered stone pas-sageway above the canal to the Via Orefici, which is full of interesting old stores. These include the Pozzo pharmacy at #1, the Bar Noce at #5, the *salumeria* at #16 with its glass jars of *mostarda* in the window and the traditional *salame mantovano* within. At #26 is Manzotti, with its fascinating collection of scales old and new that are used to measure weight and volume of food. Notice the tiny scales for weighing spices and gold. The Erboristeria La Calendula is rather modern and is well stocked with herbs and herb products. At #40 is Lo Spiedo, an excellent *rosticceria* with *faraona disossato* (boned guinea fowl stuffed with rice and herbs), roast chicken, smoked goose breast, *arrotolato di coniglio* (boneless rabbit meat rolled

with vegetables and herbs—the same preparation is done with turkey). Turn left on the Via Calvi to the Bar La Ducale.

Bar-Confetteria La Ducale, Via Calvi 25. Closed Monday.

Dating back to the 1880s, full of beautiful oak and marble details. There is a small room in the back for coffee and conversation. The atmosphere is marred by a loud radio and a red digital printout promoting the bar's offerings. The original decor is worth a look, but for coffee and pastry I would go to the *pasticceria* at Via Calvi 9.

Milano

BAKERIES

Pasticceria Confetteria Cova, Via Montenapoleone 8, tel. 02/76000578.

Since 1817, this has been one of the most elegant places in town, with fancy pastries and delicate foods to go with your tea and coffee. Very chic.

Pasticceria Garbagnati, Via Victor Hugo 3 (near the Duomo).

A classic old bakery for panettone and other yeast cakes, plus cookies, breads, *crostate,* and pasta. This should be a stop for your walk around the Via Spadari (see page 193).

Pasticceria Ranieri, Corso Garibaldi 33, tel. 02/86462211.

One of my favorite bakeries in Milano for delicate *piccola pasticceria* made with per-

fect fresh fruit and cream. The people who work here are lovely, too.

Pasticceria-Confetteria Ricci, Piazza della Repubblica (corner Viale Ferdinando di Savoia and Via Pisani). Closed Saturday.

A gracious, old-style place for coffee, tea, and nice pastries, including panettone.

Panetteria Nonsolopane, Via Bigli 21, tel. 02/76014652. Closed Saturday afternoon and Sunday.

In the building where Einstein lived from 1894 to 1900 is Nonsolopane (Not Only Bread), with a wonderful range of baked goods, including *crostate* made with apricots, cherries, blueberries, chocolate, or apples; fresh panettone; hot brioches and rolls at 17h; many kinds of focaccia and other breads.

Milano's elegant Galleria connects La Scala and the Piazza del Duomo

BARS AND CAFFÈS

In the Galleria Vittorio Emanuele that connects La Scala and the Piazza del Duomo, there are several nice bars shoulder to shoulder with others that are crassly touristic. You should select one that suits your aesthetic. Mine is Il Camparino (at the corner of the Galleria and the Piazza del Duomo). It has been serving excellent coffee and hot chocolate since 1867 and, of course, Campari, Milano's *aperitivo* of choice. Make note of the chandeliers and mosaics.

Pasticceria Confetteria Cova.

See "Bakeries," above.

Pasticceria-Confetteria Ricci.

See "Bakeries," above.

COOKING SCHOOLS

Altopalato, Piazza Aspromonte 15/4, 20125 Milano, tel. 02/2664907.

This is one of the foremost cooking schools in Italy, notable for the range and quality of its courses. One can enroll to learn practical cookery or engage in classes that emphasize food history and gastronomic culture and tradition. There is also a strong appreciation of how food and wine work together, so one finds many sommeliers among the students. The school welcomes students and instructors from around the world, and there is great sense of cultural exchange and cross-pollination of skills and ideas.

L'Angolo della Gastronomia, Piazza del Carmine 6, 20121 Milano, tel. 02/874360.

A well-regarded school run by Ada Parasiliti. She changes topics frequently in her courses, which run from October to

May. Much depends on her mood, on available ingredients, on particular celebrations, or on requests. Her food covers Milanese classics, dishes from other Italian regions, and the cuisine of other nations that captures her fancy. The school is also where many Milanese children go for their first cooking classes.

La Nostra Cucina, Corso Monforte 15, 20122 Milano, tel. 02/799204.

A school that is very popular, due in part to the charm and talents of Laura and Margherita Landra, the two sisters who run it. They are the authors of several cookbooks and have quite a following. Most courses are given one day a week for several weeks, so you need to be in or near Milano for a while to attend classes. But some courses are more concentrated, and there are classes in English. The school is open from September through June and often has guest instructors if the sisters are otherwise engaged.

Sadler, Via Ettore Troilo 14, tel. 02/ 58104451, sadler@sadler.it. The restaurant is open for dinner Monday through Saturday; closed for two weeks in January and three weeks in August. All credit cards. Expensive.

The personality of this restaurant and cooking school is that of its owner, Claudio Sadler. His is a very personal cuisine that has a devoted following in Milano. You might choose first to dine at this restaurant in the atmospheric Navigli district of Milano and then to sign up for a class if you like the food. Many of the courses are given in one long day, which makes it suitable for intensive study for someone who is in town for only a few days.

CULTURE

I don't need to tell you that La Scala is an operatic shrine equalled only by the Staatsoper in Vienna, the old Paris Opera, and the Metropolitan in New York. It used to be impossible to get tickets to La Scala without paying a hotel concierge vast sums, but things have become more orderly. Demand still far outstrips supply, but if you plan far ahead you may be lucky. Teatro alla Scala, Via dei Filodrammatici 2, 20121 Milano, tel. 02/807041; ticket office fax 02/8879297, www.teatroallascala.it.

DINING

Milano, closer to the rest of Europe than Roma is, feels more like a European capital with business hotels, high fashion, high-powered nightlife, and famous and fancy restaurants. More than any Italian city, Milano has restaurants offering foreign food from Asia, Africa, the Americas, and elsewhere in Europe. There are also many regional Italian restaurants, especially Toscana, Sicilia, and Piemonte. Prices are significantly higher in places that are popular with business people and tourists. You should plan on spending more money for a full meal in Milano than you might elsewhere, or you can eat creatively, the way most *milanesi* do. This is the city of *panini*, sandwiches filled with delicious meats, cheeses, and vegetables that are sold in a Milanese creation called *la paninoteca*. I have also listed *osterie* and good restaurants that are worth spending some extra lire for. While reserving a table is a good idea anywhere in Italy, in Milano it is essential in everything but a *paninoteca*, pizzeria, or a simple trattoria.

Savini, Galleria Vittorio Emanuele II, tel. 02/72003433, savini@thi.it. Closed Sunday, the first week of January, and most of August. All credit cards. Moderately expensive.

Marino alla Scala, Piazza della Scala 5, tel. 02/80688021, ristorante@ marino allascala.it. Closed Saturday lunch, Sunday, from Christmas to January 6, and two weeks in August. All credit cards. From moderate to expensive.

Both Savini and Marino fulfil the idea of chic Milanese dining, complete with white-gloved service and lots of velvet. While this kind of place is not the main focus of this book, it is a reality in Milan and worth knowing if you are willing to dress elegantly and indulge in the experience. I like a post-opera plate of bresaola followed by a dish of made-to-order *risotto alla milanese.*

Latteria San Marco, Via San Marco 24, tel. 02/6597653. Closed Saturday and Monday, in August, and Christmastime. No credit cards. Moderately inexpensive.

This tiny restaurant, named Latteria as in the dairy shop that used to occupy this space, specializes in food and wine from Piacenza and Milano. Superb *salumi* start a meal which should also include a risotto and, if you are still hungry, either *cotoletta alla milanese* or *parmigiana di zucchine.*

L'Osteria del Treno, Via San Gregorio 46, tel. 02/6700479. Open daily; closed for ten days in mid-August and between Christmas and New Year. No credit cards. Moderate.

Located in a former *dopolavoro ferroviario,* the place where off-duty railway workers gathered for rest and recreation before taking the next trip out of nearby Milano Centrale. The decor is vintage Italian 1940s and 1950s, yet it has unquestionable appeal. Also appealing is the food as you can sample all sorts of delicacies. These might include goose products from Mortara, *petuccia* (a minced-meat sausage from Friuli), smoked eel from Tuscany, almonds from Puglia and Sicily, and so forth. One of the specialties is *tortelli d'alpeggio con pere e cannella* (pasta filled with soft cheese, pears and cinnamon).

La Piola, Viale Abruzzi 23, tel. 02/ 29531271. Closed Sunday, August, and Christmas-time. All credit cards. Moderate.

This welcoming little place in the eastern part of the city center should be your destination if you want Milanese classics such as risotto, *cotoletta alla milanese, rostin negàa, ossobuco, cassoeula,* as well as homemade pastas.

Trattoria da Abele, Via Temperanza 5, tel. 02/2613855. Open for dinner only, Tuesday through Sunday; closed from late July to early September. All credit cards. Moderately inexpensive to moderate.

It is almost a given that you will order a risotto for your primo, though the flavoring will always be distinct (goose breast and fennel one day, chard and ricotta the next, squid ink the day after that). My favorite secondi are based on game, braised and served with polenta.

La Veneta, Via Giusti 14, tel. 02/342881. Closed Monday. All credit cards. Moderate.

This restaurant has been here since the late 1960s and, in a neighborhood that is largely Chinese, seems very much a throwback. I like the *bigoli con anatra e melograno* (long strands of wholewheat noodles tossed with duck and pomegranate). Soup, risotto and fish are all stars as well, and many dishes are accompanied by the traditional white polenta.

Bottiglieria da Pino, Via Cerva 14, tel. 02/76000532. Open for lunch only, Monday through Saturday; closed in August and for two weeks at Christmas-time. No credit cards. Inexpensive to moderately inexpensive.

Finding good food for low prices in the city center is quite rare, so the *milanesi* clamor to get into this trattoria for its set price lunches of risottos, soups, beef or poultry, and many vegetarian options. If you are part of a group of at least thirty persons, you can book the restaurant to open for a private dinner.

Joia, Via Panfilo Castaldi 18, tel. 02/ 29522124, fax 02/2049244. Closed Saturday lunch, Sunday, most of August. All credit cards. Moderately expensive to expensive.

Not far from the Giardini Pubblici is this very particular restaurant that does superb work with vegetables and fish. This is so-called *cucina creativa* that does not hew to any region or tradition, but it is delicious and people pay considerable sums to savor it.

Ristorante Piero & Pia, Piazza Aspari 2 (Via Vanvitelli), tel. 02/718541. All credit cards. Moderate to moderately expensive.

Near the Città Studi, it is worth a taxi ride to enjoy the carefully prepared food from Lombardia and Emilia. They do everything right, and the quality and

consistency of what issues from the small kitchen is laudable.

Oste del Teatro, Via Pastrengo 16, tel. 02/ 69010293. Closed Saturday lunch and Sunday. No credit cards. Moderately inexpensive.

This osteria in the Teatro Verdi near Porta Garibaldi offers a warm welcome and delicious food with a Friulian accent. Not to miss is the *prosciutto di Sauris*, which is hard to find outside of the northeast. I also like *faraona* (guinea fowl) cooked in Ramandolo wine.

Al Merluzzo Felice, Via Lazzaro Papi 6, tel. 02/5454711. Closed Sunday, Monday lunch, and three weeks in August. All credit cards. Moderate to moderately expensive.

Reservations are essential at this tiny restaurant specializing in Sicilian cookery, especially fish and seafood.

Alla Collina Pistoiese, Via Amedei 1, tel./fax 02/877248. Closed Friday, Saturday lunch, Christmastime, Easter, and mid-August. All credit cards. Moderate to moderately expensive.

Dating from 1938, when many Tuscans came to Milano to open restaurants, this classic trattoria is big on nostalgia appeal and the comfort of familiar Milanese and Tuscan specialties.

Alla Cucina delle Langhe, Corso Como 6, tel. 02/6554279, fax 02/29006859. Closed Sunday (in July also Saturday), and in August. All credit cards. Moderate to moderately expensive.

Piemontese and Lombardo food are on the menu at this restaurant that is popular with Milanese media types. The food is tasty, but one comes here to see and be seen.

FOOD SHOPPING AROUND THE VIA SPADARI

Only a few blocks from the Piazza del Duomo and Piazza Cordusio is one of the great food districts in Italy. Much of it belongs to the empire known as Peck, one of the most famous purveyors in Europe. Wander around the Via Spadari, Via Speronari, and Via Victor Hugo any morning from Monday to Saturday, or Tuesday to Saturday in the late afternoon, especially in cooler months, and you will gain a sense of what *milanese* cooks have at their disposal.

Start by visiting Gastronomia Peck at Via Spadari 9. This is the domain of elegant and refined prepared foods, and you can find delicacies to make a great meal in your hotel room, on a picnic, or for your plane trip back home. Make note of how exquisitely displayed most of the food is. This is also the place to purchase a truffle or Parmigiano-Reggiano to take home. Peck also has its *rosticceria*, which is even more dazzling than the *gastronomia*. On any given day you might find *porchetta*, roast veal, stuffed squab, quail, pheasant, rabbit, sautéed *funghi porcini*, asparagus quiche, lasagne, grilled peppers, tarts, and wonderful baked goods.

Then go to the Bottega del Maiale across from the Gastronomia Peck to see the most amazing selection of pork products anywhere. Note, too, the magnificent window display. In the winter bolts of pigskin are often arranged like draped curtains around a proscenium, so that the window display seems like a stage set. Not to everyone's liking, to be sure, but talk about turning a sow into silk! Next door is the Pescheria Spadari, with enough types of fish and seafood to make King Neptune hoist his trident with pride.

The Casa del Formaggio, on Via Speronari, is one of the best cheese shops in Italy. I love the way wedges of Parmigiano-Reggiano are arranged in the window to look like a chain of Alps. There are more than three hundred types of Italian cheese here, and it is a good place to come if you will not have a chance to tour the nation but want to become acquainted with some of its finest cheeses. On the same street is the fine Rosticceria Fontana (for roasted poultry), Panerello (for homemade panettone), Grecchi il Pane (a good bread baker), L'Ortolan (outstanding fruits and vegetables), and Vino Vino (a well-stocked wine shop).

Back up the Via Spadari are the Gelateria Passerini, serving excellent ice cream since 1921, and Le Tre Marie, which can ship its panettone to you anywhere in the world. Around the corner, on Via Victor Hugo, is the Garbagnati bakery, described in "Bakeries," above. Across the way is the Giovanni Galli sweet shop, founded in 1900 and now run by Galli's grandson Edoardo. All of the delicacies are beautifully displayed, and the staff is exceedingly courteous. The marrons glacés, chocolates, panettone, and other enticements are all perfect.

One of the most popular dining places in these parts is the Peck snack bar next door, which is, in effect, a fast-food restaurant with good dishes at moderate prices. There is great wine at the bar by the glass or bottle, and it specializes in cocktails named for beloved composers. All of them are made with spumante and fresh fruit and were devised by opera lover Mauro Bertocchi of Peck's Bottega del Vino. To list but a few, the Puccini is made with mandarin oranges, Rossini with strawberries, Wagner with raspberries, and Donizetti with pomegranate. Of course, the bar serves a Bellini made with fresh peach juice, but this one honors composer Vincenzo Bellini, while the more famous Venetian Bellini is named for a painter.

FRUIT AND VEGETABLES

Primizie Angelo Grossi, Corso Monforte 20 (near Piazza San Babila).

An old-style, very elegant fruit stand with high molded ceilings, old scales, and artful displays of excellent produce.

SWEET SHOP

Specialità Dolciarie Regionali di Maria Battimelli, Via Meravigli (in central Milano, not far from Via Dante), tel. 02/8063828. Closed Sunday.

Maria Battimelli is a lovely woman from Ravello in Campania who remembers seeing many neorealist films shot there when she was a child. She has a very unusual shop in Milano that features the best cakes and candies from every region of Italy. There are *torrone* from Cremona and Benevento, *savoiardi* from Sardegna, *pampepato* from Ferrara, *baci di San Remo, torta paradiso* from Pavia, *pandoro* from Verona, cannoli shells from Sicilia, and much, much more. This is the only shop I know in Italy that sells so many special regional sweets.

Giovanni Galli.

See "Food Shopping around the Via Spadari," above.

Monticello Brianza (Como)

COOKING SCHOOL

GI—Corsi di Cucina, Via Foppa 1, 22068 Monticello Brianza (CO), tel. 039/9205254.

This school offers an interesting combination of elements that are typical of the Brianza, the populous area between Milano and Como. The owner, Giovanna Passeri, comes from a family of coastal *abbruzzese* origin, so fish cookery is emphasized. In addition, she also teaches *brianzola* cooking, dishes that are disappearing as the Brianza has evolved from a rural agricultural zone to a constellation of bedroom communities for people who work in Milano. Brianza cookery uses many of the great cheeses of Lombardia, such as Gorgonzola, *stracchino,* and *mascarpone.*

Mortara (Pavia)

Here is a nice little town with a great food heritage. Mortara gave most of the best goose dishes to Italian cuisine. Centuries ago, this was a Jewish enclave, and the goose historically has been linked to Jewish cooking, especially in central and Eastern Europe. In Mortara, goose *(oca)* is used to make *salame* and pâté, is minced to fill ravioli, is smoked or roasted to serve as a main course, or ground to use in risotto.

If you like the flavor of goose, you owe it to yourself to visit Mortara to appreciate how versatile an ingredient it can be. Autumn is the best time to come to sample the fullest range of goose preparations. Mortara is the principal town of the Lomellina, the western part of the province of Pavia, which is famous for its rice cultivation.

DINING

Ristorante-Albergo San Michele, Corso Garibaldi 20, tel. and fax 0384/99106. Closed Saturday, end of July, much of August, and Christmas–January 6. MasterCard, Visa. Moderate to moderately expensive.

If you make a day trip to Mortara from Milano or somewhere else, this might be a good choice for sampling some special goose dishes. It is only a few steps from the train station and therefore easily located. The *ristorante* serves goose dishes from mid-September to early March, although roast goose is only available in the autumn. Antipasti include goose liver pâté, *petto d'oca affumicato* (smoked goose breast), and goose *salame*. A very nice *primo* is the *risotto con radicchio e polpa d'oca*, excellent rice cooked with radicchio and ground goose meat. A *secondo* might be goose breast with tarragon or simple roast goose. There is a *menu d'oca* that is a pretty good deal given the quality of the food.

Ristorante Torino, Corso Torino. No credit cards. Inexpensive to moderate.

About a ten-minute walk from town in the direction behind the train station is this excellent restaurant that shows off the best of regional cooking (the risotto is a very inexpensive bargain). There are all the goose specialties, as well as the *salame di duja*, the fat-wrapped delicacy from Novara that is served—in season—with succulent fresh figs. There is also lard scented with fresh rosemary. Among the risottos is one made with goose meat; another has creamy *robbiola* cheese and freshly ground green peppercorns; the *risotto alla vogherese* is made of red, green, and yellow peppers. In September the *ristorante* makes a special roast goose with rosemary and honey. There is also good grilled meat if you have tired of goose. Also consider *porcini alla milanese*, breaded wild mushrooms that are delicately sautéed. Save room for a slice of excellent Gorgonzola cheese before advancing to one of the excellent homemade desserts: *torta di marroni* (chestnut cake); apple strudel; *torta di fragole* (strawberry cake); *torta di amaretti;* and a terrific cake of pears and mascarpone cheese. This is a pleasant place, simply decorated. There is an intriguing collection of framed stock and bank notes from the 1930s and 1940s that have a peculiar beauty all their own.

FOLKLORE

La Sagra del Salame dell'Oca.

On the last Sunday of September all the producers in town offer their *salami* for tasting with local wine. There is often singing and dancing, too.

FOOD STORES

Food stores in Mortara are closed on Sunday and on Monday either in the morning or afternoon.

Salumeria Guarnaschelli, Corso Garibaldi 84, tel. 0384/98795.

Do not be fooled by the lack of showy display in this shop. It produces delicious foods based on local products such as goose, rice, and good cheeses. Guarnaschelli is especially admired for its excellent goose products: homemade *salame*, goose-liver pâté, smoked goose breast, and so on. It roasts and sells geese filled with prunes. Also available are *offelle di Parona*, small oval cakes made with flour, eggs, butter, sugar, and olive oil. These are named for a nearby town that has a folkloric event to celebrate its local specialty. (See the listing under "Parona.")

Pasta Fresca Mario Lalla, Corso Garibaldi 110, tel. 0384/92579.

Fine fresh pasta is made in this shop. In season (from December to Christmas) you can purchase goose-filled ravioli and, on order, goose-filled cannelloni. The ravioli should be boiled in water or, ideally, goose broth and served with melted butter and Parmigiano-Reggiano.

Antica Macelleria Rossi, Via San Giovanni 18.

An excellent butcher shop, with fresh goose in season and other goose products throughout the year.

Parona (Pavia)

FOLKLORE
La Sagra dell'Offella.

On the first Sunday in October, *offelle di*

Parona are served for dipping in spumante while everyone in the village turns out to sing and dance.

Pavia

Pavia is an ancient city whose greatness came more than 1,300 years ago, when it was the capital of much of the Italian peninsula. Its university is one of Italy's finest, along with those of Bologna and Padova. It is the capital of a province larger than that of Milano to the immediate north. It is also a very provincial place, despite its heritage. Aside from the University of Pavia, it is known primarily as the fur capital of Italy. Women come to Annabella and other *pavese* furriers from Milano, Torino, Parma, and elsewhere. If they arrive by rail, a car whisks them to Annabella on the Piazza Vittoria. After shopping, they are offered a cocktail at the Bar Demetrio, a provincial take on big-city elegance. In the late autumn, *pavese* women gather there wrapped in furs newly out of the vault and nibble on triangles of crustless white bread topped with mayonnaise-laden spreads while sipping pink and orange cocktails.

There is another Pavia, that of the Borgo, where one drinks wine from the nearby Oltrepò Pavese and eats risotto, frogs, river fish, and meat. The Borgo, which is the community on the quiet side of the Ticino River, used to be very rustic and full of *osterie* offering cheap wine and food to students who would stay up late debating and flirting. I was a student in Pavia for a year in the late 1970s and spent many happy hours in the *osterie,* living the life of the kind of student one sees in Middle European operettas. There are a few old-style *osterie* left, while others have been prettified and now are moderately expensive restaurants.

Pavia has several food specialties. The most famous is *zuppa pavese,* but there is also *risotto alla certosina,* created by the monks of the Certosa di Pavia. Frogs figure in local cooking, as do beef, butter, and cheese (especially the sweet-sour Certosa). There is also a distinguished baking tradition in the area.

BAKERIES

Pasticceria Medagliani, Corso Cavour 37, tel. 0382/22748. Open 8–12:30h, 15–19:30h; closed Monday.

When I was a student in Pavia I had to travel to Milano several days a week. As I walked to the train station I always managed to stop at Medagliani for a slice of *crostata* and a coffee. At the time this bakery was well stocked and homey. It has now been gussied up, but the quality of the baking is undiminished. Each day the window has several enormous *crostate,* each filled with different fruits. There are all the ones you might expect, as well as unusual flavors such as *merasca* (sour plum from the former Yugoslavia) or *ribes* (red currants). There are many other good cakes and cookies and a nice coffee bar.

Pasticceria Vigoni, Strada Nuova 110, tel. 0382/22103. Open 8–19:30h, Sunday 8–13h, 15–19:30h; closed Tuesday.

Since 1878 Vigoni has been a favorite spot in Pavia for cake, coffee, and tea in its welcoming old rooms. The famous cake is the *torta paradiso.* Vigoni also makes ice cream.

BARS AND CAFFÈS

Bar Demetrio, Corso Strada Nuova 86. Open 7–20:30h, Saturday 7–2h.

An interesting social study. This bar probably has more fur-clad women and silk- or cashmere-clad men than any spot on earth.

Pasticceria Medagliani.

See "Bakeries," above.

Bar V2, Piazza della Vittoria. Closed Tuesday.

A chic little bar with outdoor tables on one of Pavia's more attractive squares.

Pasticceria Vigoni.

See "Bakeries," above.

DINING

Antica Osteria del Previ, Via Milazzo 65, Borgo Basso, tel. 0382/26203. Closed Wednesday. MasterCard, Visa. Moderately expensive.

A nice cozy setting on the banks of the Ticino with service that is friendly and relaxed. Most of the wines are local and are labeled "O.P." (Oltrepò Pavese). Among the interesting antipasti are *anguilla al timo* (eel flavored with thyme) and *fegato d'anatra alle mele* (duck liver with apples). You should have risotto as a *primo,* which might be flavored with radicchio, speck, or frog's legs. For *secondi,* there is a genuine *cotoletta alla milanese* and several preparations of sturgeon *(storione)* and mullet *(triglie).*

Osteria della Malora, Via Milazzo 79, tel. 0382/34302. Closed Monday. American Express, MasterCard, Visa. Moderate.

A simple, unreconstructed Borgo *osteria* with respectable food and wine.

Ristorante Balin, Via Milazzo 97, tel. 0382/23164. Closed Monday. American Express, MasterCard, Visa. Moderately expensive.

A more upscale Borgo restaurant with nouvelle touches in the menu. Quite pleasant.

FOOD SHOPPING

Gastronomia Radaelli, Corso Cavour 11. Closed Monday afternoon and Sunday.

There has been a food store on this site since 1800, and Signor Radaelli has been here since 1954. You can buy many foods of the province of Pavia here, including many brands of rice, *salame d'oca,* white truffles,

and wine from the Oltrepò. *Torta paradiso* by Vigoni, *mostarda* from Cremona, saffron, and many prepared foods.

Castellami, Piazza Sabbione 4.

This is an excellent supplier of all manner of dried beans and legumes, rice, seeds, dried herbs, and spices.

ICE CREAM

Gelateria Moderna, Corso Cavour 40A. Open 6:30–12h, 14–20h; closed Thursday.

The ice cream here has a good, particularly milky flavor.

WINE

Enoteca Bolis, Corso Manzoni 27 (near the train station), tel. 0382/32328, or Via Bernardo da Pavia 9/11, tel. 0382/35575.

Two branches of a very good wine store. You can find an excellent selection of wines from the Oltrepò Pavese.

Pognana Lario (Como)

FOLKLORE

La Sagra degli Gnocchi e delle Salamelle.

On August 15 and 16 gnocchi are served

with boiled sausage, and everything is washed down with wine served from a large old barrel.

Raffa del Garda (Brescia)

OLIVE OIL AND OTHER LOCAL PRODUCTS

La Bottega del Nonno Francesco, Via Nazionale 68, tel. 0365/654281. Open daily 8–12:30h, 14–19h. American Express, MasterCard, Visa.

Some of the finest olive oil from Lago di Garda is produced in this little town on

the Lombard side of the lake. Emperor Akihito of Japan has his oil sent from here. The emperor and many other people like a very delicate oil called El Gargnà. This is made from an olive of the same name and refers to its town of origin, Gargnano, just up the road. There are other good oils here, too. This store is full of products from local farmers and cooks, including jams, pastas, pâtés, sauces, local olives, wood-roasted coffee. Look for *offelle del* *Garda,* a typical local cake made of corn-meal, orange peel, sugar, butter, and yeast.

Robbio (Pavia)

This is a town that you would never think to enter, but a great meal awaits. Robbio is actually a well-off place, thanks to the lumber mill that has provided employment to the town. But before we dine at Da Mino, there is a story to tell: Robbio is in the middle of the rice belt, and if you were to walk out of town to the *risaie* (rice fields), you would encounter a vanishing civilization. Once upon a time, rice cultivation was backbreaking work that required manual labor. During the course of the rice-growing season, the paddies must be periodically flooded. This particular phenomenon creates an environment in which some of the largest mosquitoes imaginable can breed. One of the natural predators of the mosquito is the frog, who breeds in the canals that are used to flood the paddies. In the past, men and women would go down to the canals to catch frogs, the local specialty in the cuisine of the province of Pavia. When I was a student at the University of Pavia in the late 1970s, it was possible to go to *osterie* near the Ticino River to eat rice and frog's legs while drinking Bonarda wine.

Somehow the generation of frog catchers has almost vanished, and they have not been replaced. At one time the frog population was so vast that frogs would jump out of the canals, only to be run over by cars at night. In the morning, local birds such as ravens were frequently killed as they swooped down to eat flattened frogs, only to be run over by cars themselves. But these are days long gone. At the same time, rice cultivation has become more mechanized and, in some cases, more dependent on chemicals, causing the frog population to decline at the same precipitous rate as the frog catchers. Yet as is so often the case, a food that was once an inexpensive staple of the poor has now become a luxury item. It seems that as the supply dwindles, the demand for frogs increases not only in Pavia, but on fancy tables in Milano and Torino. Frogs are harder than ever to find, and their price has skyrocketed.

In Robbio, frogs still breed in a canal that is used to flood the rice fields. Here you might find the spry old woman who told me she is the Frog Lady of Robbio. I doubt she would mind if I described her as salt-of-the-earth. She does not know of fancy restaurants in big cities, but merely goes to this waterway because it has been customary to do so in these parts for centuries. When I met her on a steamy summer's day she wore a broad straw hat and a large apron that she folded up around her waist. She carried a long pole with a short string that she dipped into the water. Imitating frog noises, she attracted her prey in short order, yanked it from the canal, and, as she sang a little song in dialect, broke its neck and dropped it into her apron. As her catch grew, so did her smile. This may sound horrific to some people, but it is a fact of life of *la civiltà contadina,* the disappearing world of rural peasant life. The frogs are sold locally, and the Frog Lady of Robbio makes a few extra lire to augment her small pension.

Even if you do not want to explore the froggy side of life in Robbio, there is a restaurant that merits a trip here all the same. Ristorante da Mino has all the sincerity and humility of country people and genuinely outstanding food that most posh city restaurants can only hope to emulate.

DINING

Ristorante da Mino, Via San Valeriano 5, tel. 0384/672216. Reservations essential. Closed Sunday evening, Monday, and in August. No credit cards. Moderate to moderately expensive.

To me, this is the summit of risotto cookery. While there are many restaurants from Pavia to Vercelli that make excellent rice dishes, Da Mino is truly special. When you dine there, you simply reserve a table, and then the food that issues from the kitchen is up to the cook. As this is right in the middle of rice country, you should expect to have risotto as the centerpiece of your meal. What I did not understand at first was why nine fabulous antipasti preceded the arrival of the rice. The answer is that (unlike most places, even those that say otherwise) risotto here is made *from scratch* and takes twenty-five to forty minutes from the time it is ordered. So first comes a parade of exquisite flavors: homemade *salame;* prosciutto of *cinghiale* (wild boar); *bresaola di cavallo* (horse) with truffle oil; lightly cooked raw beef served with oil, lemon, arugula, and shards of Parmigiano-Reggiano; vegetable carpaccio, made of white zucchini; fresh mozzarella with tomatoes and green olives;

carne alla griglia con il latte (chopped meat lightly breaded, dipped in milk, and fried); grilled eggplant with *pancetta,* mozzarella, and tomato; grilled strips of beef rolled with greens. All of this food was delicious and delicate, so that I still happily anticipated the risotto. I was not disappointed: the *risotto di funghi porcini* had perfectly cooked, slightly chewy rice with large pieces of fresh wild mushrooms. This was followed by a roasted breast of duck with zucchini. Dessert was a magnificent *macedonia di frutta.* In most restaurants, this fruit salad is made of bits of fruit that have become mushy thanks to the high amount of citric acid that is added to prevent discoloration. At Da Mino, the *macedonia* was made with large pieces of perfect, just-cut fruit that were dressed with a combination of sherry, Grand Marnier, and Rosolio (a rose-flavored liqueur). The wines were honest, which is to say that they are mostly of local production (from the Oltrepò Pavese) and marry well with the food. They are not well known, but they are delicious. While his wife cooks in the kitchen, Mino is a consummate host, serving with great pride and care. A meal here will be a pleasure that you will not soon forget.

Salò (Brescia)

This town has a famous and checkered history owing to its association with Mussolini, who made his last stand here (and was made welcome) when the rest of Italy finally rejected him. Gabriele D'Annunzio spent time here with Eleonora Duse, and many other famous Italians have used this site as a retreat for decadent love affairs. It is an attractive town, notable for the gourmet traveler because of an outstanding bakery and a very interesting hotel restaurant.

BAKERY-BAR

Pasticceria Di Novo, Via Buttirini 24, tel. 0365/20314. Closed Monday.

Carmelo di Novo is a master baker whose creations taste as good as they look. He is from Sicilia and, although he is a young man, draws from a long tradition in his native region. His cousin in Sicilia grows yeasts, and Carmelo showed me a twenty-six-year old fresh yeast that he has taken with him from Toscana to New York to the Italian pavilion at Disney World's Epcot in Orlando. His yeasty brioche and good coffee make the best breakfast in town. Among the other things I loved were the *ovis*, wonderful egg-yolk cookies with apricot, in which sensations of sweetness, softness, dryness, and butteriness are all in balance. There are beautiful marzipan roses, cakes made of rice or polenta, and many fruits. Highly recommended.

DINING

Hotel Laurin, tel. 0365/22022, fax 0365/22382. Closed December 20– January 20. All credit cards. Expensive.

This magnificent hotel was built as a villa in 1905, and the furnishings were installed between then and 1920. It became a hotel about 1960. The public rooms on the main floor are full of stunning frescoes. The dining room is one of the most splendid I know in Italy, with columns, frescoes, and handsome furniture. The room exalts the sense of power, ambition, and empire so dear to early-twentieth-century political figures as well as Brescia's industrialists today. It is possible to have the *Menu Gardesano*, made entirely with flavors drawn from the lake and the area nearby. There is perch with local olives and tomatoes, excellent *tortelli di anatra* (duck-filled pasta) with butter and truffles, and *petto di faraona con salsa di melograno*, guinea fowl with pomegranate sauce. These decadent tastes are in keeping with the setting and the mood. Other good dishes are *risotto con salamella mantovana* and *filletto di orata con cipolle rosse* (*orata* with red onions). Two good desserts are chestnut s*emifreddo* and *mousse au chocolat*. The wine list is well chosen and is moderate in price.

Ristorante 100 km; Hotel Bellerive, Via Pietro da Salò 11, tel. 0365/520410, fax 0365/290709. All credit cards. Moderate to moderately expensive.

The idea of the 100 km restaurant is that all the ingredients and wines used there be from within 100 kilometers (62 miles) of where they originated. There is lake fish, local olive oil, various polentas, meats, and fine fruit and vegetables at the peak of ripeness. A worthy meal in the restaurant devoted to what is special about the food and wine produced.

San Giorgio di Mantova (Mantova)

RICE

Riseria Campanini, Via Ghisiolo 67,   tel. 0376/340170.

Rice comes in many types, with different textures and lengths. Some of the most famous are Vialone Nano (which constitutes only 2.7 percent of national production), Carnaroli, and Arborio. Each is distinct (although connoisseurs consider Vialone Nano the best), and favorites are based purely on personal preference, much as with Beluga, Ossetra, and Sevruga caviar. These rice varieties are all grown and sold by Campanini, one of Italy's most successful producers.

Solferino (Mantova)

AGRITOURISM

Le Barche, Via Barche 6, tel. 0376/855262.
Reservations essential. Open year-round;
closed Tuesday. No credit cards.
Inexpensive.

This is a modern working farm on the fringes of town that produces salami, poultry, beef, pork, fruit, vegetables, jams, and wine. It is possible to sleep here (there are twelve beds) or to come for a meal. All the classics of Mantova's cuisine are here, and well prepared. One unusual and good dish is pasta served with a ragù of squab *(piccione)*.

Sondalo (Sondrio)

DINING AND LODGING

La Baita, Frazione Bailè—Strada
Bernardo, tel. 0342/801159. Open daily
June–December. No credit cards.
Inexpensive.

High in the mountains of the Valtellina (1,860 meters, or 6,138 feet) is a dairy farm that produces cheese, milk, and butter. It also has twelve beds and serves food to those who may want to come by for a meal. Specialties include *pizzoccheri, tortelloni* filled with spinach and ricotta, polenta with cheese, and wild forest mushrooms. You can walk off your meal with a hike in the beautiful surroundings.

Tirano (Sondrio)

FOLKLORE

On the second Sunday in September there is a festival with parades, brass bands, and consumption of polenta with melted cheese, plus grilled sausages and meats.

Tremezzo (Como)

DINING

La Fagurida, Località Rogaro di
Tremezzo, tel. 0344/40676. Closed
Monday and Christmas–February 15.
No credit cards. Moderate to moderately
expensive.

Tremezzo occupies a favored position on Lago di Como, and Rogaro is 1.5 kilometers (1 mile) above it. But La Fagurida is attractive for more than its view. There is an imposing selection of dishes that represent the food of the lake, the Alps, and the Brianza. So your *primo* might be soup or pasta or risotto, and polenta will surely come with your *secondo*, which will be braised or roasted meat or perhaps broiled fish. The flavors and the pleasant setting make this one of my preferred restaurants in the Como area, which is not blessed with an abundance of good eating places.

Uboldo (Varese)

COOKIE MUSEUM
Collezione Lazzaroni, Via IX Novembre 4,
tel. 02/967661.

In the factory where *amaretti di Saronno* and all the other famous cookies are baked is a collection relating to the history of the company and its products. You can see old utensils, cookbooks, milk containers, and all the stamps and molds used to make cookies. You will also see some of the earliest cookie-making machines.

Viganò Brianza (Como)

RESTAURANT AND
COOKING SCHOOL
Ristorante Pierino, Via XXIV Maggio 16,
22060 Viganò Brianza (CO),
tel. 039/956020.

The food here is lively, flavorful, and personable, much like Tiziana Penati, the owner. She also conducts a wide range of cooking classes, covering classical cuisine as well as dishes that appeal to newer cooks or those without a lot of time. There are special classes in fall and spring about all kinds of mushrooms. Signora Penati is very knowledgeable about wine and teaches courses about its history, its traditions, and the infinite variety and pleasures that characterize it. The cooking classes also show much more wine influence than do those at many other schools.

Vigevano (Pavia)

Vigevano is famous as one of the biggest shoemaking centers in the world and for its Piazza Ducale, one of the most beautiful squares in Italy. It is a pleasure to loll at one of the *caffès* on the piazza to drink in the intricate design and gracefulness of this high point in Renaissance town planning.

BAKERY
El Prestinè, Via G. Silva 15. Closed

Monday.

The name is a dialect corruption of *il*

prestinario, an old word for "bread baker." There is very good Gorgonzola focaccia, plus fresh breadsticks, baguettes, and other fragrant goodies.

BAR-CAFFÈ

Caffè Commercio, Piazza Ducale 24. Open 7:30–24h; closed Wednesday.

Ideal for admiring the piazza. I had a very good *granita di anguria,* a soft, cooling watermelon ice.

FOOD STORE

Macelleria di Via Dante, Via Dante 32, *tel. 0381/85797. Open 8:30–12:30h, 16–19:30h; closed Monday afternoon and Sunday.*

A very good source for the food specialties of the Lomellina, the rice-growing region at the confines of Vigevano. There are sacks of local rice that will make for a grand risotto back home. You will see bins full of dried mushrooms and different pastas. Also there are goose products from Mortara, Gorgonzola from Novara, and other fine cheeses from throughout Lombardia. The wines are from the Oltrepò Pavese.

Vighizzolo di Montichiari (Brescia)

DINING

Trattoria Rosalia Moretti, Via San Giovanni 124, tel. 030/961010. Closed Wednesday and in August. No credit cards. Moderate.

Push hard on the door to the bar that is the first of three rooms at this trattoria in the flat, fertile plains of southern Lombardia. This is not the image most travelers have of Italy, and certainly the nearby industrial complex of Montichiari does not add beauty to the landscape. Yet here people work very hard and eat the sort of substantial food served at Trattoria Rosi (as this place is called locally). Although reportedly in her midseventies, Rosalia projects a vigor and industry of someone much younger. The food, she told me, is seasonal—as it should be. Her *vitello tonnato,* for example, is only served in the summer. In most places, this ubiquitous dish is corrupted by the use of mayonnaise. Rosalia makes it in the classic version, topping cool, thin slices

of veal with a sauce made of capers, tuna, and herbs that have been blended. Enter the second room, and you will see the kitchen to the left. This trattoria seems to be owned and operated only by women. You will see them cooking, cleaning, preparing, serving, and ironing, all done with joy and assurance. To the right is a grill in a fireplace that produces excellent grilled chicken and other meats. The third room, with its vaulted brick ceiling, is the main dining room (there are two other rooms in the rear for spillover traffic). All the food I tasted was wonderful: superb *casonsei* and *tortelli di zucca,* both in sweet butter with a bit of nutmeg; very tender *stracotto* of beef with polenta; and grilled chicken served with cooked cauliflower, string beans, and salsify. The cauliflower is cooked until very soft and creamy, unusual and special. The crumbly, moist homemade walnut cake, the *torta di noci,* is a real star. Excellent coffee and service.

Villimpenta (Mantova)

FOLKLORE
Sagra del Risotto.

In May there is feasting on risotto made with meat and/or sausage.

Risotto agli Asparagi
Asparagus Risotto

Although this is not the way everyone cooks risotto, this recipe works well.

Serves 4
450 grams/1 pound thin asparagus
1½ liters/6¾ cups good beef stock
200 grams/7 ounces Vialone or other good
   Italian rice
1 tablespoon unsalted butter
1 cup freshly grated Parmigiano-Reggiano

Wash the asparagus and remove the white end from each spear. Then cut the green asparagus into 2½-centimeter (1-inch) lengths. In a large pot bring the stock to a boil. Add the asparagus. When the stock returns to a boil, add the rice and stir continuously over medium-low heat until the rice is cooked, usually about 25 minutes. Remove from the heat, stir in the butter and Parmigiano-Reggiano, and serve immediately. Have the wedge of cheese and the grater available for those who want additional cheese on their risotto.

Wine: A medium red from the Oltrepò Pavese or the Valtellina. A good white might be Bianco di Custoza or Soave from the Veneto.

Risotto agli Asparagi (alternate version)
Asparagus Risotto

Serves 4
3 tablespoons unsalted butter
450 grams/1 pound thin asparagus
1½ liters/6¾ cups good beef stock
200 grams/7 ounces Vialone or other good
   Italian rice
1 cup freshly grated Parmigiano-Reggiano

Wash the asparagus and remove the white end from each spear. Then cut the green asparagus into 2½-centimeter (1-inch) lengths. In a large pot bring the stock to a boil. Add the asparagus. Cook for a minute or so, so that the asparagus are tender but not soft. Remove the asparagus and set aside. In a large, heavy-bottomed pot melt 2 tablespoons of butter. Add the rice and brown slightly. Then add ladlefuls of stock, one at a time, stirring all the while with a wooden spoon. Once all the stock has been added, then add the asparagus, which will come somewhat undone and will color and flavor the risotto. Stir continuously over medium-low heat until the rice is cooked, usually about 25 minutes. When the rice is cooked the grains should be chewy and there should be a slight creaminess in the pot owing to the starch that has been absorbed by the remaining broth. Remove from the heat, stir in 1 tablespoon more of butter and the Parmigiano-Reggiano and serve immediately. Have the wedge of cheese and the grater available for those who want additional cheese on their risotto.

Wine: A medium red from the Oltrepò Pavese or the Valtellina. A good white might be Bianco di Custoza or Soave from the Veneto.

Cotoletta alla Milanese
Classic Milanese Breaded Veal Cutlet

This is a dish that is so weighted down with misconceptions and poor execution (outside of Milano) that I view presenting the recipe in this book as part of an effort to right many wrongs. Too often the veal is heavily breaded and the whole thing is deep-fried. Just as often, it is bathed in tomato sauce. Note that on many menus it is referred to as costoletta. Non-Milanese assume that this dish is made with a boneless veal cutlet, but it is also common to use a thin chop on the bone. Either way, the veal must be pounded before cooking to tenderize the meat. A milanese cutlet (with or without the bone) is not a thin strip like a scallopina, but is larger: at least the size of a large hand. Try to find a butcher who will cut the meat properly.

Serves 2

2 large veal cutlets, with or without bone, pounded thin
2 medium or large eggs
Unflavored bread crumbs, preferably fresh
Salt and freshly ground black pepper to taste
4 tablespoons unsalted butter
¼ lemon, halved (optional)

Pound the veal as thin as possible. Beat the eggs and then dip a veal cutlet in them. Lift it up and let any extra egg slide off. After this step, press both sides of the cutlet into a plate of bread crumbs to which a little salt and pepper have been added. The veal should be thoroughly covered but not overloaded. Lift the breaded cutlet and let any extra crumbs fall off. Repeat the process with the other cutlet. Melt the butter in a large, heavy-bottomed pan and cook the cutlets on both sides over medium heat. They should be golden brown, but not burned. Serve them immediately, accompanied by a wedge of lemon for those who want it.

Wine: A medium red from the Valtellina or the Oltrepò Pavese, or a Dolcetto.

Veneto

We are living at Danieli's Hotel, formerly a splendid Palace with marble staircase and doors and Balconies looking out on the sea covered with ships and churches and the Doge's Palace, the finest building in the world, with St. Mark's Place & Church 100 yards off. There, every night the Austrian Band plays, the finest trained I ever heard, numbering about 60 men. The whole of Venice seems to turn in there at that time. The place is like a vast drawing room lighted enough by the gas from the arcades all round the square under which sit all the Ladies & gentlemen at their coffee, iced water and cigars with a dense crowd in the centre of men, women, children, soldiers, Turks, magnificent Greek costumes and sky above studded with innumerable twinkling stars. I was walking there with John last night till past eight without any bonnet but with my hair dressed—walking about like all the rest amongst the crowd, taking our coffee under the Arcade and enjoying ourselves extremely.

EFFIE (MRS. JOHN) RUSKIN, 1849 LETTER

REGIONAL CAPITAL:
Venezia (VE).

PROVINCIAL CAPITALS:
Belluno (BL), Padova (PD), Rovigo (RO), Treviso (TV), Verona (VR), Vicenza (VI).

TOURIST INFORMATION:
Azienda Autonoma Soggiorno e Turismo, Regione Veneto, 4089 Rialto, Venezia, tel. 041/5226110.

Most visitors to the Veneto seldom venture beyond its capital, Venezia. This is not surprising, for Venezia is one of the great destinations of the world. Its unique aspects are legendary, and you certainly do not need my words to convince you to go there. I too am enchanted by its singular beauty, its past and present glory, and the feelings of fragility it provokes. This fragility is not only archi-

tectural. In Venezia I have a stronger sense of human frailty, of the evanescence of life and the desire to find meaning in it. As a native of New York City (who majored in Venetian history in college), I have often been struck by the similarities between these two cities. Both are island cities that have been seats of empire. As economic capitals, they had large mercantile classes and citizens who looked to the world beyond their mainland nation. These are cities where people are valued for genius and creativity, not merely for the ability to seize and maintain power and wealth. Each has citizens who are pragmatic and have chosen to live where they do in the face of adversity. These citizens love art, theater, spectacle, and festivity. And both New York and Venezia are places where others come, to desire, to hope, to achieve, to escape, and to disappear.

As the leading commercial city of the Italian Renaissance, Venezia imported many products from Asia and the Middle East. It looked eastward for spices and was for a long time the center of the world spice trade. On the wall of the Caffè Florian—where Mrs. Ruskin took coffee—are frescoes depicting Eastern motifs, including products such as cinnamon and coffee. Venetian cooking is a combination of the bounty from the sea and the mainland (which was part of the Venetian republic until 1797) as well as the subtle influence of the East: sweet-and-sour fish with raisins, nutmeg or cinnamon in pasta sauces, pastries perfumed with rosewater, and so forth. Visitors to Venezia seldom encounter these dishes because most of them dine at restaurants geared to tourists, where, sadly, the level of cooking is probably the lowest of any major city in Italy. Some of my restaurant recommendations are a bit afield of the main tourist districts, but you will be more likely to taste food as the Venetians know it.

As you walk around Venezia, there are two other things I would like you to bear in mind. First, this is one of the only important Italian cities that was not founded by the Romans or more ancient peoples. When Aquileia in Friuli was destroyed by Attila the Hun in the fifth century, refugees fled to more than one hundred inhospitable islands in a lagoon north of the Adriatic Sea. Through sheer will, energy, and genius, they not only survived but created a glorious city that was one of the zeniths of world civilization. Everything had to be brought to the city by boat. (The railway and vehicular bridge from the mainland was not built until 1846.)

Second, pay special attention to the acoustics of Venezia. In the absence of automobiles and much of the machinery of modern life it is possible, in this city, to hear things you otherwise would not detect. Footsteps become audible, as does the sound of raindrops hitting pavement. Speaking voices carry much farther, and so does music, which is why Effie Ruskin was so entranced. The sounds of cooking, of clattering dishes, of popping corks and clinking glasses, are all more palpable in Venezia. In other words, one hears in this city the sounds of daily life on a human scale.

For travelers who go beyond Venezia, a special region awaits. There is an impressive variety of landscapes, from the beaches of the Adriatic, to the hills in the provinces of Padova, Vicenza, and Treviso, to the beautiful if overbuilt eastern shore of Lago di Garda, through zones of intense viticulture, past some of the world's most magnificent villas, to the heights of Belluno and Cortina d'Ampezzo for alpine food and Olympic-quality skiing.

Throughout the Veneto polenta is the starch of choice, although rice and pasta dishes abound. Inland, the people are meat eaters, while at the shore, not surprisingly, fish and seafood are preferred. Many of the cities are distinct and beautiful and have food specialties of their own. Verona is the home of Romeo and Juliet, Italy's most famous opera festival, stunning architecture, and, above all, some of the most intensive wine production in the country. Bardolino, Valpolicella, Amarone, Bianco di Custoza, and Soave are but a few of the varieties produced there. Verona is full of delightful wine bars and each April is the site of Vinitaly, the largest wine exposition in Italy. Verona's province also makes superb olive oil and is one of the biggest tourist magnets in Italy because of its excellent attractions.

Radicchio from Treviso

The neighboring province of Vicenza is also full of wine, from the dependable Zonin (Italy's largest winery) to the outstanding wines made by Fausto Maculan in Breganze. Smaller towns not to miss in this province include Marostica (which produces delicious cherries and has a famous chess match on its piazza in which humans are the chess pieces) and Bassano del Grappa (which makes excellent grappa and ceramics and produces gorgeous white asparagus each spring). Vicenza itself is most noted as the laboratory of Andrea Palladio (1505–1580), the most important architect of the past five hundred years. His work is everywhere in and around Vicenza, and no lover of architecture should skip this city. Vicenza also has Italy's finest library of food history, with volumes dating back hundreds of years. In Vicenza one eats codfish and Asiago cheese.

The little-visited province of Rovigo is sandwiched between Emilia-Romagna and the rest of Veneto and draws characteristics from both regions. It is not unlike the neighboring province of Padova. The largest city in the region, Padova is the Veneto's economic center, and is the seat of one of Italy's foremost universities. Padova is full of art treasures (including the incomparable Scrovegni Chapel with its thirty-eight Giotto frescoes) and, in my opinion, has the second-best food markets in Italy after those of Bologna. In its province are the Colli Euganei, hills filled with mineral-water sources and some of Italy's leading spas.

Yet it is the city of Treviso that I have chosen as the Classic Town of the Veneto. It is charming and hardworking, with an economy that draws from industry as well as agriculture. Veneto is sometimes called the California of Italy because of the diversity of its terrain and its economy, and the province of Treviso typifies that. There are beaches, Venetian-type canals, plains, and pre-alpine hills. Fish and meat are both part of the diet, as are polenta and rice. Its most famous vegetable, radicchio, is now prized around the world. The most famous Italian dessert, *tiramisù*, was invented in Treviso and tastes better there still. There is abundant wine served in friendly *osterie*. People in Treviso speak in the lilting accent (and dialect) that so quickly identifies someone as a Veneto native. There are many small industries in Treviso that keep the economy strong, especially the world-renowned Benetton clothing company.

The province of Treviso includes Asolo, one of Italy's most charming small cities, and many rustic towns, some with excellent restaurants and others with Palladian villas. These towns, and Treviso itself, maintain a rusticity that is an important component of Veneto life. For all of the elegance of Venezia, and the economic strength of Padova and Verona, the Veneto is still a society that has close links to the land, to farm traditions, to "poor" cuisine such as polenta and codfish, and to sharing *un'ombra* (a glass of wine) and *due chiacchiere* (a chat) with a friend old or new. It was the Venetians who coined the word *ciao*, as a salutation to say hello or good-bye. You will hear *ciao!* wherever you go. The word seems to say much more about the buoyant, flirtatious, direct, and intriguing people of Italy's most diverse region.

Eating in Veneto

Because of the remarkable variety of terrain in the Veneto, it has more types of food than most Italian regions. Instead of attempting to list all of these, I have indicated local specialties under the listings for each town. The best place to get an idea of the range and quality of the food of the Veneto is in the magnificent market of Padova.

The areas near the Adriatic, along rivers, and on the shores of Lago di Garda use fish and seafood as antipasti, with pasta, and as main courses. There is also a long tradition of eating cod in numerous preparations. The people in Veneto eat a great variety of meat: beef, horse (especially in Verona and Padova), pork, calf's liver (in Venezia especially), poultry, and many types of small game birds.

Polenta is the preferred starch. It is often served soft, and what is left over is allowed to harden and served cold or grilled with later meals. The traditional method for making polenta is to use a large copper pot and stir continuously for forty minutes so that the polenta will become soft and creamy. When stirring one never scrapes the sides or the bottom of the pot. As a result, a hard crust of polenta remains that is served with salt as an appetizer with drinks.

Rice and risotto are also popular, and there are several notable pasta dishes, mostly involving seafood sauces. *Bigoli* are very long whole wheat noodles, which, when served *in salsa*, come with a sauce of anchovies and oil. In the alpine region there are several filled pastas that contain sauerkraut, beets, cabbage, or potatoes. There are also *canederli*, typical alpine bread dumplings. The best soup in the region is probably the *pasta e fagioli* from Venezia. Another is *risi e bisi*, with rice and peas.

The countryside of the Veneto produces an amazing range of high-quality fruits and vegetables, including radicchio from Treviso, asparagus from Bassano and Cavaion, many wonderful lettuces, beans, and other delights. The apples, pears, cherries, and peaches that grow near Verona are transformed into juices and jams that are consumed throughout Italy. Along the shores of Lago di Garda lemons grow not far from snow-covered mountains. Above Garda there is olive cultivation that produces some of the world's finest oil.

Probably the best cheese in Veneto is Asiago, which comes from the province of Vicenza. It comes either in a young form, in which it is firm and creamy, or *stagionato*, which is now more difficult to find, in which it is granular and pungent. I like combining it with cherries. Either way Asiago is delicious, and it deserves to be ranked among Italy's top cheeses. There are also many good mountain cheesesfrom the alpine valleys.

Desserts are prized in Veneto, owing to the abundance of good fruit and spices as well as the years of Austrian domination and the Venetian love for festive food. In the listings for bakcries in Venezia you will find descriptions of many regional specialties. It is worth noting that tiramisù, a dessert that has been abused and denatured by inferior versions sold all over the world, was created in Treviso, and, when the combination of spongy ladyfingers, strong coffee, bitter chocolate, mascarpone cheese, and cream is carefully prepared there, it can still be delicious. Also look for *pinza*, a nice cake made of cornmeal and figs.

The Wines of Veneto

Veneto is one of the foremost Italian wine regions in terms of quantity and quality of wine produced. There are seventeen DOC zones, but among these are numerous subcategories. The three most famous wines are Bardolino, Valpolicella, and Soave, but you should also look for the white Bianco di Custoza, whose quality has steadily improved; the excellent Prosecco, a sparkling wine from the province of Treviso that is a national favorite; Breganze wines; and, of course, Amarone, a rich, powerful red from the province of Verona. A novelty is the little-known Clinton, a mythical wine that is officially banned from production (because it does not conform to DOC standards) but that you can find in and around Treviso.

Asolo (Treviso)

This is a chic resort town famous for its elegantly cozy hotel Villa Cipriani. Most of the stores you will want to visit are on the Via Browning, named for Robert and Elizabeth Barrett Browning, who loved Asolo. Look for the Caffè Teatro and the Enoteca Asolo (#185, closed Monday). Be sure to stop at the Gastronomia Sgarbossa (#151, tel. 0423/529109; closed Wednesday afternoon, Sunday, and July). Aside from the pasta, breads, sauces, *salumi*, and fancy foods, you should consider the *formaggio aromatizzado*, which contains truffles and red wine. The *pinza* is a nice cake here and also at the little *forno a legna* at 344 Contrà Canova on the way to the Villa Cipriani. Good bread and biscuits are available, too. Dine at Locanda ai Due Mori (Piazza d'Annunzio 5, tel. 0423/952256; closed Wednesday; Diners Club accepted), or Ca'Derton (Piazza

D'Annunzio 11, tel. 0423/529648; closed Sunday evening and Monday, late January and mid-summer; all credit cards; moderate). Asolo has a fine chamber music festival every August and September.

Bardolino (Verona)

This is the town that gave its name to the fragrant, exuberant red wine that used to appear on tables around the world. When demand increased, so did production, and by the early 1980s quality had slipped, and its reputation was ruined. But the young wine that is consumed locally is delicious and will give you an idea of what Bardolino is supposed to taste like. Although the town has been overbuilt to respond to tourism, it still has some charm, and there is good food to be had.

BAR-BAKERY

Bar-Pasticceria Manzoni, Via Manzoni 1. Closed Tuesday.

Run by two friendly women and a baker in the back. A good place for breakfast.

DINING

Osteria Solferino, Via Solferino 18, tel. 045/7211020. All credit cards. Moderate to moderately expensive.

Delicious soups, pasta, braised meats, polenta, mushrooms, cheese, and smoked fish to pair with local wines. An ideal match for Bardolino is the *torta di patate con formaggio e prosciutto* (potatoes, cheese, and boiled ham). The owner, Mauro Braganza, is also a connoisseur of chocolate, which will inevitably turn up at the end of the meal. Ask if his special chocolate dessert is available: the *torta Savoia* is made with chocolate mousse and whipped cream plus melted chocolate. The coffee here is excellent.

Trattoria Costadoro, Via Costadoro 3, tel. 045/7210806. Closed Monday and occasional weeks (call ahead). No credit cards. Moderately inexpensive.

This trattoria is adjacent to the Costadoro farm operated by the Lonardi family. The farm is open Monday through Saturday from 8h to 12:30h and 13:30h to 19h, and you can purchase its delicious, very floral Bardolino wine and delicate olive oil. The farm is notable for experimental planting techniques supervised by the University of Milano to get better yields and quality from the olives. You can taste the wine, oil, and more at the trattoria, dining on dishes such as *spaghetti con aglio, olio e peperoncino (*salmon trout with a touch of the oil) or *spezzatino di cinghiale con rosmarino e olio d'oliva cruda* (stew of wild boar with rosemary and a drizzle of oil). I want to share with you the wisdom of Mari (the wife of the man who makes the oil and wine): "Garda oil is a condiment that should be used to give flavor, not to fry. Frying changes the whole nature of the oil. If you must use it to fry, do so on low heat, cooking very slowly. On pasta it should be used raw or slightly heated. When grilling meat or vegetables, do not grease the food, despite what you may have been told. Instead, after cooking, dress the food lightly with oil. Why? If food is greased in advance it becomes heavier and less digestible. In preparing a meat or vegetable to grill, the food should be very dry—this way it won't stick to the grill. If you do grease your food, it should be very, very light, because you don't want the oil to drip into the fire. For stews I use nonstick pots and slow-cook, adding only a drizzle of oil at the end of cooking to give flavor. What is the best way to determine the quality of an oil? Taste it on a boiled potato." Words from an expert.

FOLKLORE

Festa dell' Uva.

A grape festival held around the last weekend of September or the first weekend of October to celebrate the grape harvest.

Festa del Vino Novello.

Held around November 6 to taste the new wine.

WINE MUSEUM

Museo del Vino della Cantina Zeni, Via Costabella 9, tel. 045/7210022. Open weekdays 8–12h, 14–18h, Saturday morning in summer. All credit cards accepted for wine purchases.

The Zeni family began wine production in 1870, and you can see old equipment from the past as well as many pieces acquired from elsewhere. Notice the table full of hoes, the rudimentary hand pumps, and especially the vat that was used to make wine with one's feet. The Zenis make a very good Bardolino and also make all of the other wines of the region, although I did not sample them. You can purchase wines as well as the olive oil the family produces, although it is usually sold out by May.

Bassano del Grappa (Vicenza)

Bassano, sitting between hills and mountains, is yet another beautiful town—one of my favorites—that is too frequently ignored. It finished second to Treviso in my consideration of the most classic town of the Veneto. It is the birthplace of the great operatic baritone Tito Gobbi. Hemingway spent time here, as do those who are passionate about food and wine. There is an asparagus festival in early April—some of the most flavorful green and white asparagus grows nearby. Many dishes are flavored with excellent Asiago cheese, and meals invariably conclude with—you guessed it—a glass or two of grappa. Be sure to visit the Ponte di Bassano, the romantic bridge that spans the Brenta River, which runs through town.

DINING

Osteria al Borgo, Via Margnan 7, tel. 0424/522155. Closed Wednesday, Saturday lunch, one week in May, three weeks in August. All credit cards. Moderate.

Located in a beautiful part of town, this trattoria offers asparagus specialties, polenta with herring, and traditional secondi.

Al Giardinetto, Via Fontanelle 30, tel. 0424/502277. Closed Tuesday evening and Wednesday. All credit cards. Moderately inexpensive.

About 1.5 km (1 mile) northwest of the center of Bassano is this charming restaurant in an 18th-century building with pleasing food and a lovely setting in a garden.

FOOD SHOPING

Gastronomia Vanzo, Via Jacopo da Ponte 14, tel. 0424/522014. Closed Wednesday afternoon and Sunday.

This store has been here for nearly two hundred years, owned for the last thirty-five by Lino Santi, who is passionate about quality. There are many fine cheeses, including Asiago, Vezzena, and *malga di Posellaro*. In the meat section look for *la sorpressa*, a special fine grained *salame* from the Valle Leogra. The pigs used for this *salame* are fed chestnuts, and when the *salame* is made, only salt and pepper are added, rather than the usual assortment of spices and garlic. *La sorpressa* is considered at its best when aged. It customarily develops a black mold that is cleaned before it is sold.

Rosini—Emporio dei Fungbi, Salita Ferracina 15. Closed Tuesday.

An excellent source for dried *funghi porcini*, Marostica cherries packed in grappa, *la sorpressa*, and the local whole wheat pasta, *bigoli di bassan.*

GRAPPA

Grapperia Nardini, Ponte Veccbio 2, tel. 0424/27741, fax 0424/20477.

On the eastern side of the bridge of Bassano is this historic institution (opened 1779) that produces and sells grappa. This is the ideal place to meet locals over a glass of the smooth beverage that gives its name to the city. Walk around a bit to admire the copper vats and old-style decor of Veneto peasant crafts of another era.

Belluno

Belluno is the provincial capital of the mountainous part of the northeastern Veneto. Just to the south are the hills, wine districts, and waterways of the provnce of Treviso, to the north (in Belluno's province) are Cortina d'Ampezzo and some of the most majestic mountains in Europe.

BARS AND CAFFÉS

Caffè Manin, Piazza Martin 39. Open 7–1h, 2h in summer; closed Tuesday.

Outdoor tables on one of Belluno's main piazzas. Small pastries available.

Caffè Deon, Piazza Martin. Closed Monday.

A few doors down from the Caffè Manin. It has an attractive interior and would make a good choice in cold weather. Pastries, too.

BOOKSTORE

Libreria Mezzaterra, Via Mezzaterra 39a, tel. 0437/27765.

A very well organized bookshop that is a good source for books on local and national cuisine, plus travel books and maps for excursions in the Alps. You will find a wall full of books about mushrooms—how to recognize them, pick them, cook them. There is even a good selection of classics in English.

DINING

La Taverna, Via Cipro 7, tel. 0437/25192. Closed Sunday. No credit cards. Moderately inexpensive.

A very casual, friendly restaurant with genuine dishes and warm service. There are two rooms with wooden beams, assorted furniture and paintings, and hanging kitchen utensils. A bit of a hodgepodge, perhaps, but it all works nicely and with no forced rusticity. Among the many good dishes are *cassunziei* (pasta filled with beets and horseradish served with melted butter and poppy seeds), *canederli con lo speck* (fluffy alpine dumplings with bits of speck, served with melted butter), *schiz con polenta* (a Belluno specialty: a local cheese with a reddish tinge and a milky taste is heated and served with a cool block of polenta), wonderful *faraona al forno con la salsa peverada* (roasted guinea fowl with a peppery, creamy sauce), *finferli con polenta* (local mushrooms sautéed and served with polenta), and good apple strudel. There is also excellent coffee, made with Caffè del Moro beans.

FOOD STORES

Many of the good stores are on Piazza del Mercato, which is intimate, portico-lined, and paved with cobblestones.

Pastificio Menazza, Via Rialto 4–6 (on Piazza del Mercato).

At #6 you can see a dozen old pasta machines lined up and often at work. The adjacent store sells fresh and dried pastas, including *pizzoccheri* from the Valtellina and the many varieties made in-house. The very long spaghetti and *bigoli* are especially appealing. Jarred sauces from throughout Italy and wines from the Piave zone to the south of town are also sold.

Al Vecchio Forno—Panificio de Col, Via Rialto 9.

Fine breads, including a local specialty made with poppy seeds, walnuts, and sugar.

WINE BAR

Enoteca Mazzini, Piazza Mazzini 6–8–10.

A charming old place with two wooden tables outside, one fronted by a large comfortable bench with a high back. Good grappa and wines from near and far.

Brenzone (Verona)

OLIVE OIL

Il Frantoio dell'Alto Garda, Via Disciplina 1, tel. 045/7420658, fax 045/7420245. Open 8:30–12h, 14:30–18h; closed Saturday and Sunday.

This is the cooperative of oil producers from the northernmost part of the province of Verona that fronts Lago di Garda. Many of the six hundred members use no chemical treatments on their olives, and oil made from these is labeled "Da Agricoltura Biologica." The oil is typically delicate and should be consumed in its youth.

Caldogno (Vicenza)

DINING

Al Molin Vecio. See "Vicenza," page 252.

Castelfranco Veneto (Treviso)

This snug little town in the province of Treviso maintains regional life as it was years ago. Visit the house of Giorgione while you are there and then walk up and down the Via Francesco Maria Preti. Just down the street from Giorgione's house is the Caffè al Duomo, with its great fragrances of coffee and chocolate. In the Veneto there is a saying that dates back to the 1730s: *Caffè del collo, cioccolato del culo,* which politely translates as "Coffee from the neck, chocolate from the bottom." The idea is that the best coffee comes from the neck of the coffeemaker, while the best chocolate comes from the bottom of the pot. At #4 on this street, just across the way, pay a visit to the Pasticceria Fraccaro. In November it makes all sorts of pastries and breads with cornmeal. During the rest of the year you will find typical Veneto pastries, including some with Austrian influence, such as Sacher torte and strudel. Next door is an interesting old shop, N. Sgaravatti and Company. Here you can find all kinds of seed for local products such as radicchio and arugula. Also worth visiting are the Gastronomia Favretto (Via Canova 2a, tel. 0423/722078, closed Wednesday afternoon and Sunday), with its excellent selection of cheese and *salumi,* and the Boccanegra bakery (Piazza San Pio X 6, tel. 0423/493620), where I particularly enjoyed the dry cookies, breads, and cakes.

Cavaion (Verona)

FOLKLORE

Festa degli Asparagi.

On the third weekend of May, Cavaion consumes most of its prized asparagus, which is hard to find outside the borders of town. It is smaller than most asparagus and is a buttery white color.

Cisano (Verona)

OLIVE-OIL MUSEUM

Museo dell'Olio, Via Peschiera 54, tel. 045/6229047, fax 045/6229024. Open 8:30–12:30h, 14:30–19h, Sunday 9–12:30h; closed Wednesday.

Founded in 1987 by Umberto Turri, owner of the Oleificio Cisano del Garda (with his olive-press at Strada Campazzi 5 in Bardolino), this museum is dedicated to the history of olive-oil production, especially on

Lago di Garda. There are re-creations of olive presses from ancient Roma, and a real one from seventeenth-century southern France resembles those used in Liguria. There is a room full of old, very picturesque labels with names such as "Enrico Caruso" and "Mamma Mia," the latter be-ing from Corleone, the town in Sicilia that was the setting of *The Godfather.* The museum has a printed guide in English and German that can be used as you go through the exhibits. Mr. Turri also sells his olive oils here. All major credit cards are accepted.

Cortina d'Ampezzo (Belluno)

Because Cortina is one of the chicest ski resorts in the world, it is not a place where one would expect to find typical foods and moderate prices. This is a city of boutiques, and, in high season (summer and winter), one might feel like Cortina is a more sylvan Via Montenapoleone (in Milano). But there are places for the gourmet traveler to enjoy.

DINING

Ristorante al Camin, Loc. Alverà 99, tel. 0436/862010. Open until 24h. Moderate.

Here is good local cooking, run by a very nice lady whose son has spent time in the United States. Among the choices are *ravioli alla paesana,* filled with potatoes and carrots; *pennette alla montanara,* with a sauce of wild mushrooms, speck, and butter; *kenederli,* the local spelling for this ubiquitous dumpling; *capriolo* served with polenta; *cervo* cooked either with *funghi porcini* or wild berries; *formaggio fuso con funghi e polenta,* melted cow's-milk cheese with sauteed *finferli* mushrooms served over soft polenta. In the spring this is a good place to try dishes based on alpine herbs. As soon as the snow melts, one finds *radicchio di prato.* This is a green plant with yellow flowers that is eaten raw with hot lard (a Cortina specialty; elsewhere it is served with oil and vinegar). Soon after come *asparagi selvatici,* wild asparagus (only the tips are eaten). In May and June there is *schioppetino,* a spinachlike wild green that can be stuffed in ravioli or simply dressed with oil. The basket of bread here is special, and you should be sure to sample the *puccia secca,* a crunchy local bread made with caraway seeds. There is a short wine list with decent selections, mostly from Friuli, Trentino–Alto Adige, and Veneto. The musically sensitive may find the recorded sound track rather trying. You can dine at outdoor tables during the warmer months.

FOOD STORES
ON THE CORSO ITALIA
Except for La Cooperativa, stores are closed on Wednesday afternoon and Sunday.

#30–40: La Cooperativa. Closed Monday morning and Sunday.

(This store has the virtue of being open on Wednesday afternoon when other stores are closed.) In mountain communities in northern Italy there are general stores that often take the form of cooperatives. This all-purpose store is an indispensable resource for the people of the valley. Up a few steps is a well-stocked supermarket where you can gather provisions for mountain hikes. Note the carved crucifix at the entrance to the market—mountain people are very pious.

#42: Salumeria Oberhammer.

Homemade *salami* of pork (including *ungherese*—Hungarian), *camoscio,* and *cervo.* You can find various carpaccios as well as packages of dried *funghi porcini.*

#45: Bar-Pasticceria Lowat. Closed Wednesday.

Popular with locals who come for Italian and Austrian pastries, coffee, and hot chocolate. There are also tiny sandwiches to eat with cocktails and wine.

#124: El Zestel, tel. 0436/3467. American Express, MasterCard, Visa.

You can tell you are in a fancy international resort when you shop here. There are products from Fauchon of Paris, cookies and biscuits from England, and a huge range of gourmet items from around Italy: excellent oils, vinegars, pastas, jams, sauces, baked goods, wine. If you are staying in Cortina at a place with a kitchen, this is a fine place to stock up to make delicious meals and dinner parties at home.

#191: Panificio-Pasticceria Alverà.

Good all-purpose bread and pastry source, and the place to come to for crunchy *puccia secca,* which is made daily.

Lago di Garda (Verona, also Trento and Brescia)

Lake Garda is the largest and probably the most popular of the lakes in the lake district of northern Italy. The strong deutsche mark has made Garda a German sea. Germans arrive in May and stay through the autumn grape harvest. Because the lake offers mass tourism at a low price, much of the innate character of the place has been submerged, if not destroyed. Yet there still are things to appreciate: the lake is beautiful, and good wine and olive oil are produced on the hillsides just beyond the tourist enclaves on the shore. Towns worth visiting include Bardolino, Cisano, and Lazise (see individual listings).

Giavera del Montello (Treviso)

DINING

Antica Trattoria Agnoletti, tel. 0422/ 776009. Closed Monday and Tuesday. MasterCard, Visa. Moderately expensive.

Follow the signs in this small town near Treviso to reach this warm and welcoming place that has been receiving guests, in one form or another, since 1780. The specialties are those of the province: wild mushrooms, herbs, small game. These find their way into sauces for the delicious homemade *pappardelle* and tagliatelle. If it is available, you should taste the violet ice cream, made with real flowers.

Isola della Scala (Verona)

RICE

Antica Riseria Ferron, Via Sacco Vener 6, tel. 045/7301022.

This is thought to be the oldest rice-producing company in Italy, with records indicating cultivation and sales in 1656. It produces only one type of rice, the highly prized and little-found Vialone Nano, which discriminating palates consider the best of all. The Ferrons do not use any chemicals in the cultivation of their rice.

Isola Rizza (Verona)

DINING AND BAKERY

Ristorante Perbellini, Via Muselle, tel. 045/7135352. All credit cards.

This incongruous restaurant strikes me as a monument to 1980s consumerism. It is in the middle of the countryside, yet is a very formal room with hanging Venetian chandeliers that would seem more at home in Paris or New York. The cuisine is very refined and scarcely represents the gastronomic and agricultural traditions of the surrounding area. Yet there is delicious food, which is the reason to come here. The *torta di patate con astice e tartufo nero* has delicate slices of potato, lobster, and black truffle. Perbellini has won awards for its *zuppa di pesce*, which is very good, although it is hard to reconcile the presence of a seafood stew as the specialty in such a landlocked place. Perbellini began in the 1860s as a local bakery. In the restaurant you can see two volumes of family cake recipes, all written by hand. They are interesting, too, because measurements are in ounces and pounds, an oddity, since Italy has long been metric. In 1890 Perbellini created the *offella d'oro*, a nice cake that is made with eggs, flour, sweet almonds, and cocoa powder. The name comes from *offelleria*, which is what bakeries were then called. *Offelle* are only baked here from October to May, and you can taste them for dessert or purchase one to take away.

Lazise sul Garda (Verona)

OLIVE OIL

Frantoio per Olive Veronesi, Via Gardesana 3, tel. 045/7580030.

Not to miss, especially if you are in the area in November and December, when olives are being picked and pressed. This is one of the last of the old-style presses and is the one that will give you a sense of how olives were pressed long ago. In 1750 the Garda area had 310 olive presses, by 1880 it was down to 20, in 1943 there were 15, and now there are only 7. This one has been run by the Veronesi family since 1918, although the family has produced oil for much longer. It is the press where local farmers with small olive crops come to make oil. The Veronesis also make and sell their own oil, which is very good. You can buy olives, capers, and other vegetables packed in oil. They work in a less mechanized way than the other presses in the area, with some of the processes requiring manual labor. I also loved this place because Emanuele Veronesi and his mother, Ebe, listen to opera all day as they work. In November, when farmers bring in their olives, they watch their oil being made in this warm, peaceful environment as they listen to the sublime music of Rossini, Verdi, and Puccini.

Malcesine (Verona)

DINING

Hotel-Ristorante Cassone, Via Gardesana Sud 53/55, tel. and fax 045/6584197. All credit cards. Moderate.

Because mass tourism has pitched the quality of dining rather low along the shores of Lago di Garda, it is difficult to find good food representing local flavors that is prepared with care. That said, this is not an outstanding restaurant, but there are things to taste that are hard to find elsewhere. The hotel is situated on the Fiume Aril, which at 170 meters (about 560 feet) is said to be the world's shortest river. The *Piatto Aril* is a dish of spaghetti tossed with Garda oil and *agole,* the dialect word for *alborelle,* a small fish from Garda that is minced and salted. For *secondi* lake fish such as *lavarello* and *carpione* can be grilled or cooked with herbs.

Marostica (Vicenza)

Marostica is famous for two things: its divine cherries and its unusual chess game *(partita a scacchi)* with people and horses enacting chess pieces. A cherry festival—*la Sagra dei Ciliegi*—is held at the end of May and in the first days of June and is highly recommended. The chess game is held on the second weekend of September in odd-numbered years on the outdoor chessboard on the main square. It is necessary to reserve a place (call 0424/72127). The chess game is a reenactment of real games from history, with the one proviso that the knights be among the first to be taken because the horses become agitated.

BAKERIES-BARS

Pasticceria Chiurato, Corso Mazzin 48, tel. 0424/72134.

The popular items here are the buttery *torta regina* and the dry *focaccina della nonna* (with figs, raisins, and pine nuts), plus ice cream and coffee.

Pigato, Piazza Castello 3, tel. 0424/72022.

The *baci di Lionora* (kisses of Lionora), named for a young woman loved by two fifteenth-century cavaliers, are the famous pastries here. The two young men vied for the hand of Lionora, but her father would not let them have a duel. Rather, he proposed a chess game with living chess pieces, and that is how the famous event was born.

DINING

Trattoria Dama Bianca, Via Roma 107, tel. 0424/75096. Closed Wednesday evening, Saturday afternoon, and in August. Visa. Moderate.

Dama Bianca is the white queen in Marostica's chess match. There are excellent filled pastas here, plus grilled meats and good desserts, including some based on cherries.

WINE

Osteria della Madonetta, Via Vajenti 21.

Only wine and snacks are served at this *osteria*, which has notable wood sculptures of the walls and castles of Marostica.

Mel (Belluno)

DINING

Antica Locanda al Cappello, Piazza Papa Luciani 20, tel. 0437/753651. Closed Tuesday evening, Wednesday (except in August), and first two weeks of July. No credit cards. Moderate to moderately expensive.

This edifice once belonged to the Knights of Malta and was acquired in 1730 by Lorenzo Cappello to make an inn. Make note of the welcoming fireplace and the many seventeenth-century frescoes on the walls. When this was part of the Austrian empire, the inn was frequented by Hapsburg military men who came for a good meal and usually had a woman in tow (seldom a wife) for postprandial company. General Radetzky was a frequent visitor. There are no longer rooms for guests, but it is still an excellent restaurant. Try the *gnocchi di pane con ortiche* (bread gnocchi with nettles) or the radicchio *tortelloni.*

Montegalda (Vicenza)

DINING AND GRAPPA

Azienda Agricola Brunello, Via Giuseppe Roi 27, tel. 0444/636236. Open Friday and Saturday from 19h, Sunday from 15h. Moderately inexpensive.

Do not confuse the name "Brunello" with the great wine from Montalcino in Toscana. This is the family name of one of the better grappa producers in Italy, and you can have a look at the rather rustic machinery that produces fine spirits. This is Italy's second-oldest commercial grappa producer, in business since 1840. What I love at this farm are the delicious fruits and vegetables that are packed in jars for sale. The vegetables come in oil or vinegar; the fruits are in grappa. You can taste these and other products of the farm—fresh beans, homemade sausages and *salami,* wine, polenta from corn that grows right outside the door—in a lovely setting. After your meal visit the farm animals, which include peacocks, walk in the cornfields, or play bocce.

Padova

Padova is so often skipped by tourists who stay on the train to Venezia. This is understandable, but they are missing a lot. Padova, along with Bologna, Pavia, and Pisa, is one of the great university towns of Italy. It has, in Giotto's frescoes in the Scrovegni Chapel, some of the most important art of the early Renaissance. Padova flexes its economic muscle as the industrial hub of the Veneto. Its basilica of Sant'Antonio (Saint Anthony of Padua, who in fact was from Lisbon) makes it one of the leading pilgrimage destinations in Europe. And it should not be skipped by food lovers. In my view it has the second-best market in Italy, exceeded only by the one in Bologna. Take the walk I present below (page 225), starting at the famous Caffè Pedrocchi.

BAKERIES

Colucci già Briganti, Piazza dei Signori, tel. 049/8751560. Closed Monday and in August.

Baking has been done by various proprietors here for more than a century. Its selection reflects Veneto taste (in the use of spices and cornmeal) as well as the Austrian domination (strudel, Sacher torte, whipped cream).

Pasticceria Lilium, Via del Santo 181, tel. 049/8751107.

The major items here are the *biscotti del santo* (for Saint Anthony). While these are obviously based on a gimmick, the amaretti do taste good with coffee or a glass of Prosecco. The sweet-bitter taste seems in keeping with the mood of many pilgrims coming to pray to Saint Anthony.

THE BASILICA DI SANT'ANTONIO

A visit to the Basilica di Sant'Antonio is a chance to witness the Catholic Church in all of its majesty and mystery, operating at full tilt. Wander through the chapels full of parishioners and pilgrims to experience the depth of passion and devotion, and perhaps uncertainty, with which these worshipers practice their religion. It is much more palpable here than at the Vatican, for example. Everywhere there are lines of people waiting to confess. At the elevated tomb of Saint Anthony pictures of children and a few unwell adults are pinned, along with messages of supplication or thanks for help from Saint Anthony. People (mostly women) read these intently as they wait to walk next to the saint's tomb, where they will slide their right hand along its black stone as they silently pray. There are many young couples here, some engaged, some newly wed, who come to pray to have children. (Italy, it is interesting to note, has the lowest birth rate in the world. If things do not change, there will be no Italians within 150 years.) Pregnant women, accompanied by their husbands, mothers, or sisters, come to pray for a healthy outcome. Young mothers pray for the well-being of their children, especially if a child is ill. Older mothers pray for their children, too, especially if one has strayed into an unhealthy lifestyle. A few people have come to pray for the return of a lost object. While most of these worshipers are women, a special sanctuary on the right side of the church is dedicated specially for men to confess and pray. Within there is often a rack of white silk robes worn for special services. Outside are several stalls that sell Anthony-related memorabilia, along with candles into which the saint's image has been impressed. Behind the basilica is the Orto Botanico, botanical gardens created in 1545 that were planted for the instruction of students at the University of Padova. It was the first of its kind in the world, gathering as it now does about six thousand species of plants to use for didactic purposes. A palm tree planted in 1585 and described by Goethe during his 1786 visit is still very much alive. Aside from its historic value, the Orto Botanico merits a visit for its beauty.

BOOKSTORE

Fratelli Melita Editori, Corso Cavour, 108, tel. 0187/28196.

A good selection of cookbooks.

CAFFÈ

Caffè Pedrocchi, Piazzetta Pedrocchi, tel. 049/8752020. Closed Monday.

Opened in 1772, this is one of the oldest *caffè*s in Italy still in business. Pedrocchi was a relatively humble place until 1815, when construction began to give it the monumental neoclassical aspect we discover today. It was in 1815 that Henri Beyle, whom we know as Stendhal, spent a lot of time at the Pedrocchi in the company of a woman of Padova whose name has vanished in the mists of time. You will recognize the Pedrocchi immediately, with its facade guarded by a pair of recumbent stone lionesses. Inside, in the central room, be sure to read the *elenco* above the cashier. This is a list of the Pedrocchi's offerings in

February 1844, when Italy was not yet a nation. There are four Rhine wines, twenty-two French wines (including Chateau Lafitte), eleven Spanish and Portuguese wines, and fine wines from Asti. They also offered coffee, tea, playing cards, biscuits, candies, candles, and a tooth elixir made by one Carlo Testa. Also available was home-made chocolate served as a beverage. It came either with vanilla, with cinnamon, or as *stomachino*, which was thought to be a gastric calmant. Not all of the Pedrocchi is decorated in a manner that befits its grand past, but it is one of Italy's most famous and historic *caffè*s.

DINING

Ristorante Dotto, Via Squarcione 23, tel. 049/25055. Closed Sunday evening, Monday, January, and August. All credit cards. Moderate to expensive.

This restaurant endeavors to conserve the flavors of Padova cuisine, with an emphasis on fish, rice, polenta, and foods from the nearby market.

Osteria dei Fabbri, Via dei Fabbri 13, tel. 049/650336. Open until 1h; closed Sunday. No credit cards. Moderately inexpensive.

Not far from the Piazza delle Erbe, this is a popular place with young people who are watching their lire but still want to eat well. Good *salami*, risotto, braised meats, fish, and wine by the glass.

Osteria Speroni, Via Speroni 32–36, tel. 049/8753370. Reservations essential. Closed Sunday and August. Visa. Moderately expensive.

This is where I first tasted *spaghetti alla*

busara, made with an enormous quantity of garlic. But the garlic is cooked so that it becomes creamy and mild, and the shrimp in the dish are actually the dominant flavor. It is but one of the many fine dishes made in this creative kitchen that strives to preserve the flavors of Padova. *Tortelloni di pesce* is another. The service is correct but not overbearing, and you feel welcome to explore flavors that are new because the restaurant is proud of its dishes and the staff is ready to describe them. Reservations are essential because there are only forty seats.

Trattoria al Pero, Via Santa Lucia 72, tel. 049/8758794. Closed Sunday. No credit cards. Inexpensive.

When I asked several of the merchants in the market where they eat, most of them mentioned Al Pero. It certainly won't win any awards from globe-trotting foodies, but the genuineness of the food and the way it is served are appealing nonetheless.

Stick to simple preparations: soups, rice with vegetables, boiled beef or tongue, fried fresh sardines, and salads. The house wines are quite decent. You may wind up sitting next to someone you made a purchase from at the market. In my case, the elderly egg lady (see the "Walk," below) sat down to introduce herself. Because she only had one tooth and spoke in dialect (and usually with her mouth full), I can't tell you much of what she said. I did learn that her fiancé moved to Argentina in 1923, when fascism was tightening its grip on Italy, to start a new life making wine in Mendoza. I was very impressed with how caringly and respectfully she was treated by the young waiter.

Osteria L'Anfora, Via dei Soncin 13, tel. 049/656629. Closed Monday afternoon and Sunday. No credit cards. Moderately inexpensive.

Good food and excellent wine in a friendly setting.

A WALK THROUGH PADOVA'S MARKET

Starting from the Caffè Pedrocchi, walk down the Via Gorizia. At #20 is a nice little bakery with a wonderful array of *biscotti.* Number 16 is an unnamed wine bar with small snacks. Its charm is in its local character—it makes no effort to woo customers or tourists. At #8 is Valesio, an outstanding source for knives, chopping boards, and special equipment such as juicers, coffee makers, and slicers. Everything is well selected and beautifully displayed. Turn left to the Via Marsilio da Padova to reach the Piazza della Frutta. Stalls here are open on Monday, Tuesday, and Wednesday mornings; Thursday, Friday, and Saturday mornings and afternoons; and closed Sunday. The square is always animated, but especially at Christmas and Easter, when additional stands appear. Da Duilio, the first stand you will see, has excellent dried fruit from all over the world. Continue to the right and go under the porticoes, where shops in the market are listed by number.

#1:

A small wine bar, always crowded, that also serves *salumi*. Note the huge mortadella that often sits on the left side of the pass-through window.

#2 3,4, and 5:

Fragrant fruit stalls; a bread shop; a good fishmonger.

#7:

A well-stocked herbalist with books on philosophy, religion, massage, and books with titles such as *Artistic Creation and the Spiritual Garden*. Do you notice a wonderful fragrance of roast chicken coming from somewhere? Keep on walking.

#8 *Aglimentari Fratelli Bovo.*

Here since the start of the twentieth century. It is small and popular with an elderly clientele that receives loving attention.

Walk past the *panificio*, button store, shoe store, arms store (that caters to hunters), and you will discover a truck, so typical in Italy, that opens on one side. Called Rosticceria "Chi Magna Torna" (He Who Eats Returns), it always does a booming business selling roast chicken, guinea hen, duck, lamb, sausage, ribs, turkey, meatballs, and sparrows (popular here). This truck and its customers are a vivid sight that merit several minutes of observation. At night the truck folds up and rolls away. Near the truck is a large elderly woman selling eggs. She wears a heavy sweater and a red-and-green apron. This is one of a vanishing breed of people, usually elderly and poor, who earn a few extra cents selling whatever the land on which they live yields. Periodically the woman will stand up and walk to the *rosticceria* truck to pluck a meatball, potato croquette, or whatever has been put out for customers to sample.

Walk back under the porticoes past the man selling raffle tickets and visit the many stores under the vaults. There are too many for me to describe, but a few should not be missed. At #41 A. Borsetto has a vast selection of salami and prosciutto, including some made with goose (*oca*), deer (*cervo*), and wild boar (*cinghiale*), as well as ham from Prague, salami from Emilia Romagna, Calabria, Istria, and elsewhere, plus homemade products. These are warm, friendly people who are justifiably proud of their shop. The orderly little shop (#35) across the way sells quality canned and dried goods and contrasts with the animation all around it. Do not miss Pastificio Nello (#26), a plain, straightforward place that is all about quality rather than spectacle. But the window display is spectacular indeed. Look at the perfect tortellini, ravioli, cappelletti, gnocchi, tagliatelle, *trenette*, and *pappardelle*. The Enoteca Walter Schiavon (#23) sells bottles, but most people stop in for a glass of wine from one of the large barrels to the left. The *enoteca* also makes excellent cappuccino. Il Casaro (#22) is a fine source for cheeses from northeastern Italy.

When you have visited all of the stores on this side, walk through to the Piazza delle Erbe, where dozens more fabulous shops and stalls await. It is hard to avoid the Maceleria Equina (#4), where a whole horse's leg often hangs in the doorway. Here, for those who want them (and many people do), are horse tongue, horse sausage, and horse ribs, to mention but a few items. At #18 is an excellent cheese store, beautifully displayed. At #28 is the Bottega del Pane, an excellent bread shop.

Opposite #36, on the Piazza delle Erbe, are two superb stands offering beans, rice, chestnuts, peas, cornmeal, and seeds. There are nearly one hundred sacks here, including one containing *riso per cani* (rice for dogs). This is only a sample of what this magnificient market offers. You should devote at least two hours here to make a thorough visit.

WINE

Spaccio di Vini Carpanese, Via del Santo 44, tel. 049/30581. Open 10–13:30h, 16:30–21h; closed Sunday evening.

An excellent *enoteca* in which to drink wine by the glass and to purchase bottles. Across the way, at #95, is a wonderful *salumeria* (closed Wednesday afternoon and Sunday) with lots of good wine, excellent dried pasta, dried *funghi porcini*, and a fine selection of prosciutto and *salumi*.

Pedeguarda di Follina (Treviso)

DINING

Osteria al Castelletto, Via Castelletto 15, tel. 0438/842484. Closed Tuesday. No credit cards. Moderate.

Look for the old-fashioned pink building with TRATTORIA painted on the front. The main dining room has an open fireplace with spits turning chickens and other poultry. There is a lovely garden in the back for warm-weather dining. Try the *polenta burrata con sorpessa* as an antipasto and then choose among good primi such as *flan di zucca e spinaci* (pumpkin and spinach), *spaghetti al radicchio* or *tagliatelle all'anatra*. Secondi include grilled poultry, beef, or pork. In season, enjoy excellent *funghi porcini*.

San Polo di Piave (Treviso)

DINING

Gambrinus, tel. 0422/855042, fax 0422/855044, Closed Monday (except holidays) and two weeks in mid-January. All credit cards. Moderately expensive.

The restaurant is situated in a beautiful park with an aviary and a lovely stream nearby and is famous for *gamberi alla Gambrinus*. This is sweet, freshwater shrimp (almost impossible to find elsewhere nowadays) that are fished from the ponds and waterways of the park. They are boiled as soon as they are caught and then served on toasted polenta and topped with a sauce of parsley, celery, garlic, cloves, cinnamon (these last two a legacy of when this area was under Venetian rule), butter, and oil. Gambrinus is the name of the god of beer, and it is thought that years ago this shrimp dish was prepared with beer. But there are other specialties as well at Gambrinus, which has been open since 1847. From December to February there are *raviolini* filled with radicchio, and throughout the year there are different types of fresh fish.

San Stino di Livenza (Venezia)

DINING

Trattoria Bellomo, Via Roma 37, tel. 0421/311165. Closed Tuesday. No credit cards. Inexpensive to moderately inexpensive.

Owner Ercolina Germati is the classic *dona veneta* that one might see in a Goldoni play. Her speech is flavored with the slight lisp that characterizes Veneto diction, and she is all bubbly charm as she moves from table to table. The food is good and basic: *bigoli* with tuna and anchovies for a *primo*, red (tomato) or white (milk) *baccalà* for *secondo*, served with white polenta and fresh string beans. Fruit for dessert. The unmarked white wine will probably be Tocai.

Sirmione (Brescia, Lombardia)

DINING

Trattoria Vecchia Lugana, Piazzale Vecchia Lugana 1, tel. 030/919012. Closed Monday evening, Tuesday, and first six weeks of the year. All credit cards. Expensive.

[Included in this chapter because the flavors and influence are entirely of the Veneto.]

This well-known restaurant—considered one of the best on Lago di Garda—is in an old (1750) building on the southern shore of the lake. I particularly enjoyed a delicate *risotto di pesce del lago*, made of lake fish, tomato stock, parsley, and arugula. Also good is *luccio* (pike) served with an herb sauce. There is an excellent selection of Veneto wines.

Soave (Verona)

WINE

Enoteca del Soave, Via Roma 19, tel. 045/7681588. Closed Wednesday and in January.

The perfect place to buy fine Soave wines (as well as Bardolino, Valpolicella, and Amarone). Because Soave whites were overproduced for many years, their quality and reputation abroad diminished. Some producers have made a deliberate effort to restore the wine to its former glory. I suggest you include Pieropan and Anselmi among the producers you try.

Sottomarina Lido (Venezia)

COOKING SCHOOL

*Centro Perfezionamento Pasticceria e
Cucina L'Etoile, Hotel Airone, Lungomare
Adriatico 50, 30019 Sottomarina Lido
(VE), tel. 041/492266, fax 041/5541325.*

This hotel-school at a beach town near

Venezia is the place to come if you want to
learn the art of fancy baking. Cakes, cookies, and small pastries are the specialty here,
and, as you might expect, this is where to
learn the special baking of Venezia. You
stay at the hotel and can loll on the beach
when you are not in class.

Treviso
Classic Town

More than any region in Italy, the Veneto does not lend itself easily to the selection
of one Classic Town. The region is a blend of sea, plains, hills, and Alps. Fish and
meat are equally popular; the people are industrious and fun-loving all at once and
have a greater love of strong alcoholic beverages than do most Italians. They love
music, especially singing, and often use it as a prelude to a freewheeling amorous
adventure. Veneto people can be rustic or incredibly stylish. Only in Treviso did I
find most of these characteristics expressed, although many can be found in Padova
and Bassano del Grappa. Here, only a half hour from Venezia, is a hardworking
city (it is the home of the Benetton clothing empire and many other prosperous
businesses) that adores good food, where people drink and sing in *osterie* from
morning to night. Treviso has many canals, as does Venezia, but it is also in the pre-
alpine hills. There are good wines from this area (though those from the province
of Verona tend to be better). The *trevisani* are stylish and casual, rustic and worldly,
all at once.

BAKERY

*Pasticceria Ardizzoni, Via Nervesa della
Battaglia 83.*

One of the specialties here is *zonglada,* a
medieval sweet whose recipe was discovered and restored at this bakery. It is made
with milk, flour, eggs, butter, walnuts,
dried figs, candied apricots, raisins, pine
nuts, orange peel, and cinnamon. There
are also many traditional Veneto cakes and
cookies, all made with care.

BARS AND CAFFÈS

At the Loggia dei Cavallieri in the city center
are two bars, Biffi (closed Wednesday) and
Beltrame (closed Thursday), that are open
from 7h to 1h. They form *il salotto di Treviso*
(the grand salon of Treviso) through which
most *trevisani* pass at some point each day.
Nearby is the Cafè Hausbrandt, on Piazza
Carducci (closed Sunday), which serves excellent coffee and snacks. Also popular with
the *trevisani* is Caffè ai Soffioni at Piazza dei
Signori 26 (closed Sunday May to October,
closed Monday the rest of the year).

COOKING SCHOOLS

Gran Galà, Viale XXIV Maggio 11, 31100 Treviso, tel. 0422/430560.

Giovanna Gasparello gives much-admired training in the cuisine of Treviso and other parts of Italy in her small classes (eight students maximum) in which everyone actively participates in food preparation. Classes are held from September to June and vary in subject matter according to the season. The course in fish cookery is particularly popular. Emphasis is also given to matching food and wine.

Scuola con Renzia in Cucina, Via d'Annunzio 4, 31100 Treviso, tel. 0422/545655.

The charm of this school comes in the continuity provided by Renzia Sebellin. There is a local flavor to the place, and one often sees students returning for special classes on particular topics. It is not uncommon for a young woman to come to learn dishes to serve on holidays, at weddings, at christenings, and on other special occasions. The food is good family cooking that appeals to "real people" who care about flavor.

DINING

Trattoria Toni del Spin, Via Inferiore 7, tel. 0422/543829. Closed Sunday, Monday lunch, and in August. MasterCard, Visa. Moderate.

In many ways this is my model of what a trattoria should be. The main room has seven longish tables with thirty-six seats. Strangers often sit next to one another and become acquaintances, if not friends. (There is another room in the back.) The atmosphere is very relaxed and conducive to eating well. One finds a nice selection of wines, mostly from Veneto and Friuli. Vegetables figure prominently here, from soups with beans and barley or artichokes, to pasta with mixed greens, and excellent salads and cooked vegetables that accompany the main course. The *zuppa di carciofi* is not a cream, but rather a broth with pieces of artichoke. The broth is thickened with potato that dissolves in your mouth. The overall flavor is artichoke, and it is delicious. In the middle of the bowl is a piece of garlic toast. *Tagliolini alla verdura* is delicate egg pasta with fresh peas and tiny pieces of zucchini and carrot with bits of basil and parsley. It is delicious, marred only by a bit too much salt (you may want to ask for it *senza sale*). Main courses include excellent *baccalà* with polenta, *spiedini* with mixed meats, green and white asparagus served with a boiled egg, roast chicken, roast guinea hen, tripe, carpaccio with arugula, and steak. The mixed salad is superb, with excellent olive oil and Cabernet vinegar placed on your table for you to make your own dressing. The baked desserts are good, but I would point you to the beautiful fresh fruit or baked pears. Service is expert but friendly. Like most people in Treviso, everyone at Toni del Spin has an easy and ready smile.

Ristorante "Vecia 3 Viso," Via Sant'Antonino 131, tel. 0422/400170. Closed Wednesday. American Express, MasterCard, Visa. Moderate.

The name means "Old Treviso" with the number 3 substituting for the syllable "Tre." I wandered in here with my friend Carol

Field with the goal of finding good food in a place where tourists might never venture. This restaurant is frequented by locals who love to drink, eat, and laugh. Avoid the back room if noise disturbs you, but don't avoid the food! Antipasti such as grilled radicchio and eggplant were good, and the *antipasto di pesce* was very good, particularly the baby shrimp with arugula and the baby octopus. But the *primi* were divine: *tagliolini all'astice*, sea crayfish and bits of tomato served with perfectly cooked pasta, seemed unbeatable until the *risotto alla pescatora* arrived. Here was perfect rice served with small bits of tender seafood and a fragrant fish stock. We then had a superb platter of grilled fish. The offerings vary with the daily catch. Ours included *sarago*, fabulous *coda di rospo*, and juicy jumbo shrimp that I bet were marinated in grappa. The house salad was delicate. Desserts were not homemade, and we gave them a miss. Fruit would be a better choice. The house wine is modest, and you might prefer to choose a local bottled selection or one from Friuli. The coffee was one of the best I've ever tasted—the beans are by Treviso's own Dersut, but the coffee, like all great cups, is the product of excellent roasted beans, a good clean machine, and a watchful eye.

Antico Ristorante Beccherie, Piazza Ancillotto 11, tel. 0422/56601, fax 0422/540871. Closed Sunday evening and Monday. All credit cards. Moderate to moderately expensive.

Full of history and good food, this is the oldest restaurant in Treviso. It has been run by the Campeol family since 1944, but has been serving food since 1870. Originally an inn that served meals (it is now part of a hotel), it was frequented by the *bechèri*, the meat sellers who sold their wares on the piazza outside. Specialties include tripe in broth (a legacy perhaps of the days when butchers were the principal clients), various roast meats served from a cart, and, of course, various preparations of radicchio. You might want to try *peverada*, which is made with livers of guinea hen, *salame*, anchovy, minced green pepper, sage, rosemary, garlic, and white wine. Delicious.

Ristorante all'Antica Torre, Via Inferiore 55, tel. 0422/53694. Closed Sunday and in August. All credit cards. Moderate to expensive.

The best deal here for the visitor is the *menu tradizione*, wherein typical flavors of Treviso and Veneto can be savored. You might taste the *risotto alla sbiraglia* (with chicken and giblets), various sausages or fish with polenta, plus good vegetables. I like the very simple *patate lesse con aglio e prezzemolo* (boiled potatoes with garlic and parsley), which I mash with a little olive oil.

DRINKING AND SNACKING AT THE OSTERIE OF TREVISO

In Treviso you can taste a fabled wine called Clinton, which bears no relation to the American president. Clinton is a wine whose production is officially outlawed because it does not conform to any DOC standards. It is not a great wine, but it can be charming. Ask for it by name. Fragolino (which means "Little Strawberry") is another typical wine of Treviso. It is meant to put you in a good mood. Only 7 percent alcohol, it is not sold commercially because

Closing-up time at the Treviso fish market

it is not quite high enough in alcohol to qualify as a wine. It was, for centuries, a wine given to the sick to lift their mood. There is a very small production that is scarcely seen outside the area. It can be drunk as a dessert wine, as a meditation wine, or with desserts. In the *osterie* you ask for *un'ombra* (a glass of wine) and eat *cicheti*. Here is a list of some of the many *osterie* to visit in Treviso for tasty food, wine and company. All have variable closing times, so if one is shut move on to another:

Lindbergh, Viale 15 Luglio 1, tel. 0422/ 21037.

Good food (especially vegetables) and wine, and jazz some nights.

All'Antico Pallone, Vicolo Rialto 5, tel. 0422/540857.

Great porchetta, prosciutto and salumi.

Al Bottegon da Graziano, Piazzale Burchiellati 7, tel. 0422/548345.

Popular with young people who nibble on *cicheti*. Tripe is a specialty.

Al Dante, Piazza Garibaldi 6, tel. 0422/591897.

Sparkling Prosecco flows freely and is paired with tasty small dishes.

Corte Scura, Via Inferiore 33, tel. 0422/56683.

A formidable wine list and all kinds of fish *cicheti* and seafood.

Al Calice d'Oro, Via Pescheria 5, tel. 0422/544762.

Serves little fried fish, vegetables, and cheese.

Muscoli's, Via Pescheria 23, tel. 0422/583390.

Tasty snacks and the famous *panino al Prosecco*, with the bread doused with sparkling wine and slathered with garlic purée and a creamy cheese.

Osteria alla Pescheria, Via Pescheria 41.

Plain, unpretentious, friendly, and fun.

Trevisi, Vicolo Trevisi, no telephone.

A fine setting and good wines and *cicheti*.

Dai Naneti, Vicolo Broli 2, no telephone.

Near Piazza Indipendenza, simple and good.

Odeon alla Colonna, Vicolo Rinaldi 3, no telephone.

In a typically *trevigiano* setting, this place has become fancier through the years. It is charming nonetheless and you should opt for simpler food choices.

FOOD SHOPPING ON
THE VIA PALESTRO AND THE VIA PESCHERIA

Most food stores in Treviso are closed on Wednesday afternoon and Sunday. The market of Treviso, centered around the Pescheria and its pretty canals, is not the largest you will ever see but is one of the most atmospheric. If you shut your eyes slightly and let your vision blur, it will look like an eighteenth-century painting with smiling women, jocular men, sparkling seafood, colorful fruit and vegetables, and an overall sense of festivity. On one side of the Pescheria are *osterie* that seem little changed in decades. Be sure to make a morning visit to the market during your stay in Treviso. What follows are some places to visit near the market, plus the excellent Gastronomia Danesin, which is near the Teatro Comunale, and other stores around town.

On Via Palestro, at #23, is a pasta shop with old machines that you can observe. It also sells *canederli*, the dumplings that are popular in the Alps farther north. At #25 is Spiedo d'Oro, an excellent *rosticceria* (closed Monday) with roasted chicken and potatoes and baked pasta and vegetables. At #36 is the Casa del Caffè (closed Sunday), where you can drink coffee, buy beans, cookies, candies, and liqueurs. Next door is the Casa del Parmigiano, a good all-purpose *salumeria*.

Turn onto Via Pescheria and go immediately to #14. The Bottega del Baccalà has been in business since the mid-1920s. It is a superb source for dried cod, a staple for economical cooks everywhere, but especially in the Veneto. It also sells prepared cod in many forms. You can purchase herring, anchovies, and sardines. But this store does not stop at fish. There are sacks of beans, seeds, dried vegetables and fruits, olives, cheese (although the fishy fragrance here deters me from buying dairy products), and polenta to accompany your fish. A visit here is an education in what a Veneto cook would have in his or her pantry. The Via Pescheria is lined with fruit and vegetable stands worth investigating. In the center of the street is a bridge that extends to an island in the river that runs on either side. Here are the fish markets. As the fishmongers busily wash, clean, and fillet their wares, shoppers sniff, look fish coldly in the eye, and demand—by habit—that the fish they purchase be the freshest. Blue plastic barrels hold live eels or seafood. Occasionally one will contain water to clean fish. When the water can no longer be used it is dumped in the river. After visiting the market, repair to one of the *osterie* for a glass of wine and a snack.

FOOD STORES ELSEWHERE IN TREVISO

Gastronomia Danesin, Corso del Popolo 28, tel. 0422/540625.

A very complete *gastronomia* that sells beautiful handmade pasta, including *cappellacci* filled with asparagus. There are mountains of dried *funghi porcini,* many prepared foods that you can buy to make a nice meal, including lasagne, cannelloni, baked eggplant, and *vitello tonnato.* You can purchase excellent rice, cornmeal for polenta, *farro,* and other grains. Without being snobbish, this place has the air and quality of a first-rate emporium.

Via San Michele 7 (near the Loggia).

An excellent fruit stand, including many exotic fruits from abroad.

Drogheria Foresti, Via Martiri Libertà 66, tel. 0422/542218. Closed Wednesday afternoon and Sunday.

A very special store that should not be missed. More than a century old and maintaining its original decor, this is an emporium of spices and fragrances from throughout the world. It is owned by Mimmo Cappellaro, nephew of Giuseppe Maffioli, a famous Treviso gourmand and actor. Mixed in with exotica from Asia and

Africa are such American novelties as Bisquick and maple syrup. There is also Nin Jiom (Chinese cough syrup), *berberè* (an Ethiopian spice), tea imported directly from India rather than via India. Foreigners come to Treviso to buy rare products that they cannot locate even in the countries of their origins. It is notable that Treviso (population 84,000), a provincial capital and not usually thought of among the leading Italian cities, should have a store of this type. It bespeaks the fact that the people of the Veneto have for centuries looked outward to the world and its products and that nearby Venezia is a historic center of the spice trade.

WINE AND SPIRITS

Abbiati, Via Municipio 1, tel. 0422/52635. Closed Wednesday afternoon and Sunday. MasterCard, Visa.

On a square that was once a vibrant marketplace, where bakeries and *osterie* have given way to offices and banks as Treviso has become affluent, this store has a superb selection of grappa and spirits and a good choice of Veneto wines as well.

L'Enoteca Trevigiana, Viale IV Novembre 62.

A huge, excellent selection of Veneto wines and a friendly, knowledgeable owner.

Valeggio sul Mincio (Verona)

Valeggio is a rather astonishing place on the banks of the Mincio, a river more associated with Mantova and the third act of *Rigoletto* than with the province of Verona. There is an absolutely beautiful park on the edge of town, but for the gourmet traveler Valeggio merits a journey all by itself. I cannot think of another place in Italy of this size (population 9,300) that is so full of good restaurants. It is also notable that Valeggio remains relatively unknown to most Italians and unheard of by foreigners.

Although one naturally thinks of Bologna as the home of tortellini, Valeggio stakes a pretty good claim to being runner-up. Wherever you go in town there are artistic renderings of the navel-shaped pasta, and it seems that every street has its own shop that makes fresh tortellini each day. Another specialty is cooked or preserved fruit, including peaches, apricots, cherries, and grapes. There are easily two dozen restaurants in Valeggio, each trying to outdo the other. So the quality of the cooking is unusually high. I have only been to two restaurants in Valeggio, but I would happily return to try more.

DINING

Il Bue d'Oro, Via Sala 1, tel. 045/7950045, fax 045/6370071. Closed Monday afternoon and Tuesday. All credit cards. Moderate to moderately expensive.

This is a hotel and restaurant that has a large room in the rear where special events take place. On the evening I dined at Il Bue d'Oro with good friends, there was a huge wedding party taking place in the back, but this in way no way hampered the quality of the food and service, which were excellent. There is a beautiful table filled with fresh, inviting antipasti, vegetables, and cooked fruit. Sometimes the food on such tables looks better than it tastes, but among six of us we sampled everything and not one wrong note was sounded. All the homemade pastas were delicious: tortellini in broth, tortellini with butter and sage, *tagliatelle al ragù, tortelli di zucca,* and unusual *tortelli di stracchino,* filled with a cow's cheese that perhaps was a touch too mild but was appealing nonetheless. The second courses featured various meats: boned, stuffed guinea fowl, an excellent veal chop cooked with herbs, beef braised in Amarone wine, braised snails served with creamy polenta, grilled paillard of veal, thin slices of roasted horse meat (very popular locally and delicious if you don't conjure visions of Black Beauty or Mr. Ed). There was also tasty cod cooked in milk and served with polenta and sautéed mixed wild mushrooms and polenta. All of these were accompanied by succulent vegetables from the central table. The star dessert was a selection of cooked fruit. There is also a fine wine list. Highly recommended.

Antica Locanda Mincio, Borghetto (on the banks of the river, just outside of town; follow signs), tel. 045/7950059. Closed Tuesday evening, Wednesday, last two weeks of February, and last two weeks of October. All credit cards. Moderate to moderately expensive.

This is the most famous restaurant in Valeggio. It first opened as an inn in 1600 and has had many illustrious visitors through the years. Napoleon stopped here in 1796 during his campaign against Austria. Opera star Mirella Freni was a more recent diner. The food is very good, but I prefer Il Bue d'Oro.

Venezia

Venezia is divided into different quarters, including Castello, Cannaregio, Dorsoduro, Giudecca, San Marco, San Polo, and Santa Croce. Wherever possible in these listings the quarter will be included. Tourists often bypass the kind of places I recommend to eat because they seem too local. Unfortunately, in Venezia the tourist culture is such that restaurants that cater to visitors turn out lackluster meals at not-inexpensive prices. A few places, such as Harry's Bar and Antico Martini, capture the wealthy segment of the international set, and they do produce some good dishes. But you didn't buy this book to learn about those places. Venetians like to gather in casual places to chatter in their lilting dialect while drinking *un'ombra* and chomping on small dishes of tasty fish, liver, *salami*, polenta, and vegetables. Depending on the day, the season, and the mood of the cook, you might encounter clams in wine and herbs, *seppie, sarde in saor* (fresh sardines in a tangy acidic marinade), little veal meatballs with potatoes, grilled eggplant, or radicchio. There is usually *pasta e fagioli* or some other good soup. By eating this way you will do as the Venetians do and will more likely discover the real flavors of this city. You will also come into contact with the language and the ways of the people, and you don't have to worry about communication when you order. Most of the food is displayed on platters, and you just need to point at what looks good.

BAKERIES

Pasticceria Gilda Vio, Santa Croce 890, tel. 041/718523. Closed Wednesday.

Good small pastries and very good *tiramisù.*

Antica Pasticceria Rizzardini, San Polo 1415. Closed Tuesday.

A good source for typical Venetian cookies and pastries such as *nosea* (whole hazelnuts, cocoa, candied fruit), *pavana* (sliced almonds, amaretto), *dolce di mandorle* (ground almonds, sugar), *moro* (chocolate and almonds), *golosesso* (dark chocolate and pecans), *zaeto* (long, oval-shaped cornmeal cookies), *dogi* (amaretto, raisin, sugar, egg), and *vini* (fruit, egg, pine nuts, Prosecco wine, sugar).

Pasticceria dal Nono Colussi, Dorsoduro, Calle Lunga S. Barnaba 2867A, tel. 041/5231871. Closed Tuesday.

Every Thursday the bakery makes *focaccia alla veneziana,* which is not a bread, as in Liguria, but a fragrant and airy yeast cake. It is sold until Sunday but is best sampled on the day it is made.

Venezia

Pasticceria Fersuoch, Castello 6779, Campo S.S. Giovanni e Paolo. Closed Wednesday.

On a wonderfully typical Venetian piazza is a very old bakery/bar run by a very old woman. She makes fine coffee, and there are good pastries to be had. If you like the sweet-tangy flavor of quince, try the *fiori di mela cotogna*, which are chewy florets of quince. When you visit, take a moment to absorb the atmosphere of this old-style establishment, which is increasingly hard to come by.

Panificio Giovanni Volpe, Cannaregio 1143 (in the old Jewish Ghetto).

In addition to the usual baked specialties of Venice, Volpe makes Jewish specialties, such as *pane azimo* (unleavened bread that looks different from what American and Israeli Jews might recognize), *azime dolci* (sweet cookies made of matzo meal), *torta di mandorla* (almond cake made with soy milk to keep it kosher), large macaroons called *mandorle* and small ones called *cocco*, as in "coconut." You will also find *zuccherini* (round sugar cookies), *bisse* (seahorse-shaped cookies), and *impade*, sugared logs filled with jam or figs. Although Volpi makes traditional Jewish baked goods, you might be surprised to see pork products such as prosciutto, speck, mortadella, and *pancetta* on sale. After buying a bag of sweets you might want to walk across the street to #1236, an *osteria* where you can have a glass of *zibibbo, ramandolo*, or *moscato bianco* to accompany your *dolci*.

BARS AND CAFFÈS

Bar Rosa Salva, San Marco 4589, Campo San Luca, tel. 041/5225385. Closed Sunday.

One of my favorite places in town for breakfast—excellent coffee and brioches.

Bar-Pasticceria DalMas, Cannaregio 150/A. Closed Tuesday.

I first came here in 1973 and tasted a little triangular pastry with chocolate, butter cream, and rum. It is full of flavor but not overly sweet or alcoholic. The owner does not know what the pastry is called, but he refers to it as Arlecchino. There is a good cappuccino, too, so I have made it a custom to stop here, on the Lista di Spagna just past the train station, whenever I arrive in Venezia.

THE CAFFÈS OF
PIAZZA SAN MARCO

There are three famous *caffès* on the square that Napoleon called the Drawing Room of Europe, and you should devote some time to getting to know them.

One risk of sitting on the Piazza San Marco comes from above. Despite successful efforts to curb the Venetian pigeon population, on certain days pigeons still reach the piazza in Hitchcockian proportions. Yet it is endlessly fascinating to watch the comings and goings in the square, much as Effie Ruskin did years ago. Of course there are crowds of tourists, but there are also young lovers, wistful singles, and many school groups. With changes in world politics and the outbreak of ethnic wars, peoples who were visited by, and traded with, the Venetians during the Renaissance have made a reappearance. Just as some of their forebears came here in the sixteenth century, many now have come as immigrants and refugees from the Balkans, the Levant, and the Maghreb. These were the same people Effie Ruskin used to stare at. They add a spice and flavor to Venezia that has always made this city distinct.

Caffè Florian, Piazza San Marco 56. Closed Wednesday.

Founded in 1720 when the Venezia was still a republic, Florian witnessed the city's fall to Napoleon, Austrian occupation, and the struggle for Italian unification. Through the years, every famous person who has visited the city has had a drink here. It is hardly necessary for me to heap encomiums on this, one of the world's most famous *caffès*. It is often inundated, it is overpriced, but it is so special that you should not miss it. In warm weather sit outdoors and listen to the orchestras whose music wafts around the piazza. In the winter, occupy a spot on a slightly worn banquette indoors and take in the paintings of the famous characters who were among the most illustrious citizens of Venezia and its empire: Marco Polo, Doge Enrico Dandolo, Andrea Palladio, Titian, Casanova, and Goldoni. The decor is redolent of the oriental (that is, Byzantine) influences on Venetian art and design. The coffee, chocolate, wines, and liqueurs are excellent at Florian.

Caffè Lavena, Piazza San Marco.

The Caffè Florian may be more famous, but Lavena (opened 1750) has a following and merit all its own. Because of its location on the far side of Piazza San Marco, it is favored with more sunlight than the other *caffès* on the square. For this reason, it has always been popular with visitors from northern Europe, including Wagner, a frequent visitor to Venezia who died there in 1883. Every day, from five to six in the afternoon, Wagner came to Lavena with his family or friends for tea or cognac. His father-in-law, Franz Liszt, was another regular. The legacy of these visits is that Caffè Lavena is a required stop for every classical musician who visits town (Artur Rubenstein loved this place), and it also draws anyone attracted to sunshine.

Caffè Quadri, Piazza San Marco 120. Closed Monday.

The third of the great *caffè*s on Piazza San Marco dates back to 1775. Some Venetians avoid it because it has long been popular with—and in some years, indeed, occupied by—Germans. Nonetheless, it, too, has its beauty and history, and although this *caffè* and most everything else in central Venezia has become tourist oriented, it is still worth a look.

CATS

Cats in Venezia are revered because they saved the city from the plague in the Middle Ages by eating the rats that threatened to infest the city. To many *veneziani,* cats are descendants of the Lion of Saint Mark, who occupies a place of prominence in all representations of the patron saint of Venezia. You can see cats working their way through displays in fancy glass shops and, of course, never breaking a thing. One cat I know lives in a bookshop, where he prefers to sleep on a desk like a furry paperweight. Five cats live at the Hotel Cipriani, occupying niches in trees in the hotel's refined gardens. One seems to find blissful shade under a tree heavy with pomegranates. The more plebeian cousins of the Cipriani cats often visit the fish market near the Rialto Bridge, where they feast on morsels of Adriatic seafood that are thrown their way. You can read more about Venetian cats in Jan Morris's *A Venetian Bestiary,* a wonderful volume devoted to the birds, dogs, cats, and sea creatures that are part of the Venetian landscape.

COOKING SCHOOLS

A Scuola in Cucina, Palazzo Morosini, Castello 6140, 30100 Venezia, tel. 041/5228923.

From October through May serious courses are given that last from three hours to four weeks. Themes change all the time, so it's best to check what's being offered when you plan to visit Venezia. The real reason to come is to study the courses in ancient Venetian cuisine given by the school's director, Fulvia Sesani.

Hotel Cipriani, Isola della Giudecca 10, 30133 Venezia, tel. 041/5207744, fax 041/5203930.

In the autumn, classes are held in English in a sunny room facing a broad canal just beyond the hotel's gardens. World-famous chefs and food writers such as Julia Child, Carol Field, and Marcella Hazan give classes to hotel guests who make advance arrangements. Included in the course fee are five nights at the Cipriani, all meals (including some at selected restaurants throughout the city), three cooking classes, and an escorted tour of the Rialto market.

Marcella and Victor Hazan Cooking Classes. (In the United States, contact Hazan Classics, P.O. Box 285, Circleville, NY 10919, tel. 914/692-7104, fax 914/692-2659.)

Perhaps the best restaurant in town. Great *risotto ai frutti di mare* and *coda di rospo*. You will notice a tiny platform on the canal below. Watch how, during the course of your meal, gondolas glide by and the oarsmen pick up a glass of wine and a snack offered by the restaurant. On their next trip around, the gondoliers place their empty glass on the platform.

Cavatappi, Campo de la Guerra 525, San Marco, tel. 041/2960252. Open 9–24h; closed Sunday evening, Monday and a month in winter. No credit cards. Moderately inexpensive.

Cavatappi (corkscrew) is different from many Venetian *bàcari* because of its clean lines and airy environment. This attitude extends to the food, which includes excellent *salumi* and cheeses, and fine wines by the glass. At lunch a few dishes issue from the kitchen such as risotto or large salads. In the evenings the cooking becomes more elaborate. There are always good *cicheti* if you want a lighter repast.

Osteria agli Assassini, Rio Terà dei Assassini 3695, San Marco, tel. 041/5287986. Closed Sunday. No credit cards. Moderately inexpensive.

A good osteria with honest food and wine, and a friendly atmosphere in a part of Venezia in which these virtues are hard to find. Vegetables are excellent here, as is *fegato alla veneziana*, and there are usually interesting cheeses on hand to match with your remaining wine.

Osteria da Carla, Corte Contarin 1535 (just off Frezzeria), San Marco

Good food for a casual lunch. Soups, fish, vegetables all good, not the pastas.

The *sarde in saor* with polenta is an excellent choice. A five-minute walk from Piazza San Marco, American Express, and the Luna Hotel.

Al Bacareto, Calle de le Botteghe 3447 (Campo San Giacometto), San Marco, tel. 041/5289336. Open 7:30–23h, closed Saturday evening, Sunday, and in August. No credit cards. Moderately inexpensive to moderately expensive.

This was once a simply *bàcaro* that has expanded and now offers a moderately expensive meal for those who seek that. But one can eat well here without too much outlay of funds if you stick to the the excellent *cicheti*. At lunchtime I like to go to the bar and get a plate of whatever risotto is being served that day.

DINING IN CASTELLO

Hostaria da Franz, Fondamenta Sant' Isepo 754, Castello, tel. 041/5220861, fax 041/2419278. Closed Tuesdays, and from mid-November to just before Christmas and again in January and early February, until Carnival time. All credit cards. Moderate to moderately expensive.

This casual restaurant with very good food is a pleasant 25-minute walk from St. Mark's Square along the Riva degli Schiavoni, past the Arsenal and wonderful maritime museum. It is near the Public Gardens and a good pick if you are attending the Biennale. I really love the *moscardini* (baby octopus) cooked in Prosecco.

Alle Testiere, Calle del Mondo Novo 5801, Castello, tel./fax 041/5227220. Closed Sunday and Monday. All credit cards. Moderately expensive.

A small, cramped restaurant serving very good fish and seafood. I love the mussels cooked with ginger as an appetizer and, if they have it, *soasi* (Venetian baby turbot). Reservations are a must.

All'Aciugheta, Campo Santi Filippo e Giacomo 4357, Castello, tel. 041/ 5224292. Open daily 9–24h. No credit cards. Inexpensive.

If you can find nowhere else to eat in town, you can always eat at All' Aciugheta. The *cicheti* are tasty and the wine is excellent.

DINING IN CANNAREGIO

Fiaschetteria Toscana, San Giovanni Grisostomo 5719, Cannaregio, tel. 041/5285281, fax 041/5285521. Closed Monday lunch, all day Tuesday, and from late July to mid-August. All credit cards. Moderately expensive.

Near the Rialto bridge is one of Venezia's most consistently fine restaurants and it has perhaps the best cheese cart in the city. The risottos, soups and pastas are all very good, as is most fish preparation and the *fegato alla veneziana*. Only desserts are weak here. You might think, based on the name, that this is a Tuscan restaurant. In fact, it is on the site of a place that used to sell Tuscan wines in *fiaschi* (flasks), but the food is very Venetian.

Trattoria Ca d'Oro, Calle Ca d'Oro 3912, Cannaregio. Closed Thursday and Sunday afternoon, the two weeks after Carnival, and in August. No credit cards. Moderate.

A very welcoming place near the Strada Nova (the main thoroughfare) and the Ca d'Oro vaporetto stop. Somehow it manages to retain its very Venetian flavor.

Many local people, from professors and shopkeepers to boatmen in rubber shoes, sit or stand together chattering in dialect. They are drawn to the very good *cicheti* and tasty prepared dishes. I prefer the soups to pasta here.

Anice Stellato, Fondamenta de la Sensa 3272, Cannaregio, tel. 041/720744. Closed Monday and Tuesday, one week in late January, and two weeks in late August/early September. MasterCard, Visa. Moderate.

The name means star anise and, while that spice is not a central ingredient, this trattoria is a star on the list of many Venetians. Reservations are essential. The pastas and all seafood are delicious and there is a well-selected cheese cart. Wines are decent, not more, but few people seem deterred by that.

Trattoria dalla Marisa, Fondamenta San Giobbe 652b, Cannaregio, tel. 041/ 720211. Closed on Sunday, Monday, and Wednesday evenings, August and Christmastime. No credit cards. Moderate.

You will find this place by the crowds of Venetians who wait to get in, including gondoliers. They come here when they crave meat, which takes second place on most menus in Venezia. I have enjoyed duck, pheasant, guinea hen, and numerous game birds. If you want fish, you must reserve it ahead of time. There is no wine list and most diners drink what the owners are pouring.

DINING IN DORSODURO

Locanda Montin, Fondamenta Eremite 1147, tel. 041/5227151, fax 041/5200255. Closed Wednesday. All credit cards. Moderate to moderately expensive.

A good choice if you are seeing art at the Accademi museum or the Guggenheim gallery. Sit in the garden in the back. Good basic Venetian food. I like the *spaghetti con nero di seppie* (squid ink) and the *coda di rospo*.

Ristorante Riviera, Dorsoduro 1473, tel. 041/5227621. Closed Sunday evening and Monday. All credit cards. Moderately expensive.

If you go for a long walk on the Zattere, the broad street on the Giudecca Canal that somehow has resisted the tread of tourism, you will be able to bask in the sun and feel more connected to the older rhythms of Venetian life. At one end is this restaurant, near Venezia's only real supermarket. If you are used to the large markets in most places, this will seem puny, but Venetians flock here and then take their purchases home on the vaporetto. A few doors down is Ristorante Riviera, which has a particular following among attendees of Venezia's film festival each September. I once saw Woody Allen dining here. While not outstanding, the food is done with care. However, space limitations present a challenge: the last time I ate here, I ordered a whole fish which the waiter chose to debone for me. He placed the platter on top of a fax machine because there was no other place to put it.

La Bitta, Dorsoduro 2753, Calle Lunga San Barnaba, tel. 041/5230531. Open 18:30–1:30h; closed Sunday. No credit cards. Moderate.

This osteria is a fine place to come for meat dishes (*ossobuco, fegato alla veneziana, porchetta*) and mushrooms in season, all to be paired with red wines from the small but appealing list.

DINING IN SANTA CROCE

Osteria La Zucca, San Giacomo dell' Orio 1762, Santa Croce, tel. 041/5241570. Moderate.

This restaurant is no longer a secret and has become immensely popular. While the menu is not strictly vegetarian, the strength is in the many dishes based on the wonderful vegetables from the Veneto. There are meat and fish here too.

Rivetta, Calle Sechera 637, Santa Croce, no telephone. Open 8:30–21:30h; closed Sunday and in August. No credit cards. Inexpensive.

Near Piazzale Roma is this jumping little *bàcaro* (wine bar with *cicheti*). Apart from *salumi* and cheeses, this is a place to have a big salad.

DINING IN SAN POLO

Ristorante Antiche Carampane, Rio Terà de le Colone 1911, San Polo, tel. 041/5240165. Closed Sunday evening and Monday. American Express, Visa. Moderate.

I love the sign that hangs outside this restaurant: *No Pizza, No Lasagne, No Menù Turistico.* In Venezia so many restaurants cater to tourists that this one feels the need to assert its identity as a place where one eats serious food. Ask for an *antipasto misto* and you will receive a platter of carefully selected and beautifully cooked seafood from the Venetian lagoon and the Adriatic. If they have *linguine con lo scorfano*, a pasta with a sauce of fish, tomato, carrot, celery, onion, and parsley, do not miss it. Grilled fish is a good secondo, and save room for the *dolci della casa*. These traditional Venetian pastries are made from jealously guarded recipes that have been handed down in the family for generations.

DINING IN GIUDECCA

Hotel Cipriani, Isola della Giudecca 10, tel. 041/5207744, fax 041/5203930. All credit cards. Expensive.

There is good food to be had at this divine hotel. Prices are among the highest in this expensive city but, if this is not a problem, the setting is beautiful and the service is first-rate. If the *paupiettes* of Adriatic crab are available, go for them. I think the bitter-chocolate *gelato* is one of the finest ice creams in Italy. The wine list is well-selected but very costly.

Harry's Dolci, Fondamenta San Biagio 773, Giudecca, tel. 041/5224844. Closed Tuesday. All credit cards. Moderately expensive.

A less-expensive branch of Harry's Bar, the tourist-clogged magnet near San Marco that is vastly overrated. At Harry's Dolci, if you order simple dishes you can eat well. The house special taglierini with cheese is tasty.

DINING IN BURANO

Trattoria da Romano, Via Baldassare Galuppi 221, Burano, tel. 041/730030, www.daromano.it. Moderate to moderately expensive.

Call before setting out to see if they are open and have an available table. Take the vaporetto (line 12 from the Fondamente Nuove or line 14 from Riva degli Schiavoni) on a 35-minute ride that will help you build your appetite for Venetian classics prepared lovingly by the Barbaro family, which has run this place for almost a century. Da Romano has always been popular with artists and writers.

DINING IN MESTRE

Trattoria La Pergola, Via Fiume 42, tel.

041/974932. Closed Saturday lunch and Sunday, three weeks in January, and one week in mid-August. All credit cards. Moderately inexpensive.

If you cannot get a hotel room in the *centro storico* of Venezia, another option is to stay in Mestre on the mainland, just a short train ride away. I usually stay at the Hotel Bologna opposite the Mestre train station. I use this option too if I have an early flight from Marco Polo airport because access is much easier from Mestre. Often I have my last meal in Mestre before flying home, so I want it to be good. I love to drop in at the Trattoria La Pergola. The atmosphere is warm and convivial in winter. In the summer you might wish to sit under the pergola where workers used to play *bocce*. There are many good dishes here, including *tagliatelle con radicchio* from Treviso with *scalogno* (shallot). If *castraure* (delicate artichokes grown on the island of Sant' Erasmo) are in season, have them any way they are being prepared. Leeks, eggplants (aubergines), and various greens are deftly used in pasta, rice, meat and fish dishes.

Ostaria da Mariano, Via Spalti 49, tel. 041/615765. Closed Saturday, Sunday, Monday evening, Tuesday evening, and in August. All credit cards. Moderately inexpensive to moderate.

This is another fine choice in Mestre, where the food is centered on Venetian classics such as *sarde in saor, baccalà mantecato, bigoi con salsa peverada*, and *fegato alla veneziana*. Wine lovers should note that the list here is much more compelling than at La Pergola.

FOLKLORE

Probably no city in Italy has more festive observances than Venezia, which finds many ways to honor not only the Church but also its glorious past. Several of the events involve boat races or maritime processions down the Grand Canal. The ones listed here prominently feature food and wine.

La Sensa.

Held forty days after Easter Sunday, this is one of the most beautiful and moving of Venetian festivals. This is the day when Venezia renewed its marriage vows with the sea. The Doge would set out in a magnificent boat called the Bucintoro and then toss a gold ring into the sea. Nowadays, a laurel wreath is tossed from the Piazza San Marco, but it is still a deeply felt event.

Festa del Redentore.

On the third Sunday in June, to recall the eradication of the plague from Venezia in 1577, services are held in the Church of the Redentore, which was designed by Palladio, on Giudecca On the day before there is a huge boat procession on the Grand Canal near San Marco, followed by fireworks and feasting on fish and watermelon on Giudecca. On Sunday, after the religious services, there is a regatta in the Giudecca Canal and then more dancing and feasting.

Sagra di San Pietro di Castello.

In the last week of June there are stands offering typical Venetian dishes in the Campo di San Pietro. On Sunday evening a large dance is held in front of the church.

Sagra del Pesce di Burano.

On the third Sunday of September. Fish, polenta, and white wine are served on the island of Burano, and a regatta is held.

Sagra del Mosto di Sant'Erasmo.

Wine is actually produced in the Venetian Lagoon. On Sant'Erasmo, the first Sunday in October, the very young must is consumed along with meat and polenta, and a regatta is held in which the boat must be rowed by one man and one woman.

Festa dei Morti.

On November 1 it is a tradition to remember the dead but also to buy your beloved a bag of pink, white, and brown "beans" made of almond paste.

Festa di San Martino.

On November 11 children march through town banging ladles on frying pans and singing songs, earning a few lire from passersby. They then go to bakeries to buy pastries in the shape of San Martino on his horse.

Festa della Salute.

In remembrance of the end of the plague of 1630 on November 21 a slow candlelit procession wends its way through the Grand Canal and the Giudecca. Stands sell candles, fritters, and various sweets.

On this day it is the custom to eat a plate of Savoy cabbage and have mutton in broth.

FOOD SHOPPING

Most food stores and markets in Venezia are closed on Wednesday afternoon and Sunday. The market in Venezia, just below the Rialto Bridge, is great fun even if part of it has become touristic. Early each morning (except Sunday) you can watch fish and produce being unloaded from boats in the Grand Canal. The market is open mornings only. On the Calle de le Becarie o Panataria is the fresh fish market. This brick structure with its elegant arches is the place to learn about the fish and seafood you will be tasting in restaurants and *osterie*. On one end of the market is an old stone engraved with the minimum lengths permitted for different fish to be sold. Many of the names are in Venetian dialect. Notice, too, the six fountains that run constantly so that fish can be washed and buckets filled. Over a small bridge is the Antica Trattoria Poste Vecie, which claims to be the oldest trattoria in Venezia. It is expensive and touristy and does not merit a visit.

Drogheria Mascari, 380 Ruga dei Spezieri (near the market).

Coffee, oil, candies, and beautiful dried herbs and flavors for teas and infusions. These include Karkadè from the Sudan, chamomile flowers, calendula, flowers from cherry, apple, and pear trees, and several types of mint. This place bespeaks a time when Venezia was a major spice market, and, in fact, it is on the old street of the spice sellers.

Pastificio Giacomo Rizzo, 5778 Cannaregio, S. G. Grisostomo 5778, tel. 041/5222824.

This well-known pasta shop has been in business since 1905 and is famous for being the first place in town, and one of the first in Italy, to give pasta flavors and colors beyond tomato red and spinach green. Here you find pastas with names such as *cacao* (cocoa), curry, pizza, blue Curaçao (a robin's-egg blue), *seppie* (black ink from cuttlefish), *cipolla* (onion), green olive, cayenne, salmon, and pesto. It also sells packages with the colors of popular soccer teams, such as Milan (*seppia* and beet, black and red). This is all very festive, and therefore very Venetian, but pasta purists such as myself consider it a waste of good ingredients. When flour is blended with fancy ingredients to make pasta, those other flavors are muted. While the color is often appealing, it tastes very odd with certain sauces. On the other hand, it is fun and special (except for that weird blue pasta), and you might want to pick up a package to take home. Rizzo does sell good quality oils, vinegars, truffle paste, rice, cornmeal for polenta, Ligurian olives, and jarred vegetable sauces for pasta.

Da Lorenzo di Paparone, S. Luca 4666, tel. 041/5232682.

Excellent *salumi*, cheeses, and game. There are many products from Germany, Austria, and German-speaking Italy, reflecting not only the impact on Venetian taste of the many years of Austrian occupation, but also the strong German presence today in the city known as Venedig.

A WALK THROUGH THE SHOPPING NEXUS ON THE STRADA NOVA IN CANNAREGIO

To give you an idea of how Venetians shop in nontouristic zones, you can walk down the Strada Nova in the early evening. This is also a valuable place if you need to buy some food for a picnic or to eat in your hotel room.

#3834a:

A very capacious *drogheria* with teas, spices, many wines and other bottles. Endless canned goods, also prosciutto and cheese, especially a good Montasio. Diagonally across is a good fruit and vegetable seller.

#3843:

Next door to the *drogheria* is the Panificio F. Paronuzzi, with an extensive selection of breads, cookies, cakes, and other baked goods. Right across the way is Mauro El Forner de Canton, with more of same.

#3929:

Bellinato is an excellent source for coffeemakers and housewares. Across the way is its large appliance store, whose products seem very incongruous in this city. Imagine the effort required to bring a dishwasher here without a car or truck!

GLASS

Venezia is famous for its blown glass. Because there is so much to choose from, one can be stymied by the selection and come home empty-handed. Many shops in the old city offer tacky souvenirs and only a few feature better quality. You might consider a trip on the vaporetto from Piazza San Marco to Murano to visit some of the glassworks. One I like is Fornace Campagnol-Marega-Salvadore at Corte del Fabbro 122 (closed Sunday). Here are nice handmade glasses, chalices, plates, and bottles at fair prices.

HOUSEWARES

Bellinato, 3929 Cannaregio, at Strada Nova and Calle Ca d'Oro. All credit cards.

A basic but extensive selection of Italian cookware and kitchen equipment.

Ditta Ennio Camuffo, San Polo 2799, tel. 041/719376. Closed Saturday in summer and Sunday.

A basic lamp and hardware store, but with an excellent selection of knives, especially cheese knives, plus Italian coffeemakers from one to twelve cups, pots, pans, milk steamers, mills, grinders, slicers, truffle shavers, corkscrews, fish gutters, pasta wheels, strainers, and much more.

Domus, Calle dei Fabbri 4746, tel. 041/5226259, fax 041/5225278. Open daily. MasterCard, Visa.

A very large selection of dishes, cups, glassware, platters, and tableware. Much is ordinary, though well made, but one can find many attractive items at good prices.

ICE CREAM

Da Nico, Zattere 922, tel. 041/5225293. Closed Thursday, and late December to late January.

Outstanding *gianduia*, many other good flavors.

Da Paolin, Santo Stefano 2962 (between Teatro La Fenice and the Accademia Bridge), tel. 041/5225576. Closed Monday (except in summer).

Good flavors of melon, strawberry, *nocciola*, and *gianduia*. It has been in business since the 1930s.

THE JEWISH GHETTO

What is left of the Jewish community of Venezia (which was once one of the strongest and most creative in Europe) is centered on the Campo de Gheto Novo and the adjacent streets. You will see the Casa Israelitica di Risposo, the rest home for the Venetian Jewish community. On somedays, by prearrangement, you can have a kosher Italian meal here. To the left as you face the home are seven works by Arbit Blatas, the very fine artist whose works here evoke the horrors of the Holocaust, which devastated the city's Jews who were easily located in the Ghetto. Blatas was the husband of opera singer Regina Resnik. A number of years ago Madame Resnik directed a fine television film about the Ghetto. Across from the Casa di Riposo is a museum, the Museo Ebraico (open 10–16:30; closed Saturdays and Jewish holidays), that merits a visit. There are guided tours of the three synagogues every hour on the half hour from 10:30 to 15:30. Nearby is the studio of Gianfranco Penzo (Campo de Gheto Novo 2895, tel. 041/716313; open Monday–Thursday all day, Friday until one hour before sunset, Sunday all day in summer, morning only in winter). Signor Penzo does superb decoration of platters and chalices. Much of his work is based on Jewish themes. He receives many commissions to personalize designs for particular family remembrances or religious occasions. His works become family heirlooms. He accepts Visa and MasterCard as well as personal checks and ships his work abroad. A bit off the campo is another store, Fusetti & Mariani Arte Ebraica (Ghetto Vecchio 1218–1219, tel. 041/720092; closed Friday one hour before sundown and all day Saturday; MasterCard and Visa). This store sells Venetian glass and lace that has been specifically created for Jewish religious observance.

LINENS

A nice Venetian tablecloth with embroidered napkins makes a classic gift for someone back home or for your own table. Venezia is full of stores selling lace and embroidered cotton tablecloths, napkins, towels, aprons, and doilies, so I would never pretend to know which are the best.

Leda Fabris, Campo San Bartolomeo 5178, tel. 041/5238400. All credit cards.

This store, near the Rialto Bridge *en route* to the Piazza San Marco, has good-quality merchandise at fair prices. There is a large selection and helpful sales staff.

SPECIAL STORE

Quelchemanca, San Marco 3965, Salizzada de la Chiesa o del Teatro, tel. 041/5222681. American Express, MasterCard, Visa. Open 11–19h; closed Sunday in July and August, and Monday.

Owner Paolo Carrara has gathered an attractive and imaginative collection of antiques and bric-a-brac. Among the things you might find are beautiful old glasses and coffee cups, vases, decorative tins, and other packaging for food from the beginning of the twentieth century. The collection changes regularly, but is notable for the owner's acute taste and for your opportunity to find attractive items that filled Italian kitchens and dining rooms of old. You will likely find an object of beauty that will ultimately be more pleasing and meaningful than the usual items purchased by tourists in Venezia.

Verona

The most famous cultural festival in Italy is presented in Verona each summer, when massive productions of opera with international stars are staged at the Roman arena (tel. 045/590109, fax 045/590201) in the city center. Built in about A.D. 100, it is the second-largest after the Colosseum in Roma.

BAKERY

Pasticceria Cordioli, Via Cappello 39, tel. 045/590109, fax 045/590201. Closed Wednesday.

My favorite *pasticceria* in Verona. A good place for nice pastries with your morning coffee, which can be had at the white-and-reddish-brown marble bar. This is also the ideal place for afternoon tea. Cordioli is down the street from Juliet's balcony and serves delicious and thematic pastries honoring the two most famous personages of Verona with the *baci di Giulietta* (vanilla meringues called Juliet's kisses) and *sospiri di Romeo* (chocolate-hazelnut biscuits called Romeo's sighs). The *pasticceria* makes beautiful cakes, including such Veronese favorites as *pandoro, torta Alleanza* (with candied fruit), and various types of *colombe* (eggy cakes popular at Easter).

CAFFÈ

Caffè Dante, Piazza dei Signori 2, tel. 045/595249.

This *caffè* has occupied a corner on one of the loveliest squares in Italy since 1865. In its first few decades, it was the intellectual gathering place in town and had a large selection of periodicals whose commentaries invariably provoked debate. Here, in 1913, the decision was made that Verona should stage opera in its ancient Roman arena, thus making the city one of the great tourist destinations of Europe.

DINING

Antica Bottega del Vino, Via Scudo di Francia 3, tel. 045/8004535. Reservations essential. All credit cards. Inexpensive to moderately expensive, depending on what you order.

Journalists from the local paper (l'Arena) rub shoulders with opera lovers and oenophiles in this very popular restaurant with one of Italy's best wine lists. The environment is convivial and bustling and I always visit when I am in Verona. In recent years the quality of the cooking has declined, but *risotto all'Amarone* is still reliable, and salumi, cheese and vegetable platters are good to pair with wine.

Al Carroarmato, Vicolo Gatto 2a, tel. 045/8030175. Closed Wednesday. No credit cards. Moderately inexpensive.

A friendly *osteria* with good wine and tasty food. Gnocchi are served on Fridays.

Enoteca Cangrande, Via Dietro Listone 19d, tel. 045/595022. Closed Monday, and January. Open 16–1h. No credit cards. Moderately inexpensive.

Excellent wines, good food, especially the tortellini and the *crespelle con funghi e tartufo*.

Ristorante Il Cenacolo, Via Teatro Filarmonico 10, tel. 045/592288. All credit cards. Moderately expensive.

This restaurant is popular with celebrities, many of whom perform at or frequent Verona's indoor opera house down the street or the outdoor arena where summer opera is staged. One wall is decorated with letters of homage to the food from the likes of Jose Carreras, Luciano Pavarotti, Kiri Te Kanawa, and Ben Gazzara. Look past the copy of the fresco Leonardo's *Last Supper* to the grill where *portobello* mushrooms and small birds are being cooked. The food here is okay but one really comes to look for celebrities, so if that is your craving, feast your eyes.

Ristorante 12 Apostoli, Vicolo Corticella San Marco 3, tel. 045/596999. Closed Sunday evening and Monday, late June, and Christmas. All credit cards. Expensive.

The Ristorante 12 Apostoli is surely Verona's most famous restaurant and was, for many years, considered one of the top restaurants in Italy. It has long been the destination of well-heeled industrialists, influential politicians, and glamorous opera stars. Frankly, the quality of the food declined in the 1980s as the restaurant coasted on its reputation. But in recent years there has been a marked upswing in the kitchen's performance, making dining at the 12 Apostoli a pleasant if somewhat costly experience. Very prominently displayed is a marvelous cheese cart, with each cheese in perfect shape. Aside from such famous cheeses as Taleggio, Gorgonzola, and Asiago, there are lesser-known local varieties such as Vezzena and Mezzano. There are several outstanding dishes I have sampled recently, foremost among these the *pescatrice alle mandorle* (monkfish with almond sauce). Also worth trying is the *sogliola alle olive* (sole with a purée of green olives from nearby Lago di Garda), tortellini with local truffles, and *sorbetto rosa* (a grapefruit sorbet to which Campari is added; when pomegranates are in season, they are used instead of the Campari). For dessert, try baked peaches filled with crumbled amaretto cookies or a fig tart.

Ristorante La Greppia, Vicolo Samiritana 3, tel. 045/8004577. Closed Monday. All credit cards. Moderate.

I have been dining happily at La Greppia for more than twenty years. I return for the good food at fair prices and the friend-liness of the owners and staff. Everyone comes to this inviting room, with six vaulted arches, off an unprepossessing side street near the Piazze delle Erbe. On a re-cent visit, the happy customers included a mother with two small children, a busi-nessman with clients, and a couple of tables with young lovers. The menu is large, but I encourage first-time diners to concentrate on two items: the cart with *bollito misto* and the vast selection of raw and cooked vegetables. The *bollito misto* is a panoply of perfectly boiled meats—chicken, *cotechino* sausage, tongue, beef, pork, *tettina* (udder) and *testina* (head) of veal—that all retain their flavor. Each is sliced lovingly and offered with a range of sauces made of herbs as well as the classic *pearà*, made with marrow. It is customary to have mashed potatoes *(purè)* with this dish. In addition to the *bollito misto,* you should be sure to sample the many choice vegetables that come in a great variety of preparations. If you want pasta, the *tortelli di zucca* and the *fettuccine al sugo di fegatini* (chicken livers) are good choices. There are also *gnocchi al ragù di cavallo* for the curious.

FOOD SHOPPING

The Piazza delle Erbe is one of the most picturesque markets in Italy, but it is rather touristic and not unusual in gastronomic terms. But Verona does have good food shops.

Maculan, Via Cappello 18A.

Very carefully selected cheeses and *salumi.* There may not be as large a selection as in other stores, but the quality is very high. The ricotta is delicious.

WINE FAIR

Ente Autonomo per le Fiere di Verona, Viale del Lavoro, Casella Postale 525, 37100 Verona, tel. 045/588111, fax 045/588288.

Vinitaly, the largest wine fair in Italy, is held each April in the first or second week of the month. It is an appointment kept by almost every wine producer in Italy, the leading importers and exporters of wine from around the world, restaurateurs, and most of the journalists and writers who de-vote themselves to things enological. Vin-italy takes place at the Fiera, the gigantic fairgrounds about a kilometer south of the train station. Each of the Fiera's sixteen pa-vilions is brimming with wine makers and sellers offering tastes of the previous au-tumn's vintage. Major wine-producing regions such as Sicilia, Toscana, and Pie-monte often have pavilions to themselves, while regions that produce less, such as Umbria, Marche, and Lazio, may share a building. There are often representative wines from about twenty other wine-producing nations as well, but the focus is really Italian. Vinitaly is so huge that it is impossible, even for the most accom-plished taster, to sample more than fifty wines a day (one must spit into a bucket!). It is best to choose a particular type of wine, such as hearty reds from Piemonte or dessert wines, and taste that type for an hour or so before taking a break. One can purchase food or go to the gastronomic exhibit that is now part of the annual fair. In addition to providing a break from pure tasting, it gives you a chance to match food and wine. In recent years a prestigious wine competition has preceded the fair, with winning wines receiving their awards at a gala dinner the night before the fair opens. I have served as a judge at this competition, which is done with painstaking impartiality. One year, to everyone's surprise, the wines of Canada finished a strong second to those of Italy, which made up most of the entries. If you are a wine professional—which is to say a producer, importer or exporter, restaurateur, wine seller, or journalist—you should be sure to make Vinitaly part of your schedule. The fair is open to the public on one day, usually Sunday. If you are a traveler interested in wine, it is worth a visit. The problem is that the fair is full of people looking for free tastes of wine and snacks. But if you are developing your wine expertise, try to stay away from the crowds and visit stands offering the wines that interest you. If you plan to attend Vinitaly either as a professional or as a member of the public, you must book a hotel room months in advance or plan to stay as far away as Padova, Vicenza, or Lago di Garda and make a day trip. Restaurants are also packed, so you must reserve for the best tables. Many Vinitaly regulars go to restaurants out of town where the food is cheaper and the atmosphere more relaxed. There is often an opera festival at Verona's Teatro Filarmonico during Vinitaly that should not be missed by fans of the lyric art.

WINE

Enoteca dell'Istituto Enologico Italiano,
Via Sottoriva 7B, tel. 045/590366.

At any time of the year wine lovers who visit Verona should be sure to stop here, near the banks of the Adige. This is an expertly run wine shop where English is spoken (ask for Michael). An ideal place to learn about and acquire fine Italian wines.

Vicenza

Inevitably one thinks of architecture when one visits Vicenza, for here are many of the greatest buildings of Andrea Palladio, perhaps the most influential architect of all time. Although he was from Padova, Palladio found Vicenza a good place to work because of its *pietra tenera,* a stone that is wet when quarried and takes two years to dry. Be sure to make his magnificent Teatro Olimpico part of your visit (Piazza Matteotti, tel. 0444/323781). If a performance is being given there, so much the better. Also visit at least one Palladian villa. Vicenza is well known as the center of gold working in Italy, with more than a third of all the activity taking place here.

Despite the gold and the architectural splendor, Vicenza has also known hard economic times. A ubiquitous dish is *baccalà alla vicentina,* dried cod that has been soaked and then cooked in milk. If poorly prepared it is nothing special, but when well executed and served with polenta it can be a gratifying meal. One often finds dark bread served in Vicenza, a legacy of when fine white flour was a luxury. During the Second World War some people were so poor that they mixed sawdust into their flour. This no longer happens. And then there is the old saw about cats:

Veneziani, gran signori	Venetians are great noblemen
Padovani, gran dottori	Paduans are great doctors
Veronesi, tutti matti	Veronese are all crazy
Vicentini, mangiagatti.	Vicenzans all eat cat.

Here is the story. In the fifteenth century Vicenza was overrun with mice, and the locals applied to Venezia (their overlord) for help. Venezia, with its eternal surplus of cats, sent a bevy of felines to Vicenza to get rid of the mice. Some years later, after the problem was resolved, the Venetians asked for their cats back. "We ate them," said the grinning *vicentini*, and from that time forward the reputation stuck. I am told by local historians that at one time, during periods of privation, it was customary to eat cat in the winter, when a cat would be buried in the snow for three to seven days for proper aging. You will not find cat on local menus. One occasionally hears about certain disreputable restaurants in Vicenza, Roma, and in southern Italy that substitute cat for rabbit. This seldom happens, but there is an easy way to be sure: rib bones on rabbits are flat while those on cats are round. (With nine lives, cats give a new meaning to the term "leftovers.")

BAKERY-BAR

Antica Offelleria della Meneghina, Via Cavour 18, tel. 0444/43687 or 563687. Closed Monday.

An institution in Vicenza since 1791, attracting the *bella gente* of Vicenza , thanks largely to the *ofella*, the typical Easter cake produced here that is famous throughout Italy. It is now available year-round.

COOKING SCHOOL

La Salsiera d'Argento, Contrà Santa Caterina 14, 36100 Vicenza, tel. 0444/324162.

The school's name means "the Silver Gravy Boat," and courses are given from October to June. While all manner of cooking is taught here, the reason to come is to learn how to make *baccalà alla*

vicentina, along with other local dishes.

DINING

Al Pestello, Contra Santo Stefano 3, tel./fax 0444/323721. Closed Sunday, Monday lunch, late May, early October. All credit cards. Moderate.

Excellent Vicenza cuisine in this trattoria a short walk from the Teatro Olimpico.

Al Molin Vecio, Via Giaroni 56, Caldogno (8 km/5 miles south of Vicenza), tel. 0444/585168. Closed Monday evening and Tuesday. American Express, Master Card, Visa. Moderate.

Al Molin Vecio (the Old Mill) is named for the sixteenth-century water mill outside the building. The restaurant's owner, Amedeo Sandri (who for fifteen years was the editor in chief of *La Cucina Italiana*,

Italy's oldest food magazine), likes the idea of theme evenings, so you might arrive when tribute is being paid to writers such as Goldoni, musicians such as Rossini, to Palladio, or perhaps to Santa Maria, the local patron. You will sample many courses of local food and wine and probably be entertained by musicians or actors as you dine. This is as close as Italy gets to dinner theater. Some ancient and unusual dishes you might find are *bacalà cò poènta* (an 1852 recipe with cod, cinnamon, raisins, pine nuts, milk, and oil), *bigoli col desfrito de requeste* (with a sauce of giblets and chicken livers), *stracotto de musso* (braised mule), *portorolo* (a strong cow's-milk cheese), *poènta e fichi* (polenta and figs), and *pevarini* (cookies made with cocoa, pepper, nutmeg, and ginger).

FOOD SHOPPING
Il Ceppo Gastronomico, Corso Palladio 196, tel. 0444/544414. Closed Wednesday afternoon and Sunday.

Local specialties such as *baccalà alla vicentina*, lasagne with asparagus or mushrooms, *bigoli* pasta, Asiago cheese.

LIBRARY
Biblioteca Internazionale "La Vigna," Contrà Porta S. Croce 3, 36100 Vicenza, tel. 0444/543000. Open Tuesday and Thursday 9–12h, 15–18h; Monday, Wednesday, and Friday by appointment only with librarian Andrea Ditta.

This is one of the most outstanding libraries you will ever come across if you are interested in food and wine. There are four-hundred-year-old books of cookery and agriculture, magazines from around the world on subjects as specific as the potato, and room after room of fascinating books that the serious food writer, cook, or gourmand could peruse with great pleasure. This is a prized collection gathered by Demetrio Zaccaria, who donated it to Vicenza in 1981. He began the collection in the 1970s with a book about wine he purchased in New York. There are now books in many languages, including English, French, German, Hungarian, Polish, Russian, Spanish, and Italian. There are also rotating exhibits on subjects such as cooking and the Italian Resistance or cooking in the Fascist era.

WINE
Enoteca Berealto, Via Pedemuro S. Biagio 57, tel. 0444/322144. Closed Sunday evening in June and July, Monday, Tuesday morning, and three weeks in August.

Here is an excellent *enoteca*, ideal for tasting local and national wines accompanied by good light food. This is the place to try the wines of Fausto Maculan from nearby Breganze if you don't have another opportunity.

Villafranca (Verona)

BAKERY-CAFFÈ
Caffè-Pasticceria Fantoni, Corso Vittorio Emanuele 165.

To most people Villafranca is simply the site of Verona's airport, but there is this famous institution in town that is worth a visit. Founded in 1842 by Giovanni Fantoni to sell his delicious *sfogliatelle*, it became well known when his son Marcello took over. A great admirer of history, music, and famous figures, Marcello always seemed ready to create a cake or beverage to dedicate to a personage who inspired him. He made a *torta della pace* (peace cake) as the winds of Italian insurgence against Austria swirled. After the First World War he distilled *acqua di Fiume*, named in honor of the city where some of the worst battles of the war took place. With the advent of fascism and the annexation of Libya, *biscotti di Libia* were born. He created *dolci baci* inspired by Puccini's *Tosca*, and a liqueur named for Mascagni's opera *Iris*. Fantoni is now run by Mariarosa Ciresola Chiaramonte, the great-granddaughter of Marcello.

Fegato alla Veneziana
Calf's Liver, Venetian Style

Although I have enjoyed this dish numerous times in Venetian homes, I have seldom found examples that measure up in restaurants. While it is seemingly a simple dish to prepare, it is often ruined by carelessness. Herewith, the classic recipe. It is important to remember that the liver must be sliced very thin and that the relation of liver to onions is 2:1. If you are making more than one serving, multiply the ingredients by the number of diners.

Serves 1

1 tablespoon extra-virgin olive oil

50 grams/1¾ to 2 ounces yellow onions, sliced paper-thin

100 grams/3½ to 4 ounces calf's liver, sliced thin

Salt and freshly ground black pepper to taste

Pinch of chopped fresh parsley

Heat the oil over relatively high heat in a heavy skillet with a long handle. Once the oil is hot, add the onions and sauté for a few seconds, shaking the pan. Then add the slices of liver, salt, and pepper and sauté actively, shaking the pan, moving the ingredients around with a spatula or fork so that the liver is thoroughly cooked on both sides. The key is to work fast and not overcook the meat. Just before it is done, toss in the parsley and keep shaking the pan and moving the ingredients about with your cooking utensil. When you serve the dish, pour the pan liquid, which will have a pronounced onion flavor, on top of the meat. Serve at once.

Wine: Merlot, Refosco, or Cabernet from Veneto or Friuli.

Pescatrice alle Mandorle
Monkfish with Almond Sauce

This dish is a specialty of the 12 Apostoli restaurant in Verona.

Serves 2

For Almond Sauce

100 grams/3½ ounces peeled almonds
¼ teaspoon mustard powder
1 tablespoon freshly grated Asiago
¼ teaspoon cayenne or paprika
1 tablespoon extra-virgin olive oil
Juice of 1 lemon

1 carrot
1 teaspoon grated fresh orange peel
About 450 grams/1 pound monkfish fillet
Flour
1 tablespoon unsalted butter
Freshly ground black pepper to taste
Pinch of salt (optional)
1 cup dry white wine
*2 leaves Boston lettuce or a few leaves of
    arugula*

First prepare the almond sauce. Using a food processor or a good knife, finely chop the almonds until they are almost a powder. Combine the almonds in a bowl with the mustard powder, Asiago cheese, cayenne or paprika, olive oil, and lemon juice. Stir until all the ingredients are blended. If the sauce is of a thickness and creaminess that is to your liking, do not add water. Otherwise, stir in cold water a little bit at a time, until the proper consistency is reached. Set the sauce aside. In a separate bowl, peel and grate the carrot and combine it with the grated orange peel. Set aside.

Now cook the monkfish. The fish might be cut in 2 pieces at your fish market. Otherwise, cut the large piece of fish into two. Wash the fillets carefully, then dry them with paper towels. Lightly dip the fillets in flour. Shake the fillets to rid them of any excess flour. Melt the butter over moderately high heat in a skillet, making sure it does not turn brown. Add the monkfish fillets. Then add some pepper and, if you wish, a pinch of salt, and give the pan a good shake. Return the pan to the heat and then add the white wine. Cook until the wine evaporates, shaking the pan periodically so that the fish does not stick. Turn the fish over gently, then add enough water to just cover the bottom of the pan. Cook for 5 more minutes and then remove the pan from the heat.

Place each fillet on a leaf of Boston lettuce or next to a couple of leaves of arugula. Spoon the almond sauce atop the fish. Add some of the grated-carrot mixture on the other side of the plate, and serve immediately.

Variation: On a hot day, chill the monkfish and serve it cold, with almond sauce on top. The sauce should not be chilled.

Trentino

REGIONAL AND PROVINCIAL CAPITAL: Trento (TN).

TOURIST INFORMATION: Azienda per la Promozione Turistica del Trentino, Corso 3 Novembre 132, 38100 Trento, tel. 0461/895111 or 980000.

In Milano:
Ufficio Turismo Trentino, Piazza Diaz 5, tel. 02/874387.

In Roma:
Ufficio Turismo Trentino, Galleria Colonna 7, tel. 06/6794216.
In my opinion, the Trentino produces the best and most

 The Trentino is a much-neglected and oft-forgotten region that is full of treasures for travelers of all types, and certainly those who love food, wine, tradition, big-city restaurants, and wonderful meals in the country. It is all the more remarkable that the Trentino remains ignored because it is so close to destinations that are overflowing with tourists: Verona, Vicenza, and Lago di Garda are near (in fact, the northern tip of the lake is in the Trentino). Venezia and Milano are only two hours away.

I should first clarify something that may puzzle some readers. The Trentino and the Alto Adige are linked in the minds of many Italians as one region. You will usually see them listed as Trentino–Alto Adige. True, they are both alpine and have long pastoral traditions. They were granted autonomous status by Roma in 1948 and tend to feel rather apart from life in the rest of the nation. But for readers of this book I felt there are significant differences between the two and that they merit separate chapters, even though these two provinces are legally designated as one region. First of all, the Alto Adige, which calls itself the Südtirol, is a German-speaking region that looks north to Austria and Germany for commerce and cultural influence. By contrast, the Trentino is Italian speaking, and it conserves the best of the Tyrolean and Italian traditions. You need only visit the capitals of the two regions—Bozen/Bolzano in the Alto Adige, and Trento in the Trentino—to see the differences. The former is stiffer and more

formal, while the latter is much more easygoing and Italianate. There are similarities in the cuisines, particularly the omnipresent dumplings known as *canederli* and the extensive use of apples in local recipes, but there are many differences as well.

So the Trentino is a transitional region. Its Dolomite peaks and great ski resorts, such as Moena, San Martino di Castrozza, and Madonna di Campiglio, are strictly alpine. The central valley surrounding the Adige River may not seem impressive until you see the mountains that frame it. Other mountainous areas don't reveal the base of the mountains as the Adige Valley does, so these peaks are extraordinarily beautiful. The southern part of the region, with the very pleasing town of Rovereto and the toehold on Lago di Garda at the town of Riva, are distinctly Italian. The flavors here blend Germanic and Italian in a useful tourist materials of any Italian region. It is a region very interested in receiving more visitors, and it has made a good effort to be accessible. The maps and brochures are clear and accurate, and they anticipate questions a visitor might have rather than simply try to convince him to choose this region for his holiday.

Agritourism:

Agriturist Comitato
   Regionale,
      Via Brennero 23,

38100 Trento,
tel. 0461/824211,
or
Associazione
  Agriturismo Trentino,
  tel. 0461/235323,
  fax 0461/235333.
There are dozens of farms
  throughout the Trentino
  that offer accommodations
  and often meals. Many
  of these are in the very
  fertile Val di Non, which
  produces famous apples,
  as well as grapes, plums,
  potatoes, and other
  products. The communities
  in the valley with many
  places to stay are Coredo,
  Cunevo, Livo, Nanno,
  Revò, Romeno, Rumo,
  Sanzeno, Sporminore,
  and Tuenno.

Wine Tourism:
Vino e Turismo
  (Trentino),
  Roberto Sebastiani,
  President,
    Via Clementi 31,
    Lavis (TN),
    tel. 0461/246315,
    fax 0461/242340.

way that the Alto Adige does not, which is another reason I have accorded the Trentino its own chapter.

In the middle of the region is the Piana Rotoliana, a vast plain framed by mountains. This is an important agricultural zone, especially for wine. Here, in the town of San Michele all'Adige, is the oldest winemaking school in Italy. Teroldego Rotoliano is a wonderful medium-bodied red that takes its name from the plain. Wine producers in the Trentino wonder why this wine does not sell much abroad—perhaps it is the difficult name. But it is a very good all-purpose red at a good price that deserves wider recognition.

To learn about the history of this region you should also read my introductory words in the chapter about the Alto Adige. The Trentino has often had Teutonic influence, but with a difference. There has always been a substantial Venetian influence in the southern Trentino in towns such as Rovereto and Riva. In effect, the Trentino was a prince-bishopric from the twelfth to eighteenth centuries and was only annexed to the Tyrol in 1802. One hundred and seventeen years later, it became part of Italy after World War I. While the Alto Adige has stubbornly remained Germanic, the Trentino quickly resumed its Italian orientation. The region's capital, Trento, is a special city on its own terms. It has long had a tradition of enlightened learning and government, especially in the sixteenth century, under the reigns of Prince-Bishop Bernardo Clesio and his successor Cristoforo Madruzzo. In that century, Trento was the site for the famous Council of Trent (1546–1563), which changed the course of religious history. This was the nineteenth Ecumenical Council of the Roman Catholic Church, but it was something more. As the middle ground between Germany and Italy, Trent represented the opportunity for finding middle ground between Lutherans and Catholics. The reforms established here created a context from which a more enlightened, modern Catholic Church could emerge.

After the glory days of the Renaissance, Trento and its region quietly went their own way, being roused only by occasional incursions of foreign troops, powers, or philosophies. In the last four decades of the eighteenth century, the region was under the sway of the Hapsburgs of Vienna, and a young pianist-composer named Mozart gave his first Italian performances in Rovereto. As you will see when you visit the region, only the central Adige Valley is easily traversed. There are many other valleys and mountain passes, each with its own dialect and food culture. It is amazing that even in such a small region these differences persist. Some will be described in this chapter.

Mercato dei Funghi, Trento

A distinct feature of the Trentino is the *maso*. A *maso* is a landed estate whose name derived from the Latin *mansum* and led, I presume, to the English words "manse" and "mansion." A *mansum* denoted the amount of space that could be cultivated by a family with one plow and two oxen. The confines of a *maso* were thus delineated, and the property could be passed down from father to first-born son through the centuries. This meant that parcels were kept intact, and the land was well maintained. It also meant that younger children had to be subservient to first-born sons, but whole families tended to congregate on land, and younger sons were not necessarily sent away. One also sees the word *maso* in the Alto Adige, although there it denotes a plot of land that is now dedicated to traditional agritourism, or farm vacations.

Nowadays a *maso* remains a plot of land cultivated by a family, but there might also be food and lodging offered to travelers. Many *masi* are inexpensive and offer a good means for a traveler on a budget to get to know the Trentino and its people. The tourist office can provide a list of *masi* throughout the region. As often happens with words that connote humility, such as *maso, trattoria*, or *osteria*, someone will take the simple and make it fancy. So there are a few *masi* in the Trentino that are quite posh. One of these, the Maso Cantanghel in Civezzano, is a beautiful spot with one of the best restaurants in the region and a couple of elegant, cushy rooms for lodgers. If time and budget permit, you should have a meal there.

Eating in Trentino

As the transitional region between the German and Italian worlds, the Trentino borrows from the kitchens of both and introduces many of its own ingredients to make a robust cuisine.

Everyone in this region seems to be an expert on mushrooms. Following a rainfall, the woods are full of people gathering *funghi* for their own consumption or for sale. In the Trentino there are members of the police who are *micologi* (mushroom experts). It is their job to inspect mushrooms in the market and assure that all of those on sale are safe and edible. There is a wonderful mushroom market in

Trento that you should visit. If you are there in the autumn, your visit may coincide with the annual mushroom fair. In 2005, more than three hundred different varieties were displayed.

The Trentino is famous for many of its fruits and vegetables, particularly apples, which turn up in dishes from appetizer through dessert. Other produce of note is grapes, plums, and chestnuts. A special and unusual product that you would never expect to see in the Alps is the olive. The area around Riva del Garda is the northernmost olive-oil-production zone in the world. The cows of the region give milk that produces many wonderful cheeses. And there is superb baking as well that draws from German and Italian influences.

ANTIPASTI

As in much of Italy, pork products appear prominently in the appetizers. It is customary in some areas to eat these with *tortelli di patate*, crispy potato pancakes. A traditional sausage is the *probusto*, made in Rovereto with a mixture of pork and beef. It is smoked over a fire of beechwood before being cooked. The region also boasts a delicious form of raw beef, *carne salada* (also called *carne salà*), which is cured in vinegar and spices and served paper-thin. Some chefs also cook *carne salada* to serve as a main course.

PRIMI

Polenta is the principal staple of the region. In the early part of the twentieth century, when the Trentino was quite poor, children were often fed polenta six days a week. Only on Sunday were meals more elaborate. Mothers would make a large pot of polenta on Monday. Each day a piece would be cut off to cook with other available ingredients such as cheese, vegetables, or perhaps a stew. One typical polenta dish is *polenta smalzada,* served with butter that has been browned with a bit of anchovy. Nowadays, with more affluence, *polenta smalzada* is often a side dish rather than a centerpiece. *Canederli* are also made in this fashion, which is a traditional way to dress other pastas. A popular *primo* is polenta with melted cheese and sautéed mushrooms, *Smacafam* (which means "hunger killer" in dialect) is polenta with sausages. *Ravioli alla trentina*, a more elaborate dish, are filled with sausage, chicken, and beef—they tend to be served on special occasions. *Strangolopreti* (priest stranglers) are gnocchi.

SECONDI

This is a meat-eating region, although good fish does come from Lago di Garda, and the rivers provide abundant trout. Game, poultry, pork, and beef are all popular. Although *luganega* sausage is usually associated with Lombardia, it is found all over the Trentino. Each fine butcher shop has its own secret recipe, and most restaurants feature *luganega* with polenta on their menus.

FORMAGGI

There is an amazing amount of delicious cheese produced in this region. The only problem in giving recommendations is that these cheeses go by a few generic names, but there are distinct differences in cheeses with the same name as you move from zone to zone. Many of these cheeses are simply called *nostrano,* which implies "ours" or "homemade."

Asiago is produced near the Veneto border. Some of it is aged, which creates a different and, I believe, better cheese that should be discovered.

Grana del Trentino is this region's version of the grating cheese that is made in the Po Valley. It is often very good, but it doesn't compare with Parmigiano-Reggiano.

Vezzena is a typical cheese much prized by connoisseurs throughout Italy. It is not generally well known, and I think you should not leave the region without trying it.

Malga (plural is *malghe*) is a generic name for a category of mountain cheeses that are made with the summer milk from cows that graze in the highest valleys of the region. Only 25 percent of the region's cows are now taken up to the high Alps to make *malga* cheese. The problem is not with the cows but with the fact that it is hard to find *malgari,* cheese makers willing to journey high up for an extended period to milk the cows twice a day and then make the cheese in little huts. Until the 1970s this was not a problem, but styles have changed, and traditions are too easily abandoned. So *malga* cheese is now a luxury item rather than an essential component of Trentino life. There are about 80 *malgari* left in Trentino.

Bagoss, casolet (dialect for "homemade"), Dolomiti, Spressa, Tara, and Tosella are other Trentino cheeses to look for.

Finally, there is a strange cheese called *puzzone di Moena* (in dialect *spetz tsaorì*). *Puzzone,* loosely translated, means "big and smelly." The cheese is not so big, but it does have a rather distinct odor. If you can get past that, however, it is worth trying.

DOLCI

There are many wonderful desserts in this region. Although the apple strudel is thought of as more of the Alto Adige than the Trentino, it appears everywhere here as well. In fact, the two best examples I have found in Italy are in Rovereto and Varignano di Arco. Another great cake, which is crunchy and dry, is *torta di fregolotti,* made with butter, flour, walnuts, and almonds, a perfect match for the region's many dessert wines. *Brazadel* is a light breakfast cake. Perhaps the most famous cake is *zelten,* a traditional Christmas cake made with fruit, nuts, and a fair amount of grappa. Some bakeries make these only in the winter, but others, such as Sosì in Trento, sell it year-round. If you are in Rovereto, be sure to visit Pasticceria Andreotta, where great baking is done. Ubiquitous polenta turns up at dessert topped with raisins or other fruit that has been soaked in grappa.

The Wines of Trentino

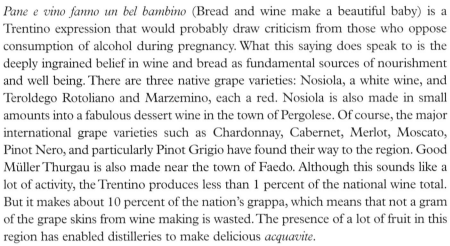

Pane e vino fanno un bel bambino (Bread and wine make a beautiful baby) is a Trentino expression that would probably draw criticism from those who oppose consumption of alcohol during pregnancy. What this saying does speak to is the deeply ingrained belief in wine and bread as fundamental sources of nourishment and well being. There are three native grape varieties: Nosiola, a white wine, and Teroldego Rotoliano and Marzemino, each a red. Nosiola is also made in small amounts into a fabulous dessert wine in the town of Pergolese. Of course, the major international grape varieties such as Chardonnay, Cabernet, Merlot, Moscato, Pinot Nero, and particularly Pinot Grigio have found their way to the region. Good Müller Thurgau is also made near the town of Faedo. Although this sounds like a lot of activity, the Trentino produces less than 1 percent of the national wine total. But it makes about 10 percent of the nation's grappa, which means that not a gram of the grape skins from wine making is wasted. The presence of a lot of fruit in this region has enabled distilleries to make delicious *acquavite*.

The Trentino is distinct from the Alto Adige in terms of wine production in an important way. In the northern region most wine is made by small family producers that sell locally and to the German-speaking countries. The Trentino has a number of fine small producers who make their own wines, but many growers bring their grapes to cooperatives such as Mezzacorona and Ca'vit, which then produce wines that taste more or less the same year in and year out. This is not a criticism: these wines sell at a reasonable price and have found a niche in the market of wine drinkers in Italy and around the world who are looking for a wine they can drink on a regular basis. Ferrari produces a fine dry sparkling wine that has been popular throughout Italy for almost a century.

An interesting case is the story of Casa Girelli, one of the largest producers in Italy. This is an established family winery that decided, after the Second World War, that the future was in markets abroad. So while other Trentino producers first attempted to sell in Italy and nearby Germany, Girelli mapped a world strategy that was subsequently emulated by other Italian wineries. The firm produces 2 million cases of wine a year, 98 percent of which is sold abroad. Girelli buys grapes from growers it has dealt with for decades so it has a good idea of what sort of grapes it will have to work with. It can also monitor the growth of grapes and encourage growers to plant new or different grape varieties as changes in international taste are detected. As the company grew, it acquired properties in Veneto, Piemonte, Toscana, and Abruzzo and became one of the first firms to sell wines from several regions. It also was innovative in promoting several quality lines of wine. So there might be economical reds and whites for one segment of the market, and certain single-vineyard wines (that is, all the grapes used to make a particular wine are grown in one vineyard rather than being a combination of grapes from several vines). This usually meant a wine with distinct characteristics that would appeal to more discerning wine drinkers. In identifying segments in the international market, the company was able to expand its reach and its marketing efforts. Only recently has the company begun to target the Italian market, where, remarkably, it is virtually unknown by consumers.

As you travel around the region to wine bars and restaurants, try to taste wines from little producers, since you can easily find the big ones at home. Smaller wine producers I like include Balter (makes a wonderfully aromatic Traminer); Battistotti (makes a fine Marzemino); Cesarini-Sforza (a consortium of fourteen producers that makes a delicious spumante); Conti Bossi Federigotti (Marzemino); Gaierhof (produces a fantastic Moscato Giallo); Maso Cantanghel; Maso Poli (which makes a nice white called Sorni Bianco that combines Nosiola, Chardonnay, and Müller Thurgau); Le Meridiane (makes a nice Riesling Renano); Pojer & Sandri.

Arco

Also see listings for Varignano di Arco and Vignole di Arco.

MEAT
Carni Rolando Pederzolli, Via della Croseta 51, tel. 0464/516756.

Makes some of the best *carne salada* in the region.

Civezzano

DINING
Maso Cantanghel, Via Madonnina 33, tel. 0461/858714, fax 0461/859050. Reservations essential. Closed Saturday, Sunday, and ten days each Christmas–New Year's, Easter, and in August. MasterCard, Visa. Moderate.

Lucia Gius is the inspired cook and Piero Zabini the inspired vintner who make this *maso* much more than typical farm cooking. A beautiful room combines streamlined but elegant table settings with wooden country furniture. There are tiny toy stoves and a few pieces of pottery about. One enters through the kitchen, always a good sign. There are only a few tables, all well served

by Piero. The only adjustment I would make is that the music is vaguely Muzak, and it falls hard on sensitive ears. The meal itself is moderate in price for such outstanding quality, but if you drink wine, as you should, the price will go up. You can order a good bottle or two for a fair price, or do what I did: have a different glass of wine with each course. The menu changes according to available ingredients and Lucia's inspiration. My recent meal was stunning: first was a *frittata di zucchine*, a dish of exquisite delicacy that was made primarily of paper-thin slices of zucchini suspended with very little egg. It was a work of art. Then came firm polenta served with chicken livers and various types of mushrooms. The livers had a slight crunch at first bite and were perfectly tender within. The mushrooms all had contrasting textures and flavors. Next was *pasta al profumo di basilico.* The silken pasta was homemade, and the sauce was delicate olive oil and basil (not pesto) over which *grana del Trentino* was grated. Next was *filetto di agnello al rosmarino con carciofi*—fabulous roast lamb with tender artichokes. Then came local cheese that was milky and fragrant. The dessert was sensational: the best hazelnut ice cream I have ever tasted. The texture was rich but not overbearing. The flavor was intense but not too much so. And the amount of sugar was perfect. This ice cream immediately ascended to my pantheon of greats. Then came wonderful *piccola pasticceria,* all made by Lucia: exemplary candied orange peel, delicate *torrone,* tiny raspberry and blackberry pastries, and a chocolate-marzipan truffle. The wines, which were all very good to excellent, can be purchased here and at fine wine shops, if you want to take some of the flavor of Maso Cantanghel with you. By advance arrangement, one can also lodge here in one of the two apartments—each furnished with antiques—in this two-hundred-year-old house.

Cognola di Trento

DINING AND LODGING
Hotel Villa Madruzzo, Loc. Ponte Alto 26, tel. 0461/986220 or 986221, fax 0461/986361. All credit cards. Closed Sunday. Moderately inexpensive to moderately expensive.

Cognola (4 kilometers [2.5 miles] from Trento on the road to Padova) has one of the most delightful hotels I have encountered in recent years. The Villa Madruzzo is run with great panache and efficiency. It is a former retirement home that has been converted into a very stylish hotel with a fashionable but unpretentious sensibility. The rooms are all different and memorable. Mine was on the top floor and had porthole windows and a sloping roof that made me feel like an artist in his atelier. It is a pleasure to dine and sleep here. The restaurant has two plush dining rooms, fine china and glassware, and superb, attentive service. Eating here is elegant but not stuffy. There is a four-course menu of *proposte trentine* (recommended regional dishes), which will give you an overview of local flavors at a very generous price, given the quality of cooking, ambience, and service. Then there is an à la carte menu, where prices move up to the moderate to moderately expensive range, depending on what you order. The Trentino menu I sampled started with an antipasto of *carne salada* (reddish pink, delicate, and delicious sliced raw beef topped with apple slivers and served with perfect baby greens and radicchio—when you are offered olive oil to dress it with, be sure to ask for *olio d'oliva del Trentino*). Next came *gnocchi di pane con verza e pancetta e burro fuso.* This was a dish of delicate bread gnocchi served with slivers of Savoy cabbage and *pancetta* and tossed lightly with melted butter. Then a *secondo* of *involtini di carne con polenta e formaggi trentini fusi,* little meat rolls served with polenta topped with melted local cheeses. A good, if high-cholesterol, combination. I ordered a small salad to lighten the flavor in my mouth. Dessert was a decent apple cake served with a glass of sparkling wine. For vegetarians there is a great option here: a very handsome rolling cart (Christofle of Paris, I seem to recall) bears dish after dish of beautifully prepared vegetables. The wine list is extensive, well chosen, and well priced. After dinner there is a good selection of Trentino grappas and distillates.

Comano

A nice town with gorgeous alpine scenery and riverside walks. There are places here to buy the cheeses of Trentino, many of which are made nearby. The Terme di Comano (tel. 0465/71277) is a popular spa for people with skin problems.

Comasine di Pejo

DINING

Ristorante Il Mulino, tel. 0463/754244. Open mid-June to the end of September (lunch and dinner), from early December through Easter (dinner only). Visa. Moderate.

Good food at this restaurant high in the mountains. Specialties include gnocchi with nettles, and *tagliata di cervo*, delicious thin slices of venison with apples, finished with grappa. Apple cake for dessert.

Faedo

You can recognize Faedo from a distance because of its two terracotta-colored steeples. It is more than six hundred meters (nearly two thousand feet) above theRotoliano plain. This is an important wine town, especially for Pinot Grigio and Müller Thurgau.

DINING

Maso Nello, Loc. Palai, tel. 0461/650384. Reservations essential for lunch, on weekends, and for certain dishes. Closed Monday. No credit cards. Inexpensive.

Above Faedo, in Località Palai, is one of the better-known *masi* of the Trentino. The fame of Cristina Arman's cooking has spread far and wide, as her guest book attests. She makes simple, traditional dishes that give you an insight into the farm cooking of the region. You may start with *tortelli di patate* made only with potatoes and flour (in some valleys cooks also add milk), which she serves topped with thin slices of speck. The *coniglio arrosto con rosmarino* (roasted rabbit with rosemary) was served with coarse, firm polenta that supported the flavorful drippings from the meat. She brought out a bowl of delicious *borlotti* beans with onions and another bowl of fresh radicchio. Fresh young *salami* and a wonderful reddish *nostrano* cheese arrived. Much of what you eat here, from the vegetables and breads to the pork and rabbit, are raised not far from where you are eating them. In general, Cristina cooks what is on hand, but it is also possible to call a day ahead and order certain dishes. These include frog's legs, snails, joint of pork *(stinco di maiale)*, rabbit, trout, homemade gnocchi, and risotto.

WINERY

Pojer & Sandri, Loc. Molini, tel. 0461/650342. Open weekdays (call first).

One of the better small wineries of the Trentino is Pojer & Sandri, which takes advantage of the range of altitudes around Faedo to cultivate a large variety of grapes. Sturdy reds grow closer to the floor of the plain, while aromatic whites such as Gewürztraminer and Müller Thurgau grow high up. You will pass all of these as you make your way to the winery.

Pergolese

This town is in the Valle dei Laghi, the valley of lakes, west of Trento. The largest and most famous of these lakes is Lago di Garda, but there are others around too. One of these is the Lago di Toblino, which makes a stunning picture with a famous castle on its bank. There is a restaurant, but it has become touristy and expensive. You may wish to stop for a coffee at the bar and a walk around the grounds. The lakes moderate the climate, making it possible in the southern part of the valley to even cultivate olives. This area is warmed by the *ora*, a wind that blows from the south. Not far beyond Toblino, if you turn south, you will reach Pergolese, where some interesting beverage making takes place. This little town produces one of the most wonderful wines I have ever tasted: Vin Santo di Nosiola. In most cases, Nosiola is a pleasant white wine typical of the Trentino, but in Pergolese the grapes go to greater glory. Only the grapes from old vines are used because the skin is firmer. They are dried for six months after the harvest (until approximately Holy Week). The grapes are then crushed to make a must, which is about 35 percent alcohol. The must remains in a barrel for five years. Because of its very high sugar concentration, it takes three years for this wine to ferment. The fermentation starts in warm weather and stops again when it gets cold, starting again when warm weather returns. The wine remains in the barrel and is in no way clarified or filtered. After five years the wine is about 13 percent alcohol and 16 to 20 percent sugar. In this process of fermentation and fining, the quantity has diminished radically: from 100 kilos (220 pounds) of grapes come fewer than 10 liters (10.5 quarts) of wine. The production of Vin Santo di Nosiola is very limited: about 300 hectoliters (7,533 gallons) per year. It is all made in and around Pergolese, half of it by the Cantina Sociale di Toblino, the rest by six small producers: Morelli, Pedrotti, Pisoni, Poli, Poli (two brothers with separate firms), and Salvetta. The cost of producing such a rare wine in small amounts is astronomical, so these producers do it more for tradition and sell this still-costly wine at a loss and make their income from other wines and grappa. The wine is best consumed at a cool room temperature (but not cold—to chill it is to kill it!) with a classic Trentino cake called *torta di fregolotti*.

WINERY-DISTILLERY
Azienda Agricola Pisoni, tel. 0461/564103, fax 0461/563163.

At harvest time the Pisoni family makes still wines and a spumante. Then, in the period from the grape harvest to Christmas, the Pisonis distill their famous grappa twenty-four hours a day using grape skins left over from wine making. The grapes here grow in unusual conditions. The *ora* that blows in the summer cools the vines, and it warms them slightly in the fall. You will see a facing mountain—Monte Casale —that reflects light early in the day, so that even though we are in a narrow mountain valley, the plants receive enough light and warmth. Some of the barrels at this winery date back to 1862, and many of them are more than one hundred years old and are handsomely carved. (These are of interest for wine lovers, but they are not used for fermentation or storage.)

The Pisonis' fame rests on their delicious grappa, which the family has made for four generations. My favorite is made with Müller Thurgau grapes, though I also liked those made with Teroldego, Moscato, and Nosiola skins. The spumante is very good as well (it is stored in the cellar that the family hid in during the First and Second World Wars). And the Pisonis' Vin Santo di Nosiola is absolutely divine. They make about a thousand bottles per year and sell them all at the winery. The cost and effort to export them would be prohibitive, and with such a limited supply they do not want to send too many bottles to one purchaser.

Riva del Garda

It is often hard to believe that the Trentino, which is essentially an alpine region, has a zone that is warm enough to grow olives. The small microclimate from the northern shore of Lago di Garda up to the valley of the lakes is strangely suited for growing olives that produce a fragrant, delicate olive oil. At a latitude higher than that of Montreal, it is the northernmost olive-oil-producing place in the world. Although there are almost a thousand oil producers, they are all tiny. The output of the area is sold almost exclusively in Italy, mostly in Trentino, Veneto, and Lombardia.

Once upon a time olives were picked from December to early March. Now harvesting starts in November and continues through mid-January. All olives are gathered by hand and are picked at the moment they turn from green to reddish brown. The flavor is light and fruity, appealing to those who think of olive oil as too heavy. Trentino oil makes an excellent condiment for cold meats, salads, pasta, and lake fish. Because of its delicacy, Trentino oil should be consumed within a year of its production.

Another delicious local food is *carne salada* (also called *carne salà* in Riva), raw beef marinated in salt, spices and vinegar. One of the best places to taste *carne salada* is at the Trattoria Belvedere in Varignano di Arco, just north of Riva.

In addition to being a special food zone, Riva del Garda is a popular summer resort with tourists, especially those from Germany and Austria.

AGRITOURISM

Agritur Eden Marone, Via Marone 11, tel. 0464/521520. Open April 1–September 30.

Tiziano Girardelli is the president of the consortium of Trentino olive-oil producers. He has olive trees on his property, and you will be able to taste his oil. There is sleeping space for thirty-two persons. Meals are available.

BAR

Pasticceria Copat, Viale Dante 37. Open 7–12:30h, 14:30–19:30h; closed Monday.

The excellent coffee and pretty good pastries make this bar a good choice for breakfast.

BREAD

Il Fornaio, Via Roma 23.

Although the name "Il Fornaio" is attached to bread bakeries all over Italy, this one is quite special. Here is the work of Giovanni Vivaldelli and family, and you should not leave Riva without coming here. If you are here during olive-pressing season, do not fail to taste the delicious *pane alle molche* (made with leftover pressings from olives). There is an excellent *pane di patate* and many other breads: *cipolle, aglio, pan de mei* (a sweet corn bread), *panini* (rolls) of walnut, sesame, olive, rosemary, caraway, onion, and even chocolate. There are magnificent, huge *grissini* made either with

flour and water or flour and oil. They come in the same flavors as the *panini*, except for chocolate. Vivaldelli makes his own panettone and strudel and more than twenty different cookies.

CULTURE

Musica Riva. (For information contact Musica Riva, Via Pilati 5, 38066 Riva del Garda (TN), tel. 0464/554073 or 516161, fax 0464/505643.)

A music festival is held in Riva every July.

FISH

Pescheria Enzo Bonetti, Via Florida 18, tel. 0464/551740.

Lago di Garda is a very large, deep lake with thirty-six varieties of fish, all of which find a place on the ice of this old fishmonger. He only sells the best and will tell you how to cook it too.

MARKET

There is a small, cute fruit and vegetable market on Piazza delle Erbe. With its flower sellers, small fountain and the slightly fading buildings, the market seems like a throwback to another time.

OLIVE OIL

Associazione Agraria, Via A. Lutti 10, tel. 0464/552133, fax 0464/553059. Open weekdays 8–12h, 15–19h, Saturday morning in winter and morning and afternoon in summer.

Most of the olive growers in Trentino bring their product to their consortium, the Associazione Agraria, where the olives are pressed into oil and sold collectively to consumers. This is the place to buy Trentino olive oil, as well as locally produced wine, plums (another local specialty), apples, chestnuts, and dairy products.

Rovereto

Rovereto is yet another of the many special towns that are completely ignored by modern travelers, both Italian and from abroad. It goes about its life comfortably and quietly. People are polite to one another and to the rare visitor. The streets are lined with old palaces and other handsome buildings. But there are advantages to Rovereto's anonymity: Because the town is not in the mainstream, it has not seen how some cities have remade themselves more glossily. So it feels like an Italian city of a few years ago—homey, gracious, and easygoing.

Rovereto is very aware of the contributions of its sons and daughters to the fight for freedom in many of Europe's wars. You will see plaques all over town dedicated in their memory, and many streets are named for these fallen heroes. In the Trentino these men and women are frequently referred to as *i martiri* (the martyrs), and they remain very much in the conscience of the citizenry. A visit to the city's war museum, Il Museo della Guerra, will explain more. The museum is actually about peace and what has been lost to preserve it.

ANTIQUES SHOP

La Porta Rossa, Via Mercerie 21, tel. 0464/421040. Open 10:30–12h, 15–19h; closed Sunday and Monday.

Michele Kiniger is an architect with a good eye for beautiful objects from the past. And in a town so rich in tradition, both Italian and Austro-Hungarian, there are many items from local kitchens and dining rooms that are of real interest and value. You might find a set of Middle European wineglasses, a Jugendstil tea set, or a wonderful nineteenth-century Italian dining table. Even if you don't buy anything, the store merits a visit to admire the owner's taste and to have a sense of the furnishings one might find in certain Rovereto homes.

BAKERY

Pasticceria Andreotta, Via Roma 9, tel. 0464/421291. Open 8–12:30h, 14:30–20h; closed Monday. No credit cards.

An outstanding bakery, the best I have encountered in the Trentino. Opened in 1875, the baking at Andreotta shows a strong Austro-Hungarian influence from when Rovereto was under the domain of the Hapsburgs, as well as the influence of Venice in the dryness and use of alcohol in some of the cakes. Some specialties: *fil di ferro* (means "thread of iron": a long roll filled with a stratum of dried fruit and rum); *vaja* (plum cake with delicious pastry cream); *heibach* (a sweet, milky yeast bread); *la bionda* (means "the blonde":

yeast bread with cream and gelatin); *nusskipferl* (rolls with ground almond paste); *crocetta con uvetta* (a yeast cake filled with raisins and sugar); *la treccina* (a braided cake with cream); *torta di carote* (carrot-almond cake); Sacher torte. There is also an excellent cappuccino, making this a fabulous place for breakfast or an afternoon pastry and coffee.

BAR

Manuel Bar, Via Tartarotti 58.
Open 7–21h; closed Sunday.

A very friendly place with good coffee.

CULTURE

Associazione Mozart Italia,
Via Mercerie 14.

Here is the site of the first concert Wolfgang Amadeus Mozart gave in Italy, on Christmas Day 1769, when he was thirteen. The building is now the headquarters of the Associazione Mozart Italia, sponsor of many concerts and other initiatives related to the composer from Salzburg. In his masterpiece, *Don Giovanni,* which takes place in Seville, the title character drinks Marzemino, the local wine of Rovereto, which probably was unknown in Spain. I suspect that Mozart became acquainted with Marzemino during his stay in Rovereto and asked Lorenzo da Ponte, his librettist, to include the wine in his text.

Rovereto is also the birthplace of Riccardo Zandonai (1883–1944). He is largely forgotten today, but in his day he was considered the successor to Puccini as Italy's leading opera composer. The Teatro Zandonai, on Corso Angelo Bettini 70–78, is truly a jewel box (a much overused term). It has a ceiling of robin's-egg blue and creamy white. The whole place looks almost like a stage set of a classical theater. It retains all of the virtues of the old, as does much of Rovereto.

DINING

E.N.D.A.S. (Circolo dell'Azione Sociale),
Scala della Torre 7, tel. 0464/437100.
Closed Sunday and holidays. No credit
cards. Moderate.

This restaurant is a popular workers' place that serves gratifying food. It may not be the sort of place tourists are directed to, but that's not what this book is about. The food here is delicious and memorable, and the welcome is warm. There are some dishes on the menu that are not specifically local, but you should look for daily specials for Trentino food such as *canederli in brodo, strangolopreti,* and *rotolo di pasta con speck e spinaci.* Second courses include many slow-cooked dishes, such as stews and braised meats, all served with a long rectangle of firm polenta. On Friday there is *baccalà alla vicentina* (the special cod dish from Vicenza)—one of the best examples I have tasted of a dish that is often served as a fishy mess. This one was creamy and tasted of cod rather than salt. Another good dish is *lumache,* braised snails. You can also have the ubiquitous polenta with *formaggio fuso e funghi* (native cheeses and mushrooms of the Trentino). The house Marzemino (Conti Bossi Federigotti) is very good. For dessert, there is a fine aged Asiago and an absolutely fabulous strudel. I tasted dozens of pieces of strudel in the research for this book, and this one was really special. The dough was crepelike, and the filling of apples, raisins, and pine nuts was full of fresh fruit flavor.

Osteria Pettirosso, Corso Bettini 24, tel. 0464/422463. Closed Sunday and July. All credit cards. Moderate.

I love the *orzotto al Marzemino*, barley cooked with the local red wine. Then proceed to alpine trout, lake fish, or *baccalà*.

FOOD SHOPPING

Rovereto's fruit and vegetable market is held in the Piazza Malfatti near Piazza delle Erbe on Thursday and Saturday mornings.

Alimentari Finarolli, Via Mercerie 9. Closed Wednesday afternoon and Sunday.

There are good hams and *salami* here, as well as a large choice of homemade pastas. It offers three types of *mostarda— mantoz'ana, cremonese, veneta*—each with its own texture. Also a good source of *funghi porcini*.

ICE CREAM

Gelateria Goccia di Latte, Via Tartarotti 56. Open summer 10:30h until late, winter 14–20h; closed Monday.

This place is very popular for its fruit ice cream. Since this is the Trentino, you should try apple ice cream. In the summer, ice cream from Goccia di Latte (Drop of Milk) is also sold down the street at the Bar Excelsior, Via Giovanni Maria della Croce 7.

SPECIALTY SHOP

Drogheria Giuseppe Micheli, Via Mercerie 16/20, tel./fax 0464/421154.

A classic *drogheria* that has been an institution in Rovereto since 1829. This is a vintage emporium that has long supplied all manner of wares to the populace. All of the furnishings are original, except for the ceiling, which has been lowered. You will immediately notice the old drawers and antique boxes used to hold herbs and spices, as well as neatly ordered sacks with dried beans, seeds, candies, and lozenges. The walls are lined with bottles of wine, oil, vinegar, elixirs, and herbal remedies. Shelves hold unusual honeys, such as dandelion and rhododendron, biscuits, cookies, cereals, and even hair dyes made from vegetable extracts. My favorite detail is the two deep indentations in the old marble floor right in front of the main counter. These have been gently worn down by nearly two centuries of customers who stood there to make purchases. You will also see the old family scale, now a decorative plant holder. Stand next to the plant and look in the rear room, and you will see vintage photographs of Micheli family members from generations past.

San Martino di Castrozza

A beautiful ski resort high in the Dolomites.

DINING

Ristorante Malga Ces, tel. 0439/68145 or

68223. Open Decembe
June–September; close

Express, Diners Club. Moderate to moderately expensive.

Three kilometers (1.9 miles) from the center of town is this comfortable restaurant that specializes in mushrooms and game.

San Michele all'Adige

This town is best known for the Enological Institute (Istituto Agrario, Via E. Mach 1, tel. 0461/650111), which has trained generations of wine makers and farmers from Trentino and elsewhere. It is the oldest wine-making school in Italy (founded in 1869) and is considered one of the best. Since 1874 wine has been produced here that is sold to the public. As you drive past or visit San Michele, you can't miss the institute—it's the huge castle that dominates the town.

DINING

Da Silvio, Via Brennero 2, tel. 0461/650324. Closed Sunday evening and Monday. All credit cards. Moderate to moderately expensive.

The homemade ravioli are delicious, there are several good preparations using mushrooms, and you can often enjoy freshwater fish.

MUSEUM

Museo degli Usi e Costumi della Gente Trentina. Open 8:30–12h, 14:30–18h; closed Sunday and Monday.

A good historical museum in the Istituto Agrario with exhibits of costumes and displays about rural agrarian life in the region.

Trento
Classic Town

Only in very few cases did I select a regional capital as a Classic Town, but Trento is a very special place that gathers within its borders great food, wine, culture, markets, stores, and history. You will find this city of 100,000 much more sophisticated than many that are much bigger and better known. There is even a place (La Rivisteria, Via San Virgilio 23) to buy the *New York Times,* which is hard to find in most major cities in Europe. Trento is also accessible to several nearby *masi,* so you can have a sense of the region without traveling far.

BAKERIES

Pasticceria Bertelli, Via Oriola 29. Open 8–12:30h, 15–19h; closed Monday.

Regarded as the top bakery in the region, although I think it has rivals in Rovereto. Also a bar, it serves an excellent cappuccino made with Illycaffè. This is a good place to have a continental breakfast.

Piazza Duomo, Trento

Pasticceria San Virgilio, Via San Virgilio 6.

A *caffè* as well. Sells *zelten* and *torta di fregolotti*.

Sosì, Via Mantova, or Piazza Venezia 40, or Via Suffragio 76. Open weekdays 7:30–12h, 15:45–19h, Saturday morning only; closed Sunday.

Famous for *zelten* and *torta di fregolotti*, but also for a broad range of breads: sunflower, olive, walnut, muesli, and others.

BARS AND CAFFÈS

Caffè Portici, Piazza Duomo 40. Open 7–1h; closed Monday.

Outdoor tables provide the best view in town, day or night.

Casa del Caffè, Via San Pietro 38. Open 7:30–12:30h, 15–20h.

A very popular place with *trentini* since 1929. You can have a cup of good coffee or buy beans roasted here. It also sells assorted teas and delicious chocolates. You will love the woman at the cash register who has a heartfelt kind word for everyone. She seems to know about the lives and families of all of her customers and is certain to inquire about their well-being and send regards.

Pasticceria Bertelli.

See "Bakeries," above.

Pasticceria San Virgilio.

See "Bakeries," above.

DINING

Osteria a Le Due Spade, Via Don Rizzi 11, tel. 0461/234343, info@leduespade. com. Closed Sunday, Monday lunch. All credit cards. Moderately expensive.

Food has been served in this room since 1545, so a papal emissary to the Council of Trent probably sat where you will. The rustic *cucina* of Trentino becomes *cuisine* as the flavors are adapted and lightened, though not diminished. So you will see a cheese-and-vegetable terrine with mountain herbs or perhaps tiny *canederli* on a bed of *finferli* mushrooms, when these are in season.

Osteria Astra, Corso Buonarroti 16, tel. 0461/829002. Open nightly, closed in August. No credit cards. Moderately inexpensive.

A unique and special place in that the osteria is part of a cinema that shows independent films to a discerning audience. On Sunday mornings one can see silent films with music. The entrance to the osteria is next to the ticket office, and after a screening filmgoers repair to the bar and tables to drink wine and eat mushroom frittatas, soups, and grilled meats while discussing the latest example of the art of the Magic Lantern.

Antica Trattoria al Vòlt, Via Santa Croce 16, tel. 0461/983776. Closed Thursday, Sunday evening, and September. All credit cards. Moderate.

Traditional dishes from the Trentino and Alto Adige, well prepared. Save room for the excellent cheeses.

Locanda Port'Aquila, Via Cervara 66 (just behind the Palazza del Buon-consiglio), tel. 0461/230420. Open 12–14h, 19–21h; closed Sunday and August. No credit cards. Inexpensive to moderately inexpensive.

Walk through the bar, past the kitchen, and into the dining room, which holds about twenty diners. The rear part is a shrine to cycling and alpinism, two sports beloved by the *trentini*. This restaurant has been in the family since 1926. The menu is the same throughout the year. You will be served a few slices of *salami* on a spade-shaped wooden cutting board as you nip into your wine. All the food is very good. I tasted *canederli* with speck and *gnocchi verdi smalzadi*. For a secondo, I tasted *luganega con crauti* (good sausage with sauerkraut). My dining companion had a paillard of *puledro* (pony), which was tender and beefy. For dessert there are cooked apples or an excellent *torta di fregolotti* with a glass of sweet *moscatello* wine.

Trattoria Semprebon, Piazza Centa 7, tel. 0461/823224. Closed Sunday. No credit cards. Moderately inexpensive.

If fish—specifically cod and stockfish—is your dish, then Semprebon will always be good. This trattoria on the north side of town specializes in numerous preparations of codfish, all of which it makes using Norwegian dried cod that is soaked and rinsed expertly so the saltiness is largely eliminated. *Baccalà* (dried cod) has been a staple of the poor in southern Europe for centuries, but just because affluence has come to this area does not mean that good preparations from the past should be forgotten. This is where you can discover them.

Enoteca La Sgeva.

See "Wine," below.

Maso Cantanghel.

See "Civezzano."

Hotel Villa Madruzzo.

See "Cognola di Trento."

FOOD STORES
Bottega del Formai, Via Calepina 33.

Excellent cheese selection from the Trentino and much of Italy, including Fontina from Valle d'Aosta, *mozzarella di bufala* from Campania, *burrata* from Puglia, and *aged* Asiago from the Veneto, which is increasingly difficult to find.

Ortofrutta Deavi, Via Suffragio 27.

A good source for Val di Non apples and other Trentino produce.

Demattè, Piazza Duomo 38.

Very choice fruits and vegetables, including dried local apples, pears, plums, and persimmons.

La Gastronomia, Via Mantova 28.

What at first looks like a miniature supermarket is in fact a well-stocked store that offers a good selection of basic ingredients. For example, there is olive oil from Lago di Garda, Liguria, Toscana, Umbria, and elsewhere. You will find most products of any interest from just about every region of Italy. There is also an unusually deep selection of products for baking. This is the source in Trento for those looking for food products from abroad, such as exotic fruit from Asia or peanut butter from the United States. A visit to La Gastronomia will give you a sense of the ingredients available to the cooks of Trento and probably will revise your view of this as a provincial city.

**Pastificio del Lago, Via Carlo Esterle 10.
Closed Saturday afternoon and Sunday.**

Beautiful handmade pasta: dainty *gnocchi di patate*, some with added speck or chives. Eggy tagliatelle, *raviolini* filled with speck and walnuts, large round *canederli* of various flavors, spinach roll, *ravioloni* filled with pumpkin, tortellini, *agnolotti.*

Mandacarù, Via Maresciallo Diaz.

An interesting example—almost an artifact—of a store with ideological underpinnings. Here one can buy food products primarily from underdeveloped countries. The notion is to support their economies by supporting their agricultural institutions. So there is coffee from Nicaragua, Guatemala, and Tanzania, herbal tea from Nepal, brown sugar from the Philippines, quinoa and cocoa powder from Bolivia, nuts from Mozambique, and hibiscus flowers from Kenya. In every case the store buys directly from food cooperatives and does not deal with governments, so you might find products from nations such as Zaire. You must remember that Italy is a very politically conscious nation—much more so than the United States—so stores such as this one flourish even when idealists in other countries have become jaded or commercial. You can certainly purchase things here if you choose, but I encourage you to at least visit the store to have a closer view of a significant and particular aspect of this nation that few outsiders acknowledge.

Gastronomia Mazzei, Via Mazzini 46.

High-end products: designer labels for oils, vinegars, and pasta. A good range of dried local mushrooms. An excellent source for *mostarda* from Cremona and the Veneto.

Salumeria Polla, Via Oss Mazzurana 33.

An institution in Trento since 1923. This place is smaller and less overflowing than most, but is distinguished by its exceedingly high quality. There are foods from around Italy, all among the best of their type: coffee from Trieste; smoked sausage from the Alto Adige; *salumi di asino* (donkey) from the Valle d'Aosta; polenta from Bergamo; truffle pasta from Alba; *bottarga* from Sardegna; *guanciale* (pork cheek) from Amatrice; tuna from Sicilia; herbs from Liguria; prosciutto from Parma, San Daniele, Valle d'Aosta, and Marche; lentils from Umbria; and *mostarda* from Cremona. The best of Italy in one store. Again, it is notable that a city the size of Trento has more than one store that stocks ingredients of such quality and scope.

Macelleria Ravagni, Piazza Duomo 45, tel. 0461/980061.

This is the oldest butcher shop in Trento. It is famous for its homemade *luganega* sausage, which can be purchased young and fresh or aged.

ICE CREAM
Gelateria Zanelli, Via Suffragio 6 (enter from Via Torre Verde). Open 11–24h; closed Wednesday.

Good ice cream, sold in warm months only.

WEEKLY MARKET
On Thursdays, just behind the Duomo on the Piazza Adamo d'Aragno (locally nicknamed the Piazzetta dei Contadini) country people sell mushrooms and whatever else they have. This includes apples, figs, chestnuts, lettuces, cheeses, honey, and many flowers. In front of the Duomo on the Via Giuseppe Verdi, stalls are set up where you can buy clothing and basic kitchenware. More stalls line Via Carlo Esterle to the left of the church as you face it. Here one often finds Costa the cheese seller, who has good local products. The market then continues on the Via Giovanni Prati.

MUSHROOM MARKET
Piazza Lodron.

In season this is the place to buy freshly picked mushrooms. If you have any fears, you can look for the police officer who is the designated mycologist on duty. This piazza also has orderly stands selling cheeses, meats, fruits, vegetables, beans, honeys, and flowers.

SPECIAL STORES
Busana, Via Suffragio 74.

A flower store that is a good source for seeds if you want to plant an Italian vegetable garden.

Erboristeria Cappelletti, Piazza Fiera 7. Open 8:30—12:15h, 14:45–19h; closed Saturday afternoon and Sunday.

Since 1909, all manner of herbal and fruit elixirs for anything that ails you. The shop also sells its own Brulè Bacchus, a spiced wine. Candies and lozenges for coughs and sore throats, other herbal pills for gastric issues.

MUSEUM

Collezione Ferrari, Via del Ponte di Ravina 15, tel. 0461/922500. Visits by appointment only.

Since 1902 Ferrari has produced a very well regarded sparkling wine that has admirers throughout Italy and beyond. It is drier than the spumante from Asti or the Oltrepò Pavese in Lombardia and appeals to people who like champagne. The museum has photographs and documents recounting the history of the firm, but I think you will be particularly drawn to the old machinery used to make sparkling wine once upon a time.

WINE

Comitato Vitivinicolo Trentino, Via del Suffragio 3, tel. 0461/235858 or 239314, fax 0464/239853. Open 8–13h, 14–17h.

Persons of serious purpose who want to learn more about the wines of Trentino should address themselves here. A wonderful resource for restaurateurs, wine writers, and wine sellers.

Via Suffragio 62. Open 8–12h, 16–19h; closed Saturday and Sunday.

This seemingly anonymous shop is an exhaustive source for equipment to make wine, beer, grappa, and *acquavita*. An education can be had here.

Enoteca Lunelli, Largo Carducci 12, tel. 0461/982496. Open 8:30–12h, 15–18h; closed Monday morning and Sunday. All credit cards.

An excellent selection of wines from every Italian region except Molise. There are also wines from fifteen foreign countries. The perfect place to purchase most Trentino wines and grappas since 1929.

Enoteca La Sgeva, Piazza Venezia 11, tel. 0461/980090. Open 8–2h; closed Sunday. No credit cards.

A vast selection of wines from Trentino and the Alto Adige, served with local cheeses, sausages, and strudel to go with spumante and dessert wines.

Varignano di Arco

DINING

Trattoria Belvedere, Via Serafini 2, tel. 0464/516144. Closed Wednesday and mid-June–September 30. No credit cards. Moderately inexpensive.

There is not a wide range of dishes here, but that is not the reason to dine at Belvedere. Since 1890 this trattoria with a beautiful view has been a mecca for lovers of *carne salada,* the Trentino's delicious raw

meat specialty. A menu is not presented here (although one is posted outside), and the day's offerings are recited by Giuseppe Santorum, whose mother is in the kitchen. Giuseppe might propose an antipasto platter of slivers of lard (very good), light *salame, prosciutto crudo,* good *prosciutto cotto,* and some *carne salada.* This platter is accompanied by *sott'aceti:* onions, string beans, red peppers, and carrots all preserved in vinegar. If you don't want all of this first, there is a nice *pasta e fagioli* soup full of red and white beans, pasta, carrots, onions, and parsley. I added some Trentino olive oil to give it extra flavor. There is one basic second course—*carne salada cotto con fasoi:* cooked *carne salada* served with *borlotti* beans and fabulous homemade ricotta cheese. The combination of meat, cheese, and beans is scrumptious, especially with a couple of drops of oil. It is served with more *sott'aceti,* but I opted for a bowl of radicchio. Dessert is very fresh homemade apple strudel. The house wine is nothing special.

Vignole di Arco

OLIVE PRESS
Luigino Bertamini, Via Mazzini 12, tel. 0464/517229.

The elderly Signor Bertamini is thought to have the last private stone olive press in the Trentino, now that most olive growers take their product to the Associazione Agraria in Riva. A few small growers in the zone prefer to use the services of Luigino. His own oil is also quite wonderful, and you may purchase some in the late autumn and winter.

Cristina Arman's Tortell di Patate
Farm-Style Potato Pancakes

These are very good when topped with a paper-thin slice of delicate meat such as speck, *prosciutto crudo, carne salada,* or even carpaccio.

Serves 2
4 medium potatoes (not new, young ones)
4 tablespoons flour
Salt and freshly ground black pepper to taste

Wash, peel, and grate the potatoes and combine them in a bowl with the flour. Add a little salt and pepper. Form large flat cakes, larger than the palm of your hand. Grease a nonstick frying pan with cooking oil (vegetable, canola, corn, or even a light olive oil), place the cakes in the pan, and fry over medium heat until golden on one side. Pour a couple of drops of oil on each cake, flip the cakes carefully, and fry the other side until golden.

Wine: Teroldego Rotoliano.

Torta con le Carote
Carrot Cake

This delicious cake is completely different from the carrot cake that is popular in the United States.

5 large eggs
225 grams/1 cup fine granulated sugar
250 grams/1 cup plus 1 tablespoon grated carrots
250 grams/1 cup plus 1 tablespoon finely ground almonds
Juice of 1 lemon
1 tablespoon flour
Unflavored bread crumbs

Preheat the oven to 160°C (300°F). Separate the egg yolks from the whites. Combine the yolks and the sugar in a mixing bowl and beat until thickened. Stir in the carrots, almonds, lemon juice, and flour. In a separate dish beat the egg whites until fluffy and then carefully combine them with the other ingredients. Pour the batter into a shallow 9-inch tart or pie plate that has been lightly buttered and sprinkled with unflavored bread crumbs. Bake for 50 minutes to an hour, until lightly browned on top. The result is like a sponge cake, which is typically served with whipped cream, although it is fine as is.

Alto Adige

Not to Miss in Alto Adige

BOZEN/BOLZANO   BRIXEN/BRESSANONE *(Classic Town)*

MERAN/MERANO   WEINSTRASSE/STRADA DEL VINO TOWNS

**REGIONAL AND
PROVINCIAL CAPITAL:**
Bozen/Bolzano (BZ).

TOURIST INFORMATION:
Ufficio Provinciale per il
    Turismo,
        Piazza Parocchia II/12,
        39100 Bozen/Bolzano,
        tel. 0461/895111.
Agritourism:
Südtiroler Bauernbund,
        Brennerstasse 7,
        39100 Bozen/Bolzano,
        tel. 0471/972145.
The Alto Adige is chock-
    full of inexpensive, clean,
    and pleasant farmhouses
    and rural homes that
    offer lodging that makes
    for perfect holidays for

Note: In this chapter, cities, towns, and addresses in the Alto Adige are listed first by their German names and then by their Italian names. The region's capital, for example, is Bozen/Bolzano.

 The Alto Adige is a region of divided loyalties and identities. To Italians the Alto Adige (the name refers to the upper reaches of the Adige River, the nation's second longest) is in every way northern and is perceived entirely differently than it is by Germans. The Alto Adige, to Italians, is a cool mountainous place that produces white wine and is full of Teutonic people. The Germans think the region is a sunny area that produces red wine and has a populace with a certain Latin temperament. Both perceptions are true. Many of the ancient peoples of the region were Ladins, the alpine "nation" that covers parts of modern Switzerland, Austria, and Italy. Their language was a corruption of Latin, and their societal roots were based in scratching out a living from the unyielding terrain of much of the Dolomites, as this portion of the Alps is known. They were deeply religious and placed crosses everywhere. You will see crucifixes in lonely mountain valleys as well as in modern offices, banks, and homes.

In medieval times, prince-bishops took residence in Brixen, Meran, and elsewhere, and their influence brought scholarship and advanced agricultural methods along with rivalries and political intrigue. Many

of these men were German speakers, and they were
the first wave of German political influence here. For
hundreds of years after, this region was linked cultur-
ally, politically, and economically to the German-
speaking lands to the north, especially the Hapsburg
territories. Because this was the southernmost area of

people on a budget. It is
often possible to arrange
for packages that include
meals.

these lands, it was called the Südtirol (the South Tyrol). Just as some of the *milanesi* and *torinesi* of northern Italy regard southern Italians with disdain or at least
with an air of superiority, so too do Prussians and Rhinelanders view the people of
the Südtirol as rustic bumpkins. Following the First World War this region was
annexed by Italy, which was one of the victorious Allies along with France, Britain, and the United States. In effect, a German-speaking minority was brought
into a new nation. When you straddle two distinct cultures but are not fully accepted in either, one choice is to go your own way. So the Südtirol/Alto Adige has
its own strong sense of identity and autonomy. In fact, the Trentino–Alto Adige
(the region was politically linked with the more southerly Italian-speaking region
in 1948) has been given special autonomous rights. The Trentino is administered
from its capital, Trento, while the Alto Adige is administered by Bozen/Bolzano.
The people here feel in every way very far from Roma, and rather than join one of

the traditional parties, they are represented in the Italian Parliament by their own, the SVP (Südtiroler Volkspartei). Television, radio, and the press are predominantly in German, although the Italian media do reach the main towns. Only Bozen/Bolzano is essentially bilingual. If you venture even a few kilometers away to one of the Wine Road towns, such as Tramin/Termeno, life is lived, for all intents and purposes, in German. I know this because many of the tourist offices there don't even print materials in Italian, which is, after all, the state language!

In examining a map of the region, you see a series of valleys and mountain ranges. There are also rivers here that create linguistic and gastronomic boundaries. The Adige (called the Etsch in German) runs south from Meran/Merano to Bozen/Bolzano and grows in force as it heads down to Trento and Verona. The Eisach/Isarco runs daintily through Brixen/Bressanone and gathers movement as it merges with the Adige at Bozen. The valleys near Meran are Venosta, Ultimo, and Passiria. Moving east from Passiria one finds the Sarentina (north of Bozen), Isarco (Brixen), Gardena (with the gorgeous Siusi Alps), Badia, and Pusteria Valleys. This last one is less frequented by visitors. Pusteria retains many Tyrolean characteristics in food and language, and Bruneck/Brunico, its principal town, is a charming place with much to recommend it. Nearby, at Amaten/Ameto, are two farms where you can dine on country cooking while looking at cows resting on tranquil hillsides.

The weather in much of the region is also quite wonderful. The air is fresh and clean, and there is a great deal of sunshine, much more than in the Italian lake district farther south and west, for example. An ideal vacation in this region is to hike in spring, summer, and fall and ski in the winter, and to then answer pangs of hunger with hearty *altoatesino* (the Italian adjective to describe this region) cuisine.

Eating in Alto Adige

Given the political, cultural, and natural components that shaped this region, you would probably expect that the cuisine would be largely Germanic with Italian influences and a great deal of milk, cream, butter, and cheese from alpine dairy cows. All of this is true, but one must also remember all the herbs that grow here during the alpine spring. Because the Austro-Hungarian Empire enjoyed flavors such as poppy seeds *(mohn/semi di papavero)*, cinnamon, horseradish *(cren)*, garlic, chive, and dill, these have all found their way into the cuisine of the Südtirol. Another flavor that appears throughout the meal is that of berries. They are generically called *mirtilli* in these parts. *Mirtilli rossi* are particular red berries that don't have a North American equivalent. They look like cranberries but have a different taste. *Mirtilli neri* are a darker version of American blueberries, but again the flavor is different.

The two most famous foods here are probably speck and *canederli*. Speck is bacon or ham that has been cured and then smoked for a few hours before being aged for about six months. Much of the speck you will find is industrially made, but there are still some fine small producers, such as Bernardi in Bruneck/Brunico. *Canederli* is the Italianization of the Germanic *knodel*, or "dumpling." Do not confuse these with gnocchi, which are smaller and more delicate. *Canederli* are a legacy of the food of poor peoples of the past who needed to fill hungry bellies inexpensively. They are made of bread and flour, and some are flavored with liver, cheese, herbs, or meat. *Canederli* are served in soup or topped with butter and cheese as a first course. They also accompany main courses such as *gulasch*. They are very tasty, but after a week in the region one does not miss them.

The Alto Adige has some of the finest breads in Italy. They represent the best of German and Italian traditions and contain seeds such as poppy or caraway, flavorings such as onion, garlic, and herbs, and use various flours, sometimes in combinations. Don't miss the *pane dei francescani* at the Panificio Franziskaner Backerei in Bozen/Bolzano. It is outstanding.

PRIMI

There are excellent soups in the Alto Adige. These include *weinsuppe/zuppa di vino*, a wonderful soup with a white-wine base. The best is from Terlan/Terlano. There is also *minestra di orzo* (barley), *crema di castagne* (chestnut), and *sauerkrautsuppe*. *Tiroler speckknodelsuppe* is a soup with *canederli* studded with speck. *Leberknodelsuppe* is made with liver-flavored *canederli*. *Meraner schneckensuppe* is the snail soup typical of Meran. *Bauernbrotsuppe* is a rye-bread soup from the Val Venosta. The filled pastas of choice are *tirtlen* (little fried pasta, which often contain vegetables or cheese) and the larger *schlutzkrapfen*, which are ravioli filled with either sauerkraut, potatoes and herbs, or cheese.

SECONDI

Meat is frequently consumed in the Alto Adige. Pork appears as speck, *kaminwurz* (a smoked sausage), *carrè di maiale affumicato* (smoked pork loin), or in chunks in *gulasch*, which can also be made with veal or beef. Blood sausages are also popular in this region. *Biroldo* is a blood sausage made with chestnuts, pine nuts, and walnuts. A veal specialty that is delicious is *sauerer kalbskopf* (called *testina di vitello all'agro* in Italian), thin slices of cooked calf's head served with a vinegar sauce and onions. Cast aside your apprehensions and sample this tasty dish. You can also have Wiener schnitzel (delicate breaded veal cutlets, cooked in butter). Game includes *hirsch/cervo* (venison), *capretto* (kid), and *hasen/lepre* (hare). A specialty throughout the region is *gröstl*, sort of like a hash of potatoes and onions to which either speck, beef, or occasionally poultry is added. What makes each *gröstl* preparation unique is the selection of flavorings. Many use garlic, but you are just as likely to find oregano, cumin, or chives as a dominant taste. The leading fish of the region is the trout from the Passirio River. It is served smoked, boiled, or sautéed.

FORMAGGI

This is a region of formidable cheese production, most of it based on cow's milk. If you find the unusual *graukäse* (gray cheese), give it a try. Others include Alpenbauerkäse, Bela Badia (a sweet, *caciotta*-like cheese), Brunecker Stangenkäse (like Tilsit), Pusterbergkäse, and Tirolerkäse. Tilsit, an Austrian cheese, is found in the areas near the border. The best cheese sources I found were in Brixen/Bressanone and Bruneck/Brunico.

DOLCI

Given the Alto Adige's proximity to Germany and Austria, it should not surprise you that the area has excellent cake. You might get tired of *apfelstrudel,* which is served everywhere. The crust here is thicker than the flaky ones in Vienna, but in good bakeries the quality of the apple filling is first-rate. Because this area grows some of the most famous apples and grapes in Europe, these flavors are everywhere. Many of the rarer varieties of apples have been eliminated in recent years, to be replaced by more generic types that are guaranteed sellers. This is a shame, and I challenge growers here to reintroduce more distinct, if less commercial, varieties. Another noteworthy cake is *torta di grano saraceno con mirtilli rossi,* a wonderful buckwheat cake with red berries. Carrot cake (often made with ground almonds or pine nuts) is light and delicious and bears no resemblance to its heavy, dark American cousin. *Zelten* is the favorite Christmas cake. Other desserts are *schmarrn,* or *kaiserschmarrn,* strips of crepes served with fruit and cream. Chestnuts also find their way into many desserts. One of them is *mohrenkoepfe,* chestnuts boiled in spiced milk and then served with cream and cherries. Handmade candies are of high quality in this region. Some of the best sweets and desserts I found were in Brixen/Bressanone and Meran/Merano.

The Wines of Alto Adige

It is customary in the Alto Adige that the local country people drink light white wine until noon (on Sunday one has white wine at an *osteria* after morning church services), and then red wine in the afternoon. We tend to think of German wine consumption as being of sweeter wines, but in the Alto Adige they drink dry wines. Italians think of the Alto Adige as the far north and associate the region with cool white wines. On the other hand, Germans and Austrians think of the Alto Adige as the Südtirol, the southernmost part of the German-speaking world. So to them this is a warm place that produces red wine. In fact, about two-thirds of the wine production in the Alto Adige is red, and this is what most local people drink.

Wine has been produced in the Südtirol for two thousand years. Since most of the sales of this wine were geared toward the north, it was a shock when the region became part of Italy in 1919. In effect, the wine had a loss of identity and only re-established its markets after each war when Germany and Austria returned to prosperity. The Alto Adige has achieved a level of consistent excellence that few places can rival. Even in 2002, when most regions had a difficult harvest, the wines produced in Alto Adige were splendid. I think that only Friuli-Venezia Giulia makes white wines that are better. Giorgio Grai of Bozen is one of the superstar enologists of Italy. His talents are sought all over the country, but he certainly has been instrumental in promoting quality in his home region.

One of the joys of a visit to this region is stopping at the gorgeous district of wine towns that start at the southern gates of Bozen and continue south for thirty-seven kilometers (twenty-three miles). The Weinstrasse/Strada del Vino is a picturesque road marked with yellow signs that lead the way. You will see Kalternsee/Lago di Caldaro, an idyllic lake surrounded by vineyards. The town of Kaltern/Caldaro has a wine museum worth visiting. Throughout the region there is the tradition of the *Törggelen*, in which people wander to a pretty place to taste new autumn wine (read more about this under the listing for the Weinstrasse). Another pleasing wine place is the Stiftkeller Neustift just outside Brixen, where wine has been made by monks for centuries. In Meran, one drinks the juice of wine grapes for their special healthful properties in an annual tradition known as the grape cure.

The Alto Adige has the highest percentage of DOC wines of any Italian region. Almost all are made by small family producers rather than the larger industrial wineries one sees farther south in parts of the Trentino and the Veneto. There are many varieties of grapes and blends in the Alto Adige, so I will list only the most prominent ones you will encounter. Where possible, the grape's name will be listed in German and then Italian.

Whites: Goldmuskateller/Moscato Giallo; Muller Thurgau; Ruländer/Pinot Grigio; Sylvaner; Terlano (a mixture of Pinot Bianco, Chardonnay, Riesling Italico, Sauvignon, Sylvaner, and Müller Thurgau); Weissburgunder/Pinot Bianco. Special mention should be made of Gewürztraminer/Traminer Aromatico. This comes from the town of Tramin/Termeno on the Wine Road. Although the grape is now found throughout the world, it is native to here and is much celebrated.

Reds: Most of the red wine consumed in the Alto Adige and sold abroad is a pleasing light red made primarily from the Vernatsch/Schiava grape. You will see many wines called St Magdalener/Santa Maddalena. This is a Vernatsch-based wine that is the house wine of almost every restaurant and bar in Bozen. Another local variety is Lagrien, and you also find Cabernet Franc, Cabernet Sauvignon, and Blauburgunder/Pinot Nero.

Amaten/Ameto

This tiny farming community is just northeast of Bruneck. If you want to make an excursion for a country lunch, this is a delightful option.

DINING

Berggasthof/Restaurant Amaten, tel. 0474/39993. Closed Tuesday and November. No credit cards. Moderately inexpensive.

You are literally on a farm when you dine here. You drive past huge cows that stand or lie on a hillside overlooking the valley. The restaurant is open to the public even if you don't choose to lodge here. The food shows more Italian influence than one generally sees in this remote part of the Alto Adige, so that the *maccheroni allo chef* (made with smoked sausage, ground beef, tomatoes, and cream) is a very good choice if you have tired of this region's ubiquitous *canederli*. There is absolutely delicious *gulasch* made of delicate beef (from one of the brothers of the cows outside, I suspect) that is all flavor. The house bread is unusual, with a pronounced cumin flavor. The special dessert is the *omelette con mirtilli rossi*, a thick, fluffy Austrian pancake made of eggs, flour, and water, filled with red berries typical of the area, and topped with powdered sugar. The wine is nothing special.

Oberraut, tel. 0474/559977. Closed Thursday (except in the summer), late January, late September, and Christmas. All credit cards. Moderate.

A restaurant with rooms in an idyllic pastoral setting. *Tirtlin* (pasta filled with sauerkraut or herbs, according to season), *weinsuppe*, venison, mushrooms, *graukäse*, and *friggilan* (little fried dumplings served with jam) are all special treats.

Bozen/Bolzano

This is the capital of the region and, with approximately 100,000 inhabitants, by far the largest city (Meran, the second largest, has 34,000 people). Other Alto Adige towns are quiet in the evening, with no Italian-style *passeggiata* (evening walk) to speak of. They are Germanic towns, neat and orderly and very still. So Bozen comes as a surprise. Young people are out at night, families stroll down the Laubengasse, mostly speaking Italian. Stores seem to prefer Italian signs, and window displays show more of the flair and carefree eye one finds farther south. Yet once one ventures up into the hills of the nearby wine towns toward the southwest or toward Brixen and Meran to the north, the German language and alpine culture and taste dominate. Bozen/Bolzano feels like an Italian city with a German accent, while the rest of the region is Tyrolean with vague hints of Italy.

Cafe Konditorei Pasticceria Heini, Laubengasse/Via dei Portici 12.

One of the city's more popular bakeries, with a large choice of German and Italian cakes and cookies. I like the *mohnstrudel* and the plum tart

Cafe Monika, Goethestrasse/Via Goethe 13. Closed Sunday.

Delicious cake and coffee.

Pasticceria Peter, Stern Durchgang/Galleria Stella. Closed Saturday afternoon, and Sunday.

Right next door to Heini, it has more refined products than its neighbor, which specializes in more typical baked goods. The *mignon* cake, with thin layers of chocolate, is very good. So too are the handmade chocolates.

Pralinè, Stern Durchgang/Galleria Stella 9.

Down the arcade from Pasticceria Peter is a tiny shop that is bursting with chocolates from Italy, Austria, Switzerland, and Germany. The window displays are made up of hundreds of boxes of chocolates.

Bar–Cafe Loreley–Bio Bar, Goethestrasse/Via Goethe 28. Closed Saturday afternoon, and Sunday.

More Milano than Bolzano, with tiny halogen lights, Keith Haring posters and funky music. A younger set comes here, and I like it because, after much of the heavy food to be had in town, one can have a cleansing, freshly juiced elixir of apple, pear, carrot, or some other fruit or vegetable.

Cafe–Bistro Vienna, Waltherplatz. Open 9–22h; closed Tuesday.

One almost feels in Vienna here. The dark wooden chairs and tables could have been designed by Josef Hoffmann. The chairs have beautiful gold Jugendstil upholstery. Adorning the walls are two framed posters from the marvelous Vienna 1900 exhibit that appeared at New York's Museum of Modern Art in 1986. In addition to the usual espresso and cappuccino one can drink a *melange*, a mix of coffee, cream, and whipped cream, as one would drink it in Vienna. *Apfelstrudel* and Sacher torte are the leading pastries, although there are other choices. There is a good choice of Alto Adige wines by the glass, plus teas, beer, mineral waters, and stronger stuff. There is a food menu, but that's best left for another place.

Cà de Bezzi, Via Andreas Hofer 30, tel. 0471/050950. Always open. All credit cards. Moderately inexpensive.

A large friendly place with music, art exhibits, freshly baked breads, delicious *crema di rafano* (horseradish soup), many pork dishes, and other enticements.

Bassenhäusel, Via Andreas Hofer 30, tel. 0471/976183. Reservations advised. Open 18:30–2h, Sunday to 1:30h; serves food until closing; closed Tuesday. No credit cards. Moderately inexpensive.

A marvelous place to eat, popular with young people who are drawn by good food at good prices. Tables fill quickly; there are about a dozen tables upstairs, which is where I prefer to eat. The presence of young people does not imply that the room is raucous or noisy. The wood-beamed ceiling and thick walls absorb sound and make dining very pleasant. And the food is delicious. To name a few dishes: *zuppa di rafano* (a creamy horseradish soup that is a bit lemony; do not prejudge this dish: it is unusual and good); *leberknodelsuppe* (a delicate liver dumpling is well integrated with the flavors of a lemony broth—superb!); *penne della casa* (tomato, cream, chopped greens, lots of black pepper, all tossed with the pasta in a small skillet, which is served to you at the table); *herrengröstl* (not the usual hash, but a skillet of cooked potatoes and onions topped with paper-thin slices of roast beef that reminded me of Japanese shabu-shabu). The meat was perfect, and the pan flavors delicious. *Herrengröstl* is served with *capucci*, cool cooked white cabbage tossed with a little bit of excellent red vinegar. *Stinco di maiale*, an oven-roasted shank of pork, is meltingly delicate and exemplary. It is served with outstanding oven-roasted potatoes, huge chips basted with oil, topped with fresh rosemary, and baked—an excellent dish. The desserts are also very good: *apfelkuchel* are delicate greaseless apple fritters served with vanilla ice cream and cinnamon. *Kaiserschmarrn* are greaselessly fried, topped with cinnamon, and served with a generous scoop of mountain berries. The house wines are good. Only the coffee is not up to snuff.

Gasthaus/Trattoria Fink, Mustergasse/Via delle Mostre 9. MasterCard, Visa. Moderate.

A charming old trattoria. The food is pretty good, the service iffy. Some typical dishes are *milzschnittensuppe/crostini di milza in brodo* (toasts with spleen pâté in broth), *kalbskopf* (calf's head, either baked or served with a vinegar sauce), *bauernplatte/piatto tirolese* (farmer's platter with sausage, smoked pork, *gulasch*, dumplings, sauerkraut, roast potatoes).

Cafe-Restaurant Gostner, Silbergasse/Via Argentieri 34 (at Piazza delle Erbe), tel. 0471/974086. No reservations accepted. Closed Saturday evening and Sunday. Moderately inexpensive.

The reason to come here is to taste excellent Alto Adige wines. There is a wine bar in the front room and tables for dining in the back. You can have wines by the bottle or the glass. I particularly like the Oxenschmid Weissburgunder that is made by the owners—curiously, it costs less than other Weissburgunder/Pinot Blancs that are not nearly as good. There are also wines produced by Haas that are worth trying. As for food, they make different types of *canederli* (plain, cheese, speck, spinach, liver, to name a few) that are good for absorbing some of the wine you will drink. The restaurant is open during the usual dining hours, but the wine bar is open all day until 21:30h.

FOOD STORES

Bozen/Bolzano has a very colorful market on Piazza delle Erbe, smack in the middle of the city. There are many markets in Italy that are much bigger and livelier, but this one so neatly fits the contours of the narrowly oval piazza that you just know that food has been sold here for centuries. Near the market, on Goethestrasse/Via Goethe to the south and Franziskanerstrasse/Via dei Franceschi to the north, are many nice little specialty shops, bars, *caffès*, and restaurants.

Panificio Franziskaner Backerei, Via dei Francescani 3.

Some of the best bread you will taste anywhere. Be sure to buy the magnificent *pane dei francescani*, which has been made by bakers on this site since 1776. This bread is full of flavors of different wheats and seeds. This is also a good place to buy *zelten*, the traditional Christmas cake of the Alto Adige.

Antica Salumeria-Selcherei Giuliano Masè, Goethestrasse/Via Goethe 15.

An outstanding small shop where the fragrances of cured pork, wild mushrooms, and tangy cheese comingle. It has all of the regional specialties and the best from throughout Italy. In the tiny room in the back is an exemplary choice of wines.

Lebensmittel-Alimentari P. Mosca, just north of Piazza delle Erbe.

A great old store with speck, cheese, and mushrooms.

HOUSEWARES, KITCHENWARE, AND EQUIPMENT

Bozen is a major shopping town for German-speaking tourists who want to buy Italian products at a favorable exchange rate. Much of this money is spent on fancy housewares. Stores are open Monday through Friday, morning and afternoon (with the customary break for lunch from 12h or 12:30h until 15h). Stores are also open Saturday morning, and many of them open in the afternoon on the first Saturday of the month. All the stores listed below accept Visa and MasterCard; some take all major credit cards.

Arcade, Goethestrasse/Via Goethe 2.

A small collection of china and housewares, artfully selected.

C. Desaler, Laubengasse/Via dei Portici 19B.

Excellent selection, and no smoking!

Electronia, Laubengasse/Via dei Portici 1, tel. 0471/976633, fax 0471/971541.

A large well-established electronics store of interest to the gourmet traveler primarily for its excellent selection of Italian coffeemakers. Almost all major brands are represented.

N. Lorenzi Il Coltellaio-Der Messerschmid, Goethestrasse/Via Goethe 36.

A good assortment of knives, cutlery, and blades.

Oberst, Bindergasse/Via dei Bottai 7.

This is not a fancy shop like those on the Laubengasse/Via dei Portici. Rather, it is a place where locals buy equipment to make juices and pulp with all the fruit that grows in these parts. Each fruit seems to have its own machine: *apfelmühlen* (for apples), *traubenmühlen* (grapes), and *obstpressen* (for stone fruits and pears). You will also find equipment for wine making and for distilling fruit to make spirits (in the Alto Adige, this machine is called a *schnaps-kessel*). Also has bulbs and seeds.

Ratschiller, Museumstrasse/Via del Museo 29.

Riedel glass, German china, and many wares from Scandinavia.

Albert Schmidt, Bindergasse/Via dei Bottai 17, tel. 0471/974489, fax 0471/972668.

You can have copper, steel, and iron cooking equipment made to order here, ranging from tiny jiggers to industrial-sized stockpots. These are things to use, not just to show. Excellent quality.

Schonhuber-Franchi, Laubengasse/Via dei Portici 56.

Alessi and other brands of plates, flatware, table settings. There are many attractive items and an outstanding selection of china.

Sudtiroler Werkstätten/Artigiani Atesini, Laubengasse/Via dei Portici 39.

This store is a showplace for the traditional crafts of the Alto Adige. The space is beautiful, with its inner atrium and balconies. Much of what is displayed could charitably be called kitschy, but if you look carefully you can find some exquisite blown glass, attractive china, and well-made linens and embroidery.

Zimmerman, Laubengasse/Via dei Portici (just off the Kornplatz/Piazza del Grano).

A mecca for cultists of Alessi products, it has other sleek tableware and kitchen equipment as well.

WINE AND WINE BARS

As the capital of a major wine-making region, the city has all the best products flowing in on a regular basis. The Weinstrasse/Strada del Vino begins just beyond the Drususallee on the south side of town.

Cafe-Restaurant Gostner.

See "Dining," above.

Left side of the arcade, near Laubengasse/Via dei Portici 30. Open 8–14h, 16–21h, Saturday 8–15h; closed Sunday.

A nameless bar that is bustling, popular, and convivial.

Vinotheque Alois Lageder, 235 Drususallee, tel. 0471/920164, fax 0471/931577.

Alois Lageder is one of the leading wine personalities of the region, and his wines have spread the name and image of the Alto Adige throughout the world. This vinotheque is not only a point of sale for Lageder wines, but includes a formidable selection of wines from all over Italy, France, and other countries, all selected by Lageder himself. Not a huge assortment, but rather a peerless selection by an authoritative palate. He told me that he first acquired these wines not to sell them but to see what other producers were doing. It was later decided that this should become the best wine shop in town. In addition you can buy jars of delicate vegetables and sauces and packages of good pasta. There was talk of changing the site of the vinotheque to a more central location by early 1997, so readers of this book should check the address before seeking this store out. Among the Lageder wines worth tasting are Pinot Bianco Hablerhof, Terlaner Sauvignon, Gewürztraminer (this sexy, perfumed wine full of apple and spices is to me the Alto Adige in a glass), St. Magde-lener Oberingram, Löwengang Cabernet, and the Moscato Rosa Alto Adige Margreid, a dessert wine that smells of roses and has a luscious flavor that fades blissfully in the mouth.

Brixen/Bressanone
Classic Town

Bozen and Meran receive more visitors, while Brixen is smaller, more beguiling, and has excellent food and hotels. This is a lovely place to stay for a few restful days of mountain walks and fine dining. It also has an imposing medieval cathedral, porticoes, palaces, cloisters, and much art and many crafts born of religious devotion. You will find that the people here are particularly involved with health and well-being. This can be seen in the Tyrolean interest in herbs, fruit teas, and long walks on demarcated paths and trails. Many people drink Plose mineral water, from a source just outside of town. Brixen is also favored by beautiful weather.

BAKERY
W. Heiss, Grosse Lauben/Via dei Portici 20. Open 8:30–12h, 15–19h, Saturday 8:30–12:45h, first Saturday of the month also 15–18h; closed Sunday.

This is the place in town to come for superb strudel and cake, as well as wonderful handmade candies and chocolates. Two outstanding cakes, both local specialties, are the *torta di carote* and *torta di grano saraceno e mirtilli rossi*. Another famous specialty is the Brixner Nüsse, marzipan-covered walnuts made only in mid-October. The bakery makes its own marrons glacés with local chestnuts and has three types of chocolate used for candies and coatings.

BARS AND CAFFÈS
Dom Cafè-Caffè Duomo, Pfarrplatz/ Piazza Parocchia. Open 8–20h; closed Monday.

Outdoor tables on a pretty piazza facing the cathedral. Good peach cake, walnut cake, and chocolate cake.

Lauben Cafè, Grosse Lauben/Via dei Portici 19. Closed Sunday.

A snug little *caffè* serving pastries from the W. Heiss bakery.

CANDLES
Ostheimer, Via Mercato Vecchio 10, tel. 0472/22203.

In a city full of churches and abbeys, candles are much in demand, and this is the place to buy them. They are also suitable for gracing your table.

CHEESE
Domgasse/Vicolo del Duomo 4B.

A wonderful milky fragrance emanates

from this tiny shop that has an excellent selection and quality cheeses from the Val Isarco. You can also buy *schuttelbrot*, the crispy rye bread typical of this area.

COFFEE AND TEA

Caracolito, Adlerbrückgasse/Via Ponte Aquila 7B.

Coffee beans are sold here, but the main attraction is thirty types of infusions and fruit teas. The dominant fragrance outside the shop is of peaches and apples.

DINING

Many restaurants in Brixen have two levels. The downstairs is usually informal, with lighter foods and some wine, while the upstairs has more formal waiter service and somewhat higher prices. It should be noted that it is easy to eat well in this town without spending much money, and for just a little more you can have delicious meals.

Alte Kapitelschenke, Domgasse/Vicolo del Duomo, tel. 0472/832344. Closed Sunday evening and Monday. No credit cards. Moderately inexpensive to moderate.

Downstairs (open 10–23h; moderately inexpensive) you can have garlic soup *(zuppa di aglio)*, fillet of marinated trout, and many cheeses. Upstairs (open 10–24h; moderate) there is wine soup, speck, *canederli* in broth, *strudel di cavolo bianco al sughetto di comino* (strudel of white cabbage and a cumin sauce), *maccheroni con ragout di selvaggina* (pasta with a game-meat sauce), gnocchi made with local cheeses, and a nice pear strudel for dessert.

Hotel Dominik, Via Terzo di Sotto 13 Unterdrittelgasse, tel. 0472/830144,

fax 0472/36554. Closed Tuesday (except in summer). All credit cards. Moderately expensive.

I am often suspicious of chefs who declare a need to reinterpret a local cuisine. This betrays a lack of confidence in the ingredients and the wisdom of tradition. Nonetheless, I admire chefs who understand the intrinsic value of ingredients and draw from tradition to create a personal style in the kitchen. One of these is Meinhard Tschurtschenthaler, who is in charge of the kitchen at the Hotel Dominik, a peaceful and perfectly run hotel on the quiet side of the Isarco River. Residents of the hotel can order from a set menu that does not in any way compromise the excitement found on the à la carte menu. Among the dishes I enjoyed was the *seezungenroulade an fenchel salat*, a delicate roulade of sole, spinach, and carrot served with a diced salad of fennel and more carrot. The wonderful *essenza di capriolo* was an intense consommé of kid, served with a dumpling of ground kid and a few small pasta dumplings filled with porcini mushrooms. Also in the soup were sautéed *finferli* mushrooms and bits of broccoli, tomato, and strips of carrot and celery. A divine pasta was *tortelloni mit steinpilzen gefüllt an schnittlauchsauce* (pasta filled with porcini, potatoes, and spinach, topped with sautéed *finferli* and a light herb-cream sauce). Two good *secondi* were *zweibelrostbraten nach tiroler art mit rostkartoffeln und blattspinat* (a steak with very flavorful roast onions and potatoes, and spinach, all mercifully low on grease) and *hirschgeschnetzeltes in leichter wacholdersauce*, an outstanding dish of tender venison fillets served in a light ginger sauce. The ginger could have easily overwhelmed

Typical Alto Adige porticoes in Brixen/Bressanone

the dish, but instead supported it nobly. The accompaniments—polenta cakes and red cabbage—were beautiful contrasts in flavor, color, and texture. The offerings on the wine list are predominantly from the Alto Adige, with some good bottles from the Trentino and some very expensive and delicious wines from Toscana.

Elefante, 4 Weisslahnstrasse/Via Rio Bianco, tel. 0472/832750. Closed November 15–March 1 and Monday (except July 30–November 10). All credit cards. Moderately expensive.

This is one of the oldest restaurants in Italy, dating way back to 1551. It is named for an elephant that was a gift from King Joao III to Emperor Ferdinand of Austria. The elephant traveled by ship from Goa in India to the port of Genova. It then had to walk to Vienna and was so tired by its climb into the Tyrol that it chose to stop in Brixen (when an elephant makes such a decision, it is hard to contradict him). The stable where this restaurant-hotel is was the biggest available, so that is where the elephant stayed. The restaurant's owner at that time painted an enormous fresco of the elephant on the outside of his building, so that long after the animal continued its walk to Vienna (where it lived a long life), the mural attracted guests to the restaurant. This is still a popular place to sleep and eat in Brixen. Many German visitors like the *Elefanten platte*, a huge plate with all sorts of food on it. The cuisine here is a mixture of German, Tyrolean, and Italian. It is good, though not outstanding.

Fink, Kleine Lauben/Via Portici Minori 4, tel. 0472/834883, fax 0472/83526. Closed

Tuesday evening, Wednesday (except late July–October), first two weeks of February, and first two weeks of July. All credit cards. Moderate to moderately expensive.

Delicious Tyrolean cuisine. You will be served zucchini bread with a creamy homemade cheese while you select your dishes. The left side of the menu, where you should look, lists local dishes. There is great soup here: *knodel di fegato in brodo* (liver dumplings in broth), *zuppa di castagne e sedano con gnocchi al burro* (chestnut-and-celery soup with small butter dumplings), and fantastic *zuppa di vino alla Val d'Isarco con crostini alla cannella* (traditional white wine soup with small cinnamon toasts). The *piatto alla Val d'Isarco* has various boiled meats served with condiments. *Gröstl alla tirolese con uova e capucci* is a hash of meat and potatoes topped with egg and served with delicate cabbage—it's quite good. There is also a fine cheese platter with specialties from throughout the Alto Adige. Good Alto Adige wines.

Finsterwert-Oste Scuro, Domgasse/ Vicolo del Duomo 3, tel. 0472/835343. Closed Sunday, Monday, three weeks in January, and late June/early July. All credit cards. Moderate.

A wine bar downstairs serves lighter dishes; upstairs is more formal fare. I particularly liked the *crema di castagne con champignons freschi*, a pureed chestnut soup with fresh mushrooms. *Testina di vitello all'agro* is a tasty local dish.

HEALTH FOOD
Euvita, Adlerbrückgasse/Via Ponte Aquila 7a.

The Germanic predilection for natural products (which forms an interesting counterpoint to the heavy, fatty nature of much German cuisine) is in evidence at this shop. There is wine in which the grapes received no chemical treatment, grains, herbal remedies, fruit teas.

HONEY
U. Rienzner, Brunogasse/Via Bruno 1.

Among the many honeys are chestnut and alpine flowers. You can buy bee pollen in jars and even toothpaste made of pollen, plus many products made of alpine herbs: skin lotions, massage oil, inhalations (made of twenty-seven herbs), and herbal spirits.

HOUSEWARES
Kerer, Erbardgasse/Via San Erardo 3b.

A full line of Alessi housewares and a good knife selection from Germany. Pots, pans, ceramics, porcelain, glassware, too.

MARKET
Pfarrplatz/Piazza Parochia.

A small outdoor market next to the cathedral, where speck, mushrooms, apples grapes, local wine, and a few other products are sold. You will be joined by families in lederhosen and nuns on bicycles. On the day I visited, there was a powerful fragrance of beans and speck from a soup being sold.

MEAT
E. Schanung Fleischhauerei-Macelleria, Adlerbrückgasse/Via Ponte Aquila 5.

Here you can purchase the cuts of wild game that find their way into local cuisine.

Seebacher Süsswaren-Dolciumi,
Albuingasse/Via San Albuino (at
Adlerbrückgasse/Via Ponte Aquila).

Walk through the Jugendstil glass door to a world of sweets from Italy, Austria, Germany, and Switzerland. A good assortment of chocolates, marrons glacés, candied fruit, jams, honeys, and spirits. Sample the local *tirolnüsse* (walnut confections) and the similar *meranernüsse*.

Bruneck/Brunico

While Bozen, Meran, and even Brixen attract many visitors who get a taste of life in the Alto Adige, Bruneck remains off the beaten path. This is a compelling reason to include this city on your visit to the region, because it has great charm and interest and has not adjusted its character to appeal to tourists. Much of what is typical about the Alto Adige, especially the Valle Pusteria area, of which Bruneck is the principal town, can be found here. The best way to get to know Bruneck is to stroll down the Stadtgasse/Via Centrale in the old city center.

A WALK DOWN THE STADTGASSE/VIA CENTRALE

#2B: Senni Bar. Closed Thursday.

Ice cream made from local milk and berries.

#4: Harrasser.

A bakery offering strudels made of apple, cherry, or poppy seeds. It also makes *kartoffelbrot* (potato bread).

#5A: G. Horvat.

This store specializes in herbs, spices, honey, seeds, and nuts. The window is full of bowls containing all of these wares, as well as the *mohn* (poppy seeds) that are ubiquitous in the cuisine of the Valle Pusteria. One also finds the fruit teas that are so popular in the Alps and the Teutonic world. These are usually dried leaves, flowers, and fruit that are infused with hot water. Some of the selections here are *pfirisch melba* (peach melba), *omas garten* ("grandma's garden"—mostly strawberry), *waldfrucht* (forest fruits), *wildkirsch* (wild cherry), and *rote grütze* (cherry and raspberry, influenced by a dessert popular in Hamburg).

#15: Frisch Brot-Pane.

Another good bakery, with a distinctive pretzel hanging outside. An unusual item here is *pane di farro* (bread made with spelt).

#26A: Stadt-Cafe. Open 8–20h; closed Sunday.

A very popular afternoon gathering spot for coffee and pastries.

#36: Gastronomia Bernardi. Open 8:30–12h, 15:15–19h, Saturday 8:30h–12h; closed Sunday. Diners Club, MasterCard, Visa.

An outstanding *gastronomia*, one of the best I know in Italy. At first look it seems like many others, until you look more closely and recognize the amazing variety and the consistently high level of quality and taste. Because we are near the Austrian border, one finds a vast selection of items that appeal to palates from Lubeck to Palermo. I suspect that many of the classically Italian foods and wines available here are sold to travelers from Germany and Austria who want the flavors of Italy in one store. The claim to fame is the homemade speck, which is of unsurpassed delicacy and flavor. There is a vast array of sausages and meats, almost all slaughtered and cured by the proprietors. One of the most popular sellers is *gulasch*, which can be purchased in cans to take home. It is made either with beef, veal, or pork. Bernardi is a great source for local cow's-milk cheeses: Alpenbauerkäse, Bela Badia, Brunecker Stangenkäse, Pusterbergkäse, and Tirolerkäse. There are magnificent olive oils, vinegars, jams, and a collection of wines and spirits that must

have been chosen by someone with real knowledge and taste. Everyone connected with Bernardi takes great pride in his work, and there is a lovely woman named Andrea who speaks excellent English.

#53: Kuntner. Open 9:30–12h, 15:30–19h, and Saturday morning; closed Sunday.

Since 1760, the factory just beyond the city center has produced ceramics that have made Bruneck famous. The patterns and colors (especially black and green) have been typical of the Valle Pusteria for centuries. Antique Kuntner creations are seen in museums in Bozen, Innsbruck, and München. One can buy vases, bowls, dishes, candleholders, but only someone with a large home will have room for the enormous stoves used for home heating. There is also a selection of ceramics from Toscana, Umbria, and Campania.

#59: Kaffee Biggi.

A nice place for coffee or afternoon tea. The rear of this café is split-level, with no smoking below. Espresso is served with a piece of semisweet chocolate. Magazines in German and Italian are available to read while you sip.

DINING
___

Hotel Post, Graben 9, tel. 0474/555127, fax 0474/31603. Closed Monday. American Express, MasterCard, Visa. Moderate to moderately expensive.

I did not dine here, but people whose taste

I trust recommend it as having typical Bruneck food. I looked at the menu and would recommend that you skip the pastas and opt instead for *gulaschsuppe* or *gemusesuppe* (vegetable soup). The kitchen is famous for its preparation of game dishes, which vary with the season. Among the desserts, *passato di castagne con gelato ai frutti di bosco* (a cream of fresh chestnuts served with mixed-berry ice cream) sounds good. The room on the street is unappealing, but in the back there is a very pleasant dining room.

LACE AND EMBROIDERY

Two stores on the main street of Bruneck offer a nice selection of typical alpine lace and embroidery, including designs of the Valle Pusteria. To my taste, those at Franz (Graben 8) are more attractive than those at Ulbrich (Graben 4A). Both stores accept all major credit cards and are open Monday through Friday from 8h to 12h and 15h to 19h. They are also open on Saturday morning.

MUSEUM

Museo degli Usi e Costumi della Provincia di Bolzano. Open 9–12h; 13–17h.

This museum, in a sixteenth-century building, houses collections of costumes, tools, ceramics, and agricultural equipment from the rural valleys of the Alto Adige.

MUSHROOMS

Frutta e Verdura Luciano Puecher, Via Stuck 4, tel. 0474/85284. Open daily.

Here is a great fruit and vegetable stand just beyond the walls of the old town. Its claim to fame is an outstanding assortment of fresh and dried mushrooms, including the *finferli* that are typical of the Dolomites, nail-shaped *chiodini*, and, of course, *funghi porcini*. All are sold at excellent prices. You can also purchase chestnuts and beautiful berries.

Gargazon

DINING

Kathi's Jausestation, Banhofstrasse 27, tel. 0473/291331. Open mid-March–end of October 10–21:30h; closed Tuesday. No credit cards. Inexpensive.

When my friend Ed and I arrived at this restaurant on a rainy Sunday in late October, we felt like immigrants in a new country. Here we were, two Americans in Italy in a place where no one speaks or thinks Italian. So remote is this place that Meran and Bozen seem like faraway big cities, and Milano and München are the stuff of dreams. On the road from Lana toward Nals/Nalles, past nothing but orchards and

vineyards, is this culinary oasis where apple farmers come to eat and socialize. The food is delicious, and the prices are amazingly low. We had *bauerngröstl* (potatoes, onions, and bits of speck sautéed with cumin and oregano), *sauerer kalbskopf,* and *frittaten suppe* (thin eggy crepes sliced in ribbons and cooked in broth—delicious, except that the broth was made with a bouillon cube). Dessert is very good apple strudel—imagine eating apple strudel in the middle of the orchard where the apples were picked! Also available are *kaminwurz, gemischter käse* (mixed cheese platter), roast potatoes with liverwurst. The beverages are fresh apple and grape juice. Beer, new wine, and coffee are available, too.

Girlan an der Weinstrasse/Cornaiano sulla Strada del Vino

DINING

Marklhof-Bellavista, tel. 0471/662407.
Closed last week of June, first week of July,
Sunday evening, and on Monday
November–June. All credit cards.
Moderate to moderately expensive.

This restaurant is famous for the astounding views from its terrace, but the food is also very good.

Innichen/San Candido

This town is just a stag's leap from the Austrian border, so it should not surprise you that the food, architecture, language, and ambience all seem more Hapsburg than Italianate.

CHEESE

Latteria Sociale di San Candido,
Via Castello 1.

The milk and cream from cows of the nearby valleys produce cheeses such as Bergkäse, *graukäse,* Tilsit, and Zieger.

WINE BAR

Uhrmacher's Weinstube, Via Tintori 1.
Open 9–24h; wine shop open 9–12h,
15–19h; closed Wednesday, though not in
high season.

A sign above the bar advises that DER IS NICHT WERT DES WEINES, DER IHN WIE WASSER TRINKT (He who drinks wine like water is not worthy of wine). Uhrmacher's is a warm, welcoming place where old men in loden coats with matching hats drink Gewürztraminer while listening to German-language radio. At harvesttime, be sure to try *frischer traubenmost,* freshly squeezed juice from wine grapes. There are good sandwiches made with speck and local cheeses. Next door is an excellent shop in which to buy wines and grappas by the bottle.

Kaltern an der Weinstrasse/Caldaro sulla Strada del Vino

DINING

Panholzerhof, Località Lago 8, tel.
0471/960259. Open 17–24h; closed Sunday
and during the harvest. Inexpensive.

An informal place where wine is the reason to come. This is one of the rare places you can sample Keil, an old and rare red wine that is produced here and very few other places. There are other wines to match with speck, cheeses, good bread, and local desserts. If there are any desserts made with walnuts (which are grown right here), those should be your pick.

Torgglkeller, Località Bichler,
tel. 0471/963421. Reserve!

One of the best places in the region for *törggelen*. It fills up quickly because the food, wine, and ambience are all very agreeable.

WINE MUSEUM

Südtiroler Weinmuseum, Goldgasse/
Via d'Oro 1, tel. 0471/963168. Open
Easter–end of October 9:30–12h, 14–18h,
Sunday 10–12h; closed Monday.

This is one of Italy's top wine museums, definitely worth a visit if you are in the area. In the first room are paintings from 1889 of the wine valleys that are just outside. Compare how they looked then and look now. There are documents dating back to 1452 about wine production in the area and books on the same from the seventeenth century. In the other rooms is a huge collection of fascinating equipment. For example, look for the bellows from 1850 that was used for blowing insects off vines. You will see a vat where wine was made with the feet. There are enormous winepresses, including one that was made in 1400. Look for the mannequin of the *saltner/saltaro*. This was an armed guard who was hired either on the day of San Giacomo (July 25) or San Lorenzo (August 10) to stand guard in the vineyards, protecting them from thieves until harvesttime. In rooms farther back you will see great old barrels and collections of bottles and labels. Look at these latter for a few minutes and notice the evolution in design from the evocation of pastoral well-being to urban high tech. Is this a positive trend? Finally, look for the collection of stamps with enological themes from around the world. Not only are there stamps from traditional wine-producing nations, but also from Afghanistan, Bolivia, China, England, Ghana, Korea, and Togo!

WINE

E&N (Erste & Neue).

Just to the right of the entrance to the Südtiroler Weinmuseum, above, is a tasting room and place to purchase wines by a well-regarded local producer.

Vinothek—Feinkost Battisti Matscher,
Goldgasse/Via d'Oro 7, tel. 0471/963299.

Excellent local selection, also a wide range of local honeys. There are unusual items, such as *aceto di prosecco,* vinegar made from the popular sparkling wine grape of the Veneto. Spacious, well ordered.

Kurtatsch an der Weinstrasse/Cortaccia sulla Strada del Vino

WINERY

Tiefenbrunner Weinstube, Via Castello 4,
tel. 0471/880122; fax 0471/880433.
Open Easter–November 10, 10–19h;
closed Sunday.

Follow the signs in town up the hill to the Tiefenbrunner winery. Drink wine by the glass and have good speck, ham, cheese, and homemade pâté in a warm room or in a nice garden with a lovely view. You can also buy bottles to take home. The Tiefenbrunners have been making wine since 1848, and wine has been made on this site for eight hundred years. For centuries, its output went to the bishop of Trento as payment of property taxes by the occupants of this castle. In recent years, their wines have come to be considered among the finest in Italy. As I have mentioned, their Müller Thurgau Feldmarschall is one of my favorite wines, and their Pinot Bianco, Pinot Grigio, Gewürztraminer, Pinot Noir, and Linticlarus Cabernet Sauvignon are all very fine.

Lana

FRUIT MUSEUM
Südtiroler Obstbaummuseum/ Museo Sudtirolese della Frutticoltura, Brandis-Warlweg 4, tel. 0473/54387. Open April–end of October, 10–12h, 14–17h, Sunday and holidays 14–18h; closed Monday.

In this area of intense cultivation of apples, pears, and grapes nine kilometers/5.6 miles south of Meran, this museum charts the history of this agriculture and its impact on the area. You will see old farm furniture and equipment and traditional costumes. You might consider lunch at Kathi's Jausestation in nearby Gargazon.

Meran/Merano

Meran has been one of Europe's leading tourist resorts for many years and has geared much of its structure and energy toward providing pleasure for the visitor. It was a favored retreat for the Hapsburgs and became a popular spa town in the mid–nineteenth century, drawing visitors from all over Germany and the Austro-Hungarian Empire. One of these was Sigmund Freud, who liked to come in early autumn for the city's famous grape cure. Although Meran can be very full of tourists, who occupy its 159 hotels, it is still possible to feel relaxed and healthy. Historically, Germanic peoples have enjoyed long walks in nature. This is not only a matter of exercise, but of spiritual communion with the elements. Lofty though this may sound, it is a genuine sentiment that millions of people pursue. For gratification of the visitor, Meran was designed as a walking city, with its beautiful promenades and designated trails along the Passirio River and in the hills around town. On the left bank of the river is the *passeggio d'estate* (summer walk); the right bank has the *passeggio d'inverno* (winter walk). There are different light and vegetation on each side, and, in truth, you can have pleasurable meanderings at any time of the year on either side. Another nice walk is on the Laubengasse/Via dei Portici, several blocks of portico-lined streets with many wonderful stores and restaurants. Many of these are listed below. (Stores in Meran are open mornings and afternoons Monday through Friday, as well as Saturday morning. Many stores also open on the first Saturday afternoon of the month.) Meran has not taken kindly to automobiles, which must be parked in lots a bit outside the city center. This is not a problem, but the traffic can be intense and is further complicated by some of the worst signage I've encountered in Italy. Print on signs is small, and by the time you have found the street or direction you need, you are forced to drive past it. I prefer to come to Meran by train or bus, leave my bag at a hotel in town, and walk everywhere. There is excellent local bus service for excursions to the countryside. If you must drive, use the car for country excursions and walk around town.

BARS AND CAFFÈS

Cafe Darling, Passaggio d'Inverno 5. Open 7:30–1h; closed Wednesday.

A lovely café on the bank of the river, and my preferred place in town for taking the grape cure. The owner, Oswald Troyer, has a vineyard outside of town and grows his own grapes, which produce my favorite juice in Meran. There is also good coffee.

Cafe Lauben, Laubengasse/Via dei Portici 120. Closed Sunday.

Fresh apple, pear, and grape juice in addition to coffee and pastries.

Cafe Maria Theresia, Rennweg/Via delle Corse 16.

Red-cheeked teenage girls drink fresh apple juice and eat cake at this quiet little café in the city center.

BEER

Forst, one of Italy's better-known beers, is brewed in Meran. It is malty and slightly bitter. It is widely available in town.

BREAD

Backerei-Panificio, Laubengasse/Via dei Portici 43.

Small but with a full range of local breads of high quality. Lines out the door.

Fine baking in Meran/Merano

DINING

Rafflkeller, Vicolo Parocchia 32, tel. 0473/232359. Closed Sunday. No credit cards. Inexpensive.

Good food year-round and a decent place in town for *törggelen.*

Rusterkeller, St. Kassian-Str./Via San Cassiano 1, Algund/Lagundo, tel. 0473/220202. Open 10–1h. No credit cards. Inexpensive.

Just outside of town is this popular place to drink young wine and eat rustic food. A platter called *misto all'agro* contains beef, calf's head, and mountain cheeses under a slightly vinegary sauce. The platter of *merende locali* contains fresh cheese, speck, *salami,* smoked trout, and fresh horseradish. There is spinach spätzle, little green gnocchi, in a sauce of cream, ham, and cheese. Of course, there are *canederli,* good ones filled with spinach and cheese. The atmosphere is friendly, and the scenery outdoors is charming.

Terlaner Weinstube, Laubengasse/ Via dei Portici 231, tel. 0473/235571. Reservations essential. Closed Wednesday and in March.

An institution since 1825 and one of the better restaurants in Meran. The wine soup, *zuppa di vino terlaner,* is a house specialty that includes cinnamon as well as white wine. The fillets of smoked trout are nice and delicate. The grilled trout fillets are also good. If you want a more substantial dish, try the *carrè di maiale affumicato con crauti e canederli,* tender smoked pork with dumplings and sauerkraut that is spiked with whole peppercorns. Be sure to save room for dessert. There are a couple of special sweets here that should not be missed. Try the *parfait al papavero con crepes di mirtilli neri.* This is an eggy poppy-seed ice cream served with crepes filled with black mountain berries. Just as good is the *terrina al latticello guarnita con frutta,* a buttermilk flan with kiwi and wild berries: simple and fabulous. There is also a very good apple strudel that seems ordinary only because of the company it keeps. I dined here with three Australians, one of whom, in assessing the meal, declared, "It's all bloody good." He's right.

FOOD STORES

Balth. Amort, Laubengasse/Via dei Portici 261.

With all the alpine and Germanic flavors preferred in Meran, this almost seems like a foreign food store. In fact, it specializes in products from all over Italy. There is *mostarda* and *torrone* from Cremona, prosciutto from Parma and San Daniele, top cheeses, cherry preserves from Modena, and chocolates from Piemonte.

Latteria, Laubengasse/Via dei Portici 235.

A milk and cheese store that sells fresh, delicious buttermilk.

Le Petit Gourmet, Pfarrplatz/Piazza Duomo 26.

One goes through a narrow passageway to reach this shop, which has a few small tables in addition to its sales counters. One can have a nice, light meal at this sleek modern place that seems very unlike the more traditional places in town. The main reason to come here is the outstanding breads (sold 7:30h to 12:30h, 16h to 19h), including *milchgipfel* (milk rolls) and whole wheat, corn, rye, and nut breads. Prepared foods are sold at another counter until 21h. You can buy *salame,* nice pâtés, and vegetables.

Seibstock, Laubengasse/Via dei Portici 223.

A fancy, well-run shop for cheese, jams, oils, wines, *funghi porcini,* plus homemade jams and condiments. It also sells small bottles (for hikers) of grappa in many herbal and fruit flavors and a *salamoia* (a mixture of coarse salt and dried herbs) that is suitable to the cuisine of this area. It would be a nice little jar to take home if you have purchased a book of Tyrolean recipes.

THE GRAPE CURE

For years before I went to Meran, I had heard of its famous grape cure. When I asked people in other parts of Italy about it, no one had a clue what it was. I imagined that one took a bath in grapes like Lucille Ball in her famous grape-picking episode or perhaps sat around feasting all day on grapes. In fact, a century ago a doctor determined that the local grapes have special qualities that benefit the digestive tract and prescribed a moderate diet abetted by drinking several glasses a day of freshly squeezed juice. The juice is naturally sweet, but not overly so. In fact, it has a very pleasant, noncloying taste. The cure (called *traubenkur* in German and *cura delle uva* in Italian) is done from mid-September to mid-October, when grapes are fresh. I suspect that the cure was invented, in part, to extend the tourist season. You usually drink three or four glasses of juice each day during the whole period when grapes are fresh. While I have not seen hard evidence about the miracle qualities of the grape cure, it is nonetheless a pleasurable autumnal activity. Many bars offer fresh juice (called *frische gepresst traubensaft*, or *spremuta di uva fresca*), as do kiosks set up along the river (look for the hexagonal stand selling juice near the Kurhaus and the bandshell on the Kurpromenade). My favorite juice is at the Cafe Darling (see "Bars and *Caffe*s," above).

HEALTH FOOD
Reformhaus/Erboristeria, Laubengasse/ Via dei Portici 4.

Here you can buy fruit teas, many herbs, and, notably, sacks of the *Kornkur*. In this health-obsessed town, this cure is in a class by itself. Portions of corn have been processed in different ways to use in drinks, soups, yogurt, and other foods. This is a popular weight-loss regime in these parts, but not for me. It does give you an insight, in gastronomic terms, into one of the realities of Meran.

HOUSEWARES
Erhart, Laubengasse/Via dei Portici 223.

A huge store with kitchenware and housewares. Vast selection, good quality.

G. Rasnelli, Laubengasse/Via dei Portici 264.

A wonderful kitchenware shop—not to be missed. One enters room after overflowing room to find thousands of items, made in places from Hamburg to Bari, reflecting the full range of culinary influences on this region. There are cannoli forms from Sicilia, Christmas-cookie shapes from Hannover, knives, coffeepots, chafing dishes, wine equipment, pots, pans, and every kitchen utensil conceivable and many you never thought of. Outside, the Rasnellis project a fully working illuminated clock on the sidewalk. Look down, and you'll know what time it is.

LINENS AND TABLECLOTHS
Lauben Zitt, Laubengasse/Via dei Portici 60.

A huge store with lots of Tyrolean handicrafts, including handmade and finished place mats, napkins, aprons, and tablecloths.

Musser, Laubengasse/Via dei Portici 197.

Gold place mats and table coverings with roseate designs. Very typical Meran designs that may appeal to some tastes.

MARKET
There is a small outdoor market for fruits and vegetables (especially grapes) on the Pfarrplatz/Piazza Duomo at one end of the Laubengasse/Via dei Portici.

MEAT
Meran has several excellent butcher shops that merit a visit to learn about how people eat around here.

Albert Egger, Laubengasse/Via dei Portici 67.

Superb assortment of *salami* and hams, many vacuum-packed to take away. The shop also makes some sandwiches.

Gögele, Laubengasse/Via dei Portici 77.
Siebenforcher, Laubengasse/Via dei Portici 168.

A bustling shop with excellent speck and *salame.*

SPIRITS

The people of Meran do not live by grape juice alone. There are all sorts of distilled spirits that end a meal. The most popular is *marillenschnaps* (apricot—it did not win me over), and there is also Williams (pear), *edelobstler* (bitter apple), *waldhimbeeren* (forest raspberry), kirsch (cherry), slivovitz (plum), and *anis* (anise). The grappa of Meran is called Treber.

WINE

Enoteca Il Carato, Via Carducci-Str. 19, tel. 0473/230623. Open 9:30–13:20h, 15:30–21:30h (or perhaps later); closed Sunday.

What a modern wine bar should be. A beautiful presentation of great wines from all over Italy, including more than two hundred reds. The room is wonderfully lit, clean, and cool. The owner is friendly and knowledgeable. A wheel of Parmigiano-Reggiano is available for nibbling while you taste wine. A wooden cover has been built to maintain the fragrance and flavor of the cheese.

Lauben Enothek, Laubengasse/Via dei Portici 112.

Small but good selection of local wines and spirits plus a large central counter for tasting. A few speck sandwiches.

Weinfachhandlung Claudia, Pfarrplatz/Piazza Duomo 13, tel. 0473/230693. Open 8:30–19:30h; closed Sunday (except in October).

Claudia is a lovely lady with a nice selection of wines by the bottle. To the right of the shop is a convivial wine bar.

Weinhandlung Winterholer, Rennweg/Via delle Corse 71.

An old store with a very nice carved-wood tasting area in the rear.

Montan/Montagna

DINING

Dorfnerhof, Gschnon/Casignano 5, tel. 0471/819798. Closed Monday. No credit cards. Inexpensive.

High, high up is a gorgeous spot to feast on scenery, wine, and food. The town of Mon-

tan is five kilometers (3 miles) away, almost completely downhill. All the classic Alto Adige dishes are here, as well as a fair amount of game. Wine is good, especially Blauburgunder/Pinot Nero. (If you are here on August 15 the town has its local festival.)

Neumarkt/Egna

This town, just off the Wine Road, is a busy little marketplace that is particularly involved in apple production. It receives almost no tourists, so it has not been prettified in the way some wine towns have. But it has a charming little market on Tuesday morning and a nice piazza. Its porticoes are very low and squat—much older and more atmospheric than those of Bozen or Meran.

DINING

Enoteca Johnson & Dipoli, Via Andreas Hofer 3, tel. 0471/820323. Open 9–16h, 18–1h; closed Monday and ten days in November. All credit cards. Moderate.

A very pretty place year-round, but especially from April to October, when you can dine outside. Good wines from the Trentino and the Alto Adige and delicate dishes to accompany them: smoked goose breast *(petto d'oca affumicato)* with a Gorgonzola cream, rack of lamb, steaks, braised beef. Good chocolate cake for dessert.

Neustift/Abbazia di Novacella

WINERY AND LIGHT SNACKS

Stifftskellerei Neustift, tel. 0472/36189. Cantina open 10–19h, guided tours of abbey and winery at 10h, 11h, 14h, 15h, 16h; closed Sunday and religious holidays.

This is a fully functioning monastery whose construction spanned from the twelfth to eighteenth centuries. Wine making began in 1142. The Augustinian monks here are learned and prosperous. They have a library with 65,000 volumes and, as is often the case, have a highly developed agricultural system that turns a good profit. You can taste their wines by the glass at the cantina operated (not by the monks) on the grounds of the monastery. The cantina is atmospheric with its stone walls, vaulted arches, round wooden tables with the center made of old wine barrels. With your wine you can have bread, cheese, speck, and *salame*. The monks also sell beer from their brothers at Augustinerkeller in München, where brewing has gone on since 1328. In season, apples are available. Nearby, at another shop, you can buy wines and apples to take home. The best wine is probably the Sylvaner. As you might expect, many tourists pass through here, but this does not detract greatly from the place's charm and interest.

Saint Michael in Eppan/San Michele in Appiano

DINING

Restaurant Zur Rose, Via Josef Innerhofer 2, tel. 0471/662249. Closed Sunday. MasterCard, Visa. Moderately expensive.

This is one of the better restaurants in the towns along the Weinstrasse. It is more expensive than most, but you will have an unusual meal. The flavors of the region are reinterpreted (not with the brilliance of the Hotel Dominik in Brixen) to create something new and pleasing. I recommend having one of the tasting menus, which will give you smaller portions of several dishes and will result in an interesting and satisfying meal. I particularly enjoyed the *lingua di vitello con insalate di canederli.* This is a plate of beautifully arranged thin disks of cold *canederli* with cool slices of calf's tongue and leaves of alpine lettuces. It was marred only by a little too much coarse salt. There was also a *strudel di coda di bue con salsa di prezzemolo* (flaky strudel filled with braised oxtail, served with an intense parsley sauce). Dessert was *frittelle di castagne con gelato a caramello,* thin pancakes of chestnut flour topped with a scoop of very good caramel ice cream. It came with a glass of a local dessert wine, Kellereigenossenschaft by Sankt Valentin Comtess, made of Gewürztraminer grapes that were picked very late so that their flavor would intensify. All the wines here are interesting and well selected, representing the best of the nearby towns.

Stern/La Villa

COOKING SCHOOL

Maso Sotciastel-Scuola di Cucina Ladina, Azienda Soggiorno di Badia, 39030 Stern/La Villa (BZ), tel. 0471/847037, fax 0471/84722.

If you are a skier who wants to study alpine cooking, this is the place for you. The Maso Sotciastel specializes in Ladin cooking, the ancient cuisine of alpine peoples before the gastronomic influences of Italy, Germany, and France arrived. You will have pastas, noodles, and dumplings made of rye flour *(segale);* rich soups; small folded pasta filled with cabbage; walnut pudding; *zelten;* and delicious *canederli.* The school opens in early December and closes around Easter. It reopens in June for summer classes through September, when the weather is warm and long hikes are rewarded by hearty food. Classes in German and Italian.

Sterzing/Vipiteno

DINING

Krone, Altstadtstrasse/Via Città Vecchia 31, tel. 0472/765210, fax 0472/766427. Moderate to moderately expensive.

This building dates back to 1540, and the restaurant is very old as well. Emperor Franz Josef, Goethe, and Heinrich Heine have all been here. There are four dining rooms, three quite homey and welcoming, the fourth done entirely in Biedermeier and somewhat more formal. The food is delicious.

Toblach/Dobbiaco

CHEESE

This area is famous for Tilsit cheese, and some of the best is made by the Latteria Sociale di Dobbiaco. You can purchase this and all the other locally produced cheeses made of milk from alpine cows at the market at #35 on the street that leads into town.

LACE AND TABLECLOTHS

Strobl, Josef Walchstrasse/Via Walch 4.

Cotton and lace napkins and tablecloths that combine the fine artistry of Venice to the south with the designs of the Tyrol.

Töllparcines

DINING

Ristorante Museumstube Bagni Egart—Onkel Taa, Via Stazione Töll 17, tel. 0473/97342. Moderate.

The building of this museum-restaurant dates back to about 1430, but nothing within remains from that era. Instead, the walls are covered with portraits of all sorts of royalty, especially Hapsburgs such as Franz Josef. The food is not unusual, but if you happen to be in this town near Meran, it is worth a look.

Tramin an der Weinstrasse/Termeno sulla Strada del Vino

The chief interest here is Traminer, the native grape that frequently appears as Gewürztraminer and is a well-known and distinctive citizen of the wine world.

DINING

Weinklause, Via Josef von Zallinger 11, tel. 0471/860112. Closed Sunday. Visa. Moderately inexpensive.

If you want to drink the local wine with good food, come here. The *weinsuppe* (made with Traminer) is delicious, as is the *piatto della casa*, consisting of spinach *canederli*, pork, wild mushrooms, and vegetables.

WINERY

J. Hofstätter Weinkellerei-Cantina Vini, Rathausplatz, tel. 0471/860161. Open 8:30–12h, 14–18h; closed Saturday and Sunday.

The Hofstätters are respected wine producers, and, as you might expect, their Gewürztraminer is their calling card. But their other wines are also worth getting to know.

Völs am Schlern/Fiè allo Sciliar

HOTEL, RESTAURANT, AND COOKING SCHOOL

Romantik Hotel Turm, 39100 Fiè allo Sciliar (BZ), tel. 0471/725014.

A marvelous and singular vacation can be had spending a week at this hotel near the Siusi Alps. The great passion of the owner, Stefan Pramstrahler, is cookery using the herbs that grow wild in the Dolomites. They are at their peak in May, so this is the time when classes are given. The fields and slopes are covered with herbs and spring flowers; days are long, warm, and sunny. You can hike to gather herbs, which will be described for their special qualities of healthfulness and flavor. The old kitchen is a beautiful setting for learning how to make pasta by hand, bread, and many typical Alto Adige dishes. The fruits and vegetables are first-rate, and the herbs elevate most dishes to unforgettable status. Although the classes are taught only in German and Italian, one can derive enough pleasure from the setting and the flavors to make a week here worthwhile.

Weinstrasse/Strada del Vino

The Wine Road south of Bozen is a beautiful thing to behold, with its perfect vineyards, charming villages, sunny valleys, and even an unspoiled lake (Kalternsee/ Lago di Caldaro) right in the middle. There are many inexpensive places to sleep and eat, and you can make a very pleasant and relaxing holiday by staying in this zone. If, during harvesttime, you see the word *Buschenschank* anywhere, this is an announcement that new wine is available to be tasted, accompanied by small snacks. A straw wheel or a bunch of fir branches are hung outside when a place is open for business. This is also announced as *törggelen,* an ancient tradition in these parts. *Törggelen* customarily begins on November 11 (Saint Martin's Day) and ends on November 25 (Saint Catherine's Day), although it often commences sooner. Most of the time a real *Törggelen* is held outside of a town because part of the custom is a good walk before and after imbibing. The traditional foods are new wine, chestnuts, and speck. Some of the towns on or near the wine road are Girlan/Cornaiano, Eppan/Appiano, Kaltern/Caldaro, Tramin/Termeno, Kurtatsch/Cortaccia, Margreid/ Magrè, Salurn/Salorno, Neumarkt/Egna, Montan/Montagna, and Auer/Ora.

Terlaner Weinsuppe/Zuppa di Vino di Terlano
Wine Soup from Terlano

This is a delicacy from the wine-producing district of the Alto Adige. While the classic wine to use is Terlaner Weissburgunder/Pinot Bianco di Terlano, you can use any dry white wine (preferably from the Alto Adige). The portion size is up to you: a cup of this rich soup might suffice, but it is so delicious that you might want more.

Serves 2 to 4
2 stale white bread rolls, or 2 thick slices stale

white bread (or a cup of unflavored croutons)

2 tablespoons unsalted butter
Ground cinnamon
½ liter/16 ounces/2 cups defatted chicken stock
5 egg yolks
375 milliliters/12 ounces/1½ cups light cream
375 milliliters/12 ounces/1½ cups Pinot Bianco
  or similar white wine

Cut the bread into cubes and sauté them in butter in a skillet until they become browned croutons (if you use commercially made croutons, they must be unflavored). Sprinkle the croutons generously with cinnamon and set aside. Heat the stock over low heat in a heavy-bottomed pot until it is just short of boiling. Briefly turn off the heat and add the yolks, start beating with a whisk, then turn on the heat to low. Add the cream, then the wine, beating all the while with the whisk. When the soup is creamy and rich, pour it into warmed bowls or dishes, top with the cinnamon croutons, and serve.

Gulasch

Goulasch (spelled without the *o* in the Alto Adige) is made many ways, depending on the meat available. It may be all beef, all veal, all pork, or in any combination. This version is with beef and has the characteristic flavors of cumin and marjoram that often provide a subtext in the cuisine of the Sudtirol.

Serves 6
5 tablespoons unsalted butter
650 grams/1½ pounds yellow onions, sliced
  into thin rings
900 grams/2 pounds boneless beef chunks
About 200 milliliters/6 ounces/¾ cup red
  wine, preferably from the Alto Adige
1 tablespoon red wine vinegar
Salt and freshly ground black pepper to taste
2 tablespoons sweet paprika
375 milliliters/12 ounces/1½ cups cold water
1 teaspoon cumin
½ teaspoon marjoram
2 cloves garlic, finely minced
½ teaspoon lemon zest
1 tablespoon fresh lemon juice

Melt 4 tablespoons of the butter in a large, heavy pot. Add the onions and sauté over medium heat until they are golden and translucent. Using a slotted spoon, push the onions to one corner of the pot and add the beef. Toss the chunks around with the spoon until they brown slightly and then combine with the onions. Continue browning the meat and allow the onions to stick slightly to the bottom of the pot. Add the wine, vinegar, and a little salt and pepper. Cook for a few more minutes until some of the liquid evaporates. Add the paprika and half of the water, cover, and cook for 90 minutes over very low heat. Check the pot periodically to assure that all of the liquid has not evaporated. Add a little more water as necessary. In the meantime, combine in a bowl the cumin, marjoram, garlic, and lemon zest with the remaining 1 tablespoon of butter. Once the *gulasch* has been cooked, add the herb-flavored butter and the lemon juice to the pot and stir just until those flavors are absorbed. Serve with polenta.

Wine: Santa Maddalena, Lagrein, or another Alto Adige red.

Friuli–Venezia Giulia

REGIONAL CAPITAL:
Trieste (TS).

PROVINCIAL CAPITALS:
Goriza (GO), Pordenone
(PN), Udine (UD).

TOURIST INFORMATION:
Azienda Regionale per la
Promozione Turistica,
Via Rossini 6,
34100 Trieste,
tel. 040/60336.

Agritourism:
Agriturist Comitato
Regionale,
Via Savorgnana 26,
33100 Udine,
tel. 0432/297068.

Wine Toursim:
Movimento del Turism del
Vino,

El vin bon,
l'omo bravo
e la dona bela,
dura poco

Good wine,
the trustworthy man
and the beautiful woman
don't last long

 This old *friulano* proverb, in my view, is all wrong, at least as regards this region. Most good wine can last long if you put it in the cellar, and there is so much good wine here that there is never a shortage. In my view, and that of many wine lovers, the wines of Friuli-Venezia Giulia (FVG, as I will refer to the region from here on) rank with those of Piemonte and Toscana, the two most famous wine-making regions of Italy. FVG is full of trustworthy men: the people of this region are amazingly hardworking and hospitable. In fact, I think that only the people of Emilia Romagna can match the *friulani* in these qualities (and for lovability). And there is a remakable abundance of beautiful women of all ages here. In *A Moveable Feast* Ernest Hemingway described the younger Gertrude Stein as a woman with a Friulian face. While he intended that as a compliment, our received notion of Gertrude Stein's appearance would lead one to think otherwise. The women of FVG are often quite beautiful, not only in their outward appearance, but also in their radiance and inner strength.

Is it possible that I gush? I believe that now that Emilia-Romagna and Piemonte have begun to receive the attention they deserve from visitors, FVG is the great undiscovered region of Italy. It has beautiful beaches on the Adriatic, stunning undiscovered Alps in Carnia, idyllic scenery in the winegrowing district known as Collio, vibrant and handsome cities such as Udine and the mysterious Trieste, historical centers such as Aquileia and Cividale del Friuli, wonderful food and wine, great coffee, good cultural facilities, and above all some of the warmest, most welcoming people you will ever meet.

When you enter a home or almost any restaurant in the region, you will see the *fogolar furlan* (Friulian hearth). It has a place of honor in the home as the site where some food is cooked and where families and friends gather for conversation, song, and conviviality. Because the hearth provided warmth, it became the focal point in a house that might otherwise be unheated. In restaurants throughout the region, one has

Sede Regionale del Friuli–Venezia Giulia, Casa del Vino— Via Poscolle 6, 33100 Udine, tel. 0432/509394, fax 0432/510180.

With so many wonderful wineries in this small region, Friuli represents a great opportunity to base yourself in one place, such as Udine, San Giovanni al Natisone, or Cormons, and then go around by car to visit wine producers. In all circumstances you should call ahead to make an appointment. Many wineries will sell by the case but might be less likely to sell a bottle or two, since these can be easily purchased in stores. At certain times of the year, most of the wineries in Friuli throw open their doors to receive all visitors as part of the initiative called Vino e Turismo.

the sense of gathering not only for food but for human and climatic warmth. In the province of Gorizia, on the border with Slovenia, there are many simple restaurants called *gostilna*, where one has fresh food and wine in a friendly setting. As one moves west toward Udine and the lands influenced by Venezia and ancient Roma, the *osteria* takes precedence.

There are more than fifty *osterie* in Udine alone, which is one reason that this city is the Classic Town for the region. The *osteria* is central to the social and spiritual life of the *udinesi*. Everyone who walks into the *osteria* is equally welcome, whether he or she is an architect or a bricklayer, a doctor or a bread baker. Titles are cast aside, unlike in southern Italy, where one's station in life is carried everywhere and is brought to bear on every social situation. In Udine and most of the region, you order a *tajut*, a small glass (usually one tenth of a liter) of wine. In the past, one would invariably be served a glass of Tocai, but now there is some variety, and you can often specify the wine you want. With *tajut* in hand you will soon make many friends to whom you might offer the next round. In the *osteria* you will find basic but delicious food such as polenta, risotto, gnocchi, cheeses, braised meats, omelettes made with wild herbs, and good baked desserts. While people eat and drink they often sing the *vilotta friulana,* the typically sad song with words in dialect, which the wine seems to elicit.

Friuli-Venezia Giulia has suffered terribly. While it had glory in ancient and early medieval times in Cividale del Friuli and Aquileia, and Udine flourished in the Renaissance, there was also privation and disaster. Once one passes Carnia, the alpine area in the northernmost part of the region, Friuli is an easily traversable land that leads to important ports and fishing on the Adriatic Sea. Every northern invader from Attila the Hun to the Nazis passed through here, and the region was the site of some of the most gruesome battles of the First World War. In most of Italy, when people talk about *la guerra* they mean the Second World War, but in Friuli it is just as often the first one, and people make the distinction in describing it to you. Gabriele D'Annunzio and Ernest Hemingway each fought and were injured in Friuli during that war. The area around Oslavia and Gorizia contains cemeteries full of the war dead. Sad as they are, they merit a visit to remind us, in our age of sanitized television wars and "strategic" attacks, what the net result of war always is.

The people of this region remain acutely aware of the issues of war and peace. In the 1980s a project was begun in the town of Cormons called *Vigneto del Mondo,* or Vineyard of the World. Grape varieties from throughout the world were planted and wine made that blends various grapes. This is called *Il Vino della Pace* (the Wine of Peace). Its labels are designed by famous artists, and bottles are sent to religious and political leaders around the world as an admonition that the preservation of peace is more important than anything that can be gained by war.

Beyond the cities there was, for centuries, grinding poverty and hunger, known locally as *la miseria.* Older people I have spoken with in FVG all remember *la mis eria* and can tell stories of relatives who went to the Americas (especially the wine-growing zones of Argentina) to start a new life. Yet these relatives who left FVG in the 1930s and returned in the 1970s were astonished to discover the economic miracle that had been wrought. Through sheer hard work the *friulani* had created well-being and relative affluence in most of the region. The area around Manzano became the chair-making capital of the world (the thinking was that everyone has to sit somewhere, so there will always be demand for the product), and much of Friuli became a world-class vineyard producing some of the best wines you will ever taste. All sorts of small crafts and industries continued to help the region prosper. When a devastating earthquake centered in Gemona destroyed much of Friuli in 1976, the people rolled up their sleeves and quickly rebuilt.

The well-being here stands in stark contrast to the hatred, wars, and misery that have raged in the bordering republics of the former Yugoslavia. Because many *friulani* have relatives or friends across the border, there is an acute sense of the pain of their neighbors. All along the border with Slovenia people talk about "over there" to refer to things in Slovenia. There are ancient family and cultural ties here: for a long time there was no border whatsoever, and when these lands were part of the Austro-Hungarian Empire they shared common identity and language. When, after the Second World War, Italy was forced to give a portion of land to what was then Yugoslavia, family holdings and vineyards were frequently divided. People here often remind themselves that man invented borders that nature disregards and, with the first glass of new wine, often drink to the health and well-being of the people "over there."

I am often amazed at how sweet and good-natured the *friulani* are despite the hardships they have endured. Only in Trieste and, to some extent, Gorizia is there a sense of *weltschmerz,* the heavy-shouldered pessimism that is the result of accumulated trouble. But this may also reflect the long Austro Hungarian influence in these areas. Trieste is a fascinating place that was the principal port of the Hapsburg Empire, and as the foods and flavors of the world passed through the harbor they influenced the cuisine. Superb coffee is everywhere in the city, and flavors such as cinnamon and dill appear here much more often than elsewhere in Italy. The city combines Italian, Slavic, and Germanic elements with a strong dose of British, making it a place like no other.

Cividale del Friuli and Aquileia are the towns of most historic interest in the region and warrant a visit to understand much about how FVG became what it is. Aquileia, founded in 181 B.C., was for a long time the second most important city in the Roman Empire. It has a museum that merits your attention and a gorgeous early Christian basilica built on ancient foundations. Its outstanding mosaics remain, although others in Aquileia were buried when the city was sacked by Attila (A.D. 452), only to be discovered early in the twentieth century. The city later became a center of Christian thought, culture, and education as well as a thriving market when Jewish merchants arrived. When FVG was an independent patriarchal state, from *circa* 1000 to 1492, Aquileia was its capital. The state had a constitution written before the Magna Carta.

Cividale del Friuli was the site of an ancient market when it was a stopping point on the trade route from the Adriatic to the Alps. A town was founded here in 50 B.C. by Julius Caesar that was called Forum Juli (Julius's Market). The market continues to this day, and you will see it in the main square when you are in town. From "Forum Juli" evolved the name "Friuli." The Romans built roads from the sea to the Alps and beyond, creating easy accessibility that would later be a source of many problems for Friuli. The chief road is called the Via Giulia Augusta, built in 150 B.C. The Romans built towns along their roads, many of which in Friuli now have the suffix "-acco."

The region also has "Venezia Giulia" (Julian Venice) as part of its name. A portion of FVG (as far east as Udine and Gradisca d'Isonzo) was for centuries a part of the Venetian Empire and still reflects some of the culinary, linguistic, and architectural influences of Venezia. Cividale became important again in the sixth century, when the Longobards (Lombards) made it one of their most important centers (along with Pavia and Milano in Lombardia). "Cividale" comes from "Civitas Australe" (it was the most eastern city of the Longobards). The Longobards left a valuable artistic legacy that can be seen in the cathedral and the museum. Copies of Longobard ornamental jewelry can be purchased at a special store in Cividale.

In much of the region, people are especially proud to speak Furlan, as the local language is called. It is not merely a dialect of Italian, but a language with Latin, Slavic, and Teutonic influences. A distinct feature of Friulians' pronunciation in Furlan or Italian is a very soft g that often appears behind an n so that the local way to say "good"—*bon*—becomes "bong," and "wine" becomes "vihng." In Trieste and elsewhere along the border with Slovenia, one hears more German, Hungarian, plus Serbo Croatian and other Slavic languages. And just as the region draws from many influences to forge a distinct linguistic and cultural tradition, so, too, does one sense this in the cuisine. As you travel around the region, try to eat in places where local people eat: the osteria in Udine, the *buffet* in Trieste, the *gostilna* in Collio, and the *frasca*. In the western part of FVG, a *frasca* is a place where wine is produced and food is served. In the past, this was a sort of private *osteria* for peasants and farmworkers that would have a seasonal permit to serve food. When a *frasca* was opened, a tree branch with leaves would be hung over the portal. The rule was that food could be sold until the leaves dried (usually by the end of the summer). Now anyone can eat at a *frasca*, which is called a *privada* in the province of Gorizia and an *osmizza* in the province of Trieste.

Eating in Friuli-Venezia Giulia

ANTIPASTI

Frico (Fricco). A sensational large fritter made of Montasio cheese. It is usually crunchy, but can occasionally be found with a crunchy top and a runny, cheesy interior. The best example of this latter version that I have tasted is at the Trattoria ai Cacciatori in Cierneglons.

Frittata con le erbe. Omelette with fresh herbs, often served cool.

Muset (Musetto) Highly spiced pork sausage that often includes cinnamon.

Prosciutto affumicato. Smoked raw ham, a specialty in the Carnia Alps.

Prosciutto di San Daniele. An exquisite air-cured ham whose flavor is only matched or exceeded (depending on your taste) by the prosciutto made in Parma. You can distinguish a San Daniele ham from a Parma one because the trotter has been removed from the latter and is still connected to the former. For the untrained palate the flavors of these two hams are hard to tell apart, and I encourage you to immerse yourself in extensive tasting until you can tell the difference. *Prosciutto di San Daniele* is customarily eaten (sliced very thin) as an antipasto, but is also an ingredient in pasta sauces, omelettes, sandwiches, and in combination with cheeses and other meats.

Speck. Smoked bacon from the Carnia Alps.

PRIMI

Cialzons. These amazing ravioli have many variations in how their name is spelled (including *cjalsons* and *cjarsons*) and even more in terms of what ingredients are used. It is traditional to use more than forty ingredients, including chocolate, lemon, cinnamon, mint, onions, dried figs, potatoes, eggs, raisins, marjoram, flour, parsley, and smoked ricotta cheese. This may sound strange to you, but I assure you that, at their best, *cialzons* are among the most delicious things you will ever taste. The best version I tasted was at the Ristorante Salon in Arta Terme.

Gnocchi di Susine. Meltingly delicious gnocchi that enclose a piece of ripe plum that softens as the pasta cooks. The best version I tried was at the restaurant of the Hotel-Ristorante Campiello in San Giovanni al Natisone. Sometimes apricots are substituted for plums, and the result is equally wonderful.

Gnocchi di Zucca con Ricotta Affumicata. A classic of this region, this is squash-flavored gnocchi served with melted butter and fragrant smoked ricotta.

Jota. A classic soup of Trieste made with cabbage and other vegetables.

Lasagne ai Semi di Papavero. Lasagne with poppy seeds.

Paparot. Spinach-and-cornmeal soup.

Toç. A generic term for a soup that is fortified with polenta and then diluted with milk.

Toç de Braide. A soup that was traditionally consumed by people working in the fields. White flour and polenta are cooked until they have the texture of a biscuit. A little water or wine is then added to dilute the mixture, resulting in a thick soup. This was the cuisine of the poor: simple but filling.

Zuppa di pesce alla gradese. A specialty of Grado, Friuli's major seaside resort. It contains the requisite fish and seafood and is flavored with garlic and vinegar.

SECONDI

Many dishes listed under "Antipasti," such as *cevapcici, muset, frittata con le erbe,* plus *zuppa di pesce,* are also served as *secondi.* In addition, Friulians enjoy all sorts of fish and seafood from the Adriatic and grilled meats and game that you will know from other regions.

Brovada. Turnips marinated with grape skins and cooked with pork sausage.

Stinco. The word means "shin," and can be applied either to pork *(maiale)* or veal *(vitello).* Either way, it is often roasted or braised to yield succulent flavor and delicacy and is a mainstay in the Friulian kitchen.

Toç de Purcit. Pork stewed with white wine, cinnamon, cloves, and other flavorings.

FORMAGGI

Formaggio di Malga. Fresh cheese made in the high Alps from the milk of cows that graze on mountain grass and herbs.

Latteria. A general term for many cow's-milk cheeses that are mild when young and more assertive when aged.

Montasio. A deceptively unpretentious cow's-milk cheese that has grand flavor. It is the essential ingredient for *frico.*

Ricotta Affumicata. Smoked ricotta cheese. The preferred grating cheese for most Friulian pasta dishes.

DOLCI

Gubana. An exquisite cake filled with ground nuts, pine nuts, dried raisins and figs, and other ingredients. A specialty of Cividale del Friuli (where it is made with puff pastry) and the Natisone Valley (where it is made with a yeast dough).

Pinza, Presnitz, and *Putizza.* Three special cakes typical of Trieste.

Strudel. As former terrain of the Austro-Hungarian Empire, Friuli is home to its versions of strudel. Some are made with apples, others with ricotta.

The Wines of Friuli-Venezia Giulia

The wines of this region represent only 2 percent of Italy's output, yet they are among the most outstanding you will encounter. Because of their high quality and relatively limited supply, FVG wines (especially whites) command prices that are higher than many others. FVG has become known for its white wines, which were produced in greater amounts in the last part of the twentieth century to occupy a commercial niche ignored by Toscana and Piemonte, which are primarily red-wine-producing regions. But there are many excellent reds in FVG as well. For a long time, they were sold young and were especially popular in Vienna and Budapest. Now many reds are aged and can take their place among the great wines of Italy. There are seven DOC zones in Friuli, all of which make excellent wine: the Grave del Friuli, Latisana, Aquileia, Carso, Isonzo, Collio, and Colli Orientali. The zones that deserve the most attention are Isonzo, Collio, and Colli Orientali.

Wine aging in barriques

Grave del Friuli. High plains with a fair amount of gravel in the soil. This is almost entirely in the province of Pordenone, and the zone respresents about 50 percent of the region's output. These are mostly good to very good wines at moder ate prices, with an emphasis on medium-weight reds, such as Merlot. The whites are also good. Grave wines have found success abroad, thanks to their good price–quality ratio.

Latisana. Closer to the Adriatic than Grave, but similar, if somewhat lighter, wines. Reds are emphasized, but whites are made, too.

Aquileia. Fruity, delightfully drinkable reds and whites.

Carso. The particular limestone and rock that characterize the soil of this zone outside Trieste give its wines a higher mineral content than most, and they are as tasty and drinkable as those of Grave, Latisana, and Aquileia.

Isonzo. This is a transitional zone between Carso and Aquileia to the south and Collio to the north. The wines resemble those of the zones they border, with subtle differences. They may have perfume, like those of Collio, but also have the flavors of the harder soils to the south. The region's foremost *enoteca* is in Gradisca d'Isonzo, a good place to try all the wines of Friuli, but especially those of Isonzo. The zone is named for the river that winds through it.

Collio (also called Collio Goriziano). This is an outstanding zone for white wines such as Tocai, Pinot Bianco, Pinot Grigio, Sauvignon Blanc, Malvasia, and

Chardonnay. It borders on Slovenia, and many vineyards were divided after the Second World War. Yet even with less terrain, the people have produced much of the best regional wine. As in most places, the wines of Collio (and the Colli Orientali) are the products not only of soils and sun but of the genius and dedication of men and women too. When I look at the name on a wine label from these two zones, I often see a face behind it. In this area the early leaders in making the wines world-class, people such as Mario Schiopetto, Livio Felluga Marco Felluga, Vittorio Puiatti, and Doro Princic, not only sought profit for themselves but also encouraged growth and success in others. The names and wine are too numerous to list here (although you will find many comments through-out this chapter), so I encourage you to visit the *enoteche* in Cormons and Gradisca and taste for yourself. If there is a wine or a producer that particularly captures your fancy, continue to explore it during your stay.

Colli Orientali. The term means "Eastern Hills," and they run along the north–south border with Slovenia. While the names here may not always be as famous as those in Collio, and the scenery a little less idyllic, the wines are every bit as good. One finds a few wineries named for the families that run them—Dorigo, Dri, Danieli, Collavini, Pighin, Zamò, for example—many others have names of land, estates, or castles. These include Abbazia di Rosazzo, Ronchi di Cialla, Ronco del Gnemiz, Vigne del Leon, Torre Rosazza, Rocca Bernarda, and others. Many in the latter group have benefited from the advice and wisdom of Walter Filiputti, a journalist, enologist, and proud Friulano who is dedicated to raising the quality of his area's wines and the visibility of Friuli's wines elsewhere in Italy and abroad. Another leader of viticulture in the Colli Orientali is the Nonino family, producers of some of Italy's finest grappa. Because the family members understand that better-quality grape skins make better grappa, they have care-fully influenced the wine producers in the area from whom they purchase the skins. The largest grape nursery in the world is in Rauscedo, and Friuli growers go there and elsewhere to find the best clonal varieties so that they get the most out of their soils.

FVG wine is remarkable not only for its quality but also for the number of grape varieties that are used. In addition to native varieties, the soil has welcomed grapes from many lands and, along with the skill of Friuli wine makers, has produced exceptional wines. Among the varieties of red wine grapes are Cabernet Franc, Cabernet Sauvignon, Collio (a blend of Cabernet Franc, Cabernet Sauvignon, and Merlot), Collio Cabernet (a blend of Franc and Sauvignon, as is also done in Bordeaux), Merlot, Pignolo (a native Friuli variety), Pinot Nero, Refosco dal Peduncolo Rosso (a native Friuli variety), Schioppettino (a native Friuli variety), Tazzelenghe (a native Friuli variety—the name means "Tongue Cutter," because of its high acidic content usually consumed in winter with pork products and game), and Terrano, the typical red of the Carso, the region immediately outside Trieste.

with the Refosco grape and grows in soil that is characteristically red. The sun and soil of the Carso contribute to the wine's particular flavor. It is low in alcohol and is often prescribed by doctors to patients with digestive problems, because it has acids that are thought to be beneficial. It is also given to anemic patients who need iron. Even the ancient Romans sought out Terrano to remedy their ills. There is a Wine Road stretching from Opicina to Visogliano dotted with wineries and restaurants that serve Terrano (see "Trieste," under "Dining on the Terrano Wine Road").

Foremost among the whites is Tocai Friulano. Because there is a grape in Hungary called Tokaj and a Tokay grape in France, the European Economic Community has demanded name changes and has said that only Hungary can keep the old name. By the year 2006 a new name will be required for the Friulian white, and it will probably be the accurate, generic, and uninspiring "Friuli Bianco." Among the many fine producers are Livio Felluga, Mario Schiopetto, and Vigne del Leon, but you will taste many more. Other whites produced in FVG include Chardonnay, Malvasia Istriana (a light, slightly metallic white that marries beautifully with Adriatic seafood. This wine should not be confused with the amber Malvasia produced in Sicilia), Müller Thurgau, Pinot Bianco, Pinot Grigio, Ribolla Gialla (a native Friuli variety), Riesling Italico, Riesling Renano (the type used in Germany), Sauvignon Blanc, Traminer Aromatico (like Gewürztraminer), and Verduzzo (a native variety that can also be produced as a dessert wine).

There are three excellent dessert wines in FVG: Picolit (a native variety that is difficult to grow, but, at its best—like that of Dorigo—is an ambrosial nectar), Ramandolo (a delicious, little-seen white; the best is generally conceded to be made by Giovanni Dri), and the dessert version of Verduzzo.

Other Beverages

Coffee. Only Piemonte rivals FVG in terms of the quality of its coffee. Take the coffee tours I have indicated for Trieste and Udine to find out more.

Grappa. With all of the wine production that happens in this region, there are a lot of grape skins available to make grappa. Some of the best is made by the Nonino family for Percoto. (Read more about grappa on page 46.)

Aiello del Friuli (Udine)

MUSEUM

Museo della Civiltà Contadina del Friuli Imperiale, Viale Vittorio Emanuele II— Via Petrarca 1, tel. 0431/99507. Open Saturday and Sunday 10–12h, 14–18h.

A fascinating collection, in four buildings, of tools, maps, machinery, art, documents, and handicrafts related to rural agriculture and life in the early nineteenth century.

Aquileia (Udine)

In the Basilica of Aquileia there are many depictions of fish and seafood on the floor mosaic. The reference is to Christ's words to his disciples that he would make fishermen of them. Centuries of shifting of the moist ground under the church have given the floor an undulating look, which only makes the piscatorial imagery more believable. Other parts of the floor depict birds, flowers, people, deer, goats, turtles, roosters, rabbit, and so on. You should devote a good hour to seeing everything in this marvelous place. The nearby Museo Archeologico, with a wonderful collection of art and objects from Roman Aquileia, is open Tuesday through Saturday (9–14h) and Sunday (9–13h). The busts of ancient people from this area look very much like some of the housewives and craftsmen you will see in Aquileia today. The garden outside the museum is a magnificent jumble of stones and capitals, as if they were part of a garage sale. The wine of Aquileia was shipped all over the world in ancient times and still is well regarded today.

DINING

Trattoria al Morar, Località Beligna (on Via Beligna on the road out of Aquileia to Grado), tel. 0431/919340. No credit cards. Inexpensive.

A very simple roadside place with some Slavic influence in the food. There is sausage with sauerkraut, *cevapcici*, and *gulasch*. Stick to meat courses, since all the available fish is frozen before use. The pastas are decent, though not special. The *affettato misto* includes delicious hams, *salame*, and cheeses.

Arta Terme (Udine)

Arta Terme is a lovely town not far from Tolmezzo on one of the roads that heads into the high Carnia Alps. There is a spa, and it is a wonderful spot to find cool air in the summer. But I would make the journey here just to taste the *cjarsons* at the Ristorante Salon.

DINING

Hotel-Ristorante Salon, Via Peresson 70, Pian di Arta Terme (upper part of town), tel. 0433/92003. American Express, Visa. Moderate.

One can feast on delicious pastas at, given the quality, amazingly moderate prices. You might consider doing a meal sampling several pastas. The *pasticcio di porcini* is a delicate, thin lasagne packed with fresh mushroom flavor. Also good are *saccottini ai funghi e tartufi* (little sacks of pasta with mushrooms, truffles, and béchamel sauce). *Gnocchi alle erbe fini*, made with forest herbs that are much more flavorful than the fines herbes found in Provence, are also delicious. *Crespelle ai fiori di zucca* are delicate crepes with cheese and zucchini flowers. But you must absolutely try the *cjarsons*, the best example that I have found in Friuli of this singular dish. It has more than forty ingredients and speaks in many flavor languages: sweet, sour, astringent, herbal, soft, buttery, toasted, smoky, and more. If you look up from your plate at all, you will notice that the dining room of this hotel has a picture window that reveals a lovely garden. Among the *secondi* are good *stinco di maiale* and *cervo al ribes rosso* (venison with red currants). As a *contorno* I recommend sticking to mixed salad. There is a delicious *torta di mandorle e noci*, with ground almonds and walnuts delicately combined with chocolate.

Buttrio (Udine)

Buttrio is easy to pass by without noticing some of FVG's best wine and good food. Top producers include Dorigo (Via del Pozzo 5, tel. 0432/674268) and Miani (Via Peruzzi 10, tel. 0432/674327).

DINING

Trattoria al Parco, Via Stretta 7, tel. 0432/ 674025. Closed Tuesday evening, Wednesday, two weeks in January, two weeks in August. All credit cards. Moderate.

The Meroi family has made wine and served food on this spot since 1920. I love the *frico* with polenta cubes and grated smoked ricotta, as well as the risotto that changes flavors with the seasons. There are all kinds of grilled meats. The famous *pollo alla griglia* is justifiably renowned and for which advance reservation is required. Save room for the excellent cheese from the Latteria di Buttrio.

Castello di Buttrio, Via Morpurgo 9, tel. 0432/673659. Closed Tuesday and November. All credit cards. Moderately inexpensive.

The kitchen here is under the control of Daniela Sestini. The *salame di oca* (goose salami), o*rzotto con le erbe* (barley with wild herbs), *frico*, game, and polenta are all outstanding and match beautifully with the wines.

Capriva del Friuli (Gorizia)

WINE

Az. Agr. Russiz Superiore di Marco Felluga, Loc. Russiz Superiore 1, tel. 0481/99164, fax 0481/960270.

Az. Agr. Mario Schiopetto, Loc. Spessa 20, tel. or fax 0481/80332.

The small town of Capriva, just down the road from Cormons, has gorgeous scenery and some of the finest wineries in the region. The names listed here are but two of the many fine producers.

Arta Terme (Udine)

DINING

Ristorante La Rotonda (Hotel Internazionale), Via Ramazzotti 2, tel. 0431/30751, fax 0431/34801. Closed Sunday evening and Monday. All credit cards. Moderate to moderately expensive.

Good food all around: *frico, frittatine con le erbe, crostini* with smoked goose breast, creamy risottos (in springtime try the one with white asparagus), are outstanding, and the breads here are special.

ICE CREAM

Gran Gelato, Via Udine 47, tel. 0431/34923. Open Sunday; closed Monday, lunch Tuesday–Saturday.

On the road to Aquileia in what looks like a tiny mall is this excellent ice-cream shop. The *pinolato* (pine-nut ice cream) is worth a detour all by itself, but all of the flavors are delicious, especially *pera rossa* (red pear) and *gianduia*. Edgardo Sgubin makes small amounts of ice cream all day. When it sells out, that's it. Anything left at closing time is thrown out.

Cerneglons (Udine)

DINING

Trattoria ai Cacciatori, Via Pradamano 28, tel. 0432/670132. Closed Monday. No credit cards. Moderately inexpensive.

This is the kind of place that would never appear in tourist guidebooks, but I commend it to you heartily. It is the social center of this small town. Young people, older men, families, and children all gather here for great food and company. Most prefer to speak in Furlan, the language of Friuli that is dear to their identity. There is a large entry room where people play cards and drink a *tajut*. Posters and announcements bring local news that people stop in to read. There is an open kitchen from which wonderful food issues forth. In the large dining room you will not see a menu and will choose from a small number of offerings. I tried the *frittata di verdura e erbe*, a tall fragrant wedge of egg, vegetables, and herbs. The *frico*, with its crunchy exterior and runny cheese center, made me happy to be alive. Just as memorable was the *minestrone di fagioli*, to which you should add olive oil and pepper but not cheese. It is an amazingly sweet bean soup, one of the best you will ever taste. There is also local *salame*, roast rabbit served with oil and herbs with polenta, and a nice sorbet. The whole meal was served with great tenderness by Ester Riello. Its cost made it even more astonishing.

Cividale del Friuli (Udine)

BAKERY

Pasticceria Ducale, Piazza Picco 18,   tel. 0432/730707.

Delicious pastries, including *crostate*, *presniz*, cigar-shaped rolls filled with ice cream, and, above all, wonderful *gubana*. There is excellent ice cream here, especially the *(pinolato)*.

DINING

Ristorante al Monastero, Via Ristoro 11, tel. 0432/700808. Closed Sunday evening and Monday. Moderate.

Good local wines and tasty dishes such as *culatello con montasio, rucole e pere* (delicate ham with Montasio, arugula, and pears), *crema di orzo e fagioli* (a soup of barley and beans), and *casunziei dello chef.*

Taverna Longobarda, Via Monastero Maggiore 5, tel. 0432/731655. Closed Tuesday evening and Wednesday. No credit cards. Moderate.

Delicious gnocchi of all types and a wonderful cart of boiled meats *(bolliti)*. Simple, fine food. Good wine, too.

Ai Tre Re, Via Stretta San Valentino 29, tel. 0432/700416. Closed Tuesday, one week in February, two weeks in June, one week in October. MasterCard, Visa. Moderately inexpensive.

Good local flavors, including *lardo alle erbe con pere* (lard with herbs and pears) and gnocchi with speck and smoked ricotta.

HERBS AND HONEY

Erboristeria Casa del Miele, Via Silvio Pellico 15, tel. 0432/733667, fax 0432/730837.

Fine honey, plus dried herbs (including chamomile, eucalyptus, and calendula), herb-based liqueurs, and other products. Gigi Nardini, who runs this store, makes his own *amaro* with herbs and a liqueur (Mirtillo) made with blueberries.

SPECIAL STORE

Bottega Longobarda, Stretta S. Maria di Corte 20, tel. 0432/730932. Closed Monday.

With its legacy as a center of Longobard culture more than twelve centuries ago, Cividale has a particular artistic style and legacy that is represented in the jewelry and crafts of Bottega Longobarda.

WINES AND SPIRITS

Sfriso, Via Stretta de Rubeis 20, tel. 0432/730574. Closed Monday afternoon, Wednesday afternoon, and Sunday.

A good source for Friuli wines and spirits, including Nonino products.

Codroipo (Udine)

Codroipo is at a major intersection of roads that lead to all parts of the region. In addition to the glorious Villa Manin and the wine museum at the Pittaro vineyards, there is the airfield of Rivolto, where the famous Freccie Tricolori reside. These acrobatic fly teams appear at air shows and are known for the streams of red, white, and green smoke that emit from their tailpipes to evoke the Italian flag.

DINING

Osteria da Marchin, Via dei Dogi, tel.   **0432/906290. Closed Tuesday. Moderate.**

Simpler, more likable than the slightly pretentious Ristorante del Doge nearby. The food is pretty good.

MUSEUM AND WINERY

Vigneti Pittaro, Via Udine 55, Zompicchia, tel. 0432/904726. Open Monday–Saturday 8–12h, 14–18h, Sunday by reservation.

The Pittaro collection includes three-hundred-year-old bottles, and some, from the early twentieth century, still have wine in them. You will also see old hand pumps, scales that weighed full barrels, barrel-making equipment, a gaily painted Sicilian cart used for transport, manual wine-presses, old demijohns, and six ancient Roman amphorae.

Cormons (Gorizia)

Cormons is the chief town of the beautiful Collio wine-growing zone. It is a pretty, leafy place with a pronounced *mittel*-European atmosphere that is reflected in some of its dishes. I was surprised to see persimmon trees everywhere, but was reminded that although Cormons is near central Europe it is also close to the sea. From houses in the hills above one can see the Adriatic in the distance. At Cormons's *enoteca* you can taste most of the wines produced in this area, and you can have magnificent meals at its two outstanding restaurants.

BAKERY

At the corner of Viale Friuli and Via Pietro Zorutti is a wonderful bakery selling great breads and basic pastries, plus *gubana*. This place, plus the nearby Frutta e Verdura da Silvana, provide a sensory feast for eye, nose, and mouth.

BARS-CAFFÈS

Caffè Massimiliano, Piazza Massimiliano. Closed Wednesday.

A cozy *caffè* with an old-fashioned feel about it.

Cafe Europa, Via Matteotti 12. Closed Sunday.

A convivial, very Viennese-type *konditorei* (pastry shop) with a chocolaty smell. Known universally as La Subida,

DINING

Trattoria "Al Cacciatore" de la Subida, Subida di Cormons (just above town), tel. 0481/60531, fax 0481/62388. Closed Tuesday, Wednesday, February, and fifteen days in July. No credit cards. Moderate to moderately expensive.

this is one of the most revered eating places in FVG. It often is ranked as the best restaurant in the region, and I have seen it appear on two lists as the best restaurant in Italy. We all know that there is no best restaurant, because food preparation and service are something that evolves and changes. Nonetheless, I have had many meals at La Subida, all of them were divine, and I would go back any time. The local pastas are all wonderful, including the *mlinci* (lightly browned fresh pasta served with a game sauce). Among the secondi, *stinco di vitello* is meltingly flavorful and should be tasted if it is on the menu. *Stinco di maiale* is just as good. Among the desserts is the unusual *pehtranova potica*, a nut cake flavored with tarragon. Meals represent outstanding value. There are three sizes of tasting menus at very fair prices. There are also some rooms here if you want to make this your idyllic base for touring Collio.

Trattoria al Giardinetto, Via Matteotti 54, tel. 0481/6 0257. Closed Monday afternoon, Tuesday, and in July. All credit cards. Moderately expensive.

A great restaurant in the center of town. The *gnocchi dell'Imperatore* (with bread, pancetta, cheese, cabbage, and *funghi porcini*) are special, as are the *gnocchi di susine*. Also great are the *zlikrofi* (*tortelli* filled with potatoes, chives, and shallots, topped with curls of aged Montasio, bits of smoked ham, and melted butter). There is an outstanding *stinco di vitello.* I also like how cheese is served here, with fig preserve and fig bread.

ENOTECA PUBLICA
Enoteca di Cormons, Palazzo Locatelli,

Piazza 24 Maggio 21, tel. 0481/630371. Open Thursday Monday 11–13h, 17–22h (24h in summer), Wednesday 17–22h (24h in summer).

A good place to taste the wines of the Collio on a friendly square in the town center. If they are available, try wines by Doro Princic.

FOOD SHOPPING
Salumi e Formaggi Marisa Tomadin, Via Cumano 5 (near Piazza Libertà).

Excellent prosciutto by Lorenzo d'Osvaldo is sold here, as are other nice *salumi*, good cheeses, and a great Montasio stagionato (aged). You can buy boxes of polenta, rice, pasta, or baked goods. There is wine, eggs are sold individually, and in the back notice shelves stacked with onions, garlic, and individually wrapped lemons.

Salumeria Lorenzo d'Osvaldo, Via Dante 40, tel. 0481/61644.

I tasted the hand-cured prosciutto of Lorenzo d'Osvaldo at practically every wine maker's house I visited in Cormons. It is delicate and very delicious.

Corno di Rosazzo (Udine)

WINE
Enoteca Gruppo Viticoltori di Corno di Rosazzo, Via Aquileia 68—Loc. Quattroventi, tel. 0432/753220. Open 8–24h; closed Tuesday.

The best place to purchase wines made

by the producers around Corno di Rosazzo.

Eugenio Collavini, Via della Ribolla Gialla 2, tel. 0432/753222, fax 0432/759792.

The Collavinis have been making wine since 1896, with Ribolla Gialla a specialty.

Giasbana (Gorizia)

DINING

Osteria-Trattoria Gostilna, Giasbana 16, tel. 0481/391633. No credit cards. Moderately inexpensive to moderate.

Giasbana is a tiny rural community surrounded by vineyards. While people sit, drink, eat, smoke, and take in the scenery, children run around playing hide-and-seek between courses. You will see a lot of basketball hoops in driveways around here. We are just over the border from Slovenia and Croatia, which produce many of Europe's top players, some of whom have had careers in the NBA in the United States. This place is interesting in that it is in a far-flung corner of Italy, very much closer to Vienna than to Roma, where people go to Sunday lunch in the country as they would elsewhere in Italy. Yet the flavors are those of central Europe. The tagliatelle were thick enough to be noodles a Hapsburg would eat. They are flavored with delicious tarragon-accented *funghi porcini*. *Cevapcici* served with onion-scented potatoes are more Slavic than Latin. They are served with a wonderful condiment of sweet red peppers. I also recommend the *capriolo*, roast venison with polenta.

Gorizia

Gorizia straddles the Italian Slovenian border. Part of the city is "on the other side," as people here say, and is called Nova Gorica. Although it never quite felt like East and West Berlin before the wall fell, there persists a certain exoticism and slight tension that comes when there is a wealthy nation on one side and a poorer, more repressed one on the other. Many Italians drive across the border to buy inexpensive gasoline, while Slovenians come to Italy to purchase goods that are hard to find at home. Until 1918, Gorizia and much of its province (including the Collio wine zone) were part of the Austro-Hungarian Empire, and many people here still recall those days with fondness. When it was mentioned to the elderly Count Attems who was part of the nobility that once governed Gorizia, that during a recent European soccer tournament there was an Austria Hungary match, he guilelessly asked, "Oh really, who are they playing?" The area around here was the site of eleven fierce battles during the First World War, and towns such as Oslavia have cemeteries filled with war dead. It is hard to believe, as you look at the quiet streets of Gorizia and the limpid scenery of the province, that so much blood was spilled here.

Gradisca d'Isonzo (Gorizia)

DINING

Ristorante al Ponte, Viale Trieste 122, tel. 0481/99213 or 99283. Closed Monday evening, Tuesday, and mid-July. All credit cards. Moderately expensive.

There are some good dishes here. Try the superb *crema di funghi porcini e cappone* (a soup of mushrooms and capon; you should not add the olive oil you are offered), delicious *ravioli con animelle e porcini* (ravioli filled with sweetbreads and porcini), and *filettino al Cabernet* (beef fillet in a Cabernet wine sauce). For dessert try the light, lemony *strudel di ricotta*, which is served warm.

Osteria Mulin Vecio, Via Gorizia 2. Open 10–14h, 17–24h; closed Wednesday and Thursday. No credit cards. Inexpensive.

A popular, unpretentious gathering place serving local wines and simple foods such as soups, freshly cut mortadella, prosciutto, cheeses, olives, mushrooms, and simple fish dishes.

Trattoria da Majda, Via Duca d'Aosta 71, tel. 0481/30871. Closed Wednesday and part of August. All credit cards. Moderately inexpensive.

Delicious *goriziano* food served by Majda, a wonderful woman.

Osteria alla Luna, Via Oberdan 13, tel. 0481/530374. Closed Sunday evening, Monday, two weeks in February, two weeks in July. All credit cards. Moderately inexpensive.

If prosciutto with *cren* (horseradish) is available, don't miss it. Soups, frittatas, and desserts are all tasty.

Rosenbar, Via Duca d'Aosta 96, tel. 0481/522700. Closed Sunday and Monday. All credit cards. Moderate.

Good meat dishes, excellent fish and seafood.

ENOTICA PUBBLICA

Enoteca Regionale del Friuli-Venezia Giulia "La Serenissima," Via Battisti, tel. and fax 0481/99528. Open 10–14h, 16–24h; closed Monday.

This is one of the nicest *enoteche pubbliche* in Italy and a good place to sample Friuli wines, especially those of the surrounding Isonzo Valley.

Gradiscutta di Varmo (Udine)

This tiny town in lower Friuli is surrounded by fields of flowers that go into perfumes and tall corn that makes polenta for the entire region.

DINING

Da Toni, Via Sentinis 1, tel. 0432/778003. Closed Monday, Tuesday lunch. All credit cards. Moderate to moderately expensive.

Run by the Morasutti family since 1926, excellent specialities include *zuppa di basilico, risotto agli asparagi* and the *oca con cren* (goose flavored with horseradish).

Latisana (Udine)

DINING AND LODGING

Hotel Residence Bella Venezia, Parco Gaspari, tel. 0431/59647, fax 0431/59649.

The restaurant, which is strong in seafood dishes, is notable for its collection of period photos of Ernest Hemingway. We see him fishing, hunting, writing, and sharing a moment with Ingrid Bergman during the filming of *For Whom the Bell Tolls*. On another wall there are photos of soccer players, Italian starlets and politicians, and a mature Joan Crawford. The old Hotel Venezia was often frequented by E.H. It was in central Latisana and was run by many of the older relatives of the current staff, many of whom have vivid memories of Hemingway. The original hotel closed in the 1970s; the new one is large and accommodating and overlooks a pretty park. It may lack the old style that Hemingway knew, but it is inviting nonetheless.

Lavariano di Mortegliano (Udine)

DINING

Ristorante Blasut, Via Aquileia 7, tel. 0432/767017. Closed Monday and mid-August to mid-September. Diners Club. Moderate to moderately expensive.

Diminutive Dante Bernardi runs a great restaurant that relies on superb local ingredients. The cuisine is creative, but always faithful to the flavors of the raw materials.

Maniago (Pordenone)

For centuries, this town near the Carnia alps has been one of Europe's major producers of knives and scissors. Shops all over town can sell you ingenious cutting tools. Local pork and game are used in specialties you can find only here: *pitina*, *peta* and *petuccia*. This latter is used for *petuccia al cao*, in which the sausage-like meat is cooked in cream.

DINING

Vecchia Maniago, Via Castello 10, tel. 0427/730583. Closed Monday evening, Tuesday, and mid-August. All credit cards. Moderate to moderately expensive.

A wonderful dining experience with a great wine list, a warm atmosphere (with garden dining in the summer), and delicious local food. There are *petuccia*, *salame* cooked with apples, risottos, *frico* with polenta, game, grilled meats and a nice cheese selection.

Monfalcone (Gorizia)

DINING

Locanda ai Campi, Via Napoli 7,
tel. 0481/481937. MasterCard. Moderate
to moderately expensive.

Fish is the reason to eat here. It is absolutely fresh, from the antipasto (which can be a bit sandy) to the *tagliatelle verdi alle seppie* to the *zuppa di pesce* (with eel, mussels, and shrimp large and small and a nice tomato-garlic base).

Mossa (Gorizia)

In Mossa, you might notice the Via Olivers. This was the site of olive trees for centuries. Olive cultivation here was at its peak during Napoleonic times but is virtually extinct now.

DINING

Trattoria Blanch, Via Blanchis 35,
tel. 0481/80020. Closed Wednesday, last
week of August, and first three weeks of
September. All credit cards. Moderate.

Elegant in its simplicity of style and food preparation, this trattoria is only five hundred meters (less than a half mile) from Slovenia. The room feels more Austrian than Italian, with lace blinds and vaguely Viennese wood paneling. Two specialties here are mushrooms (in the autumn) and *sugo di gallo* (rooster sauce), which appears on pasta. When available, the *funghi alla griglia* are exquisite. Also good is the *anatra selvaggia* (roast, stuffed wild duck). There is also good olive bread. Cheese and apple strudel make good desserts.

MEAT AND GAME

Wild, Via Isonzo 21A, tel. 0481/809611,
fax 0481/809665.

Many meats are dried or air cured here to make prosciutto and *bresaola*. The meats include elk *(alce)*, hare, partridge *(pernice)*, goose, goat, horse, wild boar, pork, chamois, venison, pheasant, duck, turkey, lamb, beef, and others.

Oleis (Udine)

I call your attention to the name of this town for its history and for its promise. The name loosely translates as "Place of Oil," because there is a particular microclimate here that favors olive growing. The trees had almost entirely disappeared due to disease and neglect, but now Walter Filiputti and others have nursed back the survivors, organized planting, and are planning to produce oil again soon. Perhaps by the time you reach Friuli there will be some. Oleis ranks along with the upper portions of Lago di Garda as the world's northernmost olive-oil-producing zones.

Osalvia (Gorizia)

WINE

Azienda Agricola Gravner, Via Lenzuolo Bianco 9, tel. 0481/30882.

Josko Gravner is a towering figure in the Friulian wine world, a sort of enological Don Quixote who tilts against tradition. He has almost completely eschewed the use of stainless steel in any phase of the ferment and age his wines in wood or even in terracotta vessels that he buries in the ground. His method have many detractors, but his wines have a legion of admirers. He is a stubborn man, but also a gentle and a kind one, and his wines rank among the best. Look for them in fine restaurants and *enoteche*. To buy a case, call before coming.

Pavia di Udine (Udine)

DINING

Trattoria La Frasca, Viale Grado 10, tel. 0432/675150. Closed Wednesday and the first three weeks of January. All credit cards. Moderately inexpensive to moderate.

In Lauzacco, just outside of Pavia di Udine, is this roadside trattoria that does not initially reveal all of the treasures to be found there. The owner is Walter Scarbolo and his particular gift is to take the products of his farm, just behind the restaurant, and offer them for sale on the side of the Viale Grado that leads to the Adriatic or to give them to his wife Mariagrazia to use in her kitchen. Walter produces excellent pork products, especially sausages and salumi, that feature prominently. His prosciutto is tossed with Mariagrazia's homemade tagliatelle. Free-range chickens and local rabbits forage on the grains and greens that grow on the farm, making them especially tasty when cooked with freshly picked herbs and served with polenta made of Walter's corn. Wines are made from the grapes that Walter grows.

Percoto (Udine)

GRAPPA

Distillerie Nonino, Via Aquileia 104, tel. 0432/676332, fax 0432/676038.

As I described earlier, the Nonino family revolutionized grappa and distilling in Italy in the 1960s, and their influence has been felt around the world. By deciding that individual grape varieties would each result in distinct flavors of grappa, the Noninos changed the approach of the past in which grape skins that remained after wine was made were blended together to produce an indistinct grappa. Now, each type of grape skin is distilled separately so that you can detect meaningful differences and flavors and the precious liquids are placed in beautiful bottles that are reminiscent of old-fashioned pharmaceutical vessels. But lest you think that all of this is gimmicky and clever marketing, you should know that this is about as good as grappa gets. Somewhere during your Friuli travels you should make a point of sampling some of the Nonino grappas and distillates of fruit in bars or restaurants. They are available for sale at major *enoteche* and gourmet shops. The Nonino family has been in business since the 1880s and is also well known for the literary prize it presents each year.

Rauscedo (Udine)

GRAPE NURSERIES

Vivai Cooperativa di Rauscedo, Via Udine 39, tel. 0427/94022.

Half the new grape plants in Italy are culti-

vated at 250 nurseries in Rauscedo. There are more than a thousand varieties and clones to be found here. These are sold to wine producers throughout Italy. You may arrange a visit by calling at least a week in advance.

Ruttars (Gorizia)

DINING

Al Castello dell'Aquila d'Oro (just outside Dolegna del Collio), tel. 0481/60545. Closed Monday and Tuesday. MasterCard, Visa. Expensive.

Set in an ancient castle whose current ap-

pearance dates back to 1600, this is a formal, elegant restaurant with delicious food. It takes many of the flavors of Friuli and reinterprets them and somewhat lightens them. There is an excellent wine list, attentive service, and outdoor dining on a nice terrace in the summer.

San Daniele del Friuli (Udine)

OSTERIA

Ai Bintars, Via Trento e Trieste 63, tel. 0432/957322. Closed Wednesday evening and Thursday.

Good wines, and a chance to sample local prosciutto and excellent cheeses.

SALUMI

Salumeria Garlatti, Piazza Vittorio Emanuele 20A.

As you would expect, an extensive line of local prosciutto, but also *salumi* and cheeses from throughout Italy. You can do a comparative tasting of San Daniele and Parma prosciutti.

San Floriano del Collio (Gorizia)

DINING

Gostilna Dvor, Via Castello 5,

tel. 0481/884035. No credit cards. Inexpensive.

A very simple and typical place without outdoor tables. I love the gnocchi here, which are filled, in the Friulian style, with either apricots, plums, or cherries. Grilled meats and local wine complete a great meal.

HOTEL, RESTAURANT, AND
WINE MUSEUM
Antica Azienda Agricola dei Conti Formentini, Via Oslavia 3, tel. 0481/ 884131 or 884034. Open 9–17h, Saturday *14–19h; closed Sunday.*

This museum is on the estate of a producer of very good Collio wines. You can see old barrels, plows, and rudimentary equipment from the era before Friuli became one of the most sophisticated wine-producing zones in the world. This estate also has rooms, a good restaurant, and even a golf course.

San Giovanni al Natisone (Udine)

DINING AND LODGING
Hotel-Ristorante Campiello, Via Nazionale 40, tel. 0432/757910, fax 0432/757426. Closed Sunday. American Express, MasterCard, Visa. Moderate to moderately expensive.

If you are planning to make a vacation of driving around to visit vineyards and wineries in the Collio and Colli Orientali, this is the perfect place to stay. The accommodations are simple but comfortable, and the restaurant is outstanding. The *gnocchi di susine* were the best I tasted in all my travels in Friuli. Also great were the *casunziei*, pasta filled with beets and topped with melted butter and poppy seeds. Until the early 1960s, it was often traditional in Friuli to drink wines made of apples or pears with the aforementioned pastas. All the food is excellent at this restaurant, the wine list is outstanding, and Dario, your host, and his family are models of hospitality.

San Lorenzo (Gorizia)

WINE
Alvaro Pecorari—Francesco Pecorari Vigneti & Cantina, Via Gavinana 10, tel. 0461/80105, fax 0461/809592.

Alvaro Pecorari is a talented winemaker who is producing vintages of real quality. Unlike most wineries in this region, whose grapes grow on hills, those of Pecorari grow on more level ground, and this presents challenges that Alvaro has faced creatively. This is a winery to watch, and I commend his Sauvignon to you now, as well as a red called Lis Neris (a blend of Merlot and Cabernet Sauvignon), and a wonderful dessert wine called Tal Lûc. It is made with Verduzzo grapes, has a cinnamony fragrance, and a creamy, peppery flavor. It goes well with young *latteria* cheese.

San Pietro al Natisone (Udine)

BAKERY

Gubane Giuditta Teresa, Ponte San Quirino, tel. 0432/727585.

A very good *gubana* is made here containing generous amounts of walnuts, raisins, grappa, rum, brandy, Marsala, almonds, pine nuts, amaretti, chestnuts, and lemon.

Sauris (Udine)

Driving through gorgeous winding valleys and tunnels blasted out of mountains, one reaches Sauris di Sotto, but you still need to climb higher to reach the smaller Sauris di Sopra, a closely huddled collection of wooden houses built so that animals could be sheltered below. There are haystacks, one little bar, and, all the way up, the store and factory of Wolf Petris.

DINING

Ristorante Kursaal, Piazzale Kursaal 91b, Sauris di Sotto, tel. 0433/86202. Closed Sunday evening and Monday (except in summer), two weeks in June, two weeks in November. All credit cards. Moderate.

Trattoria alla Pace, Via Roma 38, Sauris di Sotto, tel. 0433/86010. Closed Wednesday (except in summer), three weeks in June, ten days in November. All credit cards. Moderately inexpensive.

Little Sauris has two outstanding places to eat, offering dishes based on local pork, game, herbs, and grains.

SALUMI

Prosciuttificio-Salumificio Wolf Petris. Sauris di Sotto 86. Factory: Via Volvan 88, Sauris di Sopra, tel. 0433/86054.

Speck and prosciutto smoked with juniper, mountain herbs, and various fragrant woods are specialties, but so are *salami, ricotta affumicata,* and *formaggio di malga.*

Spilimbergo (Pordenone)

DINING

Osteria da Afro, Via Umberto 114, tel. 0427/2264. Closed Tuesday and in July. Diners Club, MasterCard. Moderately inexpensive.

There are good versions of Friuli classics such as *frico, frittata,* and *brovada.* I also recommend the *salame cotto nell'aceto.*

ENOTECA

Enoteca La Torre Orientale, Via di Mezzo 2, tel. 0427/12998. Open 10–14h,

17–24h; closed Tuesday.

The best place to taste Grave del Friuli wines as well as those from elsewhere in the western part of Friuli.

FOOD SHOPPING

Formaggio e Burro Tosoni, Via Pinzano 17.

Delicious Montasio and other cheese.

Salumificio Lovison, Via Foscolo 18.

Excellent sausages and *musetto.*

Tarvisio (Udine)

Tarvisio is nestled into the northeasternmost corner of Italy and borders both Austria and Slovenia. It is a wonderful place to ski in the winter and hike through forests along crystalline mountain lakes in the summer. The delicious cuisine here is not cognizant of borders, so dishes from neighboring countries appear on menus next to local classics. The wines, though, are mostly from FVG. A curiosity of Tarvisio is that one-third of its 5000 citizens come from Naples. Their ancestors set up the city's bustling market after the Second World War to sell Italian products to foreigners. Therefore, pizza and *pasta al pomodoro* taste better here than anywhere in the Alps.

DINING

Tschurwald, Via Roma 8, tel. 0428/2119. Closed Wednesday and Thursday. All credit cards. Moderate.

Delicious alpine food served in this warm, welcoming osteria includes *cjarsons*, game, and pork goulash with bread dumplings and sauerkraut.

Locanda Edelhof, Via Diaz 13, tel. 0428/644025, locanda.edelhof@locanda edelhof.it. Closed Monday, plus the last two weeks in March, and the last two

in October. All credit cards. Moderate.

This cozy inn has comfortable lodging and food served in a traditional *stube*.

FOOD SHOPPING

Ortofrutta, Via Cavour 10a. Closed Monday and Wednesday afternoon, and Sunday.

An excellent fruit and vegetable store with *funghi porcini*, herbs, and honey from Carnia, lettuces, beautiful apples and pears, nuts, and jellies.

Trieste

Trieste, the capital of Friuli-Venezia Giulia, became part of Italy only on October 26, 1954, as part of the postwar rearrangement of Europe. It was for many years the chief port of the Austro-Hungarian Empire and then was the principal city of Istria, which was part of Yugoslavia. *Triestini* are a mixture of Slavic, Mediterranean, and Middle European peoples and often very good-looking. They are taller than most Italians and frequently have high, prominent cheekbones. Miss Trieste is always a front-runner in the Miss Italia competition and often goes on to become a fashion model. One Miss Trieste is said to have turned the head of a famous operatic tenor. Women in Trieste tend to be very dynamic and have men who follow their lead. People in Trieste often speak with Slavic inflections, and one can hear the insistent first syllable that is typical of Hungarian.

As the chief port for goods that were destined for Vienna and Budapest, Trieste has seen many foreign flavors pass through town and influence local taste. Coffee drinking has been popular in Vienna since 1683, and that city, Trieste, and Venezia have a tradition that is more than three hundred years old. Until some time after First World War Trieste had about forty beautiful *caffès* that were a part of the social and literary life of the city. One heard a mixture of German,

Hungarian, Serbo-Croatian, and Italian with smatterings of Greek, English, and other tongues. Writers such as Italo Svevo, Umberto Saba, and James Joyce used to spend long hours at a table, immersed in writing, thought, or discourse. It is generally thought that Trieste is still *the* coffee town of Italy. Torino has the august Lavazza company, which makes an excellent product; it has magnificent *caffès*—much nicer than most of those

The coffee in Friuli is among the best in Italy

of Trieste—and it has sophisticated coffee drinkers. Napoli is famous for its dark, powerful *caffè alla napoletana*. But Trieste has coffee arriving in its harbor every day to be roasted at the plants of many of the fine firms that have solidified Trieste's reputation: Cremcaffe, Excelsior, Hausbrandt, and especially Illy. At this writing, Riccardo Illy is the president of the region of FVG and he garnered many votes as the successful former mayor of Trieste and for the respect people have for his family. Illy and Torino's Lavazza are probably the most famous brands in Italy, and during your visit to Trieste you can taste them and others for comparison. Be sure also to visit Cremcaffe on Piazza Goldoni, which has a devoted following of its own. For the listings of bars and *caffès* in Trieste I will indicate, where possible, which coffee is served where, so you can do comparative tasting. Note that a *cappuccino triestino* is something different than a cappuccino served elsewhere in Italy. It arrives in an espresso cup or even a glass, has less foamed milk, and is sometimes topped with whipped cream. A *cappuccino grande* is what you usually think of as a cappuccino.

With coffee one would often expect good baking, and Trieste does not disappoint. Go to Pasticceria La Bomboniera, which has been in business since 1856, for classic local cakes. Triestine baking often includes spices and spirits. Spice importation in Trieste is still a vibrant business. One of the largest, oldest firms is Janousek in nearby Muggia, which has been in business since 1883.

People in Trieste often tell you that there are very few choices in town in which to find authentic Trieste cooking. It is true that Trieste, an international city, has the faint air of decline that is characteristic of many seaports. What is equally true is that because of shifting borders and allegiance to old Austria-Hungary, Istria, and Slovenia that is at least as strong as fidelity to Italy, it is a dicey proposition to determine what real Triestine cooking is. Traditional dishes include *jota* (a rich soup), *canoce* (local shellfish), *persuto* (local ham), bread gnocchi, and the boiled meats that are characteristic of the buffet. To find classic food of the region, many triestini go to small country restaurants in the Carso, the rural district that surrounds the city. Look for listings under "Dining on the Terrano Wine Road," below. All have delicious, traditional food washed down with a good dry red called Terrano.

BAKERIES

Pasticceria La Bomboniera, Via Trenta Ottobre 3A. Open 9–13h, 17–20h, Sunday 9–14h; closed Monday.

Here is where to buy the three classic cakes of Trieste. *Putizza* is a Christmas cake with walnuts, melted chocolate, sultanas, honey, and rum. *Presnitz* is shaped like a script version of the letter *c*. It is a flaky Easter cake with walnuts, pine nuts, candied orange, raisins, and butter. The other Easter cake, more yeasty, is *pinza*, made with rum, vanilla, orange, lemon peel, butter, and sugar. There are many small pastries as well and a broad selection of traditional Austro-Hungarian cakes such as Sacher and Dobos. Also traditional are *fave*, bean-shaped almond-paste candies that are made prior to *Il Giorno dei Morti* (November 2), known in Italy as the Day of the Dead. Those sold around that day are known as *fave dei morti*, although they can be found during much of the year. *Fave* can be pink (made with rum), white (made with maraschino liqueur), or brown (with cocoa).

Caffè-Pasticceria Pirona.

See "Bars and *Caffè*s," below.

BARS AND CAFFÈS

In addition to the listings here, see "A Coffee Tour on the Via XX Settembre," below.

Caffè La Colombiana, Via Carducci 12. Open 7–19:30h; closed Sunday.

This large, rectangular bar is little changed since 1949 and is evocative of postwar design. Its owners and employees are also very warm and friendly, which makes it a nice place to visit. The specialty is *cappuccino viennese*, a cappuccino with fresh whipped cream and cocoa powder. The basic coffee here (La Colombiana) is not as good as some others in town, but I still recommend a visit.

Cremcaffè, Piazza Goldoni 10. Open 6–20h; closed Sunday.

Triestini love to take coffee at the long bar. Because this bar serves more than two thousand cups a day, the machines are hot, and the coffee is fresh. You might be served a *cappuccino triestino* in a glass or an espresso in a cup topped with a dollop of whipped cream. It is also possible to buy Cremcaffè in beans to take away. The other reason to come here is for the *frullati*, milkshakes with many delicious different flavors. Chocolate is great, *gianduia* is better, and *fico* (fig), almond, marrons glacés, papaya, cointreau, and banana are also grand. You will notice that bananas in Italy taste better than those sold in the United States. The reason is that bananas sold in Italy are not picked green and then gassed to ripen. Instead, bananas in Italy usually arrive from Africa full of the flavor that only older Americans remember. And because Trieste is one of the chief ports in which bananas arrive, they are even better here.

Caffè-Pasticceria Pirona, Largo Barriera Vecchia 12, tel. 040/726211.

Opened in 1900, this is one of the great surviving literary *caffè*s in Europe. It is most closely associated with James Joyce, who spent hours here each day reading, writing, drinking coffee, and eating delicious cake. It is thought that he plotted his masterpiece *Ulysses* during his days at the Pirona. I have come here often to seek similar inspiration, but I still am enslaved by commas and periods. The great pastries of Trieste, including *putizza, presnitz,* and *pinza,* and Viennese favorites are all to be enjoyed at Pirona.

Caffè San Marco, Via Gesare Battisti 18.

Opened in 1914, this is one of the most beautiful *caffès* in Italy, done in high Liberty style. It is a delight to come here for good coffee and conversation, to hear music played on the grand piano, or to read a good book.

Bar Tergesteo, Galleria Tergesteo (opposite Teatro Verdi). Closed Tuesday.

A good place to gather in winter because its "outdoor" tables are enclosed in an arcade. It is near the stock exchange and attracts many financial types.

Caffè Tommaseo, Rive Tre Novembre 5 (Piazza Tommaseo).

One of the most historic locales in Trieste. Since 1830 this *caffè* has been a center of intellectual, musical, literary, and political activity. Its history is tied to that of the city, and you owe it to yourself to pay a visit. The San Marco may be more attractive, but the Tommaseo is more legendary.

A COFFEE TOUR ON THE VIA XX SETTEMBRE

The Via XX Settembre is a lovely tree-lined promenade in the center of Trieste. It is full of *caffès* and ice-cream parlors and is a popular meeting place for people of all ages. The places listed are arranged by address. While many of these locales are not particularly unusual, the street itself is nice, and you can go from bar to bar tasting different types of coffee.

#1: Gran Bar Excelsior. Closed Monday.

This curving bar is one of the most attractive on the street. Serves Hausbrandt.

#8: Caffè Madison. Closed Monday.
Serves Lavazza.

#9: Bar Topazio. Closed Sunday.
Serves Cremcaffè.

#11: Gelateria Pipolo. Closed Wednesday.
Ice cream.

#14: Gelateria de Martin. Closed Sunday.
Ice cream.

#16: Bar Rio. Closed Sunday.

Serves Hausbrandt.

#24a:
A bar with good ice cream. Serves Excelsior.

#25: Gelateria Zampolii. Closed Monday.

Considered the best ice cream in Trieste, although I was not overwhelmed with what I sampled.

#29B: Bar la Preferita. Closed Tuesday.

Serves Cremcaffè.

#33D: Closed Sunday.

Serves Lavazza.

#35B: Closed Monday.

Next to the unmissable and quite re-markable Cinema Ambasciatori. Serves Excelsior.

#37B: Gelateria Alex. Closed Tuesday.

Right below the Mongolian consulate, in case you were looking for it. Good ice cream. Serves Cremcaffè.

COFFEE MUSEUM
Raccolta Illycaffè, Via Flavia 110,
tel. 040/3890111.
Visits by appointment only.

Within the company's plant is a collection of objects relating to coffee and to this firm's prominent role in its dissemination. In this collection are manual and electric coffee grinders, wonderful espresso cups, coffee cans, roasters, and above all a great display of packaging and advertising materials for Illycaffè through the decades. These reflect the evolution of attitudes and taste, with coffee being the unifying theme.

DINING
Ai Fiori, Piazza Hortis 7, tel/fax
040/300633. Closed Sunday and Monday.
All credit cards. Moderate to moderately
expensive.

A very warm welcome is offered at this trattoria on a leafy square in a nice part of town. The food, a combination of Triestine and Friulian specialities, is carefully pre-pared and served with pride. Some of the best cooking in the city (along with Suban, listed below) can be found here. There is also an outstanding wine list that includes many of the great bottles of Friuli-Venezia Giulia.

Buffet da Pepi, Via Cassa di Risparmio 3/B,
tel. 040/68073. Open 0900–2030. Closed
Sunday. No credit cards. Inexpensive.

Locals refer to this hundred-year old landmark as Pepi S'ciavo, which would loosely translate as "Joey the Slav". Here is one of the best examples of the Triestine buffet, a sort of hot table with splendidly prepared pork products with local names. Get a plate with *porzina*, *cotechino*, *cragno* (sausage), *lombo* and anything else you point at. Add *crauti* (delicate sauerkraut), *cren* (freshly grated horseradish) and *senape* (mustard) and have either beer or a glass of red Terrano wine for a genuine Triestine experience. Da Pepi is perfectly located near the opera house, the Roman amphitheatre, and the Piazza d'Unità d'Italia.

Città di Londra, Via Ghiberti 2,
tel. 040/365188. Closed Saturday evening,
Sunday. Visa, Master Card. Inexpensive to
moderately inexpensive.

For a genuine old Triestine experience, take the antique tram from Piazza Oberdan and travel 7 km up into the hills above the city to Opicina, just at the Slovenian border. Look for the Antica Trattoria Valeria, which has received guests since 1904 and also had them stay in the simple rooms that are a lodging option if you want to go native. Wonderful local dishes such as *jota, orzotto con le verze* (barley and Savoy cabbage), *gnocchi, blechi con la rucola* (fresh pasta with arugula), mushrooms, truffles, excellent meats, and *rigo jansci* cake.

Gran Bar Malabar at Piazza San Giovanni 6.

Not a restaurant *per se*, but one of Italy's most popular wine bars, serving tasty snacks as well. On Friday evenings, wine-makers from around Italy come to present their wines, and young *triestini* fill the triangular piazza to take part in the tastings. Even if you are not in Trieste on a Friday, this is an agreeable, centrally located spot worth a visit.

Al Bragozzo, Via Nazario Sauro 22, tel. 040/303001. Closed Sunday, Monday, December 20, January 10, and June 20–July 10. All credit cards. Moderately expensive.

A restaurant near the *molo pescheria* (fish market) with some of the best seafood in town. The best thing here is probably the self service antipasto bar.

Marasciutti, Via Cesare Battisti 2b. Open until 21h; closed Thursday. No credit cards. Inexpensive.

A typical old-style Trieste *buffet*. There is a hot table with various boiled meats, sausages, potatoes, and sauerkraut that you eat standing up. Good, basic food that doesn't seem at all Italian.

Ristorante La Marinella, Viale Miramare 323, tel. 040/410986. Closed Sunday evening and Monday. All credit cards. Moderately expensive.

Many *triestini* consider this their favorite seafood restaurant. I enjoyed the food here as well.

Antica Trattoria Suban, Via Comici 2, tel. 040/34128, fax 040/579020. Reservations essential. All credit cards. Moderately expensive.

This restaurant has been a Trieste institution since 1865. Its fame is so widespread that it is hard to get a table. For that reason, you should call or fax reservations before you get to town. The traditional flavors of the Carso— such as cabbage, caraway seeds, apricot crepes *(palacbincbe)*, horseradish *(cren)*, and robust wines—are all delicious.

Trattoria Risorta, Riva De Amicis 11a (in Muggia), tel. 040/271219. Closed Sunday evening (Sunday lunch too in July and August), Monday, and the first three weeks in January. Mastercard, Visa. Moderate to moderately expensive.

It is worth travelling 11 km south of Trieste to this engaging seaside trattoria whose seafood cookery will exceed your expectations. Be sure to taste the local olive oil from San Dorligo.

Antica Salumeria Masè, Piazza San Benco at Via del Monte, or near Piazza Goldoni at Via Giacinto Gaiini 3.

You may purchase prepared foods and local specialties. Notice the more Germanic aspect of the sausages (longer, thinner, pinker) than one usually sees in Italy. You will also find Greek cheeses and olive oil prominently sold. This appeals to the Greeks who make up yet another foreign community in Trieste.

La Società del Benessere, Via Roma 26, tel. 040/369130. Diners Club, MasterCard, Visa.

A very clean, well-stocked store filled with biological products (that is, health food). Excellent selection and service. There is an extensive selection of soy-based products from Valsoia, many herbal products, oils, grains, and liqueurs made by Franciscan monks in Assisi. One can see, with a visit to this store, how Italians who go biological can manage to eat very well.

There are four *gelaterie* on the Via XX Settembre. See "A Coffee Tour on the Via XX Settembre," above.

There are many small restaurants near Trieste in which to have traditional food of the Carso, washed down with Terrano wine. Meals are moderately inexpensive, the atmosphere is usually convivial and relaxed. Typically, credit cards are not accepted.

Basovizza. Trattoria da Pepi (Kosovel 33, tel. 040/226177).

Duino Aurisana. Trattoria al Carso (Malchina 23/A, tel. 040/299471); Trattoria Gruden (San Pelagio 49, tel. 040/200151), recommended; and Trattorria Sardoc (Precenico 1/B, tel. 040/200871).

Monrupino. Trattoria Bozo (Fernetti 3, tel. 040/211460), Trattoria Carso (Monrupino 1, tel. 040/327113), and Trattoria Krizman (Rupingrande 76, tel. 040/327002).

San Dorligo della Valle. Hotel-Restaurant Pesek (Pesek di Grozzana 38, tel. 040/226294). For exceptionally delicate oil worth sampling, visit Az. Agr. Sancin at Dolina 360.

Santa Croce. Trattoria Tipica "La Lampara" (Santa Croce 144, tel. 040/220352). Most of the menu is fish and seafood.

Sgonico. Ristorante Milic (Borgo Grotta Gigante 10, tel. 040/327330).

Udine
Classic Town

A visit to Udine is particularly agreeable on a Saturday afternoon. The shopping district near the Piazza della Libertà is full of activity as people make purchases for the Sunday meal or stroll arm in arm from bar to *gelateria* to *osteria*. The *udinesi* are very elegant: they like to dress up for the *passeggiata* and therefore engage in some very competitive people watching. On Saturday Udine is also full of Austrians who have driven across the border to purchase beautiful clothing and exquisite food.

BAKERY

Pasticceria Carli di Folegotto, Via Vittorio Veneto 36. Closed Monday.

Very nice, small pastries are served here, including a buttery little *gubana* large enough to go with a very good cappuccino at the bar.

A COFFEE TOUR OF CENTRAL UDINE

As in Trieste, it is possible to do a coffee tour through the center of Udine to sample several types and pick your favorite. You might try this one, which begins on the Via Rialto and continues to the Piazza della Libertà. You can start at one end or the other, or anywhere in between.

Bar Grosmi, Via Rialto 6A. Closed Sunday.

Serves Caffè Grosmi, also sells coffee beans and chocolates.

Udinese, Via Rialto 5B (corner of Via delle Erbe). Closed Sunday.

Serves Caffè Udinese.

Piccolo Bar, Via Rialto 2I. Closed Sunday.

Serves Ruffo Caffè. Also is a wine bar with many local varieties by the glass.

Bar-Pasticceria Panciera, Via Rialto 2E (in the Palazzo Municipale). Closed Friday.

Serves Caffè del Moro.

Bar Americano, Piazza della Libertà 7A. Closed Thursday.

Serves Caffè Hausbrandt.

Bar Cotterli, corner of Via Vittorio Veneto and Via Manin on Piazza della Libertà. Closed Sunday.

Serves Caffè Demar. One of the barmen here, Luca Tomada, took first place in a national competition for the best barman. This bar has been here since 1919.

COOKING SCHOOL

L'Arcimoboldo, Viale Palmanova 133, 33100 Udine, tel. 0432/602766.

This very popular school draws students who want to learn the classic dishes of

Friuli–Venezia Giulia as well as special gastronomic subjects from elsewhere. The head of the school, Gianna Modotti, is renowned for her knowledge of ancient Roman dishes of Aquilea as well as the Slovenian, Austrian, and other influences that make the Friulian kitchen so special. You can stay in country houses and hotels while pursuing your studies in Udine. Courses are given from September to June, and you can enroll for a weekend, a week, or up to two months.

DINING

If you plan to dine at an *osteria,* especially in the evening, it is wise to reserve. Many *osterie* fill up with regular clients, and, while you will certainly be welcome, there is limited space.

Osteria al Vecchio Stallo, Via Viola 7, tel. 0432/21296. Closed Wednesday. No credit cards.

This is an old stall where carters would arrive with their horses, stop for a meal and a rest, and then proceed with new horses. On the way back, these horses would be returned, and the first ones taken for the rest of the journey. This practice continued until the 1930s, when the first automobiles began to arrive. Soon horses were no longer used for transporting goods over long distances, but this remained a desirable place to eat and make friends. The stall was converted into another wing of the restaurant. As you walk about, notice the original wooden floor as well as the period photographs of Udine, of wine making, and particularly the ones of horses carting away snow and of the old woman leading her donkey to market as it pulls a cart—she is sort of a Friulian Mother Courage. In the warm months there is a courtyard where grapevines hang from a pergola above. The food is honest *osteria* fare, the wine is very good, prices are modest, and Maurizio Mancini and family are the very welcoming hosts. On Sunday there are delicious *cjarsons (cialzons).*

Osteria con Trattoria "Alla Ghiacciaia," Via Zanon 13, tel. 0432/508937. Open 9–15h, 17–24h; closed Monday. All credit cards. Moderate.

A popular hangout with the young, especially in summer when tables are placed outside. There are some tasty and unusual dishes here. One is *gnocchi con erba cipollina,* made with chives and flavored with smoked ricotta cheese. There is *capretto* flavored with nutmeg, an unusual combination to be sure, but it works well when washed down with the house's Cabernet Franc. The use of nutmeg dates back to when Trieste and, to a lesser extent, Venezia were ports that supplied spices to Vienna and Budapest. Most of the carts transporting spices passed through Udine, and somehow samples would fall off the carts and into the hands of local cooks. The atmosphere is quite pleasing.

Osteria La Ciacarade, Via San Francesco 6, tel. 0432/510250. Closed Sunday and in August. No credit cards. Moderately inexpensive.

There are good antipasti such as Montasio, *frico,* prosciutto, and *frittatine con le erbe.* There is some Austrian influence in the food here, the *gulasch* for example. A nice place for conversation, a little less animated than some of the others in town.

Osteria al Lepre, Via Poscolle 27, tel. 0432/295798. Closed Sunday and ten days in August. MasterCard, Visa.

One can make a nice small meal with snacks of *salumi,* prosciutto, and cheese at the bar. There is a custom here of serving risotto at the bar at 19:30h, and you will meet very nice people over a bowl. If you choose to dine here, there is some very good food. The *stinco di maiale* with polenta is delicious, and other dishes are nice, too. In the winter you can bask in the warmth of the fogolar.

Al Marinaio, Via Cisis 2, tel. 0432/ 295949. Closed Tuesday (Monday too in the summer). All credit cards. Moderate.

Its name means "The Mariner's," and fish gets more prominence here than in most of Udine. But the peasant tradition will have it that "poorer" seafood such as anchovy, herring, and mussels share the menu with fresh Adriatic fish and crustaceans that are prepared simply to bring out their flavor. In springtime, look for the *Sagra dei croz*, a festival of dishes based on local frogs.

Osteria all'Allegria, Via Grazzano 18, tel. 0432/505921. Closed Monday and in July. MasterCard. Moderately inexpensive.

The *gnocchi di zucca* are delicate, the *stinco di maiale* is succulent, and I am especially fond of the *torta di pinoli*.

Agli Amici, Via Liguria 250, tel. 0432/565411; agliamici@libero.it. Closed Sunday evening (and Sunday lunch from June through August), Monday, for a week in January, and two in July. All credit cards. Moderately expensive.

In Godia, 6 km from the city center, Agli Amici may be the best place to eat in Udine. While I love the typical *osterie*, if you want more refined cookery and excellent service, this is the place to go. If available, have the goose foie gras marinated in Verduzzo wine.

FOOD SHOPPING

Most food stores in Udine are closed on Monday afternoon, Wednesday afternoon, and Sunday.

La Baita, Via delle Erbe 1 (just off Via Rialto).

An excellent cheese store that has all the best that Friuli produces, as well as good cheeses from other regions. It also sells *frico*.

Gastronomia al Parmigiano, Via Cortazzis 6b.

Good roast chicken, vegetables, prosciutto from San Daniele and Parma, and a huge variety of other prepared foods.

Pastificio Artigianato di Stefano de Luisa, Via Poscolle 16, tel. 0432/501674.

A fascinating selection of dried pastas (forty-two types) and thirty-five different types of filled fresh pasta, one filled with *sclopit*, a local wild herb. The shop also makes excellent *cialsons*. Some of the dried pasta flavors are a bit wacky: coconut, kiwi, coffee, and rose petal. Others are interesting, such as lemon (to serve with fish) or almond (to serve with game or fowl). This store also has a *gastronomia* with prepared dishes that change seasonally. You can buy *prosciutto di San Daniele*, cheeses from Friuli, and mozzarella from Campania, a few wines, jams, honeys, and even peanut butter and Hershey's chocolate from the United States.

WINE AND SPIRITS

La Spezieria Pei Sani, Via Poscolle 13, tel. 0432/505061. Open 10–14h, 15:30–21h; closed Sunday.

A popular spot in Udine since 1939 in which to drink wine and enjoy friendship. It is across the street from an old pharmacy, which was for the sick *(per i malati)*, while this place was for the well *(pei sani)*. This happens to be a nonsmoking place, a nice relief, since many wine bars and *osterie* are smoky. Most customers here are known by their first names and are regulars, although newcomers are made very welcome. The proprietors like to follow the health and well-being of every customer and seem to know when one has been gone for a while.

You will notice old sayings printed on small dishes: L'AVARO È COME IL PORCO. È BUONO DOPO CH'È MORTO (The miser is like the pig. It's better after it is dead) or LA DONNA INTELLETUALE È COME LE SCARPE STRETTE (The intellectual woman is like tight shoes). In addition to good wine, there are small snacks. Around the corner, along the banks of a small canal, you will see stands selling cod, Montasio, fruit, and bedroom slippers. Cross back over the Via Gelso, and there is a nice bakery on the corner that sells *gubana, crostata,* and focaccia.

La Casa del Vino, Via Poscolle 6.

For serious wine drinkers and merchants, this is a resource for information about the wines of Friuli. It has 1,200 producer-members and can provide detailed information about the region's wines

Frico
Montasio-Cheese Crisp

I am a *frico* freak. This is the most delicious and addictive snack to have while drinking a pre-meal glass of wine. And once you get the knack, it is very easy to make. The version presented here is the traditional kind that becomes slightly crunchy. You will occasionally find a version that has a crunchy crust and a creamy interior, such as at Ai Cacciatori in Cierneglons, that is just as wonderful.

Serves 4

450 grams/1 pound Montasio, aged 16 to 18 months

Coarsely grate all of the cheese. If you feel your pan needs a little greasing before making the *frico,* use extra-virgin olive oil very sparingly. Hold a large frying pan with slightly curving edges over medium heat until it gets hot. Sprinkle a quarter of the cheese all over the pan, and then push any

scattered bits toward the whole so that it looks like you have a cheese crepe. Push down with the back of a fork all over the *frico* so that the fat will leave the cheese. Once the *frico* is relatively firm, turn it over and heat the other side, again pressing down to let some of the fat run out. The whole process takes about 10 minutes. Have a clean, empty wine bottle nearby. When the *frico* is done (it should be firm and have a bit of pull), press the bottom of the bottle into the middle of the *frico* and fold the edges upward around the bottle. Lift the bottle out and leave the *frico*, which is now shaped like a flower, to cool on a plate. Repeat the process 3 more times, or until you have used all of the cheese.

When the *frico* has cooled it will be crunchy. You break off a piece and eat it. (I'll bet you can't eat just one.)

Wine: The ideal match is Tocai del Friuli, but any Friulian wine will go well with *frico*.

Gnocchi di Susine
Plum Gnocchi

This is the recipe of Patrizia Filiputti, a marvelous cook whose husband, Walter, is an outstanding enologist. They are wonderful hosts (as most *friulani* are), and I have been fortunate to dine with them on several occasions. *Gnocchi di susine* is a classic Friulian dish that one can never eat enough of. You may substitute fresh apricots for plums when they are in season.

Serves 4
1 kilogram/2.2 pounds medium potatoes
Salt
1 large egg
3 handfuls (about 2 cups) unbleached flour
6 small ripe plums, washed, halved, pitted
2 tablespoons granulated sugar
8 tablespoons unsalted butter
3 tablespoons unflavored bread crumbs
Powdered cinnamon

Wash the potatoes and cook covered in boiling water for 30 minutes. Peel them while they are still hot and rice them with a fork or a potato ricer. Sprinkle on a little salt and let them cool. When they are cool, add the egg and half of the flour. Work the mixture into a dough and add more flour until you have a dough that is firm but not hard (because everyone's hand is a different size there will be some variation as to how much flour is required). Separate the dough into several pieces and roll it out gently with your hands so that you form cigar-shaped lengths. Cut a piece about 4½

centimeters (1½ inches) long, flatten it slightly in the palm of your hand, place a plum half and a pinch of sugar within the dough, and fold it around so that the plum is enclosed. Seal gently with your thumb and set aside. Repeat this process to make 12 gnocchi, reserving some sugar for sprinkling on the cooked gnocchi. Set a large pot of cold water to boil. When it reaches a boil, toss in a pinch of salt. When the water returns to a boil, put in the gnocchi and cook. When the gnocchi rise to the top, let them cook another 2 minutes and then fish them out with a slotted spoon. While they are cooking, melt the butter in a pan, add the bread crumbs, and let them toast slightly. When the gnocchi are cooked, put 3 on each of 4 plates, sprinkle some sugar and cinnamon over them, then pour on the butter-and-bread-crumb mixture.

Wine: A Friulian white of your choice, such as Sauvignon Blanc, Pinot Bianco, Ribolla Gialla, Tocai, Traminer Aromatico, or Riesling Italico.

Emilia-Romagna

REGIONAL CAPITAL:
Bologna (BO).

PROVINCIAL CAPITALS:
Ferrara (FE), Forlì (FO),
Modena (MO), Parma
(PR), Piacenza (PC),
Ravenna (RA), Reggio
Emilia (RE), Rimini (RN).

TOURIST INFORMATION,

INCLUDING AGRITOURISM:
Ente Regionale di Turismo
dell'Emilia-Romagna,
Piazzale Federico
Fellini 3,
47037 Rimini.

 In selecting what you should not miss in Emilia-Romagna, I am tempted to list at least a dozen more places. From a gastronomic point of view, and many others as well, Emilia-Romagna is the most outstanding region in Italy. It is amazing that it can have Venezia, Verona, and Milano to the immediate north and Firenze and Toscana to the south, yet be largely ignored by visitors to Italy.

This is a region of remarkable culture and energy that has produced great opera stars (such as Mirella Freni and Luciano Pavarotti), composers, conductors, popular entertainers, film makers (including Fellini), painters, writers, and fashion icons such as Giorgio Armani. Its citizens are extremely hardworking and productive, but they also devote time to pleasure and enlightenment.

Emilia-Romagna's cities routinely rank near the top of national listings for quality of life, and Modena vies with Varese in Lombardia for the title of Italy's wealthiest city. Cities are clean and safe, and the strong educational system has produced a worldly populace that is conversant in business, art, history, ethics, and politics (these last two items actually go together in Emilia-Romagna). Although Mussolini was from Forlì in Romagna, this region has a strong anti-Fascist history. Its men and women were leaders in the Italian Resistance, and museums such as the fine one in Ferrara commemorate their exploits. Bologna was the only Italian city to liberate itself from

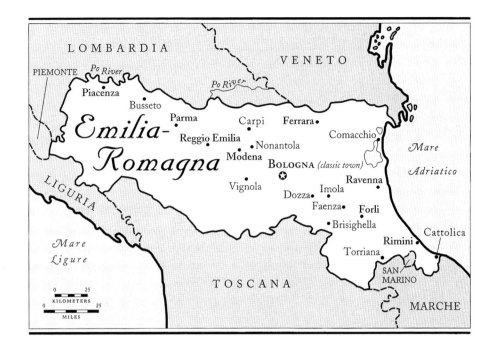

Nazi occupation without the help of the Allies. The bravery, suffering, and independence of the *bolognesi* is noted everywhere in the city, with plaques and memorials that you will see.

One conundrum in this region is that it has been, since World War II, the heartland of the Italian Communist Party and its successor, the Democratic Party of the Left, yet its citizens wear the finest clothes, eat the best food, live in beautiful homes, and are generally as bourgeois a people as you will see anywhere. The secret to this is that while the Soviet Union proclaimed itself the workers' paradise, the real workers' paradise was Emilia-Romagna. This is because the leaders who rebuilt the region following the war drew the best from Socialist thought and blended it with the incontrovertible virtues of democracy to produce a society where every citizen was cared for, but was free to do and say whatever he pleased. Collectives and cooperatives were created when they made economic sense, yet private enterprise and initiative were always encouraged.

Although Italy has lurched to the right in recent years following scandals in the governing coalition of Christian Democrats and Socialists (who are Milano-based and not in any way allied with the ex-Communists in Emilia-Romagna), the prevailing views of *emiliani* and *romagnoli* are still left wing. I mention this not as an advocate of one system or another, but to point out the fact that many foreigners who were unfamiliar with Italian Communism violently attacked it without understanding it. At the heart of life in Emilia-Romagna's ethos is a live-and-let-live attitude that would not abide totalitarian values of any kind.

And do they know how to live! Once you taste food in Emilia-Romagna, you will want to live there, too. Italians almost universally acknowledge the cuisine of this region to be the country's best. It is certainly the richest, but I think that the relaxed, happy quality of life, the relative lack of stress, and the excellent medical care mean that people here eat a lot of cheese, pork, butter, and cream yet have enviable life expectancies. Italians also acknowledge that the people of this region, especially those from Bologna, are the best lovers in this very passionate country.

I am sure that people from one town to the next in the region would debate where the best lovers are because they certainly dispute who makes the best food. If you visit Bologna, Ferrara, Modena, Reggio Emilia, and Parma you will be able to come to your own conclusions. Each town and all of the other major towns in the region have their own specialties, so that you can journey for two weeks and taste new food every day. The reason there is such a diverse gastronomic heritage is that all of the great ancient cities of the region were independent duchies and city-states that developed their own styles and preferences through the centuries. With that has come a distinct personality in each town, so that a native of the region can often figure out quickly where someone else is from. For example, the people of Parma are more reserved, while those from Modena are more vivacious.

Most of the important towns in the region lie on the Via Emilia, a road built in Roman times that leads from Piacenza through Parma, Reggio, Modena, Bologna, Faenza, Forlì, to Rimini on the Adriatic. The area from Bologna to the north and west is Emilia; the part from Bologna to the south and east is Romagna. In general the *emiliani* are thought to be more sophisticated and the *romagnoli* more rustic, yet I think that is a mistaken generalization. One need only visit Ravenna to see how classy *romagnolo* cities are. Yet I am certain that if Sir John Falstaff were an Italian, he would live in Romagna. The people there have wonderful brio and love of life and pleasure, as does Sir John, but they are also very industrious and generous. Many *romagnoli* are square-faced, with shiny black hair and green or amber eyes. A lot of the women have red hair (from the bottle) and are short and busty. You will notice that people here are often very tactile, very flirtatious, and very loving.

There is one area of Romagna that is hardly a stranger to tourism. Rimini is the capital of the Riviera di Romagna, the stretch of beach on the Adriatic that begins near Ravenna and continues to the border of the Marche and beyond. Towns such as Rimini and Riccione have been among the most popular beach resorts in Europe since the 1950s and have geared their lodgings and restaurants to the budgets of families on vacation. Therefore, one has to look harder for outstanding food at the beach, although it can be found just inland. The beach scene at Rimini is rather remarkable: in addition to families from all over the Continent, there are many beautiful young women from Scandinavia and Germany who come south looking for two-week "flirts" with local Romeos with sand between their toes. Some of them marry and stay, and I have seen more than a few heavy, middle-aged German women cooking fast food at roadside stands. Don't forget that

Fellini was from Rimini and lovingly depicted its contradictions—lust, loneliness, the eternal fascination of the sea—in most of his films. The Riviera di Romagna is an anomaly, but one worth making note of as you travel through the area.

It is interesting that the area that is now the Romagna Riviera was once the terrain of poor farmers, because this land was less fertile than the higher-yielding soil inland. Then during the postwar buildup, they sold their land and suddenly became well-off. But old attitudes die hard, and some people in Romagna still regard food and wine with older values, when production and consumption were more about quantity than quality. One certainly ate well, but the cuisine had less refinement than that produced in Emilia. Rather, it relied on the superb flavor of the raw materials.

I also hope you will develop an appreciation for the visual aspects of Emilia-Romagna. The Apennines flank the western part of the region, and there is mountain culture and good skiing. Alberto Tomba, Italy's most famous skier, is from Bologna, and his hard work and hard play are legendary. The region also has a vast, fertile plain where magnificent food is cultivated. In some parts of the year, but especially autumn, thick fogs blanket vast expanses of this plain, creating an atmosphere that some might consider gloomy, but others will find picturesque. Think of the fogs in many Fellini films, and you will find that they can be cause for sadness or nostalgia, but also for moments of revelry and awe at their beauty. The fogs and mists are especially beautiful in the cities, where people walk under porticoes and encounter one another at occasional spots of illumination. The cities also are distinct in that they have central piazzas that citizens gather in. While other regions have the *passeggiata*, in Emilia-Romagna, there is the idea of *andiamo in piazza* (let's go the main square), much as the Romans did two thousand years ago. Each day, central squares in towns large and small fill with citizens who gather for conversation and fun. Notice particularly in Bologna and Modena all the older men with hats on who stand close together in large clumps as they listen to two combatants passionately debating politics, soccer, food, or something else.

No square in Italy is more animated and endlessly fascinating than Bologna's Piazza Maggiore. Throughout the day and night it is the setting for play, conversation, music, parenting, romance, and discourse. As in most of the region (except for the beaches of Romagna) nothing in Bologna is done to appeal to what is perceived to be touristic taste, so you have a city that lives by its own codes and ethics. In this regard, it will give you a much more palpable sense of what real life is like in Italy than you will find in Milano, Venezia, Firenze, Roma, or Napoli, which is yet another reason that Bologna deserves to be visited on your first trip to Italy and revisited as often as possible.

Bologna has been selected as the Classic Town for the region because it draws characteristics and gastronomy from both Emilia and Romagna. It is the essence of this region and, I believe, the city in Italy most underestimated by tourists. Its citizens are almost as elegant as those of Parma, but have much more brio. They are openhearted, fun loving, intellectual, and sensuous. They adore good food and wine and have the best markets in Italy. Its university, founded in 1069, is the world's oldest and the best in the country. Its architecture is largely medieval, with the distinguishing characteristic being the porticoes that line most of the thoroughfares. They provide shade from the sun, shelter from the rain, and are pedestrian thoroughfares that invite social interaction.

Venezia and Firenze may have more conspicuous tourist attractions, but Bologna has better food, performing arts, nightlife, and a friendly populace that welcomes tourists with open arms, while the Venetians and Florentines have become jaded. So I encourage you, as you travel from Venezia to Firenze, to dedicate a couple of days to Bologna.

Eating in Emilia-Romagna

The quality and range of food in Emilia-Romagna is unrivaled in all of Italy. This region's citizens are also endowed with a serious knowledge of ingredients and cooking, so that food lovers will find themselves surrounded by well-nourished soulmates. What follows is a list of some of the most popular foods of the region, but I recommend, if you want to learn much more about the food of Emilia-Romagna, that you read Lynne Rossetto Kasper's excellent book *The Splendid Table*, which is so authoritative that even though the author is American, Italians use it to better understand this region's food.

ANTIPASTI

In Parma they say *Il maiale è come la musica di Verdi: tutto buono, niente da buttar via* (The pig is like the music of Verdi: it's all good, there's nothing to throw away). At the heart of Emilia-Romagna's cuisine are its many pork products.

Culatello. Another saying holds that: *A Parma si mangia due volte. Prima si mangia, poi si parla.* Which is to say that in Parma one eats twice. First you eat, then you talk. The *parmigiani* love to talk about and debate the quality and virtues of food, but perhaps no item is more discussed than *culatello.* Outside of Parma, we think of that city for its *prosciutto crudo*, but in the city the citizens are cultists of *culatello.* It comes from the leanest part of the hind leg of the pig. Usually it is the right leg, which the pig curls under itself as it sits. The other leg, used for standing, builds up muscle and therefore is not considered lean enough by the exacting *parmigiani.* As if this were not enough, the pigs used for *culatello* can only come from the flat, moist zone between Parma and the Po River. (Conversely, prosciutto is derived from pigs that are slaughtered in the Apennines—especially the town of Langhirano—because the air and humidity in that area are considered ideal for curing the ham.) Pigs used for *culatello* are slaughtered only between November and February, and then the *culatello* is aged for fifteen to eighteen months. Most people in Parma claim to have a secret source for the best *culatello* and in general are very quick to criticize any *culatello* that does not meet their standards. It it traditional to eat *culatello* as an appetizer combined with *torta fritta* (see "Breads," below).

Mortadella. The delicate sausage of Bologna that is sold in other countries in a bastardized version called bologna is in fact called mortadella. But there is no baloney here. Mortadella is a combination of pork, sometimes pork liver, spices, bits of fat, and sometimes slivers of pistachio. It must come in a large form to be good because small mortadellas, even those made with the best ingredients, dry too easily. Some are more than a meter (3.3 feet) in diameter. Other *salumi* are at their best when sliced thin, but mortadella works well both in thin slices or in chunks.

Prosciutto Cotto. Excellent boiled ham, a specialty of Parma.

Prosciutto Crudo. Usually called *prosciutto di Parma* or Parma ham, most of the most famous ham is produced in the town of Langhirano, in the Apennines above Parma. It is made under the most exacting standards imaginable. It is thought that much of the flavor of this ham comes from the whey (a by-product in the cheese-making process) that is fed to the pigs. Many people believe it is best to eat prosciutto by hand. If you tear it, the ham will invariably tear in the right place.

Salame all'Aglio. Ferrara's special *salame* is laced with garlic.

Salame di Felino. This has nothing to do with cats. The town of Felino makes some of the finest *salami* you will ever taste.

Salsiccia. A general term for "sausage," which may appear as an antipasto or cooked with vegetables as a *secondo.* In this region of pork butchers, the sausages are divine.

PRIMI

The amazing range of pasta courses in Emilia-Romagna is unmatched in all of Italy for quantity and quality. In Campania there is a marvelous selection of dried pasta, but in this region the pasta is made with flour, water, and egg, giving it a golden color. In Romagna the pasta courses are called *minestre* rather than *primi* because one so often is served more than one pasta so that the word *primo* (first course) is happily inaccurate. In different parts of the region you are often served a *tris,* which is a platter containing three different pasta courses, such as *lasagne verdi, tagliatelle al ragù,* and *tortelloni al pomodoro.*

Filled pastas can contain meat, cheese, vegetables *(zucca, patate, bietola),* or occasionally fish. Tortellini may be the most famous, and fillings differ from town to town. For example, in Modena they are filled with minced chicken, pork, veal, a little beef, butter, *prosciutto crudo,* and Parmigiano-Reggiano. In Bologna they contain turkey, veal, ground pork, mortadella, *prosciutto crudo,* Parmigiano-Reggiano, and nutmeg. The joy is going from town to town comparing the delicate flavors of tortellini. Filled pastas change name from town to town, some of them being *anolini*, cappelletti, *cappellacci, tortelli d'erbette,* tortellini, *tortelloni,* and *balanzoni.* When *sfoglia* (sheets of pasta) are cut, noodles such as tagliatelle and *tagliarini* are made, along with sheets to make lasagne and cannelloni. Also look for gnocchi, *chicchi, caramelle, garganelli, gramigna,* and especially *passatelli,* which are made with bread, lemon, and nutmeg and served in broth.

Many filled pastas are served *in brodo* (in broth), which at its best is a sublime capon broth that will make you forget every other broth you have ever had. Purists will tell you, for example, that the only way to fully appreciate tortellini is *in brodo.* Other ways to sample pasta are *alla panna* (in cream), *al ragù* (a divine meat sauce that in no way resembles what you are used to), *burro e oro* (thin tomato sauce with butter), *alla salsiccia* (sausage sauce, usually served with *gramigna*), and, of course, *al pomodoro* (tomato).

SECONDI

Cotechino. A popular minced sausage, often served with cabbage or pureed potatoes.

Cotoletta alla Bolognese. A breaded veal cutlet topped with prosciutto, Parmigiano, and, often, mozzarella and a slice of truffle.

*Salama da Sugo (*or *Salama in Sugo).* This is a specialty of Ferrara. The *salama* is a form of sausage that crumbles when it is cooked and is ideally matched with *purè* (mashed potatoes). In the summer it is cooked for less time and is served with slices of cantaloupe.

Tacchino al Cardinale. Turkey breast with prosciutto and Parmigiano, often with a slice of truffle.

Zampone con le Lenticche. Pig's trotter filled with minced pork and spices and sliced thin. This specialty of Modena is usually served with lentils, especially at New Year's, when it is thought to bring luck. Consumption of lentils is supposed to bring money in the coming year.

CONTORNI

Gratinate (grattè in Romagna). Vegetables such as zucchini are cut open and baked with oil, spices, and bread crumbs, but no cheese, as you might expect. In addition, the quality of all vegetables is outstanding.

PANE

Erbazzone. A flattish bread filled with Swiss chard, spinach, or beet tops. A specialty of Reggio Emilia.

Pane Bolognese and *Pane Ferrarese.* In Bologna and Ferrara people often eat very dry breads. They are a new taste for the uninitiated, but actually are an ideal match for the very rich dishes of these two cities.

The typical bread of Bologna

Piadina. The famous bread of Romagna, which I believe would make an excellent fast-food idea that could be sold the world over. The original formula was flour, shortening, salt, and water, although there have been some variations through the years, including the use of olive oil as the basic fat. The dough is made into thin disks about 15 centimeters (6 inches) in diameter that are cooked on a tile or another dry, hot surface. It is then wrapped around any one of many foods, from vegetables to cheese to meat to chocolate to fruit.

Torta Fritta. Made simply of flour, water, and lard, this is a delicate little fried bread that is the perfect match for *culatello* and prosciutto, especially in Parma. Sometimes a little vinegar is added to the batter to reduce the richness of the lard.

FORMAGGI

Casetto (or Cassetto). The typical cheese of Ferrara is often a mixture of cow's and sheep's milk.

Formaggio di Fossa. There is a festival honoring this cheese, the Sagra del Formaggio di Fossa, held in Sogliano Sul Rubicone (Forli) on weekends between November 17 and early December. Another festival is held around November 10 in Talamello (Forli). The cheese there is more robust.

Mascarpone. A sweet, buttery cheese that is often swirled with a liqueur and served as a dessert.

Parmigiano-Reggiano. This is what English speakers mistakenly call Parmesan, and much of what is sold abroad is a poor imitation. Once you taste the real thing, you will never again accept a substitute. In shopping for the cheese, you must buy the one that has the Parmigiano-Reggiano seal stamped on the wheel. This cheese, which is made by 737 small producers in the provinces of Parma, Reggio Emilia, and parts of three others, can make you understand the axiom that cheese is milk's leap to immortality. To make one 75lb (34kg) wheel of cheese, 154 gallons (700 liters) of milk (5 each from 30 cows) are used. Every cheese is made by hand and then is aged in carefully controlled rooms for at least twelve months and usually for two years. The result is sweet and nutty, perfect for eating or grating over pasta like a dusting of gold. Around Parma are several warehouses to store cheese for aging. Because producers need cash while their cheese matures, banks can lend up to E280 per wheel, which is repaid with interest when the cheese is sold. (The average retail price for one wheel is about E400.) Parmigiano-Reggiano has been produced for more than seven hundred years and is regarded with reverence by the people of Parma. It is among the first foods given to babies, and Parma's outstanding soccer team considers it a secret weapon as a source of protein energy. Most restaurants have a beautiful cart with a glass dome under which a wedge of the cheese lies recumbent. The cart is rolled to your table, and a piece of cheese is served with great flourish. You can go to good stores throughout the region that will vacuum-pack Parmigiano for you on the last day of your visit so that you can bring a big wedge home.

Squacquerone. A soft, easy-eating cheese popular in Romagna.

FRUIT

Cherries from Vignola (Modena) are among the best you will ever taste. In addition, all kinds of excellent fruit grown in Romagna are esteemed nationally.

DOLCI

Castagnoli con la Crema. Shaped like chestnuts, these are cream-filled fritters eaten during Carnival, particularly in Romagna.

Chiacchiere delle Monache. "Nuns' chatter," the same pasta as tagliatelle, is cut in various shapes and then fried and covered with sugar. These are Carnival sweets, especially in Romagna.

Pampepato. The origins of this Ferrara delicacy go back to the Renaissance. This "pepper bread" in fact is made with spices, chocolate, nuts, and sometimes wine.

Torta di Riso. A rice cake, a specialty of Reggio Emilia.

Torta di Tagliatelle. A dry cake baked with thin strands of pasta. Moist and crunchy.

Torta Sbrisolona. A crumbly, buttery, dry cake perfect with dessert wine.

A SPECIAL EMILIA-ROMAGNA FLAVOR

Aceto Balsamico. Balsamic vinegar is an extraordinary ingredient in the region's cuisine that is described in the section about Modena.

Wines of Emilia-Romagna

The image of the wines of this region was ruined by the Lambrusco exported in the 1970s. This bubbly wine can be tasty when well made, but what was sent abroad was inexpensive and generic and appealed to people who were just beginning to explore wine. But the Lambruschi that are consumed in Emilia-Romagna are much more subtle. Sangiovese, from the red grape that is the foundation of Chianti, is made in abundance in Romagna and, at its best, is a fine still wine. Gutturnio, from Piacenza, is another good red. Pagadebit (Pay the Debts) is a hearty grape that produces a reliable if unremarkable red. The name derives from the fact that the grape would give dependable yields. Albana was once a dusky, amber-colored white wine. It is now vinified in a much more refined way, resulting in a charming straw-colored wine. Albana is also made as *passito*, a sweet dessert wine. Pignoletto is a charming white produced in the province of Bologna. Trebbiano is a dependable white from Romagna, and Malvasia is used often in the wines of Parma.

A delicious liqueur called *sburlon*, produced in the province of Parma, is made with quince. It is not easy to find, but worth the effort.

Ancarano di Rivergaro (Piacenza)

COOKING SCHOOL
Azienda Agricola La Stoppa, 29029 Ancarano di Rivergaro (PC), tel. 0523/958159.

Not far from Piacenza is this well-known farm that produces much-admired wine.

Courses are given in spring and fall by a French chef, Georges Cogny, which is not surprising when you consider the longtime links between France and Piacenza. One must drive up a very steep hill to get there but, once arrived, finds a beautiful setting.

Bologna
Classic Town

Bologna is a sensual paradise of fragrances, flavors, beautiful smiling people who frankly love life and all of the pleasures it offers. This is the real dolce vita. Bologna shaped many of my senses and tastes. I learned its food and food culture in its markets; I learned about fashion and style, about perspective and taste. In fact, Bologna teaches you about quality in all things. Some of the earliest pages of my sentimental education were written there too. In Bologna you will understand about the visual and human integration of a city to the environment, about the sense of a civic whole in which everything has its place.

BAKERIES

Pasticceria Atti & Figli, Via Caprarie 7, or Via Drapperie 6. Closed Thursday afternoon and Sunday.

The Via Caprarie store is a beautiful old landmark with exquisite cakes and pastries. Many people consider this the finest bakery in Bologna. Around the corner, at Via Drapperie, you can get some pastries, but the real draw is a sublime assortment of breads.

Pasticceria-Panificio Soverini, Via Oberdan 13, tel. 051/224418.

When I was younger and burned calories with abandon, Soverini was my haunt. The breads, pastries, and *crostate* are all pleasing. Soverini is well regarded locally but unknown to visitors.

Pasticceria Zanarini, Piazza Galvani 1, tel. 051/222717. Closed Monday.

One of the more elegant places in town for pastries and coffee since 1919. This is where composer Pietro Mascagni took his coffee when he was in Bologna. It has superb pear ice cream.

Bar-Pasticceria Lambertini, Piazza Aldrovandi 23 (Via San Vitale), tel. 051/224726.

The Piazza Aldrovandi has yet another great food market, anchored by this fine bar-bakery.

Gamberini, Via Ugo Bassi 12.

A nice old place near the Ugo Bassi market.

BARS-CAFFÈS

Also see "Bakeries," above.

Bar Roberto, Via Orefici 9a. Closed Sunday.

Roberto Orlandi is a charming and exacting proprietor who is legendary for his devotion to quality. Long ago he banned smoking in the bar because he insisted that the smoke altered the flavors in his baked goods. The hot chocolate is made of high-quality chocolate, not from a powder. Some of the pastries are on the heavy side, but flavorful. There are also good light sandwiches.

BOOKSTORES

As the home of the world's oldest university, Bologna has many excellent bookstores. Most are open Monday through Friday 9–19:30h and Saturday 9–13h, 15:30–19:30h.

Rizzoli, Via Rizzoli at Via Fossalta.

A vast collection of cookbooks.

Messaggerie, Via Farini 6, tel. 051/267645.

Nicola Zanichelli, Via Archiginnasio 14.

COOKING SCHOOLS

International Cooking School of Italian Wine and Food. (For information, contact 201 East 28 Street, Suite 15B, New York, NY 10016-8538, tel. 212/ 7791921, fax 212/7793248)

Mary Beth Clark, an American, operates one of the better cooking schools in Italy.

She wisely placed it in Italy's gastronomic epicenter and is able to introduce her students to the best markets, ingredients, and local chefs. In addition to doing all-Emilia-Romagna courses, she also offers excursions to Piemonte and Toscana to discover the cuisines of those regions. Recommended.

Corsi di Cucina con Margherita e Valeria Simili, Via San Felice 116 (Scala G), tel. 051/554494, fax 051/523771.

At this excellent school you can enroll in one four-to-five-hour class at a moderate price as part of your stay. Margherita and Valeria are great cooks and teachers, and their repertoire is large. Contact them before you make your travel plans, so you can find out what classes are being given. This is a good choice for travelers who may not have the time for a week of classes but want to experience one. Classes are taught in Italian, but you will still get a lot out of it even if you don't understand the words—watch the technique.

CULTURE

Teatro Comunale di Bologna, Largo Respighi 1, 40126 Bologna, tel. 051/529999, fax 051/529934.

One of Italy's finest opera companies, yet as with most everything about Bologna, its praises are unsung. This theater stages a wider range of opera than other companies in Italy, with strong Wagner, and French and Russian opera performances filling out a schedule that also includes all of the Italian classics.

DINING

The *bolognesi* are such cultists about food that they develop strong attachments to their local trattoria and pay a lot of attention to rising or declining quality in their place and every other. A big topic of conversation in Bologna concerns the fate and performance of restaurants. In a city where food is so well understood (although not ponderously and solemnly analyzed), it is essential to reserve if you want to be sure to have a table. This is true anywhere, but more so in Bologna.

Trattoria Gigina, Via Stendhal 1, tel. 051/322300. Closed Saturday and August. MasterCard and Visa. Moderately inexpensive to moderate.

This old restaurant just outside the city center has changed owners, but the secrets to the recipes of the previous proprietors (including the famous Nadia) were transmitted to Carlo Cortesi, the new chef/owner and a man of talents all his own. The *tagliatelle al ragù* are as sublime as ever, and so too are all the pastas. The *lasagne verdi* are exquisite and I also think the tortelloni are great. Meat dishes are very fine and if vegetables don't quite achieve the same high stardard, they are still good.

Trattoria del Rosso, Via Augusto Righi 30, tel. 051/236730. Open daily; closed for part of August. All credit cards. Moderately inexpensive.

One can eat more lightly here than certain other spots, with a plate of *salumi* or a dish of pasta making a meal. If you wish to have a larger meal, the quality/price ratio is quite agreeable.

Osteria del Sole, Vicolo Ranocchi 1, no telephone. Open 8–14h, 19–20:45h; closed Sunday and in August. No credit cards. Inexpensive.

A classic Bolognese local, opened in 1468 and still popular with market goers and vendors. The idea is to buy food in the market and then come here to drink wine. Invariably food is passed around, and friendships are made. In egalitarian Bologna, professors with splits of champagne sit elbow to elbow with bricklayers drinking Sangiovese and eating mortadella. Luciano Spolaore, the current owner, has been pouring wine here for more than fifty years. Old traditions are stubbornly maintained. It took decades to convince Luciano to buy a dishwasher rather than wash glasses by hand. Card players are given chalk to write their scores on the table rather than using a little notepad.

Trattoria Caminetto d'Oro, Via de' Falegnami 4, tel. 051/263494. Closed Wednesday in the winter and Sunday in the summer. All credit cards. Moderate to moderately expensive.

In Bologna this is a good solid place to eat, with fine food and service. In another city it would be the top restaurant, but standards in Bologna are high. This particular place is popular with British visitors. A few recommended dishes from the vast selection: *tortellini in brodo*, tagliatelle, an excellent mixed salad, and the *torta di noci* (walnut cake).

Trattoria Meloncello, Via Saragozza 240a, tel. 051/6143947. Closed Monday evening, Tuesday, one week in January, *three weeks in August. All credit cards. Moderate.*

On a porticoed street leading up to Monte San Luca and next to the Teatro delle Celebrazioni, this is a very characteristic *bolognese* trattoria where one is made immediately welcome. All the classics are here and I especially like the nutmeg-scented *passatelli in brodo* and the chewy *gramigna con salsiccia*, a pasta with a sauce of pork sausage and tomato.

Ristorante Pappagallo, Piazza della Mercanzia 3c, tel. 051/232807. Closed Sunday and Monday lunch. All credit cards. Expensive.

Pappagallo was once considered the best restaurant in Italy, and every pope, diva, politician, and movie star who came to Bologna made sure to eat there, often leaving an autographed photograph. These portraits of wonderful old faces line the walls and give great character to the room. Pappagallo declined famously in the 1980s as it went through changes in ownership and management. More than two hundred photographs disappeared, and the Bolognese and others avoided the place as word spread of poor food and service. In recent years there has been gradual improvement. I can report, from a recent visit, that the food is now good, although the menu has abandoned the unswerving devotion to rivers of cream, cheese, and fatty meats (all delicious) that characterized Pappagallo's kitchen in the pre-cholesterol era. But you might choose to dine here for the ambience, the fine service, and the more modern flavors.

Trattoria Anna Maria, Via delle Belle Arti 17a, tel. 051/266894. Closed Monday. All credit cards. Moderate.

Near the opera house and the university you find chorus members and divas, professors, and the occasional students who come for solid food and a warm welcome from Anna Maria. The *ragù* is excellent, as are the lasagne and the tortellini, which you might have the occasion to see being made in the back room.

Trattoria Serghei, Via Piella 12, tel. 051/233533. Closed Saturday, Sunday, August, and the week around New Year. All credit cards. Moderate.

The fact that this restaurant has been in the same family for decades means that older recipes are still prepared that might have vanished elsewhere. The soups are delicious, the pasta is homemade, pork loin is slow-cooked in milk and *zucchine* (courgettes) are stuffed with meat and delicately cooked.

Osteria da Madon, Via San Vitale 75. Open Monday–Thursday until 2h, Friday and Saturday until 3h; closed Sunday. All credit cards. Moderate.

Popular with women, especially students and professors from the university. Has tasty dishes and a discreet wine list with bottles from Romagna and Trentino.

In Bologna tortellini are made by hand

FOOD SHOPPING

You are in paradise: nowhere will you find higher quality in stores and markets, nor will you ever meet people with a deeper understanding of the properties and virtues of ingredients. Most shops and markets are closed on Thursday afternoon and Sunday. There are outstanding old markets and stalls (dating back to the Middle Ages) in the streets behind Tamburini (see below) that you should devote a morning to visiting and observing. You should walk on Via Drapperie, Via Caprarie, Via Pescherie Vecchie, Via Clavature, and many more. Then walk down Via Rizzoli toward the Piazza Maggiore. Via Rizzoli changes names and becomes Via Ugo Bassi. At Via dell' Indipendenza walk past the McDonald's (the place strikes right at the heart of thousands of Bolognese gastronomes). A few blocks down Ugo Bassi is another great market (officially the Mercato delle Erbe, but more often called the Ugo Bassi market), this one covered, with even more wonderful foods in staggering abundance. Wherever you walk notice the courtesy and pride of the shopkeepers and the fierce dedication to quality on their part and on that of the shoppers. You will never shop for food in the same way again.

Tamburini, Via Caprarie 1, tel. 051/234726, fax 051/232226.

One of the best food stores you will ever set foot in. You can easily spot it because a nun or monk always sits just outside collecting contributions. This is a real emporium of cuisine, especially that of Emilia-Romagna. The goal here is to make food as it was done once upon a time: without shortcuts, without additives, and with love. The Tamburinis follow ancient traditions even if modern technology such as refrigeration may give them more opportunities. For example, they will use only pigs slaughtered in the winter because it was customary, for hygienic reasons, to do the slaughtering in cold weather. Giovanni Tamburini bemoans the disappearance of old customs that were born when farmers were poorer and therefore closer to the rhythms and dictates of nature. He is not advocating a return to poverty, but a rediscovery of the knowledge of food and agriculture that the poor farmers once had. As he said to me, "In the future the land will still be there but it will not be able to speak." The store has been in the family since 1932, but food has been sold at this site for centuries. Around 1600 the great artist Caracci had his studio across the way, and he came to this shop to paint still lifes of slaughtered meat and portraits of the butchers at work. There are more than 150 different foods to taste and purchase here at any time. Not to miss during your visit to Bologna.

Polleria, Vicolo Ranocchi 4c.

Although you probably will not buy anything here, take a look at the range of chicken, poultry, and game birds and how they are displayed. It looks like a place Caracci might have painted.

La Baita Formaggi, Via Pescherie Veccbie 3a.

This is this shop where I got much of my cheese education. I have since found shops in Italy with more selection, but this one is distinguished for the quality of the product and the enthusiasm of the owners.

Salumeria Bruno e Franco, Via Oberdan 16, tel. 051/233692.

An excellent *salumeria* with a friendly and knowledgeable staff and top-quality merchandise. It sells a fine *salamoia* (a blend of coarse salt and herbs favored in Bologna's kitchens).

ICE CREAM
Gelateria Moline, Via delle Moline 13 (three short blocks from Via dell' Indipendenza). Closed Tuesday.

Pure and simple, this is a neighborhood place that produces delicious ice cream, particularly cream flavors such as *crema, cioccolato, nocciola,* and *stracciatella.*

La Sorbetteria, Via Castiglione 44

Serves superb ice cream.

SPECIAL STORES
Ferramenta San Martino, Via Oberdan 11. Closed Saturday afternoon and Sunday.

A dazzling array of metal items huge and small, many with uses in the kitchen. There are nozzles for pastry cream decoration, butter dishes, coffeemakers, cookie molds, and much more. A wonderful showcase of the Italian creative mind.

Torrefazone Filicori e Zecchini (corner of Via Calzoliere and Via degli Orefici), tel. 051/236 720.

The fragrance sings to you as you approach.

Borgotaro (Parma)

DINING

Ristorante Sant'Adone, Porciagatone (just outside Borgotaro), tel. 0525/ 998148. Closed Wednesday October 10–June 20. No credit cards. Moderate.

Borgotaro is very famous for its *funghi* *porcini*, and you should make them a centerpiece of your meal. Be sure to try *minestra dei carbonai*, an ancient recipe from these parts that is a mushroom-and-potato soup. There are fresh pastas with mushrooms, meat with mushrooms, and grilled or fried mushrooms.

Busseto (Parma)

HOTEL AND RESTAURANT

I Due Foscari, Piazza Carlo Rossi 15, tel. 0524/92205. All credit cards. Moderate to moderately expensive.

Owned and operated by the great tenor Carlo Bergonzi and his family, this place combines a visit to Verdi sites in Roncole, Sant'Agata, and Busseto with delicious food and a friendly welcome. Try the *caramelle verdi*, which is *pasta sfoglia* wrapped around a meat filling—it looks like a wrapped candy, hence the name. The Parmigiano-Reggiano is good here, which should not surprise you— Bergonzi's father was a cheese maker. To visit Verdi's birthplace in Roncole Verdi, note that it is open 9–12h, 15–19h (March–September) and 9:30–12h, 14:30–17h (October, November). Closed Monday and December 1– February 28. Also visit the Church of San Michele, with the organ on which Verdi first learned music.

Cafragna di Talignano (Parma)

DINING

Trattoria di Cafragna, tel. 0525/2363. Closed Sunday evening (and afternoon in July), Monday, August, and from Christmas to mid-January. All credit cards. Moderate.

A pleasant country restaurant popular with people from Parma. There are many good dishes, including *risotto al tartufo* (the house specialty, with truffles and lots of Parmigiano-Reggiano), *fegato d'oca* (fresh goose liver) with *aceto balsamico, anolini in brodo*, tagliatelle with *salame di Felino*, local *faraona*, and excellent Parmigiano-Reggiano, even by local standards. Adele Camorali Padovani, who inherited this restaurant from her grandmother, has beautiful eyes and a ready smile. Her husband Giancarlo is the talented, but very thin, chef. How does he resist this food? An excellent wine list.

Cattolica (Rimini)

Many young people live and work here as waiters, cooks, and lifeguards in the summer tourist season and then go to live in colonies in Bali or India for the other eight months of the year. So if you see more than the usual amount of sarongs and tie-dyed shirts, you now know why.

BAKERY

Pasticceria Millevoglie, Via Matteotti 12 (corner of Via Corridoni), tel. 0541/954545. Closed Tuesday.

If you have been up all night at the disco on Saturday or Sunday, come here at 4h for a popular treat: *bomboloni con crema calda*, which are like large doughnuts or cream puffs filled with hot pastry cream. Sinfully delicious. There are good pastries to be had all day, and coffee too.

BAR

Caffè Gambrinus, Via Mancini, tel. 0541/960222. Closed Tuesday October–April.

A stylish bar opened in 1927 and restored in 1984. Good for breakfast, coffee, the afternoon *aperitivo*, and snacks.

MARKET

The Mercato Comunale, built in 1929, is a triumph of Fascist architecture. It is also a small, festive covered market that has excellent products, including *piadina*, baked goods, and roast chicken. Outside is a separate fish market held each morning. In addition to being a popular resort, Cattolica is a major fishing port.

Dozza (Bologna)

This little town of nine hundred citizens sits high on a hill with a view of Albana vineyards in the limpid hills below. There is good food, a restful hotel, a wonderful castle containing an interesting display of peasant life, and an excellent *enoteca* that should be on your itinerary to learn more about the little-known wines of Emilia-Romagna.

DINING

Ristorante Canè, Via XX Settembre 27, tel. 0542/678120. Closed Monday. All credit cards. Moderate.

Very good food—I am still savoring the superb *pollo alla diavola*. If you are hungry, as you should be, try the *menu degustazione*, with an antipasto, two tastes of pasta, and two *secondi,* plus dessert. The price for this is very fair.

ENOTECA PUBBLICA
Enoteca Regionale Emilia-Romagna, Rocca Sforzesca. Open 10–12h, 15–18h, Saturday and Sunday until 19h; closed Monday.

This welcoming and very well run *enoteca* is the perfect place to learn about the wines of Emilia-Romagna, which have been saddled with an undeservedly bad reputation. True, they are not up to the level of this region's fabulous cuisine, but they have improved a lot in recent years and are very fine, especially the Sangiovese, Albana, and some Lambruscos that are seldom exported. All are for sale here. There are interesting exhibits of life in former times in a section of the castle called the Museo di Civiltà Contadina. Make sure to visit the old kitchen, room 21, of the castle. Notice the ovens, old equipment, the well for water, and the dumbwaiter that was used to send food to the upper quarters. The walls of this kitchen are gray because of centuries of cooking smoke that issued from the oven.

HOTEL
Monte del Re, tel. 0542/678400, fax 0542/678444. American Express, MasterCard, Visa. Moderate to moderately expensive.

On a hill facing Dozza is this nice hotel in a villa, with fine service and tranquil views. If you have a car this is a good base for touring Romagna, but worth the price if you are seeking a restful spot. Notice the olive trees in the garden.

Faenza (Ravenna)

This city is world famous for its ceramics, known abroad as faience. You should visit the Museo Internazionale della Ceramica at Via Campidori 2 (closed Sunday afternoon and Monday) to see examples of the artistry of Faenza ceramists from the Renaissance to the present. There are many shops in town that sell ceramics. I suggest you begin at the showroom of the cooperative of ceramic producers at Corso Mazzini 72A (near Via Cavour, tel. 0546/29356, open 9h–12:30h, 15h–19:15h). This showroom has gathered some of the best of local producers since 1945 and can arrange to pack and ship your purchases for you. While in town, go to the Voltone della Molinella that connects the Piazza del Popolo and the Piazzetta Nenni (to the right of the Teatro Comunale Masini). Make note of the beautiful vaulted ceiling with two twelve-rib fans spreading from the central arch. It is a work of great beauty worthy of close inspection. Beneath it is a nice ceramics shop.

DINING
Trattoria Baia del Re, Via Marcucci 71, tel. 0546/681351. Closed Tuesday. No credit cards. Inexpensive.

This is not a dining paradise, but very much a neighborhood place down a side street that a tourist would never explore. The entrance is in the alley next to the house at #73 with the lace curtains. In addition to the kitchen, there is a grill in the dining room, where delicious sausage, ham, turkey, and steaks are cooked. For a primo, go for the minestrone or *cappelletti in brodo* instead of the pasta. The delicious olive oil is from nearby Brisighella. Here one glass serves for both wine and water, and you should hang on to your fork from one course to the next. The waitresses writes what you consume on a piece of paper that is placed under your saltshaker. At the end of the meal, take the paper to the bar to pay. This is the way things work in many inexpensive eateries in Italy, so you will also be able to absorb some local culture.

Enoteca Ristorante Astorre, Piazza della Libertà 16, tel. 0546/681417. Open 11–15h, 18–1h, ***kitchen until 23h. No credit cards. Moderately inexpensive.***

A very pleasing place for good wine and light food. The two front rooms are done in Liberty style, while the third has frescoes from the seventeenth century.

Trattoria Marianaza, Via Torricelli 21, tel. 0546/681461. Closed Wednesday, and from mid-July to mid-August. All credit cards. Moderate.

I adore the *crostini di polenta con squacquerone,* little cubes of polenta with the addictive local creamy-white cheese. The tagliatelle are excellent here too, as are the *garganelli* with prosciutto and peas. Grilled meats of all kinds are the preferred secondo, though I also admire the *coniglio ripieno* (stuffed rabbit).

Felino (Parma)

If you come to this famous *salame* making town, a good place to eat is the moderately priced Antica Osteria da Bianchini (Via Marconi 4a; tel. 0521/831165). Excellent dishes include *anolini, tortelli, stracotto, cotechino,* and, of course, *salame.*

Ferrara

As the duchy of the Este family, Ferrara was one of the most brilliant centers of the Renaissance. Writers such as Petrarch, Ariosto, and Tasso were welcomed, and architects created a city of great splendor. The city declined in the seventeenth and eighteenth centuries but later came back. It had one of the foremost Jewish communities in Italy, which was instrumental in Ferrara's reflowering. Most of the Jews were captured and killed during the Second World War, a tragedy depicted in the great film *The Garden of the Finzi Continis.* Ferrara was also one of the most important centers of the Italian Resistance, a story that is movingly documented in the Museo del Risorgimento e della Resistenza. Ferrara is a great place to eat too, starting with the pumpkin-filled *cappellacci con la zucca,* the delicious *salama da sugo,* and *pampepato.*

BAKERIES-BARS
Pasticceria Centro Storico, Corso ***Martiri della Libertà 16, tel. 0532/205785. Closed Tuesday.***

A nice bar for breakfast. Try the *pasta al riso*, a semisweet pastry with a flaky crust. You can also buy *pampepato*.

Caffè-Pasticceria Europa, Corso Giovecca 51, tel. 0532/207408. Open 7–13:30h, 15–21h; closed Wednesday.

A short walk from the Teatro Comunale is this nice place for coffee and small pastries.

DINING

Osteria al Brindisi, Via Adelardi 11, tel. 0532/209142. Open 8–20:30h; closed Monday. No credit cards. Moderately inexpensive.

The oldest *osteria* in Italy is a Ferrara institution. There is good wine and cold food to be had, but for hot dishes you need to reserve ahead. One specialty is *pasticcio di maccheroni alla ferrarese*, a baked *maccheroni* and meat sauce served in a crust. If you order it with *pasta sfoglia*, the crust has some salt. With *pasta frolla* the crust is sweet. There is also *salama da sugo*, *casetto* cheese, and several good desserts.

Antica Trattoria Volano, Via Volano 20 (corner of Via Bologna), tel. 0532/761421. Closed Friday. All credit cards. Moderate to moderately expensive.

The ideal place to taste Ferrarese food. Wonderful *salama da sugo*, very good *cappellacci di zucca*. Also good are the homemade *tagliatelle al prosciutto* and *pasticcio di maccheroni alla ferrarese, funghi e polenta*, and *bolliti* or *arrosti*. There are two good set menus at very reasonable prices, but they may not contain some of the dishes you will want to taste. Skip the house wine and order a bottle off the list from either Emilia-Romagna or Friuli.

Antica Trattoria Il Cucco, Via Voltacassotta 3, tel. 0532/760026. Closed Wednesday. No credit cards. Inexpensive.

In a very old quarter of town, where many houses are in disrepair. In fact, this place is frequented by young men with dusty shoes who are busy restoring nearby buildings. Good pastas include *cappellacci* with a creamy pumpkin filling and ravioli Giuseppe Verdi, filled with eggplant and ricotta and topped with a sauce of cream, prosciutto, mushrooms, and asparagus. *Salama da sugo* is available only by advance reservation.

FOOD SHOPPING

Most food stores in Ferrara are closed on Thursday afternoon and Sunday.

Mercato Comunale. Corner of Via del Mercato and Via Santo Stefano. Open mornings Monday–Saturday, Friday afternoon 16:30–19h.

Among the many highlights here is stand 23, a veritable showcase of vegetables in their prime, not far from at least ten stands full of gorgeous fruit. At one wall is the Carni Suini shop, where you can have an anatomy lesson on the pig and see how it is used in local cuisine.

Drogheria Bazzi, Piazza del Municipio 18.

A nice, old-style *drogheria* that sells candies, pasta, wine, cornmeal, *pampepato*, and jams from local farms.

Negozio Moccia, Via Spadari 19, tel. 0532/209772. Closed Sunday.

A famous supplier of *pampepato* since 1947. Also sells liqueurs, wines, candies, and other cakes.

Goloseria, Via Garibaldi 27, tel. 0532/25316.

A specialist in *salama al sugo*. It also has big, beautiful mortadellas, cheeses, *salame all'aglio*, superb *funghi porcini*, and other delicacies.

Salumificio Bonfatti, Via Boito 30, tel. 0532/96740.

Excellent *salama al sugo, salame all'aglio*, and other good pork products.

Salumificio Estense, Viale Volano 185, tel. 0532/61444.

Makes outstanding *salumi*, but since the shop is rather out of the way (on a tributary of the Po River), you should only journey here if you plan to purchase.

Panificio Orsatti, Via Corte Vecchia 13.

Ferrara is famous for its breads, which are often dry. They make a good counterpoint to the rich cuisine. The most typical Ferrara bread is the *coppia*, which has two curving breads joined like Siamese twins.

Bottega del Formaggio, Via Corta Vecchia 18.

An excellent source for Parmigiano-Reggiano and *cassetto*.

Fontanellato (Parma)

Come here on a Thursday morning to have a wonderful view of small-town Emilia. There is a great little market that draws people from the surrounding countryside to buy food, clothing, and housewares. That the market lines a moat that protects a castle begun around the year 1000 and occupied three centuries later is an added attraction. After walking around the market (and stopping for a sandwich or other good prepared foods at Gastronomia al Portico, Via San Vitale 5), visit the castle, which belonged to the Sanvitali family until the early part of the twentieth century. There is period furniture from 1500 and armaments from 1500 to 1800. Then go to the dining room (the Sala da Pranzo) with five-hundred-year-old ceramics, walls full of old plates, and two large still lifes by Felice Roselli (1690). All of this tells you about an important change in eating habits. Before this time, Italians ate all their food off one plate. Then around the sixteenth century there was a shift, and different courses and foods were eaten on different plates. The idea of separating foods so that they can be visually and then orally appreciated as individual entities is central to the way Italians approach food. The Sanvitalis were open-minded and progressive, so they were not oppressors of the people of the area. The agriculture of the surrounding zone served to enrich the Sanvitalis, and they used this wealth to acquire art and encourage musicians. Note the music room, and visit the seventh room, a small sitting room with a 1524 Parmigianino fresco depicting scenes from Ovid's *Metamorphosis*. If you happen to come to Fontanelleto on the third Sunday of the month (except in January), the food market will be closed, but you will find an excellent antiques market.

Forlì

COOKING SCHOOL

I Sapori, Piazzale della Vittoria 1, 47100 Forlì, tel. 0543/35770.

Pasta! This is the reason to come to I Sapori (the Flavors). You can learn to make tortellini, tortelloni, ravioli, tagliatelle, lasagne, and other fresh pastas. There are also courses in other dishes of Romagna, holiday cooking, low-fat dishes, and wine. Many foreign students enroll here.

Forlimpopoli (Forlì)

Forlimpopoli is the hometown of Pellegrino Artusi (1820–1911), author of *La Scienza in Cucina e l'Arte del Mangiar Bene (Science in the Kitchen and the Art of Eating Well)*, first published in 1891 and still very much in print. It is to Italians what *Joy of Cooking* is to Americans. Some of the recipes may seem archaic, but it is still the touchstone for anyone beginning to explore Italian cooking. Almost every household where there is someone interested in cooking has a copy of *l'Artusi*, as Italians call the book. He viewed cuisine as an ongoing discussion of science, of culture, and of art, and his influence was enormous. He was a scholar in many areas and also produced an excellent biography of Ugo Foscolo (1778–1827), one of Italy's foremost poets and patriots.

COOKING SCHOOL

Circolo Culturale Il Dibattito, Piazza Garibaldi 3, 47100 Forlimpopoli (FO), tel. 0543/68399.

This school is really an extension of the art and thinking of Artusi. Here one not only learns to cook, but engages in thought and discussion (*il dibattito* means "the debate"). Courses are given in autumn, winter, and spring, changing with the season and with the interests of the available instructors. You will invariably meet Artusian scholars in this hotbed of food cultists. Excursions to wineries and typical restaurants are part of many courses here.

Lugo (Ravenna)

DINING

Antica Trattoria del Teatro, Vicolo del Teatro 6, tel. 0545/35164. Closed Monday. All credit cards. Moderately inexpensive to moderate.

Soups are a specialty here, including *passatelli* in broth and leek soup *(zuppa di porri)*. The pasta to choose is the homemade *garganelli*, either in a *ragù* or a duck sauce *(sugo di anatra)*. *Secondi* are good roasts and boiled meats.

WINE

Enoteca La Felce, Via Tellarini 15, tel. 0545/24003. Closed Thursday afternoon, Sunday, and in August.

National wines and spirits, twenty-seven olive oils (some from nearby Brisighella), good pasta and rice.

Modena

Fancy cars, fabulous opera singers, rich Lambrusco, sensational food, and adorable people. What more can one say about Modena? *Aceto balsamico*, that's what. Balsamic vinegar has been all the rage since it was first introduced to the world a decade or so ago. But, like many great food products, it is little understood and badly misused. Calling *aceto balsamico* vinegar is like calling Pavarotti a street singer. *Aceto balsamico* is an ambrosial liquid that is used as a condiment to exalt almost anything it touches: Parmigiano-Reggiano cheese, potatoes, meat, poultry, even strawberries.

The vinegar is made only from the juice of Trebbiano grapes, and a "mother" (an old vinegar) is never used to start the process going, as it is elsewhere. Real *aceto balsamico* goes through up to twelve years of fining, being put in different barrels from year to year to absorb the essences of barrels made of different woods. The consortium that governs the quality of *aceto balsamico* grades the product, rejecting fully 80 percent as unacceptable. To assure fairness, they put tall boards up between tasters so that facial expressions cannot be read. Only *modenese balsamico* is considered by the consortium, despite justifiable complaints from producers in Reggio Emilia, where the tradition is nearly as great. Once you taste real *aceto balsamico*, which is very costly and served in drops packed with memorable flavor, you will never be able to abide the three-dollar imitations found in supermarkets outside of Italy. Buy a bottle of real *aceto balsamico* in Italy and use it at home.

COOKING SCHOOL

La Cucina di Petronilla, Via F Selmi 20, 41100 Modena, tel. 059/220789.

The cuisine of Emilia-Romagna, expertly taught. What more could one ask?

DINING

Hosteria Giusti, Vicolo Squallore 46, tel./ fax 059/222533. Reservations essential. Open for lunch only; closed Sunday, Monday, August, December. All credit cards. Moderate (but actually priceless).

As I was completing the updating of this guide in the autumn of 2005, the sad news arrived that Adriano (Nano) Morandi, the owner of Hosteria Giusti, had suddenly died at a too-young age. Nano and his wife Laura ran this place with the most incredible passion and devotion to quality. When I met him in the early 1980s he had just taken over the Salumeria Giuseppe Giusti which, since 1605, had been a purveyor of the most sublime *salumi*, Parmigiano-Reggiano, pasta and a maker of superb *aceto balsamico tradizionale*. Nano was employed by the Giustis and they entrusted him to continue the tradition so that the hosteria became a mecca for people who cared about the best of Italian products. At five tables in the back of the store one could feast on Laura's food, which Nano would lovingly serve and describe. In the spring of 2005, the city of Modena honored Hosteria Giusti and the Morandi family for their service to Italian food culture. I encourage readers to visit, to purchase their heavenly products and, if you can book a table, to savor a divine lunch. This would be a fitting tribute to one of Italy's great men of food culture and would help the Morandi family to build on the legacy he created.

Trattoria Ermes, Via Ganaceto 89, no telephone. Open for lunch only, Monday through Saturday; closed in August. No credit cards. Inexpensive.

In the Italy of a few decades ago it was common to eat lunch in trattorias such as this one, with communal tables and open bottles of wine that are passed round. The menu would be limited to a few items, all prepared with loving, accurate care by a smiling woman in the kitchen, whose name in this case is Bruna. There would be a *primo, secondo, contorno,* fruit, wine, water, and coffee. The food would be served by a smiling husband (his name is Ermes) and you felt, for an hour, like a member of an ideal family. Such places were common in my university days in the 1970s, but now are quite rare and deserve recognition and preservation as landmarks of when food was valued as sustenance and shared with a larger family, which is to say one's fellow human beings.

Trattoria Aldina, Via Albinelli 40, tel. 059/ 236106. Open for lunch only, Monday through Saturday. No credit cards. Inexpensive to moderately inexpensive.

Similar to Trattoria Ermes in being a local treasure serving lunch to a diverse crowd, but on a larger scale. The Gherardini family, with Maria Pia in the kitchen, serves excellent pastas (especially the lasagne, tortellini and ravioli, which come in a sauce of cream and pancetta). Secondi of meat and vegetable side dishes are tasty, and I enjoy the homemade fruit *crostata* to conclude a meal.

Oreste, Piazza Roma 31, tel./fax 059/ 243324. Closed Wednesday, Sunday evening, much of July, and the last week of the year. All credit cards. Moderate to moderately expensive.

Good homemade dishes are served in this restaurant which is conveniently open when many others are closed.

Nonantola (Modena)

Osteria di Rubbiara, Via Risaia 2, tel. 059/ 549019. Open for lunch Wednesday– Monday and, on Friday and Saturday, for dinner too. Closed in August and mid-Dec to mid-Jan. No credit cards. Moderate.

The excellent *aceto balsamico* is at the base of many of the traditional dishes served at this popular country restaurant.

Parma

Parma, an exquisite city of 200,000, is not to be missed by anyone who loves Italian food, elegance, hospitality, and life lived in a gracious and congenial way. The *parmigiani* are generally conceded to be the most elegant people in this very elegant nation. This is not merely a matter of wearing the latest fashions, but is owing to the fact that the city has been a style setter for centuries. The Farnese family (which counted popes among its sons) ruled from 1513 to 1727, encouraging artists and scholars to bring beauty to the Duchy of Parma. The local predisposition for refinement continued under the enlightened reign of the Bourbons (1731–1801), who brought French taste and left the local dialect with a distinctly French accent. They also had a love of grandeur and there is palpable evidence of this in the form of palaces and stately gardens that are so much a part of the cityscape. Shortly after Bourbon rule began, *La Gazzetta di Parma,* Italy's oldest newspaper, was born, offering the populace an exchange of information and ideas that made Parma a hub for thinkers and trendsetters for most of the eighteenth century. While much of Italy underwent turmoil and chaos during the revolutionary struggles of the nineteenth century, Parma rose to greater glory under the reasoned government of Napoleon's wife, Marie-Louise, who is still lovingly referred to as Maria Luigia. From 1815 to her death in 1847, Parma was renowned for her civic works. Libraries, schools, and art galleries opened, and creativity was encouraged.

In 1813, just before Maria Luigia arrived, Parma's most brilliant son was born. Giuseppe Verdi, who was from nearby Roncole, went on to become Italy's greatest composer and, ironically, one of the leaders of the national unification movement that led to the end of the glorious Duchy of Parma. Although he worked in Milano, Venezia, Paris, and other cities, Verdi remained near Parma for most of his life (he died in 1901). The citizens of Parma claim him as their own (whenever you hear someone in Parma refer to Peppino, they are talking about Giuseppe Verdi), and it is difficult to go a few steps without seeing a likeness of Verdi or hearing the strains of his music. But this being Parma, there are no tacky Verdi posters and T-shirts for tourists, but rather beautiful lithographs and carefully chiseled busts made of sublime chocolate at the city's finest sweet shop, the Pasticceria Torino.

In 1829, under the patronage of Maria Luigia, the Teatro Regio opened. This opera house is painted an egg-yolk color that is universally known as Parma yellow. Many of the public buildings are this color. They take on particular luster on sunny days and project a welcoming warmth on the misty days that enshroud Parma in late autumn. The Teatro Regio has the most knowledgeable and exacting audience in Italy, and attending a performance there is every bit as memorable as a night at La Scala or the Metropolitan Opera. Not surprisingly, productions of Verdi operas are first-rate. The Teatro Regio's fame is actually due less to Verdi than to another native son, Arturo Toscanini (1867–1957), the greatest conductor Italy has ever produced. The maestro knew Verdi, Puccini, and all of Italy's finest

Faenza, Emilia-Romagna

composers and musicians. You should not be surprised to see many music students in Parma, whose conservatory is a mecca for young singers and instrumentalists.

But how long can one describe Parma without mentioning its cuisine, which is reason enough to journey from very far away? The mere mention of the Parmigiano-Reggiano cheese, prosciutto, and superb pastas that one finds on every table in Parma is enough to make mouths water and stomachs growl with anticipation. Gourmets in Italy will tell you that Parma's only rivals in gastronomy are nearby Bologna and Modena. Indeed, one of the chief tourist attractions of Parma is its markets, food stores, and restaurants. What makes Parma distinct are its remarkable local food products. Pride of place belongs to Parmigiano Reggiano, the king of cheeses, but there is also *culatello*, sublime prosciutto, all sorts of dairy products, and excellent vegetables. There is talk of opening a museum dedicated to these products, so inquire when you are in town.

Barilla, Italy's largest pasta producer, is based in Parma. This company, the giant Parmalat food conglomerate, and the consortiums of cheese and prosciutto producers are the modern patrons who fund the arts and cultural activities for which Parma remains pre-eminent. So you may congratulate yourself with the knowledge that with every bite of cheese, ham, and pasta you have in Parma you are striking a blow for civilization. It is nearly impossible to find a bad meal in Parma and you can work off your calories by strolling through the streets of the old city. Here you will see elegant women walking arm in arm and clusters of men standing under an arcade discussing politics, sports, or, more likely, what they hope to have for dinner.

Visit the Piazza del Duomo, with the beautiful cathedral and world-famous octagonal baptistery completed in 1196. Go toward the river on any morning except Sunday to see the animated scene of the fruit and vegetable markets of the Piazza Ghiaia. Nearby is the Palazzo della Pilotta, which houses the Teatro Farnese (1617), the first theater ever designed to accommodate moving scenery. There is also a worthy art collection in the palace. At 5:00 p.m., walk down the Via Cavour or the Via Garibaldi as all of Parma comes out for its afternoon promenade. Before leaving Parma, stop at the Gastronomia Garibaldi near the train station to pick up a wedge of Parmigiano-Reggiano and some prosciutto to provide an aftertaste of this noble city that will linger in your thoughts and in your mouth long after you have gone.

BARS AND BAKERIES

Pasticceria Torino, Via Garibaldi 61. Closed Sunday afternoon and Monday.

Perhaps the best bakery in the city. Breakfast here on scrumptious pastries and perfect coffee. Except in the hot months it is possible to purchase a chocolate bust of Giuseppe Verdi. Ask for a *Peppino cioccolato.*

CULTURE

Teatro Regio, Via Garibaldi 16a, 43100 Parma, tel. 0521/795685, fax 0521/795216.

As befits the place that has given the world Verdi and Toscanini, Parma has an excellent opera season with a very discerning audience.

DINING

Ristorante Parizzi, Via Repubblica 71, tel. 0521/285952. Closed Monday, Christmas, one week in January, and three in August. All credit cards. Moderately expensive.

This restaurant is a stronghold of Parma cookery, accented with a few innovative touches. *Affettato misto* and *tortelli d'erbette* are outstanding, though I would skip the *melanzane alla parmigiana.*

Trattoria Corrieri, Via Conservatorio 1, tel. 0521/234426. Closed Sunday. All credit cards. Moderate.

A popular trattoria near Parma's excellent music conservatory.

Ristorante Coccbi, Hotel Daniel, Via Gramsci 16a, tel. 0521/995147. All credit cards. Moderately expensive.

Delicious food, lovingly prepared and served. The *tortelli di patate e funghi* are wonderful.

Trattoria del Tribunale, Vicolo Politi 5, tel. 0521/285527. Closed Tuesday and, in the summer, on Monday, plus Christmas-time and much of August. All credit cards. Moderate.

Parma's traditional dishes are all here, and I also like the *guancialetti di vitello* (braised veal cheeks). For dessert, do a *degustazione del Parmigiano-Reggiano*, sampling the cheese at different states of aging.

Antica Cereria, Borgo Tanzi 5, tel. 0521/207387. Open for dinner Tuesday through Sunday, and Sunday lunch too. All credit cards. Moderate.

Near the birth house of Arturo Toscanini is this trattoria with the Parma classics. I like the *zuppa di carote* (carrot soup).

Il Cortile, Borgo Paglia 3, tel. 0521/285779. Closed Sunday, Christmas week, and mid-August. All credit cards. Moderately inexpensive.

Another good choice for local specialties.

FOOD FAIR

Cibus, held each year in early May, is the largest in Italy and the third largest in Europe after those of Cologne and Paris.

FOOD SHOPPING

Gastronomia Garibaldi, Via Garibaldi 42, tel. 0521/235606. Closed Sunday.

Superb cheese, *salumi*, and prepared foods. You can gather the fixings for many divine meals here. The *gastronomia* will vacuum-pack your Parmigiano to take home.

Specialità di Parma, Via Farini 9c, tel. 0521/233591.

Pastas, *salumi*, and other great foods.

Piacenza

Piacenza is known as La Primogenita (the Firstborn) because it was the first city to join the united Italy of the 1860s. The city has old and strong ties to France, which ruled here about two hundred years ago. The local dialect has a distinctly French sound, and there is more than the usual amount of butter in the food. Many names in the phone book are French, and it is still customary for French people to come to Piacenza to marry local spouses.

DINING

Trattoria Santo Stefano, Cantone Santo Stefano 22, tel. 0523/27802. Closed Sunday. All credit cards. Moderately expensive.

A renowned place to dine, which may surprise you when you see how unpretentious it is. You begin with *affettate miste: coppa piacentina* (the local *salame*), lard, other *salami*, *pancetta*, and prosciutto. All the pastas and soups are excellent: lasagne, tagliatelle, *tortelli*, minestrone, *pasta e fagioli*. Then come delicately tender braised meats such as *puledro* (pony), *cavallo* (horse), *asino*. The wines and desserts are quite fine.

Polesine Parmense (Parma)

DINING

Al Cavallino Bianco, Via Sbrisi 2, tel. 0524/96136. All credit cards. Moderately expensive.

A special restaurant on the banks of the Po River. The grounds are tranquil and beautiful, full of slender trees that go right to the edge of Italy's largest river. You will often see a white pony *(cavallino bianco)* grazing nearby. If for no other reason, you should come here to taste the *culatello*, the divine ham that the proprietors make themselves. You will also be served magnificent chunks of Parmigiano-Reggiano. The pasta here is superb, especially the *tortelli d'erbette*. If you are lucky, there might be fresh sturgeon *(storione alla brace)* from the river, which is outstanding when grilled and served with a bit of olive oil and tarragon. There is a good wine list, and the homemade liqueurs are interesting, particularly the *sburlon*, which is made with quince. Service here is friendly and accurate.

Ravenna

Because Ravenna has Italy's most beautiful mosaics, a legacy of when the city was the western capital of the Byzantine Empire, visitors overlook its other charms, including excellent food and one of the foremost arts festivals in Italy. Ravenna has one of the leading music festivals early each summer, when Maestro Riccardo Muti is in residence. (For information contact Ravenna Festival, Via Gordini 27, 48100 Ravenna, tel. 0544/32577 or 482494, fax 0544/36303.) This is a provincial city of 135,000 persons, but one of remarkable sophistication.

BAKERIES-BARS

Bar Pasticceria Dolce Arte, Via IV November 20, tel. 0544/3551. Open 7–13h, 15:30–20h; closed Thursday.

Excellent coffee here accompanies delicious pastries, such as *tortelli* filled with prune jam or cream. This is a popular place with the ladies of Ravenna.

Pasticceria Calderoni, Viale Farini 28. Open 7:30–13:30h, 15:30–20h; closed Monday.

Near the train station, this is a good spot for breakfast. The coffee is delicious, and the flaky brioches are filled either with pastry cream, apricot jam, or apples.

DINING

Trattoria al Chilò, Via Maggiore 62, tel. 0544/36206. Closed Monday. All credit cards. Moderately inexpensive to moderate.

Really delicious food in an unreconstructed, old-fashioned setting. The long room seems little changed from the restaurant's opening in 1929 and has great charm. Among the delicious pastas are *cappelletti alle erbe profumate* (with herbs and a melted cheese filling) and superb *tortellaci di ricotta al vitello e carciofi* (cheese-filled pasta tossed with bits of veal and artichoke).

La Gardéla, Via Ponte Marino 3, tel. 0544/217147. Closed Thursday, mid-January, and mid-June. All credit cards. Moderately inexpensive.

Careful preparation of local specialties, especially meat and mushrooms.

Ca de Ven, Via Ricci 24, tel. 0544/30163. Closed Monday. Moderate.

A very traditional osteria. Worth visiting before or after a performance at the renowned Ravenna music festival.

FOOD SHOPPING

Mercato Comunale, Piazza Andrea Costa. Open 7–14h, Friday 16:30–19:30h; closed Sunday.

The food market is housed in a neoclassical eighteenth-century structure on Piazza Andrea Costa. At one end of the market is a shop that neatly displays all of the classical Emilia-Romagna pastas, handmade, of course. This is a good lesson in the pastas of this region. It also sells fresh hot *piadina.* To the right is a small bread and pastry shop of note. Farther right, at Box 46, is Carmen, a shop with fried goods such as nuts, beans, fruits, and herbs. Again, here is a good lesson in the names and types of different foods. Look for Box 10, where Formaggi dalla Maria has excellent wheels of aged Parmigiano and meltingly delicious fresh ricotta.

Gastronomia Marchesini, Via Mazzini 2, tel. 0544/22309.

A superb food store, worth a visit on its own. One is almost tempted to call it a supermarket because it offers everything a one-stop shopper would want, but the quality and service are those of no supermarket I've ever encountered. All along the walls hang *prosciutti di Parma,* and theirs is the dominant, inviting fragrance as you enter the store. Marchesini also has first-rate meat from its own farm. In the back are prepared foods, such as soft polenta, sautéed *funghi porcini,* and vegetables that are stuffed, baked, or grilled. In the front are beautiful handmade pastas in little wooden boxes with screens on the bottom that permit the pasta to "breathe," I was told. There are select wines, pâtés, dried pastas, fish, marvelous cheeses, and sacks of choice fruit in this, one of Italy's finest food stores.

Ovosfoglia, Via IV Novembre 11, tel. 0544/38352. Open mornings Monday–Saturday, Friday 17–19h.

Excellent handmade pasta and local color.

SPECIAL STORE

La Butèga ad Giorgioni, Via IV Novembre 43, tel. 0544/212638. Closed Thursday afternoon and Sunday (except the third Sunday of the month, when Ravenna's outstanding antiques fair takes place).

This is the finest *erboristeria* I know in Italy. It is more than a century old and somehow evokes old-fashioned virtues and contemporary values. Here you purchase herbs and spices for cooking or curing ills, much as people did decades ago. You can purchase specially blended tisanes for complaints of the stomach, liver, nerves, lungs, or skin. There are herbal elixirs for coughs and rheumatism and many types of soap for different skin conditions. There are herbal hair colorings that have none of the artificial dyes found in commercial products. For cooking there are all kinds of spices, including *salamoia,* a foundation of most Ravenna dishes. To understand the role of the herbalist in Italian life, there is no better place to visit.

Reggio Emilia

Part of the appeal of Reggio Emilia is that it has all the classic features of Emilia, but has no tourists to speak of, unlike nearby Parma and Modena. It has an ancient rivalry with both cities and has somehow been lost in the shuffle as regards its famous food products. The cheese, after all, is called Parmigiano-Reggiano, but most people equate it only with Parma. The balsamic vinegar of Reggio is every bit as good as that of Modena. Reggio remains one of the most left-wing cities in Italy (in all of Europe, in fact), and it has Italy's best schools. The people are warm and sweet and love to share their food and their little paradise with visitors.

DINING

Trattoria della Ghiara, Vicolo Folletto 1c, tel. 0522/435755. Closed Sunday, August, and the Christmas period. MasterCard, Visa. Moderate.

Lovely pastas, excellent *spalla di San Secondo* (pork shoulder that was Verdi's favorite dish), and a perfect *frittata con cipolla all'aceto balsamico tradizionale.*

Ristorante a Mangiare, Viale Montegrappa 3a, tel. 0522/433600. Closed Sunday, one week in June, late August, and Christmas. All credit cards. Moderate.

There is a set menu with local specialties that varies with the season. I love the *spuma di parmigiano reggiano* with pear *mostarda.* Pastas are delicate and pork is often cooked in milk and flavored with *aceto balsamico tradizionale.*

FOOD SHOPPING

Panificio Canazzoni Piccinini, Via Emilia San Pietro 63. Open mornings only.

People crowd into this tiny shop for bread and breakfast rolls, plus *torta di riso.*

Salumeria Capelli, Via Emilia San Pietro 57d.

The lack of abundance does not mean a lack of quality.

Baby Market al Magazzino della Bomboniera, Via Emilia San Pietro 57.

A vast array of chocolates and *confetti* in this real old-style store run by a sweet elderly couple.

Casalinga, Via Antonio Franzoni 3b.

Within is a wonderful sight: seven women with aprons and bonnets stand around a small table rolling, stuffing, and cutting *cappelletti, tortelloni,* and noodles while laughing and talking. Even if you don't buy, it is worth a look. Walk half a block and turn right onto the Via Mario Calderini. At 4b is an unnamed housewares shop with all the basic items you would see in a typical Italian family kitchen.

Antica Salumeria Giorgio Pancaldi, corner of Via Broletto and Via del Carbone.

This magnificent *salumeria* should not be missed. Fabulous products are sold by lovely people. The big scale in the middle is used to weigh whole legs of prosciutto. In the Piazza San Prospero is the fruit and vegetable market. It is a lovely sight.

Salumeria San Prospero, Piazza San Prospero 1C.

Here is the balsamic vinegar made in Reggio Emilia, which is just as good as that made in Modena.

Gastronomia La Stiva, Piazza San Prospero.

Sells canned, preserved, and dried fish, all sorts of mushrooms, olives, onions, tomatoes, and an excellent *mostarda* to go with *salumi* you might buy nearby.

Panificio Melli, Piazza San Prospero and Via del Torrazzo.

Erbazzone plus superb breads, pasta, and *tortelli.*

Rimini

Full of seaside Romeos using their *motorini* instead of a steed to sweep up German and Scandinavian girls. There is a term for this type of young man, a *ragazzo da spiaggia*, which not only suggests a boy of the beach, but also someone who should not be taken seriously.

FOOD FAIR

Mostra Internazionale dell'Alimentazione. (For information contact Ente Automna Fiera, Via della Fiera 52, C.P. 300, 47037 Rimini, tel. 0541/711711, fax 0541/786686.)

A major fair is held in Rimini every February (when there is sometimes snow on the beach) that is for food professionals, especially those who work in restaurants and hotels that cater to tourists. Originally it was a major event for hoteliers on the Romagna Riviera, but now it has more than 100,000 visitors each year.

PIADINA

Ristorante Blu Line Garden, Via Tintori (opposite Bagno 18). Closed Wednesday. Inexpensive.

By the sea, near the Grand Hotel and the Parco Federico Fellini, is this snack bar. This is a spot of interest only as a source of *piadina* with typical fillings, such as cheeses, hams, *salumi,* and vegetables, and Nutella, the chocolate-hazelnut spread loved by every Italian child.

Sant'Agata di Villanova (Parma)

DINING

Trattoria La Verdiana, tel. 0523/830209. Closed Monday. No credit cards. Moderate.

Delicious food will reward diners at La Verdiana, near the home and farm where Giuseppe Verdi spent the last half of his life and composed most of his masterpieces. All the Parma classics—*tortelli*, prosciutto, *culatello*, fabulous cheeses—are here.

Sant'Arcangelo di Romagna (Rimini)

DINING
*Osteria La Sangiovesa, Via Saffi 27,
tel. 0541/620710. Open evenings
Tuesday–Sunday. No credit cards.
Moderate.*

With its depictions of busty women and
hearty men engaged in all manner of pleasurable pursuits, this place seems the em-
bodiment of Romagna. Food is similarly
robust, the wine is abundant.

MUSEUM
*Museo di Use e Costumi della Gente di
Romagna, Via Monte Vecchi 42.*

Probably the best collection about agricultural and traditional life in old Romagna.

Torriana (Rimini)

DINING
*Osteria I Malardot, Via Castello 35,
tel. 0541/675194. No credit cards.
Moderately inexpensive.*

Here is the place where you would encounter Falstaff if he were Italian. I Malardot
(dialect for "Misplaced," because it is high
up on a hill and quite out of the way) is everything an *osteria* should be. Your host,
Giancarlo, with his firm handshake and
graying hair askew, immediately makes you
feel welcome. The atmosphere is very casual—there is a big fireplace in one corner, a
cabinet in another with fading postcards
from famous authors such as Henry Miller,
Alberto Moravia, and Marcel Proust. At
the other end of the L-shaped room is a
stove with old-fashioned underwear hanging to dry. In the past one would trudge up
the hill in rain or snow to get here and then
hang one's drawers to dry while eating and
drinking. Look behind the broad bar at the
old scale, the antique refrigerator with windows and a dim lightbulb that reveals the
silhouettes of *salami* and *prosciutti*. Past the
black-and-white TV and the vintage radio
is a piano that you are encouraged to play.
Or you might prefer the two guitars awaiting an inspired musician. The food will not
disappoint: coarsely sliced *porchetta, salame,*
and mortadella and transparent *lardo* arrives
on wax paper to go with your wine. Then
there might be *pattacucci* (noodles made
with wheat and chickpea flours) or cappelletti in broth, gnocchi with sausage and
peas, or *tortelloni* filled with chickpeas in a
fresh tomato sauce. All the pastas are good
if not excellent. But a great dish is *coratelline
con carciofi,* delicate sweetbreads, heart, and
lung served with lightly fried artichokes.
This is classic provincial cooking, and if you
cast aside your squeamishness you will be
delighted with this dish. My favorite dessert is *pere ubriache:* to make this, slow-cook
twenty pears for five hours in eight bottles
of Barbera. The result is sticky and rich.
The food here is delicious and genuine, the
wine equally so. While this is not a formal
inn, the *osteria* has a few rooms that wind up
being used if you have had too much to
drink, are too tired, or there has been a
change in the weather that discourages you
from driving down the hill.

Villa di Mamiano (Parma)

There is a good modern art museum at the Fondazione Magnani Rocca that is open from April to early November. The other reason to come here is the simple, moderately priced restaurant on the grounds. The women in the kitchen produce the best *tortelli d'erbette* I have yet tasted, and the *salumi* are also delicious.

Frittata Modenese
Omelette with Parmigiano-Reggiano and Balsamic Vinegar

An Italian frittata is different from the sort of omelette one might find in France or the United States. It is cooked longer and develops a rather firm skin. Italians often let it cool or even chill it before eating it. When a round frittata is served, it is typically cut into wedges (quarters, sixths, or even eighths) as a pizza might be. To make a proper frittata, you need a good, nonstick omelette pan and a large plate at least the size of the pan. The best demonstration of frittata cookery I have ever seen is by Marcello Mastroianni in the film *Una Giornata Particolare* (*A Special Day*), one of the high points of his long collaboration with Sophia Loren. After the eggs are vigorously beaten, they are poured into a pan that has been lined with olive oil. They are cooked at relatively high heat for about minutes, covered for part of the time so that the steam created will fluff the eggs. Then the pan is removed from the heat, a large plate is placed over it (with the cook's palm spread across the back of the plate), and the pan and plate are flipped so the egg falls out. The pan is returned to the heat and then the frittata is slipped back into the pan so that the other side can cook.

You must use outstanding balsamic vinegar for this recipe to be meaningful. The standard 3-euro *aceto balsamico* simply will not do. But if you buy excellent aged vinegar in Modena or elsewhere, then you are prepared.

Serves 4
6 *large eggs*
3 *tablespoons freshly grated Parmigiano Reggiano*
Extra-virgin olive oil
High-quality balsamic vinegar

Vigorously beat the 6 eggs and the cheese in a bowl. Cover the bottom of a medium nonstick pan with a very light layer of olive oil. Heat gently and swirl the pan so that the oil covers the sides as well. Cook the eggs for 5 minutes over medium-high heat. Use a flat wooden or plastic spatula to lift and move the frittata occasionally to prevent it from sticking. Cover the pan for the third and fourth minutes of cooking. Then flip the frittata as instructed above; cook on the other side for 3 minutes. Slide it off the pan onto a serving dish. Let it cool slightly, then pour on just a few drops of vinegar and spread them evenly with the side of a butter knife. Cut into portions and serve. This frittata is good served at room temperature, but is not good chilled. Remember, as you pour the vinegar, that a little bit goes a long way.

Risotto alla Parmigiana

Serves 6

8 tablespoons unsalted butter
1 small onion, minced
1 liter/4½ cups excellent beef stock
450 grams/1 pound Vialone or other good
*   Italian rice*
1 cup freshly grated Parmigiano-Reggiano

In a large, heavy-bottomed pot melt 2 tablespoons of the butter. Add the minced onion and cook until it is gold in color. In a separate pan bring the stock to a boil. Once the onion is cooked, add the rice to the onion and sauté it for a few seconds in the bottom of the pot. Then add half the stock and start stirring. Add more stock a little at a time, stirring all the while. When the rice is cooked (in about 25 minutes), the grains should be chewy and there should be a slight creaminess in the pot owing to the starch that has been absorbed by the remaining stock. Add the rest of the butter, which should have been cut into small pieces, and the cheese. Stir thoroughly and serve, with a wedge of cheese and a grater available for those who want to add more cheese.

Toscana

For many visitors to Italy, and those who dream of visiting this magnificent country, Toscana is the most popular region. This was the cradle of the Renaissance, the region that gave us Leonardo da Vinci, Michelangelo, Amerigo Vespucci (whose name was used to name America), Guido d'Arezzo (who invented the musical scale), Puccini, Gucci, and so many more artists, inventors, designers, and geniuses that it is fair to say that the world would be immeasurably poorer and less beautiful without their efforts.

Toscana, and images of it, have been diffused in paintings and in films such as *A Room with a View* and *Where Angels Fear to Tread*. Generations of writers, especially from Britain and Germany, have so extolled the superiority of everything Tuscan that millions of people who have never been to the region already adore it. We all have our images of Toscana: superb red wines, magnificent art, silent hill towns, gorgeous leather bags and shoes, that brief affair with someone named Lorenzo or Lorenza. For me it is the neat lines of cypress trees that crown hilltops or run along roadsides like so many exclamation points.

But however one approaches Toscana, the values invoked are beauty and perfection. This is a tall task for any place to fulfill, certainly one that receives millions of visitors each year who arrive with high expectations and enormous preconceived notions. It is complicated by the fact that Tuscans are even more oriented to their own towns and traditions than most other Italians.

REGIONAL CAPITAL:
Firenze (FI).

PROVINCIAL CAPITALS:
Arezzo (AR), Livorno (LI), Grosseto (GR), Lucca (LU), Massa (MS), Pisa (PI), Pistoia (PT), Prato (PO), Siena (SI).

TOURIST INFORMATION:
There is no regional tourist bureau. Many cities and towns have their own offices.

In Firenze the office is at Via Cavour 1, tel. 055/290832.

They will direct you to other offices in Toscana.

Wine Tourism:
Movimento del Turisom del

Vino, c/o Fattoria dei Barbi,

    53024 Montalcino (SI),

    tel. 0577/849421,

    fax 0577/849356.

Toscana has been in the fore-front of the wine tourism movement, thanks to the efforts of the Colombini

The most famous example is the deep-seated antipathy between the Florentines and the Sienese that dates back centuries. The Sienese resent the years of invasion and siege that the Florentines subjected them to, and these feelings are palpable today. If you then add to this mix the people of Pisa, Lucca, Arezzo, Livorno, and Prato, you have a region that is so socially fragmented that it is hardly the benign paradise you might have hoped for.

I believe that it is a mistake to come to Toscana full of expectations that you hope to confirm. This is not the way to travel to any place, certainly not one so fabled as this. Discard the Tuscan beauty myth and try to look at Toscana without bias. We expect the heirs of Dante, Galileo, and Machiavelli to be clever, omniscient, and reasoned. But these and others were angry, tormented men who raged as they created art and ideas. For them Toscana was as much a battleground as a paradise.

Cinelli family of the Fattoria dei Barbi in Montalcino and the Enoteca Italiana in Siena.

Many people will tell you that the Italian language is at its most perfect and exalted when spoken by Tuscans. Why then does the letter *c* turn into an *h* and you drink happuhino or Hoha-Hola? Tuscans use more foul language and scatological humor than most Italians, and if students on a year abroad to learn Italian knew what the Tuscans were saying, they would faint. Certainly they would fail their language classes.

One often reads of the simplicity and genuineness of the Tuscan diet and lifestyle. With its abundant olive oil and vegetables, Tuscan cuisine seems to embody the tenets of the so-called Mediterranean Diet. Yet Tuscans also eat a lot of meat, especially beef, but also pork, wild boar, rabbit, lamb, sausage, liver, spleen, prosciutto, and *salame*. The food of Liguria or Puglia more closely approximates what the Mediterranean Diet is all about.

As for the lifestyle, one often hears about the measured behavior and proportion in all things Tuscan, yet I find these people to be as indulgent as the Romans, except that the Romans make no effort to conceal their extravagance. Look closely in Toscana, and you will find regal opulence, an adoration of quality and luxury, and an ongoing pursuit of the good things in life. And why not?

Lest you think that I am being critical of Toscana, let me set the record straight. I, too, had my first contact with Italy in this region (in the town of San Vincenzo many years ago), and it was as a result of this experience that I chose to return to Italy to live and study. True, I chose Bologna and Emilia-Romagna as my adoptive home, but I traveled to Firenze once a week to drink from the great well of Tuscan civilization. Several of my dearest Italian friends are Tuscans, but I love them not as models of perfection but as vibrant, ironic, cultured, and adorable people with flaws like everyone else. The real Toscana lives and breathes in its citizens. You will best know this region if you try to know the Tuscans and love them not for their presumed perfection but for their brilliant idiosyncrasy.

Eating in Toscana

While the food in Toscana is not as low in fat as one might think, the appeal of its cuisine for many people is that it is not rich and elaborate in the manner of Emilia-Romagna or France. In this regard Tuscan food corresponds to our notion of eating well. A Tuscan meal will probably start with *crostini* (toasts topped with chicken liver and spleen with a hint of caper), *fettunta* (toasted bread with olive oil), or *finocchiona* (fennel-scented *salame*) and prosciutto (which a purist will tell you is cut much too thick). Soups are excellent in this region, including *pasta e fagioli*, minestrone, *pappa col pomodoro* (a puree of fresh tomatoes), *zuppa di farro* (spelt), and *acquacotta* (a few greens, leftover bread, olive oil). In Arezzo *acquacotta* is much more elaborate, including mushrooms, tomatoes, garlic, wild mint, Parmigiano-Reggiano, eggs, bread, and oil. *Ribollita* is a popular soup throughout Toscana, although it has regional variations wherever you go. It usually has beans, cabbage, and onions and, as its name suggests, is twice cooked (literally, "boiled again") to give it more depth of texture and flavor.

For the most part, Tuscan pasta is simple but flavorful. Penne are popular throughout the region, often served with a sauce of vegetables or meat (called *ragù*, as in Emilia-Romagna). Tuscans particularly like duck *(anatra)*, hare *(lepre)*, and wild boar *(cinghiale)* in their meat sauces. In southern Toscana, especially in the province of Siena, one finds chewy curled pasta called *pici*, which, though not sophisticated, are addictive nonetheless. In northern Toscana you might find filled pasta such as *tortelloni* (with cheese) or ravioli, representing respectively the influence of neighboring Emilia and Liguria. The most classic fresh pasta in Toscana are *pappardelle*, very long, flat, thin pasta (not unlike lasagne) that are notable for their curly edges.

The most characteristic main course in Toscana is *bistecca alla fiorentina*, which is as close as Italy comes to a big piece of steak. It is made with meat from Chianina cattle, a Tuscan breed, and is the perfect match for the region's superb red wines. In restaurants it is usually priced by the *etto* (hundred grams) and you will often wind up paying a small fortune. So be sure to ask before ordering. As I described above, Tuscans eat all sorts of meats, whether *alla griglia* (grilled), *arrosto* (roasted), or *bollito* (boiled). They might have a platter of mixed meats or opt for one in particular. In Firenze I often enjoy boiled tongue with spinach. Tripe *(trippa)* is particularly loved by the Tuscans when washed down with Chianti. You will also find lots of poultry and game birds. This is hardly a region of vegetarians! The most famous Tuscan fish dish is *cacciucco*, a magnificent fish-and-seafood stew from Livorno. Tradition has it that there must be at least five kinds of fish in this stew, one for each *c* in the name. Along Toscana's long coast and on the islands of Elba and Giglio are numerous seafood preparations as antipasto, with pasta and as a main course.

Vegetables are abundant and excellent in Toscana. We often associate spinach with the region (dishes abroad that are called Florentine contain spinach), but I think that beans of all types are more ubiquitous. When cooked and topped with olive oil they are delicious. White beans *(cannellini)* are often combined with tuna, onions, and olive oil for a nice light lunch. Olives (raw and cured) are also a staple and can be combined with many meats, especially chicken and rabbit. Tuscan olive oil is generally considered the world's best, and within the region there is great dispute (as in everything) about where the best oil is made. Most people will say it comes from the provinces of Lucca or Siena, but you will have to taste and decide for yourself. I should add that there is a knowledgeable minority of olive-oil connoisseurs who believe that the best olive oil comes from Liguria, Lago di Garda, or Umbria.

Tuscan bread is very popular with foreigners, who notice that it is made without salt. Tuscans have many uses for stale bread. It can be sliced, toasted, and topped with olive oil and a bit of garlic to make *bruschetta*. Another classic dish is *panzanella*, which is leftover bread soaked in vinegar, combined with vegetables, and dressed with oil. Many people consider *panzanella* a soup, while others call it an antipasto. Whatever it is, it is delicious.

There is excellent cheese in Toscana, most of it made from sheep's milk. Tuscan sheep cheese tends to be creamy and soft, or firm without being granular. Some of the best is sold in Pienza, in the province of Siena. Sheep cheeses in Toscana are often called *cacio* or *caciotta*.

Except for the Sienese, Tuscans do not go for sweet or elaborate desserts. Instead they opt for fruit, or dry cookies to accompany sweet dessert wine. The most famous are the *cantuccini* or *biscotti di Prato*, dry almond cookies. Livorno, which has ancient Jewish roots (the great artist Modigliani was a *livornese* Jew), has a dessert called *i bolli*, made with leavened dough, orange-flower water, eggs, sugar, and anise that comes from the Jewish tradition. Another dessert, Monte Sinai, is made with almonds, and *conserva di rose* is a fragrant and delicious rose preserve. The people of Lucca and Firenze like chestnuts and use them in *necci* and *castagnaccio* (a muddy chestnut pudding that often includes rosemary and is an acquired taste). Lucca has *buccellato*, a traditional doughy cake, and *brigidini* are the popular anise cakes from Pistoia. Siena is distinct for its formidable array of dense, very sweet desserts made with honey, candied fruit, almonds, and other nuts. The most famous is *panforte*, which you should not sample until you reach Siena, where it is softer, fresher, and has a broader range of flavors than what is sent to other cities. Among many other Sienese desserts, it is worth citing *ricciarelli*, delicate sugar-almond cookies.

The Wines of Toscana

So rich and wonderful is the world of Tuscan wines that you can spend several lifetimes deepening your knowledge and appreciation of them. It would be impossible to cover all of them here, but I hope to give you enough information to send you on your way. The Tuscans and the Piedmontese have an eternal argument as to which region produces the best red wine in Italy. It is really a moot point, just as a preference for Bordeaux or Burgundy is a matter of personal taste. A general distinction that can be made is that most Piedmontese reds are made with the Nebbiolo grape while most Tuscan wines use Sangiovese, often in combination with small amounts of Cabernet Sauvignon, Canaiolo, Ciliegiolo, and other grapes.

Most Tuscan wine is listed under one of the DOC or DOCG categories, but there is a new type of Tuscan red. Several producers who grew superb grapes felt confined by the DOC rules, so they decided to create wines that they modestly refer to as *vino da tavola* (table wine), but which wine experts call the Super Tuscans. These are often very expensive wines such as Sassicaia and Ornellaia that feature blends of grapes that reflect the taste of the enologist rather than the dictates of DOC law. If your budget permits, you should sample a few Super Tuscans in restaurants and *enoteche*.

It is impossible to list all of the notable Tuscan red wines here, so I will confine myself to six major types: Brunello di Montalcino, Carmignano, Chianti, Chianti Classico, Morellino di Scansano, and Vino Nobile di Montepulciano.

Brunello di Montalcino. Made in Montalcino in the province of Siena, this is sublime wine, some of the world's best. It is made entirely with the Sangiovese Grosso grape, and must be aged for at least four years before it can be sold. Among the many excellent producers are Altesino, Argiano, Banfi (owned by Americans, this is the largest producer and a consistent winner at major competitions throughout the world), Biondi-Santi (where the wine was first created in 1888), Campogiovanni (whose wine is made under the guidance of San Felice), Casanova di Neri, Case Basse, Castelgiocondo, Col d'Orcia, Fattoria dei Barbi e del Casato (its owners, the Colombini Cinelli family, are leaders in the wine-tourism movement and great advocates and defenders of Brunello di Montalcino), Tenuta Friggiali, La Poderina, San Filippo, Mastrojanni, Pieve Santa Restituta, Poggio Antico, Salvioni La Cerbaiola, and Val di Suga. Rosso di Montalcino is a lighter version of Brunello and an outstanding wine, too, sort of like what Barbaresco is to Barolo. Most of the producers listed above also make a *Rosso*.

Carmignano. Made in the town of the same name in the province of Prato, this wine was the forerunner of Chianti. It was first described in 1716, and, because the production is limited and the eight growers are very protective of their special wine, Carmignano maintains its deserved cachet even in a region that makes so much fine wine. It is 45 percent to 65 percent Sangiovese, 10 percent to 20 percent Canaiolo Nero, and the balance is made with other varieties. Capezzana, owned by Count Ugo and Countess Lisa Bonaccossi, has been a longtime leader, and Ambra and Artimino are other fine producers.

Chianti. This is the generic name for what is probably Italy's most famous wine. It has been saddled by its past reputation as a cheap wine sold in straw-covered flasks. There are many excellent Chiantis (do not confuse this with Chianti Classico, listed below) that are made in the provinces of Pisa, Firenze, Lucca, Arezzo, Pistoia, Prato, and Siena. Deserving special mention are the wines made in Rufina, northeast of Firenze, where the cooler weather gives the wine a distinct, more austere flavor.

Chianti Classico. This is the zone, in the provinces of Firenze and Siena, that has a delimited growing area, stringent DOCG rules, and meticulous wine-making methods. There is a consortium of Chianti Classico producers, who, like good Tuscans, find many things to argue about over how their wine should be made and promoted. Chianti Classico has a distinctive pink DOCG label around its neck and the symbol of a black rooster (called *il gallo nero* in Italian). In a mean and senseless lawsuit a few years ago, Gallo, the huge American wine company, went to court in San Francisco asking that wines with the *gallo nero* seal not be permitted to be sold in the United States because they were presumed to be unfair competition. In fact, Gallo's vindictive act cost Chianti Classico producers a lot of money in legal fees and served only to drive many fine wines out of the American market. Like Chianti, Chianti Classico is made with Sangiovese, Canaiolo, Ciliegiolo, Malvasia, Trebbiano, and sometimes some Cabernet Sauvignon. It would be impossible to list all of the excellent producers, but here are some: Badia a Coltibuono, San Felice, Castello di Ama, Isole e Olena, Castello di Fonterutoli, Lilliano, Ii Poggiolo, San Leonino, I Sodi, Riecine, Querciabella, Villa Cafaggio, Castello di Verrazzano, Fontodi, Castello di Vol paia, Argiano, Poggio al Sole, and Castelgreve, a large cooperative with three hundred members that I consider very *simpatico;* it organizes concerts and cultural initiatives for the grape growers, who all share in the profits from the sales. Castelgreve offers some very commendable wines at low prices. One of the nicest touristic activities in Toscana is to drive on the Strada Chiantigiana (S.S. 222) and visit wineries in the Chianti Classico zone. For a map and more information, contact the Consorzio Chianti Classico, Via Scopeti 155— Sant'Andrea in Percussina, 50026 San Casciano Val di Pesa (Fl), tel. 055/8228245, fax 055/8228173, www.chianticlassico.com.

Morellino di Scansano. A little-known wine from the province of Grosseto that has a devoted following. It is made primarily with Sangiovese, but is often more aromatic than other Sangiovese wines and goes very well with wild boar and other game found in the Maremma zone of southern and coastal Toscana.

Vino Nobile di Montepulciano. Do not confuse this with Montepulciano d'Abruzzo, where Montepulciano is the name of the grape. In Toscana it is the name of the town where this wine, made of Prugnolo Gentile and other grapes, is produced. Montepulciano is a lovely town that deserves a visit. If Vino Nobile di Montepulciano were from any other region, it would be a big star. In Toscana it is produced not far from Montalcino and therefore suffers by comparison. But it is worth discovering.

Toscana also produces a few white wines, the most notable being Vernaccia di San Gimignano. This bright, golden-yellow wine, at its best, is a wonderful comple ment to just about any dish that calls for a white wine. Two of my favorite producers are Pietrafitta (which also makes an excellent olive oil) and Pietraserena.

Other white wines to look for are Grattamacco, Bianco di Elba, Bianco di Bolgheri, Belcaro (by San Felice), Vermentino, Bianco della Val di Nievole, Galestro, and Bianco di Pitigliano (from a fascinating, ancient town in the province of Grosseto that had a vibrant Jewish community for centuries; it is described in Edda Servi Machim's *The Classic Cuisine of the Italian Jews*).

Finally, there is *vin santo*, a very famous dessert wine. I think that even some *vin santo* producers would admit that there are many Italian dessert wines of more interest, but this one does have charm and a good reputation. It is usually made of white Trebbiano grapes that are dried in an airy place until Holy Week in the spring (most wines are made in September and October). The dry grapes have more concentrated sugars, and, because there is less juice, the wine is precious because it takes more grapes to make one bottle. The *vin santo* has a variety of flavors as minor notes in the taste: honey, chestnut, vanilla, cinnamon, pepper. It is often customary to dip dry almond cookies (called *cantucci* or *biscotti di Prato*) into *vin santo*, but this should really be done only if the wine is nothing special.

Arezzo

Overlooked by many visitors, Arezzo is the birthplace of Vasari, Petrarch, and Guido d'Arezzo. It also has the biggest antiques market in Italy held on the first Sunday of each month.

BAKERIES

Pasticceria de Cenci, Via de Cenci 17, tel. 0575/23102.

This bakery specializes in *piccola pasticceria*, small *petits fours* that are as delicious as they are delicate. They are displayed in a glass case like jewels.

Pasticceria Mignon, Via Toletta 16. Closed Monday.

Nice cakes and crostata, many served at the adjoining La Saletta del Mignon, a delightful tearoom with light meals.

BARS-CAFFÈS

Caffè dei Costanti, Piazza San Francesco 19, tel. 0575/21660. Closed Monday.

A large, historic *caffè* opened in 1806. Very evocative and welcoming.

Torrefazione Sandy, Via Garibaldi 65.

Good coffee, cold coffee (lightly sugared), and *granita di caffè*. You can also buy coffee beans here.

DINING

La Torre di Gnicche, Piaggia San Martino 8, tel. 0575/352035. Closed Wednesday. All credit cards. Moderately inexpensive.

There are all manner of *crostini* to start with, and then a good selection of soups. Tripe is a popular main course, and so too are *grifi all'aretina* (braised veal cheeks) and other meat dishes. There are 400 wines on the list, many of which are local treasures. If you have any left-over wine, consult the cheese board for an ideal match.

Ristorante Il Cantuccio, Via Madonna del Prato 78, tel. 0575/26830. Closed Wednesday. No credit cards. Moderate.

Carefully made food, a cut above the average for a restaurant (really a trattoria) of this type. *Crostini* are made with toasted fresh bread rather than stale bread. The *tortelli di patate* (filled with a delicate mixture of potato and grated carrot) are delicious.

Antica Trattoria da Guido, Via Modanno del Prato 85, tel. 0575/23760. Closed Sunday (except when the antiques fair is on) and in August. All credit cards. Moderate.

A duck sauce is the condiment to either pappardelle or *tortelli di patate*, both delicious. The *crostini*, pastas and secondi are very good and the soups are excllent.

Trattoria Il Saraceno, Via Mazzini 6a, tel. 0575/27644; Antica Osteria l'Agania, Via Mazzini 10, tel. 0575/295381. All credit cards.

Serving estimable local dishes.

FOOD SHOPPING
La Mozzarella, Via Spinella 25.

A few excellent cheeses, including Pecorino, and *burrata* that arrives from Puglia.

Boutique del Pesce, Corso Italia 285. Open mornings Tuesday–Saturday.

Inside a beautiful building made from one of the five ancient doors to the city.

Casa del Parmigiano, Via Garibaldi 49.

A good basic *salumeria*.

Boscovivo Tartufi, Via Madonna del Prato 67. Open mornings on Monday, Tuesday, and Wednesday, mornings and afternoons Thursday—Saturday.

Truffles, mushrooms, cheese with truffles, and balsamic vinegars.

Gastronomia, Via Madonna del Prato 60.

A small, excellent store with a good selection of wine, cheese, *salami*, but especially prime fresh fruit.

Rosticceria Corrado, Via Madonna del Prato 54a. Closed Monday.

Roast goose, rabbit, and chicken, baked potatoes, a few vegetables.

ICE CREAM
Gelateria Soft, Via Garibaldi 10. Closed Monday.

The specialty here is carrot ice cream— in my visits to Arezzo I have found carrots featured in all sorts of dishes.

Il Gelato, Via Madonna del Prato 45a, tel. 0575/23240.

Many good flavors.

TABLEWARE
Brocante, Via A. Cesalpino (near the Church of San Francesco), tel. 0575/300476.

Among the gift items is original and beautiful glassware that would flatter many a table.

Morini, Piazza San Jacopo, tel. 0575/23277.

A vast assortment of china, crystal, glass, stainless steel.

Barga (Lucca)

Dine at Trattoria L'Altana, tel 0583/723192. Closed Wednesday and February. All credit cards. Moderate. Don't miss the olive-oil-based *zuppa frantoiana*.

Borgo San Felice (Siena)

HOTEL, RESTAURANT, AND WINERY

Hotel Relais Borgo San Felice, 53019 Castelnuovo Berardenga (SI), tel. 0577/359260, fax 0577/359089; in Italy toll-free number is 167/862060. Closed November 1–March 31. Expensive.

Borgo San Felice is as close as one might come to one's dream of what Toscana is like. This is an entire medieval village, nestled in gentle hills planted with vines and olives, that was deserted and has now been lovingly restored to become a hotel and winery. San Felice has traces of civilization dating back to the Etruscans. In 1989, when huge stones were being moved to clear ground for a vineyard, two Etruscan tombs were discovered. One had a complete skeleton with a coin in its mouth. This *borgo* (small community) has residents whose families can be traced locally back twenty-three generations. Although it is a place of perfect tranquillity, it also has a busy winery, an excellent restaurant, and a luxury hotel. What is remarkable is how seamlessly all of it fits together. The restaurant has a list of many of the finest Tuscan wines plus, of course, the "house wine," which is wonderful. Nearby is a splendid herb garden that gives flavor to everything you eat. Tennis courts are discreetly tucked away, and near the restaurant is an azure

swimming pool straight out of Matisse or David Hockney. There are horseback riding, mountain biking, and good hiking trails. The buildings of the town now are used for hotel rooms, administrative offices for the winery, and for production of wine, oil, and other agricultural products, and for housing many of the residents who also work at San Felice. Hotel rooms are comfortable and serene, and you are likely to find a volume of poetry and prose with writings about Toscana in Italian and English. The book contains a quotation from Cicero: "A room without books is like a body without a soul."

It is impossible to explain San Felice without mentioning Enzo Morganti, its guiding spirit who died suddenly in 1994. Even in the often-combative Tuscan wine world, everyone loved Morganti. He worked as a professional in forty-eight harvests and intimately understood Tuscan terrain, climate, and grapes. When he came to San Felice in 1970 after twenty-two years at Lilliano, another excellent winery, he created the Vitarium, 18 hectares (45 acres) dedicated to growing rare grapes that were nearly extinct. These grapes were made viable again by Morganti and now appear in wines by San Felice and other wineries. He created, long ago, a wine called Vigorello that was a forerunner of the so-

Borgo San Felice

called Super Tuscans such as Sassicaia and Ornellaia. He and his young enologist, Leonardo Bellaccini, conducted extensive experiments and shared their findings with other Chianti producers. Morganti arranged conferences and seminars to exchange knowledge and friendship with producers in France, California, and elsewhere. He was instrumental in a program called Progetto Chianti Classico 2000, which seeks to develop the healthiest, most flavorful grape varieties (starting with Sangiovese, the backbone of Chianti) to replace the vines planted in the late 1960s when they eventually run their course. It is hard for me to go to San Felice without thinking of Enzo Morganti, but he was generous in his instruction, and I can report that the winery remains in the good hands of people dedicated to continuing his vision.

As you might expect, a stay at San Felice is not inexpensive, but if your budget permits, this is a wonderful oasis. It is a twenty-five-minute drive from Siena and its wines are widely available and merit a taste. Look for them in *enoteche* and good restaurants.

Carmignano (Prato)

COOKING SCHOOL
Tenuta di Capezzana, Via Capezzana 100, 50042 Carmignano (FI), tel. 055/8706005, fax 055/8706005.

Classes in Italian cooking, with an emphasis on the cuisine of Toscana, are offered at the house of Conte Ugo and Contessa Lisa Contini Bonaccossi, who produce some of the finest wine in Carmignano. Five-day courses are offered in the spring and the fall that include cooking, learning about ingredients, and visiting markets in Firenze and bread bakers, cheese makers, and pastry chefs. Students reside at the Bonaccossi house.

Chianchiano Terme (Siena)

This is one of Italy's most famous spas, and its motto is *Chianciano, fegato sano,* or "Chianciano, healthy liver." It is believed that drinking the local waters will restore your liver to its fighting trim. Enough people subscribe to this to keep Chianciano a very busy place, yet there has been a change here and at other spas in Italy. Government health programs no longer provide for paid visits to thermal cures. It used to be that a diagnosis of liver or kidney trouble meant a trip to a spa. But many people used false ailments as a way of getting a free vacation. Yet the waters, for many, are soothing and relaxing and perhaps have actual therapeutic effects as well.

DINING

Hostaria Il Buco, Via della Pace 39, tel. 0578/30230; hostariailbuco@libero.it. Closed Wednesday and early November. All credit cards. Moderately inexpensive to moderate.

There are not too many notable eating establishments in this town. At the Hostaria Il Buco there are typical southern Tuscan dishes, wild mushrooms in season (not great for the liver, but delicious), and pizza each evening.

Elba (Livorno)

Elba is where Napoleon spent many years in exile, and while he must have missed the power and the glory, this was a lovely place for him to nurse his wounds. Elba is a popular destination for naturists, as it has numerous clothing-optional beaches. *Cucina elbana* is, understandably, strong on fish and seafood, though Tuscan specialties from the mainland also appear on menus. What follow are good places to eat, listed by town:

Capoliveri
Summertime, Via Roma 56, tel. 0565/935180. Closed November through March. American Express, Visa. Moderate.

Marciana Marina
La Fenicia, Viale Principe Amadeo, tel. 0565/996611. Closed Wednesday (except in summer). All credit cards. Moderate to moderately expensive.

Marciana Castello
Osteria del Noce, Via della Madonna 27, tel. 0565/901284. Closed November to March. All credit cards. Moderate to moderately expensive.

Marina di Campo
La Lucciola, Viale Nomellini 64, tel. 0565/976395. Closed Tuesday in low season. All credit cards. Moderate to moderately expensive.

Portoferraio

Stella Marina, Via Vittorio Emanuele II, tel. 0565/915983. Closed most of January, early February, and late November. All credit cards. Moderate to moderately expensive.

Rio Marina

La Canocchia, Via Palestro 1, tel. 0565/962432. Closed Monday (except in summer), November through February. All credit cards. Moderate.

Firenze

BAKERIES

Pasticceria "Dolci e Dolcezze," Piazza Beccaria 8r, tel. 055/2345458.

This wonderful establishment, whose name means "Sweets and Sweetnesses," has the sort of ambience that makes Tchaikovsky ballet music play in my head as I walk through the door. Perhaps I should be hearing his *Souvenir de Florence* instead. Chandeliers hang above domed glass cases in which baked goods are displayed like the jewels that they are. Three of my favorites are the tangy lemon *crostata*, the *torta Ilaria* (made with creamy *gianduia*), and the *torta di pere*, with fragrant pears. Many of the pastries are made in miniature form so that you can enjoy their flavor with relatively little guilt about calories.

I Dolci di Patrizio Cosi, Borgo degli Aibizi 11r, tel. 055/2480367. Open 7–13h, 15:30–20h; closed Sunday.

This place is a source for baked goods that are typically Florentine, such as *bongo*, a sort of filled puff pastry topped with chocolate syrup, and *schiacciata alla fiorentina*, an orange cake popular at Carnival time. It also makes a specialty called *pappataci*, which are filled with warm cream and raisins. This name has special resonance for opera lovers, who know that the Pappataci is a comically secret society in Rossini's riotously funny *L'Italiana in Algeri*. The clever Italian girl Isabella convinces everyone to fill their mouths with spaghetti and not talk. In this way, she is able to escape from her captors in Algiers. The *pappataci* at this bakery may also leave you at a loss for words, but for good reason.

Caffè Pasticceria Giacosa, Via Tornabuoni 83r, tel. 055/2396226. Closed Monday.

Since 1815 Giacosa has been an exclusive purveyor of chocolate, pastries, liqueurs, and coffee to royal families, diplomats, *grandes dames*, and the patrician nobility of Toscana. The Negroni cocktail, a mixture of Campari and gin, was invented here and named after a count who was a *habitué*. There is a snob appeal about coming here, but the quality is still high, and Giacosa's reputation remains intact. There is also a sort of fancy-food lunch that many *fiorentini* consume standing up.

Caffè-Pasticceria Gilli.

See "Bars and *Caffès*," below.

Florentines drink Chianti and eat panini *at open-air shops*

Robiglio, Via dei Servi 112r, tel. 055/214501, or Via dei Tosinghi 11r, tel. 055/215013. Open 7:30–13:30h, 15–20h; closed Sunday.

The two branches of Robiglio offer typical Florentine pastries, including many cookies and biscuits, *bongo, schiacciata,* and *zuccotto.*

BARS AND CAFFÈS

Caffè-Pasticceria Giacosa.

See "Bakeries," above.

Caffè-Pasticceria Gilli, Via Roma 1/R, tel. 055/2396310. Closed Tuesday. Visa.

An elegant and very beautiful *caffè* on Piazza della Repubblica. It has been in business since 1733. Within, the pink and white ceilings, wood-paneled walls, green marble bar, antique photographs, period paintings, and gentle pace recall another era. There are excellent pastries and chocolates for sale. Table service indoors and out, for an increased price, of course. I enjoy taking breakfast here.

Gran Caffè Giubbe Rosse, Piazza della Repubblica 13–14R.

Founded in 1890, this is the classic intellec-

tual *caffè* of Firenze. It was the meeting place for the futurists, Lenin spent time here, and poets feel very much at home. The Giubbe Rosse went into decline for many years but has had a resurgence recently.

Caffè Paszkowski, Piazza della Repubblica 6, tel. 055/210236.

Yet another historic (1846) *caffè* on the Piazza della Repubblica that attracted intellectuals and creative people. The Paszkowski was particularly popular with political figures such as Mussolini and the patriot Cesare Battisti.

Procacci, Via Tornabuoni 64. Closed Sunday.

Since 1885, Procacci has been serving elegant *panini tartufati*, small truffle sandwiches that you may enjoy with a glass of wine. Very chic.

Caffè Rivoire.

See "Chocolate," below.

Caffè Tornabuoni, Lungarno Corsini 12/14r, tel. 055/210751. Open 11–2h; closed Monday.

This chic locale is actually part restaurant and part bar. The dishes are made with fancy ingredients such as truffles, Gorgonzola cheese, radicchio, and succulent berries. Crepes, gnocchi, risottos, and grilled meat go well with good Chianti. This bar is also renowned for its barman, Gigi Brizzi, who has won numerous contests for best cocktail or other technical skills of running an Italian bar. Italians take these competitions seriously, and when there is a champion such as Gigi, or Luca

Tomada at the Bar Cotterli in Udine, or Renato at Camogli's Bar Primula, the barman becomes an attraction unto himself.

CHOCOLATE
Caffè Rivoire, Piazza della Signoria 4r, tel. 055/214412. Open 8–24h; closed Monday.

Since 1872, this bar has been the place for chocolate in Firenze. It is made in various shapes and degrees of sweetness. You can also buy fruit and nuts that have been covered with chocolate. Caffè Rivoire is one of the best places to discover what Italians consider hot chocolate. While in Germany, Austria, Switzerland, France, Holland, and North America, hot chocolate is a milky beverage, in Italy *la cioccolata calda in tazza* is thick and strong, almost like a hot pudding. There are nice outdoor tables where you can watch the world pass by.

DINING

There are numerous challenges to dining in Firenze. The first is that in a city so geared to tourists, the central district is filled with places offering a *menu turistico* and serving food that is prepared indifferently at best. The challenge too is that many tourists don't know the difference between the stereotypical Italian dishes and those that are emblematic of a culture and a tradition. You, as a reader of this book, are obviously more interested in finding genuine flavors, and in Firenze one must look further afield to find them. Another particular challenge in Firenze is that the local *cucina*, though appealing and rustic, can become rather repetitive because it can seem like so many variations on the themes of red wine, pungent olive oil, stale bread put to endless uses, greens and beans, and piles of cooked meat. Wherever I will send you, there will be

these factors to consider. My advice is to go into the neighborhoods, to avoid every *menu turistico* you see, to look for an *enoteca* (wine bar with light food) and to be adventurous in terms of trying things you might not know. One such thing is *lampredotto*, an organ meat from cows that is steamed or braised. In the late autumn, with the arrival of the first chill, Florentines go to outdoor stands and buy it to be served on a roll. My Florentine friends all have a different theory about which part of the bovine anatomy the *lampredotto* comes from, yet they never fail to celebrate its arrival. Also typical, though increasingly rare, is the *trippaio*, a little shop that makes tripe which you can eat with just a bit of salt and pepper or on a roll with a *salsa verde* or a sharp red-pepper sauce. You will find a list of *trippai* in these pages. When you go to an *enoteca*, you might encounter good sliced meats, excellent cheeses, vegetables cured in vinegar *(sott'aceto)* or olive oil *(sott'olio)*. They will come with salt-free *pane toscano* and you can order a superb glass of wine that is affordable even when a whole bottle of the same might be an extravagance. Of course, this city does have some good *trattorie*, but those in the know compete to get into them, so you need to reserve to be assured a table. If all else fails, go to one of the city's markets and prepare a picnic of *salumi*, cheeses, fruit, bread, and wine.

RISTORANTI E TRATTORIE
La Baraonda, Via Ghibellina 67r, tel./fax 055/2341171, labaraonda@tin.it. Open for dinner Tuesday through Sunday; closed much of August. All credit cards. Moderate to moderately expensive.

Down the street from the Casa Buonarroti, Michelangelo's house, which merits a visit is this welcoming restaurant serving good and creative food.

Trattoria del Carmine, Piazza del Carmine 18r, tel. 055/208601. Closed Sunday and mid-August. MasterCard, Visa. Moderately inexpensive to moderate.

After visiting the Masaccio masterpieces in the nearby church, this is a good place to repair to for simple food and reflection on that artist's genius.

Enoteca Pane e Vino, Via San Niccolò 70 a/r, tel./fax 055/2476956, paneevino@ yahoo.com. Open Monday through Saturday evenings; closed for two weeks in August. All credit cards. Moderate to moderately expensive.

Despite the name, this is more of a restaurant, complete with candlelight and an intimate atmosphere. It is on the far side of the Arno and offers a respite from the hubbub.

Trattoria Marione, Via della Spada, 27r, tel.055/214756.

The chief appeal is the very central location near the Via Tornabuoni.

Ruth's, Via Farini 2, tel. 055/2480888. Closed Friday evening and Saturday. Visa. Moderately inexpensive.

Italian food prepared for kosher diners, plus vegetarian and fish dishes.

Il Cibreo, Via A. del Verrocchio 8r, tel. 055/2341100, cibreo.fi@tin.it. Closed Sunday, Monday, the first week of January, and from late July to early September. All credit cards. Moderately expensive to expensive.

Osteria Cibreo-Cibreino, Via dei Macci 122r, no telephone. Same closing dates as above. Moderately inexpensive to moderate.

Il Teatro del Sale, Via dei Macci, 111r, tel. 055/2001492, www.teatrodelsale.com.

The Cibreo empire hardly needs my endorsement, as it is one of the most popular places for food lovers to gather in Firenze. Fabio Picchi and his former wife Benedetta Vitale had the idea years ago to open a restaurant that would draw ingredients daily from the nearby Mercato di Sant'Ambrogio (which I consider more interesting and typical than the overly-touristed though still valid San Lorenzo market in the city center) to create faithful versions of Tuscan classics. The restaurant became wildly successful and soon it was impossible to get in. Prices went up at the restaurant, and the bill is worth it, but the exclusivity worked against the original mission of Il Cibreo. So Picchi created an osteria nearby in which one can dine on some of the same dishes in a more casual setting, with no reservations being taken. He also opened a nearby caffé, which is a touch precious, though the coffee is good.

In 2002, he had the inspired idea to acquire a former theater down the street and create Il Teatro del Sale, which is partially a private dining club and also a place where music, dance, poetry, and other art forms are presented on most evenings. There are small additional charges to attend the cultural events and members receive frequent announcements by e-mail. Picchi also teaches occasional cooking classes, especially to children of members rather than to their parents.

Zibibbo, Via di Terzollina 3r, tel.
055/433383. Closed Sunday and part
of August. All credit cards. Moderate.

When Fabio Picchi of Il Cibreo and his
wife Benedetta Vitale (who was a crucial
part of the creation of Il Cibreo)
divorced, Benedetta went her own way,
writing a cookbook and creating her own
restaurant with very worthy food. The
dishes have touches of Toscana and
southern Italy, but reflect Benedetta's
own taste. Somewhat outside the city
center, though bus 14C from the Duomo
stops close to the restaurant.

Trattoria Bibe, Via delle Bagnese 15, tel.
055/2049085, info@trattoriabibe.com.
Closed Wednesday, Thursday lunch,
late January to early February, mid-
November. All credit cards. Moderate.

This trattoria in Galuzzo, south of the
city center, has been run by the same
family since the mid-19th century. Its
praises were sung by Eugenio Montale,
the poet who won the Nobel Prize for
Literature in the 1970s. He would still
approve of the food.

Al Tranvai, Piazza Torquato Tasso 14r,
tel. 055/225197. Closed Saturday,
Sunday and August. All credit cards.
Moderately inexpensive to moderate.

Someone once said to me here, years
ago, "Why should they try to make the
customers comfortable? If a customer
wants to be comfortable he can stay
home." Yet people flock to this one-room
trattoria on the far side of the Arno,
despite a frequently long wait to squeeze
behind a table, sit on hard benches and
stools, read from a menu scrawled onto a
chalkboard, and then eat food that
Florentines love but others might
consider intimidating. It is because
everything seems and tastes real, and the
experience is unmistakably Tuscan.
Whether it is *pappa al pomodoro*, *penne*
piccanti, tripe, pasta with tuna, or the
fabled *lampredotto* (served with leeks),
which one does not so much as savor
than allow to slither down the throat, you
are partaking of a tradition that most
tourists shy away from.

Trattoria Sostanza, Via del Porcellana
25r, tel. 055/212691. Closed Saturday,
Sunday, August. No credit cards.
Moderate.

The *pollo al burro*, a sort of Florentine
Chicken Kiev, makes me swoon. Most of
the city's classic dishes are well-prepared
here, so this has been a tough place to
reserve at since it opened in 1869. As with
many eateries of this type in Firenze, one
sits at proletarian communal tables.

Trattoria da Burde, Via Pistoiese 6r,
tel. 055/317206. Open for lunch only,
Monday through Saturday. All credit
cards. Moderately inexpensive.

Very old-fashioned, though no less
appealing for that fact. Look for
announcements for special wine dinners
done on certain evenings.

Trattoria Tre Soldi, Via D'Annunzio 4r,
tel. 055/679366. Closed Friday evening,
Saturday, and August. All credit cards.
Moderate.

It is a bit of a trip to get here, but you will
be rewarded with delicious food,
especially meat cookery, as well as a good
selection of cheeses. Service is attentive
and great care is taken that your meal be
special.

ENOTECA

Some of these places shut on certain days, others do not. I have chosen those that do not close for vacation in August (or close briefly), as that is a time when it is even more difficult to find good food and wine in Firenze.

Baldovino, Via San Giuseppe 18r, tel. 055/2347220

Boccadama, Piazza Santa Croce 25r, tel. 055/243640

Canova di Guastavino, Via della Condotta 29r, tel. 055/2399806

Cantinetta dei Verrazzano, Via dei Tavolini 18, tel. 055/268590

Le Volpi e L'Uva, Piazza de'Rossi 1r, tel. 055/2398132 (closes for a week)

Osteria del Caffè Italiano, Via Isola delle Stinche 11r, tel. 055/289368

Seidivino, Borgo Ognissanti 42r, tel. 055/217791

Zanobini, Via Sant'Antonino 47r, tel. 055/2396850 (closes for a week)

TRIPPAI

Tripe and lampredotto *sellers set up on the street, so those listed might move about a bit to find a more favorable location.*

Mario Albergucci, Piazzale di Porta Romana, closed weekends and August

Marco Bolognesi, Via Gioberti (near Piazza Beccaria), closed Sunday and August

La Trippaia, Via dell'Ariento (near Via Sant'Antonino), closed Sunday and a few days in August. Located near the San Lorenzo market

Sergio Pollini, Via de'Macci at Borgo La Croce, closed Sunday (Saturday too in July) and August. Near Il Cibreo and the Sant'Ambrogio market is one of the best of the tripe sellers

Leonardo Torrini, Viale Donato Giannotti (at Piazzetta del Bandino), closed Sunday and two weeks in August

FOOD SHOPPING

The San Lorenzo food market, which is surrounded by stalls selling leather, silk, sweaters, and T-shirts to tourists, is an excellent food source. It is open Monday through Saturday from 7h to 14h and on Saturday afternoon from 16h to 20h. While there, be sure to visit the Perini shop, with its excellent Pecorino cheeses, *crostini*, bread, baked pastas, *salumi*, prosciutto, and wine. It also has handmade pasta, including *tortellini al tartufo*. The mercato di Sant'Ambrogio, near Piazza Beccaria, has much more color and character than the one in San Lorenzo.

ICE CREAM

Gelateria Vivoli, Via Isole delle Stinche 7r (near Via Torta). Closed Monday in summer and Monday and Tuesday in winter.

This is probably the most famous *gelateria* in Italy, certainly among tourists. I don't think it is the best, but there are some good flavors. I am especially fond of the *riso* and the *gianduia*.

WINE

Bottega del Brunello, Via Ricasoli 8r, tel. 055/2398602. Open 9–19h; closed Sunday.

If you cannot travel to the province of Siena, this is the next best thing. The main attraction is the superb Brunello di Montalcino wines. This store offers more than seventy Brunellos. You can find *panforte*, the famous chewy sweet cake of Siena. There are also honeys, biscuits, olive oils, and good vegetables in jars, preserved either in oil or vinegar. It is possible to sample wines and foods on the premises.

COOKING SCHOOL,
RESTAURANT, WINERY
Badia a Coltibuono, 53013 Gaiole in Chianti (SI), tel. 0577/744812 (ask for Kelda Jones), fax 0577/749235, info @coltibuono.com, www.coltibuono.com.

Badia a Coltibuono is an eleventh-century abbey that is also a working winery and farm with a restaurant and a justifiably famous cooking school. It is an ideal place to learn about the traditions of agriculture, of seasonal influence on cuisine, and particularly about the food of Toscana while drinking fine wine and using the oil and flavors drawn from the soil outside the abbey. Students live at the Badia during their stay and make excursions to local cheese makers, wineries and other Tuscan food producers. They dine at the Badia and other private houses. The traditional curriculum is of five days of lessons. Each day has a theme: gnocchi one day, vegetables the next, breads the next, for example. Then there is a graduation dinner. The school was founded by Lorenza De'Medici (with whom I wrote *Italy Today: The Beautiful Cookbook*) and her daughter Emanuela Stucchi Prinetti, who now runs many operations at the Badia. Lorenza has retired and the school is expertly run by her son Guido Stucchi Prinetti. In addition to the traditional curriculum, which is offered between May and October, the school offers one-day classes. Classes are given in English.

DINING
Badia a Coltibuono, tel. 0577/749031. Closed Monday and mid-January–end of February. American Express, Master Card, Visa. Moderate to moderately expensive.

Good Tuscan cooking based on products grown at Badia a Coltibuono and nearby farms. An excellent dish is *bistecca alla fiorentina*. Also consider trying *risotto al limone* or *tagliolini* with zucchini and tarragon. Direct sale of wine, oil, vinegar, honey, *vin santo*, and other products, Monday through Saturday, from 10h to 18h. with a brief closure around 13:30h.

Isola del Giglio (Grosseto)

The island of Giglio has been one of my tranquil hideaways for many years. The sea is very clean, and there is a fine view of the Tuscan coast. If you travel about the island you can be favored with beautiful sunrises and sunsets over water. There are three major communities, Porto (where you will arrive), Castello (the ancient hill town), and Campese, a new town that is full of vacation homes for people from the mainland. I often stay at the Arenella Hotel (tel. 0564/809340, fax 0564/809443), which has friendly management, comfortable and simple accommodation, and decent though not outstanding food. I often dine at Ristorante Arcobalena at Castello or buy food at L'Acquolina on Via Umberto I at Porto. At

Arcobalena (tel. 0564/806106, closed Tuesday except in summer, moderately expensive, accepts American Express) you should eat fish, which the owners purchase daily from Giglio fishermen.

Greve in Chianti (Firenze)

WINERY

Castello di Verrazzano, tel. 055/854242.
Open daily. American Express, Visa.

As you approach Greve, look for signs pointing to the Castello di Verrazzano. It is thought that Giovanni di Verrazzano, an explorer for whom a bridge in New York harbor was named, was born in this castle. It is surrounded by beautiful vineyards that produce a good Chianti. *Vin santo*, extra-virgin olive oil, and honey are also available. If you give the winery at least three days' notice, tastings and a winery tour can be arranged.

MEAT STORE

Antica Macelleria Norcineria Falorni,
Piazza Matteotti 69, tel. 055/853029.

This renowned butcher shop sells its products to good restaurants throughout Toscana. In business since 1782, this is a wonderful source for all kinds of home-made sausages and *salami* (including the classic Tuscan *finocchiona*) and superb prosciutto. This being Toscana, one can also buy excellent beef, expertly cut. Occasionally one can purchase steaks from Chianina cattle.

Livorno

BOOKSTORE

Fratelli Melita Editori, Via Grande 149,
tel. 0586/893267.

A good selection of cookbooks.

BREAD

Da Cecco, Via Cavalletti 2, tel. 0586/
881074. Closed Sunday and July.

Taste the *torta di ceci*, which is not a cake, but rather a delicious bread made with chickpea flour. Some people like to wrap it with focaccia, the resulting combination being called a 5+5 *(cinque più cinque)*.

COOKING SCHOOL

Cooking, Via dell'Agave 15, 57126
Livorno, tel. 0586/505491.

A well-regarded school where you can

discover coastal Tuscan cooking. Livorno has long had a prominent Jewish community (a famous exponent being the painter Modigliani), and its influence is felt in the local cuisine, especially in the sweets. You can learn to make *cacciucco*, Livorno's famous seafood stew, or, in the spring when thoughts turn to love, the aphrodisiac menu called *Venere in cucina* (Venus in the kitchen).

DINING

Il Giro del Cane, Borgo dei Cappuccini
314, tel. 0586/812560. Closed Sunday
(and closed for lunch daily during the
summer). All credit cards. Moderate.

Very good if you stick to *il pesce del giorno* and *cacciucco*.

Cantina Nardi, Via Cambini 6, tel. 0586/808006. Open for lunch; closed Sunday and last three weeks in August. American Express, Visa. Moderate.

Very good food in a casual setting. I like the *cacciucco* and the soups.

MARKET

The covered market at the Scali Sassi is a pleasant and colorful place for morning shopping, and the selection is excellent.

WINE

Doc di Parole e Cibi, Via Goldoni 42, tel. 0586/887583. Closed Monday and in August.

Sells more than two thousand wines from all over the world. From 19:30h to 3h the place becomes a friendly wine bar.

Lucca

BAKERY

Pasticceria Marino Taddeucci, Piazza San Michele 34, tel. 0583/44933.

Lucca claims that the ring-shaped *buccellato* is native to this town, although I have seen very similar items in Pavia and throughout Liguria. The difference is that the *lucchesi* use less sugar and more anise. This is a relatively simple cake, but I enjoy it with tea or for breakfast.

BOOKSTORE

Fratelli Melita Editori, Via Filungo 169, tel. 0583/46749.

A good selection of cookbooks.

CAFFÈ

Caffè di Simo, Via Fillungo 58, tel. 0583/46234.

This place, on Lucca's most popular thoroughfare, opened in 1846 as the Caffè del Caselli. The former owners were great lovers of music and art and commissioned many paintings and drawings. The Caselli was also the preferred *caffè* of Puccini in his hometown. The Di Simo family acquired this place in 1929 and has maintained the characteristic atmosphere that makes it an institution in Lucca.

DINING

Buca di Sant'Antonio, Via della Cervia 1/5, tel. 0583/55881, fax 0583/312199. Closed Sunday evening, Monday, and most of July. All credit cards. Moderately expensive.

This restaurant was born in 1782, down the block from where Giacomo Puccini was born in 1858. Music lovers come to Lucca to visit the composer's home (now a museum), and gastronomes come to the city's most famous restaurant, where one eats very well. My only cavil is that service and food preparation sometimes slip when there is a crowd. But out of high tourist season, a meal here is a very agreeable experience.

Da Giulio in Pelleria, Piazza San Tommaso, tel. 0583/55948. Closed Sunday, Monday, twenty days in August, and Christmas-New Year. No credit cards. Moderately inexpensive.

Good food such as *baccalà con i porri* (cod with leeks) and green vegetables, all flavored with Lucca's olive oil. I like the pastas very much, including the *tacconi* (macaroni) tossed with ricotta and beef gravy; *tordelli* (filled pasta with beef and pork); and *matuffi* (cornmeal gnocchi) with meat sauce.

Massa

AGRITOURISM
Azienda Agricola Lorieri, Podere Scurtarol, Via dell'Uva, tel. 0585/831560. Reservations essential. Open late April–end of October. Moderate.

Rosanna and PierPaolo Lorieri have a remarkable farm 180 meters (about 600 feet) above the sea. There are magnificent views of the sea and the towns of Massa (to the left) and Carrara (to the right). It was from the mountains behind here that Michelangelo got the marble he used for the *David* and the *Pietà*. They produce good wines and excellent products made with honey, nuts, vegetables, and fruit. Rosanna has an outdoor wood-burning oven in which she makes a marvelous range of breads, including focaccia with cheese and herbs, tarts filled with vegetables, and *schiacciata,* a flatbread topped with black-olive spread. From this oven come *testaroli,* crepes of a sort that is cut and then tossed with oil and cheese or pesto. She also has a way with vegetables. Not to be missed is the superb *pandivino,* a cake made with wine, grapes, flour, yeast, walnuts, and eggs. Rosanna and PierPaolo have an innate understanding of the meaning of hospitality, which is, after all, an art. But like all great artists, they make their work seem effortless. This is not really a restaurant, but more of a working farm that sells its products. PierPaolo says he hopes that people who arrive as strangers will depart as friends. Reservations are indispensable, and a maximum of fifteen people can be received. Note that to reach this place one must be a careful and courageous driver, as there is only a thin, winding road that climbs along the side of a mountain.

Montalcino (Siena)

Montalcino, and the beautiful green hills that surround it, are the heartland of Brunello, considered by many to be the finest red wine in Italy, although a strong argument can be made for Barolo and Barbaresco from Piemonte and certain reds from Friuli. Nonetheless, Brunello at its best is magnificent. If you have a car, it is possible to visit many of the wineries, some of which have good restaurants too. You will undoubtedly be impressed by the beauty of this area and will embrace the chance to taste superb wine and excellent food.

CAFFÈ
Fiaschetteria Italiana, Piazza del Popolo 6,   *tel. 0577/849043. Closed Thursday.*

This *caffè* was opened by Ferruccio Biondi Santi, a young member of the family that created Brunello di Montalcino. The look of the caffè is little changed since its opening in 1888.

DINING

Castello di Banfi, località Sant'Angelo Scalo, in Poggio alle Mura, tel. 0577/816054, banfi@banfi.it.

Ristorante Il Castello, open for dinner Tuesday through Saturday. Closed January and August. All credit cards. Expensive.

Taverna Banfi, closed Sunday evening, Christmas through January, and mid-August. Moderate to moderately expensive.

Banfi produces some of the finest wines in Montalcino, and their restaurants in two price categories offer food that matches the wine well.

Taverna dei Barbi, Fattoria dei Barbi, in Podernovi, tel. 0577/841200, info@ fattoriadeibarbi.it. Closed Wednesday, plus Tuesday from October to March, the last three weeks of January. All credit cards. Moderate.

Good food and wine at one of the most important Brunello producers.

Poggio Antico, tel. 0577/849200, rist. poggio.antico@libero.it. Closed Sunday evening, Monday (except from April to October), January 7 to early February. MasterCard, Visa. Moderately expensive.

Delicate, delicious food, especially the *pappardelle* with truffles.

Azienda Agrituristica Casa Colsereno, Loc. Colsereno 31, tel. 0577/847030. Open year-round.

Good local foods, plus horseback riding, fishing, and mountain biking.

Trattoria Sciame, Via Ricasoli 9, tel. 0577/ 848017. Closed Tuesday. No credit cards. Moderately inexpensive.

This restaurant is in the town of Montalcino. Good, solid fare.

Ristorante Boccon Divino, Loc. Colombaio Tozzi, tel. 0577/848233. Closed Tuesday. Moderate.

Good basic flavors, a wonderful view.

WINE AND LOCAL PRODUCTS

Drogheria Franci, Piazzale Fortezza 5, tel. 0577/848191, fax 0577/849077. Closed Wednesday afternoon.

Good Brunello wines, cookies, truffle pasta, honeys, and other delicacies.

Montecatini Terme (Pistoia)

This is one of the world's most famous spas, immortalized in Fellini's classic film *8½*.

BAKERY

Bargilli, Via Grocco 2. Closed Monday.

The classic pastries here are the *cialde*, simple cookies made of flour, sugar, egg, and milk plus one toasted almond. A pretty box of *cialde* is the classic gift to bring home from one's sojourn. Also try the *brigidini*.

Ristorante Il Cucco, Via del Salsero 3 (near Corso Matteotti), tel. 0572/72765. Closed Tuesday, Wednesday afternoon. All credit cards. Moderate to moderately expensive.

Right in the middle of Montecatini, near the railway tracks, is this lively, youthful, tasty restaurant that is mercifully out of place. The food and environment are fun and provide a change for people spending a fortnight taking the waters and eating set menus in their hotel.

Montemerano (Grosseto)

DINING

Enoteca dell'Antico Frantoio, Piazza Solferino 7, tel. 0564/602615 or 602778, fax 0564/602620. Open 18–24h, Saturday and Sunday also for lunch; closed Monday, January, and February. All credit cards. Moderate.

Located on the grounds of an old oil press, this place is not easily forgotten. It has a magnificent view of the sea in the distance, a warm welcome from Victoria and Erik Banti, and excellent wine of their own production. The food comes entirely from local sources, and the menu varies throughout the year. The flavors, whether cheese, fruit, vegetables, oil, or bread, are vivid. There are eight rooms available for lodging if you plan to stay in this lovely town.

Locanda Laudomia, at Poderi di Montemerano, tel. 0564/620062.

American Express, MasterCard, Visa. Moderate.

A modest hotel with a good restaurant. Delicious lamb, rabbit, vegetables, Pecorino, mushrooms, and *ravioli di castagne* (with chestnuts). If you stay over, you are in for a treat at breakfast: wonderful fresh ricotta is served with homemade peach-quince jam.

WINE

Enoteca dell'Antico Frantoio.

See "Dining," above.

Enoteca Perbacco, Via Chiesa 8, tel. 0564/ 602817. Closed Wednesday. All credit cards.

An excellent selection of Tuscan wines. You can also buy delicious olive oil, honey, herbs, cookies, vegetables packed in oil, and jams made of excellent local fruit.

Montepulciano (Siena)

This town is of Etruscan origin. It dominates the hills of the Valdichiana and the Val d'Orcia. Its beauty, its geographic location, and, especially, its production of great wine made it a possession to be contested by Firenze and Siena for centuries.

DINING

Ristorante della Fattoria di Pukino, tel. 0578/758711, fax 0578/716372. No credit cards. Moderate.

A very large, casual restaurant that serves products from a farm, many of which you can also purchase to take away. There is grilled steak, chicken, kid, *Pecorino di Pienza*, a cake called *panello della Gabriella*, made from an ancient recipe of Franciscan monks using honey, whole wheat, raisins, hazelnuts, almonds, eggs, olive oil, yeast, and rosemary. Fruits, vegetables, soups, and pastas are based on whatever foods are in season.

WINE

Oinochóe, Via Voltaia nel Corso 82, tel. 0578/757524.

An interesting store that sells the best of regional wines but is also an antiques shop, with coins, prints, small furniture, and books.

WINE CELLAR

Cantine Contucci, Via San Donato 15, tel. 0578/757006. Open 8–12:30h, 14:30–19h.

A rare chance to see a huge, ancient cellar in a town. Of course, you can purchase wine, too.

Pescia (Pistoia)

Pescia is a town most tourists overlook, but its abundant charms—architecture, food, genuineness—make it irresistible.

DINING

Trattoria Cecco, Via Forti 96, tel. 0572/477955. Closed Monday, mid-January, and much of July. All credit cards. Moderate.

An almost perfect trattoria. When the homemade pasta (especially ravioli) is this good, or when the miraculous *pollo al mattone* (that is crispy on the outside and tender within) is tasted, one can only

feel gratitude for having journeyed here. *Fagioli di Sorana*, local white beans served in luscious olive oil will make you tingle with delight.

Monte a Pescia da Palmira, Via del Monte Ovest 1, tel. 0572/476887. Closed Wednesday, two weeks in July, and two weeks in October. Visa. Moderate.

Another restaurant with superb food.

Pienza (Siena)

Unlike most Tuscan cities, which are of ancient origin, Pienza was created during the Renaissance under the influence of Pope Pius II (1405-1464), for whom the city is named. The main piazza of the town is in the shape of a trapezoid and is intended to give a sense of infinity. The cathedral is at one end of the piazza, but it has been designed so that there is a clear view of the countryside in the distance. Everything about the design of Pienza is intended to exalt reason and perspective, and also the pope who was the city's patron. For the gourmet traveler the chief attraction is the Pecorino di Pienza, the superb sheep's-milk cheese that is produced just beyond the city's walls. A cheese festival is held on the first Sunday in September. There are several shops on Corso Rossellino that sell the cheese, plus little packages of dried herbs that are ideal for cooking and make great gifts. My favorite food shops on Corso Rossellino are at #15, #16, and #27. Also visit the shop of Azienda Agricola Zazzeri (Via del Giglio 4, tel. 0578/748223), which sells cheese, oil, wine, olives, jam, honey, and dried herbs, from a local farm.

DINING

La Buca delle Fate, Corso Rossellino 38a, tel. 0578/748272. Closed Monday, the last three weeks in January, the last two of June. All credit cards. Moderate.

Stick to simple dishes and be sure to have *pici* and the local Pecorino.

Trattoria Latte di Luna, Via San Carlo 2, tel. 0578/748606. Closed Tuesday, mid-February through mid-March, and July. All credit cards. Moderate.

Delicious local food and good value for money. The *maialino al forno*, roast baby pig, is delicious with *patate arrosto*.

Pisa

BOOKSTORE

Fratelli Melita Editori, Borgo Stretto 38, tel. 050/542774, or Corso Italia 97, tel. 050/45150.

A good selection of cookbooks.

DINING

Osteria dei Cavalieri, Via San Frediano 16, tel. 050/580858. Closed Saturday afternoon, Sunday, and in August.

MasterCard. Moderate.

Excellent pasta, good fish.

Vineria di Piazza, Piazza delle Vettovaglie 13, no telephone. Closed Sunday, August, and holidays. No credit cards. Moderately inexpensive.

Excellent soups and braised meats. Skip the pasta.

Pistoia

CAFFÈ-BAKERY

Caffè-Pasticceria Valiani, Via Cavour 55, tel. 0573/23034.

You can't miss the Valiani, with its distinctive black-and-white marble arch that was revealed when construction was done to open this place in 1864. Through the years, Valiani has attracted many musical luminaries, including Verdi, Puccini, Giordano, Leoncavallo, and Caruso.

DINING

Trattoria dell'Abbondanza, Via dell' Abbondanza 10, tel. 0573/368037. Closed

Wednesday, Thursday lunch, two weeks in May, and two weeks in October. All credit cards. Moderately inexpensive.

In the winter, don't miss *il carcerato* (which means "the imprisoned one", a soup recipe of the poor that has almost vanished. Stale bread is softened in veal broth flavored with black pepper and Pecorino. Throughout the year, the strength is the secondi, such as *zuppa di moscardini* (a stew of baby octopus) or *fritto di pollo e verdura* (fried chicken and vegetables).

Pitigliano (Grosseto)

AGRITOURISM

Azienda Agrituristica Podere Il Melograno, Località Formica, tel. 0564/615536.

A nice little farm that will give you an idea of small-scale, lovingly tended agriculture in southern Toscana. There are three rooms on this farm in Formica (watch for signs as you near Pitigliano). The owner, Elvezio Savelli, and his family produce olive oil, wine, cheeses made from their sheep's milk, and delicious fruit jams that you can have at breakfast. These products are for sale to the public if you don't have the occasion to stay here.

DINING

Il Tufo Allegro, Vicolo della Costituzione 1, tel. 0564/616192. Closed Tuesday, Wednesday afternoon (except in August and September); also in January, February. All credit cards. Moderate to moderately expensive.

Excellent antipasti, soups, and meats (especially lamb and boar) are complimented by wines from a well-chosen list. *Polpette con mandorle e pinoli* (small veal loaves with almonds and pine nuts) and *gnudi* (pillowy dumplings) are echoes of Pitigliano's Jewish past.

La Magica Torre, Via dei Lavatoi. No credit cards. Moderately inexpensive.

Wonderful roast chicken with rosemary.

San Gimignano (Siena)

San Gimignano is a popular tourist destination that also has a formidable gastronomic tradition. Vernaccia di San Gimignano is an excellent white wine (the first in Italy to receive a DOC designation, in 1966), and there are good olive oils and game, especially *cinghiale*.

CAFFÈ-BAKERY

Bar–Pasticceria Maria e Lucia, Via San Matteo 55, tel. 0577/940379. Closed Tuesday.

Two busy sisters make ice cream and especially cakes in the Sienese style.

Among these are *torta fiorita* with orange rind, candied fruit, and almonds, and *mandorlato*, a soft, chewy confection with delicious whole almonds, honey, and powdered sugar. Despite what you might expect, this dessert is neither heavy nor overbearingly sweet.

DINING

**Dorandò, Vicolo dell' Oro 2, tel. 0577/
941862, info@ristorantedorando.it.
Closed Monday (except in high season)
January, February. All credit cards.
Moderate to moderately expensive.**

The owners have researched
Renaissance cookbooks and have
imaginatively adapted the recipes for
modern cooking. Fine service and an
excellent wine list make this a very
appealing place to eat.

**Osteria del Carcere, Via del Castello 13,
tel. 0577/941905. Closed Wednesday,
Thursday lunch, January, and
February. No credit cards. Moderate.**

Casual dining on foods that pair well
with wines from an excellent list.

FOOD SHOPPING, WINE,
AND OIL

Gastronomia, Via San Matteo 48a.

Good sandwiches to go, excellent cheeses
and *salame*, and an assortment of local
wines. You can also buy bags of *farro*.

**La Botte e Il Frantoio, Via San Giovanni
56, tel. 0577/940353. Open 10–20h daily
in high tourist season. Diners Club,
MasterCard, Visa.**

If closed, go around the corner and up
the hill to the Enoteca Bruni on the Via
Quercecchio 61. Sells Vernaccia di San
Gimignano, Chianti, Vino Nobile di
Montepulciano, Brunello di
Montalcino, and local olive oil.

**La Buca, Via San Giovanni 16, tel.
0577/940407.**

Point of sale for the Azienda Agricola La
Buca di Montanto. It is notable
especially for homemade *cinghiale
salame*. Also sells wines and oil.

**Azienda Agricola Pietraserena, Via
Casale 5, tel. 0577/940083, fax 0577/
942045.**

Bruno and Bruna Arrigoni have a small
plot of land outside San Gimignano,
where they produce wonderful Vernaccia
and Chianti. They are a lovely couple,
and Bruna, whom I adore, is a
magnificent cook (she does not operate
a restaurant, but I have been lucky to
dine at her table on two occasions). You
can find Pietraserena wines at several
stores in San Gimignano. If you saw
Franco Zeffirelli's film *Brother Sun,
Sister Moon* you will recognize the area
where the Arrigonis live.

LODGING, OIL, WINE

**Agriturismo Fattoria di Pietrafitta,
località Cortennano 54, tel. 0577/
943200, info@pietrafitta.com. All credit
cards. Moderate.**

One of the better producers of olive oil
and Vernaccia wine has nine rooms for
travelers in its 15thcentury castle. There is
a point of sale for these products at Strada
Provinciale 1 (coming from Poggibonsi,
about 1.5 km from San Gimignano).

SPECIAL STORES

**Studio Massimo Pantani, Via
Quercecchi 13, tel. 0577/940612.**

This store sells all sorts of framed items,
including old prints of food subjects. Sig.
Pantani makes frames very quickly and
expertly. There are also nice spice racks

and other objects for the kitchen or dining room.

Giomi, Via San Matteo 39, tel. 0577/ 940331. All credit cards.

A basic electronics store that stocks extensive collection of coffee-makers, from the simplest one-cup Moka to six-cup Neapolitan pots to the most elaborate electronic machines by Pavoni and others.

Sansepolcro (Arezzo)

DINING

Da Ventura, Via Aggiunti 30, tel./fax 0575/742560. Closed Sunday evening, Monday, January 8–20, August 1–20. All credit cards. Moderate.

Well-prepared Tuscan mountain food, specializing in boiled or roasted meats and, in season, truffles and wild mushrooms. There are rooms to rent and the bed-and-board scheme is a great deal.

Sant'Andrea Percussina (Firenze)

DINING

L'Albergaccio Machiavelli, tel. 055/ 828471. No credit cards. Moderately inexpensive.

Just across the road from the office of the consortium of producers of Chianti Classico (itself worth a visit for admirers of this outstanding wine) is one of the most historic restaurants in Italy. Food has been served here since 1450, and this is most notable as the place where

Machiavelli would take refuge when things got a little hot for him in Firenze. As you would expect, the wine is marvelous, but so is the food, which is simple in the way of classic Tuscan cooking: *fettunta, ribollita, panzanellla, crostini,* and various dishes served with the house's famous *salsa verde* made of parsley, eggs, cornichons, green peppers, vinegar, capers, and mint. A perfect afternoon trip from Firenze.

San Vincenzo (Livorno)

When I first visited San Vincenzo in 1973, it was a small, very sweet town that had a little summer community of Swiss visitors. There was one cinema where everyone in town gathered on Friday night to see films such as *Via col Vento (Gone with the Wind), Prendi i Soldi e Scappa (Take the Money and Run),* and *Il Padrino (The Godfather).* Promoters helped put the town on the map, and San Vincenzo went from an innocent beach town to a resort. The cinema closed, the main street became a pedestrian mall with a video store, and the town became an international destination. One change that came was the opening, near the site of the movie theater, of the Gambero Rosso restaurant, which garnered national fame for innovative cuisine (mostly seafood) and an excellent wine list. I have dined here twice and can attest to its qualities, although I felt wistful at the disappearance of the innocence of San Vincenzo and, I suppose, of myself. But if you plan to be near San Vincenzo and want to spend a lot of money for a beautifully served, delicious meal, call ahead to Gambero Rosso.

DINING

Gambero Rosso, Piazza della Vittoria 19, tel. 0565/701021. Reservations essential. Closed Monday, Tuesday, and from late October to early January. All credit cards. Expensive.

Siena
Classic Town

Siena is a gorgeous yet odd city that is very compelling. Its people are capable of great art, wonderful kindness, and, on the day of the Palio, its world-famous horse race around the Piazza del Campo, incredible passion, anger, and exultation. The Sienese have long been expert at handling money. In the Middle Ages and the Renaissance the custom was for pilgrims from northern Europe headed for Roma to leave their money in Siena, since they were supposed to be poor and penitent. The Sienese developed banking traditions, invested the deposited money, and paid interest. Italy's oldest bank, the Monte dei Paschi di Siena, was established in 1472. You will notice that the main streets of Siena are called the Via dei Banchi di Sopra and Via dei Banchi di Sotto. For centuries they were lined with banks that held the pilgrims' money.

Siena is a place where people live in what seems like splendid contentment, but in the view of some (especially the Florentines), this contentment is born of provincialism. I have many friends in Siena in whom I find a genuine warmth and sweetness, but I notice that some of them seem very out of sorts when they are not on their home soil. There is a remarkable attachment to this place, and most visitors fall in love with it too. One does sense peace here: the province of Siena has the lowest crime rate of any in Italy. The many beautiful towns in the province produce extraordinary wine (Brunello di Montalcino, Vino Nobile di Montepulciano, Chianti Classico). The hills are full of churches, convents, refuges, and retreats. Music is taught at the famous Chigi Academy and is performed frequently in any place that has good acoustics. Curiously, I have never had an outstanding meal in Siena, primarily because simple flavors are emphasized, and inevitably the wonderful wine will be more memorable than the food. But one can eat well: I like buying bread, fruit, cheese, *salame*, and a bottle of wine and sitting at one of the many places in town that offer divine views of architecture and nature. The combination of simplicity and beauty is the essence of everything that is special about Siena.

Siena

BARS

Caffè del Corso, Via Banchi di Sopra 25. Open until 24h; closed Monday.

A small, smart bar that is open until midnight (Siena is not a late-night town). Good espresso and cappuccino.

Bar-Pasticceria Nannini, Via Banchi di Sopra 22.

Said to be the oldest bar in Siena. You can also buy pastries, gelati, *panforte*, and wine.

Bar-Gelateria Il Masgalano, Via Camporeggio 3 (opposite Enoteca San Domenico). Open 7–24h, Sunday 9:30–18:30h.

Near the buses that go to Firenze and many towns in the province of Siena, this is a good place for breakfast en route. It also has excellent ice cream. Outdoor tables provide a lovely view.

DINING

Siena is notorious for not being a great eating town. There are good meals to be had here, but it is not a given that every restaurant you visit will be memorable. So I recommend that you stick to some of my suggestions.

L'Osteria, Via dei Rossi 79/81, tel. 0577/287592. Reservations essential. Closed Sunday. No credit cards. Moderately inexpensive to moderate.

Walk down the very steep Via dei Rossi to L'Osteria for a good Tuscan meal. The *crostini* are good, the *pappa col pomodoro, ribollita, pasta e fagioli,* and the *pici* are exemplary. *Secondi* vary all the time and include pork, squab, rabbit, wild boar, and cooked vegetables. Everything is done with a sure hand. Because Siena is a seller's market and this is a relatively small restaurant, reservations are essential.

Osteria Le Logge, Via del Porrione 33, tel. 0577/48013. Closed Sunday, January. All credit cards. Moderately expensive.

Most of the dishes here serve to bring out the best in the very good wines on the list. Good choices are *mucchino con funghi* (beef with mushrooms) or *spezzatino alla chigiana* (veal with garlic, sage, black olives, cooked in white wine). The pasta here is variable.

Ristorante Mugolone, Via dei Pellegrini 8, tel. 0577/283235. Closed Thursday, Sunday evening. All credit cards. Moderate to moderately expensive.

There is excellent food to be had here, such as *agnello al forno* (roast baby lamb), *tagliolini ai funghi porcini*, and the *antipasto misto*. The wine list is very good, and service is taken seriously.

La Vecchia Taverna del Bacco, Via Beccheria 9, tel. 0577/49331. All credit cards. Moderate.

A friendly, long-established eatery very close to the Piazza del Campo. The food is generally good and basic, the atmosphere convivial.

Grotta di Santa Caterina da Bagoga, Via della Galluzza 26, tel. 0577/282208. Closed Sunday evening, Monday, February 1–15, July 24–31. All credit cards. Moderate.

Trippa alla montalcinese (tripe cooked with saffron and clove) is interesting for the adventurous. Otherwise, good straightforward cookery.

Ristorante Castelvecchio, Via Castel-vecchio 65, tel. 0577/49586. Closed Sunday. All credit cards. Moderate.

I particularly enjoy the soups as well as some meats. *Spezzato di pollo* are chunks of chicken cooked with lemon and juniper berries. Vegetables such as *zucchine ripiene* and a *terrina di zucchine, patate e melanzane* (courgette, potato, aubergine) provide a welcome break from meat if you have spent more than a few days in Toscana.

ENOTECA PUBBLICA

Enoteca Italiana di Siena, Piazza Matteotti 30, tel. 0577/288497, fax 0577/217594. Open daily 16–24h.

To call the Enoteca Italiana a place to taste wine is like calling the Vatican a place to pray. This is the most important *enoteca* in Italy, under the leadership of Sen. Riccardo Margheriti and Dr. Pasquale di Lena, and administered by a very dedicated staff, the Enoteca Italiana is a wonderful research facility with books, exhibits, all sorts of documentation about wine history and the laws that govern its production in Italy. There is an understanding here that wine is not simply a beverage, but an essential part of a culture, a heritage, and a way of life. As part of its activity the Enoteca commissions works of art, poetry, and music inspired by wine and the sociability it promotes. You will hear many people at say that wine is about friendship, and that is the premise on which the Enoteca operates. It is believed that wine promotes both interaction and meditation and therefore is an essential component in human contentment. This may sound lofty, but don't forget that Tuscans have promoted human values for five hundred years, even if there have always been ferocious rivalries among the many

Tuscan cities. One of the major annual initiatives of the Enoteca Italiana is La Settimana dei Vini (Wine Week), which has been held in Siena every June for more than thirty years. People arrive from five continents for an annual synod about wine in the world. There are meetings, conferences, papers are given and published, and participants visit wineries. Music, literature, photography, and art are presented, and each night there is a dinner featuring the food and wine of a different region of Italy. I have been fortunate enough to be a speaker at three Wine Weeks. It is here that the new DOC and DOCG wines are presented each year and then documented in one of the Enoteca's many publications. As part of its initiatives, members of the Enoteca staff travel around the world to introduce Italian wine and culture to restaurateurs, scholars, and wine lovers. A recent initiative of the Enoteca is called Vino e Turismo, in which wineries throughout Italy open their doors at appointed times throughout the year so visitors can learn more about what goes into producing wine. Many of these wineries also offer meals and lodging to paying guests. You can write to the Enoteca for details about the region you plan to visit, or you may consult the listings I have included in many of the chapters. Each night, the Enoteca Italiana is one of the more pleasant gathering places in Siena. There are more than 1,200 wines by 460 producers in its collection, and many are brought out each evening for tasting by the glass for a moderate fee. The setting, a fortress built by the Medicis is quite lovely. It should be noted that the Enoteca Italiana is a nonprofit, non-

partisan institution whose goal is to promote all Italian wine and culture. With so many changes of government in Roma, the *enoteca* is occasionally threatened with cuts in funding or even closure. This would be a dreadful mistake, because the Enoteca Italiana is an unparalleled and irreplaceable resource that does great good.

SHOPPING

Forno dei Galli, Via dei Termini 45 (from the Via Banchi di Sopra find the underpass called Via dè Pontani).

Here is an excellent selection of Tuscan breads, plus some fresh pastas and a very nice assortment of cookies and biscuits that are pretty for the eye and the mouth.

Consorzio Agrario Siena, Via Piangiani 9 (one enters at #9), tel. 0577/222368. Closed Saturday afternoon and Sunday.

The best of the agricultural production of the province of Siena: olive oil, Chianti, Vernaccia, Brunello, Vino Nobile, *vin santo*, Pecorino, *salumi*, honey, *panforte*, cookies, biscuits, *farro*, barley, jams, products made with boar, locally roasted coffee.

Drogheria Manganelli, Via di Città 71. Open 8:30–20h, Sunday 10:30–20h.

A Siena institution since 1879, this handsome store stocks good wine and oil, plus grappa, designer pastas and good local brands, honey, jams from local farmers, Pecorino in baskets. It sells *panforte* by the piece and *ricciarelli*, Siena's soft almond cookies. This store is a bit pricey but very agreeable.

WINE

*Enoteca San Domenico, Via del Paradiso
56, tel. 0577/271181. Open daily 9–20h.*

A good selection of wines produced in
the province of Siena, also honey,
cookies, sweets, and other local
products. Its business card has a vintage
chart dating back to 1928. Near the
Church of San Domenico.

Tirli (Grosseto)

HOTEL-DINING

*Locanda La Luna, Via del Podere 8, tel.
0564/945854, fax 0564/945906, info
@locanda-laluna.it. Closed Tuesday
(except in August) from Easter to
October. Restaurant open weekends
only from October to Easter; closed
most of January and early February.
Master Card, Visa. Moderate.*

Tirli is a hill town in southern Toscana
that is 6 km (up twisty roads) from
beautiful beaches, including Cala
Violina. You are immersed in beautiful
nature and can make this a base for your
local travels. Rooms are homey. The food
is excellent, including several *cinghiale*
(wild boar) dishes, filet of beef wrapped
in prosciutto, and braised rabbit.

Viareggio (Lucca)

DINING

*Ristorante Romano, Via Mazzini 120,
tel. 0584/31382. Closed Monday, also
Tuesday lunch in July and August, and
most of January. All credit cards*

Since 1970 this has been one of the most
popular purveyors of fish and seafood in
this part of Italy.

*L'Oca Bianca, Via Coppino 409, tel.
0584/388477. Open for dinner
Wednesday through Monday. Open on*

*Tuesday evenings in July and August.
MasterCard. Visa. Moderately expensive.*

Careful and creative preparation of
seafood makes this restaurant stand apart.

*La Darsena, Via Virgilio 150, tel. 0584/
392785. Closed Sunday and Christmas–
January 6. All credit cards. Moderate.*

Here one can eat well on more humble
fare: octopus, mussels, cuttlefish, whitebait, mullet, fresh anchovies, *baccalà*.

Villa a Sesta (Siena)

DINING

*La Bottega del Trenta, Via Santa
Caterina 2, tel. 0577/359226. Closed*

*Tuesday evening and Wednesday.
No credit cards. Moderate.*

Dining in a lovely rural setting. I particularly like lunch here on a warm day when one can sit outdoors and feast on light pastas, good cheeses, and excellent

secondi such as squab and rabbit. A good place to dine if you are visiting wineries just outside Siena.

Volterra (Pisa)

Volterra is of Etruscan origin and attracts visitors with its eerie silence.

DINING

Trattoria da Badò, Borgo San Lazzaro 9, tel. 0588/86477. Closed Wednesday and two weeks in June. All credit cards. Moderate.

On the periphery of town on the road that leads to Colle Val d'Elsa is this very good restaurant. Some fine dishes

include *zuppa alla volterrana* (vegetables and bread), *pappardelle alla lepre* (watch for bits of bone), excellent *penne alla boscaiola* (with slivered mushrooms that acquire the texture of a meat sauce), *coniglio a modo nostro, cinghiale in umido* (braised with tomato and herbs), tripe, Pecorino cheese, and very good coffee.

Cacciucco
Livornese Fish Stew

This dish originated with the fishermen in the port of Livorno. After selling most of their catch, they used what was left to make lunch for themselves. There is great room for improvisation in making *cacciucco*, but you must follow the guiding principle of using as many different types of fish as possible. Some should be large, others quite small. You can have *cacciucco* as a primo or as a secondo.

Serves 4 to 6
2 kilos/4½ pounds assorted fresh fish
225 ml/8 ounces extra-virgin olive oil
1 large onion, chopped coarsely
2 cloves garlic, minced
1 fresh peperoncino
350 grams/12 ounces/2 cups peeled Italian
  plum tomatoes, preferably San
  Marzano type
4 tablespoons chopped fresh parsley
6 fresh basil leaves, torn into strips
250 ml/1 cup dry white wine
180 ml/3¾ cup water

Wash all the fish carefully. Cut the bigger pieces into chunks; leave the smaller fish whole (if you are bothered by the head and tail, remove them, but remember that fish heads supply a lot of flavor). Set the fish aside. Set a large, heavy-bottomed casserole dish atop the stove, heat the oil over medium heat. Then add the onion, garlic, and *peperoncino* and sauté until the onion becomes translucent. Add the tomatoes, parsley, basil, wine, and the water and stir. Add the larger fish and cook for 5 minutes. Then add the smaller fish. Stir gently so that all the flavors combine, but be careful not to break the fish. Cover and cook over low heat until the fish is tender (about 30 minutes).

Cook's Note: It is customary to place a couple of slices of garlic-scented toasted Tuscan bread at the bottom of the diner's bowl before serving the cacciucco on top of it.

Wine: Vernaccia di San Gimignano or another Tuscan white.

Moro in Camicia
Chocolate Mousse Topped with Fresh Peach Sauce

This recipe is from the cooking school at Badia a Coltibuono. It makes a perfect dessert when fresh peaches are at their peak.

Serves 6

Cake

120 grams/4 ounces/8 tablespoons unsalted butter, plus 1 tablespoon for coating the mold
90 grams/3 ounces almonds, toasted and chopped
180 grams/6 ounces bittersweet chocolate
6 large eggs, separated
210 grams/7 ounces/¾ cup granulated sugar

Peach Sauce

500 grams/Slightly more than 1 pound fresh, fragrant peaches, peeled, pitted, and cut in pieces
60 grams/2 ounces/½ cup granulated sugar
Juice of 1 lemon

Preheat the oven to 200°C (400°F). Butter a deep mold, about 15 centimeters (6 inches) in diameter, with 1 tablespoon butter and half of the almonds. Refrigerate, covered with plastic. Melt the chocolate and the remaining butter in the top of a double boiler, stirring frequently. Let the mixture cool completely. Then beat the egg whites in a bowl until stiff. In another bowl, beat the sugar and egg yolks until fluffy, fold in the melted chocolate, and combine. Gently fold in the egg whites and the remaining almonds with a spatula. Fill the mold with the chocolate cream and bake for about 30 minutes. To make the sauce, puree the peaches with the sugar and lemon juice in a blender. When the cake is done, unmold the cake onto a large serving dish by inserting a knife around the edges. Pour the sauce around the sides of the cake and serve immediately.

Wine: Moscato d'Asti.

Marche

 Here is a region that many travelers have never heard of, and those that have would be hard put to locate it on a map. To Italians the Marche is an afterthought, something sandwiched between Umbria and Toscana on one side and the Adriatic Sea on the other. Others know it as the spillover from the Riviera Romagnola in Emilia-Romagna. Marche does have an extensive stretch of attractive Adriatic beaches that draw Italians from other regions, but most go only to those from Pesaro north. The shore is the only strip of flat terrain in the region. The *marchigiano* towns on the coast have lush green vegetation nearby and a delightful climate. There are still stretches of coastline that are undeveloped, and there is about the Marche—both at the sea and in higher elevations—a sense of peace and tranquillity.

Mountains make up 31 percent of the terrain, the other 69 percent being hills. There are many quiet hill towns, especially the city of Urbino, the Classic Town for the Marche. The hill towns of Marche stand tall, and all seem immersed in green surroundings, which distinguishes them from most of their Umbrian and Tuscan counterparts, which have beige, tan, or sparsely green outskirts. Many of the most beautiful hill towns are in the area north of Urbino called the Montefeltro, which is tucked into the border areas of Romagna and Toscana. If you go there, be sure to visit San Leo and then dine in either Carpegna or Sant'Agata Feltria.

REGIONAL CAPITAL:
Ancona (AN).

PROVINCIAL CAPITALS:
Ascoli Piceno (AP),
  Macerata (MC),
  Pesaro e Urbino (PU).
The towns of Pesaro and
  Urbino are joint provincial
  capitals, but they are
  typically listed under
  "Pesaro."

TOURIST INFORMATION:
Regione Marche,
  Servizio Turismo ed
  Attività Ricettiva,
    Via Gentile da
    Fabriano,
    60100 Ancona,
    tel. 071/8061,
    fax 071/8062154.

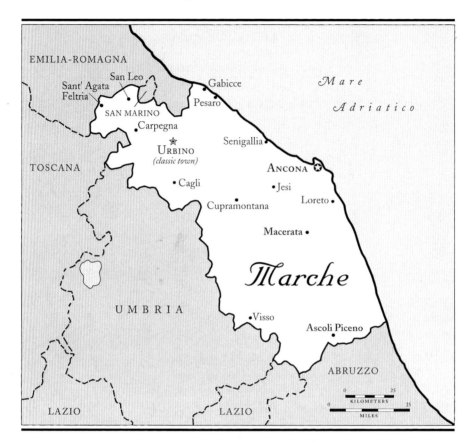

Agritourism:
Associazione Regionale
  Agriturist,
    Corso Mazzini 64,
    60100 Ancona,
    tel. 071/201751.

Why is the region so little known? It is separated from most of the rest of Italy by the Apennines. Access is either coastal, from Romagna to the north or Abruzzo to the south, or from Bologna, the only major inland city with roads that lead here. But one must plan to come to the Marche, since there is no reason to pass through there unless one is headed to or from Puglia.

Yet we know many famous *marchigiani:* artists such as Bramante, Raphael, Gentile da Fabriano, and Barocci. There is Leopardi, one of Italy's great poets, and composers such as Pergolesi, Rossini, and Gaspare Spontini (1774–1851), who composed many great operas, including *La Vestale*, and was a major figure at the Paris Opera, where he influenced Rossini, Meyerbeer, Weber, and Wagner. Few regions can claim to have produced opera stars of the caliber of Renata Tebaldi, Franco Corelli, and Beniamino Gigli.

Marchigiani are considered among the friendliest of Italians and are certainly among the best-looking. This may be due to diet or simply a fortunate gene pool. But they are also blessed with long life. Statistically they typically finish first or second in life expectancy in Italy, which usually ranks among the top three countries in the world, along with Japan and Iceland. With the exception of Urbino, Pesaro, and a couple of other beach towns, there is never the sense of the region's being overrun with tourists, so the friendly *marchigiani* often go out of their way to welcome you. Ancona, the capital and largest city, has only 105,000 people, so you will find that the cities of the Marche are of a human dimension, and that nature is always close at hand. Ancona is on a peninsula that permits you to see the sun rise and set on water. The city is elbow shaped ("Ancona" comes from the ancient Greek word for "elbow"), and the layout blocks winds from blowing south, so the part of the Marche to the south is much warmer than that to the north. There are three cities in the southern part of the region, Loreto, Macerata, and Ascoli Piceno, that deserve a visit if you are near.

Eating in the Marche

The combination of sea, hills, and mountains provides various environments for sources of food. There is superb seafood as well as excellent truffles, mushrooms, meats, olives, grapes, and especially cheeses.

ANTIPASTI

Ciauscolo (also called *Ciavuscolo*). A soft, spreadable *salame*. A specialty of Visso.
Lonza. A *salame* made of meat from a pig's neck or cheek.
Olive Ascolane. Large stuffed olives, breaded and deep-fried.
Tartufo. Truffles are a specialty in Montefeltro, the northernmost part of the region, at the Romagna border. They appear in antipasti, with pastas, and in *secondi.*

PRIMI

Maccharoncelli alla Campofilone. Thin egg noodles with a pork-and-veal sauce.
Tacconi. A pasta made of fava-bean flour. A specialty of Mondavio.
Vincisgrassi. A very rich lasagna that contains cream, a dense veal *ragù*, chicken giblets, black truffles, fresh tomatoes, butter, Parmigiano-Reggiano, mozzarella, and other ingredients. It is named for an Austrian military man named Windischgratz, who was once in residence at Macerata, where this is the local specialty.

SECONDO

Brodetto. Although *brodetto* is the name of a rich fish stew all over the Adriatic, it reaches its apex in Marche, where every little seaside town seems to have its distinct version. Classic *brodetto* uses only fish, no seafood. *Brodetto* is always made with fish, onions, garlic, herbs, oil, and is served over slices of bread. From the town of Numana north it is made with thirteen types of fish, untoasted bread rubbed with garlic, and a dash of vinegar. To the south it is made with nine types of fish, which are floured, thus thickening the soup, plus saffron and toasted bread that has not been rubbed with garlic. In both north and south sole and red and gray mullet are among the selected fish.

Coniglio in Coccio. Rabbit first marinated in white wine, then cooked in milk and spices, then browned in the oven.

Coniglio in Porchetta. Roast rabbit stuffed with wild fennel.

Garagoli. Cone-shaped mollusks cooked with wild fennel, available May through August.

Lumache a Nove Erbe. Snails cooked with nine herbs, a specialty of the northern Marche, especially Cagli.

Meats alla Brace. Charcoal-grilled meats are popular.

Oca in Potacchio. Braised goose cooked in white wine, olive oil, garlic, tomatoes, and rosemary.

Olivette. Thin rolls of meat, usually veal, that are stuffed or spread with different flavors. For example, *olivette alla pesarese* are thin veal rolls with a caper spread.

Porchetta. Roast suckling pig stuffed with herbs and garlic.

Sarde alla Marchigiana. Sardines baked with bread crumbs, rosemary, parsley, and lemon.

FORMAGGIO

Casciotta. This was the favorite cheese of Michelangelo. It is 70 percent sheep's milk, 30 percent cow's milk. His letters indicate that he always had a large supply on hand and nibbled on it while he sculpted. He also writes that he preferred cheeses that were made in the spring when the sheep grazed on tender grass. When he became wealthy, he bought a tract of land near Urbino with sheep on it to assure that he always would have cheese.

Formaggio di Fossa (also called *Formaggio di Tufo*). Pecorino cheese that is stored in caves (often made of tufaceous rock), where it loses 20 percent of its fat and concentrates its flavor. The best I have tasted is served at the Ristorante Vecchia Urbino in Urbino. The origin of this process came when barbarians invaded the region centuries ago. The shepherds hid their cheeses in caves, covering them with leafy branches. This atmosphere fostered a second fermentation of the cheese, which led to its unique flavor and, as it aged, its distorted shape.

Pecorino di Monterinaldo. Sheep's-milk cheese flavored with herbs.

Pecorino Sotto le Foglie di Noci. Pecorino cheese wrapped in leaves from a walnut tree takes on a hint of nut flavor. A specialty of Carpegna.

BREAD

Crescia Sfogliata. A popular food with students at the University of Urbino. This is a flatbread filled with cheese, eggs, or vegetables.

Piadina. Flatbread typical of Emilia-Romagna is also found in northern Marche.

DOLCI

Beccute. Little cookies from Ancona made with almonds, raisins, dried figs, olive oil, and cornmeal.

Cicerchiata. A honey cake topped with cinnamon and almonds.

Frustingolo Marchigiano. Christmas cake from Ascoli Piceno with nuts, figs, honey, and candied fruit.

The Wines of the Marche

Verdicchio. One of the most famous wines in Italy. This light white from Jesi became known because it was sold by Fazi-Battaglia in an amphora-shaped bottle that had a little scroll attached that told the story of the wine. Heavy plantings followed, and the wine boomed in the 1960s and 1970s. Quality declined in the late 1970s as most of the wines were mass-produced, but there has been a conscientious return to quality. It is made with the Verdicchio grape, although DOC rules permit using up to 15 percent Trebbiano or Malvasia grapes. One worth trying is Verdicchio Classico dei Castelli di Jesi dei Fratelli Bucci.

Bianco dei Colli Maceratesi. Made primarily of Trebbiano grapes, with the addition of Maceratino, Malvasia Toscana, and Verdicchio possible.

Bianchello del Metauro. The local white of Urbino.

Rosso Cònero and Rosso Piceno. Two excellent DOC reds. Rosso Cònero is made with Montepulciano grapes with a bit of Sangiovese. Rosso Piceno is 60 percent Sangiovese, 40 percent Montepulciano; a bit of Trebbiano may be added.

Sangiovese dei Colli Pesaresi. Another lesser-known and less forceful red.

Other Drinks

Mistrà and *Anisetta.* Two anise-based after-dinner drinks.

Moretta. Typical of the town of Fano. It is made of one part *anisetta*, one part rum, and one part cognac. It is heated, a bit of sugar is melted in, coffee is added, and then a piece of lemon peel.

Ancona

DINING

Osteria Teatro Strabacco, Via Oberdan 2a, tel. 071/56748. Closed Monday. All credit cards. Moderate.

Every political and cultural figure who passes through Ancona winds up at this restaurant, especially at night, when the kitchen is open long after most other eating places have pulled down their shutters. Stick to simple dishes here, especially *crescia sfogliata* and grilled fish and vegetables. It is possible to order a gluten-free menu by calling ahead.

La Moretta, Piazza Plebiscito 52, tel.
071/202317. Closed Sunday, early
January, and mid-August. Moderate.

Since 1897 the same family has served
marchigiano food from land and sea.

Ascoli Piceno

Here is still another Italian city that is a joy to behold yet has relatively few visitors.
It is surrounded by rivers and has stunning architecture, an imposing main square
(the Piazza del Popolo), and a nice old quarter.

CAFFÈ

Caffè Meletti Piazza del Popolo 18/22,
tel. 0736/259626.

All chandeliers, red velvet, and mirrors,
this *caffè* has been the favorite in Ascoli
since 1905. It is loved not only as a place
to meet but also as a symbol of the city.
Tenor Beniamino Gigli, from nearby
Porto Recanati, was a regular, and
Hemingway managed to get here, too.
The Meletti is often ranked among the
great *caffès* of Italy, but this too is
subjective: is a *caffè* great because of its
coffee, its decor, the people who
frequent it, or some combination of the
three? Nonetheless, the Meletti is quite
special and should not be missed. Be
sure to have *l'anisetta con la mosca,* a
glass of anisette with a coffee bean
dropped in.

DINING

Trattoria Vittoria, Via Bonaccorsi 7, tel.
0736/259535. Closed Sunday. No credit
cards. Moderately inexpensive.

Not far from the Piazza del Popolo, this
tiny and welcoming trattoria offers very
good food. The *olive ascolane* are more
delicate than most, the fresh pasta is eggy

and tastes great when *funghi porcini* are
available. The roast meats are succulent.
Decent Conero and Verdicchio wines.

Kursaal, Via Luigi Mercantini 66, tel.
0736/253140. Closed Sunday. All credit
cards. Moderate.

What was once a wine shop has
successfully expanded to become a good
place to eat and drink the best local
products.

Trattoria Corso, Corso Mazzini 277, tel.
0736/256760. Closed Sunday evening,
Monday. All credit cards. Moderate.

Come here for excellent fish and seafood.

ICE CREAM

Gelateria Veneta, Via Giudea 10 (near
the Piazza del Popolo).

Superb ice cream since 1923.

WINE

Enoteca dei Vini Regionali—Ente Sviluppo Marche, Via Alpi 20, tel. 071/8081.

This is the regional promotional center for Marche wines. Tastings are possible.

Cagli (Pesaro e Urbino)

The specialty of Cagli is snails (*lumache*), which are either braised in tomato-and-herb sauce or baked with oil, garlic, and herbs. Walk off your meal by visiting the Comune (city hall) with its beautiful small theater (il Teatro Comunale) within.

DINING

Ristorante da Rosa, Via Ospedale 11, tel. 0721/781309. Closed Monday. No credit cards. Moderately inexpensive.

Rabbit and hare are specialties here. For a *primo*, try *pappardelle al ragù di lepre* and have *coniglio in porchetta* as a secondo.

Trattoria di Luchini, tel. 0721/787231. Closed Friday. No credit cards. Inexpensive.

Good food. Snails are a specialty. Fresh pasta is good and so is the lamb.

Carpegna (Pesaro e Urbino)

This town is famous for its excellent *prosciutto crudo*. Although *prosciutti* of Parma and San Daniele are more famous, this one is delicious, too. It is saltier than the others but has a wonderful melting texture in the mouth and a sweet aftertaste. Historically the town has been famous for its foods, including poultry, eggs, cheeses, and cured meats. All sorts of wild animals live in the forest near Carpegna, including badgers, wolves, and foxes and edible ones such as partridge, magpies, hare, bucks, and boars.

DINING

Ristorante La Capinera, Via Passo Cantoniera, tel. 0722/77211 or 77458. Closed Monday. Moderately inexpensive.

Good basic food. The local prosciutto is available as an antipasto. The *coniglio ripieno* (stuffed rabbit) is moist and flavorful.

Trattoria da Silvana. Moderately inexpensive.

This place was enthusiastically recommended to me by someone whose taste I respect. He said that it looks like nothing special, what with a TV set playing soccer matches while you eat. But if you go in November, when truffles have arrived, there is a *frittata di tartufi neri* or one with *porcini* mushrooms. *Prosciutto di Carpegna* is also a major protagonist on the menu, and I'm told the pastas are great.

Cupramontana (Ancona)

FOLKLORE

Festa dell'Uva.

The grape festival is held at harvesttime in early October.

MUSEUM

Museo Internazionale dell'Etichetta, Corso Leopardi 58, tel. 0732/780199. Open 10–12h, Wednesday 10–12h, 16–19h; closed Saturday–Monday.

As of this writing, this is the only museum in the world specifically dedicated to wine labels, although one has been planned in the town of Aigle near Lausanne, Switzerland. There are about 50,000 labels in the collection, but there is only exhibition space for 4,000, so there are rotating displays. If you have a particular interest, however, you should contact the curator, Franco Rossi, who might be able to arrange a viewing of the labels that you request. There are large collections from Italy, France, Portugal, and Spain, as well as unusual labels from China, Japan, Russia, Turkey, Jordan, Israel, Egypt, Tunisia, Algeria, and many from other countries in Europe and the Americas. I find it interesting how labels are the expression of a time and place: great castles, pastoral scenery, or the more streamlined and austere labels of today.

Furlo (Pesaro e Urbino), also called Gola del Furlo

DINING

Hotel-Ristorante La Ginestra, tel. 0721/797033, fax 0721/700040. Closed Monday (except in July and August) and in January. American Express, Diners Club, Visa. Moderate to moderately expensive.

About twenty kilometers (twelve miles) from Urbino, this is considered one of the better restaurants in the region. Come in autumn, when truffles and mushrooms are in season. Good food is available, the views are superb, and the rooms at the hotel are comfortable. All in all, this is a very good base for touring the northern Marche and southern Romagna if you have a car.

Gabicce Mare (Pesaro e Urbino)

DINING

Lo Squero, Via del Porto 15, tel. 0541/967318. Closed Wednesday (except in summer). No credit cards. Moderate to moderately expensive.

Simply put, this is one of the best seafood restaurants I have eaten at in Italy. All of the food is excellent, and the prices for such a feast are moderate given the quality, but with some wine the bill may become moderately expensive. The space is vast and is simply decorated with antique photographs of fishermen. The view is of the *squero* (the place where boats are built or repaired) and the tiny harbor of Gabicce. This town is part of the Adriatic Riviera, but is not as overrun as most of its neighbors. There is a long list of antipasti, but you should sample *canocchie, sgombri bolliti,* and *pizza bianca* (which is plain crust with a bit of olive oil and rosemary). All the seafood is fresh and beautifully prepared; the *cannelloni ripieni* are thin crepes filled with fresh fish and seafood and should not be missed. The *frittura di zanchetti e calamaretti* is like tempura (which, after all, had a Mediterranean origin in Portugal). The *frittura mista* (fried mixed seafood) is delicate and greaseless; the grilled and roast fishes (which vary with the daily market) are perfectly rendered. Or try the *sauté di vongole e conchiglie crostacee* (all kinds of beautiful shellfish, including

Adriatic fish is the essential ingredient of brodetto

four types of clams). The wine list by owner Errico Tausani is well chosen and well priced. If none of this appeals to you, the restaurant also makes good pizza, but the only way I would stay away from Lo Squero would be if I were deathly allergic to fish.

Gabicce Monte (Pesaro e Urbino)

Gabicce Monte is up in the mountains that look over the sea and Gabicce Mare below. We are at the border of Romagna, and the friendly warmth of that region is palpable on this side, too. In the 1960s this place was an "in" spot for the arts and film communities; Fellini spent a lot of time here. It is now a bit *passé* as a hot spot, but perhaps this is better. As a place left behind, it has its memories and its character, but none of the frenzy.

DINING

Osteria della Miseria, Via dei Mandorli 2, tel. 0541/958308. Open evenings only; closed Wednesday. All credit cards. Moderately inexpensive.

Off the Strada Panoramica of Gabicce Monte is this prototypical *osteria.* Guido is your host, and you will be glad you came. Signora Pina, with her flour-covered hands, always seems at work making pasta or *piadine.* (She is a widow and a champion ballroom dancer with many suitors.) An open oven with a skewer for grilling and roasting warms

one room. There are long wooden tables covered with sheets of paper of the type used to wrap fish at the market. The wine is well chosen, and the food is rich and homemade. Different dishes issue from the kitchen: a pot of little clams with garlic and *peperoncino,* then transparent slices of prosciutto on *piadina.* It is nice to eat these things with your hands. Prosciutto always seems to tear in the right place, while a knife would just be too random. The fresh pasta with mushrooms or with chicken livers is better than anything you would find in the best restaurants in the United States because the flavors are intense and the pasta is perfect. But while you wait, the *salumi* are superb: sensations of pepper and sweetness and delicate fat and hints of herbs all frolic in your mouth. In the winter there is *polenta con le vongole*, an unusually satisfying combination of soft polenta with herb-scented clams. The house is famous for its *torta di cioccolato*, but there are other good desserts, too.

Jesi (Ancona)

Jesi is the epicenter of production of Verdicchio wine, one of the most famous of all Italian whites.

BAR-BAKERY
Caffè Bardi, Corso Matteotti 27.

An old-style bar from the 1930s that makes good pastries, cookies, and ice cream.

DINING
Osteria Tana Libera Tutti, Piazza Pontelli 1, tel. 0731/59237. Closed Sunday, two weeks in August, and one week in January. All credit cards. Moderate.

All the food here pairs flavorfully with Verdicchio wine. Soups such as *pasta e ceci* make a good *primo*, and I am very fond of a dish called *pollo pesce*, which is chicken cooked with capers, tuna, anchovies, and olives. Be sure to save room for *formaggio di tufo*, cheese aged in tufaceous caves. If you like it enough, they will sell you some of this precious, hard-to-find cheese to take away.

ENOTECA PUBBLICA
Enoteca Pubblica di Jesi, Via Federico Conti 5, tel. 0731/5381, fax 0731/538328. Open only July and August, Monday–Saturday 17–22h.

The setting is the Palazzo Baldeschi. One can taste and purchase wines from throughout the Marche, but especially the Verdicchio that has made Jesi famous.

Loreto (Ancona)

Loreto is a town of some religious significance, in part because many people believe that the Madonna lived here. There is a house called the Santa Casa that supposedly was transported here from Nazareth by angels, arriving in 1294 after a three-year stop in Dalmatia. The house nestles in a hill of laurels (*lauretum* in Latin, from which the name of the city derives).

DINING
Andreina, Via Buffaloreccia 14, tel. 071/970124. Closed Tuesday. All credit cards. Moderate.

Although Andreina is about 2 km (1.25 miles) from town, it is worth traveling to for the delicious *vincisgrassi*, one of the best examples I know of this ornate dish. Roast meats and poultry are wonderful. The *pollo arrosto* is juicy and fragrant with fresh herbs and garlic. Very, very good food.

Macerata

CHOCOLATE

Cioccolateria Marangoni, on Corso Cavour 159.

Makes wonderful chocolates by hand.

CULTURE

Macerata Festival: Arena Sferisterio, Casella Postale, 62100 Macerata, tel. 0733/256286, fax 0733/41603.

The Arena Sferisterio, a spherical stadium of sorts, hosts an important opera festival each year from mid-July to mid-August. Despite Macerata's relatively remote location, it attracts major stars. The opera productions are unusual because this arena is almond-shaped, so that it is long but narrow. Audience members are always near part of the action, which shifts to play to all customers at one time or another.

DINING

Da Secondo, Via Pescheria Vecchia 26, tel. 0733/44912. Closed Monday and last two weeks in August. All credit cards. Moderately expensive.

The choice of opera stars (who perform at Macerata's festival, from mid-July to mid-August) and diners, who come here for the excellent *vincisgrassi*. Lamb and grilled meats are also good.

Trattoria da Rosa, Via Armaroli 17, tel. 0733/260124. Closed Sunday, Christmas, and a couple weeks in summer. All credit cards. Moderate.

Tasty seasonal cooking, plus standbys such as *vincisgrassi*, *piccione farcito* (stuffed squab), and *baccalà in bianco con olive* (cod with olives). Be sure to have the *formaggio di fossa* for dessert.

Marina di Montemarciano (Ancona)

DINING

Ristorante delle Rose, tel. and fax 071/9198668. Closed Monday (except June–September). MasterCard, Visa. Moderately expensive.

A pretty setting not far from Ancona for classic *marchigiano* cooking. Specialties include scampi with prosciutto, *tortelloni* filled with *branzino* topped with a *ragù* of sole, delicious *crespelle* with ricotta and prosciutto, plus good braised rabbit.

Mondavio (Pesaro e Urbino)

DINING

Hotel-Ristorante La Palomba, Via Gramsci 13, tel. 0721/97105,

info@lapalomba.it. Closed Sunday evening (November– March). All credit cards. Moderate.

Good food. The specialty of Mondavio is a pasta called *tacconi*, which is made of fava-bean flour.

Osimo (Ancona)

Osimo is a little community full of good food and wine. Most of the places you might visit are on Stradale Statale (SS) 16.

DINING

La Cantinetta del Conero, Strada Statale 16 (7.5 km [4¹/₂ miles] east of Osimo), tel. 071/7108651. Closed Saturday. All credit cards. Moderate.

A trattoria across from the Umani Ronchi winery, one of the better local producers of Verdicchio and Rosso Conero. The fish here is very good.

Pesaro

Pesaro is a large, very agreeable seaside town with good restaurants and hotels. It is the birthplace of the great soprano Renata Tebaldi and the magnificent composer Gioacchino Rossini, whose operas are produced each August in a very popular festival (0721/3800294, fax 0721/3800220, www.rossinioperafestival.it). Unfortunately the Maestro's home is no longer open to the public.

CERAMICS

G. Molanari, Via Luca delta Robbia 17, tel. 0721/33181. Closed Monday morning and Sunday. No credit cards.

Some of the most beautiful and original patterns are made at Molanari, a family concern that has been going since 1880.

DINING

Hotel Principe–Ristorante da Teresa, Viale Trieste 180, tel. 0721/30222 or 0721/ 30096. Closed Sunday evening, Monday (except in high season), March, November. All credit cards. Moderately expensive to expensive.

In the past this place was well known to singers and audience members at the Rossini opera festival, but word spread and foodies arrived quickly. Otello Renzi is a genuine gastronomic scholar who also has superb taste in wine. Put this together with the delicate and assured hand of his mother, Teresa, in the kitchen, and you have a memorable dining experience. The specialties are fresh pasta and all of the fish and seafood you could ever want.

Lo Scudiero, Via Baldassare 2, tel. 0721/ 64107. Closed Sunday, July, and the first week of January. All credit cards. Moderate to moderately expensive.

Popular with critics and well-heeled fans who attend the Rossini opera festival. My favorite pasta is trout-filled ravioli. The fish is also quite fine. The large room is comfortable, and service is very capable.

La Canonica, Via Borgata (in Castel-dimezzo, 12 km [4¹/₂ miles] from the center of Pesaro), tel. 0721/209017. Open Tuesday through Saturday evening, Sunday for lunch and dinner. All credit cards. Moderate.

Pesaro's restaurants have a higher-than-usual price because they compete for a more sophisticated visitor than one sees at most beach resorts. To economize in town one can eat pizza. Or, a short ride from the center by car or taxi can lead to this osteria that specializes in fish and seafood. The *salsiccia di pesce* is a "fish sausage" that combines mackerel, tuna, and monkfish that is worth trying. So too is the excellent *brodetto*.

MUSEUM

Museo delle Ceramiche, Piazza Toschi Mosca 29, tel. 0721/31213. Closed Sunday afternoon and Monday.

A good collection of Umbrian and other ceramics of the Renaissance and later.

WINE

Enoteca Vino Vip, Viale Verdi 78, tel. 0721/31011. Closed Sunday, Thursday, and in January.

Be sure to try the Verdicchio dei Fratelli Bucci if you have not tasted it elsewhere. There are more than eight hundred different wines here, plus a nice selection of oils, vinegars, and coffees. Owned by Otello Renzi of Ristorante da Teresa (see "Dining," above).

Sant'Agata Feltria (Pesaro e Urbino)

This small town is in a beautiful hilly setting and has a lovely small theater, Il Teatro Mariani. It is practically at the border with Romagna, and its cuisine reflects the influence of its neighbor. In the autumn, there are fragrant local truffles that are worth tasting. If you are traveling here by car, be sure to visit San Leo, one of the most beautiful little towns you will see in Italy.

DINING

Ristorante Tre Castagni, Via Fonte del Maestro 12, tel. 0541/929167. Closed Monday. No credit cards. Moderate.

Truffles are the specialty here: start with antipasti such as carpaccio or *crostino al tartufo* and hot *bocconcino al pecorino e tartufo*. For a primo have *ravioli al tartufo* (although *gnocchi al cinghiale* are also fine). A secondo could be *filetto al tartufo*, boneless beef fillet with truffle sauce.

Ristorante Perlini, Piazza del Mercato 4, tel. 0541/929637. No credit cards. Moderate.

Good *salumi*, prosciutto, little *tartine* with *funghi* and truffles, homemade *tagliatelle al ragù* and *tortelloni*, *agnello alla cacciatora*, and *coniglio in porchetta*.

Trattoria Antenna dal Morino, Località Monte San Benedetto, tel. 0541/929626. Closed Monday (except in July and August), first two weeks of September, and last three weeks of January. No credit cards. Moderately expensive.

A bit out of town, this is probably the best of the three restaurants listed here. There are all sorts of fry breads for starters, but you should save room for the many dishes flavored with truffles, especially pastas. Top *secondi* are the grilled meats and poultry. For dessert, a delicious fruit *crostata*.

Senigallia (Ancona)

BAR AND ICE CREAM

Caffetteria Gelateria La Meridiana, Piazza Roma 16, tel. 071/63961. Open 6:30–4h; closed Tuesday (except in summer), ten days in October, and ten days in February.

Night or day, this is the place to be for delicious coffee, pastries, and ice cream. There are also notable wines and spirits.

DINING

Osteria del Teatro, Via Fratelli Bandiera 70, tel. 071/60517. Open evenings only, Thursday through Tuesday, and also Wednesday in summer; closed in off-season months. Visa. Moderately inexpensive.

Very fine, casual dining.

Madonnina del Pescatore, Lungomare Italia 11 (in Marzocco di Senigallia, 6 km south of Pesaro), tel. 071/698267, madonninadelpescatore@tin.it. Closed Monday, Sunday evening (in some seasons). All credit cards. Moderately expensive.

Delicious, often esoteric food with a big following.

FOOD SHOPPING

Enogastronomia La Fenice, Via Cesare Battisti 11, tel. 071/659262. Closed Thursday afternoon and Sunday.

As much a wine shop as a food store, La Fenice is a good source if you happen to be staying in the area on vacation and plan to do some cooking. There are fine local wines, excellent pasta (Latini from Osimo), wonderful olive oils from small producers, good jams, cakes, vinegars, *salumi*, cheeses (particularly *formaggio di fossa* and *pecorino con tartufo*), good vegetables packed in oil, and an amazing selection of cakes and sweets.

WINE

Enoteca Galli, Via Pisacane 15, tel. 071/ 63811. Open 8:30-12:30h, 16-20h; closed Sunday and Thursday. Diners Club, Visa.

A very well-stocked wine shop with a vast collection of Marche vintages plus an extensive selection of well-chosen wines from other regions. But this is a very good source for Marche wines at suitable prices. It also sells *ciauscolo*, the region's delicious spreadable *salame*, as well as good cakes and jams.

Sirolo (Ancona)

DINING AND LODGING

Hotel Monteconero, at Monteconero, above Sirolo, tel. 071/9330592, fax 071/ *9330365. Open daily March 15–November 15. All credit cards. Moderate to moderately expensive.*

Octopus fresh from the sea

A nice hotel set in a former abbey with fine views of the sea and good fish and pasta. Top pastas are the *strozzapreti con gamberi e asparagi*, the *molinelle al radicchio e funghi*, and the *chitarrine al nero di seppie*. Try the *grigliata del golfo* as a *secondo* for fine grilled seafood and fish.

Torrette di Ancona (Ancona)

COOKING SCHOOL
Club a Table, Via Esino 173, 60020 Torre di Ancona (AN), tel. 071/883717.

This school, with classes in Italian only, is where the people of the Marche come to learn the cuisine of the region as interpreted by Lina Morichi. In general, classes are given once a week over the course of a month, but a visitor to the area might have the opportunity to take one class. Signora Morichi is especially well known for *ripieni*, the fillings that go into pastas, vegetables, and seafood.

Urbino
Classic Town

During the Renaissance Urbino had one of the most refined courts in Italy, full of artists and scholars in the service of Federico da Montefeltro. We all know him from the famous painting by Piero della Francesca in which the artist made no attempt to hide or minimize the duke's large, misshapen nose, which was broken in a joust. Urbino is the birthplace of two outstanding artists: Raphael, whose house can be visited on Via Raffaello, and Federico Barocci (1535–1619), one of the most talented and least-known of Renaissance artists. His house was on what is now called Via Barocci. Be sure to visit the Ducal Palace and the National Gallery of the Marche, one of Italy's foremost collections, which has works by Raphael, Barocci, Gentileschi, Piero della Francesca, and others. If this museum were in a large city, it would be a major tourist attraction with lines around the block. Also walk up and down the streets of town. They are alternately steep and narrow, but through them you will often see patches of green fields and blue sky in the middle distance. Every July there is a major festival of ancient music, the Festival Internazionale di Musica Antica, held in Urbino. Probably no city in Italy with a population of 16,000 has the treasures of Urbino, but because of its smallness you are always very close to nature. This is part of what made me select it as a classic *marchigiano* town.

BAKERY-BAR

Caffè-Pasticceria Basili, Piazza Repubblica 1.

Under the portico on the main square. Try the *sacchettini al cioccolato*, which are like *pain au chocolat* except that they gush with chocolate when you bite into them.

CERAMICS

Throughout the year you can study decoration, engraving, and restoration of ceramics at the Accademia Raffaello. For information, contact the tourist office: Azienda di Promozione Turistica di Urbino, Piazza Duca Federico 35, 61029 Urbino, tel. 0722/2613, fax 0722/2441.

DINING

Nenè, Via Crocicchia 30 (2.5 km from the city center), tel. 0722/2996. Closed Monday. All credit cards. Moderately inexpensive.

The *strozzapreti* (gnocchi) are good, and, if available, so are the fresh tagliatelle with *funghi*. *Agnello arrosto* is a good secondo.

Ristorante Vecchia Urbino, Via dei Vasari 3/5, tel. 0722/4447. Closed Tuesday (except April–September). All credit cards. Moderate to moderately expensive.

This is a high-end restaurant for Urbino in terms of price, quality and attentive service; note that cover and tip are included in the prices. But one can eat very well here, and I recommend a visit during your stay in town. A grandfather clock chimes the hours, which pass blissfully as you dine. One interesting way to start the meal is to do a tasting of olive oils on the local wholewheat bread. The restaurant has a good collection of oils from most of the Italian producing regions. The primi are all good: the light *passatelli* in beef broth, the thin, eggy *tagliolini al tartufo* (tossed with sweet butter and a generous amount of truffle), or a *vincisgrassi* that is much more delicate than the version in Macerata. *Coniglio al coccio* (rabbit marinated in white wine and then cooked in milk and spices before being browned in the oven) is a good secondo, as are the grilled meats. Under no circumstance should you fail to taste the Pecorino d'Urbino, a *formaggio di fossa* made by Gabriele Monti, the restaurant's owner. This is a hard cheese with a reddish color near the rind. The flavor is rich and complex. There is a pronounced flavor of herbs in the cheese, because Signor Monti surrounds the cheese with them when he puts it in the cave. He makes forty to fifty cheeses per year, each weighing about a kilo (2.2 pounds). This is some of the best cheese you will ever taste. I sat for a half hour before having coffee to let the full impact of the cheese be felt in my mouth.

Ristorante Agripan, Via del Leone 11, tel. 0722/327448. No credit cards. Moderate.

All the products served here come from the nearby Azienda Agricola L'Aquilone. You should come here for *farro*, which is served in many guises. The ristorante also has lamb, rabbit, and *pollo ruspante* (free-range chicken). A nice, small, welcoming room that has a collection of artifacts from peasant culture.

Ristorante La Vecchia Fornarina, Via Mazzini 14, tel. 0722/320007. All credit cards. Moderate.

Good food, including cappelletti, *coniglio in porchetta, caciotta di Urbino alle brace, funghi porcini alle brace.*

Rosticceria Il Girarrosto, Piazza San Francesco 3, or Via Santa Margherita 11. Inexpensive.

Try the *crescia sfogliata.*

FOLKLORE
Festa del Duca.

Every August, there is a series of events that evoke the festivals held by Duke Federico when he headed the Duchy of Urbino. This is followed by the Cena Rinascimentale, a sumptuous meal composed of dishes that would have been consumed in Renaissance Urbino. Reservations far in advance are required. Check with the tourist office (see address under "Ceramics," above).

MARKET
The small fruit and vegetable market is on the Piazza San Francesco, open Monday through Saturday. On Saturday there is also a market for clothes, shoes, and housewares, making this the most animated and interesting day to pay a visit.

Visso (Macerata)

The specialty of Visso is the delicious *ciauscolo*, a soft *salame*. This town is close to Umbria and in many ways looks in that direction in terms of food and temperament.

DINING
Trattoria da Richetta, Piazza Garibaldi 7, tel. 0737/9339. Closed Monday and September. No credit cards. Moderate.

After sampling the *ciauscolo* (here called *ciavuscolo*), try other specialties of this trattoria that features the best mountain foods from both Marche and Umbria. Truffles from Norcia appear with tagliatelle, lentils from Castelluccio appear in *zuppa di lenticchie*, then there is excellent lamb and pork, plus trout from local rivers. Pecorino cheese and fruit are the best options for dessert.

FOOD SHOPPING
Alimentari Giuseppe Tarragoni, Via XXIV Maggio 11.

Good cheeses and *salumi*, plus truffles and lentils.

Angelo Calabrò, Piazza Capuzi 49.

The place to buy *ciauscolo*.

Maccheroncelli alla Campofilone

Despite the name, this pasta is not macaroni but thin egg noodles. You can effectively skip the labor of making these by purchasing a good Italian brand of egg pasta such as tagliatelle or tagliolini. This is a popular dish throughout the Marche.

Serves 4 to 6
100 grams/7 tablespoons unsalted butter
150 grams/6 ounces loin of pork, cut in small chunks
150 grams/6 ounces veal, cut in small chunks
450 grams/1 pound/2 cups peeled plum tomatoes
Salt and freshly ground black pepper to taste
100 grams/3½ ounces chicken livers, cleaned and minced
450 grams/1 pound dried tagliatelle or tagliolini
Freshly grated Pecorino Romano

Melt the butter in a large saucepan and add the pork and veal. Sauté on all sides until lightly browned. Add the tomatoes and salt and pepper. Cover, and cook over low heat for 90 minutes. If too much liquid evaporates, add a little water or wine (such as Rosso Conero or Verdicchio). Ten minutes before the cooking of the sauce is completed, stir in the minced chicken livers. While the sauce is cooking, set a large pot of cold water to boil. When it reaches a boil, toss in a pinch of salt. When it returns to a boil, cook the pasta according to the package directions. Time the cooking of the pasta to the completion of the sauce. Put the pasta in a warm serving bowl, toss with sauce, and serve, accompanied by freshly grated Pecorino.

Wine: Rosso Conero or Verdicchio.

Scampi al Prosciutto
Prosciutto-Wrapped Shrimp

A specialty of Ristorante delle Rose in Marina di Montemarciano. It uses prosciutto from Carpegna, but if that is unavailable you may substitute the product from Parma or San Daniele.

Serves 6 as a main course, 12 as an
    antipasto
2 kilograms/4½ pounds whole (or 1.3
    kilograms/3 pounds cleaned) medium
    shrimp or prawns
200 grams/½ pound prosciutto, sliced thin
4 to 5 tablespoons extra-virgin olive oil
1 glass/200 milliliters/⅔ cup dry white wine,
    such as Verdicchio

If you are using whole shrimp or prawns, clean them carefully and remove the shells, heads, and tails. Wrap each shrimp in a slice of prosciutto (if the slices are long, use half a slice). Pour the olive oil in a pan and heat it. Then carefully add the shrimp, shake the pan, and cover. Cook over low heat. After 5 minutes, turn the shrimp, shake the pan again, and cover. Cook for another 5 minutes. Then add the wine and let it evaporate. Serve immediately.

Variation: Marche is the home of excellent anisette. Instead of wine, you might try ½ glass/100 milliliters/⅓ cup of anisette.

Wine: Verdicchio.

Umbria

Ogni cor nasconde un mistero Every heart harbors a mystery

—VERDI, ERNANI,

LIBRETTO BY FRANCESCO MARIA PIAVE

REGIONAL CAPITAL:
Perugia (PG).

PROVINCIAL CAPITAL:
Terni (TR).

TOURIST INFORMATION:
Ufficio Regionale del
  Turismo,
    Corso Vannucci 30,
    06100 Perugia,
    tel. 075/6962483.

Agritourism:
Associazione Regionale
  Agriturist,
    Via Tuderte 30,
    06100 Perugia,
    tel. 075/30174.

Landlocked Umbria, in the center of the country, is often called the Green Heart of Italy by its boosters. It is bordered by Toscana, Lazio, and Marche and is a combination of mountains (53 percent), hills (41 percent), with the balance being the flat terrain in one of the central valleys. This is not a place without water, however. The Tevere begins just over the border in Toscana before flowing down to Roma and the sea, traversing Umbria for 210 kilometers (130 miles). The zone where it begins is called the Alto Tevere and is a fertile area of agriculture. Tributaries of the Tevere course through mountain valleys, as do other streams. Most important, though, is Lago di Trasimeno, the largest lake in central and southern Italy. As one travels its northern side, it looks like a large sea whose far shore is not visible. The lake provides a moderating influence on much of Umbria's climate. The eastern part of the region has lofty Apennine peaks, and the forests and dales of this zone are full of truffles, one of the signature flavors of the Umbrian kitchen. Despite all of the trees, there are also very high pastures where cattle and sheep graze on pure grass in fresh air. In this same area, in Norcia (the Classic Town for this region), is a gathering of superb ingredients and talented cooks that have few rivals anywhere. Norcia's pork butchers are so accomplished that they have become a noun: a *norcino* is

considered a top pork butcher, and wherever he goes he can open a *norcineria*. To distinguish a regular citizen from a butcher of the town, the townspeople call themselves *nursini* (from "Nursia," the Latin name for "Norcia").

The typical adjectives used to describe Umbria include "mystical," "serene," and "enchanted." Although it sits between the very busy regions of Toscana and Lazio, most of Umbria remains quiet and somewhat set apart. The mystery of this green heart of Italy is how it retains its quiet otherworldliness despite outside influences that would conceivably corrupt it. Only Perugia, the capital, seems at all immersed in the Italian mainstream. As Toscana became chic and overrun with summer vacationers who rented country houses, some of Umbria absorbed part of the spillover. The region may seem less rich and refined than its famous neighbor, but it too has hill towns, olive oil, young Pecorino cheese, limpid light, and medieval and Renaissance art. Americans were among the first to make the move, because many knew the region as the home of the Spoleto Festival and the Università Italiana per Stranieri in Perugia, where they took Italian classes. Now there is a very large community of foreigners and artistic Romans near Todi, which, according to a study done by the University of Kentucky, is the most livable city in the world.

Umbria is full of abbeys, monasteries, and convents in tranquil towns such as Assisi and Montefalco. Saint Francis of Assisi (1182–1226) is the most famous Umbrian of all. Many Umbrian children are named Francesco or Francesca in his honor. His belief in poverty and self-denial has been absorbed into the Umbrian ethic so that simplicity is still considered a virtue, even if voluntary poverty is excessive. Yet Francis's mysticism and his wonder at nature are enduring values in Umbria. We all know about his love of birds and trees, and when you visit Assisi you can see why. The setting looks almost exactly as it did seven hundred years ago. Umbrians are among the most environmentally conscious of all Italians, and much of the "health food" consumed in Italy is grown in this region.

Assisi is certainly full of tourists and pilgrims, as well as monks and nuns, but even at its most crowded it feels eternally peaceful. The Basilica di San Francesco has decoration by Cimabue, Simone Martini, Lorenzetti, and especially Giotto, who did twenty-eight frescoes about the life of the saint. Santa Chiara (Saint Clare) of Assisi inspires devotion almost as great as that accorded Francis. She was consecrated in 1212 by Francis and cared for him during his declining years and founded an order dedicated to the poor. She founded the second Franciscan order, known as the Order of the Poor Clares.

A visit to Perugia will give you a different sense of Umbria. The first time I went there, in 1975, it was a beautiful regional capital that was self-contained on its hill and was remarkably quiet. Its main attraction for many foreigners, aside from galleries containing works by Perugino, Piero della Francesca, Luca Signorelli, and Raphael, was the Università per Stranieri. Here is where people from throughout the world came to study Italian. Many found it such a nice place to live that they remained. As more wealth came to Umbria, Perugia grew more rapidly than any Italian city I know, so there is now a remarkable sprawl as houses and stores have colonized once-green hills. Perugia, which was always an intellectual citadel, became a major cultural and business center. It is the locale for Umbria Jazz, an annual jazz festival that is the most important in Italy. Perugia is also famous as a center for pasta production (Buitoni) and chocolate making (Perugina). The Easter eggs of Perugia are eaten the world over.

To discover what Perugia was like before it became cosmopolitan, go to smaller towns such as Gubbio, Spello, Orvieto, Todi, and Spoleto (except in June and July, when the Festival of the Two Worlds makes it the busiest town in central Italy). If you go to these towns in autumn or winter, you will detect a fragrance that to me is emblematic of Umbria: the toasty smell of burning wood. It is used for heating homes but also for some cooking. If you are lucky, you will also get to know the aphrodisiacal perfume of black truffles from Norcia and Spoleto, which elevates Umbrian cuisine to legendary status. Combine the truffles with local pasta, meat, game, delicious olive oil, and cheese, and you have a cuisine well worth discovering.

Eating in Umbria

ANTIPASTO

Bruschetta. Toasts served with olive oil and sometimes truffles.

PRIMI

Umbria makes 13 percent of the pasta made in Italy, most of it coming from Buitoni in Perugia, Italy's second-largest producer after Parma's Barilla.

Minestra di Farro. Made with *farro*, a popular local grain (see description on page 699), and cooked with a ham bone.

Spaghetti alla Norcina. Made with a sauce of black truffles, oil, and anchovies or with sausage and cream (both dishes go by the same name).

Spaghetti col Rancetto. A Spoleto specialty made with *pancetta* and marjoram.

Stringozzi (Strangozzi). Long pasta strands made with hand-milled flour. In the Middle Ages, when the area around Spoleto was part of the papal lands, the pope sent *esattari* (collectors) to gather funds from people who did not pay their taxes. Those people who did not want to pay often plotted to strangle the *esattari* with a long leather cord called the *strangozzo*. This is the source of the name of this popular noodle.

Umbricelli. Thick, chewy strand pasta, very suitable to robust pasta sauces or oil with garlic or herbs.

SECONDI

Pork is the most popular meat in Umbria, although there is good veal and lamb, too. Umbrians like poultry and fowl such as chicken, duck, squab, guinea fowl *(faraona)*, and pheasant *(fagiano)*.

Anguilla. Eel from Lago di Trasimeno, served either grilled *(alla griglia)* or braised in wine, tomatoes, onions, and garlic *(in umido)*.

Fagiano all'Uva. Pheasant cooked with grapes.

Palombacci. Wild pigeon, often served with a sauce called *la ghiotta* (see below).

Piccione alla Perugina. Squab cooked with olives.

Porchetta. Roast suckling pig with garlic, rosemary, and other herbs.

Prosciutto Cotto al Forno. Baked ham.

Salsiccia all'Uva. Fresh pork sausage cooked with grapes.

Tegamaccio. A stew of carp, pike, trout, and other fish from Lago di Trasimeno.

CONTORNO

Fave. Fava beans appear in soups, as a *contorno*, or on *crostini*.

Lenticchie. Many gourmets consider the lentils from Castelluccio the best in Italy.

These lentils are especially small compared with others and have a delicate but palpable flavor. (Read more about them under the listing for Castelluccio.)

DOLCI

Attorta. A typical Spoleto cake made with apples and a soft crust.

Cicerchiata. Traditional cake of Carnival time, made of deep-fried dough, candied fruit, almonds, honey, and pine nuts. The cake has a hole in the center.

Cioccolato. Many of the chocolate Easter eggs one eats are made in Perugia.

Fichi. Excellent figs come from Amelia, near Orvieto.

Pan Nociato. A rich dessert from Todi. Made of bread, Pecorino, raisins, walnuts, cloves, red wine, all wrapped and baked in grape leaves.

Pinoccata. A cookie made with pine nuts, lemon peel, orange peel, sugar, and sometimes chocolate.

Torcolo. A sweet roll that contains pine nuts, raisins, anise seed, and sometimes candied fruit. The dough is shaped in a coil form, so that it looks like a sleeping snake. *Torcolo* is sometimes called *il serpentone* (the big snake). It is a specialty of the Capuchin nuns of Perugia.

OTHER UMBRIAN FLAVORS

La Ghiotta. A popular sauce made of cooking juices from the meat or fowl being cooked, plus olive oil, vinegar, anchovies, olives, lemon peel, sage, salt, and pepper.

Olive Oil. The oil of Umbria is often jade green, fragrant, fruity, and sometimes very lusty. It is among the finest oils in Italy.

Tartufi Neri. Found particularly around Norcia and Spoleto. They are sniffed out either by dogs or pigs.

Torta sul Testo. A flatbread cooked on hot stones. Good with *salumi*.

The Wines of Umbria

Orvieto. This is the most famous wine in the region, a pleasant white that can range from bone-dry to buttery creaminess. It is a blend of five grapes, primarily Procanico (Trebbiano Toscano), Verdello, and Grecchetto, an Umbria variety. Fifty percent of the production is exported. Most of the production is Orvieto Secco, the dry variety, although the dryness varies from one producer to another. Orvieto Abboccato (which translates loosely as "Good in the Mouth") is a delightfully round wine that may be too sweet to have with most foods, but it is not sweet when compared with dessert wines. The result can only be described as pleasurable. In the past this wine was also exported, but wine writers, restaurateurs, and consumers did not know what to make of it because it did not fit neatly into any category. When you visit the town of Orvieto, try to taste the Abboccato wine.

Rosso di Montefalco. Made of approximately 65 percent Sangiovese, 15 to 20 percent Trebbiano Toscano, and 5 to 10 percent Sagrantino grapes, which give this wine its particular richness. It is a good wine with stews and red meats.

Torgiano. From a town of the same name. Wine has been made here since Etruscan times, and glasses and equipment from that era are part of the town's excellent wine museum. There are 113 producers of Torgiano wine, although much of it is made by Giorgio Lungarotti and his family. Their Rubesco Riserva is a particularly attractive red wine. They also run a marvelous hotel and restaurant called Le Tre Vaselle. Each year one of the nation's foremost competitions, the Banco d'Assaggio del Vino Italiano (almost always called B.A.V.I.), is held at Tre Vaselle. Judges from around the world spend five days tasting and evaluating about 800 wines in a rigorous and impartial fashion and select five winners in several categories. I was a judge in 1991 and can attest to the seriousness with which the evaluations are done and the importance that is ascribed to the winning wines.

Sagrantino di Montefalco. A wine that is well known to connoisseurs and almost unknown to everyone else. It comes in two types, each made with at least 95 percent Sagrantino grapes and perhaps a few Trebbiano Toscano grapes to lighten this intense and powerful wine. The first type is made in the traditional fashion, as grapes are crushed at picking and then vinified. Although it is intended as a wine to consume together with meat, cheese, or a rich pasta, it can often reach 14 percent alcohol, which is just below the alcohol gradation for dessert wines such as Marsala, sherry, and port. Then there is the Sagrantino di Montefalco Passito. In this case, the grapes are picked at harvesttime and then are dried for several months until they shrivel to about 45 percent of their original volume. Wine is then made from these dried grapes, a rather special, very intense, and fragrant wine to sip at the end of a meal or for meditation. It has had uses as a sacramental wine for many years in Montefalco.

Reds and Whites. Made in zones such as the Colli di Trasimeno (near the lake), Colli Perugini (near Perugia), and Altotiberini (near the source of the Tevere).

Vin Santo. As in Toscana, an amber-colored sweet wine made of dried white-wine grapes (typically Trebbiano) is often consumed at the end of a meal, sometimes with dry cookies.

Assisi (Perugia)

The law prohibits any construction (except for small changes in farm buildings) within a ten-kilometer (six-mile) radius of Assisi, so that the view you see is the same one that nourished the spirit of Saint Francis, Saint Clare, and the endless number of pilgrims who have journeyed to this small, pious town for the past seven centuries. It was G. K. Chesterton who observed that San Francesco believed that every tree is a creature of God and therefore a brother of man. Every tree here is protected from being chopped. You might think that such stasis would be oppressive, but as you reflect on Saint Francis and nature, every object, no matter how still or inanimate, suddenly seems very alive.

AGRITOURISM

Azienda Agricola La Malvarina (in Capodacqua di Assisi), tel. 075/8064280.

Near Assisi and nestled in the woods so loved by Saint Francis, here is a lovely setting for home-cooked meals from Maria Fabrizi and simple but comfortable accommodation that make this a good base to explore the area if you have a car. Maria's son Claudio raises horses that you can ride through the woods and fields, while his wife, Patrizia, gathers medicinal and cooking herbs for various preparations. You can buy products from this farm at a shop on Piazza Chiesa Nuova in Assisi.

DINING

Trattoria della Fortezza, Via della Fortezza 2b, tel. 075/812418. Closed Thursday. American Express, MasterCard, Visa. Moderate to moderately expensive.

Good Umbrian dishes, including effective use of truffles. A few modest rooms are available for lodging.

Ristorante Pallotta, Via Volta Pinta 2, tel. 075/812649. Closed Tuesday, late February, early March. All credit cards. Moderate.

Near the Piazza del Municipio and a bit removed from the most heavily touristed zones, Pallotta is all things to all diners. There is a menu of traditional dishes, another one with seasonal specialties, and yet another for vegetarians. Wine drinkers can order a glass, a small or large carafe, or a bottle. Vegetable cookery is especially good here, whether it is the soup with *farro* and peas or the numerous seasonal *contorni*. For indulgent meat eaters with cholesterol medication within reach, the *piccione alla ghiotta* (squab filled with and wrapped in pancetta) is pretty thrilling. The owners welcome you with warm Umbrian hospitality.

La Piazzetta dell'Erba, Via San Gabriele dell'Addolorata 15b, tel. 075/815352. Closed Monday and from mid-January to mid-February. All credit cards. Moderately inexpensive to moderate.

In the mornings herb and vegetable sellers often gather in the nearby little piazza (piazzetta) that gives this osteria its name. Many of these wind up in the delicious *zuppa del contadino*. Herbs are also placed on secondi of Chianina beef or with the *torta al testo* served with sausage and Pecorino cheese. The wines here are very well-chosen.

La Stalla, Via Eremo delle Carceri, tel. 075/812317 or 813636. Reservations essential. No credit cards. Inexpensive.

Just outside of town, but easily reachable, is this wonderfully rustic place that serves delicious food. It is very popular, so you need to reserve. This is a former cowshed with a low, curving roof. There is a large grill in the middle of the room, so the room is plenty warm, but cozily so. Start with a *torta* (a sort of bread) *al formaggio*— cheese is melted and served hot. There is also tasty sausage and prosciutto with the same bread. The soups and pastas are good, and then you will want to return to more grilled foods: steaks, *spiedini* (skewers with either pork, veal, or lamb). This is the sort of congenial place that merits a visit with friends so that you can sample one another's dishes. Failing that, you are sure to make friends here in short order.

Bazzano (Perugia)

FOLKLORE
Festa della Ciliegia.

Bazzano is a small town on a hill overlooking the valley between Spoleto and Trevi. Every year, for ten days in mid-June, the local cherries are honored with concerts, games, sporting events, special feasts, and lots of cherry consumption. Bazzano also produces excellent olive oil.

Castelluccio (Perugia)

AGRITOURISM
Cooperativa Agricola Castelluccio, tel. 0743/816997, fax 0743/817425.

This town is at one of the highest elevations (1,455 meters/4,800 feet) in the region and overlooks two broad plains where lentils grow. They are sown as the snow melts in April and May, and if you come to the area during June and July, you will see that the plants have sprouted white flowers. The harvest takes place at the end of July and the beginning of August. The plants are not very tall, and much of the harvesting must be done by hand because the plants are too delicate to withstand the trampling of animals or blunt machines. A new threshing machine is now being tried on some of the plants.

DINING/LODGING
Taverna Castelluccio, Via Dietro la Torre 8, tel. 0743/821158. Closed Wednesday (except in August) and from November through February. Moderately inexpensive.

Rustic but delicious food using pork, ricotta, lentils, lamb, Pecorino, and seasonal specialities. The ricotta is gorgeous and appears in tortellini and a *torta di ricotta*. One can stay in the modern but comfortable rooms and make Castelluccio a base to explore the nature of the Parco dei Monti Sibillini and to visit Norcia 30 km (18 miles) away.

Deruta (Perugia)

MAJOLICA
Since the early Renaissance some of the most beautiful majolica in Italy has been handmade in Deruta. It is particularly famous for its blue and gold colors and its evocations of scenes of knights, nobles, and courtly life. You can see many examples of antique majolica at the Museo delle Ceramica. Deruta majolica is glazed and fired twice, making it more durable than majolica from Portugal. You can buy espresso sets, pots, plates, bowls, serving dishes, egg cups, mugs, and vases. I am fond of the canisters

with covers that are used in old spice stores and apothecaries around the country. It is generally thought that the finest examples are made by Ubaldo Grazia and family, because they draw from the designs, patterns, and shapes that were first used during the Renaissance. You can visit the factory or his and all of the other pottery shops, mostly found on the Via Tiberina. Many will accept personal checks. The cost of shipping will be about 25 percent to 50 percent of the price of your purchase, depending on its weight; U.S. Customs will add a 4.5 percent tariff. Despite these additional costs, Deruta majolica will still cost less than what you would pay at home, and the selection here is greater. The majority of the shops are open from Monday through Saturday and closed for two to three hours in the afternoon.

Here are a few recommendations:
Ubaldo Grazia, Via Tiberina 181, tel. 075/9710201.

Antonio Margaritelli, Via Tiberina.

Mordenti & Nicolini, Via Tiberina Nord 2.

Cino Peccetti, Via Tiberina.

Foligno (Perugia)

DINING

Il Bacco Felice, Via Garibaldi 73, tel. 0742/ 341019 or, failing that, 335/6622659. Closed Monday. All credit cards. Moderately inexpensive to moderate.

The name of this small osteria is "Happy Bacchus," which is an apt description for Salvatore Denaro, its owner and guiding spirit. He has researched old recipes and believes that these will taste as they did once upon a time if he sources rare varieties of pork and fowl and uses organically grown vegetables. The pork appears sweet-and-sour as *maialino al forno con salsa in agrodolce* or in sausage flavored with Sagrantino wine. Chicken and peppers will seldom taste better than the *pollo con i peperoni*. In the spring, *agnello con carciofi* (lamb with artichokes) is also excellent. The *Rocciata di Foligno* is a local cake that concludes your meal nicely.

Hostaria Sparafucile, Piazzetta Duomo 30, tel. 0742/342602. Open Tuesday through Sunday evenings. All credit cards. Moderate.

People travel from far away to taste the house speciality, *le lumache al finocchio selvatico* (snails flavored with wild fennel). There are other wonderful Umbrian foods here, including red potatoes known as *patate rosse di Colfiorito*, onions from Cannara and prosciutto and *salumi* from Norcia.

Gubbio (Perugia)

DINING

Ristorante Federico da Montefeltro, Via della Repubblica 35, tel. 075/9273949. Closed Thursday (except in August and September) and in February. All credit cards. Moderate to moderately expensive.

Flavorful local dishes include *bruschetta al tartufo, umbricelli ai funghi porcini, tagliatelle al tartufo nero, piccatina all'Engubina* (turkey breast with a caper-parsley sauce), good vegetables, and wine.

Montefalco (Perugia)

Montefalco is a silent city, even by Umbrian standards. There are several religious orders here that keep to themselves, and other citizens seem to go about their lives quietly. The chief product of the city is its Sagrantino wine, which, at 14 percent alcohol, can also have a silencing effect if consumed too liberally. Another reason for the quiet is that Montefalco sits high on a hill that offers stunning views in all directions. The town is nicknamed "La Ringhiera dell'Umbria," a name that implies the railing or banister of Umbria, because of its position as the best place to view the region. It is a classic Umbrian view with gentle hills, silvery-green olive trees, neat rows of vines, and the occasional small house.

DINING

Ristorante Coccorone, Largo Tempestivi (near the Duomo), tel. 0742/79535. Closed Wednesday. Visa. Moderate to moderately expensive.

Grilled meats are very fine here and go well with the local wine. If you want a completely vinous meal, start with *pappardelle al sagrantino*, pasta with a mushroom-red wine sauce. There are also good truffle pastas.

OLIVE OIL

Giuseppe Brizi, Via Giuseppe Verdi 44, tel. 0742/79165.

Many good olive oils are produced around Montefalco. One of them is by Giuseppe Brizi. In business since 1915, here is an active oil press. I visited once in late November when the new olives were being pressed, and the fragrance was palpable out in the street. New oil is made in November and December.

Norcia (Perugia)
Classic Town

Tucked in a lovely spot in the Valnerina, a remote valley somewhat apart from the rest of Umbria, Norcia is a food lover's paradise. Here are the finest truffles in Umbria, superb pork butchers, delicate lentils, fresh river trout, fine chocolate makers, and some of the purest water you will taste anywhere in Italy. Norcia also shares the saintliness of the rest of the region. Here were born in 480 Saint Benedict, the founder of Christian monasticism, and his twin sister Scholastica. When this area was part of the Papal States, the fame of its products spread to Roma, and a commerce developed that endures to this day. Much of what is produced here is sent to the capital. If you look at the chapter on Lazio, you will discover that my favorite food store in Roma (E. Volpetti, page 481) is run by a family from Norcia.

Wherever one walks there are *norcinerie* in a number far in excess of the amount any other city of 4,912 would require. The shops are fragrant with sausages, *salame*, prosciutto, cheeses, and truffles. One special cured meat—made of pork—that you will often see is called *coglioni di mulo* ("mule's balls," so named because this is something a mule lacks). The tap and fountain water in Norcia is delicious. This means that the pasta, coffee, baked goods, and other products all taste even better. There is a nice fountain in the piazza just outside the entrance to town at the Corso Sertorio.

For some reason, Norcia is full of dogs, mostly black and white, who are very friendly and—not surprisingly—well fed. They sleep most of the time in the main square and on the steps of the Duomo and seem fully integrated into the life of the town. If you are coming to Norcia by car, you might come from Spoleto. The road (S.S. 395) is broad and well paved, but has many curves and mountain passes that make for challenging driving. Initially, you will see many of the olive groves that produce Spoleto's excellent oil. As you climb higher, olive trees give way to chestnut trees. The sights are very beautiful—classic Umbrian natural settings—for this 18-kilometer (11-mile) road. You will then pick up S.S. 209, called the Valnerina, that goes 28 kilometers (16.5 miles) to Norcia. The splendid mountain scenery continues for the whole trip through one of the largest unspoiled nature preserves in central Italy. In all directions around Norcia, the Valnerina zone is characterized by little towns that perch on hillsides. They all have views of the forest, which is full of owls, eagles, porcupines, and wolves. In the valleys, horses, sheep, cows, and goats are occasionally tended by a small boy or an old man.

BAKERY
Corso Sertorio 13, tel. 0743/816623.

What a lovely woman Anna Scolastico is! Known locally as Cocchina (Little Cook), she turns out all sorts of delicious cakes and cookies. Instead of having the finished, polished look of bakery items, these sweets are like what Mom makes. Try the *ravioli* (these are pastries, not pasta) with ricotta or cacao, the *sbronzetti* (made with flour, olive oil, and raisins), *panciallini* (chocolate, walnuts, almonds, wine must, honey), a *crostata* with ricotta and chocolate bits, and the *panpepato* (hazelnuts, figs, almonds, honey, orange, and pepper). She also makes cookies with *farro* and *biscottini a crema torroncini* (cookies with nougat cream).

BUTCHER SHOPS
Norcineria Ercole Ulivucci, Via Mazzini 4, tel. 0743/816661. Closed Tuesday.

Very nice owners and excellent products. I tasted the soft, spreadable *ciauscolo*, which was special, as are the prosciutti.

Norcineria Fratelli Ansuini, Via Anicia 105, tel. 0743/816643.

One of the finest, with outstanding sausages and other products. Lentils too.

CHEESE
Caseificio Sociale di Norcia, Vocabulo Opaco 10, tel. 0743/817050.

The cheese output from 150 local producers can be seen and purchased here. Be sure to try the *caciotta al tartufo*, a mixed-milk cheese made memorable with the addition of bits of truffle.

CHOCOLATE
Cioccolateria Vetusta Nursia (to the left of the Duomo). Open 9–13h, 15:30–17:30h; closed Monday.

All kinds of chocolate are sold here. There is chocolate-covered *torrone* and panettone, plus many sizes of Easter eggs. There is chocolate-covered *farro, tartufo al cioccolato* (chocolate with bits of truffle), a good rich cookie called *il biscotto San Benedetto* (made with chocolate, almonds, and hazelnuts). The shop also has rather substantial chocolates in the shape of a penis (don't forget, this is Italy, where such a thing is considered lusty and amusing rather than obscene). When I jokingly asked who the model was, the proprietor told me it was her four-year-old grandson.

Useful signage in Umbria

DINING

Hotel Grotta Azzurra/Ristorante Granaro del Monte, Via Alfieri 7/12, tel. 0743/816513 (hotel), 0743/816590 (restaurant), info@ bianconi.com. All credit cards. Moderately inexpensive to moderate.

Since about 1800 the Bianconi family has run this hotel-restaurant that attracts those who make Norcia their destination for its famous cuisine. In service to you, my discerning reader, my friend Laura and I tasted many dishes to assure that the food was as good as it sounded in the menu. It is. The excellent *antipasto della casa* included *lonza* (cured loin of pork), *salame di Norcia* (wonderful pork and spices with a bit of truffle), *prosciutto di cinghiale*, other local *salumi*, young fresh Pecorino, and a few pieces of melon. This was accompanied by a very good white wine, Grecante Grecchetto dei Colli Martani, made by Arnaldo Caprai. For a *primo* there are *zuppa di farro, pappardelle alla Norcina rossa* (prosciutto, sausage, tomatoes, and mushrooms), or the unusual *fettuccine al sugo di trota* (in a sauce of fresh trout). Or go all out and have the delicious but pricey *fettuccine al tartufo* or *tortellini panna e tartufo* (with cream and truffle shavings). I was very fond of the excellent homemade *tagliolini con funghi,*

burro, e tartufo. All the *primi* are delicious. Among the *secondi* there was grilled fresh trout from the Nera River flavored with rosemary and served with *turini*, the beefy mushrooms from local mountains. Not to be missed is the *salsiccia tartufata*, local sausage split, filled with truffle and cheese, wrapped in prosciutto, and then grilled. *Coniglio in porchetta* was boned rolled rabbit filled with wild fennel and other herbs. *Agnello sopravissano* (from the fields above Visso just over the border in Marche) is delicious roast lamb. It can also be had with truffle sauce, at an increased price. One of the special dishes of the house is *filetto del cavatore tartufato*, a beef fillet with a truffle sauce (the *cavatore* is the man who hunts for truffles). Another dish worth trying is *salsiccia con le lenticchie*, sausage cooked with lentils from Castelluccio. After all of this, a dessert of lemon sorbet and fresh fruit was about right. You can then have either an *amaro* or a grappa flavored with truffle. Prices depend on how much truffle you consume, but the meal is astonishingly inexpensive if you consider what this would cost you anywhere else. This is the chief hotel in town and the likely place where you will sleep if you plan to stay over in Norcia.

Trattoria dal Francese, Via Riguardati 16, tel. 0743/816290. Closed Friday (except in summer), two weeks in January and two weeks in July. All credit cards. Moderately expensive.

Serves an all-truffle feast; such a repast anywhere else would be prohibitively expensive, so you should allow yourself to be extravagant here. The meal I had was an antipasto of thin slices of smoked turkey with truffle sauce. Then came samplings of three primi; gnocchi in a Gorgonzola sauce, tortellini, and a *funghi porcini* soup. All had truffle shavings. Then there was marinated trout from nearby streams, topped with truffle sauce. After this was fillet of beef with truffle sauce and a truffled cheese sauce to dip in. For dessert there was *tartufo al cioccolato*, a gastronomic pun of sorts: a chocolate-truffle ice cream in most places is a ball of ice cream with pieces of cherry. Here it is chocolate ice cream with bits of truffle, and it is delicious. Complete the feast with *grappa al tartufo*.

DINING

Taverna d' Massari, Via Roma 13, tel./ fax 0743/816218. Closed Tuesday (except in summer). All credit cards. Moderately inexpensive to moderately expensive.

Traditional Norcia dishes, complete with pork and truffles.

LENTILS

Consorzio Agrario, Via della Stazione 2.

You can buy lentils here from nearby Castelluccio.

TRUFFLES

Tartufi Moscatelli, Via Dante 14b (corner of Corso Sertorio 42), tel. 0743/818120, fax 0743/817388.

You can buy whole truffles here, or truffle products such as creams, pastes, and oils. Those harvested in the late spring and summer are called *scorzoni*, and they are much less flavorful than those found in the autumn, which are called *pregiati*. The *pregiati* cost about four times as much as the *scorzoni*.

Tartufi Micelio, Corso Sertorio. Closed Tuesday.

Truffle products and truffles.

MUSEUM

Mostra Permanente della Civiltà Contadina, Palazzo Cavalieri di Matta (Piazza Sergio Forti 9). Open Saturday and Sunday 8–13h, 15–19h.

A nice exhibit including tools, equipment, clothing, and other effects from rural peasant life in this region.

Orvieto (Terni)

In addition to tasting Orvieto's famous wine in its place of origin, you will find a trip there is worth the effort to see its glorious cathedral, built in 1285, one of the most beautiful in Italy. It is notable that this cathedral has no known architect, but is rather the product of collective effort.

BAR-BAKERIES

Bar Pasticceria Montanucci, Corso Cavour 21.

Delicious pastries have been made here since 1917. Somehow Montanucci feels locked in time, delightfully so.

I Dolci di Moscatelli, Corso Cavour 11.

Delicious crostate and yeast cakes.

Del Moro, Via San Leonardo 7, tel 0763/342763. Closed Friday and the first two weeks of July. Moderately inexpensive.

A casual, good-value place for local flavors.

Pasticceria Adriano, Via della Pace 26.

Chocolate with hot red pepper or saffron and some of Orvieto's best pastries.

BREAD

Giuseppe Scatena, Piazza Ippolito Scalsa 6.

Try the *marsicani con Fiocchi di patate*, a fragrant potato bread. There are also good breads with figs *(fichi)* and nuts.

COOKING SCHOOL

Italian Cookery Weeks, La Cacciata (a working farm), just outside of Orvieto. (For the United States contact Jean Evers, tel./fax 0763/2080112; in the United Kingdom P.O. Box 2482, London NW10 1HW, tel. 0208/2080112.)

Courses are held from May through September. You stay at the farm among the vineyards and cook in the kitchen using local ingredients.

DINING

Enoteca Foresi, Piazza Duomo 2. No credit cards. Moderately inexpensive.

There is a fourteenth-century wine cellar and lots of good Orvieto wine to taste. There are also excellent Pecorino cheeses and good sausages, some with truffle.

Trattoria La Grotta, Via Luca Signorelli 5, tel./fax 0763/341348. Closed Tuesday, one week in July and in part of the winter. All credit cards. Moderate.

The meat here is delicious (including the *porchetta* and Chianina beef), but the vegetables are so outstanding that one can almost ignore the meat. But it is worth having both. In season, there are many truffle dishes that raise the prices somewhat, but they are still surprisingly moderate for such good quality.

La Volpe e l'Uva, Via Ripa Corsica 1, tel. 0763/341612. MasterCard, Visa. Closed Monday, Tuesday and January. Moderately inexpensive to moderate.

The dishes here change so often that one cannot list them all. Lucio Sforza is one of those cooks who relies on inspiration and the fresh market produce. But the food has great delicacy and balance of flavor: the gnocchi are like clouds, and they are flavored with wonderful fresh herbs.

Del Moro, Via San Leonardo 7, tel. 0763/342763. Closed Friday and the first two weeks of July. Moderately inexpensive.

A casual place for local flavors and good value for money.

FOOD SHOPPING

Drogheria Svizzera, Corso Cavour 35.

A good source for local products, plus spices, grains, coffee, *digestivi*.

Gastronomia Carraro, Corso Cavour 101, tel. 0763/342870.

Outstanding prepared foods, particularly *porchetta*, *baccalà*, and sweets.

Specialita di Orvieto, Via del Duomo 11.

As the name indicates, local specialties, including pasta, truffle paste, jams, honeys, oils, and wine.

ICE CREAM
Gelateria L'Archetto, Piazza Duomo.

Very good *gelati* in a prime spot opposite one of Italy's most beautiful cathedrals.

Gelateria Giuseppe Pasqualetti, Piazza Duomo 14.

A large selection of flavors, with fruit ice creams being the stars. Some people rank this *gelateria* among Italy's best.

WINE
Enoteca La Loggia, Via Mercanti 6. Open 10–13:15h, 16:30–20h; closed Wednesday morning and Sunday.

Wines, plus oils, vegetables packed in oil, jams, sauces, and truffle paste.

Enoteca Vino Vino, Via Mercanti 21. Open 10–13h, 16–20h.

A large selection of Orvieto wine.

Palazzo del Gusto, Via Ripa Serancia 16.

This is the fifteenth-century Chiostro di San Giovanni, which has been transformed into the Enoteca Regionale dell'Umbria, where you can sample and purchase wines from throughout the region. The cloister sits atop tufa rock, into which ancient caves for wine storage were carved long ago. This is also a beautiful setting with views over the hills that surround Orvieto.

Consorzio Tutela Vino Orvieto Classico e Orvieto, Corso Cavour 36, 05018 Orvieto (Terni), tel. 0763/343790.

This is the consortium of Orvieto producers. If you are interested in visiting wineries, ask for a copy of "Andar Per Vigne," which details addresses and opening hours of local producers.

Perugia

BAKERY
Caffè-Pasticceria Sandri, Corso Vannucci 32, tel. 075/61012.

Founded by a Swiss baker in 1860, this is a beautiful, chic bakery with its walnut shelves, vaulted ceilings, and subtly painted walls. Stop here for delicious pastries and coffee, as Herbert von Karajan used to when he visited Perugia.

BREAD
Panetteria Ceccarini, Piazza Matteotti 16.

Since 1917, this has been the leading bread baker in Perugia. There are more than thirty types of bread and many cookies, small pastries, and a very fine *torta di formaggio*.

DINING
Osteria del Bartolo, Via Bartolo 30,

tel. 075/5731561. Closed Sunday, mid-January, and end of July and early August. American Express, Master Card, Visa. Moderately expensive.

Delicious food. Specialties include *bottaccio* and *ravioli di ricotta di pecora con scaglie di Pecorino dolce e fondo di vitello* (ravioli filled with sheep ricotta and topped with thin pieces of sweet Pecorino and a veal sauce). Good wine list.

Osteria Il Gufo, Via della Viola 32, tel. 075/5734126. Open 20–1h; closed Sunday. No credit cards. Inexpensive.

A casual place with excellent *zuppa di lenticchie*, pork fillet with balsamic vinegar *(filetto di maiale)*, and good vegetables. Simple, but pleasing.

Il Falchetto, Via Bartolo 20, tel. 075/5731775. Closed Monday. MasterCard, Visa. Moderate.

Falchetti (plural of the restaurant's name) are spinach gnocchi. *Palombaccia al Rubesco*, squab braised in good red wine, is another signature dish. Good food.

DINING

Giò Arte e Vini, Via Ruggero D'Andreotto 19, tel. 075/5731100, hotelgio@ interbusiness.it. Closed Sunday evening, Monday lunch. All credit cards. Moderate.

Take Via San Galigano just a bit out of

Pecorino cheese

the center to this special hotel/restaurant/wine bar that is dedicated to wine tourism in every way. Food is pleasing and selected to show off wines.

FOOD SHOPPING

Spezeria Bavicchi, Piazza Matteotti 32.

Since 1897, this emporium has sold all the beans and legumes that are central to the Umbrian diet. This is your source for lentils, *farro*, and all sorts of beans.

Salumeria Fratelli Temperini, Corso Cavour 30.

Very fine *salumi* and sausages, many made by the proprietors.

WINE

Enoteca Provinciale, Via Ulisse Rocchi 18, tel. 075/24824. Open 9:30–13:30h, 16–20h, Sunday 9:30–13:30h; closed Monday.

The best place to do a tasting of Umbrian wines, which can be accompanied by small *merende* (snacks). You can also purchase bottles—a good idea, since many of these are hard to find outside Umbria.

Pierantonio (Perugia)

AGRITOURISM

Azienda Vitivinicola Agrituristica "Colle *del Sole," tel. 075/939156, fax 075/939448.*

A relaxing place to stay and eat in the countryside. There is swimming, tennis, horseback riding, and fishing in the nearby lake. It makes a line of wines under the name "Polidori"—no herbicides or pesticides are used. You can drink this wine during meals at the *azienda* or buy some to take home.

Spello (Perugia)

DINING

Ristorante La Cantina, Via Cavour 2, tel. 0743/651775. Closed Wednesday. All credit cards. Moderate.

Pasta dishes with vegetable sauces lead to sturdy meat and poultry such as lamb, baby pig *(maialino)*, rabbit, and braised squab *(piccione in casseruola)*. Good wine selection as well.

FOLKLORE

La Sagra della Bruschetta.

Held on the last Sunday in March, this is the place to have garlic toasts with olive oil, which will quickly turn you off "garlic bread," as it is known in North America.

Spoleto (Perugia)

BREAD

Forno Santini, Vicolo del Forno 2. Open mornings only; closed Sunday.

This is a wonderful old bakery that should not be missed. It seems to belong to a long-lost era when a *forno* was a place where people without an oven of their own would bring their breads to be baked. To reach it, start at the Piazza della Libertà and go up the Via Trattoria for two blocks, and you will see the tiny Vicolo del Forno on the right.

CULTURE

Associazione Festival dei Due Mondi, Piazza del Duomo 8, 06049 Spoleto (PG). tel. 0743/45028, fax 0743/220321, www. spoletofestival.it.

Founded in the late 1950s by composer Gian Carlo Menotti, this iconoclastic festival presents dance, theater, art exhibits, jazz, and classical concerts and opera from mid-June to mid-July. Events take place in churches, piazzas, theaters, and, it seems, every available space. The festival has made Spoleto a major destination that attracts beautiful people from Roma and Milano and artists from throughout the world. If you plan to visit during the festival, reserve hotel space and tickets well ahead.

DINING

Il Panciolle, Vicolo degli Eroli 1, tel. 0743/ 221241. Closed Wednesday. All credit cards. Moderate to moderately expensive.

Close by the Duomo is this well-run restaurant that specializes in meat, all kinds of Umbrian *salumi* or beef, pork,

Spoleto

and other meats cooked on the grill. Food presentation tends to be a bit fussy, but the flavors are right. In the warm season, dining on the panoramic terrace is an added pleasure.

Il Tartufo, Piazza Garibaldi 24, tel. 0743/40236, truffles@libero.it. Closed Sunday evening, Monday, and from mid-February to mid-March. All credit cards. Moderate.

As the name and the e-mail address suggest, the Umbrian truffle is the protagonist on the menu here. Given the very modest prices, you realize that there is a lot more truffle flavor (communicated through truffle pastes and truffle butters) than in fresh truffles, for the obvious reason that the truffle is a seasonal product. But if you stick to simple preparations, you can dine happily.

FOOD SHOPPING

Alimentari-Macelleria Giancarlo Padricheui, Via Aroe di Druse 22, tel. 0743/46617.

This very old *gastronomia* has been passed down from father to son since 1620. It is overflowing with quality products. There is *farro* (a saying posted in the window suggests CHI MANGIA IL FARRO NON NUTRE IL MEDICO—"He who eats *farro* doesn't feed the doctor"), *farrelle* (pasta made with *farro*), *caciottina al tartufo nero*, truffle products, *ciauscolo* from Marche, *schiacciata* (a flattened *salame* typical of Spoleto), and breads embedded with olives or walnuts. There are fine jarred sauces from La Fattoria Umbra, *strangozzi* pasta, and local oils. Another specialty is *ricotta salata* (salted sheep's-milk ricotta that is baked so that it has a crust). You eat this cheese with a dry cake called *frutto mandorlato*.

Drogheria Casale Silvano, Corso Garibaldi 61. Closed Thursday afternoon and Sunday.

This lovely old *drogheria* sells seeds for fruits and vegetables, as well as excellent dried Umbrian figs, raisins, candied citron, pine nuts, hazelnuts, almonds, coffee, herbs, spices, and dried beans and legumes.

Mini Market Silvani, Largo Ferrer 7, Corso Mazzini, tel. 0743/46657. Closed Sunday afternoon.

A friendly *gastronomia* with a good selection of local products, especially cheeses.

HOUSEWARES

Casa Idea, Via Porta Fuga 31. Closed Monday morning and Sunday.

Just below the Torre dell'Olio, the charming Via Porta Fuga is a curving street with modern boutiques and old-fashioned shoe-repair shops. At Casa Idea there is a nice selection of china, porcelain, knives, flatware, and kitchenware.

MARKETS

The Piazza del Mercato is small, with a few fruit and vegetable sellers, several clothes sellers, and Serafino, who sells *porchetta* on a roll from his truck. Nearby, on Via dell'Arco di Druso 22, is Giancarlo Padrichelli (see "Food Shopping," above), which should not be missed. In the lower part of town, there is a larger market on the Piazza Garibaldi.

PHARMACY

Farmacia Dott. Marchese, Via Brignone 5, tel. 0743/49703.

An unusual pharmacy; the floor in the front room is made of glass and reveals Roman remains below. In the rear are a Roman arch and wall in pristine shape. In this area people mix oils and extracts from fruits, vegetables, and herbs to make elixirs to respond to indigestion, high cholesterol, and other complaints.

Todi (Perugia)

DINING

Antica Hosteria de la Valle, Via Ciuffelli 19, tel./fax 075/8944848. Closed Monday. MasterCard, Visa. Moderate.

A small osteria with only a few items on the menu each day, but they are prepared with great care. Pasta with truffle sauce and beef with juniper berries are good bets.

Pane e Vino, Via Ciuffelli 33, tel. 075/ 8945448. Closed Wednesday, part of November. All credit cards. Moderate.

Good dishes include spaghetti with tomato and lemon; *zuppa di ceci* (chickpea soup) and the *filetto di maiale*, pork filet served with plums and mustard.

WINE

Enoteca dell'Accademia dei Convivanti, Via San Bonaventura 11.

A good source for Umbrian wines

Torgiano (Perugia)

HOTEL-RESTAURANT

Le Tre Vaselle, Via Garibaldi 48, tel. 075/9880447, fax 075/9880214, www.3 vaselle.it. All credit cards. Moderately expensive to expensive.

One of the loveliest and most comfortable hotels in the region. If you are on a substantial budget and are using a car to visit Umbria, this is the perfect place to make a base for touring. It is owned and operated by the Lungarotti family, whose excellent wines are available at the restaurant. If you choose to dine here without staying, you will taste good examples of Umbrian cooking in an attractive and quiet dining room.

WINE

Cantine Lungarotti, tel. 075/982348.
Open 8–13h, 15–18h; closed Saturday
and Sunday.

If you want to visit the cellar and learn about the company, call for an appointment. Purchases possible here or at the Osteria del Museo, at the wine museum.

WINE MUSEUM

Museo del Vino Cantine Lungarotti, Corso
Vittorio Emanuele 35, tel. 075/9880348.
Open daily 9–13h, 15–19h.

This is one of the world's finest wine museums. It has an outstanding collection that has been accurately displayed. You can see glasses, wine-making equipment, and other artifacts dating back to Etruscan times and all the way to the present day. There is also a good collection of art that has been inspired by wine.

Fave con i Crostini
Fava-Bean Toasts

Serves 6

300 grams/10 ounces dried fava beans
1 small onion, finely chopped
1 celery stalk, chopped in small pieces
1 large carrot, washed and peeled, chopped in
*   small pieces*
¼ teaspoon fennel seeds
Freshly ground black pepper to taste
Extra-virgin olive oil
12 slices good crusty Italian bread
2 cloves garlic, peeled and halved

Soak the fava beans overnight in 4 times as much cold water as beans. Discard any beans that float. Drain thoroughly the following day and then cook the beans, on-

ion, celery, carrot, and fennel seeds in lightly salted water to cover until the beans are soft. Drain away the liquid carefully and then lightly mash the beans, onion, celery, and carrot. Add some pepper and then stir in a little olive oil. While the beans are cooking, rub the 12 slices of bread (which can be slightly stale) with the garlic. Drizzle a little oil on each and then toast in the oven until crunchy. When they are toasted, top with the bean spread and serve.

Wine: Orvieto Secco or a light Umbrian red.

Spaghetti al Tartufo Nero
Spaghetti with Black-Truffle Sauce

Serves 4 to 6

450 grams/1 pound spaghetti or linguine
50 grams/2 ounces black truffle, chopped,
  preferably fresh, not canned or jarred
4 tablespoons extra-virgin olive oil
1 teaspoon anchovy paste

Set a large pot of cold water to boil. When it reaches a full boil, toss in a pinch of salt. When it returns to a full boil, add the pasta and cook until al dente. Place the chopped truffle in a mortar and pound until it forms a chunky paste. If you do not have a mortar, mash the truffle against a plate with the side of a knife, being careful not to touch the truffle too much with your hands. In a large skillet heat the oil until it is just below the bubbling point. Spoon in the anchovy paste and stir so that it flavors the oil. Just before the pasta is ready, spoon the truffle into the oil and give the pan a good shake. Once the pasta is cooked, drain thoroughly in a colander (do not rinse it, of course) and transfer immediately to the skillet. Remove the pan from the heat and combine the pasta thoroughly with the flavored oil. Serve immediately.

Wine: Orvieto Secco.

Lazio

Vieni a Roma, ah! vieni, o cara	Come to Rome, ah!, come my dear
dove amor, dove amore e gioia e vita:	where there is love, love and joy and life:
innebriam nostr'alme a gara del contento,	let's inebriate our souls in search of the
del contento a cui ne invita . . .	pleasure and happiness that love invites . . .
Voce in cor parlar non senti,	Don't you hear the voice in your heart
che promette del eterno ben? . . .	promising eternal joy? . . .
Ah!, dà fede a' dolci accenti . . .	Ah! trust those sweet accents . . .
Sposo tuo, sposo tuo, mi stringi al sen.	Squeeze me, your husband, tight to your bosom.

—FROM FELICE ROMANI'S LIBRETTO FOR *NORMA*,

MUSIC BY VINCENZO BELLINI

 You can take the "Roma" out of "romance," but you can't take the romance out of Roma. While a place such as Venezia or Paris may be romantic in the sentimental or nostalgic sense, there is not the erotic charge in the air that one finds in the Italian capital. It could almost be called a romantic imperative. It seems that everyone is always attuned and at the ready for an adventure. Every new person is an encounter, not simply a meeting. You will find couples being very passionate in public in ways that some people in other countries might find embarrassing or inappropriate. This is not necessarily born of exhibitionism, but rather of the fact that young people often live with their parents and cannot have privacy at home. If you walk by a car whose windows are covered with newspapers or sheets, it is very possible that a couple is in there making love. A few years ago a couple was interrupted by a car thief, who tossed them naked from their vehicular Eden like Adam and Eve, except that these two covered

REGIONAL AND NATIONAL CAPITAL:

Roma (usually listed with its full name, but sometimes "RM").

PROVINCIAL CAPITALS:

Frosinone (FR), Latina (LT), Rieti (RI), Viterbo (VT).

TOURIST INFORMATION:

Ente Provinciale di Turismo, Via Parigi 11, 00185 Roma, tel. 06/461851.

Agritourism:

Associazione Agriturist Regionale, Corso Vittorio Emanuele 101, 00186 Roma, tel. 06/6512342.

You may contact this
office for information
on agritourism all over
Italy.

Wine Tourism:

Lazio has a very active
wine tourism movement.
Numerous wineries open
their doors at certain
times of the year and you
are welcome to visit, taste,
and buy. For information,
call 06/8604694.

themselves with pages of *Il Messaggero*. While Romans identified with the humanity and cinematic humor of the incident, more than a few thought to themselves, "There but for the grace of God go I."

There is a sense of excitement in Roman social life—pleasure is derived through human interaction, even if there will not be a sexual denouement. You will find that Romans manage to find sensual and other pleasures in all things—clothing, food, flirtation, politics, driving, arguing, and making up. There is a lustiness in the food and wine of the city and, by extension, the region of Lazio that is almost unparalleled in Italy. It is true that the cuisines of other regions can be rich and substantial (such as in Emilia-Romagna, where the food is much more sophisticated), but in Lazio the delight in indulgence is as much a part of eating as the food itself. *Laziale* food is characterized by an astonishing amount of fat from pork, lamb, cheese, eggs, and organ meats. On the other hand, the region produces some of the sweetest, most exquisite vegetables you will ever taste. All of this food is swept up with dark, fragrant, crusty bread called *pane casareccio* and washed down with beguiling, drinkable, though not particularly special, white wine.

There is a popular joke in Roma: What is the difference between the ancient Romans and the modern Romans? Answer: The ancient Romans had slaves, and the modern Romans have the Milanese. People in Milano believe that they do all the work while Romans expend all of the nation's resources. This is not entirely true, of course, but it is based on attitudes born of common behaviors. It often seems that Romans are so dedicated to pleasure that they never find time to work. There is a slight arrogance in their behavior in this regard, as if it is their right to play while people in the provinces serve the capital city. This ancient attitude never quite disappeared and was significantly reinforced during the Fascist era.

Where do the Vatican and the Catholic Church figure in all of this? The presence of the sacred, I believe, almost impels Romans to be even greater voluptuaries. The Church provides a context to react against. So orgies of food and sex are not a thing of the past—many of the villas on the Via Appia Antica or at the sea are the settings for marathons of indulgence. Conversely, this sensualism can be detected in sacred Roma as well. If the men and the women of the Church usually deny themselves certain pleasures, they do indulge in the visual delights of the Eternal City, its luxuriant fountains and gardens and bluntly erotic statuary, and in the cooling *venticelli,* those particular Roman breezes that blow into the city on even the hottest day.

Ecclesiastical Romans love to eat good food and drink wine just as pagan Romans do. I have shared meals with nuns, priests, and monks who clearly delight in the pleasures of the table. It was a church figure who brought Montefiascone's wine, Est! Est!! Est!!!, to everlasting fame. Nuns and monks have played a vital role in agriculture through the centuries, tilling fields, planting crops, and improving yields. Monks were the conservators of the wine- and spirits-making tradition in the Middle Ages. There is a store in Roma called Ai Monasteri, where you can buy spirits and other products made by monks of many orders. Nuns have been among the foremost bakers and confectioners, and many orders—especially in southern Italy—support themselves through sales of their handiwork. It is important to understand that even the strictest adherent to Christianity is capable of experiencing pleasure—temporal as well as spiritual—and that the pagan and the Christian Romas are not so much adversarial as two parts of a whole.

Mamma Roma is so all encompassing that one almost forgets the rest of the region. Lazio has beautiful areas for recreation, many within an hour of the capital. One can go for picnics in the *campagna* (the nearby countryside) or among the hills and lakes of the Castelli Romani. The Ciociaria to the south is famous for its vegetables, pasta, hill towns, and beautiful women, such as Gina Lollobrigida. Viterbo is a beautiful medieval city that deserves a visit. Lago di Bolsena, one of Italy's largest lakes, is famous for recreation and for its eels. Tarquinia has an unmatched Etruscan museum and necropolis. A day at the sea is also within reach. While Roma's beaches at Ostia and Fregene are spent and overbuilt, there are pleasures to be had farther north at Santa Marinella and Tarquinia or south at Anzio and Nettuno. Wherever you go, the usually clear weather and pastoral beauty of the Lazio landscape will enchant you as much as the timeless urban beauty of Roma.

Eating in Lazio

Since most people's first contact with Lazio is in Roma, they often forget the cuisine of this region is a pastoral one born of the products of the shepherd. Lamb is the foremost meat, and practically every part of the animal is consumed. Pecorino, sheep's-milk cheese, is preferred to that made from cow's milk. Many of the recipes are born of expediency: What can a shepherd eat as he moves with his flock? The other gift the cooks of Lazio have received is a bounty of wonderful vegetables. By the seaside there is a history of good fish and seafood eating, but many of the local waters are overfished or polluted so that which is consumed must often be brought in from other waters. There is also, in Roma, an ancient Jewish community that has contributed many dishes to the regional kitchen that effectively use fish and Lazio vegetables.

People in Lazio like to eat day by day: there are certain days of the week on which most people in the region eat particular foods. It is not that they have to, but the tradition has become so comfortable that they wouldn't think not to. Tuesday often sees either fish or *bollito misto*. On Thursday there are always gnocchi. Friday brings cod and *pasta coi ceci* (with chickpeas). Saturday means tripe, usually cooked with mint and Pecorino. Sunday is the day for pork or lamb.

You will find a much more forceful presence of black pepper and salt in the Roman kitchen. Americans and others who consider themselves health conscious tend to restrict their salt intake. There are some Italians who do this, but *laziali* in particular use salt rather liberally. If you are restricting your salt consumption, simply say "Niente sale" (no salt) or "Poco sale" (just a little salt), and your wishes will be honored. Otherwise, you will certainly consume more salt in Lazio than you ever would at home.

This preference for salt dates back to ancient Roman times, when a person possessing salt was considered wealthy, and abundant dispensation of salt was viewed as a sign of generosity or, perhaps, wild extravagance. (The English words "sauce," "salad," and "sausage" all derive from the Latin *salsus,* or "salted.") The Romans got much of their salt from the Adriatic Sea, across the Italian peninsula. To transport this valuable condiment, they constructed the Via Salaria (Salt Road), which remains, after two thousand years, the most important artery from the Adriatic to Roma. The tradition of having pride in, and honoring, salt continues. In many restaurants and homes in Lazio (and other parts of Italy, too), salt is not kept in a shaker. Instead, there is a special dish called a *saliera*, which is a rounded bowl that is often encased in something more decorative. My *saliera*, for example, is an antique that was in the family of beloved friends for about 130 years. The bowl is made of blue glass, and it is covered by two metal wings. At one end of the bowl is a long metal neck that arcs upward, finishing in the head of a swan. I open the wings to take a pinch of salt and then carefully close them again. If you go to an Italian home, you will notice that the *saliera* might have a place of honor. It can be made of different materials, including gold, silver, glass, crystal, or ceramic. A *saliera* makes a nice small gift to bring home to someone special.

ANTIPASTI

Bruschetta. Toasted bread rubbed with garlic and drizzled with olive oil.

Carciofi alla Giudea. Originally a classic in the Roman Jewish kitchen, these are artichokes that are flattened and then golden fried. Not to be missed.

Carciofi alla Romana. Artichokes stuffed with mint and garlic and slow-cooked in olive oil.

Supplì al Telefono. Small balls of rice and mozzarella, deep-fried. When you bite into one, the cheese stretches like a telephone line.

PRIMI

Bucatini all'Amatriciana. Typical of Amatrice, the sauce is made with *pancetta* or *guanciale*, tomatoes, onions, garlic, and *peperoncino*. This dish is often ruined when ingredients are substituted (such as prosciutto in place of *pancetta*).

Fettuccine alla Papalina. "Papal" fettuccine with eggs, prosciutto, and peas.

Fettuccine alla Romana. Sauce of prosciutto, chicken giblets, and tomatoes.

Fettuccine Maestose al Burro. Commonly called Fettuccine Alfredo, made with lots of butter and Parmigiano-Reggiano (but no cream).

Gnocchi alla Romana. Disks of semolina baked with cheese and butter.

La Gricia (also called *pasta alla gricia*). A classic shepherd dish, made with *pancetta*, olive oil, pepper, and grated Pecorino.

Pasta a Cacio e Pepe. With grated Pecorino and freshly ground pepper. Simple and delicious.

Pasta alla Ciociara. Sauce of tomatoes, mozzarella, Pecorino, olive oil, and oregano.

Penne all'Arrabbiata. "Angry penne," similar to *amatriciana* sauce, except there is a greater presence of tomatoes and *peperoncino* and a relatively smaller amount of *pancetta* and onions.

Rigatoni alla Pajata. See *pajata* in the list of *secondi*, below.

Spaghetti alla Carbonara. Thick spaghetti tossed with beaten egg, sautéed *pancetta*, grated Pecorino, and copious amounts of freshly ground pepper.

Stracciatella alla Romana. An egg-drop soup made with chicken broth.

SECONDI

Abbacchio al Forno. Oven-roasted, milk-fed baby lamb. Made with garlic and rosemary, it is absolutely delicious.

Abbacchio a Scottadito. *Scottadito* means "burnt fingers." These are thin strips of lamb that are quickly cooked in a frying pan (perhaps with the cook turning them over manually?).

Anguille. There are very famous eels from the Lago di Bolsena in northern Lazio that one customarily consumes with Est! Est!! Est!!! or Vernaccia, the wine the eels might be cooked in. There was once, long ago, Pope Martin IV, who was a voracious eater and such a lover of eels that they did him in. This anecdote is recounted by Dante in *Purgatory*.

Coda alla Vaccinara. Oxtail-and-wine stew.

Coratella. The old-fashioned English word for this is "pluck," which implies the heart, liver, lungs, and windpipe of an animal. In Lazio, those of the lamb are used. They are minced and fried in *fritto misto alla romana,* cooked with lots of onions and pepper, or braised in wine-and-tomato sauce.

Fritto Misto alla Romana. Fried meats, organ meats, and vegetables.

Pajata. Slow-cooked lamb's intestine, often served on pasta.

Porchetta. Delicious boned suckling pig roasted with rosemary, garlic, and lots of pepper. It is served at meals, especially on Sunday, but is also sold at roadside stands in sandwiches and is often served in pieces to accompany Roman white wine.

Saltimbocca. Veal cutlets topped with fresh sage and *prosciutto crudo* and sautéed. The name means "jump in your mouth."

CONTORNI

Romans know good vegetables and go out of their way to select the freshest, most flavorful ones they can find. They are completely attuned to the seasons and look forward to the arrival of each food and enjoy it to the fullest. Roman peas are the sweetest you will ever taste, and artichokes, asparagus, spinach, and all sorts of greens are outstanding. Spinach is often served cold with a squeeze of fresh lemon juice. Also look for *puntarelle,* curly greens (from celery) served with a dressing of oil, vinegar, and mashed anchovies.

FORMAGGI

Pecorino Romano. The most popular version is the slightly salty grating cheese that is often called Romano or Pecorino stagionato. Much of it is actually made in Sardegna, and that made in Lazio is becoming harder to find all the time as Roma spreads and occupies land once devoted to grazing. Classic Pecorino from Lazio has a greenish tinge, while the one from Sardegna is whiter. The green tinge comes when the cheese is aged in tufa caves, as tradition dictates. Both cheeses belong to the Consorzio del Pecorino Romano, the producers' consortium. I recommend that you buy a piece of each at a store such as Volpetti in Roma, and you will see and taste the difference. The first taste of aged Pecorino Romano is salty, but then other flavors come forth, including milk and herbs. The cheese has a very long finish (aftertaste). As with almost all cheeses, it will taste different depending on when the milk was gathered. A one-year-old Pecorino that was made in the spring will taste younger and fresher than one made in summer or fall, because the sheep eat more tender grass in the spring. A cheese made in June, when the grass is harder, will taste stronger after a year. A popular dessert is *fave con il Pecorino*, raw fava beans served with a slice of cheese.

Ricotta Romana. This smooth, fresh creamy cheese is one of the simplest, and most addictive, in all of Italy. It is made of milk curds (cow or sheep) that are twice cooked and then cooled. I routinely eat it as a snack with cut fruit.

DOLCI

The best desserts in Lazio are the outstanding fruits one sees everywhere. An orange in February, cherries in June, a peach in July, *moscato* or *regina* grapes in September cannot be topped.

Baked goods. There are bakeries in the Castelli Romani that make nice cookies and *buccellati di vino* (rings made with wine).

Crostate. These tarts of fruit or jam, although better in Emilia and Lombardia, can be very good in Lazio when local fruits are used.

Gelato. I eat more gelato in Roma than in most places, except Sicilia. This is because there is such a festive, partylike feeling about the city that ice cream seems to be called for. Also, it is possible to find excellent gelati in many parts of town.

Ricotta desserts. Roman ricotta cheese can be very good in a light cheesecake *(torta di ricotta)*, in a mousse, or simply by itself with a little sugar or cocoa powder.

The Wines of Lazio

Unlike most wines in Italy (except Verdicchio and Soave), wine in Lazio has declined in quality. This is because Roma is a huge market that consumes most of it and wants it at low cost. In most cases the restaurants I have indicated have good or at least typical wine, but if you tire of Lazio red or whites, order a bottle from another region. People in Lazio generally drink white wine, most of it from the Castelli Romani (aka the Colli Albani), southeast of the capital. Most of it is from (and is called) Frascati, one of Italy's most famous wines. Centuries ago Frascati owners effectively captured the Roman market by opening *osterie* there to sell their wine—there were already 1,022 *osterie* in 1450! These *osterie* were leased to local franchisers, much like fast-food restaurants today. Frascati is an amiable young wine, but not always as good as it should be because producers have such a captive market. It is made of 70 percent Malvasia Bianca di Candia and/or Trebbiano Toscano, Plus 30 percent Greco and/or Malvasia di Lazio. Other wines from that area are called Marino or simply Castelli Romani.

The other famous wine of Lazio is Est! Est!! Est!!! This is one of the few wines of ancient origin whose date of birth we can trace. The wines of Montefiascone and the nearby Lago di Bolsena were admired in the region, and word of their quality spread. In the year 1000 a major religious figure (some accounts say the bishop or cardinal) of Augsburg named Defuk (or Fugger) had to go to the Vatican, and, because he had great Bacchic tendencies, he assigned his cupbearer, Martin, to travel the route before him and to mark the word *est* ("it is," in Latin) in chalk on the doors of the inns that had good wine. In Montefiascone Martin found a wine so good that a mere *est* would not suffice. So he wrote *est! est!! est!!!* When Defuk arrived he loved the wine so much that he stayed for three days before proceeding to Roma. On his way back he decided to remain in Montefiascone, where he died. He is buried at the Church of San Flaviano where, each year, a barrel of the wine is poured over the grave. Another famous Lazio beverage is Sambuca, the anise liqueur native to Viterbo. When you have it *con la mosca* (with the fly), a coffee bean is put at the bottom of your glass.

Amatrice (Rieti)

DINING

Albergo-Ristorante La Conca, Via della Madonella, tel./fax 0746/826791. Closed Monday (except in summer). No credit cards. Moderately inexpensive to moderate.

The Perilli family that owns this restaurant with rooms also has a butcher shop in which they make sausages from scratch. The herbs, vegetables, and some of the fruit they use come from their garden so they know about ingredients. As far as I am concerned, your search for the classic *bucatini all'amatriciana* should begin and end right here. Signora Perilli also makes excellent gnocchi and fettuccine and be sure to have *abbacchio al forno* as one of your *secondi*, though all of the meats are excellent. Fruit for dessert.

FOLKLORE

La Sagra degli Spaghetti.

On August 15 and 16, vast amounts of spaghetti or *bucatini all'amatriciana* are consumed to honor the local specialty.

Anzio (Roma)

Anzio is a bustling town with interesting fish markets and some beautiful villas on the hills above the port. To reach them from the port, walk up the gently sloping hill from the Piazza Garibaldi to the Via Gramsci or from the train station go left on Viale Mencacci to the Via Flora and then down into the villas. Anzio has a working port that is somewhat raffish and raunchy in the way such places are, but it is a source of great fish. There is also an ancient Roman theater and several nice beaches just beyond the old part of town. The British Second World War cemeteries are in Anzio, and may be reached from the train station. The beachhead war cemetery is better reached from the train station at Lavinio.

BAKERY-BAR

Pasticceria Partenopea, Via Gramsci 12 (near Piazza Garibaldi). Closed Thursday.

The family does the baking in the back, making good cherry and apricot tarts (*crostatine di amarene o di albicocche*). Good coffee is served, too.

DINING

La Vecchia Osteria, Via Gramsci 103, tel. 06/9846100. Closed Tuesday (except in summer) and at Christmas. All credit cards. Moderate to moderately expensive.

Very good fish and seafood that changes with the daily catch. Try the white wine based on the Cacchione grape, which is now rare.

MARKETS

Mercato Comunale, Via Matteotti (next to the Cinema Astor). Open mornings only.

A small but very vital market.

Frutti di Mare—Pescheria d'Andrassi "Io Contro Tutti," Piazza Garibaldi (near the port), tel. 06/9845362. Open 8–13h, 16–20h; closed Monday morning.

It is called "I Against Everyone" as a way of calling attention to the quality of the fish and seafood sold here. You will see some of the best the Mediterranean has to offer, many of them still moving. The Piazza Garibaldi has four palm trees and ten smaller trees, convenient stops for thousands of itinerant birds from the region. The sound of all of them chirping at once is astonishing.

Castelgandolfo (Roma)

DINING

Ristorante La Perla, Via Spiaggia al Lago 6, tel. 06/9360064. Moderate.

A lakeside restaurant with good, simple food.

Casteffi Romani (Roma)

Do you remember the famous episode of *I Love Lucy* in which our heroine goes to a small wine town outside of Roma (fictitiously called Turo) to soak up a little local color? She went to a little town in the Castelli Romani, an area southeast of the capital. True, almost all the wine making is now mechanized, but the smaller towns still have a playful innocence about them. This is where Romans go for their weekend recreation most of the year. The limpid air, deep lakes, sloping hills, and rustic cuisine are all inviting reasons to come. There are thirteen communities, all about thirty kilometers (twenty miles) from the city: Albano, Ariccia, **Castelgandolfo**, Colonna, **Frascati, Genzano, Grottaferrata, Marino**, Monte Compatri, Monte Porzio Catone, Nemi, Rocca di Papa, and Rocca Priora (those with their own listings are indicated in bold type). In addition to restaurants, trattorias, and *osterie*, the Romans enjoy stopping at roadside stands for *porchetta* on crusty *pane casareccio* and a glass of white wine. The typical Sunday meal in Castelli Romani restaurants starts with homemade fettuccine, continues with *abbacchio* or *porchetta*, accompanied by roast potatoes and good green vegetables. And, of course, rivers of white wine. When you visit these towns, go to the bakeries as well to buy hot bread, fresh from the oven—some of the best you will ever taste.

Frascati (Roma)

Frascati, only twenty-four kilometers (fifteen miles) from Roma, is the principal town of the Castelli Romani and, with Marino, the center of wine making. There are villas and beautiful gardens here, and a day trip is an easy excursion because trains leave Roma Termini about twelve times a day on weekdays (fewer on Sunday, but visiting during the week, when it is less crowded, is often interesting).

BAKING

Forno a Legna Molinari, Via Garibaldi 2.

Pane casareccio and other baked goods from a wood-burning oven.

Forno Ceralli, Piazza Bambocci 15.

Cookies, cakes, tarts, and breads, made on the premises.

DINING

Cacciani, Via Diaz 13, tel. 06/9420378, fax 06/9420440. Closed Sunday, and holiday evenings (except April–October), Monday, January 7–17, and August 17–27. All credit cards. Moderate to moderately expensive.

Good *fettuccine con regaglie* (giblets), *pollo alla diavola* (deviled chicken), lamb, *por-*

chetta, vegetables, and fruit, with pleasant Frascati wine.

Enoteca Frascati, Via Armando Diaz 42, tel. 06/9417449. Open evenings only; closed Sunday, Monday, and August. Visa. Inexpensive to moderate.

Unlike other places in Frascati that appeal to visitors, the Enoteca Frascati is strictly local. Shoulder to shoulder with *frascatani* you can sip good wine made nearby or excellent wines from elsewhere. The special soup is onion *(zuppa di cipolla);* there are good stews, excellent *salumi* and cheeses, and, as always, wonderful Roman vegetables. Save room for the *mousse di ricotta.*

Trattoria Zarazà, Via Regina Margherita 21, tel. 06/9422053. Closed Monday and in

August.Visa. Moderately inexpensive to moderate.

Very good and careful cooking of classic regional dishes. *Norcina* is pasta with excellent sausage. The *coda alla vaccinara* is very tender, and the vegetables are great. The local white is better than average.

ICE CREAM

Gelateria Belvedere, Piazza Roma 1, tel. 06/9424986.

Good ice cream and a lovely terrace with panoramic views.

Frattochie di Marino (Roma)

WINE

Azienda Vitivinicola Paola di Mauro, Via Colle Picchioni 46, tel. 06/9356329. Visits for tastings and purcbases of wine Monday–Friday, by appointment.

Paola di Mauro is a rather remarkable woman. She is a famous home cook and a guardian of the cuisine of Lazio. Chefs from Italy and abroad often come to learn secrets at her elbow in her beautiful kitchen. Enrico, her charming husband, once told me at dinner that "when I came home from the war, I weighed forty-five kilos [ninety-nine pounds]. Soon after I married Paola I started packing this valise [he pats his stomach] that I've never unpacked." Paola and her family also make some of the best wine in Lazio, most of them under the name Colli Picchioni.

Genzano di Roma (Roma)

BAKING

Da Sergio, Via Italo Belardi 13; Panificio Tosca di Iacoangeli, Via Italo Belardi 45; Bruno Ripanucci, Corso Don Minzoni 29.

Genzano's wood-oven-baked *pane casareccio* is among Italy's finest. Find it in one of the *panifici* indicated above.

DINING

Osteria La Mia Gioia, Via Ronconi 9, tel. 06/9396143. Open 17–23h; closed Wednesday and at some time each July or August. No credit cards. Moderately inexpensive to moderate.

The menu changes daily, depending on availability. Soups are consistently good as a primo, and organ meats (brains, liver, kidneys) are the traditional *secondo*. Particularly good are the vegetable preparations. In the summer try *burraggini*, leaves of greens filled with mozzarella and pitted olives, dipped in batter, and delicately fried.

Pietrino e Renata, Via Cervi 8, tel. 06/9391497. Closed Monday. All credit cards. Moderate.

Delicious, lusty food, featuring wonderful beans, greens, *bucatini all'amatriciana*, lamb, *coda alla vaccinara*, and mushrooms.

Grottaferrata (Roma)

BAKING
Panificio Cerquozzi, Via del Pratone 88.

Pane casareccio the way it should taste.

Da Valentino.

I have tasted superb breads from this bakery, but have not been to it.

DINING
La Briciola di Adriana, Via D'Annunzio 12, tel. 06/9459338. Closed Sunday evening, Monday, three weeks in August, one week in January. All credit cards. Moderate.

Adriana Montellanico makes two pasta dishes that linger in delighted memory: *ravioli ripieni di baccalà* and *gnocchetti di melanzane* (tiny eggplant gnocchi) with tomato-and-basil sauce. These are fundamentally simple foods, but prepared with such love and assurance that they are triumphant. Cooked meats are all good, particularly poultry.

ENOTECA PUBBLICA
Enoteca dei Castelli Romani, Piazza della Repubblica 1, tel. 06/9398516. Open 16–19:30h; closed Saturday and Sunday.

The easy-drinking whites and reds of the hills outside of Roma may be tasted and purchased here.

Marino (Roma)

DINING
La Credenza, Via Cola di Rienzo 4, tel. 06/9385105. Closed Sunday, August, and Christmas. No credit cards. Moderate.

You are welcomed by Massimo Lauri, who proudly serves food made by his wife Maria. The dishes combine the best of Lazio and Abruzzo and are deliciously earthy.

Montefiascone (Viterbo)

DINING
Ristorante Dante.

I have a good memory, but no notes, of this appealingly unsophisticated restaurant in the city center, with friendly waitresses in a large L-shaped room. There was good *fettuccine al ragù*, *cannelloni di formaggio, agnello al forno,* and very good *peperoni.* If you are in town, go see if my memory serves me well.

WINE
Cantina Sociale di Montefiascone, Via Cassia, tel. 0761/86148. Open weekdays during working hours to purchase Est! Est!! Est!!!

Fiera del Vino.

Every August Montefiascone has parades, displays, feasting, and lots of Est! Est!! Est!!!

Nepi (Viterbo)

MINERAL WATER

Acqua di Nepi has a creamy fizziness that makes it, to me, the most delicious mineral water in Italy. The source is Terme dei Gracchi, which is a nice place to relax and have a tall glass of water.

Nettuno (Roma)

A trip to Nettuno and nearby Anzio is interesting for several reasons. You can see some of the Lazio terrain, gaining a sense of how it relates to Roma itself. Nettuno is a retreat for Romans taking a day out of town, it is a fishing port, and it is much more. Nettuno and Anzio were the sites of Allied landings that led to some of the most ferocious battles of the Second World War, with heavy loss of life. Everyone in the two towns has a memory of those days or can tell stories that were told by older relatives. You can—and should—visit the American cemetery in Nettuno or one of the British ones in Anzio to remind yourself, in our era of sanitized, televised wars, of the real cost in human life to those who are buried and to everyone else left behind.

The one-hour train trip from Roma to Nettuno is in itself an interesting and wistful experience. There will probably be a few elderly British or American war veterans, sometimes with their wives. They sit very quietly as they travel, which contrasts with the more animated Italians on board. First you pass the squalid gypsy encampments just outside the capital and then reach gently rolling hills. In the distance you will see sheep grazing on green slopes, which to my hungry and myopic eyes looked like gnocchi in a dish of pesto. You will then pass olive groves, hills covered with trellises for grapes, and patches of land planted with peas and other vegetables. Once in a while you will see the occasional factory. As you move farther south, you will sense the sea breeze on your right side and the mountain breeze on your left. Just as the train pulls out from Marechiaro (about fifty-three kilometers/thirty-three miles from Roma) the sea will come into view, and soon you reach Nettuno.

Once there, walk down the street going straight from the train station to the port. Turn right on Viale Matteotti, and at the corner of Via Santa Maria look left, and you will see a stone turret with a Gothic portal. That is the entrance to the Borgo Medioevale, the medieval quarter of Nettuno. There, on Piazza Marconi 3, facing the church, is the Pasticceria Muzi (tel. 06/9881682; closed Tuesday). It serves homemade pastries and ice cream and sells candy and wine. Although you are not too far from Roma, the products here seem much more Neapolitan. Through the archway you can look into the kitchen as the bakers work. The *sfogliatella* is very large: it looks like a sugar-covered crustacean or some other sea creature. After a walk through the Borgo you should plan a lunch and then a visit to the American cemetery that is about a twenty-minute walk. For lunch there is a restaurant, da Rodo, that would be well worth the trip even if Nettuno offered no other reason to come.

DINING

Trattoria da Rodo, Via Santa Maria 31, tel. 06/9801154. Closed Wednesday. No credit cards. Moderate.

As I walked down the Via Santa Maria, which leads from the Borgo to the American cemetery, I could not ignore the blandishments and gaudy signs of the many restaurants on the street that call to eaters like sirens from the sea. Yet they were uninspiring. Then, near #31, I detected the most seductive fragrances, but there was only an unmarked milk-glass door that gave no indication of what was behind it. I assumed that this was a private home and began to leave when someone exited and asked, "Aren't you going to go in?" In I went, and found two absolutely plain rooms. The first one had a small refrigerator and a large open kitchen; the second had a group of men playing cards and drinking wine. They ate from magnificent plates of raw and cooked seafood antipasto. A hand truck holding the latest wine delivery stood near the refrigerator of the first room. White plates were stacked near an opened newspaper whose reader had gone into the kitchen. The reason to sit here, rather than in the room with all the card players, is that you have a clear view of the kitchen, which is where the action is. It is very clean, with its white walls mirroring those of the dining room. Two women and one man—artists all—are at work. There is a good fish fragrance, which is to say a clean fish fragrance, plus that of

tomato, garlic, and herbs. In fact, the dominant scent I noted in Nettuno as I passed kitchen windows was of tomato, that blessed but often maligned and misused food that combines the taste sensations of sweet, tart, and salty.

At da Rodo I could have had *spaghetti con pomodoro fresco*, a sauce of fresh tomatoes and herbs. There was also risotto or *spaghetti alla pescatora* (with mixed fish and seafood), but I took the advice of Francesco, the welcoming host, and had *spaghetti alle vongole*. Spaghetti with clam sauce is a ubiquitous dish in coastal Italy, so I was not prepared for the exemplary preparation that awaited me. As I watched Alicia make my dish, I was reminded of a fundamental lesson of Italian cooking: the respect and exaltation of the *materia prima*, the basic ingredients that make up any meal. She inspected every item before she used it and understood what role its flavors and textures would play. It is a lesson that should be learned by fancy cooks in America and elsewhere. At da Rodo everything, the lemons, the tomatoes, lettuce, chicory, garlic, *peperoncino*, fish, seafood, bread (with a crunchy crust and a chewy interior), the olive oil, are all perfect and are presented so that you can admire their perfection rather than the conceits of the cook.

Every clam in the pasta dish was tender and sweet, the whole cloves of garlic lent perfume rather than odor, the oil base was delicate, and the spaghetti were perfectly al dente. When Francesco suggested a grilled *orata* and a salad of greens as a *secondo*, I knew to follow his lead but ordered a sliced tomato too. What arrived was perhaps the most perfectly grilled fish I have ever tasted. The salad and tomato, which I ate after, were in peak condition and joyously flavorful. With my meal I drank the local wine, Cacchione di Nettuno, which was almost orange in color, though technically it is a white wine. At first taste it was rather harsh and rustic, but it marries well with the food. The trattoria also has bottles of Marino and Frascati wines for lighter tastes.

Francesco, a well-traveled man who has been to Spain, Argentina, Mexico, and Florida, went out to the nearby bar to get the coffee I have ordered. There is no machine here. With the coffee come delicious cookies made by Alicia: one with anise, one with almond, another with sugar and egg. As I looked up I saw her standing on a table in the kitchen scrubbing the walls now that lunchtime was over. Here is one of those cases in which the price for such a meal, if ever you could get it where you live, would be astronomical, yet at da Rodo it is by any standard moderate, which only adds to your sense of wonderment at what you have just eaten. It is after a sensual experience such as this meal that a person feels most alive and content with the world. Which makes a visit to the military cemetery that much more wrenching.

THE SICILY-ROME AMERICAN CEMETERY AND MEMORIAL
It is impossible to understand the enormity of the battles that raged here and the consequent loss of humanity until you stand in the sea of crosses and Stars of David and realize that you are the only one standing. There is something almost bibli-

The Sicily-Rome American Cemetery and Memorial, Nettuno

cal about the ancient trees that rise tall and full of life among the many tombs. Here on thirty-one hectares (seventy-seven acres) are buried 7,862 Americans who were killed in Sicilia and in the local battles that led to the liberation of Roma. They are from all fifty states and the District of Columbia. Four hundred eighty-eight of them are unknown, and their graves are headed with white crosses engraved with the words HERE RESTS IN HONORED GLORY A COMRADE IN ARMS KNOWN BUT TO GOD. It is hard to say which is more moving: to see the name of a man, where he was from, and the date of his death, or to see the grave of an anonymous hero. When a name appears, you can develop a sense of who they were, and think who they might have been. I could not help but think that Italy, the country that you and I have so freely enjoyed, is free in part because of the sacrifices of these silent heroes.

A visit here may not have been part of your vacation plans, but it will be a meaningful experience that will give you great perspective and make you grateful for many things. Open May 15–September 15 8–18h, September 15–May 15 8–17h.

Roma
Classic Town

Despite the amazing treasures Roma has accumulated in its twenty-eight centuries of life, I think what you will most remember about the city is the Romans themselves. It is as if the city were designed to be their enormous, beautiful playground. If the Milanese work hard and play hard, the Romans play hard and play harder. Social interaction seems to be their chief occupation, and they are very adept at its intricacies. They can be, by turns, gracious, playful, formal, flirtatious, confrontational, sympathetic, and sentimental, all within the space of a few minutes. They love walking down a street arm in arm, stopping to add emphasis to a particular idea in a conversation. Once that point is made they resume the gentle cadence of their gait, rocking gently right then left as they promenade down the street. They blow kisses to one another from motor scooters, yelling "Shau!"—the local pronunciation of *ciao,* that by-now universal greeting of Venetian origin.

Romans also dress very consciously. I believe that while the Milanese often dress to be stylish—a walk through that city's streets is like flipping through the pages of *Vogue*—the Romans dress to feel that they look their best. Those of modest means have one or two articles of very fine clothing that they take great care of and for the rest of the time wear colorful sweaters and sensible skirts or trousers. Even very old men make an effort to be stylish, but in a manner suitable to their age and station. Many older women choose their colors in clothes, accessories, hair, makeup, and nails with great care, and they frequently wear lots of jewelry. Young Romans are often very attractive—and seem eternally attracted. Their mode of dress is to lure the opposite (and occasionally the same) sex. Young men's trousers seem a bit tighter than elsewhere. Their shirts and jackets are tapered to flatter their physiques. They also wear ties more than other young Italians—you will be amazed at how many tie shops Roma has. Young women wear more makeup than you see in most Italian cities and dress to flatter their figures, which are realigned substantially by the high-heeled shoes they often favor. How do they walk on those cobblestone streets?

BAKERIES AND SWEET SHOPS

Forno Vincenzino Marucci, Via Amerigo Vespucci 28–30 (near Testaccio).

Signor Marucci and his son Sandro make some of the most delicious bread I have tasted in Roma.

Il Forno di Campo dei Fiori 22.

See "Campo dei Fiori," under "Markets," below.

Eredi Napoli, Via Marmorata 33, Testaccio.

Excellent *pane casareccio*, wheat breads, and *pane di farro.*

La Dolceroma, Via del Portico d'Ottavia 20B (near the old Jewish Ghetto).

An oddity: this is a bakery that specializes in Austrian and American cakes. So if you must have a brownie, pumpkin pie, *apfel strudel,* or Sacher torte, pay a visit.

La Casa del Caffè—Tazza d'Oro, Via dei Orfani 84 (near the Pantheon).
Closed Sunday.

Coffee lovers should not leave town without a visit here. In the back (to the left) is the coffee roaster, while in the middle of this Z-shaped place you can buy one of many freshly roasted varieties of beans (which you should not grind until you use it). At the front you can drink an espresso from one of the several beans they roast. In the warm months you can get a superb *granita di caffè*.

Caffè Farnese, Via dei Baullari 106, tel. 06/68802125.

A great place for breakfast if you are going marketing at the nearby Campo dei Fiori. The view from the *caffè* is the splendid Palazzo Farnese, site of the second act of Puccini's *Tosca* and now the French embassy.

Caffè-Bar Durante.

See "Food Stores: A Walk on the Via Flaminia," below.

Antico Caffè Greco, Via Condotti 86 (near the Piazza di Spagna), tel. 06/6782554.

"Il Caffè Greco è l'unico posto al mondo dove sedersi e aspettare la fine." ("The Caffè Greco is the only place in the world where to sit and await the end.") So said Giorgio De Chirico, perhaps the greatest Italian painter of the twentieth century, and one of the hundreds of artistic types who have made this place a hub for nearly 250 years. It is an ancient belief at the Caffè Greco that if a cardinal enters the *caffè* he will later become pope. This actually happened to Gioacchino Cardinal Pecci, who became Pope Leo XIII. In rooms decorated with more than 150 paintings and drawings, mostly neoclassical in theme and from the early nineteenth century, almost every notable visitor to the Eternal City has had a coffee. They include Thackeray, Stendhal, Keats, Byron, Dickens, Wagner, Goldoni, Goethe, Hawthorne, Berlioz, Mendelssohn, and Buffalo Bill. Rossini composed here, and Gogol wrote *Dead Souls* in the back room. Hans Christian Andersen lived in a rented room upstairs.

Bar Marco Polo, Largo Santa Susanna 108 (near Piazza della Repubblica).
Closed Sunday.

A typical Roman bar within reach of the Via Veneto. Not fancy or unusual, but it will give you a sense of where local people go for breakfast or cocktails. An unnamed swirled pastry filled with coconut (*cocco*) is heavenly and not too sweet, worth getting if you like this flavor. The *taralli* with almonds are also good, and the basic *cornetto* (some filled with marmalade) is kept warm and is delicious. The bar makes an excellent cappuccino, and if you want a touch of cocoa powder on it, say, "Cacao sopra per piacere." Another reason to come here is to watch how Romans interact. You will notice that they often seem aggressive with one another. They can adopt a complaining tone (listen to old films with Anna Magnani or Aldo Fabrizi and you will know what I mean), often criticizing a person present, yet who will not be directly addressed. Such a complainer is one of the barmen here, the taller one who often wears a green jacket. Don't take it personally if he is a bit brusque—he is courteous with tourists, as are most Romans.

BOOKSTORES

Anglo American Book Company, Via delle Vite 57 (near Piazza di Spagna), tel. 06/6795222.

A small but select cookbook section in English. If you have access to a kitchen in Roma, take the opportunity to use the outstanding local ingredients and make a recipe from one of these many books.

Lion Bookshop, Via del Babuino 181 (near Piazza di Spagna), tel. 06/3225837.

All the English-language books a traveler would want, including many titles not available in the United States.

Rizzoli, Largo Tritone at Piazza Colonna.

A large bookstore with one of the better food and travel selections in the city.

COOKING SCHOOLS

Associazione Enogastronomica Pepe Verde, Via Santa Caterina da Siena 46, tel. 06/ 6790528 or 06/6790779, www.pepeverdi.it. Closed in August.

An excellent, well-equipped cooking school in a *palazzo* not far from the Pantheon and the Piazza Minerva. Classes range widely from traditional Roman and regional Italian cooking to international cuisines. It is possible, by arranging at least one month in advance, to have classes in English for a day or for a series of classes during one's visit to Roma. There are also wine courses and cooking lessons for children and teenagers.

Circolo Oriele Sotgiu, Palazzo Lazzaroni 6, 00186 Roma, tel. 06/6877925.

Courses are offered in this seventeenth-century palace in the center of the Italian capital. Beginners are welcome, as are advanced cooks. Typically a course lasts for ten weeks, but you might inquire about frequenting individual lessons. There is also a popular five-lesson course on wine.

International Wine Academy of Roma:

See page 489.

See page 489.

DINING NEAR THE PIAZZA DELLA REPUBBLICA (VIA NAZIONALE, VIA VENETO, VIA XX SETTEMBRE, STAZIONE TERMINI, CHURCH OF SANTA MARIA MAGGIORE, TOWARD THE COLOSSEUM)

Agata e Romeo, Via Carlo Alberto 45, tel. 06/4466115. Closed Saturday, Sunday, two weeks in January, two weeks in August. All credit cards. Expensive.

This restaurant near the Basilica of Santa Maria Maggiore is in many ways an anomaly on the Roman dining scene. It is in a transitional neighborhood that now has more Africans and Chinese immigrants than native Italians. The decor is frilly and floral, suggesting more a tea parlor in Scotland than an excellent restaurant in Roma. There are only a few tables and the room is startlingly quiet. And yet, for many people, this is the apex of eating in the Italian capital. I certainly have eaten well here and admire the delicacy and creativity in the kitchen, the amazing wine list, the wonderful cheese cart and the care that is everywhere evident. One would not want to eat this way every day, but for a special occasion there is a lot to enjoy. The *cannelloni con ragù bianco di anatra* are delicate pasta crepes filled with a white meat sauce made with duck. The *coda di bue con crema di sedano rapa* is a deconstruction and reconstruction of Roma's earthy *coda alla vaccinara*, oxtail flavored with celery. The oven-roasted pork is exquisite. Fish preparations are excellent. And a cheese course to enjoy with the last of your wine is essential.

Ristorante dell'Arte, Palazzo delle Esposizioni (194 Via Nazionale), tel. 06/4828540. No credit cards. Inexpensive.

On top of the Palazzo delle Esposizioni is this nice restaurant. The setting is lovely, the food is really quite good for a buffet, and you have the possibility to work off your meal by seeing good art downstairs. You do not have to pay museum admission to dine here (go around to the left side of the museum to the Via Milano and look for the entrance near the tunnel). Serves lunch and dinner.

Il Quadrifoglio, Via del Boschetto 19, tel. 06/4826096. Closed Sunday and August. All credit cards. Moderately expensive.

If you want a break from Roman cuisine, here is some of the best Neapolitan food in the Italian capital.

Trattoria Monti, Via San Vito 13/a; tel./ fax 06/4466573; closed Sunday evening and Monday. All credit cards. Moderate.

Marvellous cooking from the Marche. Don't miss the flans made of cheese or vegetables, and be sure to have pasta such as *tagliatelle al ragù marchigiano*.

Bottiglieria ai Tre Scalini, Via Panisperna 251 (near Via dei Serpenti). Closed Sunday. No credit cards. Inexpensive.

A nice old place for wine and snacks.

Enoteca Cavour 313, Via Cavour 313, tel. 06/6785496. Open 12:30–14.30h; 20–24:30h, Saturday evening only; closed Sunday and in August. No credit cards. Moderately inexpensive.

A charming, cozy place, very popular with young people. Here is a wine bar with very good food to go with your wine: *affettati*, cheese, soups, salads, and particularly the *torte rustiche*, taller versions of quiche.

DINING IN CENTRAL ROMA (FROM PIAZZA DI SPAGNA TO THE TEVERE)

Trattoria La Campana, Vicolo della Campana 18 (near the Pantheon), tel. 06/6867820 or 6875273. Closed Monday and August. American Express, Diners Club, Visa. Moderate to moderately expensive.

A very old eatery with a loyal following for dishes such as *puntarelle, pasta con crema di carciofi* (artichoke-cream sauce), and *vignarola*, a vegetable stew.

Armando al Pantheon, Salita de Crescenzi (just to the right of the Pantheon as you face it). Closed Saturday evening and Sunday. Diners Club, MasterCard, Visa. Moderately inexpensive.

One of my old standbys from twenty years ago is now slightly elevated in price and decor, but it is still a worthy example of a basic Roman trattoria. There is a very good *carbonara* and daily specials such as *rigatoni con pajata* (Wednesday), gnocchi (Thursday), cod (Friday), and tripe (Saturday).

Da Gino, Vicolo Rosini 4 (between the Pantheon and the Parliament), tel. 06/6873434. Closed Sunday and in August. No credit cards. Inexpensive.

A tiny place for basic Roman food at low prices. Very good value for the price, but not a memorable gastronomic experience. Try the *tonnarelli alla ciociara*.

Da Sergio, Vicolo delle Grotte 27, tel. 06/6864293. Closed Sunday, August. All credit cards. Moderate.

Roman classics prepared with extra love and care.

International Wine Academy of Roma.

See page 489.

Osteria Fabrizio Corsi, Via del Gesù 88 (near Corso Vittorio Emanuele and Piazza Gesù), tel. 06/6 790821. Closed evenings, Saturday, and in August. No credit cards. Moderately inexpensive.

A very simple place awash in flavor. The *zuppa di ceci* (chickpea soup) and the *pollo con i peperoni* (chicken and peppers) can't be beat. The house wine is okay; if you plan to consume enough to merit it, order a bottle of the wine of your choice.

Enoteca Capranica, Piazza Capranica 100, tel. 06/69940992. Closed Saturday lunch, Sunday. All credit cards. Moderately expensive to expensive.

Near the Pantheon and loved by oenophiles for its excellent wine list. One weak link in the kitchen is soups, so skip them, but risotto is very well-prepared and the lamb dishes are outstanding. If they have herb-crusted *agnello con una crosta di erbe*, be sure to try it. Wine prices are very fair, so you can indulge in more than one bottle without finishing them, permitting you to match wines carefully with the flavors of the dishes you have ordered.

Ristorante La Matricianella, Via del Leone 4, tel. 06/6832100. Closed Sunday. All credit cards. Moderate.

The best frying in Rome is done here, whether it is mixed vegetables, potato skins, whole artichokes or divine *ricotta fritta*, little puffs of cheese. The *spaghetti cacio e pepe* is first-rate, baked lamb excellent and cooked fruit is a perfect dessert. Service is lovely too.

Trattoria Antonio Bassetti, Via del Governo Vecchio 18, tel. 333/5870779. No credit cards. Inexpensive.

A very down-home place where you share tables and enjoy great food at low prices. One must queue up, as no reservations are taken. Roast veal is exquisite, pastas are tasty, vegetables are wonderful, and fresh fruit is the best dessert.

Margutta Vegetariano-Ristorante, Via Margutta 118, tel. 06/32650577. Open daily, vacations vary from year to year. All credit cards. Moderate to moderately expensive.

The Via Margutta is one of my favorite streets in Roma. You will love the park views, the art galleries and its sense of intimacy right in the middle of a big city. This restaurant is just a few doors down from the apartment where Federico Fellini and Giulietta Masina lived during their marriage. Now the street is popular among artists and dealers who appreciate the vegetarian cookery at this enjoyable, often crowded restaurant.

Taverna Giulia, Vicolo d'Oro 23, tel. 06/6869768. Closed Sundays and in August. All credit cards. Moderate to moderately expensive.

If your trip to Italy does not include a trip to Liguria, this is one of the best places elsewhere to sample the flavors of the Italian Riviera. The pesto is quite fine, the focaccia is crisp and fragrant, and the fish and vegetables are delicious.

Hostaria della Cucagna, Via Parione 14 (just below Piazza Navona), tel. 06/6861502. MasterCard, Visa. Moderate to moderately expensive.

Roman families engage in animated bantering here until the food arrives, then they quiet down and eat. Among the good foods are walnut bread, excellent green olive bread, *gnocchi ai 4 formaggi* (on Thursday), and *abbacchio arrosto con patate*.

Fratelli Paladini, Via del Governo Vecchio 28, tel. 06/6790483. No credit cards. Very inexpensive.

A wonderful little shop for *panini*. The reason they are so good is that the bread is baked right here and then is topped with ingredients you select: fresh cheeses, fine cold cuts, and perfect vegetables.

Enoteca Il Piccolo, Via del Governo Vecchio 74, tel. 06/68801746. Open 16:30-2h; closed Tuesday, but not always. All credit cards. Moderately inexpensive.

People-watch at this *enoteca* with a good selection of Roman wines and some from other regions, plus some oddities, such as a "wine" made of wild strawberries that is available in late autumn and winter. To match the wines with different flavors, Il Piccolo serves *salami* from Calabria, Umbria, Piemonte, and the Veneto, cheeses from practically every region, plus fruit, cakes, nuts, and chocolates. A warm, comfortable little place, with jazz playing in the background.

Enoteca Cul de Sac, Piazza Pasquino 73, tel. 06/6541094. Open 12:30-15h, 19:30-0.30h; closed Monday. Inexpensive.

Many excellent wines by the glass, plus homemade pâtés such as *lepre* (hare) and *cinghiale* (wild boar). Onion soup is fine, and there are good *salumi*, cheeses, and vegetables.

La Carbonara, Campo dei Fiori 23, tel. 06/6864783. All credit cards. Moderate to moderately expensive.

It has become a bit touristy now as visitors have discovered the Campo dei Fiori, but there still is much to recommend an outdoor table on a lovely day. As trucks and handcarts from the market are moved away, more tables are put out for diners. Although the restaurant is named for a famous Roman pasta dish, I encourage you to try the *gnocchi al sugo*, perfect gnocchi in a good tomato sauce. Because of the proximity of the market, the vegetables are excellent. Try *carciofi alla giudea*, *piselli al burro* (buttered peas), *puntarelle* with anchovy dressing, and zucchini flowers filled with mozzarella, batter-dipped, and fried.

Filetti di Baccalà, Largo del Librari 88 (between Campo del Fiori and Via Arenula). Open 17–22h; closed Sunday. No credit cards. Inexpensive.

There is an old tradition, especially in Jewish Roma, of eating fried cod fillets, perhaps with a few vegetables and some wine. This is the stubbornly retro place to do it. The wine will be served from two spigots in a wooden refrigerator.

DINING NEAR THE TEVERE

Uno, Via del Portico d'Ottavia, tel. 06/6547937. Closed Saturday lunch and Friday. No credit cards.

The laws of the kosher kitchen and the available ingredients in the Roman pantry make for a great marriage: pasta with artichokes as a starter, beef in tomato sauce, fresh fish with greens, and many good vegetable dishes. Traditional Jewish pastries are served at dessert.

Pane, Vino e San Daniele, Piazza Mattei 16, tel. 06/6877147. No credit cards. Inexpensive.

For a light snack on a pretty piazza, stop here for a plate of *prosciutto di San Daniele* and a glass of Tocai from Friuli-Venezia Giulia.

Sora Margherita, Piazza delle Cinque Scole 30, tel. 06/6874216. Closed Saturday and Sunday in summer, Sunday and Monday in other months;

also closed in August. No credit cards. Moderately inexpensive.

In Rome's ancient Jewish ghetto is this trattoria that presents some traditional Jewish dishes more as a nod to tradition than religion. Cheese and meat do appear on the menu, but kosher diners can chart their own course to fidelity to the rules of *kashrut*. In season, don't miss the *carciofi alla giudia*.

Hostaria Elio.

See "Food Stores: A Walk on the Via Flaminia," below.

Antica Enoteca Beccaria.

See "Food Stores: A Walk on the Via Flaminia," below.

DINING NEAR THE VATICAN
AND IN WESTERN AND
NORTHERN ROMA

Enoteca Simposio, Piazza Cavour 16 (near the Castel Sant'Angelo), tel. 06/3203575. Open 11:30–15h, 18:30–1h; closed Saturday.

Many cheeses, salads, *affettati*, smoked fish and meat, to go with the house Frascati and other wines.

Osteria dell'Angelo, Via Giovanni Bettolo 24, tel 06/3729470. Open for dinner Monday through Saturday; lunch served on Tuesday and Friday; closed in August. No credit cards. Moderately inexpensive to moderate.

Very traditional Roman food and atmosphere, with a set meal including a modest wine. The *cacio e pepe* is great.

Il Matriciano, Via del Gracchi 49–61, tel. 06/3213040, ilmatriciano@romatour.com.

Closed Wednesdays in winter, Saturdays in summer. All credit cards. Moderate.

Pasta is the strong suit at this bustling trattoria about 10 minutes north of the Vatican. The ravioli with ricotta and spinach are wonderful, and the *bucatini all'amatriciana, spaghetti cacio e pepe, spaghetti alla carbonara* and other choices are all lusty and good. Order simply for your second courses and enjoy the nice selection of vegetables.

Enoteca del Frate, Via degli Scipioni 118, tel. 06/3236437. All credit cards. Inexpensive to moderate.

This well-stocked wine shop has an adjacent restaurant serving food that flatters the wine. At lunch is an inexpensive and good-value-for-money buffet with pasta, vegetables, fish, and local specialties such as baked ricotta. The wine list is formidable, though the mark-up can be a little steep.

DINING IN SOUTHERN ROMA (AVENTINO, PIRAMIDE, TERME DI CARACALLA, TESTACCIO, TRASTEVERE)

Tramonti & Muffati, Via S. Maria Ausiliatrice 105, tel./fax 06/7801342. Dinner only. Closed Sundays. All credit cards. Moderate.

Reservations are essential at this 7-table *osteria* that is the pride and joy of Marco Berardi and his sister Lucia. They can guide you through a meal of sublime *salumi*, cheeses, wines, and oil-cured vegetables that they find all over Italy. Before dining here, purchase some pastries at the bakery across the street, which closes at 8 pm.

La Luna Piena, Via Luca della Robbia 15/17, tel. 06/5750279. All credit cards. Moderately inexpensive to moderate.

This lively restaurant uses excellent fresh produce from the Testaccio market just across the street. The soups, pastas, and vegetable dishes are all excellent, the *pollo alla romana* (chicken with onions, tomatoes and peppers) is delectable, and the *coda alla vaccinara* (oxtail braised with celery) is superb.

Perilli a Testaccio, Via Marmorata 39, tel. 06/5742415. Closed Wednesday. All credit cards. Moderate.

Since 1911, Perilli has lovingly served Roman classics. The *carbonara* here is excellent, and lamb dishes are delectable. Artichokes, peas, spinach, and salads are wonderful, and the atmosphere is cheery.

Trattoria Lo Scopettaro, Lungotevere Testaccio 7, tel. 06/5742408. Closed Tuesday. American Express, MasterCard. Moderate to moderately expensive.

Good *pajata, bucatini all'amatriciana, carciofi alla romana*, spinach, and *puntarelle.*

Osteria del Nostri Tempi, Via Luca della Robbia 34, tel. 06/57300685. Open 13–16h, 20–24h; closed Sunday lunch and Saturday. No credit cards. Moderately inexpensive.

Choose from gnocchi, crepes, soups, and *salumi* from excellent producers throughout Italy. The cheeses and *salumi* are purchased at Volpetti on Via Marmorata. There is a good rotating wine selection.

Trattoria Zampagna, Via Ostiense 179, tel. 06/5742306. Open Monday through Saturday for lunch only; closed in August. No credit cards. Inexpensive to moderately inexpensive.

Near the Basilica di San Paolo and the site where Roma's wholesale food markets once flourished, this family-run trattoria has attracted budget-minded lovers of Roman food since 1924. It is lively and popular, but don't go if you are expecting formal restaurant service. The *pasta alla gricia*, the *petti di pollo dorati e fritti* (battered fried chicken breasts) and the *involtini* are all laudable.

Piccola Trattoria da Lucia, Vicolo del Mattonato 2, tel. 06/5803601. Closed Monday. No credit cards. Moderately inexpensive.

Years ago I wrote about this unknown place in the *New York Times*, when da Lucia was one of the few eateries that made the pasta dish called *la gricia*. In years since, da Lucia has appeared in many guidebooks, but I can still recommend it. The Vicolo del Mattonato (Little Street Paved with Bricks) is in the most typical part of Trastevere. While fancy Alfa Romeos zoom only blocks away, here the man who sharpens knives or sells fruit will arrive in a cart drawn by a donkey. A boy kicking a soccer ball down the street becomes an object of affection and concern not only to his parents, but to every neighbor. Da Lucia has been part of this scene since 1938. It was opened by Lucia Antonangeli, who died in 1967. Following the death of her daughter Silvana in 1997, her grandson

Renato is now in charge along with his family, and the food and spirit are better than ever.

La Festa de Noiantri.

In the last two weeks of July there is nightly feasting all over Trastevere, where people eat *maccheroni*, chicken, lamb, and Pecorino and drink lots of wine.

DINING AT LEORNADO DA VINCI AIRPORT

Anyone traveling by air to regional cities in Italy is likely to make a connection at Leonardo da Vinci (Fiumicino) Airport. Because of scheduling and the short duration of domestic flights, it is unlikely that a traveler will be served a meal in the air. If you are hungry, it is possible to have a very respectable meal at the restaurant above gate 7 in the domestic flights (*voli nazionali*) section of the airport (open daily 11–23h). On my last visit I had a meal of excellent pasta crepes stuffed with fresh ricotta and Swiss chard, beautifully cooked vegetables, bread, a quarter liter of Valpolicella, and some mineral water for a moderate price. If you want pasta, select the one that was most recently prepared. You can also have fine cheeses from around Italy, roast meats, salads, fresh fruit, and very good fruit tarts. Coffee should be had downstairs at the bar between gates 9 and 10. This bar sells very good *macedonia* (fruit salad), yogurt, and nice sandwiches made of mozzarella, prosciutto, *salame*, or tuna. There is a similar restaurant at the international terminal, though less good. But the food is certainly better than airline food.

ERBORISTERIE
Antica Erboristeria Romana, Via Torre Argentina 15.

An herbalist that makes elixirs, lozenges, cosmetics, oils, inhalants, soaps, and herbal preparations for gastronomic purposes.

Ai Monasteri.

See "Wines and Spirits," below.

FOLKLORE
Festa di San Giuseppe.

On March 19 in the Trionfale quarter there are stands selling *bignè* and *zeppoli*, two deep-fried batter pastries.

Festa di San Giovanni.

On June 23 and 24 in the San Giovanni quarter there are parties, light shows, singing competitions, stands selling mementos and offering games of chance. It is customary during this event to eat steamed snails and *porchetta*.

La Festa de Noiantri.

See "Dining in Southern Roma," above.

FOOD STORES
Gastronomia Volpetti, Via della Scrofa 31, tel. 06/6861940.

In 1988, I broke my foot not far from here and had to put up in a hotel across the street from Volpetti for a few days until I was allowed to walk. I therefore have a special affection for this place, which made my life more pleasurable by sending up hot delicious meals that I feasted on in my room. This is a good place to buy food in central Roma if you

Claudio Volpetti carefully tends the cheeses in his family shop in Testaccio.

want to make a picnic. I encourage you, however, to visit the Volpetti store in Testaccio, where a gastronomic education awaits you.

Gastronomia E. Volpetti, Via Marmorata 47, Testaccio, tel. 06/5742352, fax 06/5747629. Open 8-14h, 17-20:15, closed Thursday afternoon and Sunday. American Express, MasterCard, Visa.

This is one of the best food stores I know in Italy. There are others that seem fancier or have a broader selection of so-called gourmet items, but Volpetti shines through the sheer quality of its products and the fanatical devotion that the owners give to their store, to the food, and to their customers. I have acquired quite an education from Claudio Volpetti, one of the family members, during my visits. It is

Claudio who is responsible for the care and maintenance of the products. He is from Norcia, this book's Classic Town for Umbria, and comes from a long line of butchers and cheese makers. He has a climate-controlled cellar used for storing cheeses. Each day he washes the cheese rinds with whey, as his mother did in the old days, to keep the cheeses clean and uniform. He also turns each cheese once a day so that it will have even exposure to air. Few other stores still dedicate so much time to maintenance. This makes Volpetti's products more expensive, but I think you will notice the difference. This kind of store is vanishing as elderly people attached to tradition disappear. Another reason these stores are facing extinction is that Claudio works twelve hours a day, something most younger people do not want to do in the food-selling business. (Claudio's view is that "the human being doesn't live only for work, but for internal joy.") Younger people are more likely to go to a professional school to become lawyers, doctors, and businesspeople and, Claudio laments, they develop a taste for standardized commercial flavors that their elders, who know differently, would not tolerate. So one of the reasons I go to Volpetti is to understand what those older flavors are and to build a taste vocabulary in my mouth. When Claudio explains his ideas to me about cheese and prosciutto, I want to retain them and pass them to you. "Climate, terrain, and the hand of man make a cheese. The animal is the means to the cheese, but it is the land that is the source of the cheese," he says. For this rea-

son, Claudio clearly identifies the terrain where the cheese is made when he selects which ones to offer for sale. The land with better sun, air, and grass will make a better cheese. Similarly, "If you look at a pig, they all are cute and look more or less the same. You need to ask it what it ate if you want it to be a good prosciutto." So Claudio identifies the producer of the hams and investigates what the pigs are fed rather than buying from a large supplier. You will notice that he keeps truffles in a Lucite jewel box to prevent invasive air from entering. He told me that he has frequently refused to sell truffles to tourists if the travelers have two weeks of vacation ahead of them before returning home— "the truffles would become stale and the traveler would think badly of Italy." If you would like to buy cheese or pork products to take home, they can be vacuum-packed. Volpetti will put little slips of paper in many of the things you buy to instruct you how to preserve and use the food at home. Whenever during the year you visit the store, there will be cheeses, *salumi,* hams, and outstanding breads at the peak of their form, and anything you try will be vivid and exciting. On a recent visit I got to know a series of soft Pecorino cheeses from Lazio, Umbria, Marche, Toscana, and Sardegna. I bought an *etto* or two of each and exquisite breads (on Tuesday and Friday, extraordinary bread arrives from Altamura in Puglia; on the other days there is excellent bread from Roma) and had myself quite a learning experience. You should go for one too.

Food Stores
A WALK ON THE VIA FLAMINIA

I know that you have not necessarily come to the Eternal City just to go from one food store to another. Roma is so large and complicated that you could run all over town looking for a sense of neighborhood food shopping (although I encourage real food devotees to go to the Volpetti store and the market in Testaccio). I have selected one area, just beyond the Piazza del Popolo in the city center, that will give you an idea of what a typical Roman family has available and how it might live and shop. Most of these places are on the Via Flaminia, although there are detours to side streets. Take a walk to learn a few things, preferably mornings from Tuesday through Saturday. If you begin at the Piazza del Popolo, walk north under the arch to reach the Piazza Flaminio (a stop on line A of Roma's subway). Note the very old stand called Ente Comunale di Consumo, a real throwback to the 1930s with its flasks of Frascati wine. Now walk on the Via Flaminia.

Castroni, Via Flaminia 28/30. Closed Sunday.

This one store will make you realize that the average Roman has many more ingredients at his or her disposal than you might think. But do Romans use them, or is this store geared to the international community in the city? The immediate smell as you enter is coffee. On the left side of the store are six hills of beans from which to choose and purchase. To the right is a bar where you can sample some of them. The store is lined throughout with bottles of whiskey and many wines, not only those from Lazio. Then there are all the imported foods that may seem exotic or mundane: Weetabix from the U.K., canned feijoada from Brazil, halvah from Syria, salsa dip from Texas, sauerkraut from Germany, guava juice from Egypt, maple syrup from Canada, sardines from the Philippines, mole sauce from Mexico, pineapple from Malaysia, and *baba ghanouj* from Lebanon. And vitamins, which are expensive commodities in Italy, a place where people prefer to get their nutrients from their foods.

Bucci Alimentari, Via Flaminia 44.

Good prosciutto, *salumi*, wines, excellent Parmigiano-Reggiano, and breads.

Al Giardino delle Primizie, Via Flaminia 50A.

Romans are among Italy's greatest vegetable cooks (along with the people of Puglia and Liguria), and they prize *primizie*, the very first vegetables of the season, for their daintiness and delicate flavor. They are willing to pay more for these, which is why there would be a store that would sell them. Here are the first asparagus, little lettuces, baby artichokes, zucchini flowers, wonderful berries, and other fruits. You could make a nice picnic on the Tevere with these fruits and vegetables, bread and protein from Bucci, and wine and candy from Castroni.

Mercato Rionale, Via Flaminia 60–62. Open mornings only.

Behind a wall covered with movie posters is the bustling local market, where you can buy butter, cheese, produce, and soak up local color.

A block down on the same side of the street is the Accademia Filarmonica Romana. You can take a break in the lovely garden and check on upcoming performances. As you step out on the street, look out for the oncoming orange trams. Go down the block to:

Caffè-Bar Durante, Via Flaminia 101–103. Open until 21h; closed Sunday.

Roma, of course, was not only the center of an ancient empire but the seat of a putative empire during the Fascist era. With that came a style that now seems very evocative and neorealist. The white letters saying CAFFÈ DURANTE outside the bar look like a set from an early Anna Magnani film. The interior is clearly out of the 1930s—it is a smart decor, surely out of style, but with a style all its own. There are several banquettes with tables that seem designed for enjoying conversation. The dark-wood walls create a sense of coziness. There are a few unremarkable breakfast pastries, some good ice creams, and, behind the bar and overhead, are bins full of oranges and grapefruits for a *spremuta.*

Now turn around and walk back down the Via Flaminia in the direction you came from. Walk back to the

Hostaria Elio, corner of Via Flaminia and Via Pasquale Stanislao Mancini. Open

12–15h, 19:30–22h; closed Sunday. No credit cards. Moderately inexpensive.

Near one of the many Roman fountains that always drips, allowing you to rinse your flushed face with cool water. In the back is a refrigerator with a glass front that was a staple in trattorias in the 1950s and 1960s. Within are wines, meats, and other items. During your meal, Elio will retrieve items as he needs them to take into the kitchen. You can have good food here, such as a *rigatoni alla zozzona* (prosciutto, peas, cream, mushrooms, and a bit of tomato). There is fresh fish on Tuesday and Friday.

Go down the Via Flaminia and turn to the right on Via Cesare Beccaria.

Antica Enoteca Beccaria, Via Cesare Beccaria 14, tel. 06/320355. Open 8:30–15h, 17–20h; closed Sunday.

Vincenzo Gargiulo is the very friendly and informed owner. There is a nice selection of national wines by the bottle and some good wines by the glass. Many people come in for a glass of the house white (Zagarolo, from near Frascati). This small place with no tables fills easily, but convivially, and conversations are sure to start—this is what wine does. There are also thirty to forty types of *panini,* served at 13h, such as *melanzane alla parmigiana, porchetta,* and dried Calabrese tomatoes with fresh mozzarella.

You have just had a slice of life in a Roman neighborhood, meeting the sort of real people and discovering real flavors that most travelers seldom encounter.

GUIDE

Iris Carulli is often called a Roman geisha. She is deeply knowledgeable about everything Roman. It is a pleasure to walk around Roma or visit the Vatican with Iris, because she offers insights that guides who repeat things by rote could never muster. Her services are much in demand, and the fee one pays is more than worth it to discover Roma the way only the most timeless Romans can recognize it.

HEALTH FOOD

Bottega della Lungavita, Via delle Colonelle 19 (near the Pantheon), tel. 06/6787408.

This "Store of Long Life" will give you an idea about the latest in Roman notions of what health food is. This is intriguing because the Roman diet is so particular—it is full of eggs, pork, organ meats, cream, and butter, yet it also has incomparable breads, vegetables, and fruit. Romans don't seem in bad health. Most of them are very fit, although heavy Romans appear heavier than other overweight Italians. So this store seems like a beachhead acquired in a very arduous war. Most of the food is imported from Milano, which has many health-food stores. Here you can buy wholewheat pasta, sauces without additives, and biological (pesticide-free) staples such as olive oil, rice, beans, *farro*, cornmeal, couscous, and wholewheat flour. You can also buy French biological wines. There is soy milk and many products made from it (made by Valsoia in Bologna, which has seen a lot of growth in recent years as lactose-intolerant Italians have come out of their milky closets). You can also find many prepared take-out foods geared to local office workers, which represent a departure from what most food markets

do. When I last visited, the store was promoting an unusual weight-loss idea: take two glasses of water, add two teaspoons of maple syrup and a squeeze of lemon, and drink this instead of a meal.

HOUSEWARES

C.U.C.I.N.A., Via del Babuino 118a, tel. 06/6791275. All credit cards.

This store looks very much like an American housewares store such as Williams-Sonoma, Crate and Barrel, or the Pottery Barn. This gives it cachet in Italy, and you will find the contrast interesting now that your eye has become accustomed to the Italian way of presentation. This place, with an excellent selection, really seems like it landed from another hemisphere. There are few bargains, but it is notable for the depth of its selection. There are measuring cups in ounces as well as liters, and the store even has cannoli molds.

Leone Limentani, Via Portico d'Ottavia 47, tel. 06/68806686.

In the Jewish Ghetto is this shop overflowing with all sorts of kitchenware. You might be overwhelmed by the quantity, but if you like to forage, you will come up with an item of real quality.

Pisoni, Corso Vittorio Emanuele 127, tel. 06/68803531.

In a city with so many churches, it should not surprise you that candles are in constant demand. In addition to basic white, Pisoni has forty-two other colors. Candles come in many shapes, including numbers so that you can have a birthday cake that tells the truth about your age without its looking like the burning of Atlanta.

La Riggiola, Via dei Coronari 145, tel. 06/68804127.

The specialty here is tiles, antique and modern. They are really quite beautiful as decoration or for use in a kitchen.

ICE CREAM

For *granita di caffè* see La Casa del Caffè—Tazza d'Oro and Sant'Eustachio Il Caffè in "Bars and *Caffè*s," above.

Canova, Piazza del Popolo 16, tel. 06/3612231.

Part of the scene is the *caffè* life on the Piazza del Popolo, which long ago supplanted the Via Veneto as a people-watching spot. The ice cream here is delicious.

Giolitti, Via Uffici del Vicario 40 (near Piazza Colonna and Via del Corso), tel. 06/6794206. Open 7–2h; closed Monday.

The one *gelateria* not to miss. The *visciole* (an especially delicious cherry) ice cream of Giolitti occupies a special spot in my pantheon of Italian ice cream. I have often said that I would like it to be the dessert at my last meal. While I hope that such a meal will not be served for many years to come, this sentiment tells more than any tired adjective could about this delicacy. Giolitti has other wonderful flavors as well: fabulous *pompelmo rosa* (pink grapefruit), which I often pair with *visciole*, plus tropical (mango, papaya, kiwi, and grapefruit), Mozart (chocolate-almond), Grand Marnier, Champagne, *riso, gianduia, bacio* (chocolate with hazelnuts), *nocciola, noce* (walnut), *arancio* (orange), *pistacchio*, kiwi, banana, *pera* (pear, often available only on request), peach, *albicocca* (apricot), *ribes, mirtilli*

(blueberries), *fragola* (strawberry), *lampone* (raspberry), *more* (blackberries), *frutti di bosco* (a mix of blueberries, blackberries, wild strawberries, raspberries, and currants), *caffè, cioccolato, vaniglia* (vanilla), *malaga* (rum raisin), and zabaglione. All range from very good to outstanding. If you don't want ice cream, there are also handmade chocolates, pastries, cookies, and a bar for coffee. There is a rather depressing room in the back with waiter service.

Gelateria della Palma, Via della Maddalena 23, tel. 06/6540752. Open 8–1h; closed Wednesday.

This ice-cream parlor three blocks from Giolitti (see above) and the Pantheon is very popular with young people and was the "in" spot in the early 1980s. The ice cream is very good, but I prefer Giolitti.

MARKETS

Campo dei Fiori. Open mornings; closed Sunday.

This used to be the province of Romans, but it has been listed in so many travel books that people from every nation now gather at the Campo dei Fiori (Square of Flowers). It is in a lovely part of old Roma, not far from the Pantheon, the Piazza Argentina, the Jewish Ghetto, the Palazzo Farnese, and the Tiber. It is colorful and still the place in this area to buy excellent fruit, vegetables, and flowers. Look closely at how the vendors cut and handle vegetables such as celery and artichokes, and you will get lessons in how these foods should be treated. If you speak some Italian, ask the vendors for recipes. This is how I have learned local food preparations all over Italy. Since the vendors here are used to tourists, they will be disposed to take time to teach you. The side streets have interesting food shops and several clothing stores with good-quality merchandise at excellent prices; L'Antica Norcineria (Campo dei Fiori 43) uses pigs that are actually raised in Norcia, making this one of the most desirable stores for pork products in all of Roma. No less an authority than Carol Field, author of *The Italian Baker* and other fine books about Italian food and life, considers Il Forno di Campo dei Fiori 22 one of the better bread bakers in Lazio. There is *pane casareccio*, as well as breads with grapes, olives, or walnuts.

Testaccio market. Open 6-14h; closed Sunday.

The main street of Testaccio is the Via Marmorata, and the market is one block in at Piazza Testaccio. The name "Marmorata" came about because the port of ancient Roma was at the Tevere River in Testaccio. When the shipments of marble arrived that would build the city, they were transported down the Via Marmorata (Street of Marble). When shipments of oil and wine arrived to go to the Testaccio market (which was there in ancient times), these liquids were transported in amphorae, long terracotta vessels. They had a tail of sorts from which the liquid would be decanted. These tails broke, and through the centuries they were stacked up on what came to be known as Monte Testaccio, which is now 20 meters (66 feet) high. In recent times, excavation was done under this "mountain," and there are now little clubs where locals drink wine in the evenings. The Testaccio market is probably the most interesting market open to the public. It is situated in the heart of a neighborhood in the southern part of the capital and is where one can see all of the components used in the Roman kitchen.

A visit to the Testaccio market is a collection of images that resonate within me for their humanity and their attachment to a great food tradition. Here a woman diligently cuts beans and greens for soup, while another carefully skins tiny onions that she then puts in small plastic bags. I notice that many of the merchants are quite old and have a memory and knowledge of ingredients from which I hope to learn by watching and asking. One woman shows me a *pomodoro casalino*, a special tomato that is the best for making an *amatriciana* sauce. Another suddenly cries, "*Guardate questi asparagi, e a questo prezzo—è un regalo!*" ("Look at these asparagus, and at this price—it's a gift!") I cannot help but notice, in the little wooden shed, the egg lady with the bee-stung lips—When you see the term *uova da bere*, these are eggs so fresh and rich that they are best drunk straight from their shells. Walk over to the fishmongers and you will see fresh fish recumbent on their own beds of romaine lettuce, keeping cool under whirring fans and looking pristine under flattering illumination. The smells are fresh rather than fishy. For more seductive fragrances, walk to one of the herb vendors, where you will discover that Romans use several different kinds of mint in their cooking. Buy a few sprigs and bring them to your nose as you wander through the city, and you will be in an eternal good mood.

MUSEUMS

Museo Nazionale delle Paste Alimentari (National Pasta Museum), Piazza Scanderbeg 114–120. Open 9:30–12:30h, 16–19h, Saturday 9:30–12:30h; closed Sunday.

To reach the museum from the Trevi fountain, walk one block down the Via del Lavoratore to the small Vicolo Scanderbeg on the right. Walk up the gently sloping hill to the Piazza Scanderbeg.

When we think of the timeless images of Roma, there are the Colosseum, the Vatican, and the Trevi Fountain, perhaps with the sultry Anita Ekberg cooling herself under jets of water as a helpless Marcello Mastroianni looks on. An equally eternal Roman image is the heaping bowl of pasta that has fed pagans, Christians, and many Anitas and Marcellos for two thousand years.

Roma has finally created a monument to pasta with the new Museo Nazionale delle Paste Alimentari. Located on a side street near the Trevi fountain, this farinaceous shrine is a mecca for anyone who has happily twirled strands of *al dente* spaghetti in the tines of a fork. With your admission price of 12,000 lire you can borrow a recorded compact disc in English, Italian, French, German, or Spanish that will guide you through the museum's eleven rooms. While one can always debate whether noodles were originally Chinese, Italian, or from somewhere else, this exhibition approaches pasta certain that it achieved its greatest glory on the Italian peninsula. Pasta is divided into four regional schools: from Palermo, Napoli, Genova,

and Bologna. Each city produced its own style and shapes of pasta to suit local sauces. The contributions of each are amply displayed on the main floor of the museum. Because the core of this collection comes from the holdings of the Agnesi family, the leading producers of pasta in Liguria since 1824, you should not be surprised to learn about Ligurian pasta first. The centerpiece of the first room—the Sala del Grano—is a great nineteenth-century wheel made of marble and stone that was used to grind grains to make flour. We learn that two types of grains are needed to make pasta: *grano tenero* (soft wheat) becomes *farina* (flour) while *grano duro* (hard wheat) becomes *semola* (what we call semolina).

A particularly popular item in the museum's collection is the mid-twentieth-century print called *E Tempo di Pace!* or *It's Time for Peace!* Here is a cannon with a large rigatoni as its barrel, firing *farfalle* (butterfly-shaped noodles) that seem to fall to the ground like so many parachutists. In what seems to be an Italian paraphrasing of Theodore Roosevelt, the picture advocates a policy of "Speak softly and carry a big noodle." For scholars and historians, the museum also has what must be the world's most extensive library of books and documents on pasta. Access must be arranged in advance. It is probably a good idea to visit the museum in the late morning or early in the evening because you will develop quite an appetite as you tour its galleries. Don't forget to sign the visitors' log before running to the nearest trattoria for a bowl of *gnocchi alla romana* or *spagetti alla carbonara.*

Museo delle Arti e Tradizioni Popolari, Piazza Marconi 8 (in EUR; take subway line B). Open 9–14h, Sunday 9–13h; closed Monday.

This museum is chock-full of artifacts and documentation of Italian folklore and customs from every region. It is a bit forbidding in scope and presentation, but very rewarding. One can learn how different peoples observe the cycles of the year through food and festivity. There are exhibits about Italian homes, agriculture, life at sea, civic life in small towns, and music, dance, and folk art. There is much more in the collection than could ever be displayed, but what you will see will be of interest.

WINES AND SPIRITS

International Wine Academy of Roma, Vicolo del Bottino 8, tel. 06/6990878, fax 06/6791385, www.wineacademyroma. com, info@wineacademyroma.com.

This new and very exciting academy is for travelers who wish to dedicate themselves seriously to wine study. Courses change all the time and you can select from individual classes or an entire course. Some last for several weeks, so if you take up residence in the Eternal City for a while, this is a good weekly activity for learning and making friends. The Academy has a few rooms to rent as well as a restaurant featuring the cooking of young chef Antonio Martucci. In addition to doing accurate versions of Roman classics, he has developed a following for his *cucina creativa*, with dishes such as rosemary-flavored sea bass "confit" with arugula, apple, and walnuts in a caper and parsley sauce; hazelnut-encrusted tuna filet with bacon and *vin santo* sauce; *anconetana* with olives and wild fennel; and bitter chocolate tart with dried figs. Wine courses, lodging, and dining at the Wine Academy are all moderately expensive to expensive, but this makes for a memorable experience if you can splurge on a class or a meal.

Ai Monasteri, Piazza delle Cinque Lune 76, tel. 06/68802 783.

You can purchase spirits as well as honeys, herbal elixirs, soaps, creams, essences, herbal toothpastes, and jams produced at several monasteries that make this place near the Piazza Navona their point of sale.

Enoteca al Parlamento, Via dei Prefetti 15, tel. 06/6873446. Closed Monday morning and Sunday.

A large and appealing store with a vast selection of wines from all over Italy, plus Champagne, cakes, cookies, jams, honeys, truffles, herbs, mustards, fine pastas, candies, and jarred fruits and vegetables.

Enoteca Trimani, Via Goito 20, tel. 06/497971.

One of the best selections in town, in business since 1821.

Enoteca Beccaria.

See "A Walk on the Via Flaminia," above.

Enoteca Cavour 313.

One of the best wine bars in town. See "Dining near the Piazza della Repubblica".

Enoteca Cul de Sac.

See "Dining in Central Roma," above.

Enoteca Il Piccolo.

See "Dining in Central Roma," above.

Enoteca Simposio.

See "Dining near the Vatican and in Western and Northern Roma," above.

San Martino di Ciminio (Viterbo)

FOLKLORE

Festa della Castagna.

At the end of October the town holds a

chestnut festival with foods such as soups, fritters, pastas, breads, and sweets made with chestnuts and chestnut flour.

Tarquinia (Viterbo)

DINING

Arcadia, Via Mazzini 6, tel. 0766/855501. Closed Monday (except July and August) and January. All credit cards. Moderate.

Near the magnificent Etruscan museum is this appealing restaurant specializing in fish and seafood.

Tuscania (Viterbo)

FOLKOLORE

Sagra delle Frittelle.

On January 17, the day starts with a procession to the Church of Santa Maria del Riposo, where prayers are said in honor of Sant'Antonio. In the afternoon there is mass consumption of *frittelle al cavolfiore* (cauliflower fritters), which come in either a sweet *(dolce)* or salted *(salato)* version.

DINING

Palazzo Ranucci, Via della Torretta 8, tel. 0761/445067. Closed Tuesday. In August, closed for lunch. All credit cards. Moderate.

Scrumptious soups and pastas; *gnocchi al semolino con pomodorini e maggiorana* and for a secondo; *agnello con carciofi e menta* (lamb with artichokes and mint) or *pollo con verdura all'aneto*, dill-scented vegetables served with a chicken breast.

Viterbo

Viterbo, in my experience, has been curiously devoid of places to eat well. This beautiful medieval city, one hour north of Roma, sees many visitors, especially on September 4, the day of Santa Rosa. On this day, handicapped people arrive from all over Italy to pray at her shrine. Other people arrive to give money to the handicapped, this being considered a Christian thing to do. It is a very emotional day and provides a window into the level of faith that still persists in parts of Italy.

CAFFÈ

Gran Caffè Schenardi, Corso Italia 11.

This old *caffè* is replete with mirrors that have seen a lot of history. Good coffee.

DINING

La Torre, Via della Torre 5, tel. 0761/226467. Closed Sunday and in August. All credit cards. Moderate.

A wine bar first, but there is good food, including *agnolotti* that are filled either with chestnuts, artichokes, wild boar, or duck. I particularly like the *zuppa di ceci e castagne* (chickpea-chestnut soup). The wine list includes evaluations from *Gambero Rosso* and *Vini di Veronelli*, two leading Italian wine publications.

WINE AND SPIRITS

Distillerie Enoteca Viterbium, Via Garbini 1A, tel. 0761/234779. Open 8:30–13h, 14–19:30h; closed Sunday and ten days in August.

Stocks six hundred types of wine and spirits. Also sells very good olive oils from Umbria, Lazio, Toscana, and Liguria. There are cheeses, a few *salumi,* and many chocolates and other sweets.

Zagarolo (Roma)

FOLKLORE

La Sagra dell'Uva.

In the first ten days of October is a pagan bacchanale if ever I saw one. The grape harvest is celebrated very decadently with drinking, dining, singing, and romancing. Great fun and completely local—I have never seen tourists at this event.

La Gricia

La Gricia is a little-known pasta dish that was the basic meal of the shepherds of the Gricia Valley in Lazio. Since it does not call for long cooking, as might a tomato sauce, it was practical for shepherds who had to cook a meal while tending their flocks. It is made of common ingredients: pasta, olive oil, *pancetta,* Pecorino Romano, and freshly ground black pepper. This preparation is how it is served at Trattoria da Lucia in Roma. It is for one person because a shepherd would prepare it for himself. If you want to make portions for more than one person, simply multiply the ingredients by the number of diners.

Serves 1

100 grams/3½ ounces penne or vermicelli
1 tablespoon extra-virgin olive oil
100 grams/3½ ounces pancetta, cut into small cubes
1 tablespoon freshly grated Pecorino Romano
Freshly ground black pepper to taste

Set a large pot of cold water to boil. When it reaches a boil, toss in a pinch of salt. When the water returns to a boil, add the pasta and cook until al dente. While the pasta is cooking, heat the oil in a skillet and add the *pancetta.* Sauté until the *pancetta* is dark pink (be sure it does not turn crisp or golden). When the pasta is cooked, drain it well in a colander. Do not rinse. Transfer to a warm bowl. Add the Pecorino and a generous amount of black pepper. Top with the *pancetta* and oil, toss well, and serve.

Wine: Frascati, Marino, Est! Est!! Est!!!, or Castelli Romani white.

Pollo con le Olive Nere
Chicken with Black Olives

Ideally you will use olives from Gaeta, which are perfect for this preparation. Failing that, try to find medium or large black olives preserved in olive oil and not heavily salted.

Serves 4

*1 young chicken (about 1 kilo/2¼ pounds), cut
in pieces and carefully washed*
6 tablespoons extra-virgin olive oil
1 medium onion, sliced thin
*100 milliliters/½ cup Frascati, Castelli
Romani, Orvieto, or similar white wine*
1 sprig fresh rosemary
1 clove garlic, peeled
100 grams/3½ ounces Gaeta olives
1 tablespoon white or red-wine vinegar
Freshly ground black pepper (just a little bit)

First, completely wash and dry the chicken and remove whatever excess fat there is. In a heavy skillet heat the olive oil. Add the onion and sauté for a minute. Then add the chicken pieces and sauté for a few minutes on all sides until they begin to turn gold. Pour in the wine, cover, and cook over low heat for about a half hour. At this point carefully cut a piece of chicken to determine if it is cooked through. While the chicken is cooking, take the needles off the sprig of rosemary, add the garlic clove, and mince the rosemary and garlic together. Once the chicken seems done, add the olives, the garlic-rosemary combination, then the vinegar and a bit of freshly ground black pepper. Stir so the flavors penetrate, cover, and cook for 5 minutes.

Wine: Frascati, Marino, Est! Est!! Est!!!, or Castelli Romani white.

Abruzzo

Amate il pane	Love your bread
Cuore della casa	the heart of the home
Profuma della mensa	perfume of the table
Gioia dei focolari	joy of the hearths
Onorate il pane	Honor your bread
Gloria dei campi	glory of the fields
Fragranza della terra	fragrance of the earth
Festa della vita	feast of life
Rispettate il pane	Respect your bread
Sudore della fronte	sweat of the brow
Orgoglio del lavoro	pride of work
Poema di sacrificio	poem of sacrifice
Non sciupate il pane	Do not waste your bread
Ricchezza della patria	wealth of your native land
Il più santo premio alla	the holiest reward
fatica umana	for human toil

REGIONAL CAPITAL:
L'Aquila (AQ).

PROVINCIAL CAPITALS:
Chieti (CH), Pescara (PE),
Teramo (TE).

**TOURIST INFORMATION,
INCLUDING AGRITOURISM:**
For information about tour-
ism, it is necessary to con-
tact the tourist board in
one of the four provinces
of Abruzzo:
Ente Provinciale per il
Turismo,
Piazza Santa Maria
Paganica,
67100 L'Aquila,
tel. 0862/410808;
Ente Provinciale per il
Turismo,

 The linkage of bread to land, life, labor, and home depicted in this traditional poem goes back much further than the two thousand years of the Christian era. It represented survival and tradition just as much to pagan peoples as it did to Christians. The people of the mountainous inland areas of Abruzzo were cut off from one another for centuries, but also from outside influences such as Christianity. Long after other regions of Italy had accepted the Catholic Church, Abruzzo still practiced ancient pagan rituals and worshiped non-Christian gods. When Christianity began to penetrate Abruzzo effectively in the eighth and ninth centuries, it had to

Via Spaventa 29,
66100 Chieti,
tel. 0871/65231;
Ente Provinciale per il
Turismo,
Via Fabrizi,
65100 Pescara,
tel. 085/4212939; or
Ente Provinciale per il
Turismo,
Via del Castello 10,
64100 Teramo,
tel. 0861/244222.

compete with existing beliefs. Paganism never fully yielded to Christianity, but blended with it. The result was a mixture that is still experienced more intensely than in most of the rest of the country. Harvest festivals draw from pagan roots more than Christianity, and the unbridled feasting and partying are sights to behold. There are caves in the province of L'Aquila that were used for rituals by mystics. Until recently, there were regular pilgrimages to many of these sites. Lest you think that this paganism is out of step with what the real Italy is about, you should know that the name "Italia" derives from "Itali," the ancient people who lived in what is now the province of Chieti. So there is no one more Italian than an Abruzzese.

Because inland Abruzzo is largely undeveloped for tourism, with only a few restaurants where one might sample classic Abruzzese dishes, the best way to learn about the area is to go to towns on their feast days *(sagre e feste),* observe the rituals, and taste the food. On some feast days and at wedding celebrations there is a remarkable Abruzzese tradition called the *panarda.*

This is a meal that can last hours or days and have up to thirty courses. The first part (or the first night) of the *panarda* will be *magro* ("lean," which implies non-meat) and feature many courses of fish and vegetables. All of this is washed down with rosé wine. After midnight, whether the feast proceeds directly or is picked up later on, the dishes become *grasso* (fat) and will be sausages and *salumi* of many types. Then there will be soups and pastas, followed by boiled meats, fried sweetbreads and brains, then roast meats. The last of these will be roast kid, followed by cheeses, sweets, coffee, and liqueurs. Following such indulgence, it is customary to drink a *digestivo* called Centerbe, which is said to be made with a hundred herbs. If you are invited to a *panarda,* it is considered rude to decline a certain dish. So eat what you can and make gestures of fullness as you smile.

Many dishes in the *panarda* are flavored by *peperoncino* (hot red chili pepper, called *pepedinie* in local dialect). There will also be 7 *minestre,* one of them a soup called *virtù.* The superstitious *abruzzesi* consider 7 a lucky number, and the name of the soup refers to the 7 virtues taught in religious instruction. This soup was originally prepared by 7 virgins and includes 7 types of legume, 7 types of pasta, 7 types of vegetable, 7 types of meat, and 7 seasonings. A different girl puts in one of each ingredient, and the soup is then slow-cooked for 7 hours. There is a *virtù* feast in Teramo on the first day of May, associated with ancient May Day rituals of romance and mating.

Although Christian observance is now an essential component of many feasts, can you imagine Saint Francis of Assisi from neighboring Umbria honoring his religious belief with a thirty-course meal? It is important to remember that the specter of poverty hung over the inland Abruzzo until very recently, so that feasting is an act of defiance against famine, an act born of fear that hunger may return soon again. Harvest festivals were intended to give thanks to pagan gods for providing food, and many of these have attendant rituals that might be hard for the outsider to understand. If you are in a town during its festival, remember that some of the rituals you observe are not merely cute folklore, but something that is felt very deeply. So if people around you are not taking photographs, you should refrain as well.

To understand the forces that shaped the Abruzzo, it is necessary to make note of the hand of nature. This is among the most mountainous regions of Italy (62 percent), with almost all of the rest being hilly. It includes the highest peak in the Apennines, the Corno Grande (2,914 meters/9,616 feet). The many lofty mountain passes, in the days before automotive tunnels and telecommunications, meant that towns and peoples were cut off from one another. In some cases, effective contact did not exist until the mid-1960s. Although the region is in central-southern Italy (it borders Marche, Umbria, Lazio, and Molise and has a coastline on the Adriatic), the elevations inland result in snow and cold that are among the most severe in Italy. This is a popular destination for skiing for people from all over the southern half of Italy. In this region one finds the Calderone glacier, the southernmost in Europe.

Abruzzo has the highest percentage of land dedicated to national parks of any Italian region. Foremost among these is the Parco Nazionale dell'Abruzzo, which is a preserve full of bears, wolves, eagles (*aquila* means eagle in Italian, thus the name of the region's capital), chamois, and otters. The Gran Sasso d'Italia, closer to the coast, is another set of towering peaks that afford magnificent views of the sea. The region had a tradition of environmentalism and animal preservation long before most of the country. Similarly, there are many farmers who refuse to use chemicals in agriculture, in the belief that this will damage flora and fauna.

While the coastal provinces of Teramo, Pescara, and Chieti generally had enough water for agriculture, the presence and absence of water are major issues inland. Ignazio Silone, one of Italy's great writers, was from a small, poor town inland and in his book *Fontamara* wrote about the role of water in his society and how political and corrupt economic interests poisoned many wells, literally and figuratively.

In the province of L'Aquila, near Avezzano, you will hear much talk about Fucino. This is the name of the lake that was once the second largest in Italy. In A.D. 88 Emperor Claudius wanted to drain the lake to prevent the constant flooding of the towns at its edge. Much of the lake was in fact drained in an amazing feat of ancient engineering. The land that was once under the lake dried out through the years, and fertile land was sought to grow food for a starving populace. In the 1870s, it was proposed that the rest of the lake be drained. Local fishermen protested that their livelihoods would be threatened, so when the lake was drained, farmers from the Marche were brought in to teach the fishermen how to farm. In the years immediately after the Second World War, small pieces of land were given to people for cultivation. Some people think that things would have been better if cooperatives has been created, so that the high costs of farm equipment could have been pooled. There are still others who resent the fact that the lake was ever drained, and the mention of the name "Fucino" still arouses strong emotions among many people in the zone.

Agriculture is still the main source of income for this region. Produce includes potatoes (those of Avezzano are considered the best in Italy), wheat and corn, olives, wine, many vegetables, oregano, and saffron (which many cooks consider the world's best). Cattle, sheep, and goats are raised throughout the region. Sheepherding in particular is an ancient part of life. The *transumanza*, the annual migration of sheep and people from Abruzzo through Molise to Puglia, is central to understanding the pastoral life of this region. (Read about the *transumanza* in the Molise chapter to learn more about this.) Until 1963, Abruzzo and Molise were united as one region, often called Abruzzi. Nowadays, the words "Abruzzo" and "Abruzzi" are used interchangeably to describe the region of Abruzzo, which many Italians still think Molise is a part of.

In the Abruzzo it was traditional for young women to help prepare their dowries. Most of them knew how to weave blankets and spreads, as well as create lace and embroider cloths. Many stores, especially in Sulmona, sell products of this handiwork, many of which are antiques that were handed down through families and wound up in shops. The weaving tradition continues to this day.

Some of the finest weaving is found in and around Sulmona, the Classic Town for this region. Sulmona was the birthplace of Ovid (43 B.C.), a rather libertine sort and a great writer who was one of the literary giants of the Roman Empire. Abruzzo gave the world other important writers, including Gabriele Rossetti (whose son Dante was a protagonist in London's pre-Raphaelite artistic movement), Gabriele D'Annunzio (poet, lover, and patriot from Pescara), and Ignazio Silone, whose works are among the most evocative of life in this region.

Because Abruzzo is relatively close to Roma, this is a worthy region to visit even if you are a first-time traveler to Italy. It is possible to make a long day trip to L'Aquila, the region's capital and one of the most distinct cities in Italy, although I encourage you to at least remain overnight. A stay of even two or three days will give you a sense of traditional Italy that will make your understanding of the nation as a whole more rounded and meaningful. And you will eat and drink very well.

Eating in Abruzzo

ANTIPASTI

Frutti di Mare. The coastal provinces of Teramo, Pescara, and Chieti enjoy all sorts of shellfish raw, cooked in wine and herbs, or boiled and dressed with oil and vinegar to make *insalata di mare.*

Mortadelline di Campotosto (L'Aquila). Large, round *salumi* with soft pulp, similar to the *coglioni di mulo* of Norcia in Umbria.

Salsiccie di Fegato. These sausages are made with pork liver and are of delicious and memorable flavor. They come in spicy *(pazzo)* and sweet *(dolce)* versions.

Salumi. There are very good *salumi* made of pork or lamb, particularly in the province of L'Aquila.

Ventricina. A *salame* from the province of Chieti made with pork, *peperoncino*, fennel, and orange peel.

PRIMI

Some of Italy's best commercial pasta is made in Abruzzo by producers such as De Cecco and Del Verde, both in the town of Fara San Martino, which is nourished by excellent water that gives the pasta its purity.

Maccheroni alla Chitarra. This is the region's most famous pasta dish. Fresh egg pasta is cut into strips by pressing them through steel wires anchored in a wooden box. *Alla chitarra* means "guitar style," the name deriving from the appearance of the device on which the pasta is cut. It is served with a tomato-

peperoncino sauce, or with a *ragù* of either lamb or beef. In the northern part of Abruzzo it is served with a sauce of tomato and *guanciale* (pork cheek).

Ravioli all'Abruzzese. They come either sweet (filled with ricotta) or salted (with *scamorza* cheese) and often scented with saffron.

Scrippelle (also called *Crespelle*). Crepes made with flour and sometimes egg. They can be served with many types of sauce, baked with cheese and sauce, or served as *scrippelle 'mbusse,* in a rich chicken broth. This originated when Bourbon troops occupied the province of Teramo. These crepes were made for the captains and were served with sauce. Broth was made for privates, and one day a crepe slipped into the broth, and it was discovered how good this tasted.

Timballo. There are many types of *timballo,* which is a sort of casserole. It contains one starch, usually pasta, but also *scrippelle* or potatoes. Other ingredients might include fish and seafood near the coast, or lamb or pork products in the hills. A *timballo bianco* usually has cheese as its source of protein. The most famous one is probably *timballo alla teramano,* which contains lamb, pork, eggs, and is made of *scrippelle.*

Vermicelli all'Abruzzese. The sauce is made of chopped zucchini flowers, saffron, parsley, Pecorino, and onions.

Virtù. A rich minestrone with legumes, vegetables, meat, seasonings, and pastas.

SECONDI

Agnello a Cutturo (also called *Pecora a lu Cutturu*). Lamb that is boiled for two hours, defatted, and then cooked in wine, cognac, parsley, carrots, celery, onions, sage, salt, *peperoncino,* tomatoes, and lots of garlic.

Agnello all'Uovo e Limone. Lamb flavored with egg and lemon. An Easter favorite.

Brodetto. The most highly regarded *abruzzese* version of this Adriatic fish stew is served in Vasto (Chieti). *Brodetto alla pescarese* has more *peperoncino* than most preparations. In fact, it is hard to find *brodetto* as it was once classically made. In former times, fishermen on boats made *brodetto* with fish out of the water, dried sweet red pepper, oil, garlic, and *peperoncino.* Now, in general, the sweet pepper has been replaced by tomato or tomato concentrate.

'Ndocca 'ndocca. Marinated braised pork offal.

Tacchino alla Canzanese. This dish, a specialty of Canzano, requires forty-eight hours of preparation. A six-kilo (13-pound) turkey is slowly defatted with baths of hot water, and this, plus material from the turkey bones, is used to make a gelatin that dresses the slices of the turkey, which has been cooked with lots of garlic and some bay leaves. The dish is served topped with pomegranate seeds.

CONTORNI

Excellent vegetables grow near the coast in the provinces of Chieti, Pescara, and Teramo. The potatoes grown near Avezzano (L'Aquila) are very floury and make delicate gnocchi.

FORMAGGI

Scamorza. A pear-shaped shepherd's cheese. When served *ai ferri,* it has been grilled.

DOLCI

Cassata Abruzzese. Layers of sponge cake and custard, flavored with chocolate, nougat, and caramel. A specialty of Sulmona.

Confetti. These sugar-coated almonds come in many colors and are central to every sort of celebration in Abruzzo and all over Italy. Whenever you attend a wedding, an anniversary party, birthday, *onomastico* (observance of the saint's day for whom one is named), or a celebration of christening, communion, or graduation from school, you will be given a tiny package of *confetti.* The confetti-making capital is Sulmona, where most of these are still handmade and decorated. The tradition goes back many centuries, and it used to be traditional to coat the almonds in real gold to celebrate weddings and coronations. It was believed that consumption of gold would bring good fortune. For numerical observances such as birthdays and anniversaries, different colored *confetti* are used in different years: pink (one year), fuschia (five), yellow (ten), beige (fifteen), silver (twenty-five), aquamarine (thirty), dark blue (thirty-five), green (forty), red (forty-five), gold (fifty), ivory (fifty-five), and white (sixty). For university graduations, particular colors relate to different specializations: red (medicine), white (letters and philosophy), black (engineering and architecture), yellow (accounting and banking), purple (business), sky blue (languages), aquamarine (law and jurisprudence). When you are in Sulmona, be sure to visit one of the many *confetti* makers you will see in the city.

Fichi Freschi and *Uva Regina.* Figs and grapes are two especially good fruits in Abruzzo.

Parrozzo. A specialty of Pescara, this is an almond cake that is rich in butter and is covered with bitter chocolate. One of the best is made by Luigi d'Amico and can be found in much of the region.

Pepatelli. White pepper and honey cookies that are a Christmas specialty in Teramo.

Torrone ai Fichi Secchi. From Chieti, a delicious nougat laced with dried figs.

Torrone al Cioccolato. Chocolate-covered nougat, a specialty of L'Aquila.

OTHER ABRUZZESE FLAVORS

Aglio Rosso. There is a particular red garlic found near Sulmona that flavors the food of that city.

Liquirizia. Licorice is often used in local desserts, sweets, and drinks.

Zafferano. The saffron of Abruzzo is in a class by itself. The best is thought to come from the town of Navelli.

The Wines of Abruzzo

Montepulciano d'Abruzzo. This should not be confused with Vino Nobile di Montepulciano. In Abruzzo, a red wine is made from a grape called Montepulciano. In Toscana, in the province of Siena, is the town of Montepulciano, where an excellent wine is made using the Sangiovese grape. Montepulciano d'Abruzzo can range from gutsy, direct red wine good for basic drinking to examples of real class and sophistication. It is one of the most popular export wines because it represents a good value at a moderate price.

Cerasuolo. The special wine made from Montepulciano grapes is a delicate, sometimes-fragrant rosé wine that is hard to come by but should be tasted if at all possible.

Trebbiano d'Abruzzo (also called Bombino Bianco). A serviceable-to-good white wine made largely of the Trebbiano grape, although sometimes other grapes are blended in. The best is generally thought to come from the province of Chieti, where the wine is usually 100 percent Trebbiano.

Montepulciano, Cerasuolo, and Trebbiano are the only DOC wines in Abruzzo, and although they are routinely encountered, they represent only 8 percent of the wine production in Abruzzo. There are many other wines using many grapes that you will taste in your travels throughout the region.

Other Abruzzese Beverages

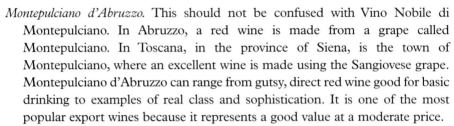

Centerbe. A delicious *digestivo* made with one hundred herbs.

Ratafia. Made in June from bitter cherries. It must stand in the sun before being bottled.

Avezzano (L'Aquila)

The most famous food product in Avezzano is its potatoes, which are uniquely flavorful. They are available only from late September to March, and you should make a point of tasting them if at all possible.

DINING

Hosteria La Lanterna, Corso della Libertà 100, tel. 330/801937 (this is the mobile phone of the owner). Open 12–1h; closed Sunday until 20h and Wednesday. No credit cards. Inexpensive.

Excellent food at low prices in this hospitable eatery. The *penne alla pecorara* (with tomato sauce and sheep's milk ricotta) and *spaghetti con aglio, olio, e peperoncino* are what good pasta eating is all about. The *zuppa di pesce* is also very fine, especially for an inland place. There are delicate *scrippelle* here, too, some of them also combined with sweet cheese, fruit, or chocolate for dessert.

from Abruzzo, Molise, and beyond. *Salumi* come from Norcia as well as the best of the province of L'Aquila. There is also a good selection of breads, pasta, and wine.

FOOD SHOPPING
Le Gastrò: Ricercatezze del Mondo, Via Marconi 20.

An excellent *gastronomia* with cheeses

HONEY
Miele Taglieri, Via delle Gardenie 10, tel. 0863/21235

Honeys and honey products.

Basciano (Teramo)

SAGRE AND FESTIVALS
La Sagra del Prosciutto e Raduno Regionale dei Ddù Bbotte.

On the first or second weekend of August

there is a prosciutto feast that coincides with a meeting of musicians who play a typical musical instrument called the *ddù bbotte*, which is like a hand organ or accordian.

Bisenti (Teramo)

SAGRE AND FESTIVALS
Montonico Estate.

On the last weekend of July there is music, dancing, and consumption of great amounts of *maccheroni alla molinara.*

Mostra Agrituristica.

On the first weekend of October there is a procession of old agricultural carts and a festival of songs traditionally sung during the harvest. There is also a lot of grape eating from the new crop.

Bolognano (Pescara)

SAGRE AND FESTIVALS
San Martino in Vino.

November 11 is Saint Martin's Day, tradi-

tionally the day when new wine is considered ready to drink. In Bolognano a feast is held to celebrate this fact.

Bucchianico (Chieti)

BREAD
Azienda Agricola Carmine Marcone, Colle

Marcone 12, tel. 0872/980421.

Signor Marcone uses no chemicals in the cultivation of wheat and other agricultural products. He uses his grains to make excellent breads in a wood oven. They go well with other products from his farm: olives, olive oil, cheeses, and grapes.

DINING

Ristorante-Pizzeria da Silvio, Corso Pierantoni 20, tel. 0871/381175. Moderately inexpensive.

Delicious local dishes. Pizza is served only on Saturday and Sunday.

SAGRE AND FESTIVALS
Feste dei Banderesi.

A series of events in late May re-creates ancient battles between local heroes and the Turks. There is great feasting, especially on the last night.

Calascio (L'Aquila)

This town is famous for a fragrant sheep cheese called *formaggio di pecora "marcetto,"* which you should look for in stores or at Trattoria da Clara. It is rather sharp in flavor and soft in texture, so it is best when spread on good bread.

DINING

Trattoria da Clara, Via Patini 9, tel. 0862/930365. Closed Tuesday (except in summer) and September. No credit cards. Inexpensive to moderately inexpensive.

A very friendly place with good rustic food. The lentil soup is rich with bread and oil and could almost make a meal in itself. Grilled lamb is the top *secondo*, washed

down by honest house wine. It is also possible to sleep here in clean, modest accommodations.

SAGRE AND FESTIVALS
Estate a Calascio.

In July and August there is a series of observances featuring particular foods, plus folkloric music and popular dances.

Campli (Teramo)

SAGRE AND FESTIVALS
Sagra della Porchetta Italica.

On the last weekend of August *porchettari* (*porchetta* makers) gather in the Piazza di

Santa Maria in Platea and near the Palazzo Farnese to compete for the best *porchetta*. The winner is hailed, and then all *porchetta* is eaten by celebrants. There is music, dancing, and other folkloric activities.

Campotosto (L'Aquila)

DINING
Ristorante Barilotto, Via Roma,

tel. 0862/900141. Closed Tuesday. No credit cards. Moderately inexpensive.

Ristorante Valle, Via Roma 57, tel. 0862/900119. Closed Monday, except from May through September. No credit cards. Moderate.

Both restaurants offer good local foods, with an emphasis on *salumi*, soups, pasta, and local trout. There are nice views as well.

SALUMI
Giovanni Deli, Via Belvedere 14.

Classic *mortadelline di Campotosto*.

Azienda Berardi, Località Poggio Cancelli.

The Berardi family makes delicious sausages, the famous *mortadelline di Campotosto*, and others.

Canzano (Teramo)

SAGRE AND FESTIVALS
Sagra del Tacchino.

In the second week of August, there is feasting and celebration of the famous local turkey dish, *tacchino alla canzanese*. This dish can be tasted for much of the year at Trattoria La Tacchinella, Via Roma 18, tel. 0861/555107.

Carpineto Sinello (Chieti)

SAGRE AND FESTIVALS
Sagra della Porchetta.

On the last weekend of July, a huge party with tasting of *porchetta* and *ventricina* is followed in the evening by dancing to the music of a local orchestra.

Festa della Birra.

On the first weekend of August, there is a large festival of beer drinking, consumption of pork products, and lots of revelry.

Castelli (Teramo)

Castelli is famous for its ceramics, which can be purchased at the Villagio Artigianato, a gathering of producers. To see the work of ceramists from centuries past, visit the Museo della Ceramica di Castelli (open 9h to 12h). In August there is Agosto Castellano, which has conferences and festivities connected to ceramics. On August 15, there is a traditional event in which all the imperfect ceramics are tossed from a height and smashed in dramatic fashion. Dine at Da Luisetta, Contrada Colledoro 1, tel. 0861/979100.

Chieti

BAKERY
Pasticceria d'Orazio, Vicolo Storto Teatro   *San Ferdinando.*

An amazing array of delicious cookies makes this bakery famous in Chieti. There are also good cakes and pastries.

Processione del Venerdi Santo.

The oldest Good Friday procession in Italy begins at 19h at the Cattedrale di San Giustino.

WINE
Enoteca Templi Romani Giannini, Via Priscilla 13, tel. 0871/69277. Closed Thursday afternoon, Sunday, August, and January.

This is one of the better-known wine sellers of the region. There is also a good selection from other regions, as well as olive oil, chocolates made with *moscato* or Barolo, honeys, and excellent coffee beans.

Cocullo (L'Aquila)

SAGRE AND FESTIVALS
La Processione dei Serpari.

On the first Thursday in May; the classic combination of pagan and Christian. Originally dedicated to the ancient goddess Angizia, ostensibly this day now honors San Domenico. It also revives the ancient ritual of snake worship in which celebrants wrap themselves in snakes and thank them for eating the pests that would ravage crops and bring disease to humans. The snakes also slither round a statue of San Domenico; in so doing they link the fate of the celebrants to that of the saint. This event must be seen to be believed.

Collelongo (L'Aquila)

SAGRE AND FESTIVALS
Festa di Sant'Antonio Abate.

On January 17 are the blessing of the *cottore* (earthenware crockery) and the distribution of *cicirocchi* (boiled corn on the cob).

Francavilla al Mare (Chieti)

DINING
Trattoria al Piatto Verde, Contrada Cerreto 3, tel. 085/817125. Closed Saturday. No credit cards. Inexpensive.

A simple trattoria with good soups, pasta, grilled meats—especially sausages.

Giulianova Lido (Teramo)

DINING
Osteria del Moro, Lungomare Spalato 74,

tel. 085/8004973. Closed Wednesday, at lunch on Monday and Tuesday, and weeks between September and October, and February and March. All credit cards. Moderate.

Lu Scucchiarelli, Via Vespucci, tel. 085/8004929. Closed Tuesday and November. MasterCard, Visa. Moderate to moderately expensive.

Da Beccaceci, Via Zola 18, tel. 085/8003550. Closed Monday, Tuesday lunch (in July/August), Sunday evening (September–June), the first two weeks of January. All credit cards. Moderately expensive.

Three excellent addresses for *abruzzese* fish and seafood.

FOOD SHOPPING
Salumeria Antonio, Via Nazario Sauro 10.

Salami, prosciutti, sausages, cheeses, pasta, wine, all of good quality.

SAGRE AND FESTIVALS
Settimana del Mare.

A week in July with concerts, dancing, and eating dedicated to the sea. As part of the event there is feasting on *pesce azzurro* (fresh anchovies and sardines).

Festa della Madonna del Porto Salvo.

In the first week of August this important religious festival has daily events in churches, squares, and by the sea.

L'Aquila

L'Aquila is a relatively young city by Italian standards. It was created in 1240 and has a profoundly medieval air that is part of its beauty. Visit the daily market in front of the Duomo, walk through the quiet picturesque quarters, and be sure to visit the famous fountain with the ninety-nine spigots.

BREAD
Panificio Eredi Celso Cioni, Via San Sisto 35.

Outstanding breads, as good as you will see anywhere. The aroma of the *pane casareccio* haunts me still. Many of the breads stay fresh several days, in the proper shepherd tradition.

DINING
Ristorante Le Tre Marie, Via Tre Marie 3, tel. 0862/413191. Closed Sunday evening, Monday, and December 24–January 6. MasterCard, Visa. Moderately expensive.

Paolo Scipioni is the guiding spirit of this famous restaurant, which is considered the best in town and, by many, the top dining place in the Abruzzo. Try the *scrippelle 'mbusse*, the *noccbette alla pastorella*, and the *scamorza alla spiedo*. Lamb, pork, trout with Avezzano potatoes and olives, and chicken breasts with truffles are all good choices. An unusual and tasty dish is the *tagliolini alla chitarra al sugo di trote e codine di gamberi*, homemade pasta with a trout-and-shrimp sauce flavored with tomato, olive oil, and *peperoncino*. When you dine here once, you will be warmly welcomed and well served. When you dine here a second time, they will bring the *Libro d'Oro*, which you will sign and thereby be considered a regular.

La Cantina del Boss, Via Castello 3, tel. 0862/413393. Closed Saturday afternoon, Sunday, and July 15–August 15. No credit cards. Inexpensive.

The name dates back to 1931, although this osteria has been in operation since 1881. Mariano Massari was a local who emigrated to the United States. Upon his return to L'Aquila in 1931, he was given the American moniker "Boss," and the name stuck. The restaurant is now operated by his heirs but has a genuinely old-fashioned feel about it. The food is tasty and meant to accompany wine, although you can make a nice meal by sampling several dishes.

L'Antico Borgo, Piazza San Vito 1, tel. 0862/22005. Closed in the first two weeks of January. All credit cards. Moderately inexpensive to moderate.

This well-located restaurant is notable for its use of local ingredients, including the great saffron of Abruzzo. Start with a platter of *salumi*, a couple of which have a dash of saffron. I love the *maltagliati con sugo di patate, rosmarino e zafferano*, pasta with a sauce of potato, rosemary and saffron. If you see *struzzo* on the menu, that is ostrich, which is now in vogue in restaurants throughout Italy, and much of it is grown in this region. Many nutritional claims have been made for this bird, and certainly it is hardly the first imported animal to enter Italian cookery (turkey, horse, cat...), and yet I hesitate to enthuse. Try it if you are interested.

ICE CREAM
Magic, Via dell'Indipendenza 25.

One of the favorite spots during the *passeggiata*.

FOLKLORE
La Sagra delle Sagre.

On the second weekend of August, all the local *sagre* of products and traditions in the province of L'Aquila gather in the capital to celebrate. If you cannot get to the *sagre* in the small towns, which are always more interesting, this is a great event for the overview it provides of local food and folklore.

La Perdonanza.

In the last week of August there are elaborate processions in full costume that are among the most extravagant to be seen in the region.

SALUMI
Salumeria Paolo Giuliani, Via Patini 21.

Wonderful *salame* is made here. It is full of pork flavor and judicious amounts of sweet fat. Each *salame* is made unique by the addition of other flavors such as *peperoncino*, black pepper, or saffron. Be sure to try the *mortadelline di Campotosto*. There are also sausages with flavors such as honey, *peperoncino*, or liver.

WINE AND SPIRITS
Enoteca Ernesto, Via Cavour 60, tel. 0862/61274. Closed Thursday.

This site was once a medieval prison and was later a place where wine was produced. Now you can purchase good wines and oils from the region and beyond, as well as several gastronomic specialties: quince (*mela cotogna*) jam, lentils from Santo Stefano, mortadella from Campotosto, Pecorino cheeses, pasta made with *farro* or *orzo* (barley), and local beans and chickpeas.

Gli Infusi delle Terre Antiche, Via Madonna del Ponte, tel. 0862/414536.

Gentian is a local flavor in this part of the Apennines, and it flavors an *amaro* called Ghentiané that is the specialty of the house. There are other drinks, syrups, and products, too, all using local herbs and plants.

Pescara

Pescara, on the Adriatic coast, is a modern city built on ancient foundations that presents a very different Abruzzo than the one seen in Sulmona, L'Aquila, or Avezzano. Here women and men interact more freely and publicly, much as they might do in Roma. There is a vibrant *passeggiata* on the Corso Umberto, a busy beach scene, and a nightlife that favors jazz and popular culture. There is excellent seafood and one restaurant, La Cantina di Jozz, that offers a wonderful introduction to the cuisine of the entire region.

BAKERIES

Pandora Dolci Artigianali, Via Pisano 33, tel. 085/77934.

Elaborate and delicious cakes and desserts, especially those made for holidays, feasts, and *sagre.*

Luigi d'Amico, Via San Tinozzo 44, tel. 085/61869.

A leading producer of *parrozzo* as well as other traditional cakes and cookies.

BARS AND CAFFÈS

Bar Camplone, Corso Umberto (opposite Gelateria Berardo). Closed Wednesday.

A very popular *caffè* that is a focal point of the *passeggiata.*

Gelateria Berardo.
See "Ice Cream," below.

BREAD

Antiche Bontà, Via Alighieri 19, tel. 085/27361.

A large variety of good breads made of various flours.

COOKING SCHOOL

Ristorante Club Nautico Pescara, Lungo Aterno Nord, 65100 Pescara, tel. 085/374230.

Most Mondays Lina Morichi comes down from her school in Torrette di Ancona (see page 431) to give classes in Pescara.

DINING

La Cantina di Jozz, Via delle Cascine 61, tel. 085/690383, fax 085/65295. Closed Sunday evening, Monday, late June to mid-July, Christmas through January 6. All credit cards. Moderate.

Giovanni Andrea Cetteo, owner of this excellent restaurant, is known to one and all as Jozz, and he runs the one restaurant you should be sure to visit in Pescara. There are differently priced menus available or an *à la carte* menu that is somewhat higher. You should come here with a good appetite and choose one of the set meals. On Saturday and Sunday, when the restaurant is very busy, large pots and platters of food are made and served to diners at all tables. One of my recent meals began with a spicy soup of corn, beans, and cereals called *li rinate*, then a delicious *spaghetti alla chitarra* in a sauce of strong duck essence, saffron, and a bit of cream. Next was *polenta con salsiccia*, soft creamy polenta with a spicy tomato sauce, grated Pecorino, and pieces of sausage. This was followed by a choice of *anatra alla scalogna* (duck in a shallot-and-wine sauce) or braised turkey breast with a sauce of herbs, pine nuts, and olive oil. They were both delicate and very flavorful. *Contorni* were sweet-and-sour peppers and whipped pumpkin. Then came a choice of *maialino arrosto* (roast baby pig) or *agnello alle mandorle* (roast lamb with an almond sauce), accompanied by roast potatoes and sautéed mushrooms. Only the dessert, *tiramisù*, was less than special. A good wine choice is the Montepulciano d'Abruzzo Duchi di Castelluccio. Part of the success of the food here is that all the vegetables come from Jozz's farm, Azienda Agricola Pompa la Pompa, and are organically grown.

La Taverna, Via del Circuito 3, tel. 085/27127. Closed Sunday and in August. No credit cards. Moderately inexpensive.

If you have time for another meal in Pescara, you might consider dining here. Do not be put off by the sign TABAC CHERIA. Simply walk through, and you will find yourself in a nice, small room with very good food waiting. The antipasti made with assorted vegetables should not be missed. *Maccheroni alla chitarra* is a worthy primo, and then mixed grilled meats are a tasty choice for a secondo.

La Lumaca, Via delle Caserme 51, tel. 085/4510880. Open for dinner Wednesday through Monday. All credit cards. Moderately inexpensive.

An excellent showcase for Abruzzese foods and wines, including rare salumi and little-seen cheeses such as *Pecorino di Farindola*.

Taverna 58, Corso Manthoné 46, tel. 085/690724. Closed Sunday, holidays, and last week of the year. American Express, MasterCard, Visa. Moderate.

If you love snails, this is the place for you. Ask for the *menù lumache*, and you will sample several snail-based dishes. Otherwise, try the *menù sapori abruzzesi*, which includes dishes made from local ingredients such as *Pecorino marcetto*, terrine made from Abruzzese duckling, trout, *maccheroni alla chitarra*, and *pecora al tegame* (a flavorful braised lamb).

FOOD SHOPPING

D'Alessandro Dolcezze, Via Fabrizi 209.

A nice store with good packaged baked goods, wines, spirits, and candies.

Salumeria di Muzio, Via Carducci 95.

The best regional *salumi* and cheeses. Try the *formaggio allo zafferano* (cheese flavored with saffron) and the *riccioli all'uovo di quaglie* (pasta made with quail eggs).

La Quercia, Viale Regina Margherita 63, tel. 085/387103.

Excellent olive oil made by the proprietors using various regional olives in blends or even as single-variety oil.

Natura Classica, Via Mazzini 140.

Many products here were grown without pesticides and produced without preservatives. These include olive oil, grains, meat, cheese, wine, and sweets.

ICE CREAM

Gelateria Berardo (under the Esplanade on Piazza 1 Maggio). Closed Monday.

A very popular and attractive *gelateria* that is one of the social hubs of Pescara. There are waiters, table service, and great views of the passing crowds. Good ice cream, too.

MUSEUMS

Casa d'Annunzio, around the corner from La Cantina di Jozz and near the Piazza Garibaldi. Open 9–14h, Sunday 9–13h; closed Monday (doors close 30 minutes before the scheduled closing time of the museum).

Gabriele d'Annunzio (1863–1938) was one of Italy's leading poets, writers, and patriots. Yet his patriotism was not necessarily to everyone's liking. While he was indisputably a hero in World War I battles, his embrace of Fascism called into question what patriotism means. He also led the life of the heroic poet, had legendary affairs with actress Eleonora Duse and others, and it is worth getting to know him through this excellent exhibit at the house of his birth. Next door is Museo delle Tradizioni Popolari Abruzzesi, an interesting collection of native costumes, agricultural tools, and objects tied to rural Abruzzese life.

WINE

Enoteca Europea, Lungofiume Paolucci 69, tel. and fax 085/28355. Closed Thursday afternoon, Sunday, and second and third weeks in August.

A very well stocked *enoteca* with more than nine hundred wines from all over Italy and abroad.

Enoteca Saper Bere, Via Guglielmo Marconi 165, tel. 085/4510965. Closed Thursday and in August.

The name means "To Know How to Drink." A very good selection of Abruzzo wines, especially those by small producers. There is also wine from around the country, plus olive oil and high-quality pastas.

Enoteca Visaggio, Via Clemente de Cesaris 44, tel. 085/4216692. Closed Thursday afternoon, Sunday, and most of January. American Express, MasterCard, Visa.

Since 1938 the Visaggio family has operated this lovely shop in the city center. There is wine from the region, elsewhere in Italy, and France and several good oils and vinegars.

Pescina (L'Aquila)

This town, in the middle of a zone frequently assaulted by earthquakes, is the birthplace of Ignazio Silone. The starkness he describes remains much in evidence, but there is beauty as well. The land is still so arid that almost the only thing that grows is oregano. Although people here certainly eat now, and the standard of living has risen, one can understand how hunger, in former times, completely affected life and led to mass emigration.

DINING

Ristorante Valle del Giovenco, Via San Rinaldi, tel. 0863/842191. No credit cards. Moderate.

Pastoral cuisine: cheeses, lamb, rich red wine, good bread.

Pollutri (Chieti)

SAGRE AND FESTIVALS

Festa di San Nicola da Bari e Sagra delle Fave.

On December 6, seven large pots of fava beans are cooked in the main square and served to all the celebrants. This event recalls a miracle by San Nicola, who made seven ships arrive from the sea, all loaded with fava beans that saved the people of Pollutri from starvation.

Rivisondoli (L'Aquila)

One of the most renowned cheese-making towns in the region. In this town one of the food traditions is that a ham cooked with pepper, cloves, cinnamon, and sugar is always served at wedding lunches. Rivisondoli is also a popular mountain resort in summer and winter.

CHEESE

Carmelo d'Orazio, Via Fonticella, tel. 0864/69115.

Fabulous handmade mozzarella.

Caseificio Bilat, Via Sulmontina 18, tel. 0864/69280.

You can find its products in many stores.

DINING

Da Giocondo, Via Suffragio 2, tel. 0864/69123. Closed Tuesday and the last two weeks of June. All credit cards. Moderately inexpensive to moderate.

Very good mountain food, richly laced with cheese.

Ristorante Al Vecchio Mulino, Via San Vito 11, tel. 0864/69296. Closed Monday. No credit cards. Moderate.

Spicy flavors and good cheese characterize the food here. Try the grilled *scamorza.*

San Vito Chietino (Chieti)

DINING

Ristorante alla Cascina Bianca, Via Quercia dei Corvi (look for the Lanciano exit on the A14 highway), tel. 0872/618625. Closed Monday. MasterCard, Visa. Moderately expensive.

A serene, artfully decorated restaurant that serves a lighter version of many Abruzzese dishes. The *scrippelle al profumo di bosco* are a specialty.

Sulmona (L'Aquila)
Classic Town

Sulmona combines excellent food, rich folklore, a cultured populace, and natural beauty in a way that makes it an expression of the mountainous part of Abruzzo. There is grand medieval and Renaissance architecture, an excellent museum of antiquity, and a lovely *passeggiata* that is more formal and less vibrant than the one in coastal Pescara. You will find several stores selling blankets, shawls, and sweaters, all made with local wool by the women of Sulmona, whose handiwork is famous. You will find that, as the birthplace of Ovid and the national source of *confetti*, Sulmona lives its history and tradition more actively than most cities you will visit.

CONFETTI

Confetti Pelino, Via Stazione Introdacqua 53–55, tel. 0864/32901 or 210047, fax 0864/55203.

Classically made *confetti*, all by hand since 1783. It also has a museum, Museo del Confetto, that is worth a look.

Confetti Giuseppe di Carlo & F., Corso Ovidio 183, tel. 0864/31385.

Confetti William di Carlo, Piazzale Stazione Centrale, tel. 0864/52693.

Confetti Ovidio, Via Sardi, tel. 0864/34147.

Confetti Pareggi, Via Corfinio 14, tel. 0864/51657.

CULTURE

The Teatro Comunale and the Auditorium dell'Annunziata are sites of frequent musical and theatrical performances of high quality. Each year, in the third week of October, there is the Maria Caniglia Singing Competition, named in honor of the great soprano of Abruzzese origin (1905–1979). All the contestants are sopranos and mezzo sopranos, and the week ends with a worthwhile concert.

DINING

Ristorante Clemente, Vico Quercia 5, tel. 0864/52284. Closed Thursday and late June to mid-July. No credit cards. Moderate.

One could do a sheep-based meal from start to finish. The *salumi* are mostly made of pork, but occasionally there is one with lamb. Then try *orecchiette alla pecorara*, made with tomato sauce and Pecorino. Lamb is either roasted, grilled, or made in stew. Be sure to have some cheese, such as *scamorza alla griglia*.

Ristorante Villa Elena, Badia Sulmonese, Contrada Quadri, tel. 0864/ 251097. Closed Monday. MasterCard. Moderate.

Several people encouraged me to dine here. It is a bit out of town, and the last stretch of the trip is on unpaved roads but it is worth the effort. You are within view of Monte Morrone in a peaceful setting. After *salumi* for antipasto, try the *ravioli di ricotta*, which have a strong hint of saffron. The *coniglio a senape e rosmarino* (rabbit with mustard and rosemary) is delicious, as is the *pecora a lu cutturu*.

Ristorante Italia da Nicola, Piazza XX Settembre 26, tel. 0864/33070. Closed Monday and July 1–15. American Express, Visa. Moderate.

Delicious *maccheroni alla chitarra* and grilled lamb.

Ristorante Rigoletto, Via Stazione Introdacqua 46, tel. 0864/55529. Closed Sunday evening, Tuesday, last two weeks

of July, and Christmas to New Year's. American Express, MasterCard, Visa. Moderate.

Just from the name I had a hunch this would be a fine place to eat. Not to be missed are the *ravioli ripieni di scamorza con zafferano*, with a cheese filling made golden by the most flavorful saffron you will ever encounter.

Gino, Piazza Plebiscito 12, tel. 0864/52289. Open for lunch Monday through Saturday. MasterCard, Visa. Moderately inexpensive.

Rustic, delicious food, including great cheeses, *zuppa di fave e cicerchie* (soup of fava beans and wild greens) and, in season, *zolle di aglio rosso di Sulmona sottâolio* (hearts of Sulmona's red garlic, preserved in olive oil).

FOOD SHOPPING

The market of Sulmona centers on the Piazza Garibaldi, which merits a visit any morning except Sunday.

Orazio Vitucci, Via Monte Santo 121.

Excellent cheeses, especially those made of sheep's milk. Be sure to try *ricotta di pecora* which should be a touchstone for what this cheese should taste like.

Pratello, Via Paradiso, tel. 0864/251485.

A good selection of regional cheeses.

Reginella d'Abruzzo, Via Aroto 1, tel. 0864/33419.

Very good mozzarella cheeses in all sizes. Try the tiny *ciliegine*.

HERBS AND SPICES

Cooperativa Il Seme, Viale Mazzini 70, tel. 0864/210213.

Many herbs and plants are grown here to be used by cooks for different dishes and by spirits makers to fashion *digestivi* and *amari*. There is also saffron, which is a good thing to buy to take home.

HONEY

Miele Fantini, Via Montesanto 37, tel. 0864/31998.

Honeys and honey products.

SAGRE AND FESTIVALS

La Madonna Che Scappa in Piazza.

On Easter Sunday many people dress in green and white (colors of peace, hope, and resurrection), and gather at 11:30h in Piazza Garibaldi. Here an ancient drama is enacted in which the Virgin Mary is notified that Christ has risen. At first incredulous, she then gradually believes the news. She exits from her doorway dressed in black and moves slowly to the fountain. Suddenly a flock of doves is released, and we see that the Madonna is now dressed in green. Bells ring, brass instruments play joyous music, the people of Sulmona wish each other a better future, and then hours of feasting begin.

Offerings in a local salumeria, *Sulmona*

Sagra Paesana.

In Introdacqua, just outside Sulmona, there is a two-week festival at the beginning of August featuring typical peasant foods and dancing every night.

WINE AND SPIRITS

Di Loreto Vinatierri, Via Gramsci 41. Closed Sunday.

The di Loreto family produces all of the typical wines of Abruzzo, as well as olive oil and saffron. In addition, you can find about six hundred other wines from the region and beyond, as well as truffles native to Abruzzo.

Luigino Cesaroni, Via Dorrucci 16.

An excellent producer of Centerbe, the classic *amaro* of Abruzzo.

Teramo

BREAD

Alberto Il Fornaio, Via Riccitelli 23.

Many breads here are worth discovering, foremost among these the *pane Altamura*, an excellent loaf made with cornmeal. The *pane casareccio* is also worth the journey.

CHEESE

Azienda Casearia de Remigis, Via Costa Sant'Agostino 53, tel. 0861/210003.

Excellent sheep's-milk cheeses are produced by this firm.

DINING

Ristorante Moderno, Via Coste Sant'Agostino, tel. 0861/414559. Closed Wednesday, mid-August, and mid-November. All credit cards. Moderate.

Good, fresh, tasty food, such as *pollo ruspante ai pomodori verdi*, free-range chicken cooked with rosemary, *peperoncino*, white wine, and green tomatoes.

FOLKLORE

Sagra delle Virtù.

All the restaurants of Teramo serve *virtù* as part of the observances of May Day, when love is in the air.

Tollo (Chieti)

FOLKLORE

Sagra del Vino.

Held on the third or fourth weekend of July, this is one of the biggest wine festivals around, sponsored by the local Cantina Sociale.

Torano Nuovo (Teramo)

WINE

Azienda Vinicola Pepe, Via Chiesa 10, tel. 0861/856493.

Emidio Pepe is one of the few wine makers who still makes it with his feet. If you want to visit, call first. Wine is made at harvest time during October.

Enoteca Centrale, Corso Cerulli 24, tel. 0861/243633. Closed Sunday evening and two weeks in August.

Many wine producers sell directly to the public

Excellent local food, including *scrippelle 'mbusse* and *virtù*.

Vasto (Chieti)

The gastronomic specialty of Vasto is *brodetto*, which is usually prepared only with flatfish and no seafood.

BAKERY

Pasticceria Argentieri, Via Madonna dell'Asilo 150, tel. 0873/2581.

Excellent sweets and pastries, especially at holiday time.

DINING

Ristorante Il Corsaro, Porto di Vasto, tel. 0873/310113. Closed Monday, November– March. MasterCard, Visa. Expensive.

Right on the beach, this is one of the better seafood restaurants on the Abruzzese coast, and a very good place to sample *brodetto di pesce alla Donna Lina.*

Trattoria Il Faro, Loc. C. da Lebba, Strada Statale 16, 69, tel. 0873/310281. Closed Sunday. No credit cards. Moderately inexpensive.

Off the beaten track, this family trattoria has delicious pasta and main courses based on local seafood.

Ristorante Villa Vignola, Località Vignola (6 km from Vasto), tel. 0873/310050, fax 0873/310060. Reservations essential. Closed one week in December. All credit cards. Moderately expensive.

A lovely restaurant that also has four rooms. Delicious seafood, artfully prepared.

All'Hostaria del Pavone, Via Barbarotta 15, tel. 0873/60227. Closed Tuesday and some weeks in January and February. All credit cards. Moderate.

Fresh fish and seafood, including *crudità* (raw shellfish) and delicious *brodetto vastese*, the local fish stew, to which you might add some pasta to the liquid after eating the fish. A rarity is *mazzancolle con lardo e miele*, an Adriatic shellfish paired with lard and honey.

SAGRE AND FESTIVALS
Festa del Ritorno.

On the first Sunday in August there is a festive and moving event that greets all of the returning emigrants who left their families to earn money in Milano, Torino, Belgium (where there is a large Abruzzese community), or other places.

Villa Santa Maria (Chieti)

Known as La Città dei Cuochi (the City of Cooks) because of a famous culinary institute—La Scuola Alberghiera—whose students have gained fame and fortune in restaurants around the world. They have cooked for czars, American presidents, Swedish kings, Fascist dictators, and in embassies, consulates, and grand hotels in every capital. The origins of this tradition date back to the sixteenth century, when the Caracciolo family ruled this area and local cooks worked in their employ. One of the Caracciolos, Ascanio (1563–1608), had a religious inclination, was beatified in 1807 by Pope Pius VII, and is now considered the patron saint of cooks. On the second weekend of October, cooks from Villa Santa Maria return for a conference and, of course, feasting.

DINING
Albergo-Ristorante Santa Maria, Piazza Maraoni 19, tel. 0872/944417. Closed Monday. No credit cards. Moderately inexpensive.

The food here is basic and flavorful, yet it seems that what is taught inside the cooking school does not filter out into the local restaurants. Nonetheless, the fare is honest, as are the prices.

Agnello all'Uovo e Limone
Lamb with Egg and Lemon

A traditional Abruzzese Easter dish.

Serves 4 to 6
4 tablespoons extra-virgin olive oil
2 cloves garlic, peeled and halved
1½ kilos/3½ pounds lamb, cut in small pieces
Salt and freshly ground black pepper to taste
170 milliliters/¾ cup dry white wine, such as
 Trebbiano d'Abruzzo
225 milliliters/1 cup light beef stock
4 egg yolks
Juice of ½ lemon

Heat the oil in a large, heavy-bottomed casserole or pot. Add the garlic and the lamb. Sauté the lamb until it is browned on all sides. When the garlic pieces become golden, remove them. Once the meat is browned, add salt and pepper and then the wine. Keep cooking over moderate heat until the wine has evaporated. Add the stock, cover, and cook until the meat is thoroughly cooked and tender. Lift the casserole or pot from the heat and, using a slotted spoon, remove all of the meat to a warmed serving dish. Return the casserole to the heat, add the egg yolks and the lemon juice, and heat until the sauce simmers, whipping it gently with a whisk. Pour the sauce onto the lamb and serve immediately, perhaps with rice or potatoes, and *peperonata alla campagnola* (recipe follows).

Wine: Trebbiano d'Abruzzo.

Peperonata alla Campagnola
Baked Mixed Peppers and Other Vegetables

Serves 6
1 small onion, sliced thin
450 grams/1 pound ripe tomatoes, peeled and
 coarsely chopped, or 2½ cups canned toma-
 toes, coarsely chopped
650 grams/1½ pounds green, red, and yellow
 peppers, washed and cut in broad strips
300 grams/10 ounces zucchini, preferably
 small ones, washed and sliced into thick
 disks
300 grams/10 ounces small potatoes, scrubbed
 and quartered
300 grams/10 ounces baby eggplant, tops re-
 moved, the rest cut into cubes
Salt and freshly ground black pepper to taste
Oregano to taste

Preheat the oven to 180° C (350° F). Lightly oil a baking dish with extra-virgin olive oil and then add all of the vegetables, in the order listed. Top with salt, pepper, and oregano, then stir to combine the ingredients well. Cover and bake for 45 minutes. The vegetables (except for the tomatoes) should be relatively firm and should retain their distinct color and flavor. Check the eggplant for doneness. If it is cooked to your satisfaction, then the dish is ready. Serve hot, tepid, or cool (but not cold).

Molise

Not to Miss in Molise

AGNONE   **CAMPOBASSO**

LARINO *(Classic Town)*

La mia terra	My land
ha mani grandi	has great hands
nodose come ceppi di quercia	knotty like stumps of oak
solitaria nella piana	all alone in a plain
segnata dal fiume	marked by a river
Nei suoi occhi	In its eyes
campi di grano maturo	fields of full-grown wheat
foglie sottili del gentile olivo	slender leaves of the gentle olive tree
La mia terra	My land
ha la voce del vento della sera	has the voice of the evening wind
quando il sole	when the sun
è già dietro la collina	is already behind the hill
e la luna alta	and the high moon
sembra ostia trasparente	is like a paper-thin host
nelle mani del cielo	in the hands of heaven
Il suo profumo	Its fragrance
è quello dell'olio di oliva	is that of olive oil

—PASQUALE DI LENA

REGIONAL CAPITAL:
Campobasso (CB).

PROVINCIAL CAPITALS:
Campobasso, Isernia (IS).

TOURIST INFORMATION:
Ente Regionale del Turismo,
   Regione Molise,
      Via Mazzini 94,
      86100 Campobasso,
      tel. 0874/949502,
      fax 0874/949523.

Agritourism:
Coop. Molise Verde a.r.l.,
   Via Cardarelli 50,
   86100 Campobasso,
   tel. 0874/62935.

 Molise is the region nobody knows. Most Italians have never been there and would be hard-pressed to locate it on a map. For many years, it was folded into the larger Abruzzo re-

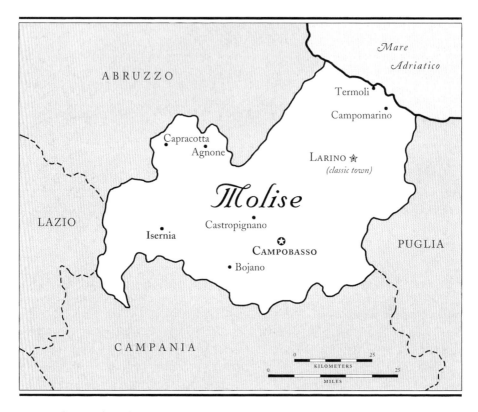

gion to the north, only gaining independence in 1963. I made this same error when I wrote *The Authentic Pasta Book* in 1985. I completely omitted Molise, thinking of it as part of Abruzzo. When I gave the book to Pasquale di Lena, the secretary of the Enoteca Italiana in Siena but a proud son of Molise, he took me to task for my oversight. Pasquale has published several volumes of poetry, much of it written in *molisano*. The verses above effectively communicate Molise: a place where the basic foods are cultivated in a beautiful but often-unyielding soil.

What is so special about Molise is that it preserves much of the culture of southern Italy at a time when other regions are assimilating with the rest of the country, acquiring the materialism and values of a wealthy nation. Molise is unmistakably poor, and its people are still very removed from the currents of modern life. Outsiders are received with a mixture of watchfulness and cordial hospitality. I encourage you to go to Molise to sample real flavors, real fragrances, and a genuine slice of life that is hard to find anywhere else.

The major cultural and historic phenomenon of Molise is something called *la transumanza*. This is a unique event that has shaped every aspect of *molisano* life. There is no suitable word in English to evoke the meaning of *la transumanza*. The literal translation is "transhumance." What it implies is a huge human migration that occurs at an appointed time each year, usually dictated by weather and available grazing terrain for one's cattle and sheep. Since prehistoric times, shepherds who grazed their flocks in the uplands of Abruzzo and Molise would migrate each September to lowlands and the sea with their animals. There are traces of *la transumanza* dating back to the fourth century B.C., the era of the Samnites, the ancient people of Molise. (Many people in Molise still call themselves *sanniti*.) The people in this region are typically shorter than elsewhere, and many of them have distinctive chestnut-colored eyes.

Most of the travelers in *la transumanza* were destined for the town of Foggia, now a principal city in Puglia. The routes they tracked were called *tratturi*. These broad green highways of antiquity exist to this day. Some *tratturi* (the word is the root of "tractor" with its implication of plowing) are 180 meters (600 feet) wide. Along their sides developed a whole civilization. Toll stations collected money or goods to permit passage. A fee was paid to the local landowner for every head of sheep that passed through. Taverns opened to receive traveling shepherds. *Masserie* (ancient estates that provided food, rest, and care for animals and humans) also became plantations where indentured peasants raised crops. A few *masserie* exist to this day, and one of them, DiMajo Norante in Campomarino, I describe in detail on page 527.

Religiosity became a deep part of these migrations. Pagan festivals related to the arrival of harvesttime or the prayer for a safe journey. With the advent of Christianity these events took on a different tone, but the emotions were the same. You will notice that many ancient churches in Molise have a series of hooks and rings attached. This is where animals were tied while the humans worshiped. Religious observances were not necessarily tied to the calendar that might be used in Roma. Rather, they took place at the times of the year when the travelers were passing by.

Research has located at least ninety-eight *tratturi* throughout Molise, and you are sure to see one in your travels. If ever you notice a wide, flattened path that is broader than most roads in the region, this is probably a *tratturo*. In the period after the Second World War, the national government created a policy of building over the *tratturi*, which was a conscious effort to eradicate a style of life that had persisted for centuries. Yet in your travels through this sparsely populated region you will find segments of *tratturi* that remain as they were centuries ago. While there are no longer the mass migrations that occurred as recently as ninety years ago, there still are shepherds and their flocks who wander for hundreds of kilometers every year.

The phenomenon corresponding to *la transumanza* is the emigration of thousands of *molisani* to the United States (notably to Cleveland), Canada (Toronto), Argentina (Buenos Aires and the winegrowing regions), and cities in northern Italy, Germany, Switzerland, and Belgium. Pasquale told me that one of his strongest memories as a boy in the early 1950s was the sound of women crying as men left to find work abroad. Many communities even now are composed primarily of women, old men, and children. While more work has come in recent years and there are signs of an agricultural revival, Molise is still a very poor place when compared with the rest of Italy. Many people live in narrow two-story houses that huddle together in small towns. Not too long ago, the family lived on the upper floor and the animals were kept below.

As in much of the rural south, the land is both a friend and a tormentor. When it is generous it provides sustenance, but it also can be stubborn and difficult. In some parts of the south water is scarce, although recent developments have alleviated the problem somewhat. Rural southerners can be even more superstitious than urban Italians (themselves a superstitious lot), and many feel that prayer is not enough. There is great fear of the *malocchio,* the "evil eye." At the mention of any potential threat, many southerners make a hand gesture intended to keep away the evil eye.

But sometimes gestures are not enough, and a ceremony called the *catechisimo del malocchio* must be performed to lift a curse. I had the unusual fortune to once witness this rite. It is almost always performed by a woman, and the victim of a curse is usually a man. A plate is filled with water, and a cup of olive oil is brought nearby. The victim is anointed with oil at various points on his face, always in a rhythmic series of gestures in the sign of the cross. All the while the woman recites a series of prayers and incantations. Then she makes several crosses on the rim of the plate by moving her hand quickly back and forth. After about twenty minutes it is time to test the effectiveness of her work. She takes a couple of drops of oil and adds them to the water. If the oil breaks up, then the curse has been lifted. If not, stronger prayers and incantations are called for. It is believed that the most powerful spell lifters are women who have borne twins. If the first woman has failed, then the mother of twins is sent for.

Another subtext in Molise life is the historical presence of an Albanian-speaking minority. Emigrants arrived from Albania centuries ago and barely assimilated into the local population. Even today it is difficult to hear Italian in some Molise towns. The chief Albanian community is in the town of Ururi. When Albania opened to the world around 1990, a new flood of Albanians arrived in Molise.

This chapter will be somewhat different than the others in the book because it is about a very unusual place. There will not be many listings because Molise is not fully developed for tourism. This is a handicap, but it is also part of its great fascination. In Molise you are venturing into uncharted terrain. There may not be attractions in the customary sense, but there is life, culture, and tradition in abundance. In Molise the fascination of the new comes in the discovery of the old.

Eating in Molise

The cuisine of Molise is also a legacy of *la transumanza.* Many dishes are prepared rapidly and simply, as they would be by people on the move. *Molisani* eat a broader range of vegetables and greens than do most Italians. These would be gathered in fields and on the fringes of the *tratturi,* boiled, and then perhaps topped with some olive oil. Pasta is simply cooked and sauced—there have never been the resources or the time for more elaborate preparations. Bread, wine, and oil are three staples. When a young man emigrates, he is sent away with a large loaf of bread to see him through his journey. The fragrance and flavor become a sensory reminder of home, a last caress from a wife or mother. Oil and wine are foods here (as in much of Italy), not merely a condiment or a beverage.

Meat was a luxury in old Molise because animals taken to Foggia on *la transumanza* were meant to be sold—every one that was consumed was a loss of income. As in much of the south, a sheep was a complete resource that had to be cared for. Its wool provided warmth; its milk and the cheese made from it provided sustenance. As for pigs, they were a prized commodity. Usually one would be slaughtered in early December, and every usable piece of it would become food: ham, bacon, sausage, *salame,* and so forth. The legacy of these traditions is that *molisani* routinely eat the sort of heart-healthy diet that is all the rage from New York to Tokyo. Pasta, grains, fruits, vegetables, olive oil, wine, and small amounts of animal fat make up what is popularly called the Mediterranean Diet. When a piece of meat, usually an inexpensive cut, is available to a *molisana,* she cooks it in tomatoes, oil, and herbs to create a pasta sauce called *ragù* (completely different than the meaty *ragù* of Bologna). Then the meat is saved for the following day to be served with cooked vegetables. As you might expect, lamb is the most frequently consumed meat.

You will certainly encounter *il diavolillo,* intensely hot *peperoncino rosso.* This small red pepper is often minced and put in olive oil, or it might be dried and ground to use as a powder. In its oil infusion, *il diavolillo* is tossed with spaghetti as a popular dish. Or it can be added to other sauces, to boiled eggs and omelettes, vegetables, fish, and meat. *Il diavolillo* is popular throughout the south (you will find a recipe on page 596 that uses it with pasta and tomatoes as is done in Puglia).

The leading agricultural products of the region (and the chief exports) are the excellent pastas and olive oil. La Molisana is considered one of Italy's best pasta brands. Colavita is the largest olive-oil producer and one of the biggest exporters in Italy. Marina Colonna is an outstanding smaller producer. In addition, many exquisite oils can be found as you journey from town to town, and you should be sure to buy some. The oil from Larino is particularly delicious. Other products include wheat, corn, potatoes, tomatoes, and the very popular fava beans. *Molisani* also dry fava beans, which become nutlike. The original intention in drying them was so they would be available in winter months when food was scarce. The lentils from Capracotta are considered among the best in Italy, exceeded only by those of Castelluccio in Umbria. Molise has also recently revealed a cache of black truffles that grow in some of its hilly forests. Unfortunately, unscrupulous merchants from

Umbria, Emilia-Romagna, and Piemonte have begun to snatch them up in such a way that the spores in the ground are disturbed, meaning that new truffles will not grow. The *molisani* are now fighting to protect this precious and lucrative resource so that it can be enjoyed in the future. But truffles figure very little in *molisano* cooking, although I have indicated one restaurant, Da Roberto in Castropignano, where you may sample them.

The rhythm of eating in Molise is dictated by ancient church traditions, but also by the practicalities of rural life, where every bit of food is used (and often reused) to be as economical as possible. Unlike in the rest of Italy, where several courses were eaten, poor people in Molise used to have a one-dish meal. Although financial well-being is slowly arriving in the region, old customs die hard. So on Monday a typical family would have a plate of cooked legumes and greens, or perhaps a minestrone. On Tuesday, fish (usually *baccalà*) would be had. Occasionally it would be accompanied by some pasta and oil. Wednesday saw the return of vegetables. Thursday was for *pasta con sugo* (a meatless tomato sauce). Friday was fish again. Saturday was a lean day: broth with noodles or bread. On Sunday there would be *pasta con ragù*, the tomato sauce that would have a hint of meat. The small piece of meat would be cut into bits and then served with vegetables. Bread was a constant at all meals, serving to fill empty stomachs.

ANTIPASTI

Bruschetta. Toasted bread with olive oil, salt, pepper, and garlic.
Capocolli. Sausage made from the head and tail of a pig.
Prosciutto affumicato. Smoked ham from Rionero Sannitico.
Salsiccie al finocchio. Fennel sausage.
Soppressata (salame).

PRIMI

Brodosini. Tagliatelle in broth with pork cheek and fat.
Calcioni di Ricotta. Fried pasta stuffed with ricotta, provolone, prosciutto, and parsley. Usually served with a *frittura mista* of artichokes, cauliflower, brains, sweetbreads, potato croquettes, and *scamorza* cheese. A specialty of Campobasso.
Cavatiegl e Patane. Gnocchi served in a meat sauce of rabbit and pork.
Pasta. Cavatelli, lasagne, or *maccheroni* served with *ragù* of lamb or goat.
Pasta e Fagioli. Pasta-and-white-bean soup cooked with pig's feet and pork rinds.
P'lenta d'iragn. "White polenta," actually made of wheat and potatoes, sauced with raw tomatoes and Pecorino.
Risotto alla Marinara. Rice with seafood.
Spaghetti col Diavolillo.
Zuppa di Cardi. Soup of cardoons, tomatoes, onions, *pancetta,* olive oil.
Zuppa di Ortiche. Soup of nettle stems, tomatoes, onions, *pancetta,* olive oil.

SECONDI

Agnello. Lamb, the most popular meat. Served *alla griglia* (grilled), *arrosto* (roasted) or *in umido* (stewed). Many organ meats of lamb, especially tripe, are popular.

Carciofi Ripieni. Artichokes stuffed with anchovies and capers.

Cipollaci con Pecorino. Fried strong onions and Pecorino cheese.

Coniglio alla Molisana. Rabbit pieces skewered with sausage and herbs, grilled.

Frittata con Basilico e Cipolle. Omelette with basil and onions.

Mazzarelle. Tightly wrapped rolls made with lung and tripe of lamb.

Ragù d'Agnello. Braised lamb with sweet peppers. A specialty of Isernia.

Torcinelli. Rolled strips of lamb tripe, sweetbreads, and liver.

Zuppa di Pesce. Fish stew, a specialty of Termoli.

FORMAGGI

Burrino. Soft, delicious, buttery cow's-milk cheese.

Manteca. Similar to *burrino.*

Pecorino. Sheep's-milk cheese, served young and soft or older and hard.

Scamorza. Bland cow's-milk cheese, often served grilled.

Caciocavallo. Sheep's-milk cheese.

DOLCI

Calciumi (also called *Caucioni*). Sweet ravioli filled with chestnuts, almonds, chocolate, vanilla, cooked wine musts, and cinnamon and then fried. A Christmas treat.

Ciambelline. Ring-shaped cakes made in the country. They may be *all'olio* (with olive oil) or *al vino rosso* (with red wine).

Ferratelle all'Anice. Anise cakes made in metal molds and stamped with special patterns.

Ricotta a Mo' di Pizza. A cake pan filled with a blend of ricotta cheese, sugar, flour, butter, maraschino liqueur, and chocolate chips.

The Wines of Molise

Oil production and wine making, which often go hand in hand, date back to ancient times in Molise, as archaeological digs have revealed with the discovery of Greek and Roman amphorae and jars as well as coins that show oil and wine activity. More than in most of Italy, wine in Molise tastes as it did years ago. The region has not benefited from the advances in wine making that have swept Italy in the past thirty years. This situation has positive and negative implications. While Molise wine would probably not fare well on the international market, it does have an honest native character that makes it distinct from the more polished product from the big wine regions. It also is perfectly suited to the honest flavors of the local cuisine. A few producers have embraced the modern style, especially DiMajo Norante, which makes a very good line of wines. Seventy-five percent of Molise wine is produced in the province of Campobasso; the rest is from the province of Isernia.

There are only two DOC wines in Molise: Biferno, which comes in red, white, and rosé (from Campobasso) and Pentro (white, also red and rosé, from Isernia). Non-DOC varieties planted in Molise include the reds Aglianico, Barbera, Bovale Grande, Cabernet Franc, Ciliegiolo, Montepulciano, Pinot Nero, and Sangiovese and the whites Bombino Bianco, Garganega, Malvasia del Chianti, Moscato, Pinot Bianco, Pinot Grigio, Riesling Italico, Riesling Renano, Sauvignon Blanc, Traminer Aromatico, Trebbiano, and Veltliner.

Agnone (Isernia)

Agnone is one of the most beautiful and important towns in Molise. It is perched on a hill surrounded by dense oak woods. It has several notable churches, including the fifteenth-century Sant'Emidio, Sant'Antonio Abate, and San Francesco. If you are particularly taken with the sound of bells here, there is a reason for that. Agnone has been the bell-making capital of the world since the year 1000. The Marinelli family began making bells in that year and has remained in business ever since. Most of the bells you hear in churches in Italy were (and are) made in Agnone. Other crafts in Agnone include excellent coppersmithing and goldsmithing. The first goldsmiths in Agnone were Venetians who emigrated here in the eleventh century. They built houses in an attractive district of town known as the Borgo Veneziano. Copper pots and pans from Agnone are among the finest around. This town also makes some of the best cheeses in southern Italy, definitely worth trying.

CHEESE SHOPS AND PRDUCERS
Antonio Dinuci, Via Roma 12, tel. 0865/ 77288.

Caseificio Fratelli di Menna, Contrada di Montagna 18, tel. 0865/77468.

Caseificio Lorenzo di Pasqua, Via Vittorio Veneto 20, tel. 0865/79275.

Try *caciocavallo stagionato.*

Alimentari di Rienzo, Piazza Vittoria 263, tel. 0865/78572.

Caseificio Mario Antenucci, Via Matteotti 17, tel. 0865/78344.

A highly regarded small producer.

DINING

Ristorante Sammartino, Largo Pietro Micca 44, tel. 0865/77577, fax 0865/ 78239. All credit cards. Moderately inexpensive.

Typical Molise flavors in this hotel-restaurant.

Boiano/Bojano (Campobasso)

CHEESE
Antonio Pulsone, Via San Bartolomeo 31, tel. 0874/773353.

The town of Boiano is almost as famous as Agnone as a cheese producer and is considered the best mozzarella maker in Molise. Here is an excellent source.

DINING
Filomena, Località Colle Pignataro 199, tel. 0874/773078. Open for lunch Tuesday through Sunday, Saturday for dinner too; dinner available on other days (except Monday) by reservation; closed in July. All credit cards. Moderate.

This eatery has been in business for more than a century and is still going strong.

One comes here for delicious local food. Since Boiano is famous for its mozzarella cheese, white *cannellini* beans, and peppers, these ingredients figure prominently. There is also a selection of honest, sturdy local wines, well-prepared pasta dishes (good gnocchi on Thursday, as is traditional in much of Italy), and roast lamb, veal, and pork.

PASTA
Pasta Bernardo, Corso Amatuzio 116, tel. 0874/773303.

This firm has been in business since 1910 and is known to use the water from one of the springs that feeds the Biferno River. They make seventy shapes of pasta.

Campobasso

This is the regional capital and the nerve center of Molise. Only Campobasso and Termoli have any sense of modernity, yet they feel like small towns in comparison with their counterparts in other regions. Don't forget, Molise became an independent region only in 1963, so it lacks the self-assurance other places have. To get a sense of the old town from a food point of view, visit the market, but also go to Via Marconi, which has some older shops. When you reach #56, go through the vaulted underpass to an area that is now a parking lot. Look closely and you can see that this was the old market of Campobasso. The *botteghe* (covered stalls) are now sealed up. Here is where meat, fish, oil, and legumes were sold. Where cars now stand used to be fruit stands. Walk through to the other entrance on the Via Palumbo (this small square is called the Piazzetta Colombo), and you will notice an ancient fountain where food would be washed.

BAKERY
Pasticceria Iannetta, Viale Elena 46a, tel. 0874/92563.

A particular alcoholic drink in Molise is called *Milk*. It is an ingredient in *milk-pan*, a sweet bread that is the specialty of the house. It is made with flour, sugar, butter, eggs, hazelnuts, and almonds and covered with a thin sheet of chocolate. The bakery also makes this cake using other local liqueurs.

BAR AND BAKERY

Lupacchioli, Piazza Prefettura (also called Piazza Gabriele Pepe) 27, tel. 0874/ 91349. Closed Tuesday. No credit cards.

This place has been a point of reference for *molisani* since 1861. Since it is one of the few institutions that is famous throughout the region, anyone who came to the capital to do business would arrange to meet people at Lupacchioli. While it lacks the elegance and *esprit* of the leading *caffès* of Torino and Napoli, it is a meaningful touchstone in this little region. Lupacchioli is well regarded for its pastries and unsweetened baked goods, such as *pinolini al crema di formaggio* (small puffs with a cheese filling). Lupacchioli also serves good ice cream; one popular flavor is *mela verde* (green apple).

BREAD

Forno Giangiacomo Felice, Via Marconi 91.

An excellent selection of breads, pastries, cakes, and *fiatoni* (large *calzoni* filled with mixed soft cheeses), which are popular at Easter.

Forno a Legno Palazzo, Via Ziccardi 5.

The last bakery in town that uses a wood-burning oven to bake bread. Various breads and pizzas with an unmistakable flavor.

DINING

Ristorante Aciniello, Via Torino 4, tel. 0874/ 94001. Closed Sunday. American Express. Inexpensive to moderately inexpensive.

Here is a nice place that rigorously serves local dishes. Most of the wine comes from other regions, except for the house wine, which goes well with the food. Among the many good things I tasted: good peppery *salame, muso di maiale* (pickled pig's cheek), *torcinelli, pizza e migliechella* (cornmeal pizza crumbled and cooked with vegetables to form a sort of thick soup). *Pantacce*, a local cut pasta, are served in lots of light tomato sauce, making the dish almost a soup. Very delicious is the *trippa d'agnello*, lamb tripe, a Molise specialty that is very hard to find. It is cooked with tomatoes, carrots, celery (considered the best vegetable grown near Campobasso), parsley, and basil and served topped with grated Pecorino cheese. You can also get a *grigliata mista* (mixed grill) of strips of lamb, sausage, a bit of tripe, and *torcinelli*.

Miseria e Nobiltà, Viale del Castello 16, tel. 0874/94268. Closed Sunday, the last week of July, and the first week of August. All credit cards. Moderate.

Very good food with intelligent use of vegetables and cheeses. *Crioli* are delicious handmade spaghetti.

Vecchia Trattoria da Tonino, Corso Vittorio Emanuele 8, tel. 0874/415200. Closed Sunday, Saturday (July/August) or Monday (September to June), last ten days of July. All credit cards. Moderate.

The pretty restaurant on the main street of town has been a popular spot since 1954. The kitchen likes to reinterpret traditional dishes for modern tastes. Some of this is done with success, but it was odd, on the day that I visited, that all the secondi were made with veal, not a meat that is widely consumed in these parts.

MARKET

Via Monforte near Via Roma. Open 7–13h; closed Sunday.

Until 1960 the market was in the picturesque Piazzetta Colombo in the historic center of town. This market, admittedly, is larger, but lacks the special character of the old one. The most interesting days to come are Wednesday and Friday, when fish arrives from Termoli. Stands 10 and 15 have cheeses from Agnone and Boiano, but you must ask. At stand 23 are cheeses and *salumi* from Abruzzo. To be certain you are getting Agnone cheese, exit the market and walk across Via Monforte to Gianfagna.

Campolieto (Campobasso)

FOLKLORE

Festa del Ritorno dell'Emigrante.

Held on the first or second weekend of August, this sad and joyous event is a product of one of the realities of life in Molise. Men return from jobs abroad and are received with traditional foods: roast lamb, fresh breads, olive oil, sweets.

Campomarino (Campobasso)

AGRITOURISM

Masseria DiMajo Norante, Contrada Ramitello, 86042 Campomarino, tel. 0875/57208 (call before coming), fax 0875/57379.

Luigi DiMajo owns this very impressive estate 3 kilometers from the sea, which is visible in the distance. He is at the leading edge of viticulture and agriculture in Molise, yet this place also has roots and tradition that go all the way back to the beginnings of civilization in Molise. A *tratturo* from the *transumanza* cuts through part of the fields where vegetables grow. This place is the site of a *masseria* that used to receive travelers on the road to Foggia. In addition to Molì (Biferno) red, rosé, and white wines, DiMajo has planted ancient vines that are a historic part of the region's heritage: Falanghina, Fiano, Greco, Apianae (a type of Moscato; the name is Latin and suggests a sweet grape that attracts *api* [bees]), Aglianico (from Basilicata), and Prugnolo. He produces red and white wines called Ramitello that use blends of some of these grapes.

Signor DiMajo described to me the agricultural traditions of the region. As recently as the 1960s, wheat was harvested by hand. Peasants would set out at dawn with sickle in hand and work all day. On the right hand would be a sort of glove made of pig's leather that would enable the peasant to hold the sickle more firmly. Each finger of the left hand would be covered with cane to prevent amputation as the wheat was cut. Now machines do this work. This, according to DiMajo, has created another form of slavery, as people without work have idle time on their hands and a sense of demoralization. After the wheat was collected, it would be placed in a pile. A heavy wheel would be anchored to oxen who would be led around in circles to grind the wheat. The wheat and good water of the region made bread and pasta, the two staples of the southern Italian poor. Peasants who worked the harvest were given a daily meal to take out to the field. It was a cooked preparation of garlic, potatoes, water, salt, a small amount of oil, and lots of *peperoncino* (which was intended to charge the workers' "batteries").

When the harvest was complete, there was a celebration called La Festa del Capo Canale. One traditional dish served at this event was *bacchieri*. These were conical pasta like cannelloni but were not filled. Rather, when cooked, they flattened and were put in a deep cauldron and topped with *ragù*. The cauldron kept the pasta and sauce hot for two hours. Another dish was tomatoes cooked with great amounts of onions and garlic. The idea of this dish was that it helped guard against malaria. This festival was to give thanks to God, to the gods, to nature or whomever, for a successful harvest. But it was also, in the minds of many, "the feast of famine." This was a chance for peasants to eat abundantly for the first time in months. Other dishes included broths, lamb, mutton, chicken, and rivers of wine. Peasants ate as much as they could and then were sent home with more food. In the winter, when fields were covered with snow, one ate what little there was at home. This usually meant bread or pasta topped with salt, oil, or sugar.

The *masseria* of DiMajo Norante is a modern farm with a strong emphasis on maintaining the classical flavors and fragrances of Molise. Wheat is but one of many crops. One of the most astonishing sensory experiences I have ever had was walking from the road to the entrance of the estate. It is not so much a walkway as a small forest of herbs. There are towering trees of wild rosemary. As you push through them you acquire their exquisite perfume. There are dozens of other herbs and plants growing in this verdant patch. Among the fruits that grow there are pomegranates, blood oranges, and *giuggiulo*, a datelike fruit. Thirty years ago there were no grapes here; now there are 60 hectares (150 acres) of vines. The wines are produced by Luigi's son Alessio.

The house as we see it today was constructed in 1974 based on the style and design of old *masserie*. There are eighteen rooms with beautiful antique furniture. But Signor DiMajo has resisted suggestions to turn this place into a wonderful hotel with great food and wine. Instead, he occasionally hosts conferences on gastronomy. The *masseria* produces an excellent line of vegetables in oil and herbs that are sold under the name Sapori della Masseria. These are very hard to find in Molise— you are more likely to see them in Roma, Milano, or specialty shops abroad. The oil is made principally with the Gentile di Larino olive. If you are staying at Termoli or somewhere else along the Adriatic, the Masseria Di Majo Norante is worth a visit to get a sense of Molise past and present and to purchase wine, vegetables, and oil.

Castropignano (Campobasso)

This town is the hub of truffle country in Molise. Other towns, including Fossalto (Campobasso), Duronia (Campobasso), Carovilli (Isernia) and San Pietro Avellana (Isernia), also have a significant supply. It is estimated that 30 percent of the region's terrain has truffles underneath, and if they are removed carefully so that spores remain to generate new ones, truffles may soon provide an important infusion of cash when they are sold for use on the tables of Umbria, Emilia-Romagna, Lombardia, and Piemonte. Black truffles are obtained from March to early October. From then on through late February the much more prized white truffles can be found. White truffles cost more than twenty times what black ones do, although the market varies each year according to supply and demand.

DINING

Ristorante Roberto, 22 Via Lacone (at Bivio Fossaltina, an intersection just outside of Castropignano), tel. 0874/503164. Closed Monday. All credit cards. Inexpensive to moderately expensive (depending if you eat truffles).

This is a noisy, animated family restaurant with lots of pink and lavender in its decor. You will have a good chance to observe families on a night out for pizza, pasta, grilled meats, but also for truffles. Ignore, if you can, the large TV screens. This is also a motel set at the edge of a forest, so there will be hotel guests in the dining room. I sampled a largely truffle meal: *bruschetta* with truffle slices; tagliatelle with truffle and *funghi porcini; a frittata con tartufi,* a delicious truffle omelette fried in good olive oil. Then came a piece of delicious grilled *scamorza* cheese from Agnone, topped with truffle for good measure. Roberto and his father hunt truffles with their dog, and you can purchase a truffle from them to take home.

Ferrazzano (Campobasso)

DINING

Ristorante da Emilio, Piazza Spensieri, tel. 0874/416576.

I did not have the occasion to visit, but this restaurant is widely considered one of the best in the region. Try *torcinelli* and *scrigni di Venere,* which are tagliatelle with truffles. The local wine of Ferrazzano is the richly aromatic Tintiglia.

Frosolone (Isernia)

CHEESE

Felice Colantuono, Contrada Acquevive,

tel. 0874/89364.

Makes delicious *burrini.*

FOLKLORE

Sagra di Peperuol e Baccalà.

Each August 1, villagers sing the song of the *prim'auste* (first of August) and eat fried cod and peppers. This is followed by a parade representing events from peasant life: planting, harvesting, knife making (a local specialty), and so forth.

Isernia

DINING

Taverna Maresca, Corso Marcelli 186, tel. 0865/3976. Closed Sunday, August, and Christmastime. All credit cards. Moderate.

FOLKLORE

Fiera di San Pietro, or La Fiera delle Cipolle (the Onion Festival).

This has been held on June 28 and 29 since the year 1200. While once devoted primarily to onions, it also features livestock, crafts, and other goods. This is the largest fair in the province of Isernia.

Larino (Campobasso)
Classic Town

Larino once had 13,000 residents, but emigration took away many of its sons, and now the population hovers around 7,000. Every August, however, the town fills up, and the streets are full of cars with license plates from Torino, Milano, Germany, and Belgium. This is always an arresting sight because otherwise Molise is not overburdened with vehicular traffic.

Originally Larino was just a small town nestled in the valley below what is now the major part of the city. The upper area was once an extensive Roman site, including an amphitheater, the remains of which you can visit. Much of the rest has been built over to create modern Larino. This is the area that has many of the hotels and services you will use, but you should devote much of your visit to the old town below. There everyone knows one another and interacts in a way that makes them seem like a large extended family. There are five churches, three haircutters, a few bars, two banks, and two public squares of any consequence.

The larger of the two squares has the *municipio*, a ninth-century Norman structure that is the center of life in the town. Here are the library, the mayor and other public officials, and the town museum (three rooms of archaeological finds from the Samnites and Romans). One walks up many steps to the central courtyard of the *municipio*, and it is here in the summer that outdoor concerts are given. Also in the *municipio* are the club Amici della Musica, where the town band rehearses, and the day center for the elderly whom you will see gathered on the street for conversation. There is also a club for sports enthusiasts.

Around the back of the *municipio*, near a small public fountain, a few fruit and vegetable vendors sell their wares. If you let your eyes blur slightly and permit sepia tones to creep in where the color is, this scene will look like turn-of-the-century photographs of life in rural southern Italy. In the old town of Larino, a few stores selling food hold out, but by now most of the commerce has moved to the upper town. While I want you to spend most of your time in the old town, most of the places that I direct you to for food purposes are now in the upper town.

Make note of something else as you stand near the *municipio*: as in much of It aly, especially the south, a great deal of love and attention is lavished on babies and children—one's own and everyone else's. If a child is bicycling on the wrong side of the street, an adult will not fail to call it to his attention, not as criticism, but as an expression of care and affection.

BAR-BAKERY
Pasticceria Federico, Via A. Morrone 8 (upper town), tel. 0874/822487. Closed Thursday.

This bar makes good coffee and serves the typical pastries of southern Italy: *sfogliatelle*, *babà*, *frolle*, and so forth. But you may want to go next door to #4, the Casa del Pane. Here is a range of excellent baked goods, including delicious local bread, pizzas, and cookies. Try the delicious *torta rustica*, a pie filled with mozzarella, eggs, boiled ham, pepper, Parmigiano, parsley, and garlic. The cookies include *uccelletti* (little birds), a Larino specialty. They get their name from their birdlike shape. These are soft cookies filled either with cooked cherries or *mosto cotto*, grape skins used in wine making that are cooked until they are reduced to an intense winy jam. Other cookies include *biscotti di uova naspretti* (rounds topped with egg white), *ferratelle* (wafflelike cookies made with stamps in different patterns), and others filled with almonds, candied fruit, or chocolate.

There is a story behind the bread you taste here. The bread of Larino is rich, fragrant, and memorable, but until the

1960s it also provided a social function. It was the story of Alfredo Federico, the paterfamilias of this family bakery. Alfredo began baking breads in 1933, when he was nine years old. Once upon a time, the women of old Larino would come by his *forno* (oven) to inform him that they needed bread the following day. At 1h he would make the rounds of town, knocking on doors to wake up the women who needed bread. It was the women's task to make the dough, which had to be kneaded for two hours. If many breads had to be made on a particular night, Alfredo would space out his knocking or spend time visiting with a family. The reason for this is that the oven could hold only so many loaves, so that he had to bake bread for the town in three shifts. He made his rounds all night so that the preparation time for every loaf would be the same.

At 4h Alfredo made a second round, returning to the women he went to at 1h and knocking on their doors to tell them to form the dough into a loaf. At 7h he would return to collect the first loaves for the *primo forno*. On his large board (called a *tavoliere*) Alfredo carried as many as six loaves on his back. How was

Gino Federico and his father, Alfredo, photographed in 1995

he able to distinguish one bread from another? Before he took the dough from a woman's kitchen, she would put an imprint of her house key on top of the loaf.

In addition to loaves of bread, he also baked fiatbreads and pizzas topped with oregano and garlic, and sometimes with tomato sauce. These pizzas were important because they lowered the temperature in the oven so that the loaves would bake properly. A loaf of bread would bake for two hours. When the loaves were ready, Alfredo brought them back to their owners and would then do the *secondo forno* and then the *terzo forno*. When the bread reached a family home, where it was intended to last several days, it was often hung from the ceiling. This was because animals were usually kept in the house, but also because the fragrance tantalized hungry children. Each day he sold the carbonized wood logs to families who used them as a source of warmth in their houses without internal heating.

Alfredo made his rounds until 1965. When he stopped, there was a notable change in the social structure of Larino. This is because he inadvertently was a gatherer of news of the town. He had heard all sorts of facts, intimacies, and private concerns from the women he encountered, much as a priest in a confessional might. He knew who had the evil curse (the *malocchio*) on them, who was being cuckolded, who was ill, and so on. He claims to have always kept his counsel, but having met this kind man, I suspect that he interceded where he could to make life easier for someone else.

It was in the 1960s that the modern town of upper Larino was being developed and much of the traditional life of the old town was being plowed under. Alfredo was also getting older, and his back ached from his labors. His son Gino was not interested in making the rounds as his father did, so it was decided that they would open a *forno* in the new town, make their own dough, and sell it in a store. So when you bite into a piece of bread that you have bought at the Federico Casa del Pane, you will know the history linked to it and to Larino.

DINING

Azienda Agricola Domenico Zeoli, Strada Statale 87 at kilometer 200, near Carpineto, tel. 0874/823685 (call first).

Good simple food is available, and you can purchase delicious Larino oil to take home.

FOLKLORE

Festa de Sant'Antonio Abate.

On January 16 and 17 a traditional porridge called *ricciata*, containing wheat and cornmeal, is cooked. The old people of town get down on their knees and press their right hand to the ground as they recite prayers and incantations while the ladle stirs the *ricciata*.

Maggio Larinese.

In the last ten days of May the most important folkloric event in Molise is held. There are concerts, religious processions, feasts, and above all the procession of San Pardo. This begins late in the afternoon on May 25 as more than 150 elaborately decorated oxdrawn carts meet in the Piazza del Duomo and Piazza del Municipio before making their way to the cemetery. Here, at 18h, a statue of San Primiano is collected and taken aboard the cart designated as the Cart of San Pardo. The procession goes all through the town and, as night falls, candles and

torches are lit. The whole journey is about 6 kilometers (3.7 miles). The carts are laden with flowers, statues, and other decorations. Each cart must have an olive branch (known in local dialect as a *tanno*) affixed to it—the cultivation of olives is sacred to the *larinesi*. Each cart is led by a *galano*, the local term for a man capable of keeping an ox in line during the long, animated event. This is no simple task on the narrow, often-slippery streets in the old quarter of Larino. Most of the oxen also have garlands on their heads, and all of them have large bells hanging from their necks. These have been passed down through the generations and remain part of the prized possessions of every Larino family. This festival lasts three days, with masses, prayers, and feasting, especially on the third day. After that, the "calling cards" left by the oxen are cleaned from the streets of Larino and life returns to normal.

ICE CREAM

Gelateria Carfagnini, Via Alberto Marra. Closed Monday.

I understand that the Carfagninis no longer produce ice cream here, but I leave this entry in this new edition as a tribute to them.

A few steps from the Federico Casa del Pane is another Larino institution, the *gelateria* owned by Giuseppe and Emma Carfagnini. They have made ice cream by hand since 1949. Giuseppe uses an ancient machine and says he wouldn't trade it in for a more modern one. I have eaten *gelato* all over Italy, and I rank this place in the top three (see "Noto" in the Sicilia chapter and Giolitti in the Roma listing for the other two). This is superb ice cream, famous throughout Molise. Giuseppe is most known for two flavors: *limone* and *crema* (the latter is made only of milk, eggs, and sugar). Giuseppe gets his milk directly from local dairies and eggs from local farmers. You will notice that the yolks of Italian eggs are almost red—in fact, in Italian they are called *i rossi di uova*. To make the lemon ice cream, he squeezes each lemon by hand, making sure that the zest goes into the ice cream as well. He uses no citric acid, as do even some of the most highly regarded *gelatai*. Unlike most strawberry ice creams, his *fragola* is not red through and through. Rather, he gathers mountain berries by hand, cooks them down, and then swirls this juice into the ice cream before chilling it. Other flavors include *stracciatella* (chocolate chip), *nocciola* (which is divine), and *cioccolato*. What is also astonishing is how low his prices are. This kind of quality, if the ice cream were to be sold in Napoli or Venezia, would cost ten times as much.

Emma and Giuseppe Carfagnini in their gelatria, *Larino*

OLIVE OIL

Centrale Oleifici Cooperativa Molisana, Contrada Torre, tel. 0874/822696.

Here is an oil press *(frantoio)* where locals bring olives to be squeezed into delicious oil. The local variety of olive, Gentile di Larino, is of exquisite flavor. There used to be twenty-five *frantoi* in Larino when it was a major regional producer. Every year the townspeople would gather each day from mid-October to near Christmas to hand-pick olives. This led to a kind of socializing that might not happen on the narrow streets of town under the watchful eyes of the elders. Each olive picker leaned a ladder against a tree, and the pickers would communicate with one another through song. It would be a sort of call and response between one man and one woman, backed up by a chorus that would chime in with commentary and then exalt *viva l'amore*. Most of the songs were about courtship and were alternately affectionate and ironic, a cat-and-mouse game of flirtation. The rhythms of the songs were the work rhythms that flowed in time with the movements of gathering the olives. The people of Larino still gather olives this way, but much less so. It is sad that such splendid olives, which would represent income for the town, go to waste.

Pescopennataro (Isernia)

FOLKLORE

La Mandrellata.

This is a footrace, named after the *mandrella*, the kerchief that *molisano* peasants.

wrap their food in before going to work in the fields. In the race, each runner is given a *mandrella* filled with food to eat during the course of the race. I wonder how long it takes to get to the finish line! Held on a different day every January.

Sagra della Ciff e Ciaff.

Lamb is roasted according to a recipe of the local shepherds. The name Ciff e Ciaff comes from the sound the meat makes as it sizzles. Held on a Sunday in mid-August.

Poggio Sannita (Isernia)

FOLKLORE
Sagra dell'Uva.

Held on or around October 17, at the end of the grape harvest. There is a parade of carts inspired by the harvest. Folksinging, dancing, wine, food.

Rionero Sannitico (Isernia)

DINING
Ristorante Pablo, Via Votacarrozza, tel. 0865/848110. No credit cards. Inexpensive.

Come here for sublime pizzas and breads from a wood-burning oven. A specialty is *fiadoni,* made with flour and cheese. Local meat, fish, vegetables, and pasta are also flavorful and genuine.

San Pietro Avellana (Isernia)

MUSEUM
Raccolta Oggetti della Civiltà Contadina, Via Tratturo 63, tel. 0865/940103.

This is a collection of kitchen equipment, farm tools, clothes, and other objects related to the rural civilization of Molise. Notice that the museum is built on a street that is an ancient *tratturo.*

Scapoli (Isernia)

FOLKLORE
Mostra Mercato della Zampogna.

What is it about bagpipes and shepherds? Why is it that pipers, whether from Scotland or Molise, also seem to enjoy feasting on sheep's innards? Maybe you will find out at this unique event. Wherever you travel in rural Italy there is the music of the shepherds. Their song has even found its way into opera (Puccini's *Tosca*). Yet a special subgroup is the *zampognari,* bagpipers who often turn up at provincial fairs throughout the country. As Italy lunges forward into the twenty-first century, the *zampognari* seem headed for extinction. Yet many who love them and their music turn up in Scapoli in the middle ten days of July. This town is the only place in mainland Italy where the *zampogna*, the bagpipe, is still produced. Pipes from Sardinia *(launeddas)*, from Hungary *(gayda)*, Scotland, and elsewhere are played. On the last night of the festival a big concert is held featuring players from here and abroad. You can also visit the Museo della Zampogna's permanent collection of bagpipes.

Termoli (Campobasso)

This is a friendly, bustling seaport and beach resort on the Adriatic that has a completely different, more relaxed air than the rest of Molise. The town is smiling, sunny, and floral. All the beachgoers like ice cream, so there are many *gelaterie* to choose from. To get a sense of Termoli as an important seaport, go down to the Mercato Ittico in the port in the early morning as the catch is brought in.

BAKERY
Pasticceria Torinese, Corso Fratelli Brigida 68, tel. 0875/3997.

This small, cool, very neat shop makes tiny, delicate pastries of the type one would find at a fine *caffè* in Torino. Ice cream, too.

CRAFTS STORE
Molise Artistico, Via Duomo 49, tel. 0875/84940. Open daily.

On a pretty street in the Borgo Vecchio, the old quarter of Termoli. Nicoletta Pietravalle has selected from the best of the region's crafts. While much is not of great interest to the gourmet traveler, there are good copper platters and pots made and decorated by hand in Agnone.

DINING
Nonna Maria, Via Oberdan 14, tel. 0875/81585. Closed Monday. All credit cards. Moderate.

Very good fish and seafood cookery in this trattoria. The *brodetto* is admirable and frying *(la frittura)* is done with delicacy.

Trattoria da Nicolino, Via Roma 13. Closed Thursday. No credit cards. Moderate.

The reason to come here is the divine *zuppa di pesce*, a wonderful balance of herbs, spices, olive oil, and other flavorings and the freshest products of the Adriatic. When you have eaten all the fish, you can ask that a portion of spaghetti be made. It will be tossed with the liquid from your *zuppa*, so the pleasure will continue for another course.

FOOD SHOPPING
There is a small outdoor market on Piazza Mercato. For a complete selection of cheese, *salumi*, bread, wine, and olives, go into the Casa del Formaggio on this same

piazza. At Via Roma 9, down the street from Trattoria da Nicolino, is a fruit and vegetable stand made special by the huge bunches of oregano and garlic sold outside. There is a nice pasta shop at Via Fratelli Brigida 80.

ICE CREAM
Bar Jolly, Corso Nazionale 73.

I liked the banana and apricot ice creams.

Pasticceria Torinese.

See "Bakery," above.

Vinchiaturo (Campobasso)

DINING
Trattoria da Netta, Contrada Coste 11 (at kilometer 217 on Strada Statale 17, the road from Boiano to Campobasso),

tel. 0874/34287. Closed Wednesday. No credit cards. Moderate.

Considered one of the best restaurants in Molise.

Coniglio Molisano
Molise-Style Rabbit

Serves 4
150 milliliters/4 ounces/½ cup extra-virgin olive oil
1 sprig fresh rosemary
1 kilo/about 2 pounds rabbit chunks
100 grams/3½ ounces prosciutto cotto (boiled ham)
500 grams/about 1 pound good Italian sausage of your choice, sliced into medium-thick disks
Salt (optional)
Freshly ground black pepper to taste

About an hour before you plan to cook, fill a glass with olive oil and immerse the rosemary in it. Swirl the sprig in the oil so that it begins to impart its flavor and fragrance. Preheat a grill to high heat as you are about to commence food preparation. Wrap each chunk of rabbit in a piece of prosciutto. Once this is done, place a chunk of rabbit on the skewer, then a disk of sausage, then rabbit. Continue until all the ingredients have been distributed on several skewers. Add pepper and, if desired, a little salt. Then brush each skewer with some rosemary oil. I like to use the sprig of rosemary as the brush. Grill until the sausage has cooked through, turning the skewers periodically to prevent burning.

Wine: Biferno Rosso.

Lenticchie alla Montanara
Mountain-Style Lentils

Serves 6

500 grams/about 1 pound dried brown lentils, preferably from Capracotta

1 bay leaf (optional)

3 tablespoons lard, or 3 tablespoons extra-virgin olive oil

15 chestnuts, roasted and chopped in small pieces

1 tablespoon tomato paste

6 tablespoons warm water

6 to 8 basil leaves

Pinch of fresh marjoram or thyme (use dried only if fresh is unavailable)

Salt and freshly ground black pepper to taste

Minced peperoncino *to taste*

The day before you prepare this dish, carefully rinse and then soak the lentils in lukewarm water. When it is time to start cooking, drain the lentils and then place them in a sturdy pot. Fill it with cold water just until the lentils are covered. Add the bay leaf if you wish. Cover and cook over low heat until the lentils are tender but not mushy—about 20 to 30 minutes. While the lentils are cooking, heat the lard or oil in a pan. When it is hot, add the chestnut pieces and cook for 5 minutes. Make sure they do not burn. Dilute the tomato paste in the warm water and then add the mixture to the chestnuts. Add the basil, marjoram or thyme, salt, pepper, and *peperoncino*. Cook over medium heat, stirring periodically, until the chestnuts soften. When the lentils are done, remove the bay leaf and then add the chestnut-tomato mixture. Stir to combine and cook over very low heat for 10 minutes. Then serve.

Campania

Not to Miss in Campania

AMALFI *(Classic Town)*

NAPOLI   **RAVELLO**

The streets of Naples present daily the appearance of a fête. The animation and gay dresses of the lower classes of the people, and the crowds who flock about, convey this impression. Nowhere does the stream of life seem to flow so rapidly as here. . . . The lower classes of Naples observe no medium between the slumber of exhaustion and the fever of excitement. . . . They are never calm or quiet. Their conversation, no matter on what topic, is carried on with an animation and gesticulation unknown to us [in England]. Their friendly salutations might, by a stranger, be mistaken for the commencement of a quarrel, so vehement and loud are their exclamations, and their disagreements are conducted with a fiery wrath which reminds one that they belong to a land in whose volcanic nature they strongly participate. . . . It is fortunate that this sensitive people are not, like ours, disposed to habits of intoxication. Lemonade here is sought with the same avidity that ardent spirits are in England; and this cooling beverage, joined by the universal use of macaroni, is happily calculated to allay the fire of their temperaments.

—COUNTESS OF BLESSINGTON,
THE IDLER IN ITALY, 1839

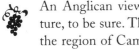 An Anglican view of the Neapolitans' nature, to be sure. The people of this city, and the region of Campania, are by turns courteous, festive, pensive, despondent, calculating, and

REGIONAL CAPITAL:
Napoli (NA).

PROVINCIAL CAPITALS:
Avellino (AV), Benevento (BN), Caserta (CE), Salerno (SA).

TOURIST INFORMATION:
Azienda Autonoma di Soggiorno e Turismo, Palazzo Reale, 80100 Napoli, tel. 081/412987.

Agritourism:
Associazione Regionale Agriturist, Via Santa Lucia 90, 80132 Napoli, tel. 081/412374.

Wine Tourism:
For information about wine

makers in Campania who will receive you for visits, tastings, and purchasing, contact Corrado D'Ambra, Delegato della Regione Campania, Movimento del Turismo del Vino,

c/o D'Ambra Vini d'Ischia,

Via M. D'Ambra,

80070 Panza d'Ischia (NA),

tel. 081/907210,

fax 081/908190.

joyous but always vibrantly alive. The astonishing natural beauty of the coastal areas and islands have made this playground a magnet for visitors for more than two thousand years. If you visit Pompei, as you should, you will find ancient kitchens, bakeries, theaters, and brothels that were centers of activity and pleasure then as their counterparts are today. People in Campania love to gather and spend time together, to drink wine, to sing, to race cars, to make love. In Campania people are everywhere: this small region has the highest population density of any region in Italy. The particular combination of beauty and animation that characterize this region make it a place you will pine for when you are gone. Napoli may be wild and chaotic, but it should be experienced before you repair to the exquisite pleasures of the small towns and the islands.

Wherever you go, Vesuvio (Mount Vesuvius), the only active volcano on continental Europe, will seem to cast its shadow. Millions of people live within its reach, and although it has been docile of late, people live with the same sense of immediacy as Californians who live along earthquake fault lines. Campania has also been subjected to severe earthquakes; if the people seem a bit jumpy, you will understand why. The volcanic soil is unusually fertile, so the fruits and vegetables that grow here are sublime.

Eating in Campania

When most people think of Italian food, it is the cuisine of Campania that comes to mind: spaghetti with tomatoes, mozzarella cheese, stuffed eggplant, seafood salad, pizza, honest wine, steaming hot espresso, crunchy pastries, and ices made of lemon or coffee. The difference is that in Campania these foods can be found at their formidable peak, while in the rest of the world they are mere imitations. Once you dine at even the most humble trattoria or pizzeria here, it will be very hard for you to swallow so-called Italian food back home. The volcanic soil gives incredible flavor to all the fruits and vegetables, so that everything from peaches to tomatoes to potatoes and lemons just seems to taste better. When the available primary materials are so outstanding, the best thing a chef can do is respect their integrity. But there is a long tradition of elaborate cooking and baking for the royal families and the nobles who have been part of the scene since antiquity (the Roman emperor Tiberius made Napoli and Capri his playgrounds). There are also, as in most of Italy, special foods for the frequent religious and pagan festivals. Pizza is the favorite nighttime meal in Napoli, as friends and families like to go out for delicious, inexpensive conviviality.

ANTIPASTI

Impepata di Cozze. Peppered mussels.

Insalata Caprese. An addictive combination of perfect mozzarella, tomatoes, and basil, with perhaps a few drops of olive oil.

Insalata di Mare. Boiled seafood, served cool with oil, vinegar or lemon, and pepper.

Melanzane Ripieni. Stuffed eggplants.

Mozzarella in Carrozza. Mozzarella "in a carriage." The cheese is placed in squares of bread, dipped in egg, and deep-fried.

Peperoni Imbottiti. Sweet peppers filled with capers, olives, anchovies, bread crumbs, basil, garlic, and parsley.

Pomodori Ripieni. Stuffed tomatoes.

PRIMI

Gnocchi alla Sorrentina. Gnocchi baked with tomato sauce, mozzarella, and sometimes eggplant.

Pasta. Campania is the heartland of dried pasta. It has given the world spaghetti, *maccheroni,* vermicelli, ziti, and many other shapes. It is topped with sauces such as *pummarola,* an incomparable sauce made of San Marzano tomatoes, a bit of garlic, and a pinch of oregano.

Pasta al Forno. Baked pasta comes in several guises in Campania. It can be lasagna or cylindrical pastas such as *maccheroni* or ziti. They are combined with tomato sauce, mozzarella, and such varied ingredients as boiled eggs, tiny meatballs, sausage, assorted vegetables, and other cheese.

Pasta e Fagioli. Some of the best pasta-and-bean soup is made in Campania.

Sartù di Riso. Rice baked with sausage, meatballs, chicken giblets, mozzarella, peas, and mushrooms.

SECONDI

There is an endless variety of fish and seafood that is the primary choice for a *secondo,* although the tradition among the poor was to have a substantial *primo* and perhaps follow it with a *contorno.* There are a few other specialties, many of which are only eaten on Sunday or religious holidays.

Baccalà con Peperoni. Salt cod cooked with sweet peppers.

Braciola. Usually served only on special occasions, in Campania this is a slice of beef that is rolled with chopped prosciutto, grated provolone cheese, eggs, and sultanas. It is tightly tied and cooked in tomatoes.

Costata alla Pizzaiola. Anything *pizzaiola* has a sauce of tomatoes, oregano, garlic, and white wine. In this case it is made with veal cutlets.

Friarelli. Tender greens that only grow in the province of Salerno. They are cooked with oil, garlic, and *peperoncino* and are often eaten as a *secondo.*

Genovese. This is a sauce of onions, carrots, and celery that tops many meat dishes and sometimes pasta.

Polpi alla Luciana. A Neapolitan favorite, made with baby octopus, tomatoes, garlic, and olive oil.

PIZZA

Pizza is one of the great culinary creations of Napoli, one that is now found in some version almost everywhere in the world. Nonetheless, one rarely finds a pizza as good as that which can be had here. The origins of pizza date back 2,500 years when flatbreads were dressed with oil, salt, herbs, and sometimes cheese. Tomatoes only arrived in Campania after Columbus's journeys to the Americas. It seems that they were not routinely baked on the flatbreads until the early nineteenth century.

An ideal pizza must have a light crust. In Napoli they often make the crust the day before, using very little yeast, and then they let it rise for twelve to fifteen hours. In lesser pizzerias around the country, lots of yeast is used to effect a quicker rise, but this toughens the crust and gives it a yeasty flavor. While there is an infinite variety of ingredients that one can use to top a pizza, in Campania the classic pizza uses very few ingredients, but of matchless quality. The best *pizza Margherita*—the type you will most often eat—uses fresh *mozzarella di bufala* (made from the milk of water buffaloes), or at least absolutely fresh mozzarella made of cow's milk. To this are added the incomparable San Marzano tomatoes from the nearby Sarno Valley. A basil leaf and perhaps a few drops of good olive oil are all that is needed otherwise. The *pizzaiolo* (pizza maker) makes an individual pie for each diner that is baked in a very hot wood-burning oven for about three minutes. A *marinara* pizza contains tomato sauce, garlic, and oregano, but no cheese. On Christmas Eve it is traditional to eat *pizza alla scarola,* topped with chopped escarole, black olives, sultanas, pine nuts, and capers. Another kind of pizza is calzone, in which the crust is folded over to enclose the ingredients. The result looks like a big shoe, which is what the word means. Neapolitans call it *oggi a otto,* meaning that you eat it today *(oggi)* and pay for it in eight days. Typically one drinks beer or mineral water or even (heaven forfend!) Coca-Cola with pizza, but one classic pizza wine is Asprinio di Aversa, if you can find it.

FORMAGGIO

Mozzarella. The fresh milkiness and soft chewy texture of this cheese are loved throughout the world, but nowhere is it made better than in Campania. Other nearby regions, such as Abruzzo and Molise, also make good mozzarella, but few mozzarellas can compare to the one produced in and around Battipaglia in the province of Salerno. The finest is called *mozzarella di bufala,* whose water-buffalo's milk produces the pungent, slightly sour but uniquely flavorful cheese that makes even the best cow's-milk mozzarella seem pallid. Because buffalo milk is precious and hard to come by, many mozzarellas are made with a mixture of cow's (70 percent) and buffalo's (30 percent) milk. The cheese is best eaten very young (unless it has been smoked) and should be stored in cool water to keep it fresh. Mozzarella finds its way onto the best Neapolitan pizza, and once you taste it with fresh tomatoes, it will be hard for you to accept anything less. A mozzarella made only from cow's milk is called *fior di latte.*

DOLCI

Campania contains such outstanding fruit that it is hard to imagine wanting anything else to end a meal. The peaches in particular are wonderfully flavorful. A traditonal way to eat them is to cut them into a glass of wine and then take a swig, letting a piece of peach roll into your mouth. Sensual and unforgettable! Nuts are also special in Campania. The best hazelnuts come from Avellino, the almonds from Nola, and the walnuts from Sorrento. These nuts find their way into many of the special baked goods in this region, although the dominant tastes are cream, ricotta, and citrus fruits.

Babà al Rhum. A pear-shaped sponge cake drowned in rum.

Granita. An ice made either with coffee or lemons that will make you forget every other version of "Italian ices" you have ever put in your mouth.

Pastiera. A special Easter cake made with flour (sometimes barley flour), ricotta, eggs, orange flavor, and candied orange or lemon peel.

Riffoli. Iced sponge cake filled with ricotta, citron, pistachio nuts, and chocolate.

Sfogliatelle. Crunchy pastries, often eaten for breakfast, filled either with ricotta or pastry cream and perhaps a cherry.

Susamelli. Pastries made with sesame seeds and honey.

Zeppole. Deep-fried dough, often served with honey. A specialty on March 19, La Festa di San Giuseppe.

The Wines of Campania

Wine has been made in Campania at least since the thirteenth century B.C. Like so much else in the region, the wines are designed for immediate pleasure rather than commercialization and sales abroad. Yet the Taurasi made by Antonio Mastroberardini is one of the best red wines in Italy, often called the Barbaresco of the South. Campania has several native grape varieties, and you should dedicate much of your tasting in the region to them because they are not easily encountered anywhere else.

Fiano. Known to the Romans as *Vitis apiana* because its particular fragrance is very attractive to bees. Grape pickers today still cover themselves to avoid being stung. It is a delicate white grape that nearly disappeared until it was brought back to viability by Antonio Mastroberardino.

Greco. A white grape that was introduced by the Greeks.

Coda di Volpe. Named by Pliny for the foxtail shape of the grape clusters.

Piedirosso. Named "Red Feet" by Pliny. The red stems resemble the feet of doves.

Some of the best wines in Campania are named for the places they come from: Capri, Ischia, Procida, Solopaca, and Ravello, for example. The small community of Furore on the Amalfi Coast produces a wine called Gran Vino del Furore, which is a hyperbolic name for a nice little wine. Many good, more substantial wines of ancient pedigree are produced inland in the provinces of Benevento and Avellino. The Fiano di Avellino is one of the best white wines in southern Italy. Look for distinct wines such as Cilento, Greco di Tufo, and Vesuvio, all worthy of investigation. The most famous wine of Campania, Lacryma Cristi or Lacrima Christi (Tears of Christ) is usually a white wine, although a red is infrequently produced. It used to be a wine of real merit, but it was so overproduced and denatured that its reputation was nearly ruined. Producers have now conscientiously made an effort to restore the wine to its former stature, so it is a wine to keep an eye on.

Other Beverages

Caffè alla Napoletana. Once upon a time, the *caffettiera alla napoletana* (Neapolitan coffee pot) was a fixture in every house and bar. Its cylindrical shape is different from the more triangular Moka coffee pot used in the rest of the country. The Neapolitan pot is designed to be turned upside down once the water has boiled, so that it passes through the canister containing ground coffee. In small restaurants you will still find coffee made this way, although larger restaurants and bars tend to have the type of machines you see everywhere in Italy. Neapolitans love their coffee, and it ranks with the best in Italy.

Limoncello. In recent years no drink has gained more popularity in Italy as an *aperitivo* or an after-dinner drink than *limoncello*, which is made with lemons from the Amalfi Coast. At its best, *limoncello* manages to capture all the freshness and sunshine of Campania in a glass. Unfortunately, the drink's popularity has made producers take shortcuts in quality in order to capitalize on the demand. The best *limoncello* has only lemon juice, alcohol, and sugar, with the canary color coming from the rind of the lemon. Read the label before buying to assure that there are no artificial colors or flavorings. At many places it is possible to have a taste before purchasing. I have recommended a few sources in the listings for Amalfi and other towns (in some places *limoncello* is called *limoncino*).

Strega. A delicious saffron-colored liqueur made with seventy herbs and spices that is a specialty of Benevento. Look for Strega ice cream, a real delicacy. The Alberti family that makes Strega also presents Il Premio Strega, one of the most important literary prizes in Italy.

Agerola (Salerno)

CHEESE

Caseificio Agerolina, Via Tutti i Santi 6.

Caseificio Fior di Agerola, Via Galli 74.

La Montanina, Via Carlo Poerio 30 bis.

This little town above the Amalfi Coast is famous for its cheeses, especially mozzarella. Here are three good cheese makers.

Amalfi (Salerno)
Classic Town

❦

Credesi che la marina da Reggio a Gaeta sia quasi la più dilettevole parte d'Italia; nella quale assai presso a Salerno è una costa sopra il mare riguardante, la quali gli abitanti chiamano la Costa d'Amalfi, piena di piccole città di giardini e di fontane.

The shore from Reggio to Gaeta is believed to be just about the most delightful part of Italy; on it, near Salerno, is a stretch of coast overlooking the sea, which the locals call the Amalfi Coast, which is full of small towns with gardens and fountains.

—BOCCACCIO, THE DECAMERON

The sun, the sea, the flavors of lemon, tomatoes, mozzarella, and herbs, the beautiful church, the playful spirit of the place all make Amalfi emblematic of the pleasures of Campania. For years, Amalfi has enchanted many visitors from the cold, unsmiling north, including Ibsen (who wrote his rollicking *Peer Gynt* here), Goethe, and Wagner. Amalfi is a former sailing power that rivaled Pisa, Genova, and Venezia. A boat race among these four cities is held each year (see "Folklore," below). The city shows Moorish influence in its flavors and its architecture. It is also one of the first places in Italy where paper was made, and there is a small museum you can visit to learn more about the history of papermaking.

BAKERIES

Pasticceria Duomo, Via Mastolo il Duca 8.

Good lemon cake.

Pasticceria Pansa, Piazza Duomo.

In business since 1830. Good lemon cake and pastries. I particularly like the *sfogliatelle all'amalfitana,* which are not like their crunchy Neapolitan cousins. They are flaky and buttery and have only a little bit of cream and cherry jam within.

Bar-Pasticceria Savoia, Via M. Camera 2.

On a central street leading from the port to the Piazza Duomo within the walls of old Amalfi. It makes delicious local pastries such as *trecce all'amalfitana,* braided pastry with hazelnuts and almond. It also makes nice *tartine al limone* (lemon tarts) and an exemplary palmier. A good place for breakfast.

BARS

Bar-Pasticceria Savoia.

See "Bakeries," above.

Il Gran Caffè, Via Marinare 37.

A large, cool bar with a good *caffelatte freddo.* There are tables across the street that overlook Amalfi's small beach. In business since 1936.

The lemons of Amalfi are the best you will ever taste

DINING

Hotel-Ristorante Santa Caterina, Strada Statale Amalfitana 9, tel. 089/871012, fax 089/871351. American Express, Diners Club, MasterCard, Visa. Expensive.

The entrance to this famous and beautiful hotel, gracious though it is, cannot prepare you for the unusual structure of this place. The hotel is built on terraces on a steep cliff high above the sea, and one encounters garden after garden during the descent to the water. There is an elevator with a glass wall providing views of all of this as you travel down to the pool, which sits just above sea level. This is a veritable garden of lemons, which grow in great profusion on terraces above the pool. I saw some friendly bees in the lemon grove, so I expect that somewhere nearby lemon honey was being made. There is an excellent herb and vegetable garden that provides, among other things, the basil that is used in the *insalata caprese*. It also yields excellent tomatoes, eggplant, *peperoni*, and zucchini. The Santa Caterina became a hotel in 1902 and for many years was a moderately priced paradise for people in the know. In recent years the hotel has upgraded some of its facilities and is now an expensive luxury hostelry that is very popular with honeymooners. If you are traveling on a generous budget, it is a lovely place to stay or at least to come to for dinner.

On a recent visit I decided to have an all-lemon meal that used the amazing lemons that grow in the garden. The dining room is formal, but it is softened by a lot of climbing vegetation and graceful windows with Gothic arch-shaped panes that afford a divine view of Amalfi and the sea. I began with *bresaola con ruchetta con salsa limoncella*, tender slices of *bresaola* with chopped arugula leaves topped with a vibrant lemon sauce. The *tagliolini freschi al limone*, my choice for a primo, was a simple but dazzling pasta dish. Delicate, thin eggy noodles are tossed in a light, lemony cream sauce and garnished with a lemon leaf. Egg is the perfect flavor match for lemon, with the cream and the flour of the noodles serving as supporting players. The dish is served with a vol-au-vent that absorbs extra sauce and is suffused with lemon. Next came *spigola* (sea bass) in a perfect lemon sauce served with steamed greens and routine potato croquettes. Dessert was a light, lovely lemon sorbet that is a perfect resolution of the meal. An excellent espresso is served (of course, without lemon peel). One does not have to do an all-lemon meal, as I did, because there are many other fine dishes as well, but if you eat at the Santa Caterina you should not miss the *tagliolini freschi al limone*.

Da Gemma, Via Fra' Gerardo Sasso 9, tel. 089/871345. Closed Wednesday and January 15–February 15. American Express, MasterCard, Visa. Moderate to moderately expensive.

Good fish and seafood. I am especially fond of the *tubetti con la pescatrice*, pasta in a monkfish sauce. For dessert, consider the *torta di limone*, using wonderful Amalfi lemons.

Cantina San Nicola, Salita Marino Sebaste 8, tel. 089/8304549. Closed Friday and between January and February. All credit cards. Moderate.

Good rustic food, including *caponata*, *crespolino* (pasta dough rolled with ricotta), fresh anchovies, cheeses, and *sfrucculata* (dried figs filled with walnuts and wild fennel).

FOLKLORE
Regatta Storica.

One of the most exciting and beautiful folkloric events in Italy. On the first weekend of June each year, as they have for centuries, boatmen from the ancient maritime republics of Amalfi, Genova, Pisa, and Venezia compete. The regatta is held in a different one of these four cities each year. Check with the tourist office for information (tel. 089/872619 or 871107). Hotel rooms will be hard to come by.

FOOD STORES
Antichi Sapori di Amalfi, Piazza Duomo 39. American Express, MasterCard, Visa.

You can buy a superb *limoncello* here. It is made by hand: women peel each lemon that will be infused with alcohol. All liqueurs are also bottled by hand. The store makes liqueurs from other fruits (including oranges, apricots, and tiny strawberries) and from herbs (basil, fennel seed). There are also honeys, jarred fruits, and *passolini* (figs or raisins and nuts wrapped in orange or lemon leaves).

Cooperativa Amalfitana Trasformazione Agrumi, Via Salita Chiarito 9.

A whole range of products, including jams, preserves, candies, and liqueurs, is produced from the lemons, citrons, oranges, tangerines, and more unusual citrus fruits that grow in the hills above Amalfi. The *limoncello* is excellent.

Nicola Anistasio, Via Lorenzo d'Amalfi 32.

A nice old store (with an ancient compass on the ceiling) that sells *passolini*, all sorts of pasta, and good hazelnuts. There are also olives, local cheeses, and sacks of beans and grains. Above all, there are wonderful bags of herbs and spices. The oregano is worth taking home even if you buy nothing else.

MUSEUM

Museo della Carta, Via Valle dei Mulini.

Open 9–13h, 17–19h. Closed Sunday and Monday.

The museum documents the history of papermaking in Amalfi and includes ancient prints, books, and manuscripts. (There are two shops on Via Fiume—Cavaliere and Amatruda—where paper is still made by hand.)

Atripalda (Avellino)

DINING

Valleverde, Via Pianodardine 112, tel. 0825/626115. Closed Sunday and in August. All credit cards. Moderate.

Delicious antipasti with vegetables and cheese precede pastas with eggplant or tomatoes. Soups are also very good, and the wide range of grilled meats makes ordering a *secondo* a pleasure.

WINE

Casa Vinicola Mastroberardino, Via Manfredi 87, tel. 0825/626123. Call before coming for tasting and purchasing.

The Mastroberardino winery is the foremost in Campania and perhaps all of southern Italy. Antonio Mastroberardino is one of the finest wine makers in Italy,

and his Taurasi reds are among the best anywhere. He also makes other reds, as well as seven different whites. The cellars have been in use since 1720 and were devastated in Second World War and again during the 1980 earthquake. Since then they have been restored with the most advanced equipment. Antonio and the rest of his family have devoted themselves to rediscovering and cultivating grape varieties that are native to Campania but had virtually disappeared. In 1952 Antonio found two abandoned wild vines with the Fiano grape and produced thirty bottles. He gradually brought it back, and Fiano is now a popular variety in Campania. A very unusual product from this house is the *passito di Aglianico*, a memorable dessert wine.

Battipaglia (Salerno)

MOZZARELLA CHEESE

Battipaglia is the center of some of the foremost mozzarella-cheese making in Italy. As you come toward town you will see white water buffalo grazing. There are many fine producers in Battipaglia.

Valtusciano Latticini d'Autore, Via Strada Statale 18—kilometer 75.6, tel. and fax 0828/300333.

A small, dedicated producer with excellent cheese, making 400 kilos each day.

Benevento

Enoteca deiVini del Sannio e della Campania, Piazza Guarrazzi 4, tel. 0824/ 47845. Open 9:30–13h, 16:30–20:30h; closed Monday.

Exhibition, information, tasting, and purchase of the wines of the province of Benevento (many of ancient origin) and of the region of Campania.

Nunzia,Via Annunziata 152, tel. 0824/ 29431. Closed Sunday and mid-August. All credit cards. Moderate.

While there is good meat to be had here, I have had splendid meals based entirely on beautiful pasta, cheeses, and vegetables.

Capri (Napoli)

Capri (pronounced KAH-pree) has been a playground for two thousand years, ever since Tiberius decided that this garden of earthly delights was the place to build his villa. The wine of Capri, light, fresh, and simple, seems to put everyone in the mood for love. People enjoy swimming in its grottoes and under the large rocks called the Faraglioni. There are two towns, Capri and Anacapri, and other communities such as Marina Grande, Marina Piccola, Damecuta, Punta Carena, and Migliara. The town of Capri is the center of activity and is full of hotels, boutiques, restaurants, shops, discos, and private villas. It is often said that on a summer's evening anyone who is anyone in Italy can be found on the tiny Piazza Umberto I. On my most recent visit,Valentino was staging a fashion show in the square that was being telecast directly around the country. Anacapri is quieter, though just as pretty, and has long been a destination for gays—especially writers— from Scandinavia, Germany, Austria, and for members of the Italian film community. The whole island is geared to recreation and tourism, so you should come here for pleasure and beauty rather than quiet and solitude.

La Capannina,Via delle Botteghe 14,Capri, tel. 081/8370732,fax 081/ 8376990. Reservations recommended. Open March 15–November 10; closed Wednesday (except in August). American Express, MasterCard,Visa. Moderate to moderately expensive.

Antonio and Aurelia de Angelis serve many delicious dishes here, among them ideal *calamari fritti, ravioli alla caprese* (delicate pillows filled with mozzarella and topped with a light tomato sauce), perfect *gnocchi alla sorrentina, spaghetti con le zucchine* (zucchini, basil, and delicate olive oil), *coniglio alla caprese* (rabbit cooked with vinegar and herbs, especially rosemary), and an *insalata caprese*, in which a tomato is partially sliced and then basil leaves and slivers of mozzarella are inserted in the openings. In the bread basket are good *taralli*, small crunchy rings seasoned with fennel.

Al Grottino, Via Longano 27, Capri, tel. 081/8370584. Closed Tuesday, January 20–March 20, and November 10–December 15. American Express, MasterCard, Visa. Moderate.

Good food.

La Rondinella, Via Orlandi 245, Anacapri, tel. 081/8371223. Closed Thursday in low season and in February. American Express, MasterCard, Visa. Moderate to moderately expensive.

A delightful restaurant with good, flavorful food and wine.

Da Gelsomina, Migliara, tel. 081/8371499. Closed Tuesday in low season and first two weeks of February. American Express, Diners Club, Master Card, Visa. Moderate.

Delicious food and fabulous views— Gelsomina is *molto simpatica*. The restaurant is a thirty-minute walk from Anacapri.

FOOD SHOPPING

Caseificio Isola di Capri, Via Roma 38, Capri.

Good mozzarella to make your own *insalata caprese*.

Capri Natura, Via Vernotto 5, Capri.

Vaguely a health-food store, but more a place to buy foods made from the fruits and vegetables of Capri. The marmalades made of lemons, citrons, oranges, and tan-gerines are unbeatable.

Sfizi di Pane, Via delle Botteghe 4, Capri.

Superb breads of all types, especially those flavored with olives, cheese, garlic, sage, sesame, or almonds.

Rosticceria–Pasticceria Scialapopolo, Via delle Botteghe, Capri, tel. 081/8370246.

All manner of cheese, *salami*, cakes, and prepared foods for picnics or if you want to skip restaurant dining.

ICE CREAM

Gelateria Buonocore, Via Vittorio Emanuele 35, Capri.

Delicious cream ice creams such as chocolate and various nut flavors.

LEMON PRODUCTS

Limoncello di Capri, Via Capodimonte, Anacapri, tel. 081/8372927.

One of the best *limoncelli* is made here, using only Capri lemons that have not received any chemical treatment. Lemons and other citrus fruits are also used to make candies and to blend with chocolate. There is a lemon marmalade that is a wonderful thing to take home. They also make herbal liqueurs and tonics.

Cava de'Tirreni (Salerno)

LIMONCELLO

Maurizio Russo produces an excellent *limoncello*, one of the best I have tasted. It remains very fresh in the mouth and has no bitter aftertaste. He calls it Elisir di Limoni. Look for it locally or in Napoli.

Foglianise (Benevento)

FOLKLORE

Sagra del Grano, tel. 0824/871008.

In mid-August a wheat festival is held, including a procession with floats made of straw, dances, music, and folk costumes.

Fontanarosa (Avellino)

FOLKLORE

Festa dell'Obelisco di Paglia,
tel. 0825/475003.

An ancient harvest ritual is reenacted in mid-August, with a thirty-meter (almost one-hundred-foot) straw obelisk constructed in the piazza serving as the focus of the celebrations.

Ischia (Napoli)

Ischia is one of the most important spa destinations in Italy, particularly famous for its mud cures. The attractive parts of Ischia are elsewhere than the port, Ischia Porto, which is geared to the lowest common denominator of tourism and is the place where most visitors stay. The port is full of hotels that offer mud treatments, and you might consider a package arrangement of meals, lodging, and cures if those are your interest. Many Germans come to Ischia for a week or two each year under this arrangement, but have very little contact with the food and culture of the island. This is not helped by the blasé tourist office, which hands out brochures without taking much interest in what the visitor is after. For example, the people in the office have absolutely no idea about the food and wine specialties of Ischia. To appreciate Ischia, travel to other towns on the island such as Lacco Ameno and, particularly, Forio. The dialect on Ischia has many words in common with the pure language of Georgia (south of Russia), although it is not clear how this came to pass.

BAKERY

Pasticceria Ciro Testone, Via Buonocore,
Ischia Porto, tel. 081/992374.

Has good *sfogliatelle* and cookies.

BARS, PASTRIES, ICE CREAM

Calise, Via F. Regine 25, Forio,
tel. 081/997283.

A nice bar with an extensive selection of pastries and good coffee. The ice cream is less interesting.

Bar Elio, Via Schioppa 27, Forio. Closed
Tuesday.

A good source for ice cream.

DINING

Da Peppina, Via Bocca 23, Forio,
tel. 081/998312. Open evenings only; closed

Wednesday (except in summer), and December–mid-March. No credit cards. Moderate.

The food is fabulous. Vegetables here are particularly outstanding; tomatoes, beans, eggplant, zucchini, and peppers appear everywhere: as antipasti; on pasta; cooked with fish, chicken, rabbit, pork; and on delicious pizzas. There is also a choice of meats that are carefully grilled.

O Porticciull, Via del Porto, Ischia Porto, tel. 081/993222. Open evenings only. American Express, MasterCard, Visa. Moderate to moderately expensive.

On this touristy island it is hard to find restaurants that avoid touristy food. This place is one of the few dining spots in Ischia Porto where one can taste local specialties. Foremost among these is the *cassuola ischitana*, a *bouillabaisse* made only of shellfish and seafood (no fish).

Aglio, Olio e Pomodoro, Via dello Stadio 67 (Spiaggia dei Maronti in Barano), tel. 081/906408. Closed from late November to Easter. No credit cards. Moderate.

"Garlic, Oil and Tomato" are only the beginning in this trattoria with good preparation of fish and seafood.

Il Focolare, Via Cretajo al Crocifisso 3, tel. 081/902944. Closed Wednesday in low season, part of December, and lunch on weekdays. All credit cards. Moderate.

Owners Loretta and Riccardo d'Ambra make rabbit a specialty and try and serve Ischia food and wines whenever possible.

FOOD SHOPPING IN ISCHIA PORTO

The communal market on I Trav. F. Buonocore (behind Via Roma) is of little interest, but olive lovers should head straight to the shop opposite the market at #7: here are excellent olives, fresh when available, or in oil or brine. The shop also sells very fine capers.

Ischiafrutta, Via Roma 24. Open 8–14h, 16–22h; closed Sunday afternoon.

An excellent selection of high-quality fruits and vegetables and a good choice of wines, vinegars, dried fruits, and liqueurs.

WINE

I have especially enjoyed the lovely Biancolella Tenuta i Frassitelli Casa d'Ambra, a long name for a delicate white (the grape's name is Biancolella), made near the Ischian town of Forio.

Enoteca Perazzo, Via Porto 23, Ischia Porto, tel. 081/991600, fax 081/982981. Open 9–13h, 14:30–23h; closed Sunday morning.

Perazzo has been producing wine on Ischia since 1880, and you can buy its wines as well as those of a few other Ischia producers. It also sells the full line of foods from Ischia Sapori, mostly oil-packed vegetables of high quality. A fine *limoncello* called Lemonis is 32 percent alcohol, while most *limoncelli* are 39 percent. There are lemon jams and honeys, and good olive oils. This is the one place in the port area where you can get a sense of Ischia's food and wine.

Napoli

Fasten your seatbelts! One can stand absolutely still in Napoli and feel like a spinning top. Everywhere you look there is constant motion. *Motorini* (mopeds) speed by on the street while people walk in crazy patterns, hands flying in wild gestures, mouths opening to receive food or make a pronouncement. Hips shake to music, pockets are deftly picked, breasts bounce, fingers scratch private areas, eyes dart. Babies are being coddled, fed, burped, powdered, diapered, and passed from one loving embrace to another. Neapolitans love interaction and may at first strike you as a bit presumptuous, perhaps too intimate, but they thrive on human contact and living in the moment. They may be rather different from what you are used to, but very few of them bite (unless you ask them to).

It is quite unfortunate that Napoli has such a poor reputation, one of organized and petty crime, pollution, chaos, and grinding urban problems. While Napoli is afflicted with many problems, it is also a city of such beauty, excitement, and drama (how many other cities of this size have an active volcano like Vesuvius in their backyard?). Napoli is probably the only Italian city that has its own modern music, and you hear it everywhere, even in the funicular. The city has produced great scholars, doctors, painters, composers, musicians, sex symbols (such as Sophia Loren), and a population that is innately theatrical and resourceful.

The spontaneity and invention of Neapolitans is part of their excitement, which is the sensation Neapolitans prize as much as Romans pursue sensual pleasure. It is true that one must be careful of pickpockets and street crime in this city, but if one is alert and stays away from quarters such as Spaccanapoli and the port at night, there should not be too much of a problem. A walk down the Via Speranzella, which runs parallel to the Via Toledo, will give you a taste of Spaccanapoli if you don't want to venture any deeper. There are excellent fruit and vegetable stands on this street—you can often perceive their fragrance many steps away. There are interesting sights to take in along the way, and you can always head back to the Via Toledo if you have had enough. To get a sense of Napoli, walk on important thoroughfares such as the Via Chiaia, the Via Toledo, and the Via Partenope. Also visit Vomero, a delightful neighborhood that is a funicular ride (as in the song "Funiculi, Funicula") from the Via Toledo.

BAKERIES

Pasticceria Pintauro, Via Roma 275, tel. 081/417339. Closed Tuesday.

A very old and famous place in Napoli, not far from the funicular. Its founder was Don Pasquale Pintauro, the prince of eighteenth-century Neapolitan pastry bakers.

This is *the* destination for *sfogliatelle.* These were made in two forms: a softer version that was favored by the Bourbons who occupied Napoli two hundred years ago and the crunchy version that is more famous. The crunchy *sfogliatella* was favored by hunters who took it with them to the woods. It kept fresher longer than its softer cousin. They topped it with sugar, which preserved it further. A variation is the classic *coda d'aragosta* (lobster's tail), a longer *sfogliatella* filled with pastry cream and cherries. At Easter, be sure to try *pastiera*, a typical Neapolitan sweet often flavored with orange. Pasticceria Pintauro is small and unassuming, with a simple gray marble counter.

Pasticceria Scaturcchio, Piazza San Domenico Maggiore 19, tel. 081/5516944. Closed Tuesday.

A wonderful sweet shop serving the Santa Chiara district of Napoli since 1920. It is very exacting in the selection and use of ingredients. Hazelnuts must be from Avellino, walnuts from Sorrento, almonds from Nola, chestnuts from Calabria, and pine nuts from San Rissola near Livorno in Toscana. These go into good ice cream and delicious pastries. Scaturcchio is famous for its Torta Ministeriale, a patented cake containing chocolate, hazelnuts, and loads of rum. You can also drink real almond milk *(latte di mandorla)* which in most places is made of an artificial syrup and water.

Pasticceria Bellavia, Via L. Giordano 158, Vomero. Closed Thursday.

The family that operates this bakery is from Palermo, which has an excellent baking tradition. It might be interesting for you to taste flavors here and compare them with Neapolitan flavors. The *cassata* and cannoli are specialties. There is also good ice cream, especially the strawberry.

Moccia.

See "A Walk on the Via Chiaia and Beyond," below.

Luigi Caflisch & Co.

See "A Walk on the Via Chiaia and Beyond," below.

BARS AND CAFFÈ

Gran Caffè Gambrinus, Via Chiaia 1/2, tel. 081/417582.

The most famous *caffè* in Napoli and perhaps all of southern Italy. Founded in 1860, it is still the place where *napolitani* come to debate politics over excellent coffee. Every writer, journalist, actor, musician, and intellectual who lives in Napoli or is passing through must make an appearance here. Outside, one might see spontaneous demonstrations in favor of or against a cause, an idea, or an individual, or perhaps an equally spontaneous performance by a musician or actor. I have never seen a mime here—the people of Napoli are too verbal to have much sympathy for someone defining space without words.

Gran Caffè La Caffettiera, Piazza Vanvitelli 10B, Vomero. Closed Sunday.

An elegant *caffè* on one of the most elegant piazzas in the city (where the Napoli subway takes you when you want to visit Vomero). Although this *caffè* opened in 1987, it feels much older and more established. There are outdoor tables and three fine rooms within for taking coffee, tea, and pastries. In a separate alcove you will find a white baby grand piano.

Bar-Tavola Calda-Pasticceria-Gelateria Mario Daniele, Via A. Scarlatti 102–104–106–108, Vomero. Closed Tuesday.

A large, busy neighborhood institution in which to buy cakes and fine candies, a half kilo of coffee beans, have a drink, breakfast, or lunch. The food is just okay, but there are delicious pastries, such as the *crostatina al gianduia*. The place has a good local atmosphere.

Bar Augustus, Via Roma 147, tel. 081/5513540, closed Sunday, or Via Petrarca 81 A/B, tel. 081/7694782, closed Monday.

A combination bar-*pasticceria* with a small *salumeria* and a *tavola calda* in the back that offers a few ready-made dishes. It makes a superb *latte di mandorla* that is rich in almond flavor but not in sugar.

Gran Caffè Cimmino.

See "A Walk on the Via Chiaia and Beyond," below.

Luigi Caflisch & Co.

See "A Walk on the Via Chiaia and Beyond," below.

Moccia.

See "A Walk on the Via Chiaia and Beyond," below.

BOOKS

Napoli is a great center of literature, culture, and scholarship and as such has many good used and antiquarian books. In the Quartiere San Giuseppe, off the Piazza Gesù Nuovo, the Via Domenico Capitelli (whose name changes to Via Maddoloni) is a great source for old books, many about the food and wine of Campania.

CHOCOLATE

Gay-Odin, factory at Via Vetriera (can be visited), stores at Via Chiaia 237, Via Roma 291, Via Roma 427, Via V. Colonna 15B, Via Luca Giordano 21, and Via Cilea 189.

Gay-Odin is an old company that produces some of the best chocolates in Italy. It is best known for a dry chocolate truffle called the *cicocí*, but you should let your desires be your guide.

Luigi Caflisch & Co.

See "A Walk on the Via Chiaia and Beyond," below.

COOKING SCHOOL

Il Peperoncino, Via del Parco Margherita 1, 80121 Napoli, tel. 081/425705.

Cooking school, family style. Michi Ambrosi is a famous food personality in Napoli, and she has engaged her husband and eight children in operating the cooking school and the catering service she owns. Come here to learn Neapolitan classics: pizza, pasta sauces based on tomatoes, seafood cookery, vegetables, and wonderful desserts and baking. Classes are given from October through June, and prices are moderate. Even if you do not understand the language, it is great fun to watch and learn.

DAIRY PRODUCTS

Soave, Via Scarlatti 130, Vomero. Closed Sunday.

It all starts with a cow. This shop is known for its dairy products: milk, fresh mozzarella, yogurt, the best-loved ice cream in Vomero, and ice-cream cakes.

DINING

Ristorante Megaris (Hotel Santa Lucia), Via Santa Lucia 175 (corner of Via

*Partenope), tel. 081/7640511. All credit
cards. Moderately expensive.*

"Megaris" was the original name of the settlement on which the famous old Castel
dell'Ovo sits across the street from the Hotel Santa Lucia. This is an elegant hotel restaurant, but the prices are not excessive for
the very good food served in a refined setting. An excellent tasting menu, called "Antichi Sapori di Napoli," reproposes the
flavors of the *cucina povera* of centuries ago.
Many good dishes based on the Neapolitan
tradition are on the regular menu, too. I particularly liked a delicious appetizer called
tignaniello, a small crock in which white
beans, clams, tomatoes, and other flavors
are cooked together. The *linguine all'imperiale* is with mixed seafood, made interesting by the addition of a judicious amount of
curry that exalts the flavors of the seafood
without coloring it. The *orata*—that great
Mediterranean fish—comes with a light
crust of bread crumbs and ground almonds.
Contorni are good, the wine list contains the
best of Campania, service is very good, and
the coffee and *limoncello* are excellent.

*Ristorante Mimì alla Ferrovia, Via Alfonso
d'Aragona 21, tel. 081/5538525. Closed
Sunday and in mid-August. American
Express, Visa. Moderate to moderately
expensive.*

Good, well-prepared Neapolitan classics in
this well-known restaurant not far from
the train station. The soups, such as *pasta e
ceci* and *pasta e fagioli,* are wonderful, the
pasta is good, and so is the fish. Service is
warm and friendly, too.

*Osteria della Mattonata, Via Giovanni
Nicotera 13 (just up from the Piazza Santa*

*Maria degli Angeli in Quartiere San
Ferdinando). Closed Sunday. Moderately
inexpensive.*

This place is what you would imagine a
small Neapolitan eatery to be like. There
has been a restaurant on this site since the
early 1800s. As you enter, the kitchen is in
full view. There are six tables flanked by
benches and a few chairs—thirty places in
all. The walls are covered with blue and
white tiles. Wine is served in pitchers made
of Vietri ceramic (unless you purchase a
bottle from the collection assembled on
three-tier shelves on the walls). There are a
couple of photographs here and there of beloved Neapolitans, such as the comic actor
Totò. There is music playing, mostly by local singers from the 1950s and 1960s, that is
alternately upbeat and soulful but always
about love. The food is classic Napoli—
pasta al pomodoro or soup with chickpeas or
beans. Then come pork chops, *polpettone*
(meat loaf), cooked vegetables, mozzarella,
and salads. All are delicious. At the end of
the meal the waiter brings you a piece of *torrone* and a soft amaretto cookie to munch on
as you sip a glass of Frangelico. Peppino is
your animated host.

*Osteria Donna Teresa, Via Kerbaker 58,
Vomero, tel. 081/5567070. Open 13–16h,
20–24h; closed Sunday. No credit cards.
Inexpensive.*

A little gem left over from another era. As
Vomero has become somewhat exclusive,
this *osteria* represents a different Napoli. It
has been in the family for a century and is
now operated by Anna and Gigione, a
beaming, enthusiastic couple who take
pride in what they do. The walls are covered with sand-colored tiles, and there are

nine simple tables for diners. In one corner is a small glass shelf with family pictures and religious icons. The kitchen is in view in the rear, and a framed menu hangs on one wall. The prices are so low that you'd think they had framed an old menu, but these are today's prices. Anna and Gigione (the name means "Big Louie") welcome a local clientele that likes the food because it reminds them of old-style Neapolitan home cooking. For a *primo*, ask for *pasta al forno*. What will come is *maccheroni* in fresh tomato sauce with cheese and whatever meat and vegetables are available at the time. That is, if some braised beef, a meatball, some eggplant, peppers, basil, and zucchini are left over from yesterday's meals, that's what you'll get in your baked pasta. The *secondo* will be the tender cooked meat of the day and more vegetables. The wine, in an unlabeled bottle, will taste right with this food. Dessert will be fruit. In my case, I was there during peach season, so I was given a slightly bruised peach that most other places would seldom serve. I began to slice it, and Gigione came over and told me I should peel it and then cut it into chunks. He said I should put the chunks into the wine glass and pour wine over it, drink the wine, pour more in, then eat the peach chunks, and finish the operation by drinking the rest of the wine. A memorable dessert indeed! The peach was also brimming with flavor, and when I observed this, Anna and Gigione proudly told me that all of the fruit, vegetables, and wine are produced at a small farm they own near Caserta. This peach variety is known as *percoca* and is particular to Campania. It has a darker flesh than usual and is very sweet. *Percoca* in Neapolitan slang also refers to a voluptuous, pretty young girl. My

delight in this meal was shared by all the regulars who were surprised to see a newcomer in their beloved little dining place. In typical Neapolitan fashion, I went from being a solo diner to a member of the family. Because Anna and Gigione don't have a coffee pot, when all the diners have finished their meal, they go around the corner (with the restaurant's owners) to the Caffè Mexico at Via Scarlatti 69 for a delicious coffee. My meal at Osteria Donna Teresa felt like I was spending the afternoon in a private home, and I remember the experience with great fondness.

Ciro a Santa Brigida, Via Santa Brigida 73 (just off Via Toledo), tel. 081/233771. Closed Saturday in July and August, Sunday, and August 15–30. American Express, MasterCard, Visa. Moderately inexpensive to moderately expensive.

Since 1932, this place has served excellent pizza and other Neapolitan specialties. The *pizza d'oro,* made with fresh tomatoes, fresh *mozzarella di bufala,* and fresh oil, should be your gold standard for what pizza should taste like. The fish, seafood, meat, and vegetables are all delicious. This is a very pleasurable restaurant in the city center, close to the Teatro San Carlo.

Osteria da Tonino, Via Santa Teresa a Chiaia 47, tel. 081/421533. Reservations essential. Open for lunch year-round 12:30–16h and October–May for lunch and dinner. No credit cards. Moderate.

Since 1880 this place has faithfully offered classic Neapolitan dishes, especially *pasta e ceci* (chickpeas), *pasta e cavoli* (cabbage), and *pasta e lenticchie* (lentils). *Secondi* are particularly strong in meat dishes. Before he became famous, Enrico Caruso used to eat pasta and beans here. There are 180 wines to choose from.

Vecchia Cantina, Vico San Nicola della Carità 13, tel. 081/5520226. Closed Sunday evening, Tuesday, and August. All credit cards. Moderate.

Cucina napoletana verace is served at this trattoria near Piazza Carità, and everything is delicious.

DINING ON PIZZA

Prices in *pizzerie* are inexpensive to moderately inexpensive.

Antica Pizzeria Brandi, Salita Santa Anna di Palazzo 1–2 (just off Via Chiaia), tel. 081/416928. Closed Monday.

Since 1800 pizza has been made in Brandi's wood-burning oven. It is said that the classic *pizza Margherita* was invented here in 1889, in honor of Queen Margherita. A note arrived from the queen's residence at Capodimonte on June 11 of that year: "*Pregiatissimo Sig. Raffaele Esposito (Brandi): Le confermo che le tre qualità di Pizze da Lei confezionate per Sua Maestà la Regina vennero trovate buonissime.*" ("Most prized Mr Raffaele Esposito: I confirm that the three types of pizza you made for Her Majesty the Queen were found to be excellent.") And thus was a reputation made, for the pizzas at Brandi were considered fit for a queen.

Ciro a Santa Brigida.

Some of the best pizzas in town. See "Dining," above.

Pizza in Napoli is baked in wood-burning ovens

Lombardi a Santa Chiara, Via Benedetto Croce 59, tel. 081/5520780. Closed Sunday. Port' Alba, Via Port' Alba 18 (near Piazza Dante), tel. 081/459713. Closed Tuesday. American Express, MasterCard, Visa.

Founded in 1830, and serving excellent pizza ever since. The only drawback is that if you sit outdoors, the roar of the motorcycles will drown out conversation.

Gorizia, Via Bernini 29, tel. 081/5782248. Closed Wednesday and in August.

This restaurant owes its unusual name to the celebration of an Italian military victory at Gorizia in Friuli in 1916, during the First World War. Gorizia is also the name of the house's special pizza, made with chunks of tomato, artichokes, and Parmigiano-Reggiano cheese.

Da Michele (also called Pizzeria Condurro), Via Cesare Sersale 1 (near Piazza Amore), tel. 081/5539204. Closed Sunday.

The figure in the neon-lit case is Sant' Antonio Abate, the patron saint of bakers.

Di Matteo, Via Tribunali 94 (near San Lorenzo Maggiore), tel. 081/455262. Closed Sunday and fifteen days in August.

Napolitani in the Pignasecca market

Capasso, Via Porta San Gennaro 2, tel. 081/456421. Closed Tuesday and fifteen days in August.

Acunzo, Via Cimarosa 60, tel. 081/5785362. Closed Sunday and in August.

FOLKLORE
Festa di San Gennaro, tel. 081/418744.

On September 19, a miracle is thought to happen when the powdered blood of San Gennaro suddenly turns to liquid. A week-long feast with street parties, processions, and abundant food.

FOOD MARKET
On the Via Pignasecca and the Piazza Pignasecca in the Quartiere Monte-calvario is a joyous, pulsating market. To visit this area, start ideally at the Piazza Carità on Via Toledo, walk past the newsstand, and work your way up the Via Pignasecca. Wherever you walk, people carry things on their shoulders or on their heads: fruit crates, ice, a refrigerator, a platter of food. Stores compete with street vendors for your attention, and proprietors will call out to you to make sure you know that their product is superior. Rather than giving you a store-by-store guide, I suggest that you devote a good hour to walking up and down the street to notice details: fish being cleaned; fruit being artfully stacked; cheeks and hooves of calves and pigs being sprayed with water to keep them fresh. Note the quiet and orderly arrangement of goods at Gelopesca (#32) and Flor do Caffè (#33) as compared with the colorful chaos all around. See the breads stacked in the window of the *panificio* at #20 and the *uova da bere* (eggs for drinking) at the chicken-and-egg store (#19). Next to the

Salumeria G. Russo on the Piazza Pignasecca is a small shrine to the Madonna Addolorata: notice how women stop to have a spirited discussion with the icon, and then perhaps leave money or a bottle of wine as an offering. Look closely and you will see photographs left by relatives of people who are sick, dead, or in serious trouble. Even with all the churches in Napoli, some people prefer to worship on the street.

ICE CREAM
Gelateria Remy, Via Ferdinando Galiani.

In business since 1919 and at the present location since 1954. Giuseppe d'Angelo and his daughter Anna Corradini make some of the best ice cream in town

Soave.

See "Dairy Products," above.

Pasticceria Bellavia.

See "Bakeries," above.

MUSEUM
Museo Nazionale della Ceramica Duca di Martina, Villa Floridiana, Vomero, tel. 081/5788418. Open 9–14h, Sunday 9–13h; closed Monday.

Campania has always made fine ceramics and some delicate china. With the arrival of the Bourbon king Charles in Napoli in 1734, there was a demand for fancy porcelain. In response to this need, the royal factory at Capodimonte was created in 1743, and its style and work subsequently influenced porcelain making in France, Spain, and Germany. This museum is one of the foremost collections of porcelain china, tea and coffee sets, and ceramics in Europe. On the upper floor, in room 5, for example, make note of the case of cups and saucers with various motifs, including castles, landscapes, courtiers, golden dueling swordsmen, trees, mosquitoes, moths, butterflies, flowers, and dancers. Room 6 (the rooms here are not numbered in a logical sequence, so you need to look for identification) has cups and saucers designed with a veritable menagerie: mallards, wild boars, cows, hunting dogs, lapdogs, sheep, goats, lions, and jackals. In room 3 (the last room), notice the oval-shaped teapot of cobalt blue, white, gold, and flaming orange that depicts what must be an eruption of Mount Vesuvius. Note, too, the golden lioness that is a handle to lift the lid of the teapot. Other rooms have work from France, Germany, and other countries that offer contrast and comparison. On the lower floor there is an extensive collection of Renaissance ceramics from Toscana, Deruta, Faenza, Venezia, Urbino, Casteldurante, Pesaro, Napoli, and Palermo. There is also crystal and glass from Venezia, Bohemia, and France.

SPECIAL STORES
Aurea, Via Vittoria Colonna 15C, tel. 081/421178. American Express, MasterCard, Visa.

Expensive, elegant, very beautiful objects in silver, crystal, ceramic, and china. Much is of exquisite taste—items purchased here will be cherished.

La Lampada di Aladino, Vicoletto Belledonne 15, tel. 081/411550. Closed Saturday and Sunday. Credit cards coming soon.

An antiques shop with old Neapolitan coffee sets, English tea sets, antique herb jars, and canisters, all in excellent taste.

A WALK ON THE VIA CHIAIA AND BEYOND

The Via Chiaia is one of the most charming and historic thoroughfares in the city, and you can get a good sense of part of Neapolitan life by traversing it. Most stores are closed on Thursday afternoon and Sunday. Start at the historic Caffè Gambrinus at #1 and walk. Note that the numbers run up on one side of the street and down on the other, so that #251 is almost at the same place as #1.

#251: Buonocore Latticini di Agerola.

Mozzarella from one of the best producing towns in Campania.

Walk past Salita S. Anna di Palazzo (unless you want to stop for a pizza at historic Pizzeria Brandi).

#94: Codrington.

A very old store that has sold spices, soaps, biscuits, and items from England such as jams, syrups, and teas. This store is an interesting artifact of a long-lost time when things English were considered a paragon of style and grace for a certain segment of the population. Nowadays this is an object of interest rather than a place where you might consider buying something Italian.

#143: Luigi Caflisch & Co.

Since 1825 this concern has made chocolates and Neapolitan pastries. It is particularly renowned for its *zeppole*. This is also a spacious bar and tearoom popular with the white-glove set.

Via Gaetano Filangieri 13: Gran Caffè Cimmino.

An old *caffè* with nice pastries that is actually a popular place for tea.

As the Via Chiaia ends, turn right, and when the street forks, go left. Just steps beyond is the Piazza Giulio Rodinò, where one finds the good all-purpose Salumeria Menichiello. Then proceed to the Via Cavallerizza a Chiaia.

10A: Mancini.

An absolutely plain and quite wonderful housewares shop that is worth a visit.

11A: Polleria Balsamo.

Good-quality chickens for sale raw or roasted. The *pollo arrosto* is delicious.

A few doors down is Salumeria Nuovo Fiore, which not only has hams, *salumi*, and cheese, but also wines, French pâtés, and other delicacies imported and domestic. Turn on Vicoletto Belledonne.

15: La Lampada di Aladino.

See "Special Stores," above.

18: Enoteca Belledonne. American Express, MasterCard, Visa.

Since 1960 this has been a source for wines from Italy, France, and California. It also sells *vino sfuso* (wine direct from the producer) that is decanted from small barrels.

Go back up to the main street, turn left, and keep walking to reach the Via San Pasquale.

31: Gastronomia Arfè.

A chic, refined *gastronomia* more like one would see in Mantova, full of hams and cheeses from the north. There are also Campania cheeses and good prepared vegetables.

21: Moccia. Closed Tuesday.

This place is a must on your visit to Napoli if you are interested in the city's

baking. A splendid *pasticceria, gelateria,* and *panificio* since 1936. You can have a coffee at the bar with all sorts of pastries, including exemplary *sfogliatelle, zeppole* and *coda d'aragosta con crema chantilly.* The *torte foreste* (flavored with strawberry, chocolate, or lemon) are beautiful cakes that look like waves or drapery. Moccia also makes a delicious *pastiera,* the Easter classic that is now available in all but the hottest months, when it is made only to order. When the late Pope John Paul II visited the city for any events, the bread and pastries for his visit always came from Moccia.

Walk hack to Gastronomia Arfè and look across to Osteria da Tonino (see "Dining," above).

WINE

Enoteca Belledonne.

See "A Walk on the Via Chiaia and Beyond," above.

Nerano (Napoli)

DINING

Taverna del Capitano, Piazze delle Sirene 10, tel. 081/8081028. Closed Monday plus Tuesday lunch (except in high season), Christmas, and most of January and February. All credit cards. Moderately expensive.

Delicious food and wine in a delightful seaside setting. Grazia Casa, the cook, makes delicious *torte rustiche* with

artichokes, zucchini, and other vegetables; homemade bread; and wonderful fish-based *antipasti.* The black-and-white *paglia e fieno* pasta is succulent; the fish-filled ravioli are delicate pillows of flavor. For a *secondo* you select a fish from its icy bed, and it will be grilled, baked, or cooked in *acqua pazza* (a water scented with tomato, garlic, and herbs). There are some rooms here if you want to spend the night.

Ponte (Benevento)

DINING

Trattoria Frangiona, Via Ocone 12, tel. 0824/874054. Closed Wednesday and early September. All credit cards. Moderately inexpensive.

WINE

Azienda Agricola Ocone, Via Monte c.p. 56, tel. 0824/874040, fax 0824/874328.

Domenico Ocone makes some of the best wines in Campania. He specializes in native varieties, many of which are difficult to find. My favorite is the Taburno Falanghina, a white wine with a green-gold color that has a fragrance reminiscent of Strega liqueur. The wine has a nice balance of acidity, sweetness, and grape flavor and has a pleasingly long and persistent finish. Another intriguing wine is the Taburno Coda di Volpe, an ancient, very rare white that is rich in flavor and has a taste a bit like a liqueur. The most popular white is the Taburno Greco and there is also a spirit, *distillato di Falanghina*, made from the same grape. Signor Ocone produces reds as well and makes an interesting sparkling wine largely from red Aglianico grapes that is very good once you get used to the unusual, slightly mushroomy fragrance.

Paestum (Salerno)

COOKING SCHOOL

Cook at Seliano, Tenuta Seliano, Capaccio-Paestum, tel./fax 0828/ 723634; in the US, tel. 718/7832626, www.arthurschwartz.com ("Cook at Seliano" section); seliano@agritur-ismo-seliano.it (for the agriturismo).

Limited to twelve people, with sessions in spring, late summer, early fall, and the week between Christmas and New Year. Custom dates available for groups of six or more. Gastronomic tours without hands-on cooking are also available.

Someone named Arthur Schwartz might not immediately suggest an expert on the food of Campania, but Arthur's legions of fans (and I count myself in that number) adore his book *Naples at Table* and admire his wonderful talents as a cooking teacher. This six-day course includes three half-day, hands-on cooking sessions in the kitchen of Baronessa Cecilia Bellelli Baratta's water-buffalo farm. You also are led to all kinds of food treasures and private homes in Campania and visit the sublime fifth- and sixth-century BC Greek temples of Paestum. Students are housed at the elegant *agriturismo* and enjoy excellent meals there and elsewhere.

Positano (Salerno)

Positano is indeed a beautiful little town, but its praises have so often been sung that it is now full of expensive boutiques and hotels and many tourists. It has long been a hangout for artists, writers, and so-called beautiful people. Tennessee Williams liked to come here, and Franco Zeffirelli has a villa above the sea. There is a small community of people who worked in the Italian film and fashion industries in the 1950s and 1960s who try to maintain a semblance of what *la dolce vita* was all about. These people may not be immediately apparent to you, but they live a sensual and pleasurably decadent life nonetheless.

BAR-BAKERY

Bar La Zagara, Via dei Mulini 8.

The best pastries and ice creams here are based on the flavors of lemon and other citrus. Good coffee, too.

COOKING SCHOOL

Hotel le Sireneuse, Via Cristoforo Colombo 30, tel. 089/875066.

You can take one-day classes in Neapolitan cuisine from chef Alfonso Mazzacano during November, December, February, and March at this famous and beautiful hotel. Advance arrangements are necessary.

DINING

La Cambusa, Piazza Vespucci 4, tel. 089/812051. Closed most of January. All credit cards. Moderately expensive.

This restaurant is an old standby for fish and the fresh flavors of vegetables, fruit, and cheeses.

Da Adolfo, Spiaggetta di Laurito, tel. 089/875022. Open daily in the warm season. No credit cards. Moderate to moderately expensive.

For a delightful trip back to the days of *la dolce vita*, go down to the small harbor of Positano and look for a little rowboat with DA ADOLFO on its sign. Climb in, and you will be taken farther down the coast to a little beach. This is something of a hangout for the artistic types from Roma who came to Positano around 1960 and set up a colony. They are all older now, a bit bored, and living very much in a different era. It seems that each one has had an affair with everyone else at some point or another. Some of their children have become part of the scene; many more have rebelled by seeking degrees in medicine, law, and business. Many people come to Adolfo and to the other restaurant down the beach for most of the day. The simple dishes are the best, such as *spaghetti al pomodoro* and grilled fish. There are two things not to miss if they are available. Start your meal by having fresh mozzarella melted on a lemon leaf—it is a taste you will never forget. At the end of the meal, have fresh peaches cut into wine. The reason to go to da Adolfo is not so much for the food, although it is fine, as to discover a little part of Italy that most tourists don't even know exists.

WINE AND SPIRITS

I Sapori di Positano, Via dei Mulini 6.

A good source for *limoncello*, made by the proprietors from their own lemons, and for wines.

Ravello (Salerno)

Ravello is the place I go when I am seeking complete relaxation. Even when the town is full of tourists, you can find a place for yourself. The gardens of Ravello, such as Villa Cimbrone and Villa Rufolo, are small paradises of beauty and tranquillity. The latter was the model for the second-act setting of Wagner's *Parsifal*. The composer wrote, upon seeing the Villa Rufolo on May 26, 1880, "I have found the enchanted gardens of Klingsor." In Ravello one delights in the wonder of nature, the limpid air, the caressing sun, and the relative absence of vehicular traffic. Such is the silence here that one morning, as I slept in the Hotel Parsifal, I was awakened by the sound of a ferocious argument that a couple was having *in the next valley*. There were no other sounds to interfere. For much of the year Ravello has concerts featuring top-notch musicians, so that the night air is filled not only with perfume but with music too. The local wine, called Ravello, is honest and pleasant, and the food here all tastes as if it has been pulled from a garden ten minutes before you eat it. Many of the hotels require that you take at least a half pension, so for your other meal you should dine at Cumpa' Cosimo or take a picnic as you go for a hike in the surrounding hills. It is inadvisable to plan an overnight stay in Ravello without hotel reservations. It is a small town with limited space. If you cannot locate accommodation, consider sleeping in Amalfi and journeying up here by day.

Ravello (Salerno)

BARS

The little bars of Ravello all have outdoor tables that are perfect places to pass the time of day.

Bar Santo Domingo, Piazza Duomo.

A popular gathering spot in this little town. Jacqueline Kennedy was a frequent patron here for granita and coffee during her beloved visits to Ravello. The piazza has a market on Tuesday morning, except in August.

Bar Klingsor, just off Piazza Duomo.

Bar Calce, Via Roma 2.

CULTURE

Ravello has a remarkable number of high-quality cultural events for a town with 2,500 inhabitants. The highlight is the music festival in July, but there are important events throughout the year. Tickets for all of these events may be booked by fax: 089/858249 or 089/857711.

DINING

Trattoria Cumpa' Cosimo, Via Roma 42, tel. 089/857156. Closed Monday, November–March only. American Express, Visa. Moderately inexpensive to moderate.

This is one of my favorite restaurants in Italy, one where I have happily dined for twenty years. Much of the reason for this pleasure is Netta Bottone, an Anne Bancroft look-alike who is the guiding spirit of the place with her warm smile and sure

Ravello

hand in the kitchen. As you dine, Netta comes forth from the kitchen, a flower in her pulled-back hair, to delight in your pleasure. You will taste all the dishes you think of as Italian food, yet here they taste as they are supposed to—light yet full of flavor. Years ago I visited the family farm in nearby Scala. There was her father, Cosimo, for whom the restaurant is named. They taught me to make mozzarella, and wine with my feet. They also slaughter their own meat and make their own sausages, one with pepper, pork, fennel seed, and cheese that is grilled and served with lemon. The farm is full of fruit, vegetables, and herbs that are used in the restaurant's kitchen. If you cannot decide which pasta to order, you might opt for the *piatto misto della casa,* with seven types of pasta. One

Da Salvatore, Via Boccaccio 2, tel. 089/857227. Closed Wednesday, November–March only. American Express, Visa.

A splendid view and a lovely garden complement very good food in this likable restaurant.

SPECIAL STORES

Ravello Gusti e Delizie, Via Roma 28, tel. 089/857716.

Giovanni and Rosa opened their store in 1991 to offer the best flavors of Ravello, in-cluding many items made with local lemons. There is excellent *limoncello*, lemon vinegar *(aceto aromatizzato al limone)*, lemon honey (made, I'm told, by Ravello's police officer), and lemon-scented candles and soaps. There are excellent pastas, including *cazzetti*, phallic noodles for the sybaritic readers of this book. You can also buy local Ravello wines, as well as many of the better wines made throughout Campania. There are many vegetables preserved in olive oil *(sott'oli)*. Look for *pomodori a piennolo*, which are tomatoes hung outside homes to dry slightly and intensify the flavor. They are served fresh, chopped, and tossed with oil and pasta. A special dessert is *passolini*, orange or lemon leaves stuffed with raisins or figs.

I Giardini di Ravello, Via Civita 14, tel. 089/872264.

Good *limoncello* and *sott'oli*.

WINE

Vini Episcopio, Via Toro 28, tel. 089/857244.

Casa Vinicola Gran Caruso, Via della Marra 13, tel. 089/857141.

These are two major producers of Ravello wine, which comes in white, rosé, and red.

Salerno

Salerno is not without its interest, yet for most people it represents the gateway to the southern portion of the Amalfi Coast. But its *lungomare*, the strand along the shore, is a nice place to take a walk before proceeding to your next destination.

DINING

Vicolo delle Neve, Vicolo della Neve 24, tel. 089/225705. Open Thursday through Tuesday evenings; closed mid-August and Christmas. All credit cards. Moderately inexpensive.

Splendid Campanian dishes, plus pizza. (For lunch, go to Il Brigante, Via Fratelli Linguiti 4, tel. 089/226592.)

FIGS

La Cilentana, Via Roma 120.

Although stuffed dried figs are a specialty of Calabria and other zones farther south, Salerno has this excellent shop in which to buy figs filled with various nuts and sometimes covered with chocolate. This is a good taste sensation if you have somehow tired of lemons. (How could you?)

Sant'Agata sui Due Golfi (Napoli)

DINING

Don Alfonso 1890, Corso Sant'Agata 11, tel. 081/8780026, donalfonso@syrene.it. Closed Monday and Tuesday (for lunch only in high season), Christmas, from mid-January to early March. All credit cards. Expensive.

This well-known restaurant near Sorrento is one of the best in southern Italy. It is in a beautiful setting with views of the sea below and the Bay of Napoli beyond. As Don Alfonso 1890 also has three attractive suites to stay in, this is a delightful if pricey option for the traveler who wants to feast on delicious food and sleep in a lovely spot. Livia and Alfonso Iaccarino and family take great pains to make the visitor happy. Livia is the smiling sunny blond; Alfonso has silver-black hair, a moustache, and memorable blue-gray eyes. The fragrances of their garden full of vegetables and herbs are a great stimulant to the appetite. I liked the *terrina di olive*, black and green olives in aspic with wild fennel leaves; fabulous *ravioli di caciotta* with fresh tomato-basil sauce; and *pesce in acqua pazza*, a preparation of fish steamed in water with tomatoes, capers, garlic, and herbs. Not to be missed is the superb *sorbetto di limone di Punta Campanella*. The lemons in this part of the world are some of the finest you will ever taste. An ancient wine cellar has an excellent selection. I drank a delicious Biancolella Tenuta i Frassitelli from Ischia.

Sorrento (Napoli)

BAKERY

Pasticceria Pollio, Corso Italia 172.

Excellent *sfogliatelle*, some filled with cream or topped with good cherries.

DINING

Sant'Anna da Emilia, Via Marina Grande 62, tel 081/8072720. Closed Tuesday (except in summer) and November. No credit cards. Moderate.

Better-than-average food in a charming though touristy town.

Telese Terme (Benevento)

SPA-HOTEL

Grand Hotel Telese, Via Cerreto 1, tel. 0824/940500, fax 0824/940504. MasterCard, Visa.

Telese is one of the most famous spas in southern Italy. The water is a bit sulfurous, but its properties have been praised for centuries. The Grand Hotel Telese, which opened in 1876, used to be a place for titled royalty, but it soon became a destination for Italian movie stars, the royalty of the postwar era. Sophia Loren and Vittorio Gassman made films here, and many other stars took the waters as well. The hotel has beautiful gardens, pools, and a good, moderately expensive restaurant.

Torrecuso (Benevento)

DINING AND ICE CREAM
Trattoria-Gelateria Sweet Garden, Via Collepiano, tel. 0824/874862. Closed Tuesday. No credit cards. Moderate.

At first sight this place does not seem like a source for special food and excellent ice cream. The *gelataio* (ice-cream maker) is Carminuccio. He makes an excellent Strega ice cream and also pours cold Strega on *fiordilatte* (a milky ice cream). Other good flavors include *cacao olandese* (Dutch chocolate), *caffè*, and pistachio. The restaurant has excellent *spaghetti all'arrabbiata* (spicy tomato) or with *aglio e olio* (garlic and oil). Good *insalata caprese*, delicious *sott'oli*, lamb, veal, and pork. There is also perfect grilled eggplant. Pizza is served in the evenings.

Vietri sul Mare (Salerno)

CERAMIC
In 1700 in little Vietri there were fifty kilns where ceramics were fired. Until 1800 many ceramists worked right by the sea so that their handiwork could dry in the sun and then be loaded onto ships destined for markets all over the country. The town is still famous for its ceramics, which are sold all over Italy and in fancy stores around the world. Vietri's main square is full of stores selling plates, vases, bowls, tureens, tiles, and so on. Some of these are of great beauty, but because there is so much to choose from, one can become overwhelmed. So look carefully and try to envision the item by itself in the place where it will be displayed. Vietri ceramics are part of daily life here and reflect the needs of the kitchen and the colors of sea and sun of the Mediterranean. So they may not be as elegant as those from Faenza or Deruta, but they give pleasure just the same. In Raito, the town up the hill from Vietri, is a nice ceramics museum (Il Museo della Ceramica; take a bus from Piazza Matteotti in Vietri, tel. 089/211835) with four centuries' worth of ceramics. Some good ceramic shops are the following:

Romolo Apicella, Piazza Matteotti 166, tel. 089/211680.

There are very nice motifs using Amalfi Coast lemons.

D'Amore, Piazza Matteotti 164, tel. 089/210504.

Pinto, Corso Umberto 127, tel. 089/210271. No credit cards.

Francesco Raimondi Ceramiche, Via Diego Taini, no telephone.

Solimene, Via Madonna degli Angeli, tel. 089/210243.

DINING
La Sosta, Piazza Matteotti. Moderate.

Good local food.

Tagliolini al Limone
Tagliolini *with Lemon Sauce*

This recipe is adapted from the dish served at the restaurant of the beautiful Hotel Santa Caterina in Amalfi. Ideally, you will have lemons of the quality of those that grow on the hotel's grounds: large, with a slightly stubbly peel and brimming with seductive fragrance. Failing that, get the very best lemons you can, preferably ones with a thicker peel than that of the usual juice lemons. One possibility is the Meyer lemon from Northern California. The portions for this dish make it a light *primo.* If you want a fuller portion, double the amounts of the ingredients.

Serves 4

2 large lemons
250 grams/½ pound De Cecco tagliolini
4 tablespoons unsalted butter
80 milliliters/⅓ cup light cream
2 tablespoons freshly grated Parmigiano-
*   Reggiano*
Pinch of minced fresh parsley

Set a large pot of cold water to boil. Wash the lemons, carefully scrubbing the peel to remove any blemishes. Peel the lemons, cutting the rind into very thin strips. Squeeze all of the juice into a measuring cup. Remove any pits. Once the water reaches a boil, toss in a pinch of salt. When the water returns to a boil, add the *tagliolini* and cook according to the package directions until al dente. As the pasta cooks, melt the butter in a heavy-bottomed skillet and then add the lemon juice and rind. Let it evaporate for 2 minutes and then add the cream and heat gently over low heat (do not boil). When the *tagliolini* are cooked, drain well and add them to the pan. Top with cheese and parsley, toss quickly to combine the ingredients, and serve.

Wine: A white such as Ravello, Ischia, or Lacrima Christi.

Granita

This classic dessert arrived with immigrants to the United States and became a corruption known as Italian ice. This is the real way to make granita, using two of the great flavors of Campania—lemon and coffee. Because the taste of the granita will be affected by any flavors in the water you use, I recommend a very clean, neutral bottled water such as Evian.

Serves 4 to 6

Granita di Caffè

225 milliliters/1 cup cold water
115 grams/½ cup granulated sugar
450 milliliters/2 cups (16 ounces) freshly
*   brewed espresso*
Freshly whipped cream (optional)

Granita di Limone

450 milliliters/2 cups cold water
230 grams/1 cup granulated sugar
225 milliliters/1 cup freshly squeezed lemon
*   juice*

Boil the water and sugar in a 2-quart saucepan over moderate heat. Stir only until the sugar dissolves. The water and sugar should boil for 5 minutes and then should be removed from the heat right away. Add either the coffee or the lemon juice (depending on which granita you are making) and then pour the mixture into a shallow bowl (preferably of metal) or perhaps an ice tray with the divider removed. Place the bowl or tray in the freezer. Every 30 minutes for the next 4 to 5 hours, stir the granita, detaching the little crystals of ice that might form and plowing them back into the mixture. In Italy the texture of granita varies from a smooth, slushy ice to one that is firmer. Make the granita to suit your taste. Serve immediately. (If you are making *granita di caffè*, many Italians like it topped with whipped cream, although I do not.)

Cook's Note: After making granita the first time, you might decide that you will want to use more or less sugar the next time. Adjust according to your preference.

Puglia

Not to Miss in Puglia

LECCE   MARTINA FRANCA *(Classic Town)*

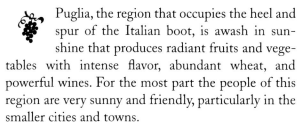

Puglia, the region that occupies the heel and spur of the Italian boot, is awash in sunshine that produces radiant fruits and vegetables with intense flavor, abundant wheat, and powerful wines. For the most part the people of this region are very sunny and friendly, particularly in the smaller cities and towns.

This is the flattest region in Italy. Fifty-three percent of the terrain is plains, another 45 percent is lowlands and low plateaus, and only 2 percent is mountainous. Although there are variations in cooking among the five provinces of Puglia, the region's cuisine is rather uniform in its reliance on the same ingredients. Because Puglia is so flat, communication and transport have never been difficult. The result is that the easy distribution of ingredients to all corners of the region has meant that cooks have had the same foods to work with. But in discovering Puglia's food, history, and culture, bear in mind one important thing: the northernmost province, that of Foggia, is distinct from those farther south (Bari, Brindisi, Taranto, Lecce). Foggia is a historic market town that was the destination of thousands of sheep and people during the *transumanza* (see page 518). It also is thought to be the mainland Italian city with the hottest weather. Foggia is the heart of a formidable wheat-growing zone (called the Tavoliere) that has given food and bread to Puglia for centuries when other southern regions were hungry. The Tavoliere is

REGIONAL CAPITAL:
Bari (BA).

PROVINCIAL CAPITALS:
Brindisi (BR), Foggia (FG),
   Lecce (LE), Taranto (TA).

TOURIST INFORMATION:
Assessorato al Turismo,
   Regione Puglia,
      Corso Italia 15,
      70123 Bari,
      tel. 080/278111.

Agritourism:
Associazione Agriturist
   Regionale,
      Via G. Petroni 23,
      70124 Bari,
      tel. 080/365025.

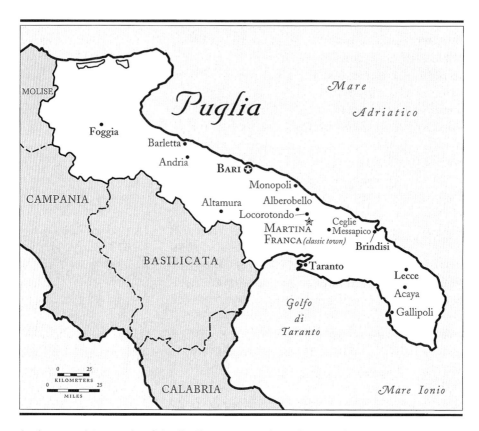

the largest plain south of the Po River in northern Italy and is traversed by rivers that flow down from the Apennines in Molise and Campania. The wheat fields of Foggia—especially near the town of San Severo—were landing stages for Allied planes that did battle in Campania, Lazio, and elsewhere farther west during World War II.

Foggia is essentially a meat and cheese town, while the rest of the region relies more on fish and seafood. Part of the reason is that almost twenty-four centuries ago, a community of shepherds was driven out of Arcadia in Greece, and they found their way to what is now Foggia. Many died during the voyage, and the survivors were very suspicious of the sea. As they were not capable fishermen, they created a meat-eating tradition that was distinct from the native peoples (the Apuli) who adeptly exploited the sea for food. Foggia is also different because it uses a lot of garlic in its kitchen. As you travel farther south in Puglia, onion gradually replaces garlic as a flavor in many dishes. By the time one reaches Gallipoli in the very deep south, the onion becomes a protagonist in dishes such as *zuppa di pesce*. There are two types of onion in Puglia's cuisine, the familiar sweet ones but also small ones that are bitter.

The soil of the provinces south of Foggia is rich in limestone (Foggia's is not), which gives particular flavor to the fruits, vegetables, and legumes that grow there. All of the sunshine serves a special function in the local cuisine. Everywhere you look during the hot months, people will have wooden boards placed in the sun to dry fruits and vegetables. These ingredients are stored for cooking in other seasons. Many are kept in their desiccated states, while others are packed in oil *(sott'olio)* or vinegar *(sott'aceto)*. When tomatoes are in season, families gather to chop them, make sauce, and then put it in jars with a few leaves of basil. You will also see tomato sauce spread on wooden boards to bask in the sun. This forms tomato concentrate the way it was made once upon a time, which is how people in Puglia like it. Women will take their boards into the sun to roll out *orecchiette* or one of the other shapes of pasta for which Puglia is famous.

Olives and almonds are central to *pugliese* agriculture and cuisine, and if you like these two flavors you will love the cuisine of this region. One-third of Italian olive-oil production happens in Puglia. The oils range from dense and rich in flavor to exceedingly delicate, making it a popular condiment as well as a cooking medium. In the nineteenth century, much of the olive oil produced in Puglia was shipped to England and elsewhere in northern Europe to power oil lamps and to grease the machines of the Industrial Revolution.

The long Puglia coastline yields a remarkable bounty of fish and seafood, the region's primary sources of protein. Taranto in particular has excellent oysters, mussels, and clams, although pollution has taken a toll. In 1994 there was a severe cholera outbreak in Puglia that serves as a cautionary warning: because of polluted waters almost everywhere in the world, it is a risky proposition to eat raw seafood. While there are a few outposts of cleaner seas, such as those near Iceland and Norway, the Mediterranean certainly is not one. So play it safe and have your seafood cooked to kill bacteria.

Of the southernmost regions of the Italian mainland, Puglia has had the most success in pulling itself up from poverty and backwardness. It has begun to draw visitors, but not nearly in the numbers it deserves. Most of them find their way to the *trulli,* the conical stuctures in and around Alberobello, and to coastal resorts along the coastline. Lovers of the baroque make pilgrimages to Lecce, but most travelers in the region begin or end their trips in Brindisi, where one catches the overnight ferry to Greece. But with its friendly people, delicious food, and abundant history, Puglia should be visited for its own merits.

Eating in Puglia

ANTIPASTI

Puglia has an amazing variety of antipasti, making this one of three regions (along with Piemonte and Emilia-Romagna) where you should include them in your meal. There are all sorts of baked, grilled, fried, or stuffed vegetables and seafood, as well as delicious *salumi* from Martina Franca.

Benedetto. An Easter antipasto in Foggia. It contains hard-boiled eggs (that must be blessed by the priest at mass), ricotta, *salame,* boiled asparagus, and sometimes oranges.

Capocollo. A tender ham from Martina Franca made with wine and peppercorns.

Cervellata. A slender sausage from Martina Franca made either with veal and pork or just pork. It is seasoned with red wine and pepper.

Panzarotti. Fried breads filled with vegetables, cheese, or meats.

Tarantello. Salted, preserved tuna.

PRIMI

Foggia eats a particular pasta, *troccoli,* which are like the *abruzzese maccheroni alla chitarra.* They probably arrived during the *transumanza,* the cultural and economic phenomenon that was a major influence in Foggia's growth. The rest of Puglia eats *orecchiette* (also called *recchietelle*), little ear-shaped pasta. *Orecchiette* are made of 80 percent semolina and 20 percent winter wheat, often from Canada. Large pasta factories make them by machine, but many people in Puglia make them by hand on a wooden board. You can often see this being done, because in warm weather people like to do it outside. *Orecchiette* are slightly concave so that they can contain cheese or sauce. There are many other styles and shapes of pasta that are peculiar to Puglia, including *lagane* and *laganelle* (sheets of pasta), *strascinate, chianchiarelle, pociacche, mignuicchie, fenesecche,* and many others. You will also see *cavatelli* (also called *cavateddi*), which are popular in much of the south.

Vegetables are the most popular ingredients for pasta sauces. These include *cime di broccoletti* (broccoli florets), cauliflower, eggplant, arugula, chickpeas, chicory, fava beans, and turnip greens *(cime di rapa).*

Ciambotto. A mixed fish sauce for pasta, a specialty of Bari.

Ciceri e Tria. Strips of fried pasta, served with chickpeas. A recipe of ancient origin that is a specialty of Lecce.

Frisella. A small hard roll soaked in a bit of water, then dressed with olive oil, salt, and fresh tomatoes.

'Ncapriata (or *Fave e Cicoria*). A fabulous dish that is positively addictive. This is a combination of cooked chicory and pureed fava beans, all flavored with olive oil. The *pugliesi* tell you that Hercules drew strength for his labors from fava-bean puree, but I think he ate it because it tasted so good.

'Ncapriata alla Martinese. Instead of chicory, the fava-bean puree is served with boiled *lampasciuni* (bitter onions).

Sagne 'Ncannulate. A long pasta with sauce and very strong ricotta. A specialty of Lecce.

SECONDI

Cozze Arrancanate. Mussels cooked with bread crumbs, garlic, oil, parsley, and tomato. A specialty of Taranto.

Gnemeridde. Lamb innards cut into strips or balls and cooked with Pecorino and
various spices.

Quagghiaride. An ancient shepherd dish found mostly in the province of Foggia,
made with sheep's stomach filled with chicken giblets, *scamorza* cheese, eggs,
and *salame.* It is baked and then served with boiled arugula. *Gnemeridde* and
quagghiaride are thought to be of Greek origin because there are almost identical dishes in the areas of Greece from where the ancestors of the people of Foggia came.

Polipetti Baresi. In Bari, when baby octopus are caught, they are immediately
beaten against rocks and then shaken in a basket to make their tentacles curl.
They are boiled and served with oil and lemon or cooked in a spicy tomato sauce.
When the dish is called *casseruola di polipetti,* it has a special sauce of olive oil, onions, white wine, pepper, parsley, and fresh tomatoes.

Spiedo Martinese. Skewers with lamb, goat, veal, and sausage cooked over a fire
that burns oak logs. A specialty of Martina Franca.

Tiella (Tiedda). The name means "baking dish." Many dishes bear this name and
are in fact casseroles containing meat or fish, vegetables, potatoes, and sometimes cheese. You will see this word on many menus. In Bari, for example, a
tiedda is made with rice, potatoes, and mussels.

Triglie di Scoglio. Rock mullet, a fish much prized in Polignano. When it is
grilled, the skin dissolves into a red liquid, which makes for an unusual natural
sauce.

Turcinieddhi. Rolls of lamb's liver, heart, and lung.

CONTORNI

In addition to all the usual vegetables found in the southern Italian kitchen, there
are additional ones that are frequently seen in Puglia. These include *fenecchiedde*
(boiled fennel cooked with oil, garlic, and anchovy fillets that are traditionally
eaten in Bari on Christmas Eve), *lampasciuni* (tiny bitter onions), *marsciuli* (bitter
greens), *paparuli* (peppery mushrooms), and *sinepi* (mustard greens).

FORMAGGI

This region makes excellent cheeses, including ricotta, *scamorza,* provolone,
Pecorino, and *caciocavallo. Cacioricotta* is aged ricotta, used for grating. There is
also a mozzarella made from the milk of water buffalo in northern Puglia, especially Andria, but it is not easy to find. The one cheese you absolutely must try is
burrata. It is round, with a shiny exterior. Handle it with care, because when you
cut into it, a rich cream will come out. Dip the skin into the cream and you will

have one of the great taste experiences. It is said that the shah of Iran used to send jets to Puglia just to bring *burrate* back to Tehran. The best are said to come from Castel del Monte.

BREAD

Pane. The hearty loaves of Puglia, especially of the town of Altamura, are well known. In a *pugliese* home, the bread is treated with respect and occupies a central place in the kitchen. There is a superstition that a loaf should always be right-side up and that it is both unlucky and disrespectful to turn a bread upside down.

Pane Purecasciu. A bread from Lecce made with oil, onions, and tomatoes.

Puccia. A bread from Lecce made with pitted black olives.

Puddica. A focaccia-type bread served with tomatoes, garlic, oil, and oregano.

Taralli. Little round breads with a hole in the middle. They can be as tiny as crackers or the size of a small loaf. They are frequently flavored with pepper or wild fennel or, for dessert, with cinnamon.

DOLCI

Although Puglia produces outstanding fruit, especially grapes, the people of this region tend not to eat them for dessert. Instead, they opt for a plate of raw vegetables, including radishes, fennel, carrots, and celery. The one fruit that is a popular dessert is the *mellone.* This is not cantaloupe, but a very sweet watermelon that is native to the region. Taste it if possible.

Cotognata. A specialty of Lecce, this is a sweet that is made when quinces are cooked down to their pulp and form a concentrate that is placed into molds. When it cools, the result is the *cotognata.*

Scarteddate. A Christmas sweet made of strips of dough soaked in white wine and olive oil and then topped with honey and cinnamon.

Bari U Grane Cuotte. On All Saints' Day, a sweet is made with flour, chopped almonds and walnuts, chocolate, citron, cinnamon, pomegranate seeds, and small sugar-coated almonds, all cooked in wine. In Ban this is called *colva.*

To learn more about this region's food, read *The Flavors of Puglia* by Nancy Harmon Jenkins.

The Wines of Puglia

Puglia produces more grapes and wine than any other region, usually about 17 percent of the national total. For a long time, much of the wine was sent to Torino to make vermouth or to France where it was blended to give structure to French wines in the years when the output was thin. When wine was used for vermouth or blending, the preferred type was rich in grape flavor and low in acidity. In recent years, *pugliese* vintners have changed their view and now seek wines suitable for drinking with food. Current *pugliese* wines more effectively balance sweetness, acid, alcohol content, and density. Eighty-two percent of the wine produced is red (a little of this is rosé), and the rest is white. There are twenty-four different DOC designations, several of them named for the towns where they are grown. These include Brindisi, Castel del Monte, and Gioia del Colle (these two are among the nicest), Locorotondo, Martina Franca (a rather charming white wine), Ostuni, and San Severo. Special mention should be made of Salice Salentino, from the Salentine Peninsula in the province of Lecce. It is made primarily with the Negro Amaro grape and is a wine that has gained a following abroad because it represents excellent value for a wine buyer on a budget. There are many restaurants abroad that feature it as their house wine. Some of the best are made by Cosimo Taurino, Conti Zecca and Leone de Castris. Taurino also makes a wine called Brindisi Patriglione, which is one of the best reds in southern Italy. The most famous dessert wine is probably the Aleatico di Puglia, most of which is made in the province of Bari. There is not much of it, but if you find it in your travels, give it a try. When it is *dolce naturale*, it is of moderate sweetness. When it is *liquoroso*, it is made of grapes that have been dried to concentrate the sugars.

Acaya (Lecce)

Acaya was a futuristic, idealized town when it was built in 1535. The castle here is connected underground to that of Carlo V in Lecce, 10 kilometers (6 miles) away. The town jealously preserves its particular look, and the marshes just outside its walls are a protected site of the World Wildlife Fund.

DINING

Locanda del Gallo, Piazza Castello 1, tel. 0832/861102. Closed at lunchtime from May to September. All credit cards. Moderate.

Owned by the Sozzo family. Enzo and Carlo are the artists who did the paintings on the walls of the restaurant. There is a set-price menu whose offerings change daily. You start with abundant, delicious antipasti and go on to good pasta such as *farfalle alla Gian Giacomo* (with *funghi porcini*, three types of sausage, olive oil, Pecorino, *peperoncino*, and onions), or *tubettini con salsa di cernia* (tomatoes and grouper). There might be grilled shrimp or sardines, or delicate pork chops in a light tomato sauce. In typical *pugliese* style, you end not with fruit but with fresh vegetables such as radishes. A delicious dessert is *fagottini della nonna*, a hot pastry filled with hazelnuts and raisins.

Alberobello (Bari)

Twenty or thirty years ago it was the unusual and audacious travelers who found their way to Alberobello to observe the *trulli*, the unique conical structures that top most of the dwellings. Now tour buses trundle through every day, and much of the town has sold its soul to tourism. Nonetheless, the *trulli* deserve to be seen, and I recommend that you stay in Martina Franca and make a day trip to Alberobello, with a stop at Locorotondo *en route*. Alberobello can be mercilessly hot in the summer, which the dark, cooling *trulli* help counteract. You will notice that old men like to take shade under the ten trees that form a triangle next to the *municipio* at the beginning of the Corso Vittorio Emanuele. The trees stand so close and have been pruned in such a way that they form an impenetrable barrier to even the strongest rays of sun.

DINING

Il Poeta Contadino, Via Indipendenza 21, tel./fax 080/4321917. Closed Mondays (except in July, August, September), January 7–31. All credit cards. Moderately expensive.

A fancy eatery in a *trullo*. The restaurant is almost painfully formal for such a rustic setting. The brocaded chairs with designs of birds and flowers and the cardinal-red tablecloths all seem incongruous, as does the moody piped-in-piano-bar-type music. The wine list has top national labels and good bottles from France and the United States, but local wine is poorly represented. Nonetheless, once one overcomes the incongruities, it must be acknowledged that the wine list is indeed excellent, and the menu is promising. The service by black jacketed waiters is attentive to a fault. All the food I tasted was delicious: *burrata* with a *timballo di cicoria selvatica* (a sort of wild-chicory custard) was scrumptious, and the sensational *pureé di fave* with *cicorielle selvatiche* was the best example of this classic dish that I have tasted. *Filetto di capretto al vino rosso*, kid in a red-wine sauce, was also quite fine. Desserts are fancy and draw heavily on chocolate and excellent local almonds. So here is a

The *trulli of Alberobello*

quandary: how much do all the externals in a restaurant contribute to the appreciation of the food? We have an accomplished cook at work here, but all of the surroundings are so studied that it almost takes away from one's ability to concentrate on the good food. A restaurant comparable to this is the Gambero Rosso in San Vincenzo (Toscana). Yet Gambero Rosso's food tastes better because the settings there become a soothing backdrop rather than a protagonist in the meal.

L'Arbatro, Via Monte San Michele 23, tel. 080/4322789. Closed Monday and January 10–30. All credit cards. Moderate.

Vegetable cookery is especially strong here, as is pasta.

FOLKLORE
Città dei Trulli Festival.

The festival of Italian folk music also features tasting of local food and wine. Held on the third weekend of August.

ICE CREAM
Gelateria Arte Fredda, Piazza Girolamo 1. Closed Monday.

While I have had better, less sugary ice cream, the product here is made by hand by the talented and serious Caterina di Pietro. I can heartily recommend the *anguria* (watermelon), *fico* (fig), and *noce di cocco* (coconut) flavors. This is also an attractive shop. The eighteen metal containers of ice cream are each topped with formidable metal domes that look like helmets for Kaiser Wilhelm.

OLIVE OIL
Antico Frantoio, Via Monte Sabotino 119 (in the trulli district). Always open in summer, less often in other seasons.

Try *il mosto*, that is, the oil that comes when olives are lightly mashed rather than pressed. The oil from pressed olives is less interesting.

WINE
Enoteca Puglia, Largo Martalotta 84, tel. 080/721034.

Of the touristy shops near the *trulli*, this one has the best selection of *pugliese* wines.

Altamura (Bari)

BREAD

The bread in Altamura is ranked among the best in Italy. Good sources are Francesco Picerno (Corso Umberto 15), Gaetano Altamura (Via del Carmine 22), Forno all'Antica (Via Giannuzzi 71), Forno a Legna San Giovanni Bosco (Via Gradisca 9), and Forno dei Fratelli di Gesù (Via Pimentel 15).

CAFFÈ
Caffè Striccoli, Corso Federico II di Svevia 73.

More than 150 years old, this is one of the most historic *caffès* in Puglia. It is also famous for its Elisir Nocino, a strong walnut liqueur.

DINING
Tre Archi, Via M. Direnzo 4, tel. 080/ 715569. Open evenings only; closed Wednesday.

The pizza here is excellent, but one can make a great meal from the many vegetable preparations, which vary according to the season.

Andria (Bari)

CHEESE
Caseificio Baffone, Via Sant'Andrea 2.

Exquisite *burrata* is the reason to come here, although all the cheeses are excellent.

DINING
Ristorante La Siepe, Via Bonomo 97, tel. 0883/24413. Closed Wednesday, last ten days in July, and first ten days in August. American Express, MasterCard, Visa.

Be sure to try the *cavatelli con fagioli e cozze,* a delicate mixture of pasta, beans, and mussels. Fish is a good *secondo,* as is grilled local cheese.

FOLKLORE
Sagra della Burrata.

At some point each September this festival honors Andria's wonderful local cheese. At the same time there is the *corteo storico,* a parade in medieval costume.

OLIVE OIL
The area around Andria is heavily planted with olive trees (some more than two hundred years old that still flower), and there are many fine oil producers. Improved irrigation has meant good yields most every year. One oil I tasted that I was particularly enthusiastic about was the Grotte de Angelis *da affioramento* made by Azienda Agricola Liso (Via Gioacchino Poli 62, tel. 0883/81242).

SWEETS
Antica Fabbrica di Confetti Mucci, Via Gammarota 12.

With almonds an essential part of *pugliese* agriculture, it should not surprise you that they form the base of many of the sweets here. Mucci is famous for its *confetti*—there are many historians who think that *confetti* were born in Puglia, although those of Abruzzo are more famous—and the marzipan is excellent, too.

Bari

The capital of Puglia is a busy place with broad boulevards as well as a labyrinthine old quarter called Vecchia Bari or the Città Vecchia. Recently there has been a spate of purse snatchings and robberies in this quarter, and tourists have stayed away in droves, especially at night. City officials have begun to act, but in the meantime it is probably advisable to come to this area with a group or at least to be as inconspicuous a visitor as possible. Bari has some of the best fish and seafood you will taste anywhere, although you should not eat it raw.

CAFFÈ
Caffè Stoppani, Via Roberto da Bari 79, tel. 080/5213563.

Since 1860, the most famous *caffè* in Bari and perhaps all of Puglia. It was here that sympathizers gathered to discuss their participation in the campaigns of Garibaldi for the unification of Italy. In addition to coffee and pastries, there are excellent chocolates.

COOKING SCHOOL

Nouvelle Ecole de Cuisine Bari, Via Amoruso 7, 70124 Bari, tel. 080/513498.

Despite the French name, this school is all Italian, specializing in the cuisine of Puglia, with its wonderful antipasti, vegetables, olive oil, and seafood. Unlike many schools, it is also open in the summer. Classes (in Italian only) are given to beginners and to advanced students, and you can do a five- or six-week course, if you plan to be in the area for a while, that will give you a solid foundation in the cooking of this region.

DINING

Lo Sprofondo, Corso Vittorio Emanuele 111, tel. 080/5213697. Closed Saturday lunch (in July and August), Sunday, and August 9–20. All credit cards. Moderate.

Good seafood dishes include *cozze al gratin* (mussels stuffed with breadcrumbs, a little cheese, and several herbs), *tagliatelle alla vongole*, and grilled fish. In the summer there is air-conditioning, which should appeal to diners who don't suffer heat well.

Terranima, Via Putignani 213, tel. 080/

5219725. *Closed Sunday evening, August. All credit cards. Moderately inexpensive.*

Classic Pugliese cuisine. I love the *pignatino alberobellese*, chunks of veal cooked with carrots.

Al Focolare da Emilio, Via Principe Amedeo 173, tel. 080/5235887. Closed Sunday evening, Monday, August. All credit cards. Moderate.

A lively place in the city center with seafood being the strong suit. In the evening there is good pizza too.

FOOD SHOPPING

Antica Salumenia D.C.A., Corso Vittorio Emanuele 28.

A first-rate store with cheeses, *salumi*, many types of pasta, and bread, including that of Altamura.

WINE

Enoteca Domus, Via de Vitofrancesco 6, tel. 080/5225481. Closed Sunday, Thursday afternoon, and in August.

This *enoteca* stocks many of the great wines of the world, and there is a good selection of jams, chocolates, and sweets.

Barletta (Bari)

DINING

Baccosteria, Via San Giorgio 5, tel. 0883/534000. Closed Sunday evening, Monday, the first three weeks of August. All credit cards. Moderate.

Regional flavors are presented here with care and delicacy, and the results are excellent. Try the *gamberi tiepidi al*

profumo di basilico (basil-scented prawns) and *calamaro gratinato* with ricotta.

Antica Cucina, Via Milano 75, tel. 0883/521718. Closed Monday, January 1–10, June 20–30, November 1–10. Moderate.

The dining room was once a place where olives were pressed to make oil.

Bitonto (Bari)

The almonds and olives grown in Bitonto are considered among the best in the region. There are many candies and pastries made with the almonds at the Pasticceria dei Portici on the Via Repubblica Italiana.

Brindisi

Brindisi is not the most enchanting city in Italy, but it is very well known to back-packers and other travelers on a budget as the place to catch the overnight ferry to Greece. If you are taking this trip, I recommend a good meal on land rather than the fare aboard ship. To wine drinkers, *brindisi* has another meaning, one that is very pleasing: it means "toast." *Fare un brindisi* means "to propose a toast."

DINING

Trattoria Pantagruele, Via Salita di Ripalta 1, tel. 0831/560605. Closed Sunday evening and Monday in winter, Saturday and Sunday in summer, two weeks in August. All credit cards. Moderate.

The *zuppa di scorfano* is a rockfish stew in which the secret flavor is ginger. *Lagane con gli scampi* are broad noodles with prawns. *Alici con scalogno* are delicious fresh anchovies scented with shallot.

WINE

Enoteca Bacco's Shop, Via Masaniello 18, tel 0831/526411. Closed Thursday afternoon and Sunday.

Cosimo Flores, the proprietor, has a knowledge of Champagne, Bordeaux, fortified wines such as sherry and port, and Scotch whisky, thanks to years of experience in the UK. There are also excellent wines from all over Italy, so if you want to pick up a bottle before setting sail, this is the place to do it.

Castel del Monte (Bari)

Famous for its castle, this is also a place with good wines and excellent cheeses.

DINING

Ostello di Federico (near the castle), tel. 0883/569877. Closed Monday, January, and November. No credit cards. Moderate.

Try *strascinete*, wholewheat noodles served with ricotta and arugula. Vegetable dishes are good, too.

Ceglie Messapico (Brindisi)

DINING

Al Fornello—da Ricci, Contrada

Montevicoli, tel. 0831/377104. Closed Monday evening, Tuesday, February 1–10,

September 10–30. All credit cards.
Moderate to moderately expensive.

One starts with a magnficent antipasto that is worth the trip all by itself: *melanzane soffrito* (roasted eggplant), *fior di zucca ripiena* (zucchini flowers filled with cheese), fava-bean purée, *salame*, *peperoni*, breaded cheese balls, and meltingly light, warm *ricotta di pecora*. For pasta you might try *fruseinddati* (longish tubular pasta) with a sauce of tomatoes and arugula. For a *secondo* there is delicious kid, *capretto e fegatino al fornello*.

Cisternino (Brindisi)

DINING
Trattoria dell'Emigrante, Via Regina Elena 8, tel. 080/716821. Closed Thursday. No credit cards. Inexpensive.

This trattoria is called the Emigrant because its owner, Vincenzo Picoco, lived for many years in Switzerland before returning to his native town. The dishes are of peasant origin. For example, the *gnumereddeianche* are rolled tripe cooked in a celery broth. There is a vast selection of antipasti, mostly based on vegetables, many of which seem not even to have names. *Orecchiette* are served with a very spicy tomato sauce. *Coniglio al forno* (roast rabbit) is very special because it is unusually juicy and tender. The wines are as rustic as the food—some are made by Signor Picoco.

Corato (Bari)

Some of the best examples of *burrata*, the wonderful creamy-buttery cheese of Puglia, come from Corato. One source is the Cooperativa Caseificio Pugliese, just out of town, on the Strada Statale 98. It was founded in 1946 and is now one of the top producers in the region. It is particularly famous for its mozzarella. There are several stores in town that sell the cooperative's cheeses.

Foggia

BREAD
Panificio Montrano, Via Isonzo 2.

Excellent breads, pizza, and *taralli*.

COOKING SCHOOL
Ecu Scuola Effetto Cucina, Via La Rosa 6, 71100 Foggia, tel. 0881/70970.

A school popular with young students but lessons are given year-round, and instruction is serious.

DINING
Hotel-Ristorante Cicolella, Viale XXIV Maggio 60, tel. 0881/688890, fax

0881/678984. Closed Sunday, most of August, and December 23–January 6. American Express, MasterCard, Visa. Moderate to moderately expensive.

The leading hotel in Foggia also has what is generally considered the leading restaurant. You can sample good pasta and meat dishes here.

Da Pompeo, Vico al Piano 14, tel. 0881/724640. Closed Sunday, August 15–31. No credit cards. Moderate.

Everything here is about the food, and it is wonderful. Fresh pasta (*troccoli, cavatelli, orecchiette*) topped with vegetables or *pomodorini* and cheese; *lagane* (broad noodles) with *fava purè* and fried onion; *tiella di agnello*, lamb with mushrooms and potatoes; fresh fish; sweets based on divine almonds.

Gallipoli (Lecce)

DINING

Ristorante Il Capriccio, Viale Bovio 14, tel. 0833/261545. Closed Monday (except June 15–September 15) and in October. American Express, MasterCard, Visa. Moderate to moderately expensive.

Maria Negro runs her restaurant with a firm hand and cooks her seafood with a gentle one. The *tubettini con le cozze* is a simple but delicious *primo*, the *pesce alla griglia* is perfect, and all the other dishes I sampled were quite good.

Grottaglie (Taranto)

This city is famous for its pottery. Shops line both sides of the Via Crispi.

Lecce

Here is a city of great beauty and history that was completely forgotten until a British architect, Martin Briggs, arrived there in 1902 and described it in his book *An Unknown City*. Most of Lecce's great buildings were built between 1660 and 1720 in high-baroque style using a golden stone called *pietra di Lecce*. The city is nick-named the "Florence of the South," because of its architectural unity and the studiousness of many of its young people. Although Lecce and Firenze really have very little in common, the city does deserve to be seen if you are in Puglia. In the summer, music and dance performances are held in the baroque palaces and piazzas throughout the city. Not surprisingly, much of the music is from the baroque era.

CAFFÈS

Caffè Tito Schipa, Via dei Fedeli 14 (near Psz. S. Oronzo).

A wonderful *caffè* dedicated to Lecce's famous *tenore di grazia*. You will see artifacts from the singer's career and probably hear old recordings of his while you sip good coffee or a cocktail.

Caffè Alvino, Piazza San Oronzo.

An old *caffè* with an attractive crowd drinking rich coffee and eating excellent *granita di caffè*.

DINING

Trattoria Casareccia, Via Costadura 19, tel. 0832/245178. Closed Sunday evening, Monday, and early September. Master Card, Visa. Moderately inexpensive.

Typical homemade *leccese* cuisine served with love and pride. Vegetables appear everywhere in the menu and you should favor them. I also love the *polpettoni di vitello*, little veal meatballs filled with cheese and cooked with white wine.

Osteria degli Spiriti, Via Battisti 4, tel. 0832/246274. Closed Sunday evening, July 15–31. All credit cards. Moderate.

Similar cuisine to Trattoria Casareccia,

plus excellent *agnello al forno coi carciofi*, baked lamb with artichokes, in springtime.

FOOD SHOPPING

Giuseppe Marazia, Piazza Mazzini 50.

Excellent cheeses: mozzarella, Pecorino, *scamorza, ricotta ascante* (salted and aged).

WINE

Enoteca Caffetteria Carlo V, Via Palmieri 42, tel. 0832/44425. Closed Sunday and Monday. American Express, MasterCard, Visa.

A fine selection of local and national wines and an impressive selection of olive oils from Puglia, Toscana, and Liguria. There are also many local food products.

Enoteca Internazionale, Via Cesare Battisti 23, tel. 0832/302832. Closed Sunday and in August.

Owner Raffaele Rollo knows wine and loves opera, so he is a man of real taste.

Locorotondo (Bari)

A DOC wine is named for the town, which is one reason to come here. Another is the views of the *trulli*, with Martina Franca in one direction and Alberobello in the other. Locorotondo's *centro storico* (the old city center) is certainly worth a look.

DINING

Trattoria Centro Storico, Via Eroi di Dogali 6, tel. 080/4315473. Closed Wednesday (except in summer). American Express,

MasterCard, Visa. Moderate.

All the classic *pugliese* dishes are found here.

Martina Franca (Taranto)
Classic Town

Martina Franca is not only a Classic Town for Puglia but in many ways embodies much of what is fun, joyous, beautiful, and timeless about all of Italy. You are close enough to the famous *trulli* of Alberobello, but you don't feel like you are in a tourist trap. Martina Franca goes about its business, but also makes visitors very welcome, especially during the excellent Valle d'Itria Festival of music and folklore in the summer (tel. 080/4805100; fax 080/4805120; www.festivaldellavalleditria.it).

Although I had been to Martina Franca before, for the research purposes of this book I arrived there at dusk on a day in late June 1994. The city was full of people and animation, and I decided to have a look at the town during the hour of the *passeggiata*. Cars and motorcycles sped around in the streets where they were permitted (much of central Martina Franca is a pedestrian zone). I walked under the arch that leads to the *centro storico* and found myself in the triangular Piazza Roma, one of the most beautiful public spaces I know in Italy. The long leg of the triangle is dominated by the Palazzo Ducale (1668), a dramatic though not overbearingly baroque palace. This is the site of the friendly tourist office. In the center of the piazza is a lovely fountain surrounded by bright green grass. A happily recumbent dog embodied the cool serenity the Piazza Roma evokes. I ventured farther into the quarter, which is very much like an operatic set. The Piazza Plebescito, with its richly baroque church, would make a perfect setting for *Cavalleria Rusticana* even though that opera is set in Sicilia. I have witnessed baptisms, weddings, and funerals in this church, which is the spiritual center of the city. I headed toward Trattoria ai Portici, the restaurant I intended to visit, only to find that it was closed. I walked down side streets all fragrant with delicious cooking smells, but these were in private homes. Nowhere could I find an open restaurant, because Italy's national soccer team was about to face Norway in a World Cup match being played in New York. Having been upset by Ireland in the opening match, Italy had this last major chance to advance to the second round. Everywhere I looked Italian flags hung from windows, and soon this busy town went silent, and streets that were crowded thirty minutes before were suddenly vacant. The nation was watching the World Cup. I, however, had not had lunch after traveling all day to get here. Down a narrow side street I spotted a white light and went toward it. As I drew near, I found a butcher shop, Macelleria-Rosticceria Ricci (see "Dining," below), that grilled its own sausages (for which Martina Franca is renowned) to serve to diners at a few tables in the back. The decor was absolutely Spartan, and the only diners were three Belgians and a multigenerational Italian family. While this is not the sort of place tourists generally gravitate to, it is the real Italy and therefore of interest. I began with pickled local onions, green and black olives, roasted eggplant, a slice of local *salame*, and then tasted various grilled meats that were brought forth from the kitchen. There was a good salad, but my only cavil is the industrial-tasting oil and vinegar that were placed on the table. The waiter encouraged white wine instead of red, and it was decent. This was a very inexpensive meal, with the free entertainment of the nearby family enjoying a night out. As I walked back through the vacant streets under a full moon, I had Martina Franca all to myself—the Piazza Roma was even more astonishing when it was empty and silent.

Under the arch that led from the *centro storico* was a plaque that bore the words of Pope John Paul II, who visited here on October 29, 1989:

Popolo diletto di Martina Franca, accoglie le tue nuove generazioni con costante e coraggiose amore alla vita. Nel fiducioso ascolto della parola di Dio saprai così resistere alla tentazione del consumismo e alla seduzione del secolarismo. . . .

Beloved people of Martina Franca, welcome your new generations with constant and courageous love of life. In faithful listening to the word of God you will thus know how to resist the temptation of consumerism and the seduction of secularism. . . .

The seduction of secularism was very much present two hours later, when, at midnight, Italy claimed a 1–0 victory over Norway. Suddenly the Piazza XX Settembre filled with hundreds of cars, motorcycles, and bicycles, all circling the piazza, honking horns, waving the Italian colors, and singing victory songs. People from eight months to eighty years took part in the festivities, which were peaceful and joyous. That happy Italian family at dinner was a microcosm of the city of Martina Franca, whose 45,000 souls manage to find festivity in sacred and secular contexts.

BARS AND CAFFÈS

Caffè Derna, Piazza XX Settembre 4. Closed Tuesday.

This octagon-shaped bar-*pasticceria* at the portal near the Piazza Roma is a good place for breakfast. The coffee and pastries are excellent. The specialty is *bocconotti*, pastries shaped like mandarins' hats filled with fresh ricotta or *amarena* (sour cherry).

Caffè Tripoli, Via Garibaldi 9/10. Open 6–14h, 15–22h; closed Thursday.

Opened in 1911 and named for the capital of Libya, which at that point was being conquered by Italy. Excellent *granita di caffè* and people watching.

Bar Carriero, Piazza Roma 9. Open until 0:30h; closed Wednesday.

The reason to come here is the excellent *torta rustica*, which is not the tall quiche-like pie one sees in Liguria, but rather a puff pastry filled with different ingredients. It comes from a nearby baker (the bar's owner wouldn't reveal the source) and is delicious, especially if you get one that is newly delivered and piping hot. I had one with ricotta, mozzarella, and a touch of tomato—delicious, creamy, tangy cheese in delicate pastry.

Bar Adua, Via Paisiello 60 (corner of Corso Italia).

Stop here for a refreshing if rather sweet *latte di mandorle* (almond milk made with fresh almonds) or a *granita di caffè*. There are good creamy pastries, but I particularly liked the *pasticceria secca*, made with almonds, hazelnuts, and other "dry" ingredients.

BREAD

Sfornatutto, Via Lanucara 12–13 (just off Via Paisiello).

A wonderful bread shop. The *pane casareccio* is crunchy and fragrant. There is *puccia di patate* (made of potato flour), *filoni* (long loaves), *panini al burro* ("butter rolls," a very unusual thing for this region), *frise* (popular small rounds of whole wheat that are moistened with water, then dressed with garlic, olive oil, and fresh tomatoes; they also can be made of white flour or barley), *taralli* (made of white wine or milk), and immense loaves from which pieces can be cut. You can get an education on the bread of southern Italy in this store.

Panificio San Marco, Via Vittorio Emanuele 8 (near Piazza Roma).

Taralli of several types, good bread, pizza, and calzone.

CHEESE

Centro Formaggi, Corso Italia 1, tel. 080/8806961.

Shelves from floor to ceiling filled with cheeses of wonderful fragrance and quality. A special shop whose strong suit is aged cheeses.

La Nuova Casearia, Via Paisiello 17.

While Centro Formaggi specializes in older cheeses, this store has excellent fresh cheese such as ricotta and mozzarella.

DINING

Trattoria ai Portici, Piazza Immacolata 6, tel. 080/701702. Closed Tuesday lunch and at some point during the summer. MasterCard, Visa.

Two days after Italy's World Cup victory (see above) was one of the many feast days observed in Martina Franca. From May until the end of August these feast days occur about once a week. This particular day celebrated the hearts of Jesus and Mary. A mass was said at the Duomo, and a huge illuminated image of mother and son was placed near the altar. All day long and well into the night citizens came to pray. This was also a day for weddings: two elaborate celebrations were held in the city, one at the Duomo, the other at the church next to the Hotel Villa Ducale. In the spring and summer a fourteen-sided green-and-white gazebo is placed in the Piazza Immacolata, near the Duomo. The piazza is mostly circular, and 75 percent of it is ringed by graceful porticoes. Here one finds the Trattoria ai Portici, which has outdoor tables. It is often the case that restaurants with good locations are either pretentious or deficient in the kitchen, but here is a happy exception. Service is friendly but unobtrusive, and the food represents the best of local cuisine. The *antipasto locale* is a corrucopia of sausage, *salumi*, cheeses, olives, and vegetables—one portion can easily serve two persons. The *fave e cicoria* is very fine and the *orecchiette alla contadina* is poetry: the pasta is perfectly cooked, and each ingredient—fresh tomatoes, oil, and basil—is an example of how it should taste. The house wine is an easygoing Martina Franca DOC white. On my visit the *secondo* was a *grigliata mista* including veal sausage, chicken livers wrapped in *pancetta*, and various unfamiliar but delicious parts of a lamb; dessert was a delicate lemon sorbet. On the particular day I had this meal, a visiting band from nearby Bracigliano occupied the gazebo to play music as part of the feast day.

These bands travel from town to town to perform classical and local music. Such bands are popular throughout Italy, especially in the south. If you ever see the words AMICI DELLA MUSICA on a plaque, this is often where the band meets. On the other side of the piazza from where I happily dined a crowd listened attentively. Here was an example of the magic of Italy: a beautiful setting, lovely people, great food and wine, wonderful music. The whole experience evoked humanity and served as a reminder that, despite the incongruities and inconveniences that Italy often creates, there is very little that can outshine this nation at its best.

Al Ritrovo degli Amici, Corso Messapia 8, tel. 080/4839249. Closed Sunday evening and Monday (in summer all day Sunday). All credit cards. Moderate.

Wonderful food. Don't miss the *capocollo, frittatine di zucchine, timballo di melanzane,* and so much more.

Macelleria-Rosticceria Ricci, Via Cavour 19, tel. 080/903241. Closed Sunday. No credit cards. Inexpensive.

Good basic food, excellent meat.

Trattoria Renzo Ceci, Via Valle d'Istria 99, tel. 080/705245. No credit cards. Inexpensive.

Although this restaurant is an easy ten-minute walk from the Piazza XX Settembre, the Via Valle d'Istria can be a little desolate at night. While the walk is not unsafe in terms of crime, there is a stretch of road that is without a sidewalk,

and cars race by quickly. So walk carefully, but do not be deterred. From the terrace of this large, friendly restaurant is a splendid view of the Valle d'Istria, the area where much of the bounty is grown. By day this view is of beautiful hills and fields; by night it is an amphitheater of sparkling lights. All the typical local dishes are here: *orecchiette,* fava beans and chicory, lamb, veal and pork sausage, potatoes, salads, good fruit. This is simple fare, well prepared. The wine is Martina Franca DOC. At night, pizza is also made. Service is friendly, if somewhat relaxed. There is no menu; dishes are simply recited.

Pizzeria, Via Vittorio Emanuele 7. Closed Wednesday. No credit cards. Inexpensive.

Good pizzas served at long outdoor tables in a delightful setting. Open quite late on summer weekend nights.

FOLKLORE
Sagra dell'Arrosto.

Under the motto *Mang v'v schirz e r'r* (the local dialect's way of saying "Eat, drink, joke, and laugh"), the people of Martina Franca feast on roast lamb and lamb innards on the last Sunday in August.

Sagra della Porchetta e del Maiale.

The finest pork products in Puglia are made in Martina Franca. On the first weekend of December (the time when historically there would be the slaughtering of a pig by families that had only one), the city holds a festival highlighting the sausages, hams, and *porchetta* of this area.

PASTA

Pastificio Nuova Antichi Sapori, Viale della Libertà (corner of Via Fanelli—en route to the train station).

You can find typical *pugliese* pastas such as *strascinate, orecchiette, cavatelli,* and others. You can buy dried pasta to bring home with you.

WINE

Enoteca Semeraro, Piazza XX Settembre 7. Closed Sunday.

A large good selection of wines from Puglia and elsewhere.

Monopoli (Bari)

BAR

Caffè Roma, Piazza Vescovado 1.

An old, atmospheric *caffè* with good pastries, excellent ice cream.

DINING AND LODGING

Hotel Melograno, Contrada Torricella 345, tel. 080/6909030, fax 080/747908. Closed in February. American Express, Diners Club, MasterCard, Visa. Expensive.

If you are on a big budget, this is one of the nicest places to stay in southern Italy. Set on an ancient *masseria* (agricultural estate) with whitewashed buildings, tropical vegetation, and comfortable accommodations. The food is also quite fine and service is excellent.

Trattoria del Procaccia, Via Ariosto 16, tel. 080/777936. Reservations essential. No credit cards. Moderate.

Owner Stefano Gilberti runs a very popular restaurant near the port where a great seafood meal can be had at very reasonable prices.

FOOD SHOPPING

There is a delightful market in Monopoli in front of the cathedral, open Monday

Bringing in the catch near Monopoli

through Friday 8h to 13h and Saturday 8h to 13h and 17h to 21h. Sellers enthusiastically trumpet the quality of their wares, and you will quicky agree. Between the market and the port is the Quartiere Peugezia, a wonderful maze of streets with good food stores, old bars, and many, many barber shops that seem to be social centers for the men of the town. The port is full of fishermen young and old, many of whom sit in outdoor *caffè*s and *osterie*. Unlike many port towns, Monopoli is very clean and amicable. There are several appealing food shops in Peugezia to look for, including the following.

Forno Santa Caterina, Via Santa Caterina 4.

There is a great tart made of Swiss chard, onions, and black olives, and the many interesting biscuits include *diavolacci* (made with flour, almonds, pepper, clove, and cinnamon).

Salumeria Esposito, Via Magenta 4.

Well known since 1922 for its many good food products, including prepared dishes to take out.

Old fishermen, Monopoli

Lo Sfizietto, Piazza A. Diaz 16m.

This store overflows with good flavors: *salumi,* cheeses, breads, conserves, olives, and jarred vegetables.

WINE
Enoteca Il Tralcio, Via Daniele Manin 33, tel. 080/9301366.

Wines, oils, vinegars, sweets, jams, pastas, crystal, and ceramics.

Ostuni (Brindisi)

AGRITOURISM
Masseria Lo Spagnulo, tel. 0831/333756 or 970209.

About six kilometers (four miles) from Ostuni is this marvelous estate built in 1600 that is now a working farm. There are sheep, rabbit, chickens (and eggs, of course), beans, chickpeas, fava beans, figs, wonderful grapes, cheeses, olives, and wines. You are also very close to the coast (Rosa Marina), so that you can make a nice vacation combining land and sea.

COOKING SCHOOL
Italian Cookery Weeks, Lo Spagnulo (a sixteenth-century castle-farmhouse), just outside Orvieto. (For information contact in the United States Jean Evers, tel. 602/204-2458; in the United Kingdom P.O. Box 2482, London NW10 1HW, tel. 081/208 0112.)

Course are held from May through September, alternating with classes given in Orvieto in Umbria. There are orange and lemon trees, olive oil, cheese, fabulous vegetables, and local seafood, all of which will be prepared during classes. The instructor is Susanna Gelmetti, who teaches in English.

Otranto (Lecce)

DINING

Taverna Leone Marino, Corso Garibaldi 5, no telephone. Closed Monday and October 15–November 15. No credit cards. Moderately inexpensive to moderate.

Unlike most places in this pretty but touristy town, here is food prepared with care and attention, and at moderate prices. I particularly enjoyed the *orecchiette* with ricotta and *peperoncino*. Good seafood, too.

Il Duca d'Aragona, Via Scupoli 32, tel. 0836/801322. Closed Tuesday. Master Card, Visa. Moderate.

Good local food, including *risotto con le seppie*, *spiedino di pesce* (skewered fish), and a delicious *torta di mandorle*.

ICE CREAM

Gelateria Artigianale, Corso Garibaldi 18.

Top flavors include *mandorla* and *fico*.

Polignano a Mare (Bari)

DINING

Grotta Palazzese, Via Narciso 59, tel. 080/4240677. Always open. Visa, MasterCard. Expensive.

This is a special place on many counts. It is set in a natural grotto that is cool and atmospheric and that often reverberates with the sound of musicians engaged to play while you dine. This grotto has been a site of banquets and (occasional) orgies for centuries; the food is delicious, but the activities are now more tame. The seafood is excellent, including the *zuppa di frutta di mare*, the *risotto alla pescatora*, and the grilled *triglie di scoglio*. There are fourteen rooms here, if you wish to use this as a place to stay.

Taranto

Taranto is not, to put it mildly, a place that puts on its best face for the visitor. As one approaches it from any direction, the lush vegetation yields to parched terrain, much of it sullied by industry. Some of the largest oil refineries and steel mills in Italy may be found here, and when the economy is healthy they provide much-needed employment. Most of the town is filled with demoralizingly similar apartment flats. Mangy dogs congregate outside the train station, and, as you walk through the *centro storico*, you will find it run-down but without the raffish animation of similar areas in Palermo, Napoli, or Genova. Taranto is one of the chief ports of the Italian navy, so the town is full of randy young sailors, most of them with lots of energy and no way to expend it. But there is one essential reason to visit Taranto, at least on a day trip. The Museo Nazionale has a stupendous collection of Greek antiquities, as well as artifacts dating back to the Paleolithicera. Because Taranto is so little frequented, you will be able to take in this collection undisturbed by crowds. Among the many things to observe are the gold wreaths, meant to be worn on the head, that represent leaves of ivy. It was thought that a person who wore ivy while drinking wine would not become drunk. In the same room (the Sala degli Specchi) are earrings that represent a bunch of grapes.

DINING

Gesù Cristo, Via Battisti 8, tel. 099/ 4777253. Closed Sunday evening, Monday (except in August). All credit cards. Moderate.

Naming a trattoria for the son of God can make for high expectations, which are for the most part met here. You won't quite walk on water, but you will taste delicious seafood. I particularly like the *tubettini con le cozze*, stubby little pasta with mussels, as well as the *frittura di pesce*, delicately fried fish. Many diners enjoy *pesce crudo* (raw fish) here, but I suggest caution. Not all of us can be resurrected.

Trani (Bari)

BAR

Bar-Pasticceria La Parisienne, Via E. de Nicola (at the corner of Via Bachelet).

A good breakfast place with fresh pastries and strong coffee.

DINING

Antica Osteria del Teatro, Via Statuti Marittimi 60, tel. 0883/41210. Closed Sunday evening and Monday. Master Card, Visa. Moderate.

Excellent vegetable antipasti, good seafood, breads, and cheeses.

FOOD SHOPPING

Lo Sfizio alla Casa del San Daniele, Corso Vittorio Emanuele 95, tel. 0883/583558.

In addition to regional specialties are good cheeses and ham from around the country. Seafood is also especially good, and pasta.

Vieste (Foggia)

BAKERY

Cannarutiz'i, Via Milano 9.

Be sure to try the *cannoli con marmellata d'arance*, made with homemade orange marmalade. Other interesting pastries and candies are a *base di mandorle* (almond-based).

DINING

Enoteca Vesta, Via Duomo 14, tel. 0884/ 706154. Open Easter–end of September, 10–14h, 18–2h. Visa. Moderately inexpensive.

This inviting *enoteca* (set in a grotto) sells wine by the bottle and serves *salumi*, grilled shrimp, soups, vegetables, salads, seafood, grilled cheese.

Fave e Cicoria
Fava-Bean Puree with Chicory

Known in dialect as *'ncapriata,* this is the classic *primo* of Puglia. In many parts of the region the beans are served as is, although I prefer them pureed. To make this an attractive presentation, spoon the puree onto the left side of a shallow bowl and place the chicory on the right to achieve a yin-and-yang look. The diner can then add more olive oil at will and either blend the puree and the chicory or pick at one and then the other.

Serves 4
450 grams/1½ cups dried fava beans
Salt to taste (optional)
4 tablespoons extra-virgin olive oil
450 grams/1 pound fresh chicory (the approximate weight of 1 head)

Wash the beans carefully to rid them of any dirt or foreign matter. Place them in a large bowl, cover them with water, then cover the bowl and soak them overnight. The next day, when the beans have plumped, remove the outer shells and rinse the beans in cool water. Place the beans in a pot, cover with water, and cook over medium heat. When the water reaches a boil, turn down the heat to low, cover the pot, and cook for about an hour. The beans are ready when they can be easily mashed. Remove them from the heat, add a little salt if you wish, and set aside for 15 minutes. Then mash the beans, add the oil, stir (I like to use an eggbeater to fluff the bean puree), and cover. Chop off the base of the chicory, wash the greens well, and separate them. Cook them in a large pot of boiling water for about 4 minutes, then drain them. Serve the puree and the chicory as I described above. Have olive oil available to drizzle on the chicory, if you wish.

Wine: A white or red from Castel del Monte, Gioia del Colle, or Locorotondo.

Spaghetti con il Diavolicchio e Pomodoro
Spaghetti with Hot Pepper, Garlic, and Tomato Sauce

Call the fire department! Some like it hot, and if you are one of those fire-breathing eaters, this is the dish for you. The amount of *peperoncino* you use is up to you.

Serves 4 to 6
Extra-virgin olive oil
1 or 2 peperoncini, minced
2 cloves garlic, minced (optional)
450 grams/1 pound spaghetti or linguine
800 grams (a 28-ounce can) peeled Italian plum tomatoes, preferably San Marzano type, coarsely chopped with all excess liquid removed
Minced fresh parsley, or several torn fresh basil leaves (optional)

You first need to make the intensely flavored oil. Three days before you plan to make this dish, take a clean, dry jar (approx. 2 deciliters/7 ounces—whatever you have available) with a lid that closes tightly. Fill it about three-quarters of the way full with olive oil. Then add the *peperoncino* and, if you wish, the garlic, to the oil. Close the lid tightly and store in a dark, cool place. When it is time to make the dish, set a large pot of cold water to a boil. When it reaches a boil, toss in a pinch of salt if you wish. When the water returns to a boil, add the pasta and cook until al dente. Consult the pasta's package for guidance about cooking time. While the pasta is cooking, pour the flavored oil into a skillet and heat gently (do not boil, and make sure that the garlic does not burn). Add the chopped tomatoes and combine until the tomatoes are warm to somewhat hot and have slightly broken apart. This should not take more than five minutes. When the pasta is done, drain it into a colander, shake quickly, and then transfer to the skillet. Toss well to combine the sauce and the pasta. Serve in pasta bowls, topped perhaps with parsley or basil, and eat immediately.

Cook's Note: Some people add a little grated Pecorino or Parmigiano-Reggiano. To me, cheese flattens the dish and robs it of its power.

Wine: A fresh, delicate white from Castel del Monte, Gioia del Colle, or Locorotondo.

Basilicata

Not to Miss in Basilicata

MATERA *(Classic Town)*

REGIONAL CAPITAL:
Potenza (PZ).

PROVINCIAL CAPITAL:
Matera (MT).

TOURIST INFORMATION:
Ente Provinciale per il
Turismo,
Via Cavour 15,
85100 Potenza,
tel. 0971/21839.

Agritourism:
Associazione Regionale
Agriturist,
Via XX Settembre 39,
75100 Matera,
tel. 0835/214565.

Dalle ringhiere del balcone pendevano e dondolavano pigre al vento le trecce dei fichi, nere di mosche che correvano a sorbirne gli ultimi umori, prima che la vampa del sole li avesse tutti succhiati. Davanti all'uscio, sulle strade sotto agli stendardi neri seccavano al sole, su tavole dai bordi sporgenti, liquide distese color del sangue di conserva di pomodoro. . . . Il grande silenzio della campagna pesava nella cucina, e il mormorio continuato delle mosche segnava il passare delle ore, come la musica senza fine del tempo vuoto. Ma a un tratto, dalla chiesa vicina, cominciava a suonare la campana, per qualche santo ignoto, o per qualche funzione deserta, e il suono riempiva lamentoso la stanza.

From the railings of the balcony, braids of figs hung and swayed lazily in the wind. They were black with flies that ran to drink the figs' last humors before the blaze of the sun sucked them all dry. In front of the door, on streets beneath black banners, liquid expanses of tomato preserve the color of blood dried in the sun on jagged-edged boards. . . . The great silence of the countryside hung over the kitchen, and the continuous murmur of the flies marked the passing of the hours like the endless music of empty time. But suddenly, from the nearby church, the bell started to ring for some unknown saint or for some lonely function, and the sound filled the room mournfully.

—CARLO LEVI, CRISTO SI È FERMATO AD EBOLI

(CHRIST STOPPED AT EBOLI), 1945

The impression most people have of Basilicata, if they have any impression at all, is the one of bleak desolation described by Carlo Levi in 1945 when he published one of the great Italian novels of the twentieth century. Levi, who was from Torino, was among the many Italian Jews and anti-Fascists sent by Mussolini to internal exile in Basilicata. The title refers to the town of Eboli, in southern Campania, and suggests that even Christ would not (or could not) have ventured into this godforsaken region. Levi was first sent to Aliano and then lived in Matera for many years like a stranger in a strange land, finding eloquent words to describe a place a few hundred kilometers and centuries away from the sophisticated cities of the north. Even sixty years later his book reflects some aspects of this relatively impoverished region that is disconnected from the currents of modern life that most other Italians enjoy.

Basilicata is the instep of the Italian boot, bordered by Puglia (the heel) to the east, Calabria (the toe) to the west and south, and Campania and Molise to the north. The region is 47 percent mountains, 45 percent hills, and 8 percent plains and shore, primarily near Metaponto on the Gulf of Taranto and Maratea on the Tyrrhenian. Although it is cut through by four rivers, much of the land is parched and unyielding.

The original name of the region is "Lucania." There are various theories about the origin of this name. It might come from the word "Lyki," the name of the people who came from Anatolia in Asia Minor to settle here around 1300 B.C. The root might also be in the Latin *lucus* (woods) or from the Greek *lukus* or *lykos* (wolf). The Lyki lived inland and had developed a civilized democratic society. The Greeks arrived on the coast in the eighth century B.C. and had colonies for five hundred years in places such as Metaponto. The Greeks were succeeded by the Romans, who dominated the Lyki and all the other peoples living in the region. After the fall of Rome, the region fell into the hands of the Byzantine Empire.

The name "Basilicata" was thought to come from *basileus,* the job of the functionary in the Byzantine Empire who was posted in the area. More recent thought suggests that the name is linked to the basilica in the town of Acerenza. The earliest documentation in print of the name "Basilicata" dates to 1154. From that time until 1932 the region was called Basilicata, when Mussolini ordered that it go by the more ancient Lucania. In 1947, in the post-Fascist era, the region's other name was restored, yet the natives of the region are called *lucani.*

The prevailing impression in recent centuries has been of an impoverished, rural backwater. In the nineteenth century and well into the twentieth, the region was subject to mass emigration, leaving some towns practically empty. Percentually, Basilicata had the highest level of emigration of any Italian region. In fact, 270,000 left between 1945 and 1955 alone. The region now has about 600,000 people, with Potenza and Matera being the only towns with more than 50,000 residents.

One can travel long distances without seeing another person. There is only one train line, the 107-kilometer/65-mile journey from Metaponto to Potenza. Only the occasional bus reaches Matera, and if the driver decides there won't be passengers that day, he won't make the trip. The best way to get to Matera is by the ninety-minute train ride from Bari (the capital of Puglia), or you can drive there if you have a car.

You should not be deterred by the seeming isolation and desolation of Basilicata. The empty spaces can be starkly beautiful and come as quite a change in a nation with high population density. (Italy, with 57 million people, is about the same size as New Mexico, which has fewer than 2 million.) The interest in coming to Basilicata is to feel like an explorer in a new world, even though this is an ancient, nearly forgotten civilization. And Matera, Classic Town for this region, is as singular in its way as is Venezia.

Eating in Basilicata

Needless to say, the cuisine of Basilicata is *cucina povera.* But poor does not equal bad. The cooks of the region took what meager ingredients were available to them and created delicious dishes. With them they drink Aglianico, one of the great red wines made south of Toscana. Historically, meat was eaten only on Christmas,

Easter, at weddings, and on the saint's day for the patron of a particular community. Typically the meat was chicken or rabbit. Sheep were only eaten when they died of old age. The way the lamb was prepared was *cutturiedd,* in which it was cooked very slowly to try to eliminate some of the toughness of the old meat. Every family had a pig each year. If they were too poor to own it outright, they would raise it for a wealthier family and keep half of it (usually the less desirable cuts) at slaughter time. Since ancient times the *lucani* have been skilled at slaughtering pigs and making their meat last as long as possible in different forms. Once upon a time, cured meats were the principal source of animal protein and were eaten in small amounts to make them last for as long as possible. Although Basilicata still ranks among the poorest regions in Italy, many of the cured meats that became specialties now function principally as antipasti.

ANTIPASTI

Lucanica (Luganiga, Laganega, or *Luganega).* The most famous food product of Basilicata, this spiced sausage is renowned throughout Italy, although imitations elsewhere cannot compare with the original. The Roman writer Varro spoke of the local sausage that was consumed by Roman soldiers who were stationed in Lucania. In Lombardia and Trentino it is usually said that the *luganega* that is popular in those regions is an old adaptation of the *lucanica.* Because the Longobards occupied Lucania in the middle of the ninth century, it is possible that these sausages were brought north and took root in Pavia, Milano, Cividale, and other Longobard centers.

Pezzente. The word means "beggars." This is a *salame* made of the less desirable parts of the pig that are not put to other uses. The notion is that these meats are what would be given to beggars. They are finely minced and combined, and do make for a tasty *salame.*

Soppressata. Blood sausage.

Sugna Piccante. Lard flavored with *peperoncino.* It is stored in jars and is used to cook or to spread on bread.

PRIMI

Grano e Ceci. A soup made with chickpeas, barley, and wheat with a touch of oil, tomato, and rosemary.

Lagane. Broad flat noodles. The word's root is similar to that of "lasagne," but these noodles are usually tossed with tomato sauce or with lentils and beans rather than being baked. *Lagane con lenticchie e fagioli* is always eaten on March 19, Saint Joseph's Day, and is offered to the poor.

Maccheroni di Fuoco. This fiery dish is made with *bucatini* tossed with red-hot *diavolicchio* (see page 596).

Minestra Strascinata. A specialty of Potenza, this is square pasta tossed with tomato sauce and aged Pecorino.

Minuich. Short spaghetti with a hole in the middle that are served either with tomato and *cima di cola* (boiled green cauliflower) or with oil and *peperoncino.*

Zuppa di Legumi. A soup of various beans, peas, and chickpeas.

CONTORNI

In this region it is common to serve vegetables after the *primo.* Until recently, this was all that would be eaten, because meat dishes were reserved only for special occasions. Almost every vegetable consumed in Italy is eaten in Basilicata. Look for *lampasciuoli* (local bitter onions) and many local mushrooms, particularly *funghi cardoncelli.* One customary way to serve vegetables is in calzone, a folded savory pastry in which dough is wrapped around cooked vegetables and then baked. Other specialties include *ciammotta* (mixed fried vegetables), *ciaudedda* (fava beans, onions, artichokes, and potatoes cooked in olive oil), and *mandorlata di peperoni* (peppers, almonds, and *peperoncino* stew).

SECONDI

As in much of the rural south, the standard diet is pasta and vegetables, with meat being reserved for special occasions. As affluence has begun to reach even this very poor region, lamb and goat now are eaten periodically. Fish and seafood are available primarily near the two coasts.

Agnello e Funghi Cardoncelli. Lamb and mushrooms sautéed or stewed. A specialty of Matera.

Beccacce in Salmì con Prosciutto Crudo, Acciughe, Capperi, e Marsala Secca. Jugged snipe with prosciutto, capers, and dry Marsala wine. A specialty of Potenza.

Ciammaruchedde. Pan-cooked snails with mint, garlic, *peperoncino,* and tomatoes.

Cutturiedd. Slow-cooked lamb flavored with numerous herbs.

Pastizz. A half-moon-shape calzone filled with meat (pork, kid, or lamb).

Pigneti. A stew made with chunks of kid, lamb, or mutton with sliced *salame,* tomatoes, onions, potatoes, celery, carrots, aged Pecorino cheese, *peperoncino,* wine, and water and cooked over a tiny flame all night.

Scapice. Fresh anchovies fried and flavored with mint.

Zuppa di Pesce. A stew of mixed fish, spiked with *diavolicchio.*

FORMAGGI

Burrata, burrini, and *mozzarella* are delicious soft cow's-milk cheeses. There is also soft and aged Pecorino.

DOLCI

In addition to local sweets, people in Basilicata eat a lot of fruit. The oranges and lemons of the region are very flavorful.

Focaccia al Miele. A dessert dough drenched in honey.

Imbottiti. Pastries filled with quince jam.

Linguette. Flour, sugar, wine, and yeast.

Mennu'l Atturat'. Toasted almonds.

Paparotta. A sweet made with wine must during harvesttime.

Qur'sam'. Easter cookies.

Rococò. Filled with a mixture of flour, almonds, and sugar.

Stozze. Filled with a mixture of flour, eggs, almonds, and sugar.

Strazzate. Chocolate-almond cookies.

Torta di Latticini. "Cake of cheeses" is the literal translation of this rather unusual pastry that often is served as a sweet but is more of a savory. A sweet crust is filled with ricotta, grated Pecorino, mozzarella, egg, prosciutto, salt, and pepper.

The Wines of Basilicata

Although Basilicata has only one DOC wine, it is of sufficient fame and quality to be ranked in the forefront of Italian reds, certainly in the view of wine lovers. The name of the grape—Aglianico—is a corruption of the word "Hellenic." While Aglianico is not technically a grape native to Basilicata (there are none), it was planted by the Greeks so long ago (seventh to sixth century B.C.) that it has been vinified longer than most native varieties in more northerly regions. The Greeks planted many vines near Monte Vulture, and this is the area where most of the best Aglianico is grown today. The Aglianico harvest, in late October to early November, is one of the latest in Italy. The wine tastes closed and often harsh when it is fewer than two years old, but it opens up very nicely after that and displays pleasing flavor, color, character, and persistence. The most prominent non-DOC wines are called Colli Lucani, and they are made in both white and red. White-wine production in Basilicata is modest in quality and quantity.

Other Beverages

Amaro Lucano. This is one of the more popular *digestivi* in southern Italy.

Vena. A coffee-flavored cordial.

Atella (Potenza)

FOLKLORE

La Festa del Ritorno.

Held in July, this is the celebration of the return of emigrants to the family and to the culture. There are exhibitions and parties, but the air is tinged with remorse.

Avigliano (Potenza)

BAKERIES

Panfido Caterina Lovallo, Via Petruccelli 2, tel. 0971/700112.

I loved the focaccia with fresh tomatoes, olive oil, and oregano. There is a small selection of good bread as well.

Pasticceria Maria Giovanna Lucia, Via Petruccelli, tel. 0971/81366.

This is one of the best places I discovered in Basilicata for classic regional pastries.

CASTLE-MUSEUM

Lagopesole.

Built by Frederick II of Swabia, this castle is generally considered the most beautiful in the region. It contains an exhibit of peasant tools and furniture in Basilicata that were used as recently as the 1960s, even though they look like rudimentary antiques.

DINING

Trattoria Vecchio Lume, Frazione Sarnelli, tel. 0971/87000. Closed Friday and first ten days in September. No credit cards.

Sarnelli is near Avigliano. Delicious *pasta e fagioli*, *capretto*, and in winter the *cutturiedd*.

Pietra del Sale, Contrada Pietra del Sale (Monte Carmine), tel. 0971/87063. Closed Monday. All credit cards. Moderately inexpensive.

The former stables of Frederick II of Swabia on Monte Carmine in the castle of Lagopesole is a microcosm of *lucano* food culture, with production of meats and cheeses. There is tasty, rustic food here and the *cauzuni* (ravioli with ricotta and mint) are not to miss. Call before coming.

Bernalda (Matera)

Bernalda has one of the most characteristic central districts of any town in Basilicata. It is notable for the case *minime* (minimal houses) that are clustered together to make narrow two-story whitewashed dwellings.

DINING

Da Fifina, Corso Umberto 63/65, tel. 0835/743134. Closed Sundays (except in August) and September. No credit cards. Moderately inexpensive.

The family that operates this restaurant owns the butcher shop next door. The *lucanica* should not be missed, and other good meats and vegetables are cooked simply to honor their flavor.

Filiano (Potenza)

CHEESE

Caseificio Piano della Spina, tel. 0971/808500, fax 0971/808508.

One of the better cheese factories in Basilicata, it is notable also because it ships cheese around the world. While its *burrata*, which is very good, does not travel, firmer cheeses such as *Caciocavallo*, Pecorino, and *ricotta dura* (harder, aged ricotta good for grating) can make the trip. If you are driving around, pick up a *burrata* to eat during your journey.

Maratea (Potenza)

Sandwiched between Campania and Calabria, Maratea is a very pretty beach town that is Basilicata's tiny window on the Mediterranean. It has more in common with its neighbors than with its home region farther inland.

BAKERY

Antica Pasticceria Iannini, Vicoletto Rovita 9.

The *pasta di cedro* (citron pastry) is delicious, as are the nut pastries and chocolate.

DINING

Trattoria da Cesare, Contrada Cersuta 52, tel. 0973/878241. Reservations advised in summer. Closed Thursday (except in summer). No credit cards. Moderate to moderately expensive.

Delicious seafood that varies with the day's catch. Tuna and grouper *(cernia)* are specialties.

Matera
Classic Town

Because Basilicata is so poorly served by public transportation—the federal railways don't come to Matera, and the city is connected to Potenza only by one bus a day—it is essential to have a car. However, there is a way to come to Matera without an automobile. There are nine trains that leave Bari (in Puglia) each day on the private Ferrovie Apulo-Lucane. Therefore, if you are traveling in Puglia, you should use that occasion to visit Matera.

Matera is like no other city you will ever see. The center of the city is a giant bowl surrounded by a newer city. This "bowl" is made of soft rock in which caves (called *sassi*) were hollowed out centuries ago and used for habitation. They were cleared out during the Fascist and postwar eras, in part because people lived in close quarters and diseases became epidemics. In recent years people have begun to return to the *sassi*. With electrification, telecommunications, and indoor plumbing, some of these *sassi* are now very desirable places to live. Yet there are only seven hundred inhabitants, and most of the *sassi* are still empty. Besides the dwellings, there are more than 120 *chiese rupestri*, which are cave churches carved from the stone. The *sassi* are connected by narrow paths and form a labyrinth not unlike a Moroccan souk. There are young boys whom you can (perhaps should)

Street scene

hire to lead you around, because it is very easy to get lost. But you should visit them: the *sassi* are an extraordinary, singular sight that once seen is never forgotten. You should not walk around the *sassi* at night, because you will never find your way out, and it can be rather frightening. All of the restaurants, stores, and sights that I have directed you to in this chapter are not in the *sassi*. Aside from all of the interesting sites and foods, it would be worth coming to Matera only to take part in the *passeggiata*, which is far and away the most interesting and exciting I have encountered anywhere in Italy.

BARS AND CAFFÈS

For other bars and *caffès*, see "La Passeggiata," below.

Gran Caffè, Piazza Vittorio Veneto 3, tel. 0835/332302. Closed Tuesday.

A good central spot for breakfast. Makes a delicious *caffè latte freddo*.

Caffè Schiuma, Via Tommaso Stigliani 92.

Although it has no outdoor tables, this is everything you would want from a place to stop during the *passeggiata*. There are more than thirty flavors of ice cream, all well made. (Try *veleno* [poison], which is a mix of zuppa inglese and coffee flavors.) There are fresh strawberries, cherries, kiwi, pineapple, and other fruits to mix with your ice cream. You will also see a huge case filled with sumptuous pastries. I particularly liked the *bignè al cioccolato,* a dry chocolate pastry filled with dark chocolate. This treat was rich in chocolate flavor but not oppressively sweet. Beyond the pastries is a small, green marble bar that is very swanky.

Bar-Gelateria Hemingway, Via Ridola 44. Closed Tuesday.

During the warm weather, this bar is open until 3:30h. On other nights it also stays open quite late, depending on the traffic. Down the block from the Museo Nazionale Ridola, Bar Hemingway sets out more than thirty tables with large canvas director's chairs. There is bar service, beer on tap, but many people come here for the ice cream—the *torrone* is very good. The chocolate, good. And the hazelnut is also good. The Via Ridola is the favored block at one end of Matera's superb *passeggiata*. Fathers hold their babies, giving mothers a brief respite from their work. Everyone looks at everyone else, openly or discreetly. The *passeggiata* continues on the Corso, where the traffic and socializing are intense.

DINING

Trattoria Lucana, Via Lucana 48, tel. 0835/336117. Closed Sunday (except in high season) and a week in September. All credit cards. Moderate.

Justifiably popular for its regional specialties and friendly atmosphere.

Lucanerie, Via Santo Stefano 61, tel. 0835/ 332133. Closed Sunday evening, Monday, August. All credit cards. Moderate.

I like the *orecchiette con cardoncelli, mollica fritta e pecorino di Moliterno*, the pasta being tossed with wild cardoons, breadcrumbs and tangy pecorino. You must reserve ahead for the *pastorale*, a complex and fascinating local dish in which various parts of sheep are braised with vegetables.

Venusio, Via Lussemburgo 2, tel. 0835/259081. Closed Sunday evening, Monday, August 1–15. All credit cards.

Moderate to moderately expensive.

You must travel 7 km/4 miles to Borgo Venusio if you wish to enjoy the fish and seafood on offer here. It makes a nice change from the meat-oriented dishes of Matera.

Il Cantuccio, Via delle Beccherie 33, tel. 0835/332090. Closed Monday and early September. All credit cards. Moderately inexpensive.

Casual dining on very tasty food, with an emphasis on local cheeses, grilled or pan-cooked vegetables (try the *peperoni cruschi*) and lamb prepared in many ways. *Agnello alla contadina* is simply lamb with onions and tomatoes, but it is genius.

Le Botteghe, Piazza San Pietro Barisano 22, tel. 0835/344072. Open nightly and at lunch on Saturday, Sunday, Monday. All credit cards. Moderate.

Delicious dishes with an accent on local vegetables, including *cicorielle selvatiche, cime di rapa, cardoncelli* and more. The crostata, whose flavor changes often, is not to miss at the end of the meal.

Ristorante Mateola, Vico Lombardi 52 (off Via Beccherie), tel. 0835/336910. Closed Wednesday. Moderate.

A very attractive restaurant with a superb view of the *sassi*. It prepares a cross-section of Italian dishes and has Lucanian specialties as well.

FOLKLORE

Luglio Materano.

Throughout the month of July, starting with the Festa della Madonna Bruna, Matera is the site of cultural events drawn from local customs and traditions. This is a good month to visit the city.

Festa della Madonna Bruna.

One of the great religious/pagan events in southern Italy. On July 2 each year since 1380, a cart *(carro)*, a symbol of peasant labor, bearing a statue of the Madonna is transported to various quarters of the city. The *carro* is traditionally made by the Pentasuglia and Epifania families, and it takes four months to construct. It is adorned with papier-mâché statues and friezes that depict a scene from the Old or New Testament. At dawn it begins its journey through the city, drawn by eight mules and guarded by young men wearing helmets, breastplates, and ornate costumes. The cart finally reaches the Duomo, where it is taken for three trips round the square, then the Madonna is removed and brought into the church for blessing and veneration. The townspeople then attack and destroy the cart and seize all of the objects it carried, which become relics much in the way a piece of clothing that is presumed to have been worn by a saint would be saved and cherished. In the evening there is great feasting and a fireworks display.

La Crappiata.

On August 1 this harvest festival is held to thank the earth for its bounty. One always eats mashed broad beans and boiled chicory and other foods.

FOOD STORES

Be sure to visit Matera's colorful market on the Via Persio just off Piazza Vittoria Veneto. Here, under the shade of a large tree, the old men of town gather to talk.

Sign outside an alimentari, *Matera*

Il Buongustaio, Piazza Vittorio Veneto 1, tel. 0835/211732.

Owner Samuele Olivieri lived in Toronto for many years and speaks very good English. You can make this an opportunity to learn about the specialties of Basilicata in his attractive, well-stocked shop. In addition, there are specialties from throughout Italy, but you haven't journeyed all the way to Matera for that!

Drogheria Latorre, Via del Corso 42. Closed Thursday morning. MasterCard, Visa.

The bright picture windows are full of candies, liqueurs—especially Amaro Lucano—and other blandishments. Inside is a bazaar of candies, cookies, cakes, wine, coffee, imported teas, and liqueurs. An institution since 1915.

MUSEUMS

Fondazione Carlo Levi, Palazzo Lanfranchi (Piazza Pascoli), tel. 0835/310137. Open 9–13h; closed Monday.

A collection dedicated to the life of Carlo Levi and his particular relationship with Basilicata. You can see his paintings of life in the region and, if you look out the window, there is a remarkable view of the *sassi*.

Museo Nazionale D. Ridola, Via Ridola 24, tel. 0835/311239.

A four-part collection that displays archaeological finds from the prehistoric, Iron Age, Greek, and Roman eras in the area around Matera.

LA PASSEGGIATA

The evening stroll is one of the great Italian traditions and is practiced in one form or another in just about every community in Italy. It is as if there is an almost primal urge to step out-of-doors as the sun starts to go down to have a coffee, see friends, and gather news. Nowhere in all of my travels have I encountered a *passeggiata* that rivals the one in Matera. It seems as if the whole town comes out, and the streets and *caffès* fill up for hours. In the rest of the country the *passeggiata* lasts about an hour. In Matera, it lasts from 20h to 23h in the summer and from 19:30h to 22h the rest of the year. Great amounts of wine, coffee, ice cream, and pastries are consumed, babies are passed from arms to loving arms, and the whole thing feels like a spontaneous street festival. Remarkably, this event happens every night. It is the city's principal form of entertainment, and no one wants to miss it. The *passeggiata* is quite long, extending from the triangular park at Via Stigliani all the way down the Via XX Settembre, through the Piazza Vittorio Verieto, up the Via del Corso, and on to the Via Ridola. Once you have completed the walk, you turn around and go back for more. There is a good bar at each end—the Hemingway (see page 607) and especially the Caffè Schiuma (see page 606).

Bar-Pasticceria Sottozero, Via XX Settembre 51.

Caffè Tripoli, Piazza Vittorio Veneto.

Outdoor tables and a huge palm tree.

Bar del Corso.

A popular place on the Corso where young people buy ice cream.

The Via Roma, just off the Piazza Veneto, is the province of adolescents who have their own separate *passeggiata*, during which they meet tentatively or affectionately.

Melfi (Potenza)

DINING

Trattoria Vaddone, Contrada Sant'Abruzzese, tel. 0972/24323. Closed *Monday evening. All credit cards. Moderately inexpensive.*

The best pasta I tasted in the region was at Trattoria Vaddone. The *cavatelli* with ricotta and a *ragù* of veal and lamb are delicious. More delicate, but no less special, are the *cavatelli* with *finocchio selvatico* (wild fennel). *Orecchiette* are also delicious, and, though I did not taste the baked pastas, I hope one day to do so. There is a terrific *zuppa di legumi*, with peas, beans, chick-peas, and other legumes. The roast lamb and goat are expertly done.

FOLKLORE
La Sagra della Varola.

On the third weekend in August the town celebrates the *varola*, a chestnut pastry that is typical of Melfi.

Metaponto (Matera)

In ancient times this town, founded in the seventh century B.C., was an important outpost of Hellenic civilization. Pythagoras and Cicero came here, as did Hannibal in Roman times. The nearby Bradano River valley, called the Tavole Palatine, is a treasure trove of remains from antiquity, many of which appear in the local Museum of Antiquities (open summer 9–13h, 15:30–18:30h; winter 9–12h, 14–17h) or in the stupendous museums of Taranto and Reggio Calabria. The Tavole Palatine is also a fertile plain where recently introduced modern agricultural methods have made this a promised land for the economic future of the region. There are stunning beaches that are virtually unknown except to people from Basilicata and Taranto, plus a few adventurous Germans. At this writing there were a couple of hotels with decent food, but not yet special enough to merit a journey unless you are a beach person.

Montescaglioso (Matera)

As part of the agricultural revolution in the Bradano River valley (described under "Metaponto"), there is a segment that has devoted itself to organic farming, which in Italian is called *coltivazione biologica*. These foods have found a market in big cities and have brought cash to the area. The two sources below only deal in organic foods.

FOOD STORES
Rocco Contangelo, Via Matteotti 4,
tel. 0835/207332.

Signor Contangelo makes excellent oil from local olives and sells vegetables and lamb.

Ortosano, Via San Francesco 34.

Fruit, vegetables, and grains. The oranges and lemons are wonderful.

Potenza

This is the region's capital, but Matera is the cultural and spiritual heart of Basilicata. In fact, Matera was the principal city until 1806, when the occupying French made Potenza the capital because it was closer to Napoli. The city was one of the most active centers of the liberal movement that led to the unification of Italy: it was the first city on the Italian mainland to rise up against the Bourbons. The most interesting aspects of Potenza nowadays are the Good Friday observances and a walk down the Via Pretoria, one of the oldest thoroughfares in Italy. Much of the town was destroyed in the 1980 earthquake, so many of its original sites of interest are gone. At 822 meters (2,713 feet) Potenza is the highest regional capital in Italy, and winters can be very cold despite the southern latitude.

BAKERY

Panetteria Giovanna Salvatore, Contrada Poggio Cavallo 84b, tel. 0971/56100.

Outstanding baked goods, including breads, rolls, focaccia, pizza, and pastries made with ingredients such as almond paste and olive oil.

CHEESE

Latteria Rizzo, Vicolo Fratelli Assisi.

Sensational *burrata* cheese, plus many other classic cheeses of southern Italy.

DINING

La Tettoia, Via Due Torri 1, tel. 0971/24123. Closed Sunday. All credit cards. Moderate.

The menu is divided in three parts: *lucano*, vegetarian, fish, and all are worthy.

Salumi *for sale in Potenza*

GRAINS

Mulino Lo Schiavo, Via dei Mille 103, tel. 0971/470866.

Bread, pasta, and beans are essential components in the cuisine of Basilicata. Here you can buy freshly milled flour of wheat, corn, or semolina, as well as dried beans, chickpeas, and lentils. A pleasing shop.

Rapone (Potenza)

FOLKLORE

La Sagra del Caciocavallo.

Each August the town celebrates its *caciocavallo* cheese and *soppressata salame* with festivity and fair amounts of eating.

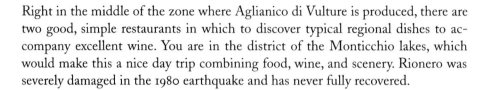

Rionero in Vulture (Potenza)

Right in the middle of the zone where Aglianico di Vulture is produced, there are two good, simple restaurants in which to discover typical regional dishes to accompany excellent wine. You are in the district of the Monticchio lakes, which would make this a nice day trip combining food, wine, and scenery. Rionero was severely damaged in the 1980 earthquake and has never fully recovered.

CHEESE

Casa della Mozzarella Donato Corbo, Piazza XX Settembre.

Braided mozzarella is called *il treccio* and is made from fresh local milk. You can also buy popular silken *burrata* cheese here, but the supplies vanish early in the day.

DINING

Di Lucchio, Via Monticchio 15, tel. 0972/721081. Closed Friday. No credit cards. Moderately inexpensive.

Local food, good wine, nice views.

Marziano, Via Nazionale, tel. 0972/721027. Closed January and February. No credit cards. Moderately inexpensive to moderate.

The proprietors make their own wine, which goes well with the numerous dishes made with *funghi,* along with the delicious grilled *salsicce.*

WINE

Casa Vinicola Donato D'Angelo, Via Provinciale, tel. 0972/721517. Call before coming.

Just outside of town is probably the most famous wine maker in Basilicata. The Aglianico here combines careful grape cultivation with modern wine-making techniques. Some English spoken.

Casa Vinicola Armando Martino, Via La Vista 2A, tel. 0972/721422. Call for an appointment. Closed Sunday and Monday.

San Giorgio Lucano (Matera)

FOLKLORE

Festa del Raccolto.

This ancient pagan ritual, held in late June to early July, is regarded as an act of apology to the land after harvesting, which was once thought of as theft. A man dresses up as a wild goat, hides in the newly harvested food, and is chased by the townspeople. This ceremony is viewed as a reconciliation with nature.

Orecchiette al Tegamino
Baked Orecchiette

The *orecchiette* in Matera are larger than those of Puglia and are called *scorze di mandorla* (almond skins). If you can not find these, you may substitute smaller *orecchiette* from Puglia.

Serves 2

300 grams/10 ounces orecchiette

100 grams/1 cup tomato puree, preferably made with fresh tomatoes

100 grams/4 ounces cooked lucanica, *cut in little bits (see note)*

100 grams/4 ounces fresh unsalted mozzarella, cut in bits

2 tablespoons freshly grated aged Pecorino Romano

Preheat the oven to 210°C (425°F). Set a large pot of cold water to boil. When it reaches a boil, toss in a pinch of salt. When it returns to a boil, toss in a pinch of salt. When it again returns to a boil, add the *orecchiette*. As soon as the *orecchiette* are half cooked (they should be quite chewy and still have a slightly floury taste), drain them in a colander. Combine them with the tomato puree and bits of *lucanica* in a pan, perhaps the one you used to cook the sausage. Heat and stir until the flavors combine (about 3 minutes). Pour this mixture into a terra-cotta or glass baking dish. Add the mozzarella pieces and stir. Then top with the grated cheese. Bake in the hot oven for 10 to 15 minutes, until the mixture bubbles. Serve immediately and be careful not to burn your mouth!

Variation: Instead of sausage, some cooks make tiny, fingertip-sized meatballs of beef, garlic, egg, parsley, salt (and I add a drop of fresh lemon juice).

Note: Buy *lucanica* or other sausage laced with *peperoncino* at a good Italian market or during your stay in Basilicata.

Strazzate
Lucanian Chocolate–Almond Sweets

I have changed this recipe just a bit. As eaten in Matera, these cookies become very hard and are intended for dipping in sweet wine. Even at that, you need good bicuspids. So I recommend baking them for slightly less time, so they are still slightly chewy.

1 kilogram/2.2 pounds toasted almonds, coarsely chopped
1 kilogram/2.2 pounds unbleached flour
1 kilogram/2.2 pounds granulated sugar
50 grams/2 ounces cocoa powder
50 grams/2 ounces baking chocolate, shaved in strips
1 cup Strega liqueur

Preheat the oven to 200°C (400°F). Combine all of the ingredients, except the Strega. Then add half the liqueur and make a rather firm dough. Add more Strega as you see fit, making sure that the dough is relatively firm. If you use all the Strega and need more liquid, use water a bit at a time. Form little squares of dough (about 2.5 centimeters [1 inch]) and place them on a greased (with corn or vegetable oil) baking sheet. Allow some room between each cookie. Bake for 10 to 20 minutes. The cookies should be slightly chewy and springy, and not browned. Let them cool before serving.

Wine: A dessert wine such as Moscato del Vulture or *vin santo*. I like these with a glass of Strega.

Calabria

Not to Miss in Calabria

COSENZA   SAN GIOVANNI IN FIORE/SILA

TROPEA *(Classic Town)*

Vigna piantata da me	A vineyard planted by me
olivo da mio padre	an olive tree by my father
e castagno da mio nonno	and a chestnut tree by
	my grandfather

 For many people Calabria, the toe of the Italian boot, is only the long coastal jouney that separates Campania from Sicilia. Most visitors see only this part of the 800-kilometer (496-mile) coastline, but there is more to discover on the shoreand within. Calabria remains one of the poorest, most backward rcgions of the country, but no less interesting because of that. The coast is notable because it is much less developed than farther north. Calabria has some of the cleanest water on the whole Italian coastline, owing in part to the lack of development. The Ionian coast in particular has vast expanses of virgin beach and scrub and a fertile agricultural plain that yields sublime produce, especially figs.

The story of Calabria, I believe, can be told in its trees. Near the shore one finds palm, lemon, oleander, and almond trees. In the hills just up from the shore are citron and bergamot. Citron *(cedro)* is a large citrus fruit in the lemon family. It is prized above all for its skin, which is boiled and then candied, and winds up in fruitcake the world over, pastries in Sicilia, and panettone in Milano. The skin is rougher than that of a lemon, with indentations that are referred to as "Adam's bites." Legend has it that the citron was the forbidden fruit eaten by Adam and Eve in the Garden of Eden. Citron is also important to the Jews, who customarily eat it as part

REGIONAL CAPITAL:

Catanzaro (CZ).

PROVINCIAL CAPITALS:

Cosenza (CS), Crotone (KR), Reggio Calabria (RC) and Vibo Valentia (VV)

TOURIST IMFORMATION:

I have found that the best tourist information about Calabria is actually in Milano. This office can give you detailed contacts for the places you want to see in Calabria: Regione Calabria, Via Broletto 16, Milano, tel. 02/874993 or 02/807877.

AGRITOURISM:

Associazione Agriturist, Via XX Settembre 41, 88100 Catanzaro, tel 0961/45084.

of the celebration of Succoth. In Israel the fruit is known as *etrog*, and much of the citron consumed there has always come from Calabria.

Bergamot *(bergamotto)* is often associated mistakenly with the Lombard city of Bergamo. In fact, the name derives from "Berga," the place in Spain where the plant is thought to have originated. It, too, is a citrus fruit, although closer to the orange than the lemon, that is particularly prized for its spicy fragrance. It is exported to France for use in perfumery and to England, where it provides the unmistakable fragrance and taste of Earl Grey tea. The low hills near Reggio Calabria, the regional capital, have most of the bergamot, and you will also see date palms, magnolias, bananas, and even rubber trees.

The higher hills beyond are where many of the important towns are—in centuries past people did not live near the shore, fearing malaria and invasions by pirates and foreign occupiers. Here are the vines and olive trees that provide the wine and olive oil that have been central to sustenance in Calabria since its earliest inhabitants. Grapevines and, in particular, olive trees represent the people of Calabria to me. They have been bent and twisted by the elements, yet they endure and produce and never break.

In the center of the region are the Calabrese Apennines, three ranges of high peaks and plateaus known as the Sila, Serre, and Aspromonte. Here are enormous forests that are little touched and sparsely inhabited. You can see beech, fir, oak, and pine trees, many green all year and covered in snow for much of the winter. There is a distinct tree in the Serre called the *calabrese* pine, which has silvery scales on the bark that reach all the way up to the needles. Visit these forests—especially the Sila—and you will think you are in Scandinavia rather than an hour's flight from Tunisia.

During the long winters people in the Sila and the other mountain areas create handicrafts that have always been necessities and only now seem geared to tourists. The men are adept wood-carvers, and the women weave beautiful blankets. Women in this area wear a rather somber-looking traditional costume, and many of them carry things atop their heads rather than in their arms or on their backs. But mountain people in Calabria have always been more self-sufficient than people in the lowlands. Many of them worked on landed estates called *latifundia* as serfs and later peasants. They toiled in abysmal conditions that often verged on starvation, while a few lords became wealthy on the backs of the poor. *Latifundia* existed as far back as the Roman era, and many lasted until the 1940s. In 1948 during land reform there were bloody riots in the town of Melissa as it was being determined how the land would be parceled. The strife occurred because Melissa produces an excellent wine, and there was competition for the best terrain.

Calabria was inhabited in Paleolithic times. It was an important piece of Magna Graecia, the Greek Empire, and was a supplier of foodstuffs and raw materials to Athens. Cities such as Sibari, Crotone, and Locri were founded on the Ionian Sea between 744 and 650 B.C. Sibari was the home of the Sybarites, a people for whom I have great affection. This was a group that understood pleasure in life, and the word "sybaritic" is a testament to their outlook. Pythagoras was the most famous resident of Crotone, making it a center of science and culture in the sixth century B.C. He also was influential in helping his city destroy the Sybarites, striking a blow for the Apollonians in their constant struggle against the Dionysians. (Can't we all just get along?)

The Romans followed the Greeks, and then came centuries of foreign occupiers—Goths, Byzantines (who collected silkworms from mulberry trees, which were prized in Constantinople), Lombards, Saracens, the Catholic Church (which consolidated the latifundia), Normans, and the Swabians, who tried to develop commerce and check the power of the latifundia. Jewish traders arrived and encouraged cultivation of citron and other crops. Then came the French and the Spanish, the kingdom of Naples, and the Austrians.

In effect, *calabresi* were seldom self-governing and never had a chance to develop civic institutions of their own. Family members became the only people one could trust, and people sought protection from outsiders. This led to the rise of the *'n dranghetta,* which is an organization similar to the Sicilian Mafia. It is seldom acknowledged that this phenomenon developed not for the commission of crime but as a form of protection from it. With the *'n dranghetta* came a code of ethics whereby one did not betray the protector. As a result, the person who provided protection gained power, and thus was created a structure parallel to the latifundia. Rivalries between towns and interfamilial quarrels meant that local disputes could last for generations. When *calabresi* emigrated to new lands, the ancient feuds would continue, and this explains in part the perceptions that peoples of other ethnic groups had of immigrants from rural southern Italy. Many *calabresi* seem more reserved in their dealings with visitors because of the defensiveness that has evolved over centuries.

But the lack of polish, of modernity, and development in Calabria is part of its interest to the visitor. The underdevelopment has meant less desecration of the land. A city such as Cosenza (with 100,000 residents) is much more old-fashioned than northern cities of similar size, such as Lucca in Toscana or Piacenza in Emilia. You get the feeling that people cling to the old in Calabria because it is comprehensible and it is *theirs.* Anything introduced from the outside, even a genuine improvement, might be seen as a threat to a way of life that has stood tall, with roots deeply planted, like the trees that can tell the story of Calabria.

Eating in Calabria

As in much of mainland southern Italy, the cuisine of Calabria is one born in kitchens that had few available ingredients, yet they were used resourcefully. In this region people were often isolated for long periods because of weather or because they were seeking refuge from invaders. Pasta with vegetables is the region's staple, and there are many variations on this theme. *Peperoncino* is a dominant flavor in much of the cuisine, and superb vegetables, especially sweet peppers, artichokes, zucchini, onions, mushrooms, and eggplants, are ubiquitous. People who live near the sea feast on delicious swordfish and seafood, while people inland get much of their animal protein from lamb, kid, pork sausage, and cheeses such as

Olive trees are a part of the Calabria landscape

caciocavallo and *provolone*. Citrus flavors occasionally appear in different parts of a meal, including sauces for fish and for baking. In addition to citrus, the excellent figs of Calabria turn up everywhere. Eaten fresh, they are the perfect dessert. When dried, they are stuffed with almonds, chocolate, fruit, or other nuts and appear at any festive event. The mountains produce some chestnuts, although many are sold to markets in Roma and Piemonte.

ANTIPASTI

Capocollo. The most typical *salame*, it appears in all antipasti.

Lagrumuse. This means "lachrymose," because this *salame* weeps a drop of fat when you cut it.

'Nduja. Pork sausage heavily spiked with *peperoncino*.

Sopressata. A blood sausage, often tightly pressed and dried.

Melanzane a Scapece. Pickled eggplant.

Ovotarica. These are dried tuna eggs, like the Sardinian *bottarga*, served on bread with olive oil and tomatoes.

Sardella. Fish fry (baby fish) of all types, minced with powdered *peperoncino* and olive oil and spread on bread. A specialty of Crotone.

PRIMI

It is traditional that *calabrese* brides-to-be know how to make at least a dozen different pasta shapes. They have names such as *pizzicotti* (which are round), *ricci di donna* (woman's curls), *paternostri* (small cubes with holes in them), *rascatelli* (long, thick-cut pasta), and *cannaruozzoli* (bent canes). Some specialties are listed below.

Bucatini con la Mollica. Bucatini with olive oil, mashed anchovies, and bread crumbs.
Fileia (or filej). A pasta that gets its shape by being rolled around wire or sticks. It is served with a spicy pork sauce. A specialty of Vibo Valentia.
Millecosedde. "A thousand things"—a soup with rigatoni, fava beans, chickpeas, red and white beans, and lentils.
Perciatelli con le Marozze or con le Monacelle. Perciatelli with different types of snails.
Rigatoni alla Toranese. Rigatoni with onions, grated Pecorino, and a touch of lard.
Sagne Chine. Lasagne filled with different flavorings, including sausage, tiny meatballs, hard-boiled eggs, artichokes, cheeses, fresh tomato sauce.
Zite. With lard, *prosciutto crudo,* parsley, tomatoes, garlic, and basil.

SECONDI

Alici a Beccafico. Fresh anchovies stuffed and fried.
Alici all'Involtino. Fresh anchovy fillets stuffed and rolled.
Frittula. Hot pig's skin eaten with warm bread, a specialty of Reggio Calabria.
Melanzane alla Parmigiana. Breaded, fried eggplant baked with tomatoes, mozzarella, and Parmigiano-Reggiano. Often a main course in Calabria.
Mursiellu (Morsello, Morzello, or Murzeddu). Fried or stewed tripe with giblets and other organ meats, red wine, tomatoes, *peperoncino,* and herbs. A specialty of Catanzaro.
Mustica. Sun-dried whitebait, peppered and preserved in oil.
Pescespada. Swordfish, cooked in many ways. This best is caught at Bagnara and Scilla.
Scilatelle. Stuffed eggplant.
Tonno. Tuna steaks are served in many ways. One is *in agrodolce* (sweet and sour); another is with *salsa verde,* a slightly sharp green herb sauce. The best tuna is caught in the beautiful little town of Pizzo, just north of Tropea. The expedition to catch tuna is called *la tonnara,* and it is an impressive, if sometimes bloody, thing to watch. Much of the best tuna is canned in Pizzo.

CONTORNI

All of the *calabrese* vegetables, especially eggplant, are cooked in numerous ways, including grilling, frying, baking, stuffing, and stewing. The oddly named *melanzane stupide* are baked eggplant seasoned with oil, parsley, salt, and cheese.

Cipolle di Tropea. The sweet red-purple onions from Tropea.
Insalata Calabrese. A mixture of boiled and raw greens, tossed and dressed with olive oil.

FORMAGGI

Mozzarella, *scamorza, provola,* provolone, *caciocavallo* are all excellent cow's-milk cheeses. The last two are especially popular. Fine cow's-milk cheese is made in small quantities by the monks at the San Bruno Monastery in Serra San Bruno. Buttiri is a creamy, buttery cheese from the Sila made with milk from cows that have not calved for a year. The region also is famous for goat's-milk cheeses such as those from the towns of Bova, Roccaforte del Greco, Staiti, Motta San Giovanni, and Roghudi.

DOLCI

There are all sorts of sweets in Calabria, most of them connected with the observances of Easter and Christmas. This is because in the past, when the region was very poor, the luxury of sweets was only permitted for holidays.

Brioche con il Gelato. In warm weather in Reggio it is customary to fill a large roll with ice cream and have it at breakfast with the morning coffee.

Cumpittu. Of Arab origin, a soft nougat with honey, sesame seeds, and almonds.

Fichi alla Sibarita. From Sibari, these are dried figs filled with almonds, hazelnuts, cocoa powder, *sapa* (cooked wine must), sugar, cinnamon, and candied fruits.

Fichi Ripieni. From Cosenza, dried figs with a single filling, such as one of the items listed for *fichi alla sibarita* or perhaps something else.

Mostaccioli. Made of flour, honey, and almonds. A specialty of Soriano Calabro.

'Nzuddi. Made with flour, white wine, honey, and spices. *Mostaccioli* and *'nzuddi* are often made in pagan motifs called *babbaluti* or in the shape of early Christian fish and bird symbols.

Nacatula. Flour and spices, fried in olive oil. This was once a cake eaten at weddings and during Carnival.

Torrone Gelato. From Reggio Calabria, a cylinder made with candied tangerine, orange, and lime mixed with ground almonds and coated with chocolate. Despite the name, this is not an iced dessert.

The Wines of Calabria

The Greeks gave considerable impetus to viticulture in Calabria, bringing various grape varieties and wine-making techniques. The indigenous people became so adept at wine making that soon the wine of Calabria was considered better than that made in Greece. The Greeks had originally called this area Enotria (Land of Wine), although the name was later applied to much of the Italian peninsula. Cremissa, a wine from Krimisa (between Sibari and Crotone), was used to toast victorious athletes at the ancient Olympic Games. Cirò, made in the same place, is said to be the oldest wine in the world, although I think that is impossible to deter-

mine. But the area unquestionably is one of the places in Italy with the longest enological traditions. (Cirò was the wine offered to the athletes at the 1968 Olympics
in Mexico City.) It was mostly produced around Sibari, and archaeologists have
discovered an ancient vinoduct, a system of pipes that carried the wine from the
producing areas to the thirsty Sybarites. After the fall of Rome, *calabrese* wines were
basically forgotten, although by the fourteenth century there was considerable
export to cities on the North Sea. Cirò, made in red, rosé, and white, is the major
DOC wine of the region and the one that is the most produced. Melissa, another
good DOC wine, comes in white, red, and the better *rosso superiore*. Another wine
of note is Greco di Bianco, an amber-colored sweet dessert wine that has a powerful citrus fragrance with herbal undertones. It is quite outstanding, and very hard
to find. The best producer is generally thought to be Umberto Ceratti in Caraffa
del Bianco (Reggio Calabria). The wine is from the town of Bianco (Reggio
Calabria), and its traditional name is Bianco di Gerace.

Bagnara Calabra (Reggio Calabria)

This town is famous for its swordfish catch, which is prominent in local cuisine.

DINING

*Taverna Kerkira, Corso Vittorio
Emanuele 217, tel. 0966/372260. Closed
Monday, Tuesday, August 1–Sept 15,
December 20–January 15. All credit cards.
Moderate.*

"Kerkira" means "Corfu" in Greek. The
owners are originally from Corfu, so the
flavors mix the influences of Greece and
Calabria. There are moussaka, *tzatziki*,
stuffed grape leaves *(foglie di vite)*, feta
cheese, and olives. But you can also have
local fish and seafood in many guises. Be
sure to try the homemade *gelato al miele*
(honey ice cream).

Caraffa del Bianco (Reggio Calabria)

WINE

*Azienda Agricola Umberto Ceratti, Via
degli Uffizzi 5, tel. 0964/913073.*

The top producer of Greco di Bianco,
one of the most memorable dessert
wines you will ever taste.

Catanzaro

s

The farms, forests, and fields of the province of Catanzaro are famous above all
for chestnuts and figs. The chestnuts are shipped all over Italy and are often sold
roasted at outdoor stands in Roma or as *marrons glacés* in Torino. The nuts also

are used to make chestnut flour for pancakes, breads, and crepes in Liguria and Toscana as well as preparations in Calabria. The Catanzaro province is known for its gutsy red and white wines, wild mushrooms, citrus fruits, tuna from nearby seas, vegetables preserved in oil and vinegar, and sausages spiked with *peperoncino rosso*. The most famous dish is *mursiellu* (also called *morzello* or *murzeddu*), a sort of slow-cooked stew made with tripe, tongue, spleen, and other organ meats, tomato, oregano, and bay leaf. It is served with a round bread called *pitta* with a hole in the middle where the stew is placed. It is eaten in bites (*morsi*, which is the origin of the name). In the past, cod *mursiellu* was made on Friday, when meat was forbidden by the Church. It is occasionally possible to taste cod *mursiellu* nowadays. The places where *mursiellu* is served used to be very humble locales called *putiche*. There are still a few around today.

DINING

Da Salvatore, Salita I del Rosario 28, tel. 0961/724318. Closed Monday and last three weeks in August. All credit cards. Moderately inexpensive.

Very good eating: lasagne, fried cod, *mursiellu*, and pizza. A happy ambience.

Osteria La Stella del Sud, Via Cilea 44, no telephone. Open 9–14h; closed Sunday, holidays, and mid-July–end of August. No credit cards. Moderately inexpensive.

Very good *mursiellu*.

Cicala (Catanzaro)

CHESNUTS

Fratelli Muraca, via Garibaldi 129, tel. 0968/85305, fax 0968/85313.

The Muraca brothers like to extol the healthful properties of chestnuts, which contain potassium, phosphorus, magnesium, calcium, iron, sodium, protein, vita-mins B_1, B_2, and C. They claim that

Grandma Carmela lived to ninety-nine years old thanks to chestnuts, and that Grandma Annina made it to ninety-seven the same way. They sell chestnuts in many forms—fresh, dried, puréed, candied, in syrup, and as chestnut flour, which can be used to make bread, fritters, or gnocchi. They will ship all but fresh chestnuts.

Cosenza

Although Cosenza is an ancient city (it was Cosentia to the Romans), I find it interesting because much of the old city, the *centro storico*, seems locked in about 1910 to 1940. It looks much like our immigrant grandparents from Calabria might have known it. Take a walk up the Corso Telesio (described under "A Walk Through Old Cosenza," below). The new city of Cosenza, at the foot of the *centro storico*, is modern, but it too feels slightly old-fashioned, as if it were locked in the 1960s. Cosenza is a city that almost never sees tourists, except those who are passing through *en route* to the Sila. It has relatively few hotels and restaurants that would be acceptable in cities with more traffic. The Hotel Centrale, usually considered the leading place to stay, is mediocre at best. I prefer the Excelsior, which is all faded charm, not bad, but not for every taste. There are brand-new hotels outside of town that have meeting facilities, but you need a car or a taxi to get around.

CAFFÈ

Gran Caffè Renzelli, Corso Telesio 46, tel. 0894/26814. Open until 12h or later depending on the traffic; closed Tuesday.

Opened in 1800 as the Caffè Gallicchio, the Renzelli has been restored faithfully to its old style. It absolutely merits a visit if you are in Cosenza. At its outdoor tables you can have a nice view of the back of the Duomo and, to the right, the hills beyond. Inside is a cash register from 1910 (the year the Renzelli family became the owner), an antique coffee grinder, cups and dishes from long ago, diplomas and other forms of recognition that would be at home on the walls of Gabriele d'Annunzio because of their florid language and design that is part monumental, part Pre-Raphaelite. There is even a certificate of merit from King Vittorio Emanuele III dated 6 March 1929, and a Mussolinian diploma from 1928.

DINING

L'Arco Vecchio, Piazza Archi di Ciaccio 21, tel. 0984/72564. Closed Sunday, mid-August. All credit cards. Moderate.

A pleasing restaurant in the old town that is faithful to the Calabrese tradition.

Al Frantoio, Via Ternesa, tel. 0984/31131. Closed for three weeks in August. All credit cards. Moderate.

Just outside Cosenza is this restaurant built inside a former olive oil press that specializes in seafood and also serves pizza in the evening.

FIGS

Luigi Bertini & Figli, Corso Mazzini 92, tel. 0984/22517, fax 0984/76910. Closed Saturday afternoon and Sunday.

Some of the best stuffed figs in Calabria can be had at this small, inviting store on Cosenza's main thoroughfare. It ships to all of Italy and abroad. It has baked figs *(crocetti)* filled with either walnuts or almonds, and the latter also can be had chocolate-covered. Candied fruits *(fruttini)* such as citron, orange, tangerine, cherry, or chestnut are sold covered with chocolate. There are many other delicacies as well, and mixed boxes can be made, so you can taste an assortment.

FOOD AND SPECIALTY SHOPS

Via Piave (off Corso Mazzini) has fish markets most mornings.

Rondinella, Via Piave 37, tel. 0984/26850. Closed Saturday and Sunday.

This is the best store I found in Calabria to purchase calabrese food and wines, especially from the Sila. There are all kinds of mountain mushrooms, fresh, dried, and preserved in oil. You can find other vegetables in jars, including black olives, tomatoes, wild chicory, *lampascioni* (little onions), and various vegetable sauces. There are many types of pasta, all made in Calabria, including *peperonella*, which is made with *peperoncino*. There are cans of excellent Tonno Callipo, pink tuna from Pizzo. Little jars called Rosamarina contain tiny baby anchovies. All of the cheeses are made by the owners. These include a fresh ricotta made of a mixture of goat's and sheep's milks. This cheese is also sold smoked and stored in a basket that gives it a cylindrical shape. Also available are provolone, Pecorino, and mozzarella. There are numerous *salami*, including *salamino calabrese* (spiked with *peperoncino*) and *pancetta* rolled in *peperoncino*. The many honeys include *mandarino*. Very popular here is *mosto cotto*, known elsewhere as *sapa*, which is a concentrated syrup made from the juice of wine grapes. You can also buy locally roasted coffees made by Gugliemo Sesso.

A WALK THROUGH OLD COSENZA

Start at the Piazza Matteotti, opposite the old train station. You can see how this station was situated to carry goods to and from the old city of Cosenza. This station was recently rendered obsolete by the clean, modern station that seems to be the model of new Italian railway terminals (there is one that is almost identical in Pescara). The new railway station, unfortunately, is far from the city center. Near the Piazza Matteotti, be sure to visit the old Excelsior Hotel (now called the Nuovo Excelsior Hotel), a whiff of the early twentieth century that was, in effect, a southern Italian equivalent of the French Grand Hotel de la Gare. Look in its lobby and the adjoining bar, and you will be impressed by its faded grandeur. Then walk toward the old city, and you will find Mazzuca, a store on Piazza Tommaso Campanella (next to the Church of San Domenico) that is worth a look. The sign says that it has been in business since 1930, but in fact it has been much longer. This store has all kinds of corks, from tiny to huge. Many of these are appealingly displayed on a rack to the left of the main door as you enter. There are also demijohns, bottles, and all manner of wine-making equipment, some of it rather rustic. You get a sense of how people make wine at home in the rural south. Go over the bridge called the Ponte Martire to the Piazza Valdesi, a busy intersection with fruit and vegetable stalls. This is the beginning of the *centro storico*, the old section of Cosenza. It is interesting to walk up the Corso Telesio, which is a street undergoing transition. There are traces of many old family businesses whose signs and shutters bespeak respectability. One notices that most of the storefronts represent services based on artisanal work—watch repair, shoemaking, tailoring. Many are now closed, but one sees the beginnings of a revival, with the opening of a few art galleries bravely trying to survive like flowers pushing through a late-spring snowfall. After visiting the Duomo, walk up to the Piazza Parrasio, where you will see the historic Gran Caffè Renzelli (see *"Caffè,"* above). It has been restructured but preserves its old style and merits a visit. At its outdoor tables you have a nice view of the back of the Duomo and, to the right, the hills beyond. After your coffee, walk farther up the Corso Telesio to the Piazza XV Marzo. Here are the prefecture, the interesting Museo Civico Archeologico in the Palazzo dell' Accademia Cosentina, and, above all, the Teatro Comunale Rendano near the lush gardens of the Villa Comunale, where young couples go to bill and coo. The theater, which opened in 1903, has an imposing exterior and a gracious auditorium within. Although it has three tiers, the 830-seat theater is quite intimate. The elaborately painted curtain brings to mind the old one at La Fenice in Venezia, except that instead of depicting exploits at sea, this one is all castles and cavalry. This walk you have completed is a rare view, largely unaltered, of what life must have been like in a remote provincial capital in the Italian south a century ago. Try to think what a peasant from a small village in the Sila must have thought arriving at the old station and making his way up this same hill to the center of power at the Villa Comunale.

Diamante (Cosenza)

Diamante has some of the most pristine beaches in Italy, and the air is made fragrant by the many citron trees in the area. This is where many Jewish merchants came to purchase the fruit for religious observances.

DINING

Azienda Agricola Il Corvino, Contrada Fiumara, tel. 0985/876325. Reservations essential. Open daily. No credit cards. Moderate.

This is a farm easily reached from Diamante where you can have a delicious meal. Rosalba de Marco works wonders with eggplant, peppers, and pasta, above all *lagana e ceci* (lasagne with chickpeas). There is also excellent grilled meat, espe-

cially pork. The ambience is very friendly. Rosalba makes her own *digestivo* of citron that is the perfect way to end a meal.

SPECIALTY FOOD STORE

Sapore Calabria, Via Amendola 3.

One of the better sources in the region for the typical flavors that are hard to find elsewhere. There are more than three hundred items, including *liquore di cedro* (citron liqueur), citron jam, *salami*, cheeses, pastas, and so on. Worth a visit.

Maida (Catanzaro)

OLIVE OIL

Antico Frantoio Fratelli Anania, tel. 0968/71402, fax 0968/71401.

This producer makes a particularly fruity olive oil, unusual for this part of Italy.

Reggio Calabria

Reggio Calabria is a dispirited and dispiriting place that has only two things that inspire. The Lungomare Matteotti is a seaside promenade with attractive stretches and the Museo Nazionale has a world-class artistic treasure in the Bronzes of Riace, the famous bronze statues found on the sea's floor in 1972. The museum also has a superb collection of the antiquities of Magna Grecia, including numerous amphorae that were used to transport oil and wine in ancient Greek ships. Otherwise, Reggio Calabria is a transit point to and from Sicilia for rail and vehicular traffic that takes the ferry across the Straits of Messina.

DINING

Baylik, Vico Leone 1, tel. 0965/48624. Closed Thursday, mid-August. All credit cards. Moderate.

With a view of the Straits of Messina and carefully rendered local food, this is the place to eat. Try the *parmigiana di pesce* if they have it.

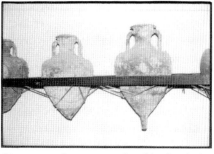

Terracotta amphorae were used to ship oil and wine in ancient times

MUSEUM

Museo Nazionale, Piazza De Nava and Piazza Indipendenza. Closed Monday.

If you want to visit the museum before catching a train north or a ferry to Sicilia, take a train to the Stazione Lido, and the museum will be in front of you. Later, to get the ferry, you need to take a train north to Villa San Giovanni. On your way to the room leading to Bronzes of Riace, stop to look at the thirty-five amphorae, many dating from 400 B.C. They are shaped as they are so that they could be stacked closely in holds so that a ship could carry many of them.

WINE

Enoteca Vintripodi, Via Vittorio Veneto 46a (near Via Roma), tel. 0965/895009.

Fausto Tripodi is a knowledgeable wine maker who makes good Greco di Bianco and other wines and sells fine wine from throughout Calabria and beyond.

Riace (Reggio Calabria)

Off the coast here in August 1972, the magnificent Riace bronze statues were fished out of the sea and given a home in the Museo Nazionale in Reggio Calabria. If you are here the last weekend of September (around 25 to 27), go to La Festa per i Santi Cosima e Damiano. This is a festival honoring two revered saints who are the Christian stand-ins for Castor and Pollux, local figures of note from the age of antiquity. Pilgrims come from all over the region for this major event, where they will eat and then dance the tarantella all night.

San Giovanni in Fiore and Sila (Cosenza)

The Sila (from *silva brutta*, or "wild forest") has five-hundred-year-old pine trees that are 2 meters (6.6 feet) in diameter and more than 40 meters (132 feet) high. The trees, at Fallistro, near Camigliatello, are known as the Giants of Sila and are famous throughout Italy. The Sila is laced with six rivers—the Mucone, Corace, Tacina, Trionto, Crati, and Neto that flow into great artificial lakes such as Lago Cecita near Camigliatello. These lakes were created at the beginning of the twentieth century and make the Sila distinct because so much of inland southern Italy has always been short of water. The forests of the Sila are so green in part because there is so much water present. The Sila forests are full of animals such as deer, foxes, squirrels, hare, owls, woodpeckers, and wild boars. But the most notable species is the Apennine wolf, of which fewer than one hundred remain. They are very shy, so it is unlikely you will see one, but at night there is the haunting sound of their baying, which contrasts with the hooting of the many species of owl.

Unless you have a car, the best way to journey through the Sila is to take the old cog railway or the bus *(pullman)* that departs from the new train station in Cosenza. In the past the railway was the only way to go, but now the buses are rapidly making the train obsolete. The road climbs quickly into the mountains over spectacular passes spanned by bridges that are audacious feats of engineering. Many people choose to get off and perhaps stay in Camigliatello, which is a charming town in a lovely situation, but I prefer to go to higher ground to San Giovanni in Fiore. About 300 meters (990 feet) from the start of the road from Camigliatello to San Giovanni is a stand at the turn of the road where you can buy delicious mountain cheeses made of sheep's or cow's milk. It also sells jarred mushrooms and very good honey. Try some on a slice of Pecorino for a novel taste sensation.

As you journey toward San Giovanni, you will pass cattle grazing in high pastures of grass and purple, red, and yellow flowers that make a beautiful contrast to the deep lakes and towering trees beyond. As I traveled this route and reached San Giovanni, I thought of the touring players in the opera *I Pagliacci*, who might have traveled in this area a century ago. Now for entertainment the citizens gather in front of the screen of the Cinema Italia to watch televised soccer matches.

BAR

Birreria Passepartout, Via Roma 39.

In this alpine part of southern Italy it is possible to drink Danish and German beer on tap in this local hangout where young people engage in very competitive games of chess. The whole thing seems very out of place, yet it is real.

DINING

Osteria Bologna (also called Il Cuore della Sila), Via Gramsci 329, tel. 0984/991533. Closed Monday. Moderately inexpensive.

Good food. Porcini mushrooms are found in many dishes, including *sciacatielli* (long, quill-shaped pasta) *alla boscaiola* and *cotoletta alla Silena* (veal with mushrooms and mozzarella). An order of large roasted porcini *(porcini arrosti)* is another pick. They also appear in the antipasto *Silano*, along with many types of *salumi.* The local white and red wines are called Silanello. There are also some Bolognese dishes, but I would stick to local food.

FOOD STORES AND SPECIALTY SHOPS

Mulino a Cilindri Belsito, 235 Via Roma.

Not to be missed. An old mill for grain and flour. The door is often open and you can have a discreet look inside at this large cylinder-powered mill that must have seemed remarkably advanced in this far-away place when it opened in the 1920s. Next door, at #233, is the Panificio Belsito, where you can get local *pane casareccio* made with the flour from the mill.

Caseificio Sociale Croce di Magra, Via Roma 225.

Fresh cheeses made in the Sila, including ricotta, *scamorza,* and mozzarella.

Panificio Fratelli Mancini, Via Panoramico 83.

Excellent bread, including the typical *pitta mpaigliata.*

Pizzicheria, Via della Repubblica 1.

Isabella, a very sweet woman, can make you a delicious *panino* with many local ingredients. Mine had fresh mozzarella topped with *peperoncino*-spiked grilled eggplant and was scrumptious. If you want provisions for a mountain hike, this is where to come.

Centro Artigianato Tiano, Via Vallone 225, tel. 0984/991515.

Sila wood carvings, blankets, and other crafts.

Tropea (Vibo Valentia)
Classic Town

For a small town (population seven thousand), Tropea has many food specialties, thanks to fertile land and a generous sea. The red onions of Tropea are the most famous specialty, and the eggplants, capers, tomatoes, and fish are also excellent. The local pasta is *filej,* short macaroni that look like thick string beans and are chewy in texture. They are served with a spicy pork sauce. Other specialties are *pasta con nero di seppie* (with cuttlefish ink), swordfish, *peperonata* (cooked peppers), almonds, and almond paste *(pasta di mandorle).* Add to this abundance the town's relative isolation from the main byways of Calabria (so that a local culture could develop without outside influences), and you have a place to be treasured. Tropea receives enough tourism to have a steady income, but it has not sacrificed its values and virtues. The Piazza Vittorio Veneto still fills with locals each evening. Hotels run north and south of town, and though there is some tackiness, the ambience is nice.

BARS AND CAFFÈS

The Piazza Vittorio Veneto, with its big outdoor *caffès*, pulsates with life. This is the place where the people of Tropea meet.

Caffè del Corso, Corso Vittorio Emanuele 14.

A nice place for morning coffee with good *paste* (breakfast rolls). They also sell local almond paste.

DINING

During high tourist season most restaurants are open every day.

Trattoria al Timone, Piazza del Duomo. No telephone. No credit cards. Moderately inexpensive.

This nice place faces the attractive Duomo on what is a relatively quiet piazza, except for the occasional passing *motorino* and the sound of children playing soccer in the courtyard. There are outdoor tables and good fragrances that greet your arrival. Start with *bruschetta all'inferno*, a toast topped with a spread of tomatoes, oil, and *peperoncino*. The *filej*, instead of being sauced with pork, come with a delicate combination of tomato, garlic, piquant green pepper, and grated Pecorino. The *spaghetti al nero di seppie* (with cuttlefish ink) is very good. The trattoria also serves *spaghetti al uova di pescespada* (swordfish roe), which I did not sample. You should certainly have the *insalata tropeana*—tomatoes, olives, bits of cheese, oregano, and

the famous onions. The *secondi* feature all the local seafood. I was encouraged to try the *sùrici*, delicious little white fish caught locally and delicately batter-fried. You must beware of bones. Some people eat these fish whole; I preferred to cut off the head, split the fish lengthwise, lift out the bones, squeeze some lemon, and then eat. (The fish heads were a princely meal for a mendicant cat.) Local fruit was a good dessert. The waiters were the young sons of the family, barely into their teens, who are already more expert than many professionals.

Osteria del Pescatore, Via del Monte 7, tel. 0963/603018. Closed October to April. No credit cards. Moderate.

The fish is good and the *spaghetti alla cipolla rossa* (red onion) or *tropeana* (mixed vegetables) is great.

Trattoria Vecchia Tropea, Largo Barone. No telephone. No credit cards. Moderately inexpensive.

Go down Largo Duomo to Via Vulcano. Turn left and go past the doorway where the old lady and small children are watching TV. You will reach a small piazza at Largo Barone. This back alley is a spot that probably matches some preconceived idea you've had about what small-town Italy looks like. This is a great spot for outdoor dining on local specialties.

Ristorante Pimms, Largo Migliaresi, tel. 0963/666105. Closed Monday. Master Card, Visa. Moderately expensive.

The food is good but the main reason to come is the panoramic view of the Norman castle and beautiful sunsets over the sea.

FOLKLORE

Sagra del Pesce Azzurro e della Cipolla Rossa di Tropea.

On July 4 Tropea celebrates its famous on-ion and the *pesce azzurro*, one of the favor-ite fishes from local waters. You can sample dishes with these ingredients at many local restaurants.

FOOD SHOPPING

Prodotti Casarecci, Largo Vaccari (just beyond the Piazzetta Panoramica that leads to the city center).

Cesarina Stupia sells all kinds of local specialties: onions, anchovies, sun-dried tomatoes, olives, eggplants, local tuna in oil, artichokes, capers, dried or baked figs, olive spread, *peperoncino* (dried or in oil), and *'nduja*.

Ditta F. Schiariti, Via Campo Superiore 13, 88038 Tropea (Vibo Valentia), tel. and fax 0963/61675.

Just outside of town, a leading grower and shipper of Tropea's red onions.

Fruit and vegetable stand, Corso Vittorio Emanuele 6 (corner of Viale Regina Margherita).

Here is the place to buy red onions and *local* fruit. The flavors will amaze you. It also sells local wine and almond paste.

LODGING

Hotel Rocca Nettuno, Via Annunziata, tel. 0963/61580 or 61612, fax 0963/62717, www.roccanettuno.com. MasterCard, Visa.

The Hotel Rocca Nettuno, where I stayed on my most recent visit, is a study in sociology and the trends of European tourism. Namely, it is the Germans who often call the shots because they are far and away the most numerous travelers. The Rocca Nettuno is just south of town in a beautiful setting: the hotel and gardens are perched 36 meters (120 feet) above a stunning beach with white sand and clean water. Because Tropea is much farther from Germany than Lago di Garda or Rimini, the Germans who come here are those in the know. The food is of much better quality than the spaghetti-and-tomato-sauce/ breaded-veal-cutlet set meals one finds up north. There is a good selection of fish, vegetables, pasta, meats, and fresh fruit. Breakfasts are more traditionally German, with eggs, cheeses, wursts, dark breads, and cereals. There are many planned activities—something very un-Italian—as well as a health spa, a doctor, a masseur, and a children's pool. The tropical gardens are gorgeous, the rooms are large and comfortable, and the prices are moderate. I do not mean to suggest that a non-German is unwelcome, but rather that very few seem to come here. German is the first language, with Italian spoken among the staff. The non-German traveler might feel a bit out of place at the Rocca Nettuno, but should not avoid it for that reason.

La Minestra di Castagne, Latte, e Riso di Nonna Annina
Grandma Annina's Chestnut, Milk, and Rice Soup

Annina dalla Cutura of Cicala lived to the age of ninety-seven and claimed that this soup was one of her secrets to good health.

Serves 4

200 grams/7 ounces fresh chestnuts
2 liters/slightly more than 2 quarts cold water
Salt to taste
150 grams/¾ cup Italian rice
½ liter/2 cups milk
1 tablespoon unsalted butter

Boil some water, peel the outer skin off the chestnuts, and plunge them in the hot water for a few minutes. You will then be able to peel off the second skin. Put the peeled chestnuts in a pot containing the cold water, add some salt to taste, cover, and cook over medium-low heat for 3 hours. Then add the rice and cook for half the projected cooking time of the rice (typically 12 to 15 minutes). Then add the milk and butter and keep cooking until the rice is done (use projected cooking time as a guide but check for doneness). The soup should be quite dense.

Variation: I added a little sugar and cinnamon before eating this soup. It was delicious, but I don't know if Grandma Annina would approve.

Fichi Freschi Ripieni
Stuffed Fresh Figs

Serves 4

12 perfectly ripe fresh figs
1 tablespoon candied citron or other fruit, cut in bits
30 grams/1 ounce/¼ cup finely chopped almonds
1 tablespoon honey
1 tablespoon bittersweet or semisweet chocolate shavings
1 tablespoon confectioners' sugar (optional)

Cut the figs in half vertically and scoop out a teaspoonful of the pulp. Combine thoroughly the fig pulp, candied fruit, almonds, honey, and chocolate in a bowl. Be careful not to stir aggressively or the fig pulp will liquefy. Fill the fig halves with the filling. If you wish, dust lightly with the sugar.

Sicilia

O tu, Palermo, terra adorata,	O, Palermo, you adored land,
A me sì caro sorriso d'amor, ah!	like a dear smile of love to me!
Alza la fronte tanto oltreggiata	Raise your outraged brow
Il tuo ripiglia primier splendor!	and take back your previous splendor!
Chiesi aita a straniere nazioni	I sought aid from foreign lands
Ramingai per castella e città	I wandered through castles and cities
Ma insensibil al fervido sprone	but, unmoved by my ardent prompting,
Dicea ciascun: Siciliani	everyone asked: "Sicilians,
Ov'è il prisco valor?	Where is your long-lost glorious valor?
Su, sorgete a vittoria, all'onor!	Rise, rise up to victory, to honor!"

—E. SCRIBE AND C. DUVEYRIER, ORIGINAL FRENCH
LIBRETTO, VERDI'S I VESPRI SICILIANI

REGIONAL CAPITAL:
Palermo (PA).

PROVINCIAL CAPITALS:
Agrigento (AG), Caltanissetta (CL), Catania (CT), Enna (EN), Messina (ME), Ragusa (RG), Siracusa (SR), Trapani (TP).

TOURIST INFORMATION:
There are tourist offices for each province. Those for Agrigento, Catania, Messina, Palermo, Ragusa, Siracusa, and Trapani are listed under the headings for those cities. If you need information about a place in the province, contact the provincial office (for

 The rising and falling fates of Sicilia through many centuries seem to be mirrored in Palermo, the capital of Italy's largest region. Here is a city of great beauty and terrible squalor that reflects the legacies of Siculi, Greek, Roman, Arab, Norman, Spanish, and Italian civilizations. You will see splendid churches, squares, monuments, and architecture. There is a vibrant market, delicious food can be had at all prices, and

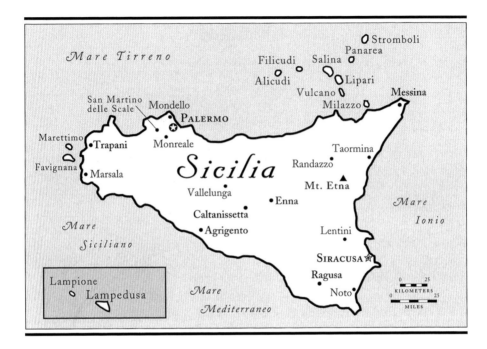

example, contact Siracusa if you want information about Noto).

Agritourism:

Associazione Agriturist
Regionale,
Via Alessio di
Giovanni 14,
90144 Palermo,
tel. 091/346046.

there is a strong cultural and political tradition. Yet parts of the city have never been restored following the destruction wreaked in World War II. Unemployment is high, and many people are disenchanted and disaffected. The Mafia makes its presence felt in frequent conflicts among clans and occasionally with government officials. In recent years, the great majority of *palermitani* have risen to reclaim their city from governmental corruption and organized crime.

Sicilia has endured so much oppression from foreign rulers and domination that it often drew inward, seeking to protect itself from harm. So it is its great achievement that it has built a magnificently complex culture with sublime food, great music (Vincenzo Bellini), literature from writers such as Sciascia, Lampedusa, and Pirandello, and painters such as De Chirico and Guttoso. Sicilian life is full of color and spectacle, as is evident in the religious observances at Easter and in the famous medieval puppet shows in Palermo. It is also full of tragedy, of families separated by immigration, by war, by feuds, by men who leave in search of work. The opera *Cavalleria Rusticana* perfectly depicts all of this conflicting festivity and drama.

Sicilians love titles and honorifics as part of their formal, somewhat-baroque way of interacting. Once, in a restaurant in Siracusa, I heard the phone ring, and the proprietor answered by saying "Buona sera, ingegnere!" ("Good evening, engineer"). A second call prompted a "Buona sera, avvocato!" ("Good evening, lawyer"). The third time a caller asked for one of the diners. He was summoned to the phone with "Barone, é per Lei" ("Baron, it is for you"). A not-particularly-distinguished man took the call. Whether he was a baron, I do not know. Nowadays, barons and baronesses look like everyone else. What is of interest is that this behavior—part deferential respect, part tradition, part fear—is indicative of the way people in Sicilia interact. They are courteous, formal, and a bit wary of anyone they do not know intimately.

What makes the travel experience in Sicilia so meaningful is that it is not, for the most part, oriented to tourism. Taormina is a splendid vacation spot, and islands such as Pantelleria and Lipari receive a select clientele from northern Italy. A few visitors come to Sicilia for the architectural sites and perhaps Mount Etna. So if you go to Palermo, Marsala, Siracusa, and other towns, you will find a people, and a place, going about their lives as they normally do. The food you eat will be their food, and if you have to struggle a bit to fit in, your effort will be rewarded. If you are dealt with coolly or formally, you will know the reason why. You are as new to them as they are to you.

Eating in Sicilia

In my regional discussions of the cuisines of many parts of southern Italy, I use the term *cucina povera* to describe peasant cuisine or the cooking of the poor. This simply means that there were few ingredients and flavors available to impoverished people who nonetheless used creativity and ingenuity to create tasty and substantial dishes. The story of eating in Sicilia is something else again. Here is one of the foremost kitchens in Italy, bursting with flavor, color, fragrance, and high drama. In addition to the creative poor who had unusual ingredients available to them, Sicilia had two other important strains in its culinary evolution. The monks and especially the nuns in convents become proficient pastry chefs who sold their products to support their orders. They were among the first to preserve and candy citrus and other fruits, and they were the guardians of the tradition of making ice cream. At certain points in Sicilian history when nuns left the convent they were engaged by wealthy families to make sweets for daily consumption and festive occasions. This explains in part why Sicilian Easter and Christmas desserts are unrivaled. As the nuns' work was appreciated by a wider segment of the population, sweet making became an honored profession on the island. During the period of the Bourbon occupation (at the end of the eighteenth century) the noble families of Sicilia wanted professional French chefs in their homes. A class of chef called the *monzù* (the word is a corruption of the French *monsieur*) entered Sicilian kitchens (carrying butter) and developed a refined culinary tradition that is distinct from the peasant food that is usually associated with southern Italy. There

Outstanding vegetables grow in Sicilia

are still some *monzù* extant today, including Mario Lo Menzo, the chef at the Regaleali cooking school in Vallelunga.

But the success of poor cooks, monastic cooks, and the *monzù* owed a great deal
to the fact that Sicilia is blessed with amazing raw materials. Unlike Sardinians, who
avoided the sea until recent decades, Sicilians have feasted on the magnificent fruits
of the sea since antiquity. Luscious vegetables that flavor many of the pasta sauces
and main courses grow throughout the island. The citrus fruits (called *agrumi* or *za-
garà*) that grow near Palermo are sublime eaten alone and are regular protagonists in
every part of the meal. Exotic combinations of nuts, fruit, fish, herbs, and bread produce dishes of unself-conscious sophistication. They flavor memorable *primi* using
pasta, rice, and couscous (a legacy of Sicilia's many centuries of contact with North
Africa). Powerful wines add assertive flavors to many recipes. One would think that
all the high-powered, intensely flavored ingredients would implode when combined, yet they succeed brilliantly. Sicilian baking is unmatched in its richness and is
one of the most appreciated of any Italian region. And the ice cream of Sicilia, at its
best, is poetry in the mouth. It is impossible to list even a small number of the great
foods of the island, so I commend anyone who wants a deeper knowledge of Sicilian
cooking to read books by Mary Taylor Simeti, Anna Tasca Lanza, Mimmetta Lo
Monte, and Anna Muffoletto. In selecting Siracusa as the Classic Town for the region, I have included nearby itineraries for you to get a sense of the food of that province, which offers many of the most essential Sicilian flavors.

A few words about Sicilian restaurants: There was not a real restaurant tradition in Sicilia until recent years. People with money always had their own chefs, and those without money cooked at home. Many people without proper cooking facilities also went to fry shops to buy delicious but humble precooked foods. After the Second World War, out-of-work chefs from wealthy families became teachers of cooking. Their students cooked in the first restaurants of consequence that opened on the island, but theirs was a sort of fancy international style of cooking that excluded the treasures of Sicilian home cooking. Only recently has that sort of food been afforded the glory it deserves, and I have tried to list restaurants and trattorias that are exponents of the home tradition.

ANTIPASTI E MERENDE (APPETIZERS AND SNACKS)

There is no tradition of antipasti in Sicilia. The snacks typical of fry shops now appear as antipasti, as do dishes that have been appropriated from other courses.

Arancini. Crunchy rice balls flavored with ground beef, chicken, or vegetables.

Cacio all'Argintera. Fried or roast cheese with a dressing of oil, anchovies, and oregano.

Guasteddu (also called *Pani Ca' Meusa*). A Palermo specialty: a sesame-seed roll is filled with spleen and *caciocavallo* cheese.

Panelle. Chickpea fritters.

Sarde a Beccafico. Boneless fillets of fresh sardines filled with bread crumbs, cheese, raisins, and herbs.

Sfincioni. Light, pizzalike snacks with onion and tomato.

PRIMI

Cuscus (Cuscusu). Couscous is a legacy of the many years of Arab influence in Sicilia.

Pasta alla Norma. With tomato sauce, *ricotta salata,* and fried eggplant. A specialty of Catania.

Pasta or *Risotto con Frutti di Mare.* Many varieties of seafood are served with pasta or rice.

Paste con le Sarde. Fresh sardines, wild fennel, chopped onions, tomato sauce, olive oil, black currants, pine nuts, sea salt, and sugar. A Palermo specialty.

Spaghetti alla Siracusana. With bread crumbs and anchovies.

Zuppa di Aragoste. Lobster soup, a specialty of Trapani.

SECONDI

There is an old Sicilian proverb: *Quannu 'u piscaturi pigghia pisci, magari passa Cristu 'un lu canusci* (When a fisherman catches a fish, he wouldn't even notice if Christ passed by). The waters that surround Sicilia provide an amazing bounty of fish and seafood. If a fisherman has a good day, he can feed his family and earn money. One of the most dramatic and, yes, upsetting things to observe in Sicilia, especially near Trapani, is *la mattanza,* as fishermen in small boats encircle a school of tuna and stab wildly to kill as many as they can. As the water turns red with blood, the fishermen pull in their catch. The two most prized fish are *tonno* (tuna) and *pescespada* (swordfish), which appear in many guises in Sicilian fish cookery. "Poorer" fish such as *alici* (fresh anchovies, which taste nothing like salted ones) and *sarde* (fresh sardines) are no less flavorful or nutritious than their larger cousins. If you see the word *neonata* (*nunnata* in dialect), this refers to one of the many types of delicate newborn fish. Seafood includes *ricci* (sea urchins), *gamberoni* (large shrimp), *vongole* (clams), *cozze* (mussels), *polpo* (octopus), *seppie* (cuttlefish), calamari (squid).

Beef and veal are precious commodities in Sicilia, and goats and lambs are prized (although the latter are always consumed at Easter). Chickens and rabbit are the most common sources of animal protein.

CONTORNI

Sicilia is blessed with vegetables of amazing variety and quality. Eggplant reigns, particularly in the eastern part of the island, and tomatoes, onions, zucchini, capers, garlic, olives (and olive oil), broccoli, peppers, and cauliflower are wonderful. Look for the unusual purple cauliflower.

FORMAGGI

Many of the classic cheeses of the South are found in Sicilia, too. Listed below are a few that are especially popular.

Caciocavallo Siciliano (also called *Casciavaddu Rausanu*). A large, long cheese with a rounded bottom. Made primarily of cow's milk. A specialty of Ragusa. Sometimes fried or grilled and served with oil and pepper.

Canestrato (also called *Incanestrato*). A sheep's-milk cheese that, when fresh, is sold under the name *tuma*. Most *tuma* is put in small wicker baskets and aged. The rind of the harder cheese shows the imprint of the basket. The cheese is used for eating and for grating into fillings.

Majorchino. A Pecorino heavily spiked with black pepper. A specialty of Messina.

Piacentino. A *canestrato* with pepper.

Ragusano. A 100 percent cow's-milk cheese from Ragusa. It can be eaten young and smooth or aged and granular.

DOLCI

Read more about sweets in "Ice Cream and Pastries" in "Noto" (page 647) and the convent of the Church of Santa Maria dell'Ammiriraglio (La Martorana) in "Palermo" (page 649).

Cannoli. Traditional at Carnival, although you can find them most of the year. These are deep-fried cylinders of dough that are filled with luscious ricotta cheese and, often, chocolate chips or bits of candied fruit.

Cassata Siciliana. Made of *pan di Spagna* (sort of a sponge cake) with ricotta, sugar, vanilla, chocolate, pistachios, and cinnamon, icing, candied fruit, and marzipan. The origin of this is that once upon a time the ingredients were *incassate* (encased), as ricotta and sugar were put in a little wooden box and pressed. Then candied citrus would be churned in, and it was ready. Modifications in time saw the *cassata* become round and surrounded with a marzipan wrapping.

Fruit. Despite all of the wonderful desserts, little can rival Sicilian fruit: the figs and grapes are delicious, and the *agrumi—limoni* (lemons), *cedri* (citrons), *mandarini* (tangerines), and *tarocchi* (blood oranges)—rank with the best in the world. Every month during the winter a new kind of orange seems to be harvested, and if you are there you should try them all.

Gelato. Much of Italy's best ice cream is made in Sicilia, especially Noto.

Pasta Reale. Almond paste (marzipan). Sicilian almonds are unsurpassed in flavor, and their taste can be found in many desserts. The best almonds are said to come from Avola, in the province of Siracusa. At Easter Sicilians like to eat a marzipan lamb filled with quince jam. It is called *pasta reale* (royal almond paste) because the extraordinarily beautiful confections made with this marzipan were considered suitable for a king.

BREAKFAST

Many Sicilians like to have a strong espresso accompanied by a dish of *granita di mandorle* (almond granita) and a sweet brioche. They either fill the brioche with some of the granita, or they consume the three items separately.

The Wines of Sicilia

Sicilia has more vineyards than any other region and in most years produces more wine. Yet *per capita*, Sicilians consume less wine than any other Italians. Many grapes go to make raisins, which are a key ingredient in Sicilian cooking, and for dessert wines, which require higher concentrations of grapes and are consumed in smaller amounts than table wine. Sicilia's claim to fame comes in its outstanding dessert wines, though in recent years its table wines have improved radically.

Marsala is one of the most famous dessert wines in the world. It is produced in the western tip of Sicilia in the province of Trapani, particularly in the town of Marsala. Vines have been cultivated in the Marsala area at least since the Phoenicians established colonies there in the eighth to sixth century B.C. The system for making the fortified (higher-alcohol) dessert wine that we know today was introduced in 1770 by John Woodhouse, an English wine merchant who had a background in sherry and port wines. Within thirty years or so, it became a viable product to sell in place of sherry, which was unavailable because the Napoleonic Wars were raging.

Nowadays there is intense grape cultivation (you will see vines much closer together than elsewhere in Italy) by the 3,065 local growers who supply their grapes to the eighteen Marsala producers. The wine is made of grape varieties that are native to Sicilia. To most wine drinkers outside of the region, Marsala is the rich, sweet dessert wine sold by Florio. If you travel to the area, you will discover that there are many variations in the wines that all come under the name "Marsala." Some are lean and dry; others rich and robust. There are two different types of Marsala, one lighter and one darker, and for each there is a choice of different grapes that can be used to make them. The lighter-colored wines, Ora and Ambra, are made from Catarratto and/or Ansonica (also called Inzolia) and/or Damaschino. The ruby-red wine called Rubino is made from Perricone grapes (known locally as Pignatello) and/or Calabrese (known locally as Nero d'Avola) and/or Nerello Mascalese. The types of Marsala change style and name, depending on their age. *Fino,* 17 percent alcohol, is aged for one year. It is sometimes labeled "LP" (London Particular) and comes either *dolce* (sweet), *semisecco* (semidry), or *secco* (dry). *Superiore* is aged in wood for four years and is 18 percent alcohol. It is sometimes labeled "SOM" (Superior Old Marsala), "LP," or "GD" (Garibaldi Dolce). *Vergine* or *solera* is aged in wood for five years to make a *secco* and spends ten years in the barrel to become *stravecchio* (extra aged).

Florio is by far the largest producer. Marco de Bartoli is an outstanding smaller producer. Others to look for are Fratelli Lombardo, Marino, Mirabella, Fratelli Montalto, Carlo Pellegrino, and Nuova Rallo.

Moscato di Pantelleria and Passito di Pantelleria are rich, spicy dessert wines made on the intensely sunny Sicilian island of Pantelleria, which is near Tunisia. Donnafugata and Salvatore Murana are good producers. Malvasia delle Lipari is an exceptional dessert wine made on Salina by Carlo Hauner. (See the listing for that island.)

Red and white table wines are found all over the island. Good ones are made by large producers such as Duca di Salaparuta, which makes Corvo; Regaleali; Rapi-talà; and smaller ones of quality such as Donnafugata, Fontanarossa, Consorzio Agrario Provinciale di Trapani, Planita, and Cooperativa Agricola Le Torn. In parts of Sicilia a celebration is held on November 11, the name day of San Martino, because this is the day when the wine is considered ready. The related expression is *Al giorno di San Martino il mosto diventa vino* (On Saint Martin's Day the must becomes wine). If you are in the region then, look around for signs announcing the local Festa del Vino.

Averna, one of Italy's favorite *digestivi,* is a product of Sicilia.

Agrigento

Agrigento has some of the finest Greek ruins anywhere, and there is a stupendous view of the temples and the sea. The city of Agrigento is only moderately interesting, and there has not been a great effort to create tourist facilities that meet the level of the principal attractions. But the temples are among the most moving things you will ever see.

DINING

Tratttoria dei Templi, Via Panoramica dei Templi 15, tel. 0922/403110. Closed Sunday (July–August), Friday (September –June), first ten days of July. All credit cards. Moderate.

The food is good, but the selling point here is the view of the temples.

Leon d'Oro, Viale Emporium 102, tel. 0922/414400. Closed Monday. All credit cards. Moderate.

In San Leone, 7 km (4 miles) from Agrigento but close to the temple district, is a good source of local flavors. The *casarecce con pescespada, pistacchio e pomodoro fresco* is wonderful fresh pasta with swordfish, pistachios and fresh tomato.

FOLKLORE

Sagra del Mandorlo in Fiore.

One of Sicilia's favorite festivals is the one each February that marks the flowering of the almond trees. There are concerts, parades, and feasts.

TOURIST OFFICE

Azienda Provinciale Turismo, Viale della Vittoria 255, 92100 Agrigento, tel. 0922/401352, fax 0922/25185.

Calascibetta (Enna)

FOLKLORE

Sagra di Buon Riposo.

A popular harvest festival in early September that includes races, music, and the Sagra della Salsiccia, with lots of feasting on sausages.

Catania

Catania is a hard city for the visitor to love. It is Sicilia's second-largest city, but lacks the splendor of Palermo. Crime and poverty are higher here than in most of Italy, and it has been viewed as so hopeless that it suffers from terrible neglect. It has been destroyed or damaged numerous times by the eruptions of Mount Etna and by war. One's impression of Catania will be especially grim if arriving at the train station or coming through the southern part of the city from the airport. It seems particularly depressed and desperate on a hot day as people wander about without direction or sprawl in grassless parks. But by the time one reaches the Via Etnea, there is a sense of a city that still retains some grandeur. The Duomo (dedicated to Sant'Agata) has curving arches that lead to an unexpected Gothic arch above the altar that pulls the eye upward from the view offered by the rest of the space. This visual command to look up is a metaphor for all of Catania. The farther one climbs, the more attractive the city becomes. The Corso Italia has some flash and charm, and some of the side streets above it are quite pleasant. The people of Catania are forthright and determined, and one admires their resilience. The city has a superb cultural tradition: there is an ancient Greek theater (Teatro Greco), where concerts, operas, and plays are given during the warm months. This is the birthplace of Vincenzo Bellini (1801–1835), whose sublime melodies in bel canto operas such as *Norma* and *I Puritani* have moved audiences and provided vehicles for divas such as Maria Callas, Joan Sutherland, and Montserrat Caballé. One of Italy's most popular pasta dishes, *spaghetti alla Norma*, is from Catania and named for the Bellini masterpiece. The Teatro Bellini is the finest opera house in Sicilia and, despite severe budgetary constraints, presents some of the best productions in Europe with top artists, conductors, and stage directors.

BAR-PASTICCERIA

Al Caprice, Via Etnea 30–32–34, tel. 095/ 320555. Closed Monday.

This *pasticceria-gastronomia* has classic Sicilian pastries such as cheesecake and *cannoli*, many cookies, and snacks such as *arancini* (with chicken, beef, or *alla Norma*). There is also excellent ice cream: I particularly liked *gelso* (mulberry) and *cedro* (citron). The Bar al Caprice dates back to the 1920s, although it was restored in 1976. While some of the art in the back room is of marginal quality, you should be sure to see the collection of drawings and lithographs by Renato Guttoso, a Sicilian who was one of the leading Italian artists of the twentieth century.

CULTURE

Teatro Bellini, Via G. Perrotta 12, tel. 095/312024.

Built in 1890, the theater has a memorable exterior: eleven busts of famous composers, with Bellini being the most prominent. Verdi and Rossini receive places of honor on either side, while Donizetti,

Bellini's bel canto rival, is on the rear right, as far out of view as is possible.

DINING

Trattoria La Paglia, Via Pardo 23, tel. 095/346838. Closed Sunday. No credit cards. Inexpensive.

I love this place right in the fish market of Catania. You should allow yourself to be guided by Maria, the lovely woman who is the spirit of La Paglia. Do not skip, as a *primo, la triaca pasta* (pasta in a fresh bean sauce). For a *secondo*, take the best fish available. If there's nothing you like (which I doubt) step outside, buy a fish, and Maria will cook it.

Ambasciata del Mare, Piazza Duomo 6, tel. 095/341003. Closed Monday and September. All credit cards. Moderate.

The "Embassy of the Sea" represents Neptune's realm well, drawing its bounty from Catania's nearby *pescheria* (fish market). The many good choices include *sarde a beccafico, tagliolini con bottarga di tonno*, and *cernia* (grouper). The *caponata* is also excellent.

TOURIST OFFICE
Ente Provinciale Per il Turismo, Largo *Paisiello 5, 95100 Catania, tel.* *095/312124.*

Gangi (Palermo)

FOLKLORE
Festa della Spiga e Corteo di Cerere.

In the second week of August an ancient harvest festival reenacts the devotion to Ceres, goddess of grain (from whom we get the word "cereal"). Music, dance, processions, and lots of food.

Lentini (Siracusa)

AGRITOURISM
Azienda Agricola Casabianca, tel. 095/497477.

Giovanna Notarbartolo grows oranges andother citrus and makes good jams and other products with them. There is also good wine, ricotta, and homemade bread. Food only; no lodging.

Lipari (Messina)

BAR-BAKERY
Bar-Pasticceria Subba, Via Vittorio Emanuele 92.

Excellent coffee, pastries, ice cream, and granita since 1930.

DINING
Filippino, Piazza Municipio, tel. 090/9811002, fax 090/9812878. Closed Monday (except June–September) and mid-November–mid-December. All credit cards. Moderate to moderately expensive.

This is the most famous restaurant in the Isole Eolie, and its good reputation is deserved. Filippino opened in the 1930s and quickly became the place where anti-Fascists who were exiled to Lipari would gather. The seafood is typically superb, but you should also try the *maccheroni alla Filippino,* pasta baked with meat sauce, egg-plant, mozzarella, Parmigiano-Reggiano, prosciutto, and hard-boiled eggs. There is a moderate to moderately expensive fixed-price meal, but there is so much to eat that it seems like a bargain. But you must be hungry.

Le Macine, Via Stradale 5 (in Pianoconte), tel. 090/9822387. Closed Tuesday (except in summer), February. All credit cards. Moderate.

Upon request when you call, a vehicle is sent to bring you to this restaurant a bit out of the center of Lipari. The view *en route* is gorgeous. The food has an exoticism that would seem forced in a restaurant in London or New York, but makes sense here. For example, *risotto con fichi e crostacei* combines figs and shellfish to great effect. Swordfish marinated in pistachio and mint works well, as does a salad of octopus and cantaloupe. Afterwards, try the *semifreddo allâ arancia con crema di bergamotto* (divine Sicilian orange *semifreddo* with bergamot cream).

A Loggia, Pianoconte, tel. 090/9822387. Visa. Expensive.

One must take an expensive taxi ride up to A Loggia, which occupies a lofty spot in Pianoconte in the hills above the town of Lipari. This is a very fancy restaurant with nouvelle pretentions, but there is an accurate and thorough understanding of flavor that one finds in dishes such as paper-thin slices of swordfish with tomato, eggplant, and fresh mint. The star pasta is *spaghetti con capperi e pomodori secchi sott'olio.*

Marsala (Trapani)

This place looks like North Africa. White and beige buildings sit low and flat under a broad, hot, cloudless sky. The fields of vines have a wild, unmanicured look about them, and you can imagine that these qualities are essential elements in the local wines.

DINING

Trattoria Garibaldi, Piazza dell' Addolorata 35, tel. 0923/953006. Closed Saturday lunch, Sunday dinner. All credit cards. Moderately inexpensive.

Good, simple fish preparation, including an excellent *cuscus di pesce.* At the end of the meal, *tagliancozzi* biscuits in Marsala.

MUSEUM

Museo Florio, Via Vincenzo Florio 1, tel. 0923/781111. Visits by appointment only.

This museum gathers equipment from the 1880s to the 1940s that was used in cultivation of grapes as well as in wine making. Notice the carts that were used back when for transporting grapes from the fields and barrels to the port for export.

WINE

Cantine Florio, Via Vincenzo Florio 1, tel. 0923/951122. Call for an appointment. Open 9–12:45h, 15–17:30h; closed Sunday.

Florio is the largest and most famous producer of Marsala, and one should not come to this area without visiting this winery and its museum (see listing above).

Azienda Agricola Vecchio Samperi—de Bartoli, Contrada Fornara Samperi 292, tel. 0923/962093. Visits in the afternoon, by appointment.

Marco de Bartoli likes to follow his own drummer in all things he does. He makes his wines largely using the Grillo grape, while most of the other producers use Catarratto. He calls Grillo "the Sicilian Chardonnay," and he harvests it a month before everyone else does, but makes his wines a month later than the others. De Bartoli's Grillo is one of the better white wines you will taste in Sicilia. The Marsalas have a clean taste and are rich in flavor— this is due in part to the fact that de Bartoli does not fortify his wine with added alcohol as most producers do. He produces an unusual dessert wine with *zibibbo* grapes from Pantelleria that he calls Bukkuram. He ages his older wines in chestnut, the younger ones in stainless steel or oak. Da Bartoli has also been a professional auto-rally and race-car driver and has an extraordinary collection of old cars that share space with his wine barrels. As he told me, "Wine making, like cars, is about control and about contact with the past."

Messina

DINING

Trattoria Piero, Via Ghibellina 121, tel. 090/718365. Closed Sunday and in August. MasterCard, Visa. Moderate to moderately expensive.

Very good *pasta 'ncaciata* (baked pasta with tomatoes, ricotta, eggplant, and basil) and daily seafood specials.

TOURIST OFFICE

Azienda Autonoma Soggiorno e Turismo, Piazza Cairoli 45, 98100 Messina, tel. 090/694780.

Milazzo (Messina)

Milazzo is the port for boats and hydrofoils to the Isole Eolie, including Lipari and Salina.

ENOTECA

Al Pescatore, Via Marina Garibaldi 176, tel. 090/9286595. Closed Tuesday, November. All credit cards. Moderate to moderately expensive.

Good fish and seafood cookery

Mondello (Palermo)

Mondello is the affluent suburb of Palermo that is the city's summer resort of choice. The beach is lined with bathing stations where cabanas are rented months in advance. The young people, many of them the *jeunesse dorée* of Sicilia, congregate each night in the Piazza Mondello and the surrounding restaurants before going to private parties in nearby villas. The bay is also full of windsurfers, many of them European champions.

DINING

Ristorante da Sariddu e Figli, Piazza Mondello 48, tel. 091/451922. Moderately expensive.

A very casual place with good seafood. If you would like to try *ricci* (raw sea urchins) this is the place to do it. If you don't want them raw, they can also be had hot with spaghetti. *Risotto con frutti di mare* and spaghetti with swordfish and baby shrimp are also admirable.

Trattoria Gambero Rosso, Via Piano Gallo 30–32, tel. 091/454685. Closed Monday and last two weeks in November. Moderate.

Very good seafood. The antipasti, including little fried fishes, *zuppa di cozze*, tiny fried calamari, cold seafood salad, are all yummy. *Risotto alla marinara* is flavored with tomato and *peperoncino* in addition to seafood, and the *spaghetti con le cozze* is rich in garlic. Grilled fish and shrimp are good secondi.

Pizzeria–Trattoria Marechiaro, Via Torre 28. Closed Wednesday. No credit cards. Inexpensive.

I had a superb *pizza greca* (olives, mushrooms, mozzarella, tomato, *peperoncino*, and eggplant).

ICE CREAM

Gelateria Antico Chiosco, Piazza Mondello. Closed Tuesday.

A popular hangout for good *gelato, semifreddo,* sugar-free ice cream, and brioches filled with ice cream.

MUSEUM

Museo Etnografico Pitre, next to Villa La Favorita.

The island's best collection of native costumes, carriages, donkey carts, puppets, and utensils.

Noto (Siracusa)

Noto was destroyed by an earthquake on January 11, 1693, a time when baroque architecture was all the rage. The result is a city center of great architectural unity. Be sure to walk up the Via Corrado Nicolacci, which is crowned by the Church of Montevergini. The street is filled with outrageous baroque carvings under its balconies—all sorts of creatures, plus putti and bare-breasted women. The next street over is the Via Rocco Pirri. On this street, between the Corso Vittorio Emanuele and the Via Cavour, is the Loggia del Mercato, the old market with stalls and a central fountain. A memorable bit of once upon a time. Film lovers will remember parts of Noto as the setting for Michelangelo Antonioni's classic *L'Avventura* with Monica Vitti.

CAFFÈ

Caffè Sicilia, Corso Vittorio Emanuele 125. Closed Monday.

This historic *caffè,* opened in 1892, sells good coffee and has a popular following for its *gelati, granite* and *cannoli.* Try them here for comparitive purposes before sampling their counterparts at Costanzo.

DINING

Trattoria del Carmine, Via Ducezio 9, tel. 0931/838705. Closed Monday (except in summer). No credit cards. Inexpensive.

A fine meal can be had at this unassuming place near the Church of the Carmine. In the winter there is homemade *ravioli di ricotta.* In the rest of the year, choose penne, maccheroni or spaghetti with one of four sauces: *capricciosa* (a delicious vegetable pesto), *pomodoro fresco*, Norma, or Pirandello. The best secondo is *coniglio alla stimpirata*, tender rabbit cooked in olive oil, *peperoncino*, carrots, olives, tomatoes, celery, and basil.

Trattoria del Crocifisso da Baglieri, Via Principe Umberto 46, tel. 0931/571151. Closed Wednesday, the week after Easter, and Sept 15–30. All credit cards. Moderate.

A rich antipasto platter leads the way to homey pasta and a selection of typical meat and fish. In season have *tonno e cipollata*, an excellent tuna/onion combination.

Ristorante al Barocco, Ronco Corrado Sgadari 8 (off Via Cavour), tel./fax 0931/573309. Closed Monday. American Express, Visa. Moderate.

The tradition in this restaurant, especially in the cooler months, is to recreate baroque dishes of the past. Chef Giuseppe di Palma does these menus on advance request, but you will also be pleased with his standard menu. His secret ingredient is what he calls *acqua di mare*. This is not sea-water, but the piquant liquid found when he opens sea urchins. It flavors soups, certain pasta sauces, and many of his fish preparations. His *spaghetti allo scoglio*, with baby squid and shrimp, mussels, clams, and *acqua di mare*, is delicious.

ICE CREAM AND PASTRIES

Corrado Costanzo, Via Silvio Spaventa 7/9, tel. 0931/835243. Closed Wednesday.

Few tastings of anything anywhere matched the morning I spent discovering the artistry of the late Corrado Costanzo, a maestro sweet maker whose legacy is maintained by his children. He knew and honored Sicilia's ancient tradition of *gelati*, *granita* and pastries and shared some of his knowledge with me. He was a man of genuine humility, despite all the acclaim he received, and made the act of work seem noble and spiritually fulfilling. He was also a passionate opera lover.

Maestro Costanzo told me that the origin of his craft began more than a thousand years ago, when the Arabs brought sherbet and sweet making with them to Sicilia. They planted citrus and almonds throughout the island and in this area, which is closer to North Africa than anywhere on the island, sugarcane. At the time, the pharmacist was called *lo speziale* (the spice seller) and was the person in town who sold sugar, which was thought to have health-giving properties. Later, nuns throughout the island became the master sweet makers, and monks made sweet liqueurs using sugar, citrus, and almonds. Although the nuns of Palermo are now more famous, those in Noto were at least accomplished. The demand for their products rose as this area and the rest of Sicilia saw the rise of a professional class that wanted private sweet makers. Many of them were ex-religious figures. When convents were closed, nuns exited and found work. It was at this point that the career of sweet making, called *artigianato del dolce*, came to be. Teachers passed knowledge from one generation to the next through the centuries, and Maestro Costanzo was

Corrado Costanzo, master ice-cream maker, Noto

the most important teacher in Sicilia. He began his work at age 9 in 1940 and worked until his recent death.

As good as his sweets are, his sorbet and ice cream are better. The Arabs made a confection called *sharbat*, which was snow with essence of rose or jasmine that they used to refresh themselves on hot afternoons. This original sweet, similar to sherbet, evolved in time and saw the addition of sugar and milk (and later cream). Maestro Costanzo lamented the fact that "we've reached the year 2000 and make a thousand flavors of ice cream in modern machines." He strove to make sorbet and ice cream that use flavors native to the area, and these are the things you should taste. I would travel across oceans to again taste the *sorbetto di mandarino* (tangerine sorbet), which he described as "a little bit of Sicilia in your mouth." This was one of the great taste experiences of my life. Almost as good were mulberry

(gelso), lemon, and strawberry sorbets and a granita made with almond milk.

Gelato also is sublime here. The first local *gelati* were made with local flavors such as almonds, pistachios, hazelnuts. Chocolate arrived in the 1890s. Maestro Costanzo followed ancient tradition and made ice cream with roses and jasmine *(gelsomino)*. The *gelate alle rose* is divine, the jasmine almost as good, and there is wonderful *mandarino*, although I preferred this flavor in the sorbet. His ice cream feels different on the tongue. This is due, in part, to the fact that he did not use gums to thicken his product (as all but the most fanatical *gelatai* do), but opted for the more classical egg white. He pointed out that ice cream in America has more air and butter-fat and less concentrated flavor than ice cream in Italy, and you only need to taste his artistry to understand the difference.

Paceco (Trapani)

SALT MUSEUM

Museo del Sale, c/o Saline di Trapani, tel. 0923/8674422. Open 9–17h in winter, 9–18h in summer; closed Sunday.

Near the salt flats, this museum gives a good idea of the atmosphere in which salt workers have labored for generations. You can take a guided tour to see how sea salt is made from the waters of the Mediterranean.

Palermo

Also see listings for Mondello.

BAR-BAKERY

Bar Italia, Via Benedetto d'Acquisto 1, Monreale, tel. 091/6402421. Closed Tuesday.

A good place to relax after your visit to Monreale. Less conspicuous than other places near the Duomo, but more serious about what it sells. All the cookies I tried were relatively plain but full of flavor and freshness. There is good cappuccino, too.

CERAMICS

Ceramiche Nino Parrucca, Via San Lorenzo 291r, tel. 091/6790484, fax 091/241149.

Cheerfully bright ceramics and tiles at good prices will make a nice Sicilian souvenir.

CHURCH

Church of Santa Maria dell' Ammiriraglio (La Martorana), Piazza Bellini.

This historic and beautiful church, built in 1173, became attached to a convent in 1233 founded by Eloisa Martorana. It is generally conceded that it was in this convent that the Sicilian art of dessert making reached its early heights. *Frutti*

alla martorana are made of marzipan shaped in many forms: oranges, cherries, prickly pears, bananas, and so on. The name *martorana* is often thought to be the root of the word "marzipan."

DINING

Enoteca Cibus, Via Emerico Amari 64, tel. 091/323062. Open daily 12h–1h in the morning. Visa. Inexpensive.

Get a the ticket at the cashier, move to where the food is, and point. There is wonderful pizza, fine seafood, and superb vegetables. You will also find a small grocery.

Capricci di Sicilia, Via Istituto Pignatelli 6 (at Piazza Sturzo), tel. 091/327777. Closed Monday. Master Card, Visa. Moderate.

A restaurant that makes classical Sicilian dishes, especially those of Palermo, with great care. The pastas are all delicious: ravioli, *pasta c'anciuova* (anchovies, tomato concentrate, breadcrumbs), all sorts of seafood sauces.

Trattoria Shanghai, in the Vucciria market.
No credit cards. Inexpensive.

The first time I came to Palermo I thought this was a Chinese restaurant, and I skipped it. What a mistake! Shanghai is a very raffish, rough-and-tumble place with good food at low prices. It is the right place for lunch after visiting the market, but you should not expect anything fancy.

Lo Strascino (U' Strascinu), Viale Regione
Sicilia 2286, tel. 091/401292. Closed
Sunday and in August. American Express,
Diners Club. Moderate.

Classic Sicilian cooking, especially fish. Good pizza in the evening; a charming atmosphere with scenic outdoor dining in warm weather.

Antica Focacceria San Francesco,
58 Via Paternostro, tel. 091/320264.
No credit cards. Inexpensive.

One of the most historic places in Palermo, definitely worth a visit. Here you have Sicilian fast food, and part of the spectacle is watching it being prepared. One of the specialties is *guasteddu,* a roll with slices of spleen and caciocavallo, and hands fly quickly as it is made and served. Also look for *arancini, sfincioni,* and *panelle.* You pay, place a number, and wait to be called. It is said that Garibaldi ate here after liberating Palermo. Nowadays it is full of parents and children who frequent the Church of San Francesco, which is opposite the *focacceria.*

Trattoria Macco, Via Benedetto Gravina
85 (near Piazza Politeama),
tel. 091/6114302. Closed Sunday.
No credit cards. Moderate.

Very good vegetable dishes at this small eatery near the Politeama, where maybe, just maybe, an opera will be playing.

FOOD SHOPPING AND MARKETS
Il Mercato della Vucciria.

The dazzling market of Palermo, an exhilarating mixture of Italian market and North African souk. Everywhere you go in its alleyways and illuminated streets you will see vendors eager to offer you their wares: an amazing variety of seafood, fragrant breads, fruits and vegetables of every hue, including purple cauliflower. I am particularly drawn to the perfumes of wild fennel, saffron, sweet and bitter almonds, pepper, and capers. There are wandering vendors of cooked tripe and all manner of fried food. Vucciria is different from most markets in Italy because it is on a series of little streets rather than under a pavilion or in a square. You should be aware of pickpockets and hold your bag and camera close to you. This said, it should also be noted that Palermo has a lower crime rate than many northern cities and that Italy is still a safer country than many others.

Salumeria Gastronomia Mangia, Via
Principe di Belmonte.

Good all-purpose source of cheeses, *salumi,* tuna, and breads.

Salumeria da Filippo, Via Mariano Stabile
19.

An excellent selection of wine, cheeses, and *salumi.*

ICE CREAM
Gelateria Ilardo, Foro Umberto I 6.

Good Sicilian ice creams. Be sure to try *limone, mandarino,* and other citrus flavors.

Pasticceria Oscar, Via Migliaccio 39.

Very good cakes, especially those made of citrus, and outstanding ice cream, especially strawberry.

SWEETS

Convento di San Benedetto, Piazza Venezia 38A.

This is a rare experience: you place your order with a novitiate in this silent order of nuns and wait for a package that will come to you on a wheel from within the convent. As their sisters did centuries ago, these Benedictines support themselves by making cannoli, *grappolo di uva* (marzipan and pistachio paste shaped like a bunch of grapes), *minne di Vergini* (breasts of the Virgin: appropriately shaped, anatomically correct, and made of marzipan!), *il trionfo della gola* (the triumph of gluttony: *pan di Spagna* with almond and pistachio paste), and lambs and fish made of marzipan.

Most of these require a two-kilogram minimum, but they're worth it.

TOURIST OFFICE

Azienda Autonoma di Turismo Per Palermo e Monreale, Via Belmonte 43, 90100 Palermo, tel. 091/540122.

WINE

Enoteca Picone, Via Marconi 36, tel. 091/331300. Open 7:30–14h, 16–21h; closed Sunday and two weeks in August.

There are more than 750 wines in the two rooms of this charming, somewhat-crowded place. A real Palermo landmark and a must-see for wine lovers.

Enoteca Miceli, Via Gagini 103, tel. 091/306805, or Via Generale Streva 18A, tel. 091/584728. Open 9–13h, 16:30–19:30h; closed Sunday and Wednesday afternoon.

Two branches of a very established wine seller that is also a good source for buying Sicilian cakes and sweets.

Ragusa

DINING

Trattoria La Rusticana, Via XXV Aprile 68, tel. 0932/27981. Closed Tuesday and three weeks in September. Inexpensive.

In the Ibla quarter you can find this eatery where pork is a specialty: as a pasta sauce, or as a *secondo*, where it is roasted, served in

chops, or as sausage. The people here are very nice and make you feel immediately at home.

TOURIST OFFICE

Azienda Autonoma Provinciale per l'Incremento Turistico, Via Bocchieri 33, 97100 Ragusa, tel. 0932/621421.

Randazzo (Catania)

DINING

Trattoria Veneziano, Via del Romano 8, tel.

095/7991353. Reservations advised. Closed Sunday evening, Monday,

Christmas week, and first three weeks of July. American Express, MasterCard, Visa. Moderately inexpensive.

A popular restaurant with visitors to Mount Etna, so reservations are advised. The food is good, particularly antipasti and soups.

Salina (Messina)

This island of volcanic origin is part of the Isole Eolie (Aeolian Islands). Unlike Lipari, the most famous of the islands, Salina is distinctly low-key and not oriented to tourism. For that reason, the few hotels are not fancy, the restaurants are unpretentious (although one eats very well), and one can have a sense of life in the Isole Eolie that has not yet sold its soul to the touristic devil. So you should not expect the sort of accommodations and facilities you have become accustomed to. The best hotel is the Signum, in the community of Malfa (tel. 090/9844222, fax 090/9844102). If you are willing to rough it a bit, you will find Salina quite rewarding. It has 2,500 residents, most of whom are engaged in agriculture. The capers are often called the world's best, and there is a famous wine, Malvasia delle Lipari, that is worth knowing. On Salina one sees small bunches of cherry tomatoes hanging on porches. They are not quite sun-dried, but rather are used for their more concentrated flavor. There was a huge volcanic eruption around 700 B.C., and half the volcanic wall collapsed into the sea, leaving Salina with an impressive wall of cutaway rock (at the Baia di Pollara) and a small plain near the shore. This is, in fact, the world's largest half volcano. You will notice holes cut in the volcanic rock: these were refuges years ago for the men who built the treacherously winding roads that hug the island's mountains. The best way to explore Salina is on a *motorino*. It can be rented at Motonoleggio Antonio Buongiorno, Via Risorgimento, at Santa Marina, where you arrive on the island (tel. 090/9843308). There is some fishing here, but not much. Many of Salina's sons went to Milano to find work, so you will see more women, children, and the elderly during your visit. Many people on Salina look North African in appearance. Like North Africa, Salina has almost endless sunshine.

DINING

Ristorante Porto Bello, Santa Marina, tel. 090/9843125. Closed Wednesday (except June–September) and October 15–31. American Express, MasterCard, Visa. Moderate.

The best place on the island for local food. This is also the only restaurant that sells bottled wine: the rest sell *vino sfuso* (carafe wine). You must try the *calamaretti con mal-* *vasia e cipolla:* the baby squid are stuffed with bread crumbs, Pecorino, and basil and are cooked with onions and the local Malvasia. This may sound like a strange combination, but it is absolutely delicious. Other dishes worth trying are *spaghetti in bianco* (capers, anchovies, eggplant, onions, basil, and tuna), *farfalle con le mandorle* (wild fennel, tomato, onions, crushed almonds, vodka), and *spaghetti al fuoco* (Salina's small tomatoes with garlic, basil, baked ricotta, and *peperoncino*). Boiled seafood is a good *secondo*. Also try the *ricotta salata con miele*, sheep's-milk cheese with warm carob honey, pine nuts, and raisins. There are many small pastries with orange peel or almond paste that are served with Malvasia. Marilena Cataffo is the inspired cook, and her husband, Teodoro, is the welcoming host.

FOOD SHOPPING
Mr. Luschiero's Store, Via Risorgimento 28, tel. 090/9843053. Closed Wednesday afternoon and Sunday.

Cheese, *salumi*, eggs, wine, and beer. English spoken.

WINE AND AGRICULTURAL PRODUCTS
Azienda Agricola Carlo Hauner, Via Umberto 1, tel. 090/9843141.

Carlo Hauner left life in Milano as an architect and found paradise in Salina. He makes a spicy dessert wine, Malvasia delle Lipari, that is like nectar. I imagine that this dark amber wine is closer to what the ancient Greeks drank than most of the wines we see today. There are many taste sensations in a sip: honey, eucalyptus, walnut, walnut shell, and privet. These are all unusual tastes in a wine, so you should not use your previous wine-tasting experience for comparative purposes. Hauner also produces delicious vegetables that he packs in oil. The onions in particular are outstanding, and the capers, like all of those on Salina, are among the best you will ever taste. His products are packed under the name Sapori del Mediterraneo. Also look for *miele di carubo* (carob honey).

San Martino alle Scale (Palermo)

DINING
Ai Pini, Località Villaggio Montano, tel. 091/418198. Open daily. American Express, Visa. Moderate.

The setting of this restaurant—750 meters (2,475 feet) up—is so unlikely when you stop to think that you are in Sicilia, not terribly far from the temperate coastline where oranges and lemons grow. The location in pine trees (which give the restaurant its name) is a breath of cool, fresh air that is welcome relief on a hot summer's day in Palermo. The food is good and basic: *pastasciutta*, grilled meat and fish, *cassata* for dessert. Ai Pini is spacious but also very popular, so you should dine on the scenery first with the food a close second.

Santa Domenica Vittoria (Messina)

FOLKLORE
Festa di Sant'Antonio Abate.

In early September, a huge local feast cele-

brates the patron saint with a *spaghettata* (lots of spaghetti) and a *salsicciata* (lots of sausage).

Siracusa
Classic Town

Not only is Siracusa the classic town for Sicilia, but I count it among the top destinations in Italy. As a city that was once the greatest in the Mediterranean, it has eighteen centuries of glorious history. Founded in 734 B.C. by settlers from Corinth, it grew in power and wealth and was a center of knowledge that spawned geniuses such as Archimedes. It has some of the best remaining treasures of antiquity in the Neapolis Archeological Park. The regional museum has a sensational collection of ancient art and artifacts, all much better organized and displayed than you will see in most places. The new city of Siracusa is vibrant and well laid out. After the earthquake of 1693, it was rebuilt on a rational grid. But the biggest delight is probably Ortigia, the small island that was the original Greek settlement. Here are wonderful restaurants, *caffès*, a great market, and marvelous nightlife. The people in Siracusa are very friendly and welcoming and considerably more open than most Sicilians. And the food of Siracusa is sublime: the swordfish and tuna are incomparable; vegetables, fruit, and ice cream are first-rate. And you are close enough to Noto to have the best ice cream of your life.

BARS-BAKERIES
Pasticceria Cassarino e Midolo, Corso Umberto 86, tel. 0931/68046. Closed Monday.

A good place for breakfast: the brioches and rolls are excellent, as is the Segafredo coffee.

Bar Marciante, Via Landolina 9, Ortigia. Open 7–14h, 16–00:30h; closed Monday.

There are good brioches filled with almond granita, honey, jam, or ricotta and chocolate.

Pasticceria L. Marciante, Via della Maestranza 39, tel. 0931/67303. Closed Monday.

Marzipan in every form, plus *buccellati* filled with dried figs, and *cubbaita*, a sesame brittle of Arab origin.

Pasticceria-Gelateria Leonardi.

See "Food Shopping," below.

BREAD
Panificio Bianco, Via Roma 42.

One of the best little bread shops you will see in Italy. It bakes breads in whimsical shapes such as the sun, sea horses, and loaves of fishes. With twenty-four hours' notice you can special order the shape of your choice.

CULTURE
Every other year in even years since 1914, a festival of Greek tragedies is held at the ancient amphitheater in the Neapolis. In odd years visiting dance companies such as the Bolshoi and Martha Graham's troupe appear. May to mid-June.

DINING
It would be unwise to dine in Siracusa during the first forty days of the year if you are a fish eater. This is the period of *fermo pesca*, when fishing is banned so that fish can breed and replenish their stocks.

Trattoria Archimede, Via Gemellaro 8, Ortigia, tel. 0931/169701. Closed Sunday. American Express, Visa. Moderate.

A place that has acquired a fair amount of fame among visitors. Although it offers meat dishes, I would come here for seafood, especially swordfish. Start with *involtini di pescespada*, outstanding swordfish fillets, rolled and filled with raisins, pine nuts, and other ingredients. The vegetable antipasti are very good, particularly the grilled eggplant and potatoes. Do not miss the *olive snocciolate*, wonderful pitted green olives with basil, mint, celery, and carrot topped with olive oil. The *primi* are all manner of good seafood and pasta or a fine *zuppa di pesce*. *Secondi* are all good, especially tuna and swordfish. Fruit is beautifully displayed and is the best dessert. What I particularly like about Trattoria Archimede is that it is very anchored to its community. People come in from the narrow street to greet owner Antonio Zammitti, patrons are made to feel at home, and there always seems to be room for everyone of whatever station. When I spent a lot of time in Roma in the 1970s there was a woman with large sad eyes and slumped shoulders who trudged from restaurant to restaurant offering crumpled, tired-looking flowers for sale. She always wore one in her unwashed black hair, and this effort to be pretty was affecting and a bit pathetic. Usually she passed by each table in a restaurant without waiting for an answer, since 98 percent of the time it was no. Later, after restaurants closed, she trudged down the Via Veneto, offering her flowers to tourists seated in

Siracusa

caffès. I have not seen her in recent years, and there has never been someone to replace her—restaurateurs knew her and indulged her. Yet in the old section of Siracusa there is another such woman, a bit younger and more energetic. She is a link to an older Italy that you will not see elsewhere, and it is heartwarming to see that she is made welcome in places such as the Trattoria Archimede.

Trattoria da Mariano, Vicolo Zuccolà 9, tel. 0931/66366. Closed Monday and late July. All credit cards. Moderate to moderately expensive.

Homey dining on local flavors. The antipasto platter includes ricotta with almonds and pistachios, and peppers, eggs, potato, eggplant and olives. Among the primi, in season, is *pasta con tenerumi*, the delicate flowers of zucchine and some mint. Meat predominates, including pork, veal, liver and rabbit. The *lumache al pomodoro* are plump delicious snails in tomato sauce.

Minosse, Via Mirabella 6, Ortigia, tel. 0931/66366. Closed Monday and late July. All credit cards. Moderate to moderately expensive.

Very fine fish and seafood.

Ristorante Don Camillo, Via Maestranza 96, tel. 0931/67133. Closed Sunday. American Express, Diners Club, MasterCard, Visa. Moderate to moderately expensive.

I was on a Siracusan swordfish binge when I came here, but there is a lot of good food to be had in this large restaurant. Seafood tops all kinds of pasta, and in main courses fresh tuna is the star. I began with *penne con pescespada*, cubes of swordfish with oil, tomato, pine nuts, parsley, basil, and dark tiny raisins: a great contrast of flavor, texture, and color. I had swordfish *alla siracusana* in a sauce of green olives, fresh tomatoes, basil, garlic, and capers. Fish can be grilled, steamed, fried, poached, or cooked *al cartoccio*

(wrapped in foil with herbs and vegetables and cooked to create steam). The good house wine was Rapitalà from Alcamo, and fruit was the perfect dessert.

Taverna Aretusa, Via Santa Teresa 32, Ortigia, tel. 0931/464992. Open daily; closed forty days in January and early February. American Express. Moderately inexpensive.

Save one night for the Taverna Aretusa. Deep in Ortigia, past the busy Via Capodieci, is this restaurant with a main room of about thirty seats and an outdoor terrace of equal size, where a mandolin player and a guitarist might be playing. The musicians seem not to be playing for tips and never tour the restaurant as so many do. They seem to be playing for the pleasure of it (and perhaps a meal). The inescapable centerpiece of the indoor room is a table supporting a dozen platters with delicious antipasti. Most of them are vegetable-based: fried artichokes; sautéed zucchini; grilled eggplant; a salad of celery, black olives, and carrots; grilled tomatoes; pickled onions. The pastas include *pasta con le sarde, pasta con frutti di mare*, and the restaurant's version of *spaghetti alla siracusana*, which is made with tomatoes, anchovies, olive oil, and basil, topped with toasted breadcrumbs. You will also find a whole clove of garlic, which you can eat or ignore. I smashed mine and its flavor permeated the dish. Secondi are all fish: swordfish, tuna, fresh cod, and sea bass (*spigola*) were the choices on my most recent visit. I opted for *tonno alla griglia con limone*: two paillards of tuna—tender and flavorful—

that are finished with olive oil and a toss of sea salt. There is no printed menu; everything is recited, so if the waiter is talking too fast, say, "Piano, più piano, per cortesia." You will be brought a couple of delicate almond pastries at the end of the meal. The restaurant serves good Lavazza coffee (but in plastic cups). A great meal.

Bar-Ristorante Casablanca, Viale Teracati 106, tel. 0931/35316. Closed Sunday. Inexpensive.

The two restaurants just outside the grounds of the Neapolis are tourist traps with poor food. I suggest instead that you walk about 250 meters (a few blocks) from the amphitheater up the Via Romagnoli or up from the corner of Viale Teocrito where the Corso Gelone becomes Viale Teracati. You will soon see the very simple-looking Bar-Ristorante Casablanca. Despite its plain appearance, there is good food to be had if you stick to the local preparations (that is, skip the salmon, the tortellini, and other foreign ingredients). I had a very respectable *penne alla Norma* with a very piquant and chunky tomato sauce. The cubes of eggplant were perfectly cooked. Chilled, cooked spinach rounded out a lunch that was hard to top and made nicer by its very low price.

Ristorante-Pizzeria al Delfino, Riva Porto Lachio, Sbarcadero Santa Lucia, tel. 0931/68229. Closed Monday. No credit cards. Moderately inexpensive.

A place full of fun and romance with a matchless view of Ortigia. Families park here to admire the setting, which includes a few small fishing craft in dry dock. At one of the outdoor tables near me, 5 ten-year-olds were having a boys' night out of pizza,

French fries, and Fanta (no adult supervision). At another table a young couple had bites of pizza between kisses and small talk. He discussed soccer, and she indulged him. My waiter's girlfriend sprawled atop her motorcycle, purring and stretching like a cat. She exuded a mixture of boredom, alienation, and desire that would do Michelangelo Antonioni or Tennessee Williams proud. Oh yes, the food. . . . Pizza is only served at night, and that is the dish I would come for. You can top it with many ingredients, including fresh seafood and great vegetables. There is decent pasta during the day, but there are better ones elsewhere in town.

Pizzeria Minerva, Piazza Duomo, Ortigia. No credit cards. Inexpensive.

A popular place for pizza in a gorgeous setting.

Il Panino di Notte.

See "Food Shopping," below.

FOOD SHOPPING

The food market in Ortigia, though not huge, is one of the most delightful and animated in Italy. It has crowded byways like the Vucciria in Palermo, but this one is open and easygoing. The heart of the market is Via deBenedictis, where stands flank both sides of the narrow street as shoppers hurtle through. Sellers hawk their wares, flirt, and cajole shamelessly and are as appealing as the products they sell. It is all very festive and not particularly claustrophobic. Make note of the high quality of the food, such as the eggplants called *violette di seta* (silken violets) and the mussels that glisten in the sun. Do you see that the vendors have placed halved lemons and to-matoes among the mussels to heighten the visual contrast and to subtly reassure the buyer by presenting a combination that she would like at home? Wherever you turn, magnificent fresh tuna and swordfish beckon, as do the children underfoot who sell the fresh herbs they have gathered. The market is open Monday through Saturday mornings and is especially lively on Satur-day. Before leaving, go around the corner to the Via Trento. At #21 is a special store called Randazzo that has a dazzling collec-tion of scales and other means of measure-ment that would do Archimedes proud.

The Viale Teocrito is a major thor-oughfare near many of the antiquities that make Siracusa a not-to-be-missed destina-tion. If, between visiting the sites at the Neapolis Archeological Park, the Cata-combs, and the Museo Regionale, you want to restore a bit, there are several spots on the Viale Teocrito that merit attention. Most stores are closed on Wednesday af-ternoon and on Sunday.

Boutique della Frutta da Luciano, at the corner of Viale Teracati, has excellent fruits and vegetables.

La Pizzicheria, at the corner of Via Socrate, is a very good all-purpose *alimen-tari* that sells wine, bread, cheeses, *salumi,* olives, and some prepared foods.

Pasticceria-Gelateria Leonardi, at #123, has many notable offerings, including al-mond and chocolate granita and *maritozzi,* slightly sweet rolls filled with raisins. There are also lunch items such as *cartocciate* (folded pastries with either spinach, mush-rooms, or onions) and *arancini* filled with either ground beef, cheese, or spinach.

Il Spaghettaro, next door, is a restaurant-pizzeria that sells good pizza by the slice.

If you would prefer a place to sit down to eat, go to the nearby Bar-Ristorante Casablanca on the Viale Teracati (see "Dining," above).

Another good area for food shopping is on either side of the underpass separating the Largo Gilippo and the Piazza Eu-ripide. Largo Gilippo is a good place to come late at night for a snack. There is a great fruit stand on one side with marvel-ous watermelon. Next door is a superb *salumeria* in the form of a roadside stand. Opposite is Il Panino di Notte, which has a grill and makes excellent sandwiches.

Gastronomia Le Bontà, Piazza Euripide 13, has a good selection of cheese, *salumi,* and prepared foods. *Le bontà* means, more or less, "the good things in life." This is an area (at least as night falls) that is of slightly mar-ginal safety, where prostitutes gather to offer their services. One of them, standing in front of this store, called out, "Oh! Ma tu vuoi vedere le bontà davvero?" which trans-lates loosely (very loosely) as "Hey, do you want to see the real good things in life?"

ICE CREAM
Caffè Minerva, Via Minerva 15, Ortigia, tel. 0931/22606.

Excellent lemon ice cream and small al-mond pastries. Also a very charming coffee bar with lovely outdoor tables and late-night service.

Pasticceria-Gelateria Leonardi, #123 Viale Teocrito.

See "Food Shopping," above.

LA PASSEGGIATA
Siracusa has one of the most beguiling *passeggiate* in Italy. During the early eve-

ning, many of the town's young people gather on the Via Tevere in the Piazza Aldo Moro, one block off the Corso Gelone in the city center. They stand close together by the hundreds, creating a great din much like penguins on an Antarctic beach. It is interesting how close they stand given the great amount of space available to them. Later on, much of the socializing moves to several areas of Ortigia, a serene backdrop that makes for a most relaxed and pleasant way of meeting people. Start at the soigné Caffè Minerva (see "Ice Cream," above) and move toward the memorable Piazza Duomo, down the narrow Via Picherali to the Fonte Aretusa, once used by Lord Nelson to water his troops. It is now a place where graceful papyrus plants brought long ago from the Middle East grow in an elegant fountain. Some people walk down the adjacent Lungomare Alfeo for a drink at one of the bars or clubs or move to one of the side streets to neck. It is all so very romantic and congenial—could this be where *la dolce vita* moved to?

TOURIST OFFICE
Azienda Provinciale Turismo di Siracusa, Via San Sebastiano 43, 96100 Siracusa, tel. 0931/461477, fax 0931/67803.

WINE
Enoteca Solaria, Via Roma 86,

tel. 0931/463007. Open 9:30–13:30h, 16–20h; closed Wednesday afternoon and ten days in September.

A good spot in Ortigia to sample local wines by the glass. Also look for the excellent dessert wines and olive oil by Donnafugata.

A GASTRONOME'S DRIVE
NEAR SIRACUSA
If you have a car at your disposal, there are many places near Siracusa with gastronomic specialties. While many of these appear in Siracusa, you might want to go to their place of origin.

Buccheri. Fresh sausages, almond pastries.
Carlentini. *A 'empanata,* a turnover stuffed with cauliflower, black olives, garlic, Pecorino, and anchovies.
Leontinoi, Monte Pancali, and **Francofonte.** Superb oranges.
Melilli. Sheep farming; from February to May there is fresh hot ricotta and homemade bread.
Palazzolo. Excellent trout from the Manghisi River, served *alle erbe* (with herbs), grilled, baked, or *al cartoccio* (steamed in foil with herbs), *affumicato* (smoked with juniper).
Rosolini. The Cantina Cooperativa Elorina makes good red wine and dessert wines from *moscato* or *zibibbo* grapes.
Sortino. Honey.

Taormina (Messina)

The unmatched beauties of Taormina have been sung about for centuries. Despite rather intense tourism and lots of construction, Taormina remains extraordinary and merits a visit as you travel to or from Siracusa. The splendid Greek theater in Taormina is the setting for performances of dance, opera, instrumental music, theater, and jazz from July to September (contact Taormina Arte, Via Pirandello 31, 98039 Taormina (ME), tel. 0942/21142 or 0942/23220, fax 0942/23348).

BAR-BARKERY

Pasticceria Etna, Corco Umberto 112.

The specialty is *pignolata*, a black-and-white cake made of sugar, flour, alcohol, almonds, chocolate, egg whites, and lemon but, despite the name, no *pinoli* (pine nuts). There are also *torta Taormina*, made with ricotta, almonds, chocolate, and candied fruit; *n'zuddi*, dry almond cookies; and marzipan sculpted in many shapes. Have a strong espresso with one of the sweets you buy here.

DINING

Ristorante al Feudo, Contrada Feo Coniglio, tel. 0942/58042. Closed Monday. Moderate.

An old standby with consistently good food. The homemade *maccheroncini alla Norma* are exquisite. The specialty of the house is the *grigliata di carni miste*, a large platter of grilled meats. Fresh fruit is the best dessert: in season try the peaches in wine.

Al Duomo, Vico Ebrei 11, tel. 0942/625656. Closed Wednesday. All credit cards. Moderate to moderately expensive.

There are many excellent vegetables in different guises here, and good seafood too. Two meat dishes are wonderful: *polpette avvolte nella foglia di limone* (ground meat wrapped in lemon leaves that impart a bewitching perfume) and

agnello 'ngrassatu, chunks of lamb with delicious vegetables.

Villa Sant'Andrea, tel. 0942/23125, fax 0942/24838. All credit cards. Moderately expensive.

This hotel in Mazzarò, the seaside community below Taormina, has good food in a gorgeous setting. Stick to simple, local dishes such as *linguine alle vongole* and calamari cooked in tomatoes, garlic, and capers. As you dine under luxuriant trees you have a great view of the nearby bay.

FOOD SHOPPING

La Bottega del Buongustaio, Via di Giovanni 17, tel. 0942/28691. Open 8:30–13h, 16–20:30h; closed Tuesday.

A range of local products and good sandwiches to take away.

HOUSEWARES

Emporio Auteri, Via di Giovanni 18.

Kitchenware, cooking equipment, and Alessi products.

WINE

La Torinese, Corso Umberto 54. Open daily 9–13h, 16–21h.

In business since 1936, this store is a good source for Sicilian table wines, plus a large selection of Marsala. There is also *vino liquoroso alla mandorla*, a high-powered almond wine. At #59 are sweets, cheese, *salumi*, and prepared dishes.

Trapani

ENOTECA

Enoteca Bourbon Street, Via Gian Battista Fardello 207, tel. 0923/871188. Open 8:30–13:30h, 16:30–20:30h; closed Sunday and Wednesday afternoon.

Anna Maria Mazzara is a passionate collector of wine and has more than two thousand old bottles of historic interest. In addition, she has more than a thousand different wines for sale, not only from Italy but also from most major wine-producing countries. As this is the land of Marsala wine, it is interesting that you can find good port, sherry, Madeira, and other fortified wines. You can also purchase oil, vinegar, chocolate, coffee, and many sweets.

DINING

Cantina Siciliana, Via Giudecca 32, tel. 0923/28673

Trattoria Fontana, Via San Giovanni Bosco 22, tel. 0923/24056.

WINE

Eno Museum, Contrada Bérbero, tel. 0923/969697. Open weekdays 9–13h, 15–19h, Saturday 9–13h, and Sunday in summer.

A museum where you can also taste some wines of the province of Trapani.

Vallelunga (Caltanissetta)

COOKING SCHOOL/
WINERY/DINING

Regaleali. www.tascadalmerita.it. For wine tastings and dining: welcome @tascadalmerita.it or Lilly Lo Cascio at 091/6459711. For cooking classes: e-mail antalan@tin.it or call 091/450727.

Regaleali, half way between Palermo and Agrigento, is 600 meters (1,980 feet) above sea level and surrounded by hills that are even higher. You travel through rather dry, rough terrain to get to what seems like an oasis. There are vineyards, palm trees, cacti with prickly pears, 4,000 olive trees and a small lake. Sheep graze everywhere, feeding on pristine grass and herbs that flavor their meat and milk. This country estate (485 hectares/1,200 acres) has been in the Tasca family since 1830, and its residents welcome you into

their world in several ways. One can come for a tasting of some of Sicily's best wine, for a wonderful five-course wine lunch using products from the estate, or cooking classes with the formidable Anna Tasca Lanza, renowned for her vibrant and faithful books on Sicilian cookery. In some parts of the year, a five-day course is offered, including lodging on the estate and day trips to Agrigento and elsewhere. Prince Charles's cook came here to study in 1991. Opera lovers will enjoy the company of Anna's sister Costanza, who is knowledgeable and passionate, especially about the works of Wagner, who was a friend of the family's forebears. He wrote much of the first act of *Parsifal* in the gardens of the family home in Palermo.

Zafferana Etnea (Catania)

FOLKLORE

Ottobrata Zafferanese.

On weekends in October there are festivals celebrating different local foods: grapes, mushrooms, honey, wine, and chestnuts.

Involtini di Pescespada
Swordfish Rolls

This is the recipe of chef Salvatore di Mauro of the Trattoria Archimede in Siracusa. He serves his *involtini* with a *salsa aurora*, but I prefer simply squeezing fresh lemon juice over them just before I eat them. For the record, chef Salvatore's *salsa aurora* contains ketchup, mustard, sugar, Tabasco, Worcestershire sauce, and Grand Marnier that you can combine in amounts that appeal to you. Once the ingredients are combined, fold in enough mayonnaise to make the sauce creamy but not heavy. (I'll stick to lemon.) What is very important is that you assure that your fish seller slice your swordfish fillets to the correct measurement, especially as regards the thickness.

Serves 4 as an antipasto

Filling
Extra-virgin olive oil
1 medium onion, minced
2 tablespoons pine nuts, lightly chopped
4 tablespoons raisins
4 tablespoons dry Marsala
110 grams/¾ cup unflavored bread crumbs
4 tablespoons freshly squeezed orange juice,
*   ideally from blood oranges*
1 teaspoon freshly grated Parmigiano-
*   Reggiano*
8 slices swordfish fillet, about 7 centimeters
*   (3 inches) wide and ½ centimeter*
*   (¼ inch) thick*

Breading
Extra-virgin olive oil
Salt and freshly ground black pepper to taste
Unflavored bread crumbs

Preheat the oven to 200°C (400°F). For the filling, pour a couple of drops of olive oil in a skillet. When it is hot, add the onion, pine nuts, and raisins and sauté for about 5 minutes, or until the onion is golden. Stir continuously to prevent sticking. Add the Marsala and cook for a half minute or so, until it has partially evaporated, although there can be a fair amount of liquid left. Let cool. Combine this mixture in a bowl with the bread crumbs, orange juice, and Parmigiano-Reggiano. The result should be a moist filling. Adjust with either juice or bread crumbs until it reaches the right consistency.

After you have washed and patted dry the swordfish fillets, lay them down on a clean surface. Do not pound them or attempt to flatten them in any way. Fill each with about 1 tablespoon of filling and then roll it so that the filling is contained. If necessary, crimp the sides of the rolls slightly. For the breading, set out 2 plates. In one, put some olive oil, salt, and pepper. In the other put bread crumbs. Gently dip each roll in the oil and then transfer it to the bread-crumb plate, dipping it so that it will be lightly covered in crumbs. Place each roll in a lightly oiled baking dish and bake for 15 minutes.

Patate con Capperi di Salina
Potatoes with Capers from Salina

I sampled this wonderful dish on a sunny terrace overlooking the sea at the home of Carlo Hauner, who not only produces famous wine but cultivates delicious vegetables. Many cooks consider the capers of Salina the world's best, so if you travel in Sicilia you should pick some up to use at home. Failing that, use large capers that are either packed in salt or unflavored vinegar.

Serves 6

1 kilo/2¼ pounds medium potatoes, preferably red-skinned or waxy
1 medium red onion, cut in ½-inch bits
4 tablespoons capers, preferably from Salina, rinsed
2 teaspoons dried oregano
8 tablespoons extra-virgin olive oil
3 tablespoons red-wine vinegar
Freshly ground black pepper to taste

Carefully wash the potatoes and cook them in boiling water until tender. The cooking time depends on the size of the potatoes, but you can test them by poking one with a fork. When the tines enter without too much resistance, they are done. Let the potatoes cool and then cut them into cubes or half-moon slices. If they are waxy or small brown-skinned potatoes, you might want to peel them first. Transfer the potato pieces to a bowl and add the onion, capers, and oregano. In a jar or cruet pour the oil and vinegar, and grind in pepper to taste. Close and shake vigorously. Pour the dressing over the potatoes, toss, and serve.

Note: If you want this dish to be cold rather than lukewarm, chill the potatoes before cutting them.

Sardegna

Not to Miss in Sardegna

ALGHERO   CAGLIARI

NUORO *(Classic Town)*   OLBIA

REGIONAL CAPITAL:
Cagliari (CA).

PROVINCIAL CAPITALS:
Nuoro (NU), Oristano (OR),
    Sassari (SS).

TOURIST INFORMATION:
Ente Sardo Industrie
    Turistiche,
        Via Mameli 97,
        09124 Cagliari,
        tel. 070/60231,
        fax 070/664636.
I consider the tourist
    information and brochures
    produced by the Sardinian
    tourist authorities to be
    the second best in Italy,
    exceeded only by those of
    Trentino.

"Adattarsi bisogna," disse Efix versandogli da bere. "Guarda tu l'acqua: perché dicono che è saggia? Perché prende la forma del vaso ove la si versa."

"One must adapt," said Efix as he poured himself something to drink. "Look at water: why do they say that it is wise? Because it takes the shape of the vessel in which it is poured."

"Anche il vino, mi pare!"

"So does wine, it seems to me!"

"Anche il vino, sì! Solo che il vino qualche volta spumeggia e scappa, e l'acqua no."

"So does wine, yes! Except that wine sometimes bubbles over, and water does not."

"Anche l'acqua, se è messa sul fuoco a bollire," disse Natòlia.

"So does water, if it is put on a flame to boil," said Natòlia.

 This discourse is from the novel *Canne al Vento (Reeds in the Wind)*, for which Sardinian writer Grazia Deledda became the first woman to win the Nobel Prize for literature in 1926. This book is the classic work of Sardinian literature, the one in which the people of this island region see themselves even today. Wherever you go in Sardegna, but especially in the author's native Nuoro, you find hotels, bars, and restaurants named either Grazia Deledda or Canne al Vento.

The Sardinians are reeds to the wind, standing exposed to the elements and being tossed about but

never broken. This particular passage from the book also makes something clear about *i sardi*. They can adapt to different situations, sometimes showing rare moments of mirth, but just as readily showing flashes of heated temperament. More than anywhere else I have been in Italy, one can detect distinct characteristics in the nature of people here, especially those that separate the sexes.

Agritourism:
Terranostra—Associazione
  Regionale
    Sarda Per
    L'Agriturismo,
    Via Sassari 3,
    09124 Cagliari,
    tel. 070668367.

While most Sardinian men still show the courtesy one finds throughout Italy, they can often be either withdrawn or abrupt in their dealings with strangers —although they always have time and interest if approached by a child. Sardinian women, by contrast, are very intriguing: they are strong, self-reliant, have a ready smile, and show great warmth and interest to someone new. I suspect that part of the explanation for this is that many Sardinian women have had to spend a great deal of time alone if their husbands are either shepherds or fishermen, two leading occupations on the island. So they develop skills to support themselves emotionally and often financially. You will find many women as shopkeepers, restaurateurs, bartenders, hotel owners, newsagents, and so on.

This certainly counteracts the image—a mistaken one, I believe—of Italian women as submissive. Some do revert to submissive roles in certain settings, but I know of many throughout the country who think and act for themselves. The difference is that in other parts of Italy this is a relatively recent behavior that has evolved, while in Sardegna I think it has been around for a long time. This contradicts what one would imagine upon seeing the many Sardinian women dressed in black, even wearing black kerchiefs around their heads. But once they smile, a special radiance emerges. They may be widows, but they are not dead!

In thinking of Sardegna, one must never forget that it is an island in the middle of the Mediterranean, isolated from the rest of Italy and Europe. When Sardinians talk about the rest of Italy, they refer to it as *il continente* (the continent). But there is another crucial thing to remember: unlike Sicilia and most other islands, Sardegna has become oriented to the sea only in the past sixty years. Except for the ancient port cities of Cagliari (the region's capital, on the south end of Sardegna) and Alghero (at the northwest corner), very little of the shore was inhabited. Much of Sardegna's coast was a marshy breeding ground for the malaria that afflicted the island for centuries. The disease was eradicated only in 1950. Because of this, most of the population lived inland to escape the plague. Foreigners, from the Phoenicians to the Piemontese, arrived through the centuries, but had very little impact. Pirates plied the sea for many years, posing another threat to anyone who might live on the coast. Only the Catalans made cultural inroads, arriving in Alghero in 1353 and bringing a new language and culinary influences to that city, which had previously been under the control of the Republic of Genova. People in Alghero speak an older, purer form of Catalan, and philologists from the University of Barcelona regularly arrive to dip into the linguistic well. The rest of the island speaks Sardinian, a language that evolved directly from Latin. In addition, of course, almost everyone speaks Italian.

When the native people of the island moved to the hills and mountains of the interior thousands of years ago, they encountered a terrain that is strangely beautiful and very forbidding. A living had to be scratched out the land, and the cuisine of Sardegna is a direct result of that. Because people lived in tiny communities separated by natural boundaries, there was very little communication and exchange from place to place. So dialects and recipes, though similar, had marked differences even in nearby areas. What was similar among all these communities was that this was a pastoral society, with sheep providing the milk, cheese, wool, meat, and companionship for shepherds who would take their flock out for weeks at a time. Breads (such as *pane carasau*) were developed that could last a long time, so that *il pastore* would subsist on bread, cheese, wine, and whatever fruit or vegetables he might find during his travels. It used to be that the virtue a

Sardinian man sought in a prospective bride was her skill at baking bread rather than any more alluring charms. Many of the shepherds played pipes and other musical instruments. The most famous is the *launedda*, a wind instrument whose origins date back to the fourteenth century B.C. (See the listing for the town of Tadasuni for more information.) Women in the small communities cooked, cleaned, made clothing and handicrafts that

The vine-ripened tomatoes of Sardegna are prized throughout Italy

had practical applications, raised children, and prayed. Their crafts, referred to as *artigianato,* are still made and used today. The best of these are sold in stores (called I.S.O.L.A.) that are run by the region. Cork has always been a typical product of northern Sardegna, and many of the products women made there used that material. As they sat in circles and worked, the women also sang, creating a plaintive and haunting choral music that remains part of the island's cultural heritage.

The center of the region, much of it called La Barbagia, is in the province of Nuoro, which is the Classic Town for Sardegna. You can still hear ancient Sardinian choral music there and visit the sites that Grazia Deledda wrote of. The town is not of exceeding beauty, but the surrounding area is a powerful display of nature that has conditioned the people who live there. Deledda lived in Nuoro until she was twenty-five and often journeyed deep into the nearby hills and valleys. The winds, the clouds, the forests, the hills, the many rocks, all of these became her points of reference. As she traveled she absorbed local dialects and learned fables, historic tales, and native music from the people who lived in the various isolated communities around Nuoro. When she wrote of these places, they were otherworldly. Now, with the automobile and regional bus lines, these valley people do come to Nuoro, bringing their culture with them. You should make visits to Barùmini, Oliena, and Orgosolo part of your stay in the province of Nuoro.

When you meet the people of Nuoro and elsewhere, you will find that they are proud. Proud and severe, a legacy of the insularity and the need to survive in harsh elements. Somehow Sardegna, despite areas of great beauty and an absolutely gorgeous coastline, is not romantic in the way that so much of Italy is. This too is part of its being a world apart, and my observations are not a criticism but an acknowledgment of a rich and fascinating culture that grew up by its own rules and exigencies.

There are other fascinating elements to the Sardinian landscape. First and foremost are the *nuraghe,* amazing cylindrical stone structures that date back at least to 1800 B.C. (the early Bronze Age). Some of these were sites for the veneration of pre-Christian deities. Others were places to live or to keep one's flock during bad weather. Ancient sculptures and tools are found all the time in *nuraghe,* and many of these now are in fine museums in Sassari and Cagliari. Sheep still graze in the hills and take refuge in the *nuraghe*. In 1992, Sardegna had 3.8 million head of sheep and only 1.6 million people. Pecorino, the sheep cheese of the region, is one of the most outstanding cheeses in Italy. It comes in many forms, from soft ricotta to very aged, granular cheese, and you should make it a regular part of your dining during a visit. Most of the best cheese never leaves the island. Sardegna also has outstanding honeys, which are served with many of the cheeses, and are used in meat and dessert cookery.

Sardinians have now made the sea part of their lives. Fish and seafood have entered the cuisine in much of the region, while for centuries they figured in the cooking of only a few places. Cagliari has a nice repertoire of dishes from the sea, and Alghero is famous all over Italy for its lobsters, which are prepared in a way that someone from Maine would never comprehend.

The part of Sardegna that has changed the most is the northern coast from Castelsardo to just north of Olbia. Because of its proximity to northern Italy, this area was ripe for touristic development. There are some magnificent beaches and scuba-diving possibilities, and this coastal part of the province of Sassari has boomed in the last quarter of the twentieth century. A zone in the northeast called La Costa Smeralda (the Emerald Coast) was developed in the 1960s and 1970s to become one of the most chic resorts in Europe. You will find relatively little coverage of La Costa Smeralda in this chapter because there is not much that is typically Sardinian about it. Most of the excellent seafood is cooked in the same way it would be in Liguria, Campania, Sicilia, or the Adriatic. The architecture and the hotel facilities are not distinct: they resemble fine resorts throughout the Mediterranean, the Caribbean, and Hawaii. I am not discouraging you from going to La Costa Smeralda, but I remind you that if this is your only exposure to this island you cannot say you know Sardegna.

Eating in Sardegna

In major cities on the island there are usually one or two restaurants that have become shrines for the specialties of their provinces. You will find listings in this chapter for the leading restaurants of Cagliari, Oristano, Nuoro, and Sassari, the four provincial capitals, as well as places worth going out of your way for in Olbia and Alghero. Aside from these places (and everything on the Costa Smeralda), the selection on many menus tends to be rather limited. You will find offerings that rise out of the local tradition of the place you are in, but in most cases these will be variations of the themes of bread, lamb, cheese, honey, certain vegetables, wine, and very sweet almond pastries that are a legacy of the Moorish presence on the island centuries ago. But the food you will eat will invariably be fresh, flavorful, unpretentious, and served with pride.

PRIMI (AND BREAD)

Culungiones. Delicate pasta pillows filled with potato and pepper.

Impanadas. Baked meat-filled pasta; a specialty of Nuoro.

Malloreddus. Tiny gnocchi with saffron in the dough. An old dialect name meaning "little bulls."

Pane Carasau (Carta da Musica). This crisp bread of the shepherds is a Sardinian classic that can last for a long time. You might want to bring some home and make Sardinian dishes such as *pane frattau.*

Pane Frattau. *Pane carasau* is soaked in hot water, layered, topped with tomato sauce, grated Pecorino, and a fried egg. This classic dish of the poor is outstanding.

Zuppa Cuatta. A casserole made with bread, meat, cheeses, and broth.

SECONDI

Aragosta. Lobster, a specialty of Alghero. It is often served *in insalata,* lobster chunks tossed with lemon juice and olive oil, or *all'algherese,* tossed with oil, lemon juice, tomatoes, and onions. When grilled, it is *alla griglia.*

Arselle. A local type of clam with a delicate flavor.

Bottarga (or *Bottariga*). This specialty of Cabras is also called the poor man's caviar. Bottarga is made of the eggs of tuna or gray mullet. They are soaked in salt water, dried, and compressed so that they form a deep orange-colored block. It is used as a condiment with vegetables or blended with butter to flavor breads and pastas. You can also have shavings of *bottarga* topped with lemon juice. *Bottarga* has acquired a following in continental Italy, especially in Liguria.

Burrida. Sweet-and-sour catfish or eel with a sauce of oil and almonds or walnuts.

Cefalo and *Muggine.* Two types of mullet.

Monzette. Snails, loved in Sassari.

Porceddu. Spit-roasted suckling pig seasoned with herbs. One of the region's great specialties.

Sa Cassola. Of Catalan origin, this is a stew with many types of fish and seafood.

FORMAGGI

The cheeses of Sardegna are among the best in Italy. While regions in the north such as Lombardia tend to make cheeses from cow's milk, Sardegna is renowned above all for its cheeses made from ewe's milk. The general term is "Pecorino," but every cheese is different, depending on where it is made. The cheese can be very soft and creamy when young, but it becomes hard and granular when aged and is perfect for grating over pasta. Much of the Pecorino Romano that is grated over pasta in Lazio (that Americans call Romano cheese) is actually produced in Sardegna.

Pecorino Sardo. A great eating cheese. It is usually aged for two months, and no two are alike. Each one has the flavor of the herbs and grasses that a ewe consumed as she made the milk from which the cheese was produced. Many of the best are made in Macomer and elsewhere in the province of Nuoro, although towns throughout the region boast great cheese. You should devote some calories each day of your visit in Sardegna to getting to know new types of Pecorino Sardo.

Fiore Sardo. A one-year-old Pecorino that is shipped to Liguria for use in pesto.

Ricotta. Delicious soft cheese, which in Sardegna is almost always made of ewe's milk.

Other cheeses are made with the milk of a *vacca* or *mucca* (cow), or *capra* (goat).

DOLCI

Sardegna is famous for its pastries, which arrive at the end of almost every meal. Many are made with the delicious honeys whose fame extends far beyond the island. Many of the honeys are more bitter than sweet and make unusual combinations with other ingredients. *Seadas* is the ubiquitous dessert throughout Sardegna. The use of honeys, almonds, and other nuts is a legacy of the Arabic presence on the island centuries ago.

Aranciata Nuorese (or *Aranzata*). Candied orange peel flavored with honey and tossed with almonds.

Ciccioneddas. Pastry filled with cherry jam.

Copulletas. Whatever they are they seem to multiply.

Pabassine (or *Papassine*). Pastry filled with raisins and almonds.

Seadas (or *Sebadas*). A ravioli-shaped dessert filled with a tangy, soft sheep's-milk cheese. The *seadas* is fried and topped with either sweet or bitter honey.

Sospiri. Small, soft rolls filled either with *mirto,* chocolate, or almond paste.

Tilicas (or *Tillicas*). Crown-shaped pastries filled with marzipan.

OTHER SARDINIAN FLAVORS

Miele. There are many flavors of honey in Sardegna. Many of the most famous ones are seasonal, based on when particular flowers and plants are in bloom. These include *corbezzolo* (strawberry plants) from October to December; *lavanda* (lavender) and mountain flowers in springtime; *cardo* (thistle) from the end of April through May; *agrumi* (citrus) in May, and eucalyptus in summer.

Pinzimonio. Generally associated with Toscana, this is a palate-cleansing combination of chopped raw vegetables.

Sapa (or *Saba*). A syrup made with wine must from Nuragus grapes. Ten liters of must produce one liter of *sapa.* It can be used to flavor baked goods or other foods, or diluted with water and chilled to make a beverage.

Zafferano. Saffron.

The Wines of Sardegna

It would be commonly assumed that the wines of Sardegna are rough, heavy, and, to use a mistaken and unflattering euphemism, peasantlike. There was a time when the island did produce *vini da taglio* (wines for cutting) that were used to blend with others in France or for making vermouth in Piemonte. But old beliefs die hard. The Piedmontese have had a positive influence in Sardegna, with the result that there is a tradition of fine wine making. Producers such as Sella & Mosca in Alghero have been in business for almost a century, and other smaller producers (such as Giovanni Cherchi in Usini) have raised the quality of Sardinian wine much higher than its image. One good way to get to know some of the region's best wines is to dine at the Ristorante dal Corsaro in Cagliari and to allow Giuseppina Deidda to guide you through a wonderful tasting experience.

There are eighteen DOC wines in Sardegna, but the two names you should be sure to remember are Cannonau and Vermentino.

Cannonau. A medium- to full-bodied red that is made of 75 percent Cannonau grapes and is blended with others, such as Bovale di Spagna, Bovale Sardo, Carignano, Pascale di Cagliari, or Monica (and up to 5 percent Vernaccia, a white grape). These other grapes are also made into wines of their own names, as well as blends.

Vermentino. A grape that is also found in Liguria and Toscana. It makes a delicious white wine to go with seafood. There are two varieties: Vermentino di Gallura (which is more prized) and Vermentino di Sardegna.

Nuragus. Actually the white grape that is the most cultivated in Sardegna. It has a floral bouquet and produces a dry, slightly acidic wine.

Vernaccia di Oristano. Vernaccia is a white-wine grape that shares its name with several others in Italy, but this one is not related to the others. It makes an intense, slightly liquorlike dessert wine.

Malvasia, Nasco, and *Moscato.* Other grapes used for dessert wines.

Other Beverages

Filo di Ferro (or *Filu Ferru*). This means "iron string." It is a high-powered alcoholic beverage (45 percent alcohol) that was contraband because it was not made under government supervision and no taxes were paid on it. The name derives from the fact that bottles were buried in the ground, with the string sticking out, to be hidden from the police. Nowadays *filo a ferro* is made under more careful supervision and might be offered to you as an after-dinner *digestivo.*

Mirto. Myrtle used to flavor food (meat might be wrapped around a myrtle twig, or steaks and chops might be cooked over a fire made with myrtle wood). A very popular after-dinner liqueur is *mirto,* which may be red or white.

Alghero (Sassari)

Alghero is a delightful city in the northwestern corner of Sardegna. It spent many years under the domination of Spain (particularly Catalonia), from the fourteenth century to the mid-eighteenth century, and the cuisine and language reflect that influence. People here use expressions such as *mas o menos* and bon di that reflect Spanish influence. Every Saturday at 19:30h, mass is held in Algherese, the local dialect with heavy Spanish overtones. There are lovely beaches here that attract day-trippers from Sassari as well as vacationers from the Continent who can't afford the Costa Smeralda. I prefer Alghero to the famous resorts because one finds good local food (especially lobster and paella) and wine, intriguing architecture and culture, and all the beach life anyone could ask for. The surrounding area has spectacular grottoes and rock formations that have been formed by centuries of winds blowing from Provence.

BAR AND CAFFÈS

Cafe Latino, at #6 opposite the cathedral. Open 8–13:30h, 16–2h; closed Sunday.

There is a terrace with a grand view of Alghero. Stop for a drink at one of the outdoor tables.

DINING

Il Pavone, Piazza Sulis 3, tel. 079/979584. Closed Sunday (lunch June–October; all day November–May), Nov 1–10. All credit cards. Moderately expensive.

Be sure to try the *lumache*. These snails are simply cooked in salt, with the result that you taste their flavor rather than the garlic or butter that they are usually drowned in. Good shrimp and lobster, *polpo con patate* (octopus with potatoes), *acciughe farcite di formaggio* (fresh anchovies stuffed with cheese), *melanzane ripiene di pesce* (fish-filled eggplant), and *cozze fritte* (fried mussels). Very good food all around.

Ristorante La Lepanto, Via Carlo Alberto 135, tel. 079/979116. Closed

Monday (except mid-June–September). All credit cards. Moderate to moderately expensive.

Owner Moreno Cecchini, originally from Lucca, has lived here for many years and is an ambassador for the food of Alghero. The very large menu is full of pastas and many types of fish. *Spaghetti all'algherese* is made with clams and green olives. There are all sorts of mixed fried seafood platters and some good meat dishes. For dessert are *sebadas*, or you can select from a large table with more than twenty types of cookies and biscuits. Service is very good, and there is a well-chosen wine list at reasonable prices. If you do not eat lobster, a fine meal can be had without excessive expenditure. But lobster is the raison d'être of a seafood restaurant in Alghero, so you should indulge. It is sold by the *etto*, and the average portion is 350 grams. The typical preparation is lobster that is steamed, cut in pieces with the shell attached, tossed with oil, white vinegar, onions, tomatoes, and served with orange slices. You can also have grilled lobster *(aragosta alla griglia)*.

Trattoria La Singular, Via Arduino 45, tel. 079/982098. Closed Monday (except in summer). No credit cards. Moderately inexpensive.

The tunnel-shaped room is a former wine cellar. The food features local specialties of Alghero. Among these are *bouvel* (large snails), *caragol* (small snails), and *cordula di luna* (rolled sheep innards). For dessert be sure to try *manja en branc*, a light cake of sugar and egg yolk that is an Alghero specialty.

Da Zia Maria, Strada dei Due Mari, Malai, tel. 079/951884. Reservations essential. Always open. No credit cards. Moderate.

Maria Floris operates a simple but delightful *agriturismo* not far from Alghero. It is possible to sleep here or to come only for a meal. The food is great. Her homemade ravioli are deli-cate, and she does wonders with rabbit, *porceddu*, and kid *(capretto con il mirto)*.

FOOD SHOPPING

The small market in the center of Alghero is between Via Sassari and Via Cagliari and continues around the Via Genova and the Via Mazzini. There is a much bigger market on Wednesday, where you can buy food, clothing, housewares, and flowers. This market is about a twenty-minute walk from the city center: the nicest route is to leave the Piazza Sulis and walk along the shoreline of the Lungomare Dante and the Lungomare Valencia. At the Via Toda go inland and you will soon reach the market. If you want to visit only the food sellers, you can return to town on Via

Giovanni XXIII. If you want to see the whole market, keep walking and return to the center on the Via Valverde. The last stretch is where flowers are sold, but there is also the Panetteria Sarda, an excellent bread bakery.

Casa del Formaggio, Via Mazzini 43. Closed Monday afternoon in winter, and Sunday.

There is a glorious fragrance in this store that sells a variety of Pecorino, plus cow and goat cheese. You will see shelves stacked with rounds of cheese, while above hang *salami*, sausages, and other cheeses. Local cheeses include *maristella* (a sweet cheese), *sandalio* (can be two to three months old or one year old, each with a pleasing flavor), *cabriol* (two-year-old Pecorino), *bonassai* (a triangular soft sheep cheese), and a local mozzarella. You can also buy *bottarga*, sausages, oils, honey, local wines, and sometimes *porceddu*. Sausages in Alghero are different from others in Sardegna because they have no anise, fennel seed, or *peperoncino*.

Enodolciaria, Via Simon 24, tel. 079/979741. Open summer 9–13h, 17–23h, closed Sunday morning; winter: 9–13h, 16–20h, closed Sunday.

Alghero is a wine-producing area of great renown. Many of the wines are called Aragosta, which are whites well suited to lobster. This store sells local wines, plus *mirto* (twelve types), *filo di ferro*, honeys, breads, *malloreddus*, and pastries.

La Fantasia della Pasta Fresca, Via XX Settembre 68, tel. 079/979497.

Fresh pasta here includes *ravioli di*

ricotta (filled with local cheese), *malloreddus*, *fregola* (tiny pin-dot-sized pasta often used in soup), *arizangnas* (the local equivalent of long, broad noodles such as *pappardelle*), and *seadas* made with fresh cheese and the zest of lemon and orange.

Barùmini (Cagliari)

One of the best-preserved Nuraghic communities is Barùmini, which refers to itself as Su Nuraxi. Many of the *nuraghe* date from 1700 B.C. If you are in Oristano and have not seen any *nuraghe*, you should make an excursion to Barùmini. Eat at Sa Lolla, Via Cavour 49, tel. 070/9368419.

Borore (Sassari)

SWEET SHOP
Carmina Medde, Via Martini 13, tel. 0789/86207.

Some of the best Sardinian pastries you will taste anywhere.

Bortigali (Nuoro)

Some places, for no particularly explainable reason, have an innate charm and likability. Such a place is Bortigali, a small town near Macomer on the road to Nuoro. The town is built into a long curve in a hillock so that almost every house has a view of the valley below and the distant mountains. It is a pleasing sight to round the curve from the west that leads into town, and suddenly all of Bortigali appears. Townspeople like to gather in the tiny triangular piazza and in *caffès* along the main street. They are very friendly to the visitor. At the fringes of Bortigali one sees dairy cows, certainly a minority animal in this region where the ovine is prized more than the bovine. At about 20h the main street of town fills with trucks carrying steel cans holding the results of the evening milking. If one travels a few kilometers beyond Bortigali, old *nuraghi* and more recent brick dwellings come into view. These simple constructions—descendants of *nuraghe*—are used by itinerant shepherds to rest while their herds graze. This is a place where a fifteen-year-old shepherd and his flock still have right-of-way on narrow country roads.

Bosa (Nuoro)

DINING/HOTEL
Sa Pischedda, Via Roma 2–8, tel. 0785/373065. Closed Tuesday (except April–October), January. All credit cards. Moderate.

Bosa is a beautiful seaside town with a famous *carnevale* each winter, and here is a good place to eat and stay. An antipasto of *frutti di mare* paves the way to pasta such as *anguleddas con la bottarga* or *tagliatelle alle granseola* (crab). Then grilled fish or *sa cassola* (fragrant poached fish).

HONEY

Costantino Brisi, Viale Repubblica, tel. 0785/374591.

Many varieties, including *asfodelo* (asphodel—which is narcissus to the Greeks and daffodil to the French and English), rosemary, cardoon, eucalyptus, *corbezzolo* (a pinkish flower that is also the state flower of Massachusetts).

Cabras (Oristano)

BOTARGA, FISH, SEAFOOD

Fratelli Manca, Via Cima, tel. 0783/290848.

DINING

Ristorante Zia Belledda, Via Amsicora 77, tel. 0783/290801. Closed Wednesday. No credit cards. Inexpensive.

Elisabetta Trincas, known to all as Zia (Aunt) Belledda, seems like the archetype of the older Sardinian woman: clothed all in black, with pulled-back silver hair. Yet she is neither dour nor mournful, as the cliché might dictate. Rather, she is joyous and welcoming. She choreographs an operation that involves four other women (one older, three younger). Zia Belledda proposes dishes and then supervises their preparation. She is also involved in selecting the fish that arrive each morning from the sea and the nearby lagoon. Each morning Zia Belledda makes any dish that can be prepared in advance. The other women peel, clean, cook, tally checks, talk, and laugh among themselves. The scene brings to mind Lina Wertmüller's play *Amore e Magia nella Cucina di Mamma (Love and Magic in Mama's Kitchen)*.

Zia Belledda in her restaurant, Cabras

Because *bottarga* is the local delicacy, you might consider *spaghetti alla bottarga* as your first course. But she also makes a good *risotto alla pescatora* and an unusual *pesto di pesce*, in which various types of fish are filleted, cooked, mashed, and combined with tomato and herbs. This pesto is delicious on spaghetti. *Secondi* include *muggine* (gray mullet) from the lagoon that can be grilled or poached and is often available chilled. As a side dish, ask for the *cipolle*, soft onions cooked in oil and vinegar that have an unexpected sweetness and delicacy. Dessert can be fruit, homemade *sebadas*, and some Sardinian sweets. Belledda also makes an excellent, smooth *mirto* liqueur. You will remember Belledda for a long time.

Sa Funtà, Via Garibaldi 25, tel. 0783/290685. You must reserve 24 hours ahead. Closed Sunday, December 15–February. No credit cards. Expensive.

Gigi Ledda is an inspired cook who uses *bottarga* and other local ingredients to make exciting dishes. Among the specialties are *anguilla con carciofi* (eel with artichokes), *fregola con arselle*, and *formaggi freschi arrosti* (delicious roasted cheeses).

Cagliari

BARS AND CAFFÈS

City Bar, Largo Carlo Felice 3 (at the corner of Via Sardegna). Closed Sunday.

This is where I had the best espresso in Sardegna, which is served with a small piece of semisweet chocolate.

Caffè Genovese, Piazza Costituzione 10. Closed Thursday.

For more than 150 years this square-shaped, very solid *caffè* with an intimate outdoor terrace has been a focal point in Cagliari. It sits near the town's main landmark, the imposing Bastione St Remy, yet somehow feels just as important. A historic place that should be listed with the great old *caffès* of Italy.

DINING

Dal Corsaro, Viale Regina Margherita 28, tel. 070/664318. Closed Sunday (except August), December 23–January 6. All credit cards. Moderately expensive.

Ristorante dal Corsaro is considered one of the best restaurants in Sardegna, and my visit there certainly bears out that assessment. Owners Giuseppina and Gianluigi Deidda run their restaurant with great love and care. The dishes are all in the classic Sardinian tradition, beautifully cooked and served. Everything I tasted was excellent. I urge you to try the *minestr'e cocciula e fregolina*, delicate tiny clams served with pasta the size of the head of a pin. The *culingionis di cibudda con il pecorino stagionato*, a flat square raviolo filled with onions and topped with butter and aged sheep cheese, is divine. As good as all the food is, the star of this restaurant is Giuseppina and her wine list. She has one of the most refined palates I have ever encountered, and my visit became an opportunity to get to know wonderful Sardinian wines that are hard to find anywhere else. Here are five wines worth sampling:

Nuragus di Cagliari "Dolianova." A light, fresh white.

Vermentino di Gallura "Funtana Liras," Cantina Sociale di Monti. An almost peppery flavor that is a good match with the *culingionis*. This white wine has a clean taste, complex flavors, and a nice finish.

Tuvaoes Vermentino di Sardegna Riserva, Giovanni Cherchi. A wine of very limited production. Its fragrance is most subtle, the first taste is fresh and clean, and it has a long and exciting finish in the mouth.

Carignano del Sulcis "Rocca Rubia," Riserva Cantina Sociale Santadi. A big, power-ful, but not overpowering wine. Carig-nano is an ancient Sardinian grape variety that is usually blended with other grapes to make Cannonau. This is a rare chance to taste it on its own.

Donna Jolanda Moscato di Cagliari (Meloni). An award-winning dessert wine, and deservedly so. Golden in color, tempered in sweetness, and a perfect match for sweet Sardinian pastries.

One can have an excellent tasting menu at Ristorante dal Corsaro at a moderately ex-pensive price. If you order *à la carte* and have several wines (all reasonably priced), your meal will be more expensive, but very worth the cost.

Lillicu, Via Sardegna 78, tel. 070/652970. Closed Sunday, last three weeks of August. All credit cards. Moderate.

A popular local trattoria that specializes in fish and seafood. It has characteristic gray marble tables and a simple white decor. There is *bottarga* as an antipasto or served with spaghetti. *Burrida* is another house specialty. Pasta is also served with *arselle*, which I recommend. Also excellent is the *zuppa di pesce*, a bowl brimming with assorted fish and sea-food. Raw fish is brought to your table for inspection before it is cooked for you and is priced by the *etto*. Other than this, prices are moderate.

Basilio, Via Satta 112, tel. 070/480330. Closed Sunday, January, August. All credit cards. Moderate.

One can enjoy food from land or sea, or a bit of both. The *fregola con le arselle*, tiny Sardinian pasta with clams, is delicious. *Funghi*, when available, are a speciality. Save calories and skip dessert here.

FOOD SHOPPING

Centro FOS (Formaggic Ovini Sardi), Via Sassari 50, tel. 070/650745. Closed Saturday afternoon and Sunday.

If I were to pick one store in all of Sardegna to give you a sense of the range and quality of Sardinian food, this would be the place. Upon entering you are immediately struck by the intoxicating fragrance of many different Pecorino cheeses. It is a beguiling smell that brings to mind pastures, herbs, grass, fresh milk, and fresh air. A refrigerator case contains various Pecorino spreads and jars of *bottariga*. There is a large selection of honeys, many in flavors you have never seen before. Look for Sardinian pastas such as *culungiones, malloreddus,* and ravioli filled with sheep cheese. There are fresh and dried sausages, dried fruit, many regional wines and liqueurs, including *mirto* and *filo di ferro*. Toward the front of the store (behind the cheese counter) are shelves with enormous loaves of bread as well as smaller *pani*. Farther toward the front, near the good selection of olive oils, is *pane saba*, an intense fruit-and-nut loaf flavored with wine must. Everywhere you look are typical *dolci sardi: ciccioneddas, pabassine, tillicas, copulettas, sospiri*. At the cashier are a lovely mother and daughter. In front of them is a large basket of fresh brown eggs and a few packages of saffron.

A WALK ON THE VIA BAYLLE

As in most cities, there is a street in Cagliari that is of particular interest to the gourmet traveler. The stores are closed on Saturday afternoon, and, except for Gastronomia Pisu, credit cards are not accepted.

#19: Sini.

An excellent selection of knives and cutlery, many made locally.

#25: Salumeria Paghi.

Since 1902 this has been the leading *salumeria* of Cagliari, although for Sardinian products I would direct you to Centro FOS. Paghi has fancy foods from the Continent and from around the world.

#29: Vittorio Sini Lame da Collezione.

This man is the cousin of the knife sellers at #19. Here you can buy modern knives and antique ones from the nineteenth century. Many of these come from the town of Pattada (Sassari), which is famous for its knife making.

#39: Gastronomia Pisu.

All manner of foods from Italy and Sardegna. Many dishes are cooked here throughout the day and are available for take out. There is *pescespada* (swordfish) *alla Carlofortina*, grilled and finished with tomatoes, olive oil, parsley, and other spices. In the winter the *gastronomia* makes *porchetta alla romana*, which is set up in the window and sold directly to passersby. On Friday the specialty is paella (don't forget that there has always been Spanish influence in Sardegna). Each day there are many salads, vegetables, and cheeses. You may want to sample Casu de Binu, an unusual local cheese. You may have heard about Sardegna's *formaggio alle verme* (cheese with worms). This is a cheese in which worms grow as the cheese ages. When the cheese is spread on bread the worms become, shall we say, an additional sort of protein. If you do not feel up to the task of sampling cheese with worms, then try Casu de Binu. This cheese tastes very similar to *formaggio alle verme,* but does not contain the offending little squirmers. It is made of soft sheep's-milk cheese that is blended with high-powered *filo de ferro.*

#42: Panificio.

A small, good selection of Sardinian breads. In the morning you can see bakers at work in the back.

MARKET

Although it's called the San Benedetto market, Cagliari's lively market (open Monday through Saturday 7h to 13:30h) is actually off the Piazza San Rocco, bounded by the Via Tiziano and Via Cocco Ortu. On Monday, the fish market is rather quiet, but it picks up on Tuesday and gets better through the week. Much of the seafood is still alive: eels, lobsters, and many flipping fish. Each fishmonger, many of whom caught the fish themselves, vies for your attention in this very animated market. Upstairs are the stalls selling fruit, vegetables, cheese, and meat. You may find it notable how many meat sellers there are here compared with other markets in Italy. Wherever you look, lamb, pork, beef, poultry, and horse meat are being sold. Historically Sardinians are big meat eaters because most of them lived inland, tending sheep. The carnivorous tradition continues.

The fish market, Cagliari

Castelsardo (Sassari)

A small town founded by the Dorias of Genova in 1102, who named it "Castelgenovese." It became Castelaragonese under Spanish rule. The basket makers of Castelsardo are considered the best in the region and among the best in Italy.

BASKETS (CESTINI)

Cooperativa Cestinaie Castelsardo (I.S.O.L.A.), Via Sant'Antonio.

Anna Maria Sanna, Via Carlo Alberto.

Franco Sardartis di Marras, Via Sedini.

Three good sources.

Il Cavalluccio, Località Punta Tramontina, tel. 079/474510. Closed Tuesday. MasterCard, Visa. Moderate to moderately expensive.

A restaurant that offers delicious fish and seafood. There is a hot appetizer *(antipasto caldo di mare)*, good *risotto ai frutti di mare*, a grilled fish of the day, nice local wines, homemade cakes and, in season, delicious peaches soaked in wine.

Nuoro
Classic Town

Nuoro gathers within its borders and nearby towns of Oliena and Orgosolo so much of what is classically Sardinian: pastoral culture and cuisine, *nuraghe*, literature, music, handicrafts, and the rugged beauty of the mountains. The town becomes very festive on Shrove Tuesday during Carnival, and there are processions to the statue of the Redeemer on the last Sunday in August.

CULTURE

On most Tuesdays and Fridays, at 20:30h, a local chorus rehearses typical music of the Barbagia, this zone of the province of Nuoro. Rehearsals are held at the Funtana Buddia and are open to the public, and to appreciate the sound of this ancient music, you need to hear it. To get there, either take a taxi or start at the Piazza Vittorio Emanuele and take bus 4. Ask the driver to leave you at the *cabina telefonica* (phone booth) and ask for directions from there to the Funtana Buddia.

DINING

Ristorante Canne al Vento, Via Repubblica 66, tel. 0784/201762. Closed Sunday. American Express, MasterCard, Visa. Moderate to moderately expensive.

The anonymous milky-glass door does not suggest the large, airy restaurant behind it. There is a broad selection of Sardinian specialties from land and sea, but I would stick to foods from the land. The *primo, spaghetti Canne al Vento* (with tomato, cream, Pecorino cheese, sausage, and prosciutto), is rich and delicious, but if you have not yet sampled the *pane frattau*, this is the place to do it. The must-taste *secondo* is the *porceddu*, which is perhaps the best roast suckling pig I have ever tasted. The meat was buttery soft and remarkably free of grease. The skin was crisp and crunchy, not leathery. Unlike on the mainland, where pigs in Lazio, Umbria, Marche, and Abruzzo are laced with oil, garlic, and rosemary and are a hedonistic bath of decadent grease, this Sardinian pig was a triumph because of the flavor of the meat and how well it was prepared. I ate it with *pinzimonio*. With this I drank Nepente d'Oliena, a nice medium-weight red wine. Dessert was *caschettas*, little wisps of chewy nuttiness served with *aranciata*, the other local dessert. Friendly service.

Il Rifugio, Via Mereu 28, tel. 0784/232355. Closed Wednesday. All credit cards. Moderate.

There is good *salumi di pecora* (salami made with lamb) and lamb appears elsewhere on the menu, including in *cassola alla nuorese* and the rare and wonderful *su filindeu* (which must be ordered ahead), handmade pasta cooked in lamb broth. There is also excellent fish if you prefer.

RESTAURANTS WITH A VIEW

Just outside of Nuoro is the Monte Ortobene, with gorgeous views of the nearby valleys and a gigantic statue of Christ the Redeemer (which is the site of an important folklore festival in August). To reach this statue, you can take bus 5, which departs from the Piazza Vittorio Emanuele every forty-five minutes. Have lunch at Hotel-Ristorante Fratelli Sacchi (tel. 0784/31200) or Albergo E.S.I.T. (tel. 0784/33172), which is also a hotel school.

FOOD SHOPPING

As in most of Sardegna, food stores in Nuoro are closed on Saturday afternoon and Sunday.

Formaggi Sardi e Salumi, Piazza G. Marghinotti.

A good selection of cheeses, *salumi*, olives, *pane carasau*. Because Sardinians claim they can detect subtle differences, each product is labeled with its town of origin. You, too, can taste and discover subtle differences in seemingly identical foods.

Latteria Marianna, Corso Garibaldi 174.

Owner Marianna Floris is animated, knowledgeable, and proud. I noticed that younger people who enter the shop refer to the owner as Zia Marianna. I have heard many older Sardinian women referred to as "Aunt" even if they are not a relative, much in the way that older women in Rus-sian plays and novels are called "Mother." You can sample a wide range of cheeses in this excellent shop. Buy an *etto* of each and compare. The Casi Solu is made by shepherds in the fields and brought into town to be sold. They hang along one wall and look like bongo drums. Among the Pecorino cheeses, many are labeled by the town. Try those from Bonassai, Nuoro, Orgosolo, and Siamanna and notice the differences. Marianna also sells a wide range of Sardinian pork products (those from the town of Irgoli are considered the best; Oliena also makes a good prosciutto). Marianna's fully packed but neatly organized store also has honeys, *sapa*, cookies, sweets, breads, wines, and *mirto*. But the one thing you must try is *latte di pecora*. This is fresh ewe's milk: an interesting taste on its own, but keep in mind this is the ingredient that ultimately makes the sheep's-milk cheeses for which Sardegna is so renowned.

HANDICRAFTS

I.S.O.L.A., Via Monsignor Bua 10, tel. 0784/31507. Open 9:30–13h, 16:30–20:30h.

The opening and closing times are somewhat elastic. An excellent selection of the best of Sardinian crafts, including pottery and beautifully embroidered cloths.

MUSEUMS

Museo della Vita e delle Tradizioni Popolari Sarde, Via Meru 56 (near Viale San Onofrio), tel. 0784/31426. Open 9–13h, 15–18h, Sunday 9–13h; closed Monday.

An outstanding exhibit of Sardinian costumes, cookware, utensils, furniture, musical instruments. This will give you great insights into the roots of Sardinian life as you witness it today.

Casa di Grazia Deledda, Via Grazia Deledda 42, tel. 0784/34571. Open 9–13h, 15–18h, Sunday 9–13h; closed Monday.

The home of the author whose writings are the voice of Sardegna. A simple collection, but worth a visit.

SWEET SHOPS

Casa del Dolce, Corso Garibaldi 105.

Homemade typical sweets, including a very good *aranciata nuorese* and *torrone* (made with honey, hazelnuts, and almonds) from Tonara, a small town in central Sardegna.

Ladu, Corso Garibaldi 43. Closed Tuesday.

An old sweet shop with elixirs and confections and a charming proprietress.

Pasticceria Il Golosastro, Corso Garibaldi 173–177.

The Mele-Cadinu sisters make all sorts of local sweets, cakes, cookies, and sell cheese and honey as well.

Olbia (Sassari)

Olbia's airport is the gateway to the Costa Smeralda. The city itself is not particularly interesting, but it does have an extraordinary restaurant that I would travel for many hours to reach. If you are not as dedicated as I am, at least plan a meal at the Ristorante Gallura as you transit to or from the Costa Smeralda.

DINING

Hotel-Ristorante Gallura, Corso Umberto 145, tel. 0789/24648. Closed Monday, October 15–31, December 20–January 6. All credit cards. Moderately expensive to expensive.

Here is that rarity: a restaurant in which the chef is so original and audacious that tasting her food is like hearing a new language or seeing a new color in the spectrum. Rita d'Enza makes daring and unusual flavor combinations, but cooks with such knowledge, insight, and

a sense of proportion that everything succeeds. One can only regard her with awe and gratitude. In service to you, the reader, and in a fit of blissful indulgence, I tasted nineteen dishes and four wines and can report that I had two of the most sublime meals of my life. Rita draws from many sources and inspirations: her fundamental ingredients may be local, but her spices and flavorings are from all corners of the world. Unless you dine with a marine biologist you will not recognize half the things you are eating. When you enter the small, attractive dining room with its vaguely nautical air, you will see a central table stacked with up to forty bowls containing special foods. You will also pass a crock with the soup of the day. Although the menu changes with the season, here are some of the amazing dishes you may get to sample:

Tiny lobsters, steamed, tossed with onions and tiny ripe tomatoes

Delicate Olbia mussels with basil leaves, red onions, tiny sesame seeds, and oil and vinegar

Red *cappelloti*, white *pentini*, green *anemoni:* all delicious little sea creatures ever so lightly battered and fried so all their texture and flavor remain (on the plate they look like a little Italian flag)

Alghe di mare, ever-so-light batter-fried seaweed with lemon—superb!

Gattuccio al cioccolato, catfish with strong vinegar, orange peel, cardamom, pine nuts, raisins, and bitter chocolate

Olbia mussels with saffron and coriander —creamy and wonderful

Tortino di carne, a thin crust surrounding delicately seasoned meat—sublime

Maltagliati (fresh pasta) with *funghi,* oysters, and a healthy dose of thyme

Sorbet of pink grapefruit with a light sauce of honey and orange peel

Crostata of fresh figs with a raspberry-vinegar sauce

The flavors dazzle, but they are all rational and not mere showmanship. When I dined at the Gallura, it was 40°C (104°F), but the dining room was air-conditioned. The hotel, which is modest, is not cooled, so you should bear this in mind if you book a room. Rita and her waiters make sure you are having fun, but are affectionate and not overbearing. Follow her wine recommendations, too. Her selection is exceeded only by that of the Ristorante dal Corsaro in Cagliari. A meal at Ristorante Gallura can be expensive, but it will be a dining experience that will open your eyes and imagination to things you have never even dreamed of.

HANDICRAFTS

I.S.O.L.A., Corso Umberto I 28–34. Open 9:30–13h, 17–20:15h; closed Sunday.

Oliena (Nuoro)

This community not far from Nuoro offers a total immersion into Sardinian flavors and folkways. Women often wear native costumes and jewelry. Everyone in town gets into costume on August 21, San Lussorio's Day, when there are celebrations of Oliena's patron. The cheeses, breads, ham, and Cannonau wine here are among the best in the region.

BREAD

Raimonda Zola, Via E. Matteri 7, tel. 0784/287208.

Makes *pane carasau* in a wood-burning oven.

DINING AND HOTEL

Su Gologone, tel. 0784/287512, fax 0784/287668. Open March–October. All credit cards. Moderate.

This very nice hotel in a beautiful setting is

a good place to settle in for a couple of days to eat Signora Palomera's excellent cooking, which you can work off by taking excursions in the surrounding hills and mountains or by walking the 12 kilometers (7½ miles) to Nuoro.

SALUMI

Giovanni Puddu, Località Orbuddai, tel. 0784/288457.

Produces fine *salumi*, including *prosciutto di cinghiale*.

SWEET SHOP

Anna P., Viale Italia 100, tel. 0784/287610.

Makes outstanding confections, including *aranciata* (here called *aranzada*).

Orgosolo (Nuoro)

DINING

Ai Monti del Gennargentu, Località Settiles, tel. 0784/402374. Closed Tuesday, December, and January. All credit cards. Moderately inexpensive.

Authentic local dishes in a beautiful mountain setting. Owner Maria Giovanna Ruggiu makes a special dish, *vitella al miele* (veal lightly flavored with honey).

Oristano

BAKERY-SWEET SHOP

Franca Tocco, Località Is Antas, tel. 0783/73311.

Makes a regional specialty called *mostaccioli oristanesi*, referred to locally as *su mustazzolu*. These are of ancient origin and are made with flour, yeast, sugar, and zest of lemon. The dough sits for twenty days be-fore being baked.

BARS AND CAFFÈS

Tonietto Arru and l'Azzuro are the two spots on the Piazza Roma that draw most of the *oristanesi* for coffee, pastries, and ice cream in the evening.

DINING

Il Faro, Via Bellini 25, tel. 0783/70002. Closed Sunday, December 22–January 20. All credit cards. Expensive.

I visited Oristano in July, when Il Faro was closed. This is a famous restaurant that is generally thought to do honor to Sardinian cooking, although I have heard from several people that the dishes are excessively fancy and sacrifice genuineness for elegance.

Antica Trattoria del Teatro, Via Parpaglia 11, tel. 0783/71672. Closed Wednesday (except in August), October. All credit cards. Moderate.

Try *lorighittas*, a typical pasta of Oristano, that is served with a sauce of various white meats plus Pecorino. Fish, lamb, and pork are all good here, as are desserts such as *seadas* flavored with pistachio or *semifreddo al mirto.*

Palau (Sassari)

DINING

Da Robertino, Via Nazionale 20, tel. 0789/709610. Closed Monday and first six weeks of the year. All credit cards. Moderate to moderately expensive.

Very good fish and seafood, including *arselle, bottarga,* lobster, and mussels.

San Gavino Monreale (Cagliari)

SAFFRON

Su Zafferanu, Via Sauro 12, tel. 070/9339207.

A good source for this expensive ingredient that is used in *malloreddus* and other Sardinian preparations.

Sassari

Sassari, with its pink and ocher buildings, its leafiness, and its student population, is quite pleasant if you have spent a lot of time in the stark central section of Sardegna. The Piazza d'Italia is one of the better-known squares in Italy. The nearby Piazza Castello is the hub for many nice *caffès* (Cafezinho, Mokador, Sechi), as is the Via Roma (Maraviglie, Florian, Tre "B").

BARS AND CAFFÈS

Bar Mokador, Largo Cavallotti 2.

Nice outdoor tables; skip the ice cream.

Bar Rau, Piazza d'Italia 27.

Famous for its homemade *mirto.*

Bar-Pasticceria Sechi, Piazza Castello.

The oldest *gelateria* in town, but the pastries are more interesting.

DINING

Ristorante Pizzeria da Nanni, Viale Dante 31, tel. 079/275556. Closed Saturday. American Express, Master Card, Visa. Moderately inexpensive.

A very nice place about a ten-minute walk from either the Museo Archeologico Sanna or the Mostra di Artigianato Sardo, your two main reasons for visiting Sassari. It is also down the block from the city's best hotel, the Grazia Deledda. If you reserve a day in advance at da Nanni you can have a very good *zuppa di pesce* with mussels, clams, and various fish made to order. On some days, depending on what the cook finds in the market, *zuppa di pesce* will be on the menu. There are good seafood pastas, fresh fish, and *monzette* (local snails cooked either with tomatoes and herbs, with oil and garlic, or with wine). In the evening there is pizza from a wood-burning oven. Have fruit for dessert and skip the commercially made *tiramisù*. After my coffee I was asked if I wanted an *ammazzacaffè* (coffee destroyer), not knowing this meant a *digestivo*, in this case a good, strong white *mirto* served ice-cold. Service is friendly, decor is simple, and you will notice neighborhood people coming and going as they pick up orders they have called in.

Trattoria da Gesuino, Via Torres 17g, tel. 079/273392. Closed Sunday, mid-August. All credit cards. Moderate.

Various fresh pastas with delicious sauces that come and go with each season. Summer might have fish and vegetables, fall brings *funghi*, winter has meat sauces. Every Wednesday has succulent *porcetto al forno*, other meats and fish. Save room for a cheese plate from the tantalizing cart.

Trattoria da Tommaso—L'Assassino, Vico Ospizio Cappuccini 1 (from Piazza Tola walk down Via Pettenadu), tel. 079/235041. Reservations advised. Closed Sunday. American Express, MasterCard, Visa. Moderately inexpensive.

A popular place in town. One receives a very friendly reception, and as you walk to your table you might see an opulent display of antipasti. Grilled vegetables are very good. So is creamy *melanzane al forno*, baked eggplant. For a primo, you might try the *raviolone con formaggio e verdure*. This is one very large raviolo filled with ricotta, Pecorino, and minced spinach, topped with a creamy tomato sauce. Also good are the penne alla sarda (with sausage, tomatoes, and Pecorino cheese). For a secondo, tender *spiedino*, veal chunks with slices of red pepper, is tasty, but a bit bland if you don't add black pepper. This restaurant is well regarded for its seafood, but if you are going to one of the nearby coastal towns you may want to wait until you reach the shore before eating fish. The food here is good, not outstanding, and the service is very good.

one very large raviolo filled with ricotta, Pecorino, and minced spinach, topped with a creamy tomato sauce. Also good are the penne alla sarda (with sausage, tomatoes, and Pecorino cheese). For a secondo, tender spiedino, veal chunks with slices of red pepper, is tasty, but a bit bland if you don't add black pepper. This restaurant is well regarded for its seafood, but if you are going to one of the nearby coastal towns you may want to wait until you reach the shore before eating fish.

Museo Archeologico Etnografico G. A. Sanna, Via Roma.

A beautifully organized museum of Sardinian civilization. Among the many appealing exhibits are pottery, plates, cooking utensils, and equipment for cooking, eating, and food preservation. Some of these date back to before Roman times. In room 12 notice the two mosaics from the Roman era (A.D. 1–200) with lobsters, fish, octopuses, and sea horses. If you leave out the sea horses (perhaps) you can see what ancient peoples might have had in their *zuppa di pesce.*

SPECIAL STORES
Caprice, Via Carmelo 1, tel. 079/234388.

Ceramics, china, crystal, and silver, including many antique pieces. Most of the items are not Sardinian, but represent the refined taste of the nice woman who owns the shop.

Drogheria Piras, Largo Cavaiotti 8, tel. 079/233302.

A fascinating and amusing all-purpose *drogheria.* A close look will be a rewarding insight into what people in Sassari use at home to make food and drink. One sees teas, coffees, candles, bug sprays, soaps, and ironing-board covers upon entering, but then one discovers a dream world of fancy and unusual items: sherry vinegar from Spain, Japanese toothpicks, the house's own pure alcohol if you want to make your own elixir, using perhaps one of the many fragrances and flavors sold here. Notice behind the rear right counter (behind the rice) the little white boxes holding *essenze per la preparazione dei liquori*: bitter almond, chocolate, raspberry, caraway, walnut, and many more. Then look at all the bins and bags: popcorn, Mexican black beans, red beans from Lombardia, white beans from Toscana, peas, lentils, chickpeas, almonds (sweet and bitter), soybeans, honeys, dried foods such as ginger, figs, papaya, mango, apple, kumquat, pineapple, peaches, and coconut. There are bags of sugar from various countries, canisters of many types of rice, bottles of tamarind syrup, bags of wheat, oats, cornmeal, sunflower seeds, and *misto canarino*, a combination of seeds for that special yellow bird in your life. You can also buy excellent Sardinian saffron. All the way in the back are pantyhose and dish soap.

Tadasuni (Oristano)

MUSEUM
Don Giovanni Dore is the parish priest in

this little town. He has spent more than thirty years gathering 360 examples of 75 different native musical instruments that are products of the Sardinian folkloric tradition. The oldest *launedda* he has is about one hundred years old, and Don Giovanni (who does not resemble his namesake from Molière and Mozart) can play it and other instruments for you. His collection is a re-markable testament to the native musical tradition of Sardegna. If you arrive in Tadasuni unannounced, you should look for Don Giovanni at the church. If you speak Italian, it would be wise to call ahead (tel. 0785/50113).

Aranciata Nuorese

This delicacy from Nuoro is addictive and easy to make. Try to find the best-quality oranges possible. Make fresh juice or a salad with the leftover oranges. As you can see, it is possible to increase or decrease the amount of ingredients to suit your needs.

225 grams/½ pound of fresh orange peel (from about 1,000 grams/2 pounds oranges)
225 grams/½ pound/8 ounces honey, preferably from Sardegna
225 grams/½ pound almond slivers, lightly toasted

Carefully wash the oranges in cool water to get rid of any blemishes. Use a very sharp knife to remove the peel from the oranges, and then eliminate as much of the white part as possible. Cut the peel into strips as long and as thin as possible so that they do not break. Place the peel in a covered dish, fill with water, cover, and store at room tem-perature. After one day, drain and then fill with fresh water. Cover and store. On the second day, drain completely and pat dry with paper toweling. Put the honey and the peels in a saucepan and heat over moderate heat for 30 minutes, stirring periodically so that the peels are well coated and do not stick. Add the toasted almonds and stir so that the ingredients are thoroughly combined. Transfer to a plate and let cool. It is possible when eating *aranciata nuorese* to either grab a piece or cut a chunk away. For a more formal presentation, you should separate the peels into little clusters as you remove them from the saucepan.

Penne con Ricotta e Noci

If at all possible, the ricotta you use should be made of sheep's milk. Failing that, you should find the best possible cow's-milk ricotta. Similarly, use the best Pecorino Romano you can find. It must be imported: American imitations simply will not do.

Serves 4 to 6

350 grams/about 12 ounces unsalted walnut meats

450 grams/1 pound penne

350 grams/about 12 ounces fresh ricotta

75 grams/2 to 3 ounces freshly grated Pecorino Romano

Set a large pot of cold water to boil. When it reaches a boil, toss in a pinch of salt and let it return to a boil. While the water is boiling, mash the walnuts until they form a creamy puree. This is classically done with a mortar and pestle, although you may use a blender or food processor to do the job. Once this is done, start cooking the pasta according to the directions on the package. Put the walnut cream and the ricotta in a large bowl and combine with a spoon. When the penne are al dente, drain well and add them to the walnut-ricotta mixture. Toss well and serve, topping each portion with some grated Pecorino Romano.

Wine: This dish goes well with a Cannonau red wine.

A GLOSSARY OF
ITALIAN FOOD AND
WINE TERMS

The food-loving traveler in Italy will encounter an almost endless array of terms on menus and in stores that reflect the great range of Italian gastronomy. In addition to the many words and phrases in Italian, there are hundreds of modes of expression that come from regional dialect. While it is impossible to cover all of these, this directory should prove fairly comprehensive as you travel the length and breadth of the Italian peninsula.

Abbacchio Spring lamb, typically of Lazio, Abruzzo, and Sardegna. (Someone who is considered *abbacchiato* is sheepish or bashful.)

Acciughe Anchovies, usually salted for preservation. Fresh anchovies are *alici.*

Aceto balsamico Balsamic vinegar, a specialty of Modena.

Aceto di vino Wine vinegar.

Acqua Water. The term is used interchangeably with *acqua minerale,* at least in restaurants. Tap water is known as *acqua del rubinetto* and is, in most of Italy, perfectly safe. If you see *acqua non potabile,* don't drink it.

Acqua cotta A thin vegetable soup, typically of the Maremma area in southern coastal Toscana.

Acqua minerale Mineral water. When served *con gas* or *gassata,* it is bubbly or carbonated. When served *naturale* or *non gassata,* it is still.

Affettato Sliced. *Affettato misto* is the common term referring to a mixed platter of sliced cold cuts, usually served as an an-

tipasto. *Una fetta* or *fesa* means "a slice."

Affumicato Smoked.

Aglio Garlic.

Agnello Lamb.

Agnolotti Large, folded, stuffed pasta similar to ravioli. Found throughout Italy, but typical of Piemonte.

Agretti A delicate, delicious grasslike vegetable popular in Umbria that has a very brief season in late spring.

Agrodolce Sweet and sour. Usually vegetables cooked in vinegar and sugar.

Agrumi A generic term referring to citrus fruit such as oranges, lemons, grapefruit.

Albicocca (plural *albicocche*) Apricot.

Alcolico Containing alcohol.

Al dente Chewy, toothsome. The proper way for pasta to be cooked.

Alici Fresh anchovies, popular in coastal regions such as Liguria and Sicilia.

Alimentari A grocery store where you can purchase most basic food items you might need.

Alloro Laurel.

Amabile In wine terms, semisweet. The word also means "pleasant" or "amiable."

Amarena (plural *amarene*) Sour cherry, a specialty of Bologna and Modena in Emilia.

Amaretti Bitter macaroons, typically made with almond. A specialty in Piemonte and Lombardia.

Amaro Bitter. This can be an adjective or can describe one of a group of after-dinner drinks thought to aid digestion.

Amatriciana, all' A pasta sauce from Amatrice in Lazio, made with tomatoes, *pancetta* or *guanciale*, onion, and *peperoncino rosso*. Usually served with *bucatini*.

Analcolico Not containing alcohol.

Ananas Pineapple.

Anatra Duck. *Petto di anatra* is duck breast.

Anatra in porchetta A typical dish of Umbria and southern Toscana. The duck is stuffed with prosciutto, duck liver, rosemary, fennel seed, and garlic.

Anguilla Freshwater eel. A specialty of Comacchio in Romagna.

Anguria Watermelon. (The preferred term in northern Italy; in the center-south it is often called *cocomero*.)

Animelle Sweetbreads.

Anitra Duck (not to be confused with the character in Ibsen's *Peer Gynt*).

Antipasto Starters, appetizers, or hors d'oeuvres. This catchall term only begins to suggest the endless selection of delicious foods that are meant to take the edge off your appetite and make your mouth water while you are waiting for your *primo piatto* of pasta, rice, or soup. In much of Italy antipasti are vegetable based (Piemonte and Puglia are the stars in this category), although you will find seafood in coastal areas (Liguria, Veneto, Friuli, Campania, Sicilia). Regions that specialize in prosciutto and *salumi* (Emilia-Romagna, Friuli, Toscana, Umbria, among others) will typically present a platter of *affettato misto*, a combination of the best local cold cuts. While it is not obligatory to begin your meal with an antipasto (which means, literally, "before the meal"), it has become increasingly popular as Italy has become more affluent. Many Italians will now select an antipasto and either a *primo piatto* or *secondo piatto* as a gesture toward the waistline or, in some cases, the pocketbook. But in a complete meal, the antipasto will be the first of many courses.

Aperitivo Aperitif or cocktail. A drink to consume before a meal.

Apribottiglia Bottle opener.

Aragosta Crayfish or small lobster. A specialty of Sardegna.

Aranciata Orangeade or orange soda.

Aranciata nuorese. A typical dessert in Sardegna.

Arancini Literally, "little oranges." These are actually deep-fried rice balls that are a classic antipasto in Sicilia. *Arancini* are often stuffed with a bit of meat or vegetables in addition to the rice. They are sometimes served with a bit of *sugo* (tomato sauce).

Arancio (plural *arance*) Oranges. Italian oranges appear first in the winter, usually from Sicilia. They are intensely flavorful, especially the type known as *tarocchi* or *sanguinelle*, which have blood-red flesh and hints of raspberry in their taste. A *spremuta d'arancio*, available for a price at most Italian bars, is delicious freshly squeezed orange juice.

Arista A roasted loin of meat, either pork *(maiale)* or veal *(vitello)*. This is usually an excellent cut of meat, roasted lovingly with added olive oil, rosemary, garlic, pepper, and salt. It is found all over central and northern Italy and is often the center of a glorious meal in Toscana and Friuli.

Arrabbiata, all' Literally, "in an angry style." A very spicy pasta sauce made of olive oil, tomatoes, and copious amounts of *peperoncino rosso*. It is often served atop penne and is popular in Lazio, Abruzzo, Molise, and elsewhere in the south.

Arrosto Roast or roasted. *Un arrosto* is a roast meat, usually veal.

Arrosto misto A platter of mixed roasted meats, including *vitello* (veal), *maiale* (pork), *coniglio* (rabbit), and *capretto* (kid). Popular in Toscana and Umbria.

Arsella (plural *arselle*) A type of clam.

Asiago A popular and delicious cow's-milk cheese from Vicenza in the Veneto.

Asino Donkey.

Asparagi Asparagus. Delicious throughout Italy, but most prized in Bassano del Grappa in the Veneto, where an asparagus festival is held every April.

Assaggio A taste. When you ask for *assaggi*, you will receive little tastes of various foods.

Astice Larger lobster, as opposed to *aragosta*.

Baccalà (or *Bacalà*) Dried salt cod. This word is usually spelled with one *c* in the Veneto and two in other regions. This is a classic food of the poor that provides great nutrition and, when carefully prepared, fine flavor. In Lazio *baccalà* is soaked in water, batter dipped, and deep-fried *(dorato)*. *Bacalà alla vicentina*, from Vicenza, is cooked with milk and onions and served with polenta. Since the Renaissance, most of the *baccalà* consumed in Italy has come from Bergen and the Lofoten Islands in Norway.

Bacelli The Tuscan term for fava beans.

Baci Kisses. These are a popular candy made of chocolate and chopped hazelnuts. In a bakery, *baci* are also small sandwich cookies that vary from one baker to another. These are often called *baci di dama* (lady's kisses). As an ice-cream flavor *(bacio)* this is chocolate with pieces of hazelnut.

Bagna cauda (or *bagna caöda*) A classic antipasto from Piemonte, particularly good in Alba. Olive oil is heated with garlic, anchovies, and occasionally a bit of truffle. Fresh vegetables (especially cardoons, fennel, and sweet red and yellow peppers) at the peak of their beauty are dipped into this exquisite oil.

Bagnet A term in Piemonte to denote a sauce served as an accompaniment to meats, eggs, or fish. A *bagnet verde* has a base of chopped parsley and includes olive oil, anchovies, bread crumbs, garlic, and lemon or vinegar.

Bar Not a dark room for hard drinking, but rather an Italian social institution where one can have coffee, juice, a glass of wine, a stiff drink, a sandwich, or a sweet. You will find that a visit to a bar several times a day will become a pleasurable part of your routine while you are in Italy.

Barbietola Beet.

Basilico Basil. A pungent, aromatic herb that is found throughout Italy but at its most sublime in Liguria, where it is used in pesto.

Beccaccia Woodcock.

Bellini A cocktail created at Harry's Bar in Venezia that is a combination of Asti Spumante and fresh peach juice.

Bel Paese A common, industrially produced cow's-milk cheese from Lombardia. Very mild in flavor, popular with babies and unadventurous tourists.

Besciamella (sometimes called *balsamella*) Béchamel sauce, popular in the cooking of Emilia-Romagna.

Bianco White, as in wine. Something cooked *in bianco* is plain, without fats or flavorings, such as a poached fish or simple boiled pasta or rice to which a bit of Parmigiano-Reggiano might be added.

Bicchiere A glass for drinking.

Bietola Chard.

Bigné Cream puffs. When they are served on March 19 (Saint Joseph's Day), they are deep-fried, filled with custard, and rolled in sugar and called *bigné di San Giuseppe.* Do not confuse these with *zeppole*, which are not cream filled.

Bigoli Very long, thin whole wheat pasta popular in the Veneto. When served as *bigoli in salsa,* they come with an anchovy sauce.

Birra Beer. *Birra alla spina* is draft beer.

Biscotti Cookies, biscuits.

Biscotti di Prato See *"Cantucci."*

Bistecca Steak or beefsteak. This almost always refers to steaks served on the bone in Toscana, most famously the *bistecca alla fiorentina*, made from Chianina beef, rubbed with olive oil, and grilled.

Bitto A delicious cow's-milk cheese from the Valtellina in Lombardia. This is the cheese of choice in Valtellina pasta dishes such as *pizzoccheri.*

Bocconcini Chunks or bits, typically of veal. In Emilia and Lombardia they are cooked in white wine with onions, peas, and sometimes mushrooms.

Bollito Boiled.

Bollito misto An elaborate and magnificent main course popular in the colder months in the Veneto, Emilia, Lombardia, and Piemonte. Various meats, including pork, chicken or capon, *cotechino* and other sausages, oxtail, tongue, and veal, are boiled and served with a variety of sauces. In a restaurant a cart is rolled to your table for you to select the meats you prefer. Sauces include *salsa verde* (an herb-and-caper sauce) and *peará* (a bone-marrow sauce from Verona). The classic *bollito misto* will always be served with *mostarda*, wonderful pickled fruit typical of Cremona and Mantova in Lombardia.

Bolognese, alla In the style of Bologna. This usually refers to the rich and exquisite meat sauce known as *ragù* that is served with tagliatelle. It can refer to any Bolognese dish, including *cotoletta alla bolognese*, which is a veal cutlet topped with prosciutto and Parmigiano-Reggiano cheese.

Bonet A delicate, wonderful custard or pudding from Piemonte. It usually contains chocolate and may also feature flavors such as coffee, almond, or hazelnut.

Borlotti Red and white beans used in soups and pasta sauces. Popular in Mantova and elsewhere in the North.

Borragine Borage, greens popular in Liguria for filling *pansôti.*

Boscaiola, alla In the style of the woodsman. The word derives from *bosco*, meaning "forest" or "woods." Since mushrooms are often found on the forest floor, a sauce in the style of the woodsman invariably features wild mushrooms and other ingredients, including tomatoes, ham, and certain herbs.

Bottarga (or *bottariga*) Occasionally referred to as "poor man's caviar." *Bottarga* is the dried pressed roe of tuna or mullet. It is most popular in Sardegna and Liguria, although it is now a chic item among foodies throughout Italy. It is usually served in shaved curls over pasta, although it also appears as an antipasto served with generous amounts of lemon. In Calabria, *bottarga* is known as *ovotarica.*

Bottega A shop. This word is commonly used in the Veneto.

Bottiglia Bottle.

Brace, alla Charcoal grilled.

Braciola Shoulder chop, usually of pork *(maiale)*, veal *(vitello)*, or lamb *(agnello)*.

Branzino Sea bass.

Brasato Braised. A *brasato* is also a term for "braised beef," usually in red wine. In Piemonte, the *brasato* is often made with Barolo, the king of Italian red wines.

Bresaola Dried, air-cured beef from the Valtellina in Lombardia. This is now a chic appetizer in Milano.

Brioche A breakfast roll sold in most Italian bars along with your cappuccino.

Broccoletti Turnip tops. A bitter, leafy green vegetable popular in Puglia. Not to be confused with broccoli.

Brodetto di pesce A fish soup or stew found in coastal areas throughout Italy. In the Veneto it is spelled *brodeto*. A particularly good example is found in the Marche. When this dish includes shellfish, it is often called *zuppa di pesce*.

Brodo Broth. When something is served *in brodo*, such as filled pasta in Emilia-Romagna, it usually is in a rich capon broth. Of course, you can find beef and vegetable broths as well, but the assumption should be made that a broth is poultry based unless you learn otherwise.

Bruschetta Toasted bread topped with delicious fruity olive oil and garlic. Popular in Toscana, Umbria, the Marche, and Lazio.

Brutti e buoni (or *brutti ma buoni*) Ugly but good. The name does not derive from a Sergio Leone western, but suggests instead some delicious dry cookies, often made with hazelnuts, that are not aesthetic masterpieces but taste great.

Bucatini (also known as *perciatelli*) From *bucato*, meaning "with a hole." Long, spaghetti-like pasta with a hollow center. Typically served *all'amatriciana*.

Budino Pudding.

Buridda A fish stew popular in Liguria. Contains tomatoes and other vegetables. In Sardegna this refers to a fish steak topped with garlic, nuts, bread crumbs, and nutmeg.

Burrata An exquisite cow's-milk cheese in southern Italy that has a buttery, almost liquid center. It must be eaten carefully, but it is one of a kind.

Burrida A Sardinian sweet-and-sour catfish or eel preparation.

Burrino (plural *burrini*) Small cow's-milk cheese from the South, usually filled with butter.

Burro Butter. In Italy most butter is sweet (unsalted). When something is *al burro*, it is cooked in butter.

Busecca A Milanese specialty made of tripe, vegetables, tomato sauce, butter, and white beans. It is topped with grated Parmigiano-Reggiano.

Cacciagione Game.

Cacciatora, alla In the style of the hunter. Usually chicken *(pollo)*, rabbit *(coniglio)*, or lamb *(agnello)* made with olive oil, rosemary, garlic, and sometimes tomatoes. A popular preparation throughout Italy, but especially in Piemonte and Toscana.

Cacciucco A fish soup typical of Livorno (in Toscana). It usually includes *triglie* (red mullet), shellfish, and tomatoes.

Cacio Cheese. A generic term in the South.

Caciocavallo A mild-to-sharp pear-shaped cheese, traditionally hung to mature. Its fragrance is very typical of *salumerie* in southern Italy.

Cacio e pepe Cheese and pepper. A popular topping for pasta in southern Italy.

Caciotta Soft sheep's-milk cheese, often eaten with olives. *Caciotta* is a generic term to describe many small cheeses made in central and southern Italy. They weigh less than a kilo (2.2 pounds) and can be made from cow's, sheep's, or goat's milk or a combination of these milks. In Marche the cheese is often called *casciotta*.

Caco (plural *cachi*) Persimmon. Sometimes this fruit is called *diaspora*.

Caffè Coffee. While this is the generic term, if you order *un caffè* in a bar, you will receive a small cup of rich, intensely flavored coffee English speakers call an espresso.

Caffè corretto An espresso to which a bit of brandy or grappa has been added.

Caffè decaffeinato Decaffeinated coffee.

Caffè d'orzo A coffee made with barley.

Caffè Hag Italy's most popular brand of decaffeinated espresso.

Caffelatte What we might call café au lait. Espresso combined with at least an equal amount of hot milk. This is different than a cappuccino, in which a layer of steamed milk is poured on top of coffee. A *caffelatte freddo* is a delicious concoction in central and southern Italy—especially in Roma—that combines intense, cold coffee with rich, cold milk. If you want this without sugar, be sure to say "Senza zucchero."

Caffè macchiato Literally, "stained coffee." An espresso to which a bit of hot milk has been added.

Calamari Squid. *Calamari ripieni* are stuffed, usually with bread crumbs, capers, garlic, and anchovies. *Calamaretti* are baby squid.

Caldo Hot.

Calzone A pizza that has been folded. Popular in Napoli.

Cameriere Waiter. It is better to address your waiter as "Signore" (Sir).

Camomila Chamomile tea. Italians drink this to induce sleep.

Camoscio Chamois. Popular in stews,

sauces, and dried in the kitchens of Valle d'Aosta.

Canederli (or *kenederli*) Wonderful dumplings made with cheese, bread crumbs, herbs, and sometimes nutmeg and ham and served with melted butter. Typical of the Trentino–Alto Adige.

Cannella Cinnamon.

Cannellini White beans, popular in Toscana when served with tuna, onions, and olive oil.

Cannoli Scrumptious Sicilian pastries. These cylinders of fried dough are filled with a cream of whipped ricotta cheese, sugar, candied fruit, and, occasionally, bits of chocolate.

Cantina A wine cellar. Also, in a winery, the place where wine is produced.

Cantucci (also called *biscotti di Prato*) Popular almond cookies from northern Toscana, traditionally served as a dessert with a glass of *vin santo*.

Capelli d'angelo Angel's hair. The thinnest of all pastas, served with delicate sauces or in broth.

Capellini Long, very thin spaghetti-type pasta.

Capesante Scallops.

Capitone Saltwater eel, popular in southern Italy. It is traditionally eaten in Napoli at Christmastime, cooked in tomato sauce.

Capocollo A spicy *salame* from Calabria.

Caponata A delicious vegetable dish from Sicilia, served hot or cold. It usually contains eggplant, zucchini, olives, sultanas, *pinoli*, vinegar, and sugar. Served as part of an antipasto, over pasta, or as a side dish.

Capperi Capers. The very best come from the island of Salina off the coast of Sicilia.

Cappone Capon. Delicious and popular in Emilia-Romagna. Often used as the basis for broth *(brodo)*.

Cappon Magro An elaborate cold dish of poached fish and cooked vegetables that is traditionally served on nonmeat feast days (such as Lent) in Liguria. It includes several vegetables, an herb sauce, and shrimp.

Cappuccino A popular morning coffee with steamed milk.

Capra Goat.

Capretto Kid (baby goat). Usually served roasted *(arrosto)*, especially at Eastertime.

Caprino Goat cheese.

Capriolo Venison.

Carbonada A braised-beef dish popular in the Valle d'Aosta.

Carbonara, alla A Roman style of preparing spaghetti with raw eggs, *pancetta*, Pecorino cheese, and abundant freshly ground black pepper. Delicious if not exactly advisable for heart patients.

Carciofo (plural *carciofi*) Artichoke. Superb in Italy, especially in Roma and Liguria. In Roma it is served *alla Giudia* (Jewish style), deep-fried, or *alla romana* (stuffed with garlic, mint, and parsley).

Cardi Cardoons, a vegetable popular in Piemonte.

Carne Meat. When unspecified, this usually refers to beef.

Carne cruda Raw veal or beef. Popular in Piemonte.

Carne macinata Ground meat.

Carne salada (or *carne salà*) Salted, raw beef that is a specialty of Trentino.

Carpaccio Raw, air-cured beef popular as an antipasto, especially in Lombardia. It is often served with chopped greens, olive oil, lemon juice, and slivers of Parmigiano-Reggiano.

Carpione, in Pickled, usually with vinegar, lemon juice, wine, and herbs.

Carta di musica Sheet music—thin unleavened bread from Sardegna.

Cartoccio, in When something is served *in cartoccio*, it is usually cooked in a foil wrap. A popular way of preparing fish.

Casalinga Housewife. A restaurant that offers *cucina casalinga* serves home-style dishes.

Casalinghi Housewares, or a store where these are sold.

Cassa The cashier, as in a bar or food store. Traditionally, one pays the cashier before having a drink or taking one's purchase. The cashier will give you a receipt to show to the person behind the counter.

Cassata A rich Sicilian dessert made with sugar, ricotta cheese, lots of candied fruit, sponge cake, almond paste, and liqueur.

Cassoeula A classic dish from Milano made of pork spare ribs, sausage, cabbage, and vegetables. It is eaten all winter, but especially on January 17, the feast day of San Antonio.

Cassola A stew from Cagliari in Sardegna, made with fish, octopus, tomatoes, onions, *peperoncino rosso*, and garlic.

Castagna (plural *castagne*) Chestnut.

Castagnaccio A dessert from Toscana that is a cross between a cake and a pudding. It is made with chestnut flour, olive oil, rosemary, and *pinoli*. It should be tried, but I've never met anyone who really loves it (or maybe I've never had a great example of *castagnaccio*).

Castagnole Little balls of fried dough, rolled in sugar. A traditional sweet served in the Carnival period, prior to Lent.

Castrato A generic term referring to any emasculated male animal, be it a horse, a bull, or a ram. In general, *castrato* on a menu implies mutton, but it is worth asking if you have any doubt.

Cavallo Horse. This meat, also called *carne equina*, is eaten in certain parts of

Italy, especially in the provinces of Verona and Vicenza.

Cavatappi Corkscrew.

Cavatelli (or *cavateddi*) A popular small pasta shape in the South.

Caviale Caviar. Not typically an Italian product, except for that which is taken from Po River sturgeon.

Cavolfiore Cauliflower.

Cavolo Cabbage. This word is often used as an expression of surprise or disbelief.

Ceci Chickpeas. *Farina di ceci* is chickpea flour, popular in Puglia.

Cedro (plural *cedri*) Citron. A popular citrus fruit in Calabria and Sicilia.

Cena Supper (the evening meal).

Cernia Grouper.

Cervello Brains, usually calf's brains. Often served in Roma with fried artichokes.

Cervo Deer or venison.

Chiacchiere Literally, "chatter" or "small talk." In food terms it refers to the strips of dough topped with honey that are popular as a sweet during Carnival, in the period before Lent.

Chinotto A bitter soft drink, vaguely reminiscent of Dr. Pepper. In Liguria a *chinotto* is an orange with myrtle leaves that is used to make jams or to be candied.

Chiodini Literally, "little nails." A type of small mushroom, often pickled and sold in jars.

Chiuso Closed. Most Italian restaurants close one day each week.

Ciabatta A crusty loaf of flatbread.

Cialzons (cjalsons, cjarsons) This word has many spellings. These are wonderful dumplings made in the Carnia Mountains in the northern part of Friuli. They contain forty ingredients, including smoked ricotta, bitter chocolate, and cinnamon.

Ciambelle (or *ciambelline*) Ring-shaped cakes or cookies, usually topped with confectioners' sugar. They are sometimes made with wine and are very popular at the end of the meal.

Cicoria Chicory. Served raw or cooked.

Ciliege Cherries.

Cima ripiena Stuffed veal, popular in Liguria. It contains vegetables, eggs, and cheese.

Cime di rapa Turnip greens.

Cinghiale Wild boar. Though found in various regions of Italy, *cinghiale* is particularly popular in Toscana, especially in and around the town of San Gimignano. It is served roasted, braised, in pasta sauces, or air-dried in the manner of prosciutto.

Cioccolato Chocolate. *Cioccolatini* are individual chocolate candies.

Ciociara, alla Either a pasta sauce made with tomatoes, mozzarella, Pecorino, olive oil, and oregano or a pasta sauce to which cream has been added. The Ciociaria, a fertile agricultural region south of Roma that produces the best peas you will ever taste, is also famous for its beautiful women. *La Ciociara* was the book by Alberto Moravia that served as the basis of *Two Women*, the film for which Sophia Loren won an Oscar.

Cipolla (plural *cipolle*) Onion.

Ciuppin A fish soup from Liguria.

Cocco (or *noce di cocco*) Coconut.

Cocomero Watermelon. This word is used in southern Italy.

Coda alla vaccinara An oxtail stew popular in Roma.

Colazione Breakfast. Also called *prima colazione* or *piccola colazione*. In older usage, *la colazione* can also mean "the midday meal."

Colomba Dove. This is actually a dove-shaped Easter cake popular throughout Italy.

Coltello Knife.

Con With. (*Senza* means "without.")

Confetti Sugar-coated almonds. The most famous come from Sulmona, in Abruzzo. They come in several colors and are given in pretty little packages at special occasions: first communions and weddings (white), engagements (green), anniversaries (silver and gold), and graduations (red).

Coniglio Rabbit. A popular meat throughout Italy, with good versions made in Piemonte, Liguria, Toscana, Campania, and Sardegna.

Cono An ice-cream cone.

Conto The bill or check.

Contorno A side dish that comes with the *secondo piatto*. This may be any vegetable, including potatoes, beans, or cooked greens. In Italy, rice or pasta is almost never served as a *contorno* because it forms the basis of the *primo piatto*.

Coperto Cover charge. This is added to the bill at most Italian restaurants.

Coppa A cup, as for ice cream. Also, a term describing salt-cured boneless ham.

Cornetto A croissant.

Corzetti A typical Ligurian pasta made either in the shape of the number eight or as a square of pasta stamped with a design recalling the Republic of Genova.

Coscia Thigh, usually referring to a piece of poultry.

Costata di manzo Entrecôte of beef.

Costoletta Cutlet. See *"Cotoletta."*

Costoletta di agnello Lamb chops.

Cotechino A minced, spicy pork sausage popular in Emilia and the Veneto. *Cotechino* is often part of a *bollito misto*, in which it is boiled and sliced. The classic accompaniment for *cotechino* is a dish of lentils.

Cotoletta A cutlet, usually of veal.

Cotoletta alla milanese The famous preparation of a veal cutlet or, occasionally, a veal chop that is dipped in egg and bread crumbs and then fried in butter.

Cotoletta alla valdostana Typical dish of the Valle d'Aosta. A breaded veal cutlet that is stuffed with Fontina cheese and a slice of prosciutto.

Cotto Cooked. In the *salumeria*, when you ask for *cotto*, you receive delicious *prosciutto cotto* (boiled ham). *Frutta cotta* (such as a *pera cotta*, "baked pear") refers to cooked fruit that is usually baked or poached.

Cozze Mussels.

Crauti Sauerkraut.

Crema A term that has various uses in Italian gastronomy. It can loosely be thought of as cream, but this is not very exact. In soups, the term implies "cream of," as in spinach, broccoli, mushrooms, or asparagus (in fact, this is a velvety soup that may or may not have added cream). In a *gelateria*, *crema* is rich plain ice cream, often made with egg yolk. When a dish is *alla crema*, it means "in a cream sauce." Note that cream used for whipping is called *panna*.

Crema fritta A fried custard dessert popular in Venezia.

Cren (or **Kren**) Horseradish.

Crescione Watercress.

Crespelle Crepes. Especially popular in Abruzzo, where they are also called *scripelle*.

Crocchette Potato croquettes. Often sold in *rosticerrie* to accompany roast chicken.

Crostata A fruit or jam tart, usually open-faced but occasionally with lattice. This classic Italian dessert can be made with most fruits, although apple *(mela)*, pear *(pera)*, cherry *(ciliegia* or *amarena)*, apricot *(albicocca)*, peach *(pesca)*, plum *(prugna)*, and fig *(fico)* are most commonly used. *Crostatine* are small tarts that are individual portions.

Crostini Toasts served as an appetizer. The most popular are from Toscana, where they come topped with chopped chicken liver and spleen, or with a puree of olives or artichokes.

Crudo Raw. *Prosciutto crudo* is what English speakers simply call prosciutto.

Cucchiaio Spoon. *Cucchiaino* is a teaspoon.

Cucina Kitchen, cuisine, cookery.

Culatello The most delicate part of a *prosciutto crudo*. A specialty of Parma. (The rest of the prosciutto is called the *fiocchetto*.)

Cuscus (or *cuscusu*) Couscous, popular in Sicilia.

Datteri di mare Sea dates. Delicious brown-shelled crustaceans that are wonderful in Trieste and also quite fine in Liguria.

Dattero Date.

Degustazione A tasting, as in wine.

Diavola, alla Deviled. *Pollo alla diavola* is chicken prepared with herbs and lots of *peperoncino rosso.*

Diavolillo (or *diavolicchio*) A fiery sauce or condiment made with *peperoncino* that is popular in Abruzzo, Molise, Puglia, Basilicata, and Calabria.

Distillato Distillate, any clear eau-de-vie, usually derived from fruit.

Distilleria Distillery.

Dolce Sweet.

Dorato Meaning "covered in gold." Usually batter-dipped and then deep-fried or sautéed.

Dragoncello Tarragon.

Drogheria A dry-goods store. In Italy, this is a place that may sell bottled, packaged, and canned goods. It also may carry spices, candies, and detergents. *Drogherie* are often very interesting places that merit a visit, such as the Drogheria Giuseppe Micheli in Rovereto in the Trentino.

Emmenthal The popular cheese that Americans call Swiss cheese. But it can also come from France, Austria, Germany, Finland, and elsewhere. Italians sometimes use it as one of the cheeses in a *quattro formaggi* sauce.

Enoteca A wine store. Also a place to drink wine, often with small snacks.

Erba (plural *erbe*) Herb.

Erbazzone A flatbread, typical of Reggio Emilia, filled with Swiss chard or other greens.

Erbette Swiss chard. In Parma, the typical pasta is *tortelli d'erbette*, filled with ricotta cheese and Swiss chard.

Erboristeria Literally, "herb store." *Erboristerie* are very intriguing, typically Italian stores that specialize in herb-based products. These might be soaps, hair dyes, liqueurs, elixirs, medicinal remedies. You will find an endless assortment of herbal teas and, in the Alto Adige, fruit teas. Of course, fresh and dried herbs are also sold, alone or in combination. A visit to an *erboristeria* will tell you a lot about how Italians use herbs in their lives. My favorite is in Ravenna.

Etto (plural *etti*) A common unit of measurement in Italian stores. It equals 100 grams, or about 3½ ounces.

Fagiano Pheasant.

Fagiolino (plural *fagiolini*) String bean, or *haricot vert.*

Fagiolo (plural *fagioli*) Bean. This is a generic term, although it often refers to white beans.

Falso magro A Sicilian meat roll filled with cheese, sausage, and boiled eggs.

Faraona Guinea fowl.

Farcito Stuffed.

Farina Flour.

Farinata A Ligurian crepe made of chickpea flour.

Farro Emmer or spelt, a grain popular in Umbria. This grain was a staple in ancient times, when its Latin name was *far*. Part of the wedding rites of ancient Roman nobility was that the bride and groom sacrificed a *far* cake to Jupiter Farreus. Their marital state was called *confarreatio*. A divorce was termed *disfarreatio*.

Farsu magru See *"Falso magro."*

Fave Fava beans. Romans like to eat these with chunks of Pecorino cheese.

Fegatelli Pieces of liver, usually pig's liver.

Fegatini Chicken livers.

Fegato Liver, usually calf's liver. *Fegato alla veneziana* is a classic Venetian preparation using onions and white wine.

Fernet A dark, bitter after-dinner *digestivo*.

Fettuccine Strips of egg pasta that are favored in Roma. Fettuccine Alfredo are made with sweet butter and heaps of freshly grated Parmigiano-Reggiano.

Fettunta Literally, "oiled slice." A piece of toasted Tuscan bread doused with olive oil.

Fico (plural *fichi*) Fig.

Fico d'India Prickly pear.

Fiera Fair, festival, open-air market.

Filo di Ferro (or *Filu Ferru*) A high-powered Sardinian liqueur that is named for the steel thread that would stick out of the ground when bottles of this drink were buried during periods of prohibition.

Finanziera, alla Financier style. You probably would think that this preparation would be found in Milano, the financial capital of Italy, but it is actually from Torino. This is a sauce made with chicken livers, mushrooms, onions, and white wine.

Finferli Small, delicious wild mushrooms found in the Alps.

Finocchiella An Umbrian *salame* containing fennel seed.

Finocchio Fennel. In purchasing fennel in the market, you will notice that those with the more bulbous heads are called *maschio* (male) while the *femmina* (female) are flatter. The *maschio* is usually more tender and can be eaten raw, with just a bit of olive oil and some fresh lemon juice. The *femmina* is firmer and is better suited to cookery. In common Italian usage, *un finocchio* is also a frequently used term for "a gay man." So when you ask for a *finocchio,* be sure you know which one you want. I am unsure whether the gender classification in the vegetable market had any influence on the word's second flowering as slang.

Finocchiona A *salame* from Toscana containing fennel seed.

Fior di latte A cow's-milk cheese similar to mozzarella, though milder and less distinct in flavor. *Fior di latte* is also a plain ice cream made with milk or cream and sugar.

Fiori di zucca (also called *fiori di zucchini*) Zucchini flowers. These are delicious when stuffed with mozzarella, batter dipped, and carefully fried.

Focaccia The classic, delicious bread of Liguria. It is baked plain or with onion, rosemary, or cheese.

Focolare An open hearth. In Friuli, where it is called the *fogolar,* this is a traditional place where family and friends gather in the home.

Fonduta The Italian equivalent of fondue, this is popular in Valle d'Aosta, Piemonte, and northern Lombardia. The cheese of choice is wonderful Fontina.

Fontina The classic cheese of Valle d'Aosta. It melts perfectly, has a slightly nutty taste, and is one of the world's great cheeses. When shopping, bear in mind that Fontina from Scandinavia is not an acceptable substitute for Italian Fontina.

Forchetta Fork.

Formaggio Cheese.

Forno Oven, typically where bread is baked. *Al forno* means "baked."

Fragola (plural *fragole*) Strawberry. Italian strawberries are exquisitely flavorful. Little wild strawberries *(fragoline)* are delectable. Occasionally you will find giant strawberries *(fragoloni)*.

Frantoio A press to make olive oil.

Frasca An informal restaurant in Friuli, often outdoors and near a vineyard. Similar to an *osteria*.

Frattaglie Giblets.

Freddo Cold.

Fresco Cool.

Friarelli The tips of *broccoletti*. In Napoli they are sautéed and often served with sausages.

Frico (or *fricco*) A wonderful melted cheese appetizer typical of Friuli.

Friggitoria A fry shop.

Frigo (frigorifero) Refrigerator.

Frittata (plural *frittate*) The Italian version of an omelette. Eggs are cooked in olive oil instead of butter, and ingredients, usually vegetables and cheese, are added. In Friuli, a *frittata con le erbe* is made with seven or more herbs.

Frittelle Fritters.

Fritto (fritta, fritti, fritte) Fried, usually deep-fried.

Fritto misto A combination of fried foods. When ordered in coastal areas, this usually contains fish and seafood. When you see *fritto misto all'italiana*, this refers to a mixture of organ meats, lamb, and batter-dipped vegetables such as zucchini, eggplants, and artichokes.

Frittura di mare Mixed fried seafood.

Frittura di paranza Paranza is a type of fishing boat with sails, but the word also means "group" or "society." In Napoli it refers specifically to a group of criminals. In terms of food, this refers to the group of fish that are not the stars of the catch. This does not mean they are less desirable, but simply that the fisherman would likely be able to sell the larger fish first. So a *frittura di paranza* will be a mixture of delectable tiny fried fish.

Frittura di pesce Another term for *fritto misto*. This will include fried fish, squid, octopus, and perhaps a few shrimp.

Frullato A whipped or blended drink made with milk and either fruit or another flavoring, such as chocolate.

Frutta Fruit.

Frutta cotta Cooked or stewed fruit.

Frutti di bosco Literally, "forest fruits." This refers mostly to berries: *fragoline, lampone, mirtilli, more, ribes*. Many restaurants offer these in a bowl, dressed with lemon juice and sugar, and call it *sottobosco* (from under the forest).

Frutti di mare Shellfish.

Funghi Mushrooms. So enamored of *funghi* are many Italians that in an Italian bookstore you can find many shelves filled with books about them. The most famous type is *funghi porcini*, which have large caps that can be grilled and eaten like steaks. *Funghi* can form the base of pasta sauces (often called *alla boscaiola*).

Funghi trifolati Sliced mushrooms cooked with garlic in either butter or oil.

Fusilli A corkscrew-shaped pasta.

Fuso Melted, as in cheese or chocolate.

Gallina Hen.

Gamberi Prawns. *Gamberetti* are small prawns; *gamberoni* are jumbo prawns.

Gastronomia A food store, generally one where cold cuts, cheeses, and olives are featured, as well as delectable prepared dishes.

Gelateria Ice-cream parlor.

Gelato (plural *gelati*) Ice cream.

Gelso Mulberry.

Genovese, alla This term has two meanings. In Genova, it is a dish such as pasta or minestrone to which pesto has been added. In Napoli, it is an onion sauce served with meat.

Germano Mallard.

Ghiaccio Ice.

Ghiotta, alla A style of grilling meat or fish in which the meat's juices are blended with prosciutto, olive oil, wine, garlic, and other flavorings. This dressing is then used for basting.

Gianduia A wonderful combination of chocolate and hazelnuts. A specialty of Piemonte.

Ginepro Juniper.

Gnocchi Pillowy dumplings made with flour and, sometimes, riced potatoes. Gnocchi are among the oldest foods in Italy. Their ancestors appeared in the kitchens of ancient Roma. *Gnocchetti* are tiny, thimble-sized gnocchi.

Gnocchi alla romana Disks of semolina baked with butter and cheese.

Gorgonzola Wonderful blue-veined cheese native to Lombardia, although most of it is now produced in Piemonte. It comes in milder *(dolce)* and sharper *(piccante)* forms.

Grana A hard grating cheese found in the Po River valley in Lombardia, Emilia, Veneto, and Trentino. Much of it is produced in the city of Lodi. It is often called *grana padana* (grana of the Po) and has a nice, nutty flavor. You should not confuse this cheese with Parmigiano-Reggiano, which is to grana what silk is to polyester. This is not to suggest that grana (or polyester) is bad, but simply that the king of cheeses is in a class by itself. What is further confusing is that in the delimited production zone of Parmigiano-Reggiano (the provinces of Parma, Reggio-Emilia, and parts of the provinces of Bologna, Modena, and Mantova), locals often refer to their cheese as "grana," which is a generic term for the typical grating cheese of the region.

Granchio Crab.

Granita Water ices, most often flavored with coffee or lemon. The American dessert called Italian ice is a dreadful corruption of granita.

Grano Wheat or grain.

Grano saraceno Buckwheat. Popular in foods from Valtellina in Lombardia.

Granoturco Maize.

Granseola A large crab found in the Adriatic Sea.

Grappa A powerful spirit distilled from grape skins and pits. Grappa originated in Veneto and Friuli, but imitations have popped up all over Italy. The best still comes from traditional makers such as Nonino and Brunello in the northeast.

Grattugia A grater, usually for cheese or nutmeg.

Gremolada (or *gremolata*) A mixture of garlic, rosemary, and lemon used to flavor osso buco.

Griglia, alla Grilled.

Grigliata mista Mixed grill of meats. A *grigliata di legumi* would comprise mixed grilled vegetables.

Grissini Breadsticks, typical of Torino and the rest of Piemonte, where they are often made by hand.

Guanciale Pork cheek, used in *amatriciana* sauce.

Gubana A fragrant, delicious breadlike cake, filled with raisins and nuts, that is typical of Cividale del Friuli.

Gulasch (or *Goulasch*) Similar to its Hungarian cousin, this spicy meat stew is found in Friuli and the Alto Adige.

Indivia A pungent, curly salad green.

Indivia belga Endive.

Insaccati Dried, hard *salami*.

Insalata Salad or salad greens. When ordering it in a restaurant, you will get mixed greens.

Insalata caprese A Capri salad. This popular dish, served as an antipasto or as a light main course, contains fresh mozzarella cheese, tomatoes, and basil, plus a few drops of olive oil.

Insalata di mare A delicious mixture of cold seafood, dressed with oil and lemon.

Insalata di riso A popular summer dish, this cold rice salad is often found in Piemonte and Lombardia. It includes rice, vegetables, and, occasionally, meat.

Insalata mista A mixed salad, typically containing mixed greens and tomatoes, plus whatever else the chef fancies. This will be a *contorno* rather than a main course.

Integrale Whole wheat.

Involtini Rolled meat or fish fillets stuffed with vegetables or other fillings. Typical of southern Italy.

Jota A thick soup found in Trieste, Gorizia, and elsewhere in Friuli. Its main ingredients are beans, cabbage or sauerkraut, onions, sage, and garlic. Sometimes pork is added.

Lampasciuoli (lampascioni, lampascioli, lampasciuni) Small, bitter onions found in southern Italy.

Lampone (plural *lamponi*) Raspberry.

Lardo Salt-cured lard, sometimes scented with rosemary or other herbs. Popular to eat in Piemonte and Valle d'Aosta, it has less cholesterol than butter and fewer calories than olive oil.

Lasagne Sheets of pasta that are layered in baking dishes with various sauces and other ingredients. The classic lasagne is from Bologna, and Napoli also produces a commendable version.

Latte Milk.

Latte di mandorla Almond milk, a sweetened drink popular in southern Italy that is very refreshing when served cold on a hot day.

Latteria A dairy or store that sells milk, cream, butter, and cheese. In Friuli, *latteria* is a common type of cow's-milk cheese.

Latterini Little poached fish served with lemon juice and olive oil.

Latticini The term means "milk products." It usually refers to fresh cheeses made in Campania and elsewhere in southern Italy.

Lattuga Lettuce.

Lauro Bay leaf.

Lenticchie Lentils. Eaten year-round, but always on New Year's Eve. They are said to look like little coins, and it is said that eating them will bring money in the coming year.

Lepre Hare. This meat is the basis of a pasta sauce from Arezzo, in Toscana.

Lepre in salmi Jugged hare, popular in the north.

Lesso Boiled.

Limonata Lemonade or lemon soda.

Limoncello A lemon liqueur from the Amalfi Coast that has become immensely popular.

Limone (plural *limoni*) Lemon.

Lingua Tongue.

Linguine Long, flat spaghetti.

Lombata Sirloin.

Lombata di maiale A grilled pork chop.

Lombatina Veal chop.

Lonza A freshly cured *salame*, popular in the fall and the winter, eaten young.

Luccio Pike, popular in Mantova and at Lago di Garda.

Luganega A sausage that originated in Basilicata. There are also versions in Lombardia and Trentino.

Lumache Snails.

Maccheroni We call it macaroni.

Maccheroni alla chitarra Fresh pasta typical of Abruzzo. They look like squared spaghetti, made on a device that looks like the strings of a guitar *(chitarra).*

Macedonia Fresh fruit salad. A popular dessert throughout Italy.

Maiale Pork.

Mais Corn.

Malaga Rum raisin (an ice-cream flavor).

Malloreddus Gnocchi typical of Sardegna. Often scented with saffron.

Mandarino Mandarin orange from Sicilia. Often described interchangeably with tangerines.

Mandorla (plural *mandorle*) Almond. *Pasta di mandorla* is almond paste.

Manzo Beef.

Marinato Marinated.

Maritozzi Sweet buns, often filled with whipped cream. Popular in Roma. In Sicilia *maritozzi* are often filled with raisins.

Marmellata Jam or marmalade.

Marroni Chestnuts.

Marrons glacés Candied chestnuts.

Marzolino A fresh, delicate sheep's-milk cheese, customarily made in March *(marzo).*

Mascarpone (also called *mascherpone*) A rich, sweet, buttery, very perishable dessert cheese typical of Lombardia and Emilia-Romagna.

Mattarello Rolling pin. In Italy this is usually a wooden cylinder without handles.

Mazzancolle Giant prawns.

Mela (plural *mele*) Apple.

Mela cotogna Quince.

Melanzane Eggplant, aubergine.

Melanzane alla parmigiana Breaded, fried slices of eggplant, baked with fresh tomato sauce, mozzarella, and Parmigiano-Reggiano.

Melograno Pomegranate.

Melone Melon. This usually implies cantaloupe.

Menta Mint.

Merasca Sour plum.

Mercato Market.

Merenda Snack.

Merluzzo Cod.

Mesciüa A Ligurian soup made with beans and chickpeas.

Mezzafegato A raw sausage made with pig's liver, pepper, sugar, raisins, *pinoli*, and orange peel.

Mezzo (mezza) Half. As in *litro* (liter) or *bottiglia* (bottle).

Midollo Marrow.

Miele Honey. There are many honeys made in Italy, and each region likes to brag that its honey is the best. Those from Sardegna, Valle d'Aosta, Trentino, Alto Adige, and Toscana are ones I am fond of, but you should explore them on your own, too.

Milza Spleen.

Minestra Soup. This term also suggests the first course of a meal.

Minestrone A rich soup with vegetables, beans, and either rice, pasta, or, in Friuli, barley. Although it originated in Lombardia, versions now appear throughout Italy. The best are probably found in Milano and Genova.

Mirtilli Blueberries. (In the Alto Adige, a generic term for "berries.") *Mirtilli rossi* are red, while *mirtilli neri* are blue.

Mirto Myrtle. A popular flavor in Sardinian cooking. This also refers to a liqueur made with myrtle that is served at the end of meals in Sardegna.

Missultitt A dish made from dried fish, typical of Lago di Como in Lombardia.

Misticanza Mixed greens, mostly bitter.

Mocetta Dried veal, chamois, or other meat, typical of the Valle d'Aosta.

Moleche Soft-shell crabs.

Montasio The typical cheese of Friuli. Used to make *frico*.

Monte Bianco Mont Blanc. A sweet, rich pastry made with cream, meringue, and chestnut paste.

Montone Mutton.

More Blackberries.

Mortadella A wonderful, inexpensive royal cousin of bologna that hails from the city of Bologna. It is made with pork, spices, pieces of fat, and, sometimes, pistachios. It is served either in chunks or in thin slices. It can also be minced and used as part of a pasta filling.

Mostarda Mixed fruit pickled with mustard seed. It is served with boiled meats or fine cold cuts. The best *mostarda* is from Cremona and Mantova. *Mostarda veneta* is more like a spicy puree of fruits.

Mosto del vino Wine must. This is the fresh juice of wine grapes. In Meran (Alto Adige) it is consumed in September and early October in what is called the grape cure. In other regions, such as Toscana and Basilicata, it is sometimes used as a flavoring in cooking and baking.

Mozzarella One of the great cheeses. Handmade from the milk of water buffalo *(mozzarella di bufala)* or in combination with cow's milk. The best mozzarella comes from Battipaglia, Benevento, and other towns in Campania.

Mozzarella in carrozza Deep-fried mozzarella between two pieces of bread that has been dipped in egg. Sometimes a small piece of anchovy is added.

Muscoli The Ligurian word for mussels. In the rest of Italy *cozze* are mussels and *muscoli* are muscles.

Nervetti Chilled, boiled calf's foot. A rustic specialty of Lombardia.

Nespola Medlar.

Nocciola (plural *nocciole*) Hazelnut.

Noccioline This means "little nuts" and usually refers to peanuts. The other word for these is *arachidi*.

Noce (plural *noci*) Walnut. This is also a generic term for nut.

Noce moscato Nutmeg.

Nocepesca Nectarine

Nocino Walnut liqueur. When it is made in Toscana, the walnuts are always picked in the last days of June.

Nonna, della Grandma's style. This term appears on menus throughout Italy. While we are certain that every cook in Italy does not have the same grandmother, any dish that is *della nonna* suggests that it is made with loving care. Once, years ago in Verona, when I was still very new to Italy, I had a very poorly executed dish of *tortellini della nonna*. When I left the restaurant, I told the confused restaurant owner that I hoped Grandma would be feeling better soon. I had not yet realized that there was a *nonna's* dish on almost every menu in Italy.

Norcina, alla (or *alla nursina*). In the style of the city of Norcia. This town, in Umbria, is famous for its pork butchers. Pastas and other dishes that are *alla norcina* usually contain spicy sausage and, sometimes, a piece of truffle. A *norcineria* is a quality pork butcher, presumably someone from Norcia.

Norma, alla A style of pasta sauce named for the opera *Norma* by Vincenzo Bellini, native son of Catania, Sicilia. The sauce includes eggplant, basil, tomato, and cheese.

Oca Goose. *Petto di oca* is goose breast.

Offella (plural *offelle*) Soft round or oval cakes popular in northern Italy. Famous examples come from Vicenza and Parona (Pavia).

Olio Oil.

Olio di semi Seed oil.

Olio d'oliva Olive oil, the principal cooking fat in most of Italy, from Liguria and Toscana on south. If you are used to the harsh or overprocessed oils one finds in most markets at home, you will be delighted by the quality of the oil consumed in Italy. The northernmost production zone is at the northern end of Lago di Garda in the alpine region of Trentino. About 33 percent of the oil is produced in the region of Puglia, and other excellent oils come from Liguria, Toscana, Veneto, Lombardia, Umbria, Marche, Lazio, Abruzzo, Molise, Campania, Sicilia, and Sardegna. Ideally, you should only use and consume extra-virgin oil, which is from the first pressing of the olives. Oil is used not only for cooking and dressing salads, but also as a condiment. You might be offered *un filo d'olio,* a "thread of oil," that will flavor *pasta e fagioli* soup, boiled fish, or pasta. A classic pasta dish is *aglio e olio,* in which a plate of spaghetti is tossed with olive oil and garlic. This is a fundamental dish of *la cucina povera,* the ancient diet of the poor that we now consider among the most suitable and appealing for all tastes. Olive oil is the healthiest of oils and, along with wine and good bread, one of the reasons why the diet in Mediterranean countries is considered a model for correct eating. Whenever I go to Italy, I always buy olive oil to take home either as a gift or for use in my own kitchen. In stores you must rely on the advice of the seller, your awareness of geography (for example, do you prefer the lighter oils of Garda and Liguria or the lustier oils of Umbria and Lazio?), and recommendations from friends. If you go to an oil producer, it is a good idea to taste a bit before purchasing a few bottles. The ideal way to taste oil is not, as is often thought, to dip bread in it. Instead, pour a little into a cup. Look at it to examine the color and the clarity. Then hold the cup in your hands to warm the oil slightly so that the natural esters release its fragrance. Is it pleasing? Then put a bit of oil on the tip of your tongue and on the sides so that the taste buds can sense it. Bring your tongue to the roof of your mouth and let the taste permeate your mouth. Is it smooth, peppery, tart, harsh, or some other sensation? You should select the one that has the attributes that please you. That slight harshness in the back of the throat is often considered a virtue in that it sometimes indicates a youthfulness that will even out as it ages. Oil should be stored in a dark, dry place, and most bottles are only good for about a year. You will find nowadays that many oils have vintage dates the way wine does. If you see bottles of oil in a store that are dusty, this is usually a sign of low turnover—it is best to avoid these oils.

Oliva (plural *olive*) Olive.

Olive ascolane Stuffed olives, a typical antipasto of Ascoli Piceno in the Marche.

Orata Gilthead. One of the most prized and delicious of Mediterranean fish. *Orata alla griglia,* made with a fish in pristine condition, is one of the more delicious things you can eat.

Orecchiette (or *recchietelle*). Ear-shaped pasta popular in Puglia.

Origano Oregano.

Orzata A nonalcoholic beverage made with barley.

Orzo Barley.

Ossobuco Braised marrow-bone veal steaks, cooked in butter, wine, and *gremolada.* A classic dish from Milano.

Osteria (plural *osterie*) A tavern or humble

restaurant where wine is served as the main attraction and tasty food is prepared to wash it down. In certain cities there are now very upscale restaurants that call themselves *osterie,* so if there is a pricey menu displayed, you are not in a real *osteria.* These are great places to meet and enjoy the company of Italians you would never encounter in your customary travels as a tourist.

Ostrica (plural *ostriche*) Oyster.

Padella Frying pan or skillet. Something that is *in padella* is pan-cooked.

Pajata Calf's or lamb's intestines cooked in a piquant tomato sauce and served with rigatoni. This is an old Roman dish that is served in Testaccio and other neighborhoods in the Eternal City.

Pancetta Salt-cured, unsmoked bacon.

Pandoro A yeasty cake from Verona that many Italians eat at Christmastime.

Pane Bread.

Panettone A scrumptious yeast cake from Milano made with raisins, candied fruit, and eggs. This is popular during the Christmas period, starting on December 7, the feast day of San Ambrogio, patron of Milano.

Panficio Bread bakery.

Panforte A thick, delicious cake made of nuts, spices, candied fruit, and a dusting of confectioners' sugar. A little bit of this specialty from Siena goes a long way.

Panino Sandwich.

Paninoteca Sandwich shop.

Paniscia (or *panissa*) In the provinces of Vercelli and Novara in Piemonte, this is a rice dish made with sausage and vegetables. In the Valle d'Aosta, this combination appears in a more souplike form.

Panissa (or *paniccia*) Do not confuse this with the rice dish in Piemonte. In Liguria *panissa* is a chickpea tart.

Panna Cream.

Panna cotta Cooked cream. A rich, delicious dessert often served with pureed berries.

Panna montata Whipped cream.

Pansôti Ligurian pasta filled with greens and herbs and served with walnut sauce.

Papera (papero) Duckling. ("Paperino" is the Italian name of Donald Duck.)

Pappa col pomodoro A bread, tomato, and oil soup from Toscana.

Pappardelle Broad, flat noodles that are popular in Toscana and served with meat sauces such as duck, goose, or hare.

Parmigiano-Reggiano Italy's finest cheese and perhaps the greatest in the world. It is produced, as it has been for seven hundred years, in the provinces of Parma, Reggio Emilia, Modena, Bologna, and Mantova. Accept no substitute that passes itself off as "Parmesan." See "*Grana*" for more background.

Passatelli Fresh noodles for soup made with bread crumbs, lemon, egg, and nutmeg. A specialty of the Marche and Romagna.

Passato A puree that is either blended or passed through a sieve. *Passato di pomodoro* is the basis for tomato sauce. A *passato* of vegetables is usually a soup.

Passeggiata A stroll that is taken in late afternoon or early evening by almost every Italian. *Fare la passeggiata* does not simply mean "to go for a walk," which can be done at any time, but to partake in this ritual in which one likes to see and be seen. During the *passeggiata* one runs into friends, relatives, and business associates who will be invited for a coffee, an *aperitivo,* or an ice cream. While the *passeggiata* is not conspicuous in large, busy cities such as Milano, there is in every city a place where one partakes in the *passeggiata.* Torino has a nice one on the Via Roma, and Bologna's Piazza Maggiore fills with people. Lucca, La Spezia, and Siracusa also have very nice ones. But the best one I know is unquestionably that of Matera in Basilicata. This one goes on for hours, and the whole city turns out every evening. I would say that Matera would merit a visit just for its *passeggiata,* but it has numerous other virtues and blandishments as well. Wherever you are in Italy, you should make a point of noticing where people congregate in the late afternoon for the *passeggiata* and then be sure to join in.

Pasta A general term for the great variety of noodles for which Italy is duly famous. *Una pasta,* when ordered at a bakery or a bar, is a pastry.

Pasta al forno Baked pasta. This category includes lasagne, cannelloni, *timballi,* manicotti, and baked ziti.

Pasta con le sarde A Sicilian specialty, made with sardines, pasta, sultanas, *pinoli,* onions, anchovies, wild fennel, and saffron.

Pasta e fagioli A soup of pasta and beans. There are popular versions from Venezia to Palermo.

Pasta fresca Fresh pasta. This is usually made with flour, egg, and water. Among the most popular are tagliatelle, fettuccine, *pappardelle,* and various filled pastas.

Pasta 'ncasciata A Sicilian baked pasta dish made with *salame,* hard-boiled eggs, mozzarella, eggplant, and other ingredients.

Pasta reale Magnificent Sicilian marzipan.

Pasta ripiena Filled or stuffed pasta. These include tortellini, *tortelloni, anolini,* and ravioli.

Pastasciutta Dried pasta, usually industrially produced but of high quality. Popular varieties include spaghetti, *maccheroni,* penne, and rigatoni.

Paste reali Neapolitan marzipan cakes served at Christmas.

Pasticcieria Pastry shop.

Pastiera napoletana A delicious lemony Neapolitan ricotta cake served at Easter.

Patata (plural *patate*) Potato.

Pearà A marrow-based sauce served with *bollito misto* in Verona and nearby.

Pecorino Sheep's-milk cheese. The versions produced in Sardegna and Lazio (Pecorino Romano) are hard grating cheeses. These are sharper than Parmigiano-Reggiano and are better suited for the spicier pasta sauces of central and southern Italy. In Toscana, especially the town of Pienza, one can find delicious fresh Pecorino that is wonderful to eat.

Penne Short, versatile quill-shaped pasta.

Pepe Pepper.

Peperonata A side dish made of cooked sweet peppers that marries well with many roasted or boiled meats.

Peperoncino Hot pepper. These small, intense peppers, usually red, are essential in the cuisines of Calabria, Basilicata, Molise, and Abruzzo, and they turn up frequently in other kitchens in central and southern Italy.

Peperoni Sweet peppers, as in *verde* (green), *rosso* (red), *giallo* (yellow).

Pera (plural *pere*) Pear.

Pernice Partridge.

Pesca (plural *pesche*) Peach (this also means "fishing," from the verb *pescare*).

Pescatora, alla A general term that suggests the use of a combination of seafood and fish (as opposed to just seafood, which is called *ai frutti di mare*).

Pesce (plural *pesci*) Fish.

Pescespada Swordfish. Popular in Sicilia and Calabria.

Pescheria Fishmonger. Also called *pescivendolo.*

Pesto A world-famous Ligurian sauce made of fresh basil, garlic, pine nuts, olive oil, and Pecorino or Parmigiano-Reggiano.

Petto Breast, as in *pollo* (chicken), *oca* (goose), *anatra* (duck), or *tacchino* (turkey).

Peverada A sauce for poultry popular in the Veneto. It is made with anchovy fillets, chicken livers, pickles, parsley, garlic, grated cheese, vinegar, and olive oil.

Pezzente A sausage of the poor, made with leftover bits of pork after all the good parts are used. It is highly seasoned with pepper and very good. Yet another food of the poor that now pleases all palates.

Piadina A soft flatbread that is ubiquitous in Romagna. It is used to wrap prosciutto, cheese, or other ingredients, making a great fast food. I predict it will one day catch on worldwide.

Piccante Sharp or spicy.

Piccata A meat cooked in butter and lemon, typically thin veal cutlets.

Piccione Squab.

Pignolata A black and white cake from Sicilia.

Pinolata A pine-nut cake, especially popular in Toscana and Liguria.

Pinolati Pine-nut cookies, a specialty of Liguria.

Pinoli Pine nuts.

Pinzimonio Raw vegetables that are dipped in olive oil. Similar to crudités, except *pinzimonio* usually follows the heavy courses of a meal to freshen your mouth rather than preceding a meal to stave off hunger.

Piselli Peas.

Pistacchio Pistachio.

Pitta Pizza as served in Calabria. It is usually topped with tuna, hard-boiled eggs, tomatoes, olives, capers, and *peperoncino*.

Pizza Simply put, the world's most popular fast food. It began in Napoli, where the best pizza is still made. Once you taste it there, very little will ever match it. Real Neapolitan pizza is made in a wood-burning oven, has a thinner crust than that in America, and is topped with scrumptious tomatoes, milky buffalo's-milk mozzarella, a couple of basil leaves, and a few drops of olive oil.

Pizza di Pasqua An Umbrian specialty, originally served only at Easter, that is a bread flavored with Pecorino.

Pizzaiola, alla Literally, "pizza maker's sauce." It contains fresh tomatoes, oregano, garlic, and oil and is used for cooking meat.

Pizzella Small, thin-crusted pizzas. Sometimes the crust is cooked alone and dipped in honey or sugar to make a dessert.

Pizzoccheri Buckwheat pasta that is a specialty of the Valtellina in northern Lombardia.

Polenta Cornmeal that is served as a mush or hardened and cut into blocks. It is popular in the Veneto, Friuli, Trentino, Alto Adige, Lombardia, and Valle d'Aosta and is becoming more conspicuous on tables throughout the country. Read more about it on page 37.

Pollo Chicken.

Polmone Lung.

Polpa Pulp. (This also implies ground meat, such as *polpa di oca*—"ground goose meat.")

Polpetta (plural *polpette*) Meatball. These meatballs are fingertip-sized, despite one's preconceptions.

Polpettone Meat loaf. Particularly popular in Napoli and southern Italy.

Polpo (or *polipo*) Octopus. *Polpetti* (or *polipetti*) are baby octopus.

Pomodoro (plural *pomodori*) Tomato.

Pompelmo Grapefruit.

Porceddu Whole roast baby pig as prepared in Sardegna.

Porchetta Roast suckling pig. This is a wonderful dish in central Italy, particularly in Lazio and Umbria. Many Romans leave their city on Sunday afternoons to go to outdoor trattorias in the nearby hills to eat *porchetta alla romana* and rosemary-scented potatoes, all washed down with fresh white wine. *In porchetta* refers to a meat that is stuffed and cooked in the style of roast pork.

Porcini See *Funghi.*

Porro (plural *porri*) Leek.

Prezzemolo Parsley.

Primo The first course of a meal, although if it follows an antipasto it is technically the second course but still referred to as the *primo.* A dish of pasta is the most familiar *primo,* but one can also have soup, risotto, or soft polenta.

Prosciutto cotto Boiled ham. It is often referred to simply as *cotto.* The best comes from Emilia and should be sliced transparently thin to truly appreciate its flavor.

Prosciutto crudo Literally, "raw ham." In fact, this is dried air-cured ham that is one of the great ingredients in Italian cuisine. It is generally agreed that the best comes from Parma (actually, from the nearby town of Langhirano) in Emilia, although there is a conspicuous minority that prefers the prosciutto from San Daniele in the province of Udine in Friuli. There is also a good prosciutto made in Carpegna, in the province of Pesaro in the Marche. I must add a little-known prosciutto from San Marcel in the Valle d'Aosta. This ham is cured with eighteen mountain herbs in addition to the fresh alpine air. *Prosciutto crudo* should be served paper-thin (which is not how it is done in Toscana) and is usually served with *melone* (cantaloupe), fresh ripe figs *(fichi freschi),* or simply with plain breadsticks *(grissini).*

Provola A semisoft cheese of central and southern Italy that is classically made of buffalo's milk, but now also is made of cow's milk. It is often lightly smoked.

Provolone One of the most popular cheeses of southern Italy. It can be mild or sharp, is usually firm and aged, and is a familiar sight in cheese shops because of its characteristic pear shape. It also comes in other forms, including that of a piglet.

Prugna (plural *prugne*) Plum.

Prugna secca (plural *prugne secche*) Prune.

Puledro Pony.

Puntarelle A popular dark-green Roman vegetable found in winter and spring. They are plunged in ice water to make them curl and then served with a dressing of oil, vinegar, and anchovy. They are addictive.

Purè Mashed potatoes.

Puttanesca, alla Literally, "in the style of the prostitute." This is a pasta sauce found throughout the country but typical of the area from Roma to Napoli. It is made with garlic, capers, black olives, anchovies, and tomatoes. Would you kiss someone who has just consumed a bowl of this? It is generally thought that the name originated with the idea that this dish is of rapid preparation and that a prostitute could make herself a tasty meal between clients.

Quaglia Quail.

Quattro formaggi, ai Literally, "with four cheeses." This is a pasta sauce that varies according to the preferences of the chef, but it often contains Fontina, Parmigiano-Reggiano, Emmenthal, and Groviera (Gruyère).

Rabarbaro A bitter-tasting rhubarb liqueur.

Radicchio A red-leaf lettuce from Treviso that is now an international superstar. It is best known abroad as a tight little ball, but in Treviso it is often found in a long-stalk version shaped like romaine lettuce.

Ragù This is a meat sauce for pasta. The best comes from Bologna, where it is made with various meats and results in something spectacular. In Napoli and the rest of the south, a *ragù* is usually a meat-flavored tomato sauce—that is, it is the gravy from meat in tomatoes. This sauce is then served on pasta.

Rana (plural *rane*) Frog. *Cosce di rane* are frog's legs. Popular in Pavia and in the Po Valley.

Ravanada A sauce used for *bollito misto* in the Trentino. It contains horseradish, apples, vinegar, and sugar.

Ravanello (plural *ravanelli*) Radish.

Ravioli Famous filled pasta, native to Liguria but now found everywhere. They typically contain ricotta cheese or chopped meat, although numerous other fillings are possible. *Raviolini* are tiny, and *ravioloni* are very large—there may be only one or two on a plate.

Ribes Currants.

Ribollita A thick soup made of old bread, vegetables, and olive oil. It is twice cooked. (*Ribollita* means "boiled a second time.")

Ricciarelli Small almond cookies topped with confectioners' sugar, typical of Siena.

Ricevuta Receipt (usually used for fiscal purposes). See also *"Scontrino."*

Ricotta romana "Ricotta" means "cooked again." This is whey from cheese making that is heated a second time. The result is a wonderful, soft creamy cheese that is eaten cool by itself or with flavorings such as fruit, sugar, or even freshly ground coffee. *Ricotta romana* is also used in cheesecakes and in fillings for pasta or for dessert cannoli.

Ricotta salata A salted, firmer ricotta.

Rigatoni Large tubular pasta with grooves. *Rigato* means "with lines."

Ripieno (plural *ripieni*) The word means "filling" or "filled" and suggests either what you would put in a pasta, such as ravioli or tortellini, or the sort of stuffed vegetables you find in Liguria.

Ris e verz A rice-and-cabbage soup from Lombardia.

Risi e bisi Rice and peas—a classic Venetian dish.

Riso Rice.

Risotto A creamy rice dish usually served as a *primo*. Its most famous preparation is *alla milanese* (with saffron and Parmigiano-Reggiano), but it has been made in literally hundreds of ways. There is a restaurant in Milano called La Risotteria that has eighty-five different risottos in its repertoire. In the mountains, risotto is often made with wild mushrooms, while in Venezia it is made with fish and seafood. The classic zone of risotto is Piemonte, Lombardia, and Veneto, but the dish is now prepared—with less proficiency—throughout Italy.

Ristorante Restaurant. In general, this is a more formal establishment with waiters, printed menus, wine lists, and so on. This does not make it better than a trattoria or an *osteria*, but the style of eating is often more ambitious, and prices are correspondingly higher.

Robbiola A general term for the delicious soft cheeses that are made in the mountains of Lombardia.

Rognone (plural *rognoni*) Kidney.

Rosato Rosé, as in wine. The most famous is probably Chiaretto di Bardolino from Lago di Garda in the Veneto.

Rosmarino Rosemary. In Puglia, *rosmarino* also denotes a type of pasta shaped like a large grain of rice.

Rospo Monkfish. (*Coda di rospo* is monkfish tail, an excellent Venetian specialty.)

Rosso Red, as in "red wine."

Rosticceria A store that sells excellent roasted chicken and other poultry.

Rucola (sometimes called *rughetta*) Arugula.

Salama al sugo A delicate, crumbly cooked sausage that is typical of Ferrara.

Salame (plural *salami*) What in English is called salami. This is any chopped meat (pork, goose, game) combined with fat and spices and stuffed in membrane. It is cured with salt (*salame* as a word comes from *sale*, or "salt"). There are countless *salami* throughout Italy, flavored with *peperoncino rosso* in the south, fennel seed in central Italy, sometimes with wine in Piemonte, and so on. They are usually served sliced thin and are popular food to accompany wine at an *osteria*. This was food of the poor—while the better parts of a pig became prosciutto that was sold, *salame* used the less desirable parts.

Sale Salt.

Salmone Salmon. *Salmone affumicato* is smoked salmon.

Salsa Sauce.

Salsiccia (plural *salsicce*) Sausage.

Saltato (or *saltata*) Sautéed.

Saltimbocca Literally, "jump in the mouth." A Roman specialty made with veal *scaloppine*, fresh sage, and prosciutto.

Salumeria (or *salsamentaria*) A store that sells cold cuts, including *salami*, prosciutto, and other sliced meats. Cheeses might be sold as well. A lot of *salumerie* also carry olives, tuna, sardines, anchovies, and vegetables such as mushrooms, eggplants, onions, peppers that are preserved either in oil or vinegar. This is a good place to put together a tasty, all-purpose meal or to buy delicious if somewhat-fragrant ingredients for a food to take on a train trip.

Salumi Cold cuts.

Salvia Sage.

Sambuca A syrupy anise-flavored liqueur popular in Roma. Elsewhere in Italy, especially in the Marche, it is referred to generically as *anisetta*.

Sanguinaccio Blood sausage. This also refers to a specialty in the south made with pig's blood, chocolate, sugar, vanilla, cinnamon, and candied citrus peel.

San Pietro A wonderful fish from the eastern Mediterranean. Highly recommended.

Saor, in Typically a Venetian preparation in which a fish is marinated in vinegar, onions, raisins, and *pinoli*.

Sarde Sardines. In Italy, they are often eaten fresh (especially in Sicilia).

Sarde a beccaficcu A Sicilian classic. Fresh sardines are boned, filled with a filling that varies from town to town and chef to chef, then folded, dipped in egg and flour, then fried. The filling might be raisins, pine nuts, cheese, bread crumbs, or a vegetable.

Sartù di riso An elaborate Neapolitan rice tart made with mozzarella, sausage, peas, a *ragù*, mushrooms, hard-boiled eggs, and chicken livers.

Sbrisolona A crumbly, buttery cake typical of Mantova.

Scaloppine Thin boneless slices of meat, usually veal.

Scamorza A popular cheese in southern Italy. It is firmer than mozzarella and is often grilled.

Scampi Large shrimp or prawns.

Sciatt Fritters filled with *bitto* cheese and cooked with butter and grappa. This is a specialty of the Valtellina in Lombardia.

Sciroppo Syrup.

Sconto Discount.

Scontrino The type of receipt you receive in a bar or food store after you have paid.

You must then hand this to the barman or the person who filled your order before you can receive your coffee or your goods.

Seadas (or *sebadas*) These look like ravioli, and they are filled with cheese. But they are deep-fried and served with excellent honey. This is the classic dessert of Sardegna.

Secondo The main course of a meal, it follows the *primo.*

Sedano Celery.

Senape Mustard.

Senza Without. (*Con* means "with.")

Seppie Cuttlefish. (*Nero di seppie* is squid ink.)

Sfoglia A sheet of fresh pasta or pastry dough.

Sfogliatelle In Napoli pastry dough is filled with ricotta cheese and candied fruit and baked to create this delectable pastry to accompany your morning coffee.

Sfuso Loose. This specifically applies to wine. When you order *vino sfuso,* you are likely to receive house wine in a carafe that has already been decanted. It is wine that is purchased in large quantities and kept in a demijohn. *Vino sfuso* is not necessarily bad wine. It simply means that you are not receiving a labeled bottle of wine that will be uncorked before being poured.

Sgavecio A specialty of Liguria. Small fish are fried and then pickled in vinegar, wine, onions, and spices.

Sopa cauda A soup from the Veneto made of layers of bread and squab, topped with broth.

Soppressata A typical *salame* of Toscana in which pieces of pig's head and tongue are pressed with spices and pistachio nuts. Other versions of this are to be found in southern Italy.

Sorbetto Sorbet or sherbet.

Sorrentina, alla In the style of Sorrento.

This is a dish made with mozzarella cheese and tomato sauce (and sometimes eggplant).

Sott'aceti Vegetables preserved in vinegar, often served with cold cuts.

Sottobosco See *"Frutti di bosco."*

Sott'olio Preserved in olive oil. (This usually refers to vegetables.)

Spaghetti Long, thin strands of pasta, native to Napoli.

Spalla cotta Boiled pork shoulder, served cold and transparently sliced.

Speck Smoked cured ham or bacon from the Alto Adige.

Spezie Spices.

Spezzatino Stew, usually chunks of veal cooked with peas, onions, and wine.

Spiedino (plural *spiedini*) Literally "skewer." This is a kebab made of meat or fish with vegetables.

Spigola Sea bass.

Spina, alla On tap (as in beer).

Spremuta A squeezed juice, typically orange, lemon, or grapefruit.

Spuntino A little snack.

Stinco A roast joint of meat. The most popular are pork *(maiale)* and veal *(vitello).*

Stoccafisso Stockfish—imported dried cod from Norway.

Storione Sturgeon.

Stracchino Creamy delicious cheese from Lombardia made with milk from cows who are tired *(stracchi)* after a long day of grazing.

Stracciatella Technically, an egg-drop soup, but this almost always refers to chocolate-chip flavor, as in ice cream.

Stracotto Literally, "overcooked." This implies beef that has been cooked for many hours, usually with a lot of wine. Typical of Piemonte, Lombardia, and Emilia.

Strangolopreti Priest stranglers. This is what gnocchi are called in Trentino.

Strudel Typically made with apples, the most popular dessert in Trentino and Alto Adige.

Struffoli Tiny fried balls of dough with honey. A Neapolitan Christmas treat.

Strutto Pork fat.

Struzzo Ostrich. This has become a voguish, if not exactly classical, meat on Italian tables.

Succo Juice, typically of fruit or vegetables.

Sugo Juice, but more accurately the juices of meat. This term is often used to imply tomato sauce that is used on pasta.

Supplì Rice balls made with chopped meat, tomato sauce, and sometimes raisins and pine nuts. A Roman specialty but found in one form or another in much of southern Italy.

Surgelato Deep frozen. Restaurants are obliged to indicate on a menu when they are using an ingredient—usually fish and seafood—that was frozen and then thawed before being cooked.

Tacchino Turkey.

Taleggio A rich creamy cheese from Lombardia.

Taralli Small bread rounds with a hole in the middle. These are popular in Puglia and elsewhere in southern Italy and are often flavored with pepper or other spices.

Tarocco (plural *tarocchi*) Blood orange from Sicilia.

Tartine Little tarts filled with truffle, meat, fish, vegetables, or cheese and served with an *aperitivo*.

Tartufo Truffle. This is the fragrant gift of the earth found principally in Piemonte and Umbria, but also in Veneto, Molise, and elsewhere. It improves any pasta or rice it is tossed with. *Tartufo* also is a ball of ice cream with chopped cherries and nuts that has been dipped in melted chocolate and then frozen.

Tavola calda Literally, "hot table." Prepared foods—pasta, roast meats, good vegetables—that can be purchased and casually eaten standing up, at a table, or taken out.

Thè (or *tè*) Tea.

Tiella (or *tiedda*) A baking dish used in Puglia in which potatoes and other vegetables are combined and baked.

Timo Thyme.

Tiramisù Literally, "pick-me-up." This dessert of mascarpone, cocoa powder, and espresso originated in Treviso and is seldom made well. Look for it in Treviso, Asolo, and Venezia, and you are more likely to find the genuine article.

Toma A word for "cheese" in Piemonte and Valle d'Aosta. It is usually made with cow's or goat's milk and takes the name of the town where the cheese is made.

Tomini Little cheeses from Piemonte, often of goat's milk, that are marinated in olive oil, pepper, and other flavors.

Tonno Tuna.

Torrone Nougat. A specialty of Cremona in Lombardia and Benevento in Campania.

Torta Cake.

Torta pasqualina Liguria's famous Easter dish. It is made with vegetables, eggs, and all sorts of ingredients. It is classically made with thirty-three layers, each representing a year in the life of Christ.

Tortelli Filled pasta typical of Emilia. May be filled with potatoes, cheese, vegetables, herbs, *zucca*, or some combination of these.

Tortellini Wonderful little meat-filled, belly-button-shaped pasta that is the pride of Bologna. Another version is made in Valeggio sul Mincio, in the province of Verona.

Tortelloni Larger filled pasta of Bologna, typically containing cheese.

Totani Similar to squid and found in various preparations all around coastal Italy.

Tozzetti Small, hard nut cookies made in Toscana.

Trattoria (plural *trattorie*) One of the most popular eating institutions in Italy. A trattoria is usually family run, and the food and service are usually more casual than in *ristoranti* but also warmer and more personal. Clients become regulars at trattorie because their tastes and preferences become known, and they become part of the family. While the standard of cooking in trattorie is usually of good quality—certainly by American standards—I have tried in this book to include ones that are special.

Trenette Flat strands of pasta, like linguine, that are popular in Liguria.

Triglie Red mullet. Popular in Livorno.

Trippa Tripe.

Trofie (or *troffie*) Short, skinny Ligurian pasta ideally suited for pesto.

Trota Trout.

Umido, in Poached or steamed.

Uova Eggs.

Uva Grapes.

Uvetta Raisins.

Vaniglia Vanilla.

Vapore, al Steamed.

Verace Literally, "truthful." The word is popular in Napoli but is used throughout the country to imply genuineness. This is particularly true with *vongole.*

Verdura Greens, as in vegetables. *Verdura cotta* are cooked greens.

Vincisgrassi A very rich and elaborate lasagne typical of the city of Macerata in the Marche.

Vino Wine.

Vin santo Literally, "holy wine." This is typically made in Toscana or Umbria, although small amounts of superb *vin santo* are made in Trentino, too. White-wine grapes are harvested late and then air-dried until Holy Week, before they will be used to make wine.

Virtù A classic Abruzzo soup with forty-nine ingredients.

Visciole (or *marasche*) Black sour cherries, much beloved by the author of this book.

Vitello (sometimes called *vitella*) Veal.

Vitello tonnato A popular warm-weather dish in northern Italy. Roast veal is chilled, sliced paper-thin, and topped with a sauce of pureed tuna, capers, and other flavors. The sauce typically contains mayonnaise nowadays, but it did not originally.

Vongole Clams.

Weinsuppe A white-wine soup from Alto Adige.

Würstel A generic word for Germanic-type sausages. The closest example an American might know is called Vienna sausage. I think that in Italy what is sold as *würstel* is of poor quality, and you are better advised to stick to all of the wonderful *salsiccie* and *insaccati* that are made in Italy.

Zabaglione (or *zabaione*) A delicious dessert made with Marsala or some other dessert wine, plus sugar and egg yolks. May be served hot or cold.

Zafferano Saffron.

Zampone Stuffed pig's trotter, boiled and sliced. A specialty of Modena that is usually served with lentils *(zampone con le lenticche)* and is a centerpiece of a New Year's meal.

Zelten A typical Christmas cake with candied fruit that is served in the Trentino and Alto Adige.

Zeppole Deep-fried batter balls that are

made throughout southern Italy for much of the year but invariably on March 19, which is La Festa di San Giuseppe (the Feast of Saint Joseph).

Ziti The word literally means "bridegrooms," and these are the firm, elongated noodles that are popular in Napoli. Come to your own conclusions as to the origin of the name.

Zucca An orange squash akin to pumpkin.

Zucchero Sugar. *Zuccherato* means "sugared," and *non zuccherato* means "sugar free."

Zucchini The long, green squash called the same thing in English.

Zuppa Soup. In the Valle d'Aosta it is often called *seuppa* or *seuppetta*.

Zuppa di pesce A fish soup or stew, popular throughout the country but especially on the Adriatic coast. In the Marche this is often called *brodeto* or *brodetto*.

Zuppa di verdura Vegetable soup.

Zuppa inglese Trifle.

Zuppa pavese A soup from Pavia with chicken broth, eggs, and Parmigiano-Reggiano.

AN INDEX OF CITIES COVERED IN
ITALY FOR THE GOURMET TRAVELER

Every city listed in this book is indicated by its Italian name. Cities that have names in English (Florence, for example) are cross-referenced to their Italian names. Cities in the Alto Adige are cross-referenced from their Italian to their German names if there are significant differences (such as Bressanone and Brixen). Otherwise, Alto Adige cities will be listed by their German names first, such as Meran/Merano.

The listings of those cities that are not provincial capitals will be followed by the name of their provincial capital in parentheses. After this, the region in which the city is located will be indicated. For example: San Remo (Imperia), Liguria. Note that all cities in Alto Adige have Bozen/Bolzano as their regional capital, all cities in Trentino have Trento as their regional capital, and all cities in Valle d'Aosta have Aosta as their regional capital. The names of those cities that have been designated "Not to Miss" are printed in bold type.

A LIST OF RECIPES FOR THE GOURMET TRAVELER